Karl Marx

ALSO BY JONATHAN SPERBER

Europe, 1850–1914: Progress, Participation and Apprehension

Property and Civil Society in South-Western Germany, 1820–1914

Germany 1800–1870 (editor)

Europe in 1848: Revolution and Reform (co-editor)

Revolutionary Europe, 1780–1850

The Kaiser's Voters: Electors and Elections in Imperial Germany

The European Revolutions, 1848–1851

Rhineland Radicals: The Democratic Movement and the Revolution of 1848–1849

Popular Catholicism in Nineteenth-Century Germany

Karl Marx

A NINETEENTH-CENTURY LIFE

JONATHAN SPERBER

LIVERIGHT PUBLISHING CORPORATION

A Division of W. W. Norton & Company

New York · London

For information about permission to reproduce selections from this book,
write to Permissions, Liveright Publishing Corporation,
a division of W. W. Norton & Company, Inc.,
500 Fifth Avenue, New York, NY 10110

For information about special discounts for bulk purchases, please contact
W. W. Norton Special Sales at specialsales@wwnorton.com or 800-233-4830

Manufacturing by Courier Westford
Book design by Ellen Cipriano Design
Production manager: Julia Druskin

Library of Congress Cataloging-in-Publication Data

Sperber, Jonathan, 1952–
Karl Marx : a nineteenth-century life / Jonathan Sperber. — First edition
p. cm.
Includes bibliographical references (p.   ) and index.
ISBN 978-0-87140-467-1 (hardcover)
1. Marx, Karl, 1818–1883. 2. Communists—Germany—Biography. 3. Philosophers—
Germany—Biography. I. Title.
HX39.5.S67 2013
335.4092—dc23
[B]
2012044951

Liveright Publishing Corporation
500 Fifth Avenue, New York, N.Y. 10110
www.wwnorton.com

W. W. Norton & Company Ltd.
Castle House, 75/76 Wells Street, London W1T 3QT

1 2 3 4 5 6 7 8 9 0

This book is dedicated to the memory of

my father

LOUIS SPERBER

Contents

PART III: LEGACY

Introduction

·=])[c··

EARLY IN THE WINTER of 1848 in the Belgian capital of Brussels, a man, short but broad-shouldered, still youthful-looking, his dark hair and beard nonetheless showing the first streaks of gray, sat at a desk in a poorly furnished apartment. He was writing, as he usually did, in fits and starts. For a while his pen moved across the paper, in a barely legible left-handed scrawl, then he would break off, stand up and pace around his desk, before returning, crossing out parts of what he had written, and starting again. His family members—a wife a few years older than he was, two small daughters, and an infant son, along with a single servant, her presence testifying to the gap between her employers' social expectations and their financial circumstances—left him alone in his labors. They knew that the piece was overdue for delivery to the publishers, a chronic problem for his literary work.

The man and father was Karl Marx, and his writing, past its deadline to be sent to the Central Authority of the Communist League in London, was the League's new political statement, its *Communist Manifesto*. For so many historians and biographers, this *Manifesto* and the life of intellectual inquiry and political struggle to which it was connected was that of a modern contemporary, a nineteenth-century figure who had looked deeply into the future and helped to shape that future, whether for good or for ill. This understanding of Marx as a controversial contemporary appears in one of the very first biographies of him, published in 1936 but still well worth reading. It is rarely cited, for its title is embarrassing to current sensibilities: Boris Nicolaievsky and Otto Maenchen-Helfen's *Karl Marx: Man and Fighter*:

> Strife has raged about Karl Marx for decades, and never has it been so embittered as at the present day. He has impressed his image on the time as no other man has done. To some he is a fiend, the arch-enemy of human civilization, and the prince of chaos, while to others he is a far-seeing and beloved leader, guiding the human race towards a brighter future. In Russia his teachings are the official doctrines of the state, while Fascist countries wish them extermi-nated. In the areas under the sway of the Chinese Soviets Marx's portraits appears upon the bank-notes, while in Germany they have burned his books.[1]

Viewed positively, Marx is a far-seeing prophet of social and economic developments and an advocate of the emancipatory transformation of state and society. From a negative viewpoint, Marx is one of those most responsible for the pernicious and evil features of the modern world.

As the passage from Nicolaievsky and Maenchen-Helfen's book suggests, these strongly polarized opinions about Marx were a reflec-tion of the major twentieth-century conflicts between communist regimes and their opponents, both totalitarian and democratic. Yet even after the end of most communist regimes in 1989, this view of Marx as our contemporary has remained. In 1998, at the time of the 150th anniversary of the *Communist Manifesto*, there were frequent references to Marx as someone who had predicted the consumerist future; the eminent historian Eric Hobsbawm suggested that Marx and Engel's 1848 treatise had foreseen the age of globalized capitalism. One might

expect Hobsbawm, himself a Marxist, to assert the continued validity
of the ideas he espoused over the course of his long lifetime. Yet in the
global economic crisis of the fall of 2008, the headline in *The Times* of
London, a newspaper above any suspicions of communist sympathies,
screamed: "He's back!" France's right-wing president, Nicolas Sarkozy,
was photographed thumbing through *Capital*. Apparently Marx's status as a contemporary is very long lasting.[2]

Here it seems appropriate to ask how a mortal human being, and
not a wizard—Karl Marx, and not Gandalf the Grey—could successfully look 150 or 160 years into the future. A closer examination of
the *Communist Manifesto* itself, with its vision of a recurrence of the
French Revolution of 1789, its reiteration of the theories of early
nineteenth-century political economists, its veiled references both to
the philosophy of G. W. F. Hegel and to the new anti-Hegelian ideas
of positivist scholarship, its many insider references to Marx's own
past and to what are today obscure features of the European politics
of the 1840s, suggests something quite different. The view of Marx as
a contemporary whose ideas are shaping the modern world has run its
course and it is time for a new understanding of him as a figure of a
past historical epoch, one increasingly distant from our own: the age
of the French Revolution, of Hegel's philosophy, of the early years of
English industrialization and the political economy stemming from it.
It might even be that Marx is more usefully understood as a backward-
looking figure, who took the circumstances of the first half of the nineteenth century and projected them into the future, than as a surefooted
and foresighted interpreter of historical trends. Such are the premises
underlying this biography.

Complementing these new premises is a remarkable fresh source
for Marx's life and thought, the complete edition of the writings of Karl
Marx and Friedrich Engels, generally known by its German acronym
as the *MEGA*. This enormous project began in the Soviet Union during
the 1920s. Its very energetic first editor, David Rjazanov, was arrested

in one of Stalin's great purges and later shot, bringing the first phase of the project to an end. Work resumed in 1975, sponsored by the Institutes of Marxism-Leninism in East Berlin and Moscow. After 1989 and the end of communism in Eastern Europe, the project has continued, housed in the Berlin-Brandenburg Academy of Sciences, and directed by the International Marx-Engels Foundation. The edition's finances come from the government of a united Germany, initially thanks to the project's endorsement by the conservative architect of German unification Chancellor Helmut Kohl, himself by training a historian. This very large scale scholarly undertaking, still ongoing today, aims to publish everything Marx and Engels ever wrote, including the notes they scribbled on the backs of envelopes. Unlike less complete editions of the two men's works, it does not just print the letters Marx and Engels themselves composed, but the letters addressed to them as well. This new source contains no smoking gun, no single document that completely alters existing understandings of Marx; but it does bring to light hundreds of small details that subtly change our picture of him.[3]

The *MEGA* was originally part of a broader Cold War publishing competition that pitted the communist heirs of Marx's ideas in East Berlin and Moscow against his social democratic ones at the International Institute of Social History in Amsterdam, the Friedrich Ebert Foundation in Bad Godesberg, and the Karl Marx House in Trier. Unlike most Cold War competitions, this one had useful results, including a flood of source publications, narrowly focused monographs, and highly detailed scholarly articles providing a mass of information about Marx's life and times—often printed in obscure venues and little used or not at all in previous biographies.

Alongside this new information about Marx's life have been historians' initiatives to rethink Marx's times. Usually below the radar screen of the general public, these specialized works have been reconceptualizing and rethinking the nineteenth century, and doing so in ways that are eminently relevant to an understanding of Marx. Recent historical scholarship has downplayed the extent and significance of the industrial revolution, observing that conflicts between social classes have been just one feature shaping political confrontations in general and the socialist and labor movements in particular, pointing out the long-lasting and continuing influence of ideas and forms of political action from the French Revolution of 1789, the key role that religion played in interpreting the world, the considerable if complex and convoluted effect of nationalism, and the significance of family life and relations between men and women for the organization of society. The upshot of all these investigations has been to delineate an era rather different from our own.

Putting Marx into that era means remembering that what Marx meant by "capitalism" was not the contemporary version of it, that the bourgeoisie Marx critically dissected was not today's class of global capitalists, that Marx's understanding of science and scholarship, contained in the German word *Wissenschaft*, had connotations different from contemporary usage. Unfortunately, the common practice of citing Marx's words in standard translations that do not always do justice to the original context of his writings has frequently obscured their meanings. In this book, I have consistently gone back to the original versions of Marx's writings and devised my own, new translations: some of them will sound familiar, others rather different.

All too often, works about Marx focus on his ideas, his philosophical, historical, and economic theories. This biography will certainly have a lot to say about Marx's theories, but it will describe them in their own contemporary context, as interventions in ongoing debates and as critical comments on—and Marx was always very proud of his role as a critic—thinkers of the time. Some of those thinkers, such as Charles Darwin, are well known today; others, like Bruno Bauer or Moses Hess, are more obscure. Such an exposition of Marx's ideas in its contemporary context will include a consideration of the canonical Marxist texts—the *Communist Manifesto*, *The Eighteenth Brumaire*, and *Capital*, for instance—but also the stranger writings, often passed over or dismissed as personal idiosyncrasies, such as *Herr Vogt* or *The Secret Diplomatic History of the Eighteenth Century*. Interesting in their own right, these lesser-known works also cast a new light on the classic Marxist texts.

To understand Marx's ideas, it is not enough to know their intellectual context; it is also necessary to see them in the broader framework of his life. This biography will discuss, in some detail, his private life: his family, education, and upbringing, his courtship and marriage to Jenny von Westphalen, his relations with his children, his friendships and his enmities, his chronic financial problems. It will describe Marx as a public figure: his extensive work as a journalist—all too often ignored or not given its due—his political activities during and after the Revolution of 1848–49, and his role in creating and destroying the International Working Men's Association, the so-called First International. The portrait of Marx will be found at the interaction of his private life, public actions, and intellectual formulations.

As with Marx's theories, this book will place his private life and political actions in their nineteenth-century context. As such, it will be a portrait, not just of Marx but of the many people surrounding him. Two of these individuals are obvious choices: Marx's loyal friend, political associate, intellectual collaborator, and chief disciple, Friedrich Engels, and his wife and lifelong love, Jenny von Westphalen. Others are less well known but have an intriguing story to tell. There are family members: Marx's parents Heinrich and Henriette Marx, and his daughters Jenny, Laura, and Eleanor. His communist colleagues and rivals are another fascinating group—the dreamy Moses Hess and the flamboyant Ferdinand Lassalle. August Willich was a Prussian army officer turned Spartan communist, with strange sexual proclivities; Wilhelm Liebknecht a loyal follower, who secretly and stubbornly had a mind of his own. Marx's rivals and allies included non- or even anti-communists, such as the democratic and nationalist revolutionaries of 1848, Giuseppe Mazzini, Gottfried Kinkel, and Lajos Kossuth, or the eccentric, pro-Islamic and anti-Russian British politician David Urquhart. Most of these people were, one might say, part of the underground of the nineteenth century: dissidents, insurgents, nonconformists, outside the circles of privilege, influence, and power. Their world was Marx's as well.

But Marx's life also intersected with figures of greater power and renown. Moving through these pages will be the British prime minister Lord Palmerston, the Prussian king Friedrich Wilhelm IV, the French emperor Napoleon III, and the German chancellor Otto von Bismarck, all men whose policies and actions profoundly affected Marx's life, and about whom he had his own acerbic opinions. Prominent figures of science and scholarship also shaped his story: Adam Smith's most important follower, the economist David Ricardo, and the towering scientific genius of the century, Charles Darwin.

In looking for models of a biography placing a complex individual in the context of his or her time, I have found previous lives of Marx less useful. Two marvelous works on important figures of central European history—both very different from Marx and living in very different historical periods—have offered some helpful ideas: Heiko Obermann's life of Martin Luther, which perceives the architect of the Reformation more as a late-medieval than a modern figure, and Ian Kershaw's celebrated biography of Adolf Hitler, situating the Nazi dictator squarely within the twentieth century age of total war. When it comes to the nineteenth century, two excellent studies of German academics (neither, unfortunately, translated into English) emphasize the interplay between personal, professional, political, and private life: Constantin Goschler's biography of the great physiologist and political activist Rudolf Virchow; and Friedrich Lenger's engaging life of the sociologist and economist Werner Sombart. The approaches of these biographers to their subjects are quite suggestive for a life of Marx, who was, of course, not an academic, although at one point in his life he had aspired to become one, and always maintained many of the habits and practices of a nineteenth-century German scholar.[4]

Almost unavoidably, the author of any book about Marx, even one setting him in his nineteenth-century context, is going to be asked for an opinion about his contemporary relevance. Two versions of doing so go under the general heading of "Marxology," or Marxist theory. One is the attempt to update Marx, to make his ideas more relevant by adding to them or reinterpreting them in the light of psychoanalysis, existentialism, structuralism, post-structuralism, or elements of any other intellectual movement emerging in the years between Marx's death in 1883 and the present. The second version is the study of Marx's own ideas, so that revisions and later accretions can be erased and Marxism can be returned to its original purity: a project more suited to adherents of revealed religion than proponents of a purportedly secular and rationalist theoretical framework.

Speaking as a historian, someone committed to understanding the past on its own terms, and reserved about judging it by present conceptions, I find these versions of Marxology singularly useless pastimes. Marx's life, his systems of thought, his political strivings and aspirations, belonged primarily to the nineteenth century, a period of human history that occupies a strange place in relation to the present: neither evidently distant and alien, like the Middle Ages, nor still within living memory as, for instance, the world of the age of total war, or communist regimes of the Eastern bloc in the years 1945–89. Every once in a while, the nineteenth century suddenly emerges into the present, with an eerie clarity and familiarity. A prime example are the revolutions of 1848, whose rapid spread from country to country in a few months was a central political event of the nineteenth century, but since then have been known only to historical specialists. All at once, these obscure uprisings seemed current and familiar during the fall of 1989, as revolutions moved through communist Eastern Europe, or in the winter of 2011 as they raced through the Arab world. Much the same can be said about the relationship of Marx's life and thought to the present: there are moments of familiarity, but more often than not, I am struck by the differences—between Marx's world and the contemporary one, or between his system of thought and his political aspirations and those of his twentieth-century successors, who called themselves "Marxists."

Critics of these Marxists see Marx as a proponent of twentieth-century totalitarian terrorism, as intellectually responsible for the Russian Revolution and Stalin's mass murders. Defenders of Marx's ideas vigorously reject these assertions, often interpreting Marx as a democrat and proponent of emancipatory political change. Both these views project back onto the nineteenth century controversies of later times. Marx was a proponent of a violent, perhaps even terrorist revolution, but one that had many more similarities with the actions of Robespierre than those of Stalin. In a similar way, adherents of contemporary economic orthodoxy, the so-called neoclassical economic theorists, dismiss Marx's economics as old-fashioned and unscientific, while his proponents suggest that Marx understood crucial features of capitalism, such as regularly recurring economic crises, that orthodox economists cannot explain. Marx certainly did understand crucial features of capitalism, but those of the capitalism that existed in the early decades of the nineteenth century, which both in its central elements and in the debates of political economists trying to understand it is distinctly removed from today's circumstances.

If Marx was not our contemporary, more a figure of the past than a prophet of the present, one might ask why anyone should write a new biography of him, or, once that biography exists, bother reading it. One answer is that the nineteenth century itself remains fascinating and important, even if it does belong to an increasingly distant past. Explicating Charles Darwin's ideas remains significant, even though Darwin lacked modern knowledge of genetics. The life and struggles of Mazzini and his right-hand man Giuseppe Garibaldi continue to be intriguing, even if the political issues crucial to them have long been

resolved. Bismarck's diplomatic maneuvering and his skillful states-
manship attract attention, although their framework, that of the five
European great powers, has been obsolete for almost one hundred
years. But the value of studying the nineteenth century goes beyond
the good stories to tell about it. It is precisely by perceiving the contrasts between that century and the present that the latter appears in its
own distinct light. Seeing Marx in his contemporary context, not ours,
helps illuminate our current situation and is one of the major intellectual virtues of a biography in the early decades of the twenty-first
century.

PART I

Shaping

1

The Son

KARL MARX WAS BORN in the southwest German city of Trier in
1818, at the end of three decades of revolutionary upheaval and counterrevolutionary response that shaped the lives of his parents, strongly
influenced his upbringing and education, and created political passions and political enemies that would remain with him throughout
his life. Trier remains today, even as it was in Marx's youth, a very
old city, a Roman foundation, like many urban centers on Germany's
western fringes. It had reached its high point in the third century AD,
when it glimmered briefly as the capital of the Roman Empire, but had
been in almost continuous decline for the next 1,500 years. As late as
the 1840s, the city seemed like the wraith of a past civilization, large
vacant spaces within its walls—some employed for farming, some just
empty and unused—eloquent testimony to a distant past overshadowing a modest present.[1]

The economic changes of the modern world seemed to have passed
the city by. Eighteenth- and nineteenth-century Trier possessed no
industry; the railroad only reached it in 1860. Commerce was equally
unavailing; the peasants of the Eifel and Hunsrück highlands, to the
north and south of Trier respectively, were badly impoverished and

had few goods to bring to market. Perhaps more promising was the viticulture practiced in the valley of the Moselle River, where Trier is situated, but for most of this era Moselle Valley winegrowing was either faring poorly or its product was being sold directly by producers, bypassing the city and its merchants.

What remained for the city was another Roman legacy, its close ties to the Catholic Church. A center of Christianity since Roman times, with a resident bishop from the third century onward, Trier was a deeply and profoundly Catholic city, whose inhabitants had vehemently rejected the Reformation. Yet even there, the city's eighteenth-century archbishops, who were also Electors, worldly princes of the Holy Roman Empire, moved their capital city to Koblenz, on the Rhine River, abandoning Trier to a declining university and its many monasteries. The city council's 1788 complaint made all too clear the lack of economic prospects: "neither court nor nobility nor garrison and absolutely no manufacturing is present in Trier; the few persons of quality and the university, currently lying buried under its upheaval, are worth little; in current circumstances, there are simply no sources of earning a living on which we can count, so that we can foresee, with all certainty, that the unusually large number of poor burghers will be increased still more."[2]

Social and political institutions in the city of Trier, in the Electorate to which it belonged, and in the Holy Roman Empire, the governing body loosely tying together the hundreds of small, medium-sized, and a few large states in central Europe, as was generally the case in continental Europe before the French Revolution of 1789, were organized in an arrangement that historians call "the society of orders." In this sociopolitical world, rights and privileges, as well as obligations and restrictions, pertained not to individuals but to groups, whose membership came from status derived at birth, or from membership in a religious confession. Members of different groups possessed very different rights and privileges, generally set down in legally binding charters, such as the privileges of the Catholic burghers of the Catholic city of Trier to practice crafts and to deny Protestants residence there. The Catholic clergy and the many petty nobles residing in the vicinity in Trier had the privilege of collecting seigneurial dues from peasants whose land lay in their jurisdictions. Although the practices of the society of orders in Trier and its vicinity, as was true in Western Europe more generally, were not so fierce and harsh as they were in the eastern reaches of the Continent, they were far removed from contemporary, or even nineteenth-century conceptions of fairness and equity.

There was one particular group within this society of orders whose legal position was determined by its religious peculiarity, namely, the Jews. For Europeans of the eighteenth century, Jews formed a "nation," whose members were spread all across Europe. This Jewish "nation" should not be confused with its modern namesake, in a world of nation-states, since pre-1789 European states were the patrimony of their rulers, not the product of nations. Rather, it was one of many groups within the society of orders, whose place was guaranteed by its own charters, although these tended to contain more obligations and restrictions than rights and privileges. Jews had to pay special taxes and dues to their lords for the privilege of residing within their territory, and were generally restricted in their choice of occupation to commercial and financial enterprises. There were often special restrictions on Jews' place of residence, and their social relations with Christians. Today, we would say that the Jews were victims of discrimination; but in a society of orders, where different rights and privileges pertained to members of different groups, there was no ideal of equality from which complaints of discriminatory treatment could be derived.[3]

This was certainly the case in Trier, some of whose Jewish inhabitants paid their "protection money" and yearly "New Years Donation" to the Elector, while others paid these funds to the cathedral chapter, monastic communities, or local noblemen, who were their overlords. The Elector's "Regulation of the Jews" carefully circumscribed occupational prospects, limited the rate of interest Jews could charge for loans, and regulated their financial transactions. It set down the yearly taxes the Jewish community had to pay, and made the Jews jointly responsible for the collection of these taxes—a typical procedure of a society of orders, based on groups rather than individuals. The Jewish population of the Trier Electorate was small, mostly residing in little towns and villages, eking out a meager living dealing in cattle. The Jewish community of Trier itself was even smaller, numbering on the order of one hundred people, just over 1 percent of the municipal population. Like the city itself, the Jewish community was marginal and undistinguished, not to be compared with the larger and more active Jewish settlements in such western German cities as Frankfurt, Worms, or Mainz. Trier's Jewry did, however, include a handful of families who were somewhat more affluent and influential, wholesale merchants or professionals.[4]

Karl Marx's paternal ancestors came from this group, and Marx is usually described as being descended from a long line of Trier rabbis. As so often with instances of common knowledge about Marx's life, this one is only half-true. Marx's paternal ancestors did include Aaron Lwow, a seventeenth-century Trier rabbi, and his son, Joshua Heschel, rabbi in Trier from 1723 to 1734. This line ended with Joshua Heschel's son Moses Lwow, Trier rabbi from 1764 to 1788. It was his daughter Chaje, also called Ewa, who was Karl Marx's grandmother. Her husband, Mordechai or Marx Lewy, was not from Trier at all, but came from the little town of Postolprti in distant Bohemia, today's Czech Republic. His antecedents show how the Jewish "nation" was spread out across state boundaries in old regime Europe. This feature of Jewish life also appears in Marx Lewy's initial residence in Western Europe, in the city of Saarlouis, not far from Trier, an eastern outpost of the kingdom of France, seized in the wars of Louis XIV. Marx Lewy was the rabbi of the town's Jewish community; in 1777, his son,

Heschel (at different points in his life calling himself Henri or Hein-rich), Karl Marx's father, was born there.[5]

The Electorate of Trier, the Holy Roman Empire, the society of orders, and the place of Jews in this social hierarchy all came to a sud-den, drastic, and violent end in the decade of the 1790s. The outbreak of war in 1792 between the revolutionary government of France and the Holy Roman Empire—actually, between France and virtually all the powers of Europe—put Trier on the front lines, as it had been in wars over the previous century and a half. On August 8, 1794, French armies, fighting on behalf of a revolutionary republic, stormed the Aus-trian positions on the heights overlooking the city, and, the following day, marched into Trier. The Austrian defenders had retreated and the Electors' officials all fled, leaving the city fathers on their own. Dressed in festive regalia, they came out and ceremonially presented the keys of the city to the commanding French general.[6]

Unlike the soldiers of the French kings, who had previously occu-pied Trier in order to seize territory and to gain strategic advantages in a wider war, the troops of the revolutionary French Republic were determined to combine military occupation with political and socio-economic transformation, to bring their revolution, by force of arms, to the lands they conquered. It would be, as the jurist Michael Franz Müller remembered twenty-five years later:

> a just about total upheaval in the constitution of the church and state, in the relationship between church and state, in the admin-istration of justice, in commerce, manufacturing and crafts, in cus-toms and the national mode of thought, in the arts and sciences in land cultivation and much besides.[7]

If anything, Müller understated the extent of upheaval during two decades of French rule in Trier. The occupiers abolished the Electorate of Trier, tore the city and its surrounding territory out of the Holy Roman Empire, and, in 1797, formally annexed it to the French Republic. Chartered privileges of the society of orders were replaced by a government in which all citizens were equal under the law, and in which the basis of sovereignty was no longer the hereditary property of a monarch but the will of the nation. Guilds were abolished and occupational freedom instituted; seigneurial dues came to an end. The property of monasteries and the nobility was confiscated and sold at auction—in Trier and vicinity, about 9,000 hectares (the use of metric measures was another revolutionary step), or 14 percent of useful agricultural land, including most of the very best vineyards.

Although initiated by the occupiers, these measures found a modest degree of support within Trier itself. Unlike larger cities in the Rhineland, such as Cologne, Mainz, and Koblenz, where the adherents of the new, revolutionary principles organized political clubs and tried to mobilize popular support, Trier's sympathizers with the imported revolution were fewer in number and less well organized. Most of them were intellectuals and even former public officials, servants of the Archbishop/Elector, adherents of the reforming ideas of the Enlightenment. These included Johann Heinrich Wyttenbach, who had dropped out of the theological seminary in Trier when his teachers rejected the ideas of Kant, and had been a member of Trier's reading club, in which Enlightened ideas were exchanged, until the Elector dissolved it as potentially subversive. Decades later, Wyttenbach would be an important influence on the young Karl Marx.[8]

The results of the efforts of the French occupiers and their local sympathizers to turn the burghers of Trier into citizens of a revolutionary republic were less than they had hoped. In spite of the publication of revolutionary newspapers, the organization of patriotic festivals, and the planting of trees of liberty, enthusiasm for the new state of affairs was conspicuously lacking. Living off the land, the French revolutionary army seized its supplies from the areas it had conquered. No sooner had the occupying troops liberated Trier from the tyranny of the old regime than they demanded the enormous sum of 1.5 million livres from the city's inhabitants to support the war effort. When the municipality could not raise the sum, the French confiscated all the gold and silver they could find, even seizing people's shoe buckles. Finally, the municipal government had to take out a loan to meet the rest of the imposition; almost thirty years later, in 1823, the city still owed the depressingly large sum of 56,000 Prussian talers on the loan.

An even more unpopular group of measures taken by the new revolutionary regime stemmed from its anti-clericalism. Rejecting a Catholic Church that had been closely tied to the society of orders the revolutionaries were determined to destroy, they created their own Deist religion appropriate to a republic of equal citizens, disestablished the Catholic Church, sold its properties, prohibited its public religious functions, and turned Trier's many monasteries into hospitals, barracks, jails, or ammunition storehouses. The city's cathedral housed the barrels of wine the French army confiscated from the monks. Trier's deeply Catholic inhabitants boycotted the patriotic festivals of the republic and its new religion, and continued to engage in the prohibited processions of their strongly held faith.

Napoleon Bonaparte, who ended the revolutionary regime in France, took measures aimed at reconciling the inhabitants of Trier and of western Germany more generally with French rule. Following on Napoleon's victories in the field, French armies and their requisitions moved deep into central and Southern Europe, meaning that the burghers of Trier would no longer have to meet their demands. The city received administrative functions in the Napoleonic imperium as the seat of the prefect, the chief administrative office of the Department of the Saare, and a court of appeals—such government offices providing potential income and jobs the Trier city council had decried as lacking at the end of the 1780s. When Napoleon, having declared himself emperor, toured the eastern marches of his realm in 1804, he received a tumultuous welcome almost everywhere and certainly in Trier itself. Perhaps the most important feature of consolidating his rule, Napoleon reconciled with the Catholic Church, signing a Concordat with the Pope in 1801. The agreement did not restore the privileged position of the Church as it existed in the old regime; most church lands remained seized; indeed, the emperor, needing funds for his wars, hastened their auction. But Trier was once again the home of a bishop—one who actually resided in the city, unlike his predecessor. In 1810, Trier's Catholics publicly demonstrated their faith by celebrating the return of their most precious sacred relic, hustled out of the city before the appearance of the revolutionary armies in the 1790s—the Holy Shroud, the seamless garment of the crucified Christ, described in the Gospel of St. John— with a public exhibition and a enormous pilgrimage drawing tens of thousands of the faithful. The relic has remained in its case in Trier Cathedral ever since. Its public exhibition and pilgrimage have been repeated on a number of occasions, most recently in 1996.[9]

The upheavals of two decades of revolutionary and Napoleonic rule would create an exceptionally turbulent period for Trier's Jewish minority, one in which the tantalizing possibility of a fundamentally different position for the Jews in state and society was promised, subjected to public observation and critical scrutiny, but never quite realized. The promise of the revolution to the Jews was the abolition of the society of orders and its replacement with a regime of free and equal citizens, one in which religious affiliation was not politically relevant. As the first prefect of the Department of the Saare, Joseph Bexon d'Ormechville, put it at the end of 1801, "all distinctions between citizens on account of the religion they profess" were "absolutely contrary to the principles of the government."[10] In theory—although the practice, especially as interpreted by state officials at the local level, did not always turn out quite so positively—the old regime restriction on Jews' occupations, on their residence, on their relations with Christians, and the special taxes Jews had to pay, were to disappear.

The redefinition of political belonging that accompanied the new, revolutionary concept of citizenship went along with a new, revolutionary understanding of the nation, as a body of free and equal citizens, as the source of sovereignty. There was no room in such a concept for the old regime Jewish nation, a separate corporate body of the society of orders. Exactly what the end of this old regime nation would mean for Jews was not always clear and remained in dispute for much of the nineteenth century. For the Jews of Trier, it was the emperor Napoleon who offered the first answer to this question. Jews in his realm would have to conform to cultural norms of the society in which they lived: abandon their laws of ritual purity when they served in the armed forces, take family names rather than referring to themselves by their patronymic, organize their religious practice in a system of consistories based on the Protestants of his realm. Most controversially, in 1808, Napoleon issued his "infamous decree," which required Jewish businessmen to obtain a "certificate of morality," with the authorities testifying to the legitimacy of their business practices, particularly that they lent money in honest and above-board fashion, in order to engage in commerce. This decree strongly encouraged Jews to bring up their children to work in more "useful" and "productive" occupations than lending money or acting as middlemen.

The emperor's conditions for joining the French nation were difficult and controversial, leading to a split in Jewish ranks. Jews living in the countryside rejected the idea, clinging to their long-established religious practices and way of life. In Trier itself, by contrast, particularly among the Jewish community's leading families, Napoleon's demands found a more favorable hearing. Trier's rabbi, Samuel Marx—son of Marx Lewy, the family choosing to take Marx as a surname, which is why Karl Marx's paternal ancestors were not named Marx—was a delegate to the Sanhedrin, the 1806 gathering of Jewish notables from across Napoleon's empire that created the new system of Jewish consistories. Under Samuel Marx's leadership, the Trier Consistory called on the Jews of the Saare Department to be loyal citizens of the nation, to serve their emperor in the armed forces, to avoid usury and questionable business practices, and to bring their sons up to learn a craft. An important ally of Samuel in this task was his younger brother Heinrich, who was the Consistory's secretary.

Heinrich found his job difficult and frustrating. He was responsible for collecting the assessments on the Jewish population of the Saare Department, not only for the work of the consistory and the salary of his brother the rabbi but also for the debts that the old regime Jewry of the Electorate of Trier had accumulated to make their annual tribute payments to the Elector. Jews living in the rural areas, not very well off to start with, not particularly sympathetic to the consistory's aspirations, and facing a threat to their livelihood from Napoleon's infamous decree, refused to pay. At the same time, the central consistory in Paris delivered a constant stream of orders and requests for information and for funds, complaining about the inability of the Jews in the province to follow their orders. The central consistory was particularly hard on Heinrich, their officials asserting that he lacked the capability with the French language to carry out his task as Trier Consistory secretary.[11]

Difficult as the Napoleonic administration and the differences among the Jewish population were for Heinrich and the members of the consistory, the attitudes of the Christian inhabitants of Trier and its vicinity were an even greater problem. As the consistory complained to the prefect in 1811, Christians were unwilling to accept Jews as equal: "to be named a Jew is all that is needed to be rejected everywhere."[12] The Jews' identification with the new regime, which for all its problematic features promised an improvement in their condition, meant that opposition to Napoleonic rule would be focused on the Jews.

The year 1809 had been a difficult one for the emperor. Many of his soldiers were bogged down fighting a guerrilla war in Spain, and the Austrians had once again gone to war with him. Caught short of troops, he was forced to increase the draft call sharply, a broadly

unpopular move. While there were draft riots in rural areas, disturbances in Trier, where gendarmes and soldiers were stationed, never
came to pass—until August 15, as the Jews were decorating their synagogue in celebration of Napoleon's birthday. That day and evening,
hostile crowds gathered in the streets, beating up the Jews and smashing the synagogue windows with stones. The police were nowhere to
be seen, evidently content to let hostility to the regime be deflected
onto the Jews.[13]

Just how much these difficulties and evident hostility played a role
in Heinrich Marx's decision to leave Trier around 1811 is unclear. But it
does seem likely that the frustrations of his position, and its low salary—
about that of a primary schoolteacher, a notoriously badly paid occupation, even assuming he was paid regularly, which he probably was
not—played a role in his move to the Westphalian city of Osnabrück,
at the northern end of Napoleon's empire. He worked there as a court
translator, and had plans to obtain a position as a notary—an important position, then as today, in Roman Law countries, where notaries
do much of the work of drawing up contracts and wills performed by
attorneys in Common Law jurisdictions. But leaving Trier did not mean
leaving hostility to the Jews behind. The municipality of Osnabrück
refused to grant Heinrich permission to establish a permanent domi-
cile, a necessity if he wished to be a notary.[14] At the beginning of 1813
he moved again, returning to the Rhineland to study at the School of
Law in Koblenz, which the French had set up to train practitioners in
the new legal system they had created. If he followed the standard curriculum, in his ten months of studies he would have taken classes on
Roman Law, an introduction to criminal and civil law, and a course on
civil and criminal procedure. At the conclusion of his studies, he was
granted a "certificate of capacity"—the lowest level of course completion offered at the school, taken only by a small number of its students,
primarily older ones from a more modest background who could not
afford a full three- or four-year course of study.[15]

For Heinrich Marx, the French Revolution and its aftermath offered an opportunity to escape the narrowly circumscribed social and political position of Jews in the society of orders. He would no longer be a member of the Jewish nation but a French citizen of the Jewish religion, no longer a moneylender or middleman but a productive citizen, practicing a legal profession—one of the many barred to Jews before 1789. His path to that end was hard for him to follow: most of his fellow Jews rejected his redefinition of Jewishness; the Christian inhabitants of Trier and Osnabrück did not seem ready to welcome him into the ranks of free and equal citizens. His aspirations to study law—marked by almost certainly false claims to have studied at the School of Law in Koblenz before he was enrolled there, and to have studied law in Berlin before the University of Berlin was actually founded—were greater than his ability to do so.[16]

In November 1813, he seemed close to having reached his goal, only to see it dissolve in the fortunes of great power warfare. In the ten months Heinrich Marx was peacefully studying law in Koblenz, Napoleon's empire, which had provided the entire legal framework for the new possibilities Jews might have, was collapsing. The emperor's hubristic decision to invade Russia in 1812 met its nemesis in the winter of 1812–13 when his invading *Grande Armée* was destroyed. Although he raised new armies in the spring and summer of 1813, at the famous Battle of the Nations in Leipzig that October the allied European powers completely defeated the emperor's forces and forced them to retreat westward toward the French borders. Heinrich Marx was the very last student to complete a course of study at the School of Law in Koblenz; just six weeks later, Prussian troops reached and crossed the Rhine River, bringing Napoleon's rule in western Germany to an end.[17]

THE CONGRESS OF VIENNA of 1814–15 that reorganized Europe following Napoleon's defeat granted Trier and most of Germany west of the Rhine to the Prussian kingdom. The initial decades of Prussian rule would prove extraordinarily unpopular in Trier. While the French may have been godless subversives, they were, at least, Catholic godless subversives. The Prussian ruling house and its leading officials and generals were Protestants, a religion most inhabitants of deeply Catholic Trier viewed with suspicion and hostility. The first three decades of Prussian rule were marked by large incidents and small, in which the officials of the Protestant kingdom insulted the sensibilities of their Catholic subjects.

More profane reasons complemented spiritual ones in inciting hostility to Prussian domination. The Prussians actually increased taxes over their already high Napoleonic levels. Property taxes doubled, which led to especially bad feelings, since the property of large, noble landowners in the eastern provinces of the Prussian monarchy was exempt from taxation. An excise tax on food entering the city walls increased the cost of basic essentials. Following the initiation of the Prussian-sponsored all-German tariff union of 1834, the *Zollverein*, Moselle Valley wines faced strong competition from climatically more favorable viticultural regions in southern Germany, leading to a collapse in wine prices. The tax on wine, though, did not decline as prices did. While the defeat of Napoleon meant a long period of peace in Europe, the Prussians continued the French practice of military conscription, only their policy was actually rather more onerous since, unlike the French, they did not allow draftees to purchase a substitute to serve in their stead.

Prussian rule in Trier was colonial in nature, the oppressive domination of an alien government, backed up by a heavily armed garrison, engaging in economic exploitation for the benefit of the inhabitants of Prussia's eastern, core provinces. The reckoning with such a regime would come in the Revolution of 1848, when Trier's inhabitants would smash the insignia of Prussian authority, drive off the tax collectors, assault government officials, openly and vociferously demand that

Trier secede from Prussia, and engage in a series of brawls with soldiers from the garrison, ultimately escalating into a full-blown insurrection. It was only suppressed when the general commanding the
fortress turned his artillery on the town and threatened to blow it up.[18]

Understanding some of the problems they would face in incorporating the Rhineland into their kingdom, the Prussians proved surprisingly conciliatory about employing officials of the former Napoleonic
regime. Johann Heinrich Wyttenbach, the sympathizer with the revolutionary republican government of the 1790s, had spent most of the
Napoleonic era as principal of the Collège de Trèves, Trier's secondary
school, as the French called it. Following 1815, he became the director
of the renamed secondary school: the Friedrich-Wilhelm *Gymnasium*.
This policy of taking over into Prussian service former Napoleonic officials was particularly pronounced in the judiciary.[19]

Such a policy offered Heinrich Marx his chance. In 1814, he moved
back to Trier and set himself up as an attorney, quickly being admitted
to practice before the court of appeals. The Prussians transferred the
court of appeals from Trier to Cologne, but they created a midlevel
court in its place, a *Landgericht*, and Heinrich Marx continued his practice with it. Like other graduates of the Koblenz School of Law, Marx
strove to reconcile the Napoleonic judicial past with the present reality
of Prussian rule, sending a memorandum to the Prussian authorities
calling for the retention of the Napoleonic Code as the basis of the
legal system in Prussia's new Rhine Province. This was a hotly debated
question for a number of decades; but in the end, the Napoleonic Code
of Civil Law remained in force in Prussia's Rhenish possessions until
the introduction of the All-German Code of Civil Law in 1900.[20]

There was just one problem with Heinrich Marx's plans: his religion. Ironically, this problem emerged from measures the Prussian
government had taken to improve the status of Jews under its rule. In
1812, the reforming Prussian chancellor Prince von Hardenberg had
issued an Edict of Emancipation for the Jews of the Prussian kingdom,

granting them freedom of residence and occupation, and the right to serve in the armed forces. The edict had reserved for future decision the question of whether Jews would be allowed to work as government officials. By the end of the decade of the 1810s, the Prussian government had decided that they would not, including attorneys in private practice such as Heinrich Marx in the category of government officials.[21]

Marx hoped that an exception would be made in his case, and the Prussian commissioner in charge of reorganization of the judiciary in the Rhineland did recommend that Marx and the two other Jews working in legal occupations be allowed to continue; but the authorities refused to reconsider, part of an increasingly conservative turn in Prussian government policy. In these circumstances, Heinrich Marx took the decision to change his religion: at some time in the late 1810s or early 1820s, most probably toward the end of 1819, he converted to Protestantism.[22]

Historians have sometimes made a lot of this decision, some suggesting that Karl Marx deeply despised his father as an unprincipled sellout because of it, and seeing this contempt for his father as integral to Marx's future radicalism.[23] Even if we ignore very convincing evidence of Karl's filial devotion, this whole line of reasoning involves projecting twentieth-century identity politics back into a previous era. Conversion was a common option for central European Jews interested in engaging in public life during the first half of the nineteenth century. There were numerous examples on the left and center of the political spectrum, and even some on the right. Friedrich Julius Stahl, one of the most important figures among Prussia's conservatives, both a political and a parliamentary leader, and a constitutional theorist, an important intellectual influence on Bismarck, was a converted Jew. In Trier itself, most of the members of the leading families of the eighteenth-century Jewish community had converted to Christianity by the 1830s.[24]

In August and September 1819, the Hep Hep riots broke out in central Europe, in which mobs attacked Jews, their businesses and their homes. Particularly pronounced in the cities of Würzburg, Frankfurt, and Hamburg, although occurring elsewhere, anti-Semitic assaults centered on retail establishments that Jews had not been privileged to run before 1789, and on expelling Jews from public spaces previously reserved for Christians. In other words, the rioters intended to thrust Jews back into their subordinate condition of the society of orders. Although there were no disturbances in the vicinity of Trier and little in the Rhineland more generally, the riots were major news, discussed and portrayed in detail in the press, and there can be no doubt that Heinrich Marx would have known about them. For someone whose life over the previous decade had been one long effort to escape the limited circumstances of the society of orders, to enjoy new possibilities for his occupation and his citizenship, the prospect of being forced to return to old regime conditions must have been the final impetus in making his decision to become a Christian.[25]

Heinrich Marx could have stuck with his Judaism and renounced practicing law, although that would have meant grave economic difficulties for himself and his newly started family. There was a younger contemporary who took such a step, the Hamburg jurist Gabriel Riesser, the leading advocate of Jewish emancipation in Germany during the first half of the nineteenth century. After receiving his law degree from the University of Heidelberg in 1826, Riesser was barred from practicing law because of his religion. Instead, he published a periodical, *Der Jude* (*The Jew*), devoted to demanding equal rights for Jews in central Europe. Riesser, though, came from a much more affluent and better-connected family than Marx did, and could afford not to practice his profession. He also lived in the city-state of Hamburg, a relatively liberal polity, where his magazine could appear, not in the strictly governed, highly censored Prussian kingdom.[26]

A more interesting question is why Heinrich Marx, in converting to Christianity, chose to become a Protestant rather than a Catholic.

The other members of Trier's onetime leading Jewish families who converted all chose Catholicism, as did Heinrich's brother Cerf (or Hirsch).[27] Going from Judaism to Protestantism in deeply Catholic Trier meant exchanging one form of minority existence for another.

The answer to this question brings us to the heart of Heinrich Marx's views on the world that helped shape the outlook of his son. As might be expected from someone who had accepted the principles of the French Revolution in their Napoleonic form, Heinrich was a strong adherent of the Enlightenment. Karl Marx's youngest daughter, Eleanor, reported after her father's death that Heinrich had read Voltaire aloud to the young Karl Marx. We can take this secondhand reminiscence as we wish, but we also find Heinrich writing to Karl when he was at the university, praising the Deist beliefs of Leibnitz, Locke, and Newton—a veritable Enlightenment trinity. After Heinrich Marx died, a notary meticulously inventoried his private library. The list contained mostly law books, but also a copy of Thomas Paine's *The Rights of Man*.[28]

In early nineteenth-century Germany, Protestantism would have been the religion of choice for a supporter of rationalist, Enlightened ideas. By no means all Protestant theologians, to say nothing of ordinary pastors or laypeople, supported the Enlightenment, and by the early nineteenth century there was a strong countertendency in the making: "the Awakening" (contemporaries also described it using the older term "Pietism"), a central European version of born-again Christianity. Still, particularly among the Protestant intellectual middle class, the wish to reconcile the rationalism and empiricism of the Enlightenment with the tenets of revealed religion was very widespread. There certainly were Enlightened Catholics, such as Trier's first bishop under Prussian rule, Joseph von Hommer, but opponents of Enlightenment rationalism were gathering strength and influence in the Catholic Church. Heinrich Marx witnessed firsthand one of their first public demonstrations, the pilgrimage to the Holy Shroud of Trier in 1810. Its repetition in 1844 would spur an angry and massive reaction among Germany's rationalist and Enlightened intellectuals.[29]

This connection between Protestantism and Enlightenment was already evident in Heinrich Marx's thinking some years before his conversion. In 1815, he wrote a memorandum to the new Prussian authorities in the Rhineland, calling on them to abolish Napoleon's infamous decree against the Jews. In the course of that essay he noted that "the mild spirit of Christianity could often be darkened by fanaticism, and the pure morality of the Gospels polluted by ignorant priests."[30] Both the sentiments and, particularly, the language in which they were expressed—"fanaticism," "pure morality of the Gospels," "ignorant priests"—reinterpreted Protestant criticisms of Catholicism in Enlightened terms, pointing toward a liberal and Enlightened Protestantism, not entirely separate from Deism, that would become Heinrich Marx's Christianity of choice.

Trier's Protestants were ready to welcome the new convert. The Protestant Prussian officials, many of them thinking along Enlightened lines, ruling a disaffected Catholic Rhineland, needed all the allies they could get, and took them in the form of Enlightened Catholics, such as Trier's bishop, or the attorney with a Napoleonic past willing to renounce his formal allegiance to Judaism. Continuing in this vein would require that the connections between Enlightened and rationalist ways of thinking, the Protestant Church, and the Prussian state be preserved. Even in Heinrich Marx's lifetime, this connection would prove increasingly strained; in the life and times of his son, it would collapse completely.

A NECESSARY PRECONDITION TO setting himself up as a practicing attorney was another step Heinrich Marx took in 1814: he got married. His bride, Henriette Presburg, eleven years his junior, was from Nijmegen, in the Netherlands, member of a Jewish family which,

as the name shows, was originally from Hungary (the city of Press-
burg, today's Slovak capital of Bratislava), who had settled in the Netherlands during the eighteenth century and had been quite successful in
their mercantile ventures. Henriette's younger sister, Sophie, married
the businessman Lion Philips, who handled his sister-in-law's finances
after her husband's death, and became a friend and confidant of the
adult Karl Marx. Sophie and Lion's grandsons were the founders of
the electrical equipment and electronics multinational that bears the
family name.[31]

It is not at all clear how Heinrich and Henriette met. Most likely, it
was through his mother Ewa, whose second marriage, five years after
the death of her first husband Samuel Levi, was to the rabbi of the
German-language congregation in Amsterdam, Moses Löwenstamm.
If so, then Heinrich and Henriette had an arranged marriage, a common practice among the Jewish middle class in central Europe through
the beginning of the twentieth century.[32]

Henriette brought to this marriage a necessary foundation for Heinrich's practice of law in Trier: a substantial dowry. It included cash,
8,100 guilders, or about 4,500 Prussian talers—quite a bit of money,
considering that a day laborer or poor artisan would have earned about
100 talers per year. Along with the money went the household furnishings, which included, decades later, at the time of Heinrich's death, 68
bedsheets, 69 decorated tablecloths, 200 napkins, and 118 towels. It
was only with the assets of his bride that Heinrich was able to establish
his own household and practice his profession—a very common state
of affairs in the nineteenth-century German middle class. In his own
private life, Karl Marx would reject this approach and take a very different path, paved with financial insecurity for himself, his wife, and
his family.[33]

Henriette Marx née Presburg has not had a good press from historians and biographers. They have taken their cues from Karl Marx
himself, who was very much his father's son. Years after his death, his

daughter Eleanor reported that her father was deeply devoted to his own father's memory and never tired of speaking of him. He always carried around with him a daguerreotype of Heinrich, which the family placed with Karl Marx in his grave.[34] There was no mention of Karl keeping a picture of his mother with him. Quite the opposite; he got along badly with her, seeing her as a philistine, with no interest in intellectual questions, quarreling constantly with her over his inheritance, and showing little emotion at the news of her death.

Marx's mother is usually described as an uncultured woman, who could neither speak nor write proper German, someone completely devoted to her home, obsessed with the health of her family members—"modest, even primitive," "one of those Dutch housewives who live entirely for their family," or even a "yiddische Mama."[35] Her surviving correspondence reveals a very broken German, but considering that Dutch was her native language and she only began to learn German when she got married at the age of twenty-six, this lack of facility is not particularly surprising. Her efforts at writing in a foreign language, as poorly as they may have turned out, testify to her above average literacy, especially for a woman of the time. Her concern for the health of family members—the chief topic of her letters to Karl when he was at the university—is understandable when we realize that her husband and four of their children died of tuberculosis.[36] If Henriette was taken up with her household, and all its bedsheets, tablecloths, and napkins, and if she persistently refused Karl an advance on his inheritance, this was all about preserving her dowry, a central element of her commitment to her marriage and family.

Henriette Marx was a person caught up in the middle of a social transformation: from the Jewish nation of the society of orders, spread across the borders of pre-1789 European states, to the emerging nineteenth-century world of nation-states, in which Jews aspired to be citizens. Heinrich Marx's father, Marx Lewy, had come all the way from Bohemia to be a rabbi in Saarlouis and Trier, without anyone see-

ing it as peculiar. But then, Jews were largely limited in their public
life and sociability to themselves. Heinrich Marx wanted a career and
a public life in Prussia, a German state; his Dutch wife, despite her
impressive dowry, did not fit very well in such a social world. When the
attitudes of the Prussian government made it necessary for Heinrich
to become a Christian, Henriette's devotion to her household, and the
very household-oriented version of female Jewish piety that accompanied it, was also a poor match for these new circumstances. Henriette
was evidently reluctant to convert, and held out on the conversion of her
children as well. Karl Marx was only baptized in 1824, five years after
his father; Henriette finally accepted her baptism the following year.[37]

Whatever the degree of social compatibility, religious tension, or
romantic involvement between Heinrich and Henriette Marx, their
marriage was very fruitful. Their first son, Mauritz David, was born
at the end of October 1815, a little more than a year after his parents'
nuptials. He died three and a half years later, their only child to pass
away before reaching adolescence—an impressive result for the time,
and one that Karl Marx, founding a family under much less favorable circumstances than his father had, would not be able to match. In
November 1816, Heinrich and Henriette's daughter Sophia was born;
in May 1818, their son Karl. August 1819 saw the birth of their son
Hermann, October 1820 the birth of their daughter Henriette; Louise
was born in November 1821, Emilie in October 1822, Caroline in July
1824, and their last child, Eduard, in April 1826, at which point Henriette Marx was a few months short of her thirty-eighth birthday. The
Marxes had nine children in less than eleven years. This very rapid
pace of reproduction excluded any possibility of practicing contraception, which was basically unknown in central Europe at the time. It
also rather suggests that Henriette employed a wet-nurse to feed her
infants, for if she had breast-fed them herself, her lactation would have
reduced her fertility.[38]

Heinrich could support his large and rapidly growing family

because his law practice was flourishing—a success in middle age, after a long and difficult period in his youth. In 1820, he was appointed an *Advokat-Anwalt*, enabling him to represent clients in lucrative civil cases and not just the less remunerative criminal ones. His clients included the peasants of a number of villages in the vicinity of Trier and the municipal government of Trier itself. The family's finances reflected the success of his legal work. A special levy on the city's propertied citizens, imposed to fund measures taken against the cholera epidemic of 1831 (Heinrich Marx represented one affluent inhabitant of Trier who sued the city because she thought she was over-assessed), shows that Heinrich had a yearly income of 1,500 talers, not in the same league as Trier's wealthiest merchants, bankers, and landed property owners, but still placing the household in the top 5 percent of the city. Heinrich put the family's assets, stemming from his wife's dowry and a later inheritance, into different forms of property: a house in Trier, a vineyard overlooking the city, loans to Trier businessmen and to nearby villagers, and 540 talers' worth of 5 percent Russian government bonds.[39]

The family enjoyed esteem as well as affluence. In 1831, Heinrich Marx received from the Prussian government the title of *Justizrat*, judicial councilor, a highly desired honorific, awarded by the authorities, following careful investigation, to well-regarded attorneys. He was a member of the Casino, Trier's exclusive social club. We might leave the final word on Heinrich Marx's position in Trier society to Karl Marx's younger sister Louise. Married to a Dutchman who owned a publishing house for Protestant literature in Capetown, South Africa, and extremely embarrassed to have a communist leader for a brother, she would always emphasize to anyone who would listen her antecedents in "a respected and well-loved Trier attorney's family."[40]

We do not know much about the place of the young Karl Marx in a prosperous but fast-growing and increasingly crowded household. Perhaps his mother's constant succession of pregnancies made it difficult for Karl to develop a strong emotional relationship to her, foreshadowing their later estrangement—although the property disputes between them after Heinrich Marx's death would have been cause enough. Marx's daughter Eleanor related after her father's death that her aunts had told her Karl as a boy had been a "terrible tyrant," always ordering his sisters around.[41] Since one of Eleanor's sources would have been the same Aunt Louise who disapproved of her brother's communist life, we might want to take that assertion with a grain of salt—or several. It seems likely that Karl did not attend elementary school, but received private lessons at home. At the very least, a Trier book dealer, Eduard Montigny, instructed him in writing.[42]

The young Karl Marx really only emerges into any sort of light in 1830, when he began his course of studies at the Trier *Gymnasium*. This university-preparatory secondary school, the crown jewel of education in Germany from the early nineteenth century to the present day, was, in its initial phases, characterized by a very heavy emphasis on the classics, with most hours of instruction devoted to the study of Latin and Greek.[43] It was not an entirely appealing curriculum for the adolescents subjected to it (exclusively young men, until the beginning of the twentieth century), and generations of sensitive German intellectuals have penned lengthy complaints about a youth wasted in tedious memorization of meaningless texts, classes led by pedantic and authoritarian teachers and populated by dim-witted and careerist pupils. Concisely summing up a rich and evocative literature of complaint are the remarks of the dramatist and theatrical critic Alfred Kerr: "Three things—the relationship with the teachers, the relationship with the other pupils, and the smell in the lavatories—can be summarized in one word: abominable."[44]

We will never know what Marx thought about the lavatories—outhouses, then—but all his writings, throughout his life, loaded as they are with Greek and Latin phrases and allusions to the classics, suggest that his school experience was more positive than that of complaining memoirists. Marx's appreciation of the classics and understanding of their modern relevance appeared in his private as well as his public life. February 1861 was a particularly difficult time for Marx. His income was threatened by the loss of his lucrative position as a European correspondent for the *New York Tribune*; his family life was still shaken by the near death of his wife from smallpox; and his political future remained undecided between returning to Germany and resuming political agitation there, or staying as an exile in London. In this period of personal stress, he relaxed by reading Appian's book on the Roman civil wars in the original Greek text, and making comparisons between the leading personalities of ancient Rome and his European contemporaries. The form of Marx's instruction made every bit as much of an impression as the content. Wilhelm Liebknecht, one of the founders of the Social Democratic Party in Germany, and a close political ally and friend, recalled how in 1850, Marx had taught a class on political economy to the German Workers' Educational Association in London:

> Marx proceeded methodically. He put forth a proposition—as short as possible—and explained it in a longer exposition, in the course of which he took the greatest care to avoid all expressions that the workers would not understand. Then he demanded of his listeners that they pose him questions. If they did not, then he began to examine them, and did it with such pedagogical skill that no gap, no misunderstanding evaded him.[45]

It is easy to see Marx here making use of the teaching style he had encountered in the *Gymnasium*.

The secondary education Marx enjoyed was just for a small portion of the population; his graduating class of 1835 counted all of thirty-two pupils, from Trier itself as well as towns and villages in the vicinity. His classmates were divided into two groups, largely by religion. Most of the Catholics were from modest backgrounds, typically intending to go on to the Trier Theological Seminary and become priests. By contrast, the seven Protestants in the class were from families of government officials, professionals, or army officers: they were heading for the university to study law, medicine, or public administration. Forty years later, Marx would remember the Catholic pupils in his class as a bunch of "peasant dolts," probably reflecting the opinion their Protestant classmates from more affluent and better-educated families had of them. Marx himself was a good but not superb pupil, receiving high grades on his German and Latin exams but doing poorly in math.

For his third foreign language, after Latin and Greek, Marx chose French rather than Hebrew. This choice reflected the wishes of Heinrich Marx that his son prepare for a legal rather than a theological career. An aspiring Protestant pastor would have learned the language of the Old Testament, but an attorney who was to practice in the Rhineland would need to know the language of the Napoleonic Code that was still, as Heinrich had advocated, the basis of the legal system. Although Karl's plans would veer off in a quite different direction from his father's wishes, his capabilities in the French language, and his knowledge of French culture and history—both sharpened by lengthy stays in Paris and Brussels—would be a central fixture of his intellectual world.[46]

There was another more political aspect to Marx's educational experience. The *Gymnasium* director, Johann Heinrich Wyttenbach, no longer expressed the youthful radical enthusiasm he felt in the 1790s, when he had worked closely with the revolutionary French occupiers (Napoleonic rule had been, for him, a sobering experience), but the Prussian authorities were convinced that his basic political sympathies had not changed, and that he was unwilling to keep the younger teachers in line. A number of these teachers advocated subversive causes—the union of the different central European monarchies into a German nation-state, the introduction of a constitution in the Prussian kingdom, perhaps even a democratic and republican government—or advocated

freethinking points of view, like the science teacher who was accused
of emphasizing differences between geological findings and biblical
revelation. The authorities suspected that the teachers were indoctri-
nating their pupils with such subversive ideas. Their suspicions were
not entirely unjustified. A number of the *Gymnasium* graduates became
leftists, including the director's son, Friedrich Anton Wyttenbach, who
was imprisoned in a fortress for his radical ideas and activities. Ludwig Simon, son of one of the politically questionable teachers, became
a fiery opponent of Prussian rule and represented the city of Trier in
the German National Assembly during the Revolution of 1848 as a
prominent member of the Assembly's extreme left. Viktor Valdenaire,
from the nearby town of Saarburg, was another left-wing activist in the
midcentury revolution.[47]

School was not the only place that the young Karl Marx would
have been exposed to politically questionable ideas. There was another
source, a good deal closer to home. On January 25, 1834, his father
Heinrich was involved in a notorious episode at the Trier Casino. Following the founders' day dinner, a group of fifteen members sitting
around the table began to sing revolutionary songs: the Polish national
anthem and the *Parisienne*, anthem of the 1830 Revolution in France,
when an authoritarian conservative monarch, not entirely unlike
Prussia's king, was overthrown and replaced by a liberal regime. The
outburst culminated in repeated renditions of the *Marseillaise*, accompanied by shouting, pounding on the table, and waving around a tricolor
handkerchief containing scenes of the July 1830 barricade fighting in
Paris. A Prussian army officer who had witnessed the scene denounced
the group to the government, creating a scandal. There was an investigation and charges of revolutionary subversion were brought against
some of the participants, although they were all ultimately acquitted by
a jury. The Casino itself was dissolved, and replaced with two social
clubs. One of them had a membership mostly consisting of army officers and government officials; the other counted among its founders

(including Heinrich Marx) the more affluent and esteemed burghers of Trier.

In the course of the investigation, the accused all claimed to have left before the most subversive aspects of the singing. It was also reported that the singers had consumed rather more wine than was good for them. If there was ever a scene to which the Latin motto, *In vino veritas*, applies, it was this one. Those who joined in the singing included affluent merchants, attorneys, a notary, physicians, a teacher at the *Gymnasium*, and even a few lower-ranking state officials—the sorts of people on whom the Prussian authorities relied to work with them in their colonial regime in western Germany, ruling over a discontented lower-class Catholic population. Yet even the Prussians' allies, once their inhibitions were lowered, despised them. For Karl Marx, who was fifteen at the time, and would have known about and understood the event and its ramifications, it must have been a revelation, about both the Prussian government and his father. The Protestant, the good Prussian, proud bearer of the title of *Justizrat* and respected and prosperous attorney, was, at least for a brief alcoholic interlude, a sympathizer with ideas diametrically opposed to Prussia's authoritarian regime.[48]

About a year and a half after the founders' day outburst, Marx completed his courses and sat for the graduation exam, the *Abitur*. The essays he wrote for his religion class and for his German class are his very first writings to be preserved. As might be expected from a seventeen-year-old writing his graduation exam, they largely reflected the ideas of his teachers and of the adults around him. But they also contain initial glimmerings of Marx's own ideas and aspirations.

The essay on religion had as assigned topic, "The Union of the Faithful with Christ, According to John, 15:1–14." Marx began his essay by considering the pre-Christian peoples of antiquity, and concluded that in spite of their cultural, artistic, and scientific progress, they could never "throw off the fetters of superstition, develop true and dignified concepts of either themselves or of Divinity," and that even their ethics and morality were never free of "alien admixtures of ignoble limitations. . . ." And the ancients were aware of this: "Even the greatest sage of antiquity, the divine Plato, speaks in more than one place of a deep yearning for a higher being, whose appearance the unsatisfied aspiration to truth and light fulfills." These aspirations, Marx suggested, could be fulfilled only by the union with Christ, without which humans are "condemned by God," a condition "from which only He is capable of redeeming us." The union with Christ takes the form of passionate love for Him, which also makes humans virtuous, causing them to love their brothers. The result is virtuous behavior, a virtue that stems from "love of Christ, from love of a divine being, and when virtue arises from this pure source, it appears liberated from everything worldly and truly divine . . . it is simultaneously milder and more human."[49]

The idea of Christ's love liberating mankind from its sinful condition was a classic piece of Christian doctrine, but Marx's interpretation of it makes clear that he was taught an Enlightened version of Christianity. One of the burdens of the pre-Christian world that Christ's love could lift was superstition—a major enemy of Enlightened thinking. Plato's yearning for "truth and light," a yearning that only Christ could fulfill, was another clue, since those terms, "light" in particular, were code words used by central Europe's Enlightened Protestants. While Marx did mention human sinfulness and depravity that could only be redeemed by Christ, he did not dwell on it. Nor did he emphasize the transforming experience of Christ's redemption, the believer being born again, an experience that Germany's Pietists found every bit as central to their religion as their American counterparts did. These sentiments are redolent of the intellectual influence of Heinrich Marx, of the *Gymnasium*'s director Johann Heinrich Wyttenbach, a lifelong adherent of Kantian ideas, and of Johann Ludwig von Westphalen, privy councilor of the Prussian district administration and a family friend. By contrast, the ideas of Marx's actual religion teacher, a Protestant pastor who was skeptical of the Enlightenment and had some modest sympathies for the Awakening, seem less prevalent in his pupil's essay.[50]

The theme of Marx's essay for his German class was "Observation of a Young Man on the Choice of Profession." He began by suggesting that young men should base their choice on their most profound inclinations: "the deepest conviction, the innermost voice of the heart . . . for the Divinity never leaves the mortal completely without a guide. . . ." He then introduced two groups of qualifications. One concerned the validity of an individual's inward voice. Perhaps his inclination toward an occupation was just a temporary enthusiasm. Young men could consider the advice of their more knowledgeable elders, such as their parents—a suggestion Marx blew through in one sentence and to which he never returned. Most of all, they must trust to their own experience, to see if their inclination is a permanent one.

Marx then pointed out another problem for following one's heart: "our relationships in society." We might want to see the future socialist here, but the example he used was choosing an occupation for which an individual lacked physical capacity or talent. This inability to perform one's chosen occupation would be shaming, proof of a person's cosmic and social uselessness, leading to self-contempt, "a snake that, eternally undermining, gnaws at the breast, sucks the lifeblood from the heart and mixes it with the poison of hatred of humanity and despair."

Yet, and this was the main point of the essay, it did not suffice to follow an occupation for which one had both the inclination and the ability. Rather, the chosen occupation should be one that "grants us the greatest dignity, that is founded on ideas, about whose truth we are convinced, that offers the greatest field, in which to act for humanity, and even to approach the universal goal, completeness and perfection. Every occupation is just a means to that goal." Marx suggested that such completeness and perfection occurs at the intersection of the fulfillment of individual inclinations and abilities, and the improvement of the human condition:

The main consideration that must steer us in our choice of occupation is the welfare of humanity, our own completion. One should not
delude oneself to imagine that these two interests could be in hostile
conflict, that one must annihilate the other. Rather, the nature of
man is so arranged that he can only reach his perfection when he
acts on behalf of completion, for the welfare of the world around
him. If he just creates for himself, he can certainly be a famous
scholar, a great sage, an excellent poet, but never a completed truly
great man. . . . When we have chosen the profession in which we can
do the most for humanity, then burdens can never press us down for
they are sacrifices on behalf of all. Then we will not enjoy a poor,
limited egoistical joy, but our good fortune will belong to millions,
our deeds will live on silently but their effects will be eternal and
our ashes will be moistened by the glowing tears of noble men.[51]

In this essay, we can see, besides an excessive use of mixed meta-
phors, once again the influence of Johann Heinrich Wyttenbach and
the Kantian ideas he professed. Another important influence was the
Olympian German literary figure of the day, Johann Wolfgang von
Goethe, whose poetry, novels, plays, and collected personal conversations all articulated the ideals of completion and perfection as goals of
human striving. Known to virtually every educated speaker of German, Goethe's works were required reading for the students in the
Trier *Gymnasium*. The principal Wyttenbach was a personal acquaintance of the celebrated poet.

One feature of this essay was Marx's choice of examples for individual accomplishment: a scholar, sage, and poet. He did not mention
being a soldier, administrator, businessman, or lawyer—all fields of
accomplishment to which young men of his social class in Prussia might
aspire. The last was his father's choice, and at this time Marx's own, for
his career. The intellectual and artistic pursuits he mentioned instead
reflected the influence of Wyttenbach, who was all those things, and

whose presence loomed large on the modest stage of Trier, even though it was not of any great import in the broader central European cultural world. The pursuit of intellectual investigation as a means to the betterment of the condition of humanity was a theme that would recur throughout Marx's life—one need only think of his constant insistence that communist politics and communist aspirations for humanity had to be based on *Wissenschaft*, systematic scholarship—and found its first naive, adolescent expression in this essay.

If the two graduation exam essays showed aspects of Marx's formal, intellectual education, another feature of the graduation suggests something of his informal, political one. In this same year the Prussian authorities, tired of what they saw as Wyttenbach's inability or unwillingness to counter subversive political currents, installed a classics teacher with reliably conservative ideas, a man named Vitus Loers, as co-director of the school. This move was both a personal affront and a political gesture. Marx responded in kind. He snubbed the new co-director, refusing to pay a farewell visit to Loers, one of only two members of his graduating class who behaved this way. Shortly after Marx left Trier for his university studies in November 1835, there was a banquet in Loers's honor. Heinrich Marx was present, and saw that the right-wing teacher was visibly angry about his son's behavior. Heinrich attempted to pacify Loers by telling him that Karl had paid him a visit but found him out of the office. At the banquet, Heinrich also met Wyttenbach, visibly depressed by the affront of Loers's appointment. Heinrich tried to pacify him as well, informing him of Karl's admiration and devotion to him, remarks that evidently cheered him up.[52]

Heinrich Marx's two actions at the banquet might sum up much of his son's early life. Karl Marx was born into and grew up in a family seeking to leave the constrained and cramped environment of the Jewish "nation" in a Europe of the society of orders. In its place, family members would put a life based on the doctrines of the Enlightenment: a rationalist approach to the world, a Deist religion and belief in human equality and basic rights, an aspiration toward being a productive citizen in a community of such citizens. As Heinrich's own experiences had shown, the path to such a life was tortuous and difficult, filled with compromises, and affected by the vicissitudes of war and revolution over which the inhabitants of the small, marginal city of Trier had little control.

In following this path, Heinrich had become first a Frenchman and a supporter of the emperor Napoleon, and then a Prussian and Protestant, both distancing him from the social environment of deeply Catholic Trier. He had obtained a modest affluence and social respectability. But there were incidents, like the singing in the Casino or his son's snubbing of Vitus Loers, that brought into sharp relief the difficulties encountered in being both a good Prussian and a supporter of the doctrines of the Enlightenment. It is perhaps characteristic of the differences between Heinrich and Karl, or maybe just of the contrast between a cautious and reticent middle-aged paterfamilias and a brash adolescent, that the former made his doubts about Prussian rule known when he was drunk, the latter when he was sober.

Karl was certainly rasher than his father in 1835; but one might wonder if he was politically more radical, if he was willing to oppose the Prussian monarchy consistently and fundamentally, rather than just at specific times and on particular issues. The answer is probably not yet, and we might see that by comparison to another student and future revolutionary at the Trier *Gymnasium*, Ludwig Simon. Simon was a year behind Marx, and the German essay assignment for his *Abitur* in 1836 was to write about love of the fatherland. In his essay, Simon insisted that only Germany could be his fatherland, but never Prussia—a radical repudiation of the monarchy that fit the dominant attitude in Catholic Trier. Neither Heinrich nor Karl was quite ready to take that step.

We can take this comparison a little further. Simon was a revolutionary in 1848 and remained true to his revolutionary views in French and Swiss exile, where he lived until his death in 1872. But Simon's revolutionary ideals were very much those of the Jacobins of the French Revolution of 1789—nationalist, republican, and democratic, perhaps given to social reform, but certainly not an opponent of capitalism or private property. While in exile, Simon worked as a banker.[53] Karl Marx would be a revolutionary as well, one who would share many of Simon's Jacobin tendencies, a point often lost in discussions of Marx's revolutionary ideas and aspirations; but his version of revolution would involve the demand for changes in economic structure and property relations. The path to combining Jacobin politics and communist economics would go through a distinctly Prussian form of intellectual life that Marx encountered in his university studies. In the fall of 1835, this encounter still lay in the future.

2

The Student

··✺··

AS KARL MARX TRAVELED down the Moselle from Trier to Koblenz, and then by steamboat north along the Rhine to Bonn to begin his university studies in October 1835, he could have seen Halley's Comet, high in the night sky. In mystical thinking, comets are portents of great deeds, although an ever rationalist Marx would have rejected any connection between astral signs and his own destiny. The realities of university study in central Europe during the 1830s supported such perceptions, suggesting not great deeds ahead of the new student but a long and tortuous career path, with an uncertain outcome. A young man in Prussia beginning a legal career faced years of university study, an unpaid apprenticeship, and two state exams, before there was even the possibility of an appointment as a state's attorney, judge, or lawyer in private practice. For a decade or more, the student and aspiring jurist would be without any income and dependent on his family for support. Other career paths for students, including those leading to a position at a *Gymnasium* or a university, were just as long, difficult, and stressful.[1]

While secondary and higher education had expanded substantially in the German states during the first decades of the nineteenth cen-

tury, funding of government positions to employ the growing number
of graduates had not kept pace. Between about 1820 and 1840, the
number of law graduates in Prussia holding unpaid positions tripled,
but salaried state judicial posts increased by only 20 percent. This mismatch has been a chronic problem in central Europe, recurring at regular intervals over the last two centuries, but the difficulties created by
the disjuncture between graduates and state-funded positions for them
were probably worse in the 1830s and 1840s than at any other time.
Slow economic growth in the German states meant that governments
lacked the tax revenues to expand the number of public service positions available for graduates, but also that the private sector, struggling
with hard times, could not provide adequate alternatives.[2]

Karl Marx's legal studies required a long-term family financial
commitment to him. Women were not admitted to German universities until the beginning of the twentieth century, so that Karl's sisters
would receive a different kind of commitment, albeit also financially
substantial—a prospect, Heinrich Marx, asserted, that "made his hair
stand on end"—namely, a dowry enabling them to make a good marriage. Karl's younger brother Hermann, "a deeply good heart" but "not
much in his head," as Heinrich described him, did not attend a university but was instead sent to Brussels and apprenticed to a merchant.[3]

The years 1835 to 1842, which marked Marx's transition from
adolescence to adulthood, were dominated by the difficulties of his
projected career and the long-term financial dependence on his family it implied. The prospect of dependence itself was difficult enough
for a self-assertive young man like Karl, and conflicts with his family seemed inevitable. Within a year of leaving home, the difficulties
of this path and the conflicts with his family expanded, almost to the
breaking point.

As a good Prussian subject, Heinrich sent his son to the university
in Bonn. The Prussian government had founded it in 1818 in this little
Rhenish town—then as today in the shadow of its much larger northern

neighbor Cologne—as an act of political integration and reconciliation. Young men from the middle and upper classes of the Rhineland, suspicious of and potentially hostile to their new overlords, would be transformed into future members of a loyal provincial elite by spending their formative years with students, many Protestant noblemen, from the kingdom's core eastern provinces. In practice, this combination of Rhenish students—often with liberal, democratic, or Catholic conservative but anti-Prussian political sympathies—and young Prussian noblemen led more to conflict and exacerbation than to the creation of Prussian loyalties.

Such conflicts shaped Marx's first year at the University of Bonn. He attended lectures "industriously," as his professors attested, and took part in the League of Poets, a group of young men (including some future revolutionary leaders) who met to discuss literary and aesthetic questions, and to try their hand at writing poetry. But Marx's chief activity was his extracurricular association with an informal circle of students from Trier and other cities in the southwestern part of the Rhineland, whose members spent their time in Bonn's taverns, drinking heavily, and then brawling with other students. It was among these students that Marx acquired his nickname, "The Moor," from his swarthy complexion, by which he would be known to friends and family for the rest of his life.[4]

Drinking, brawling, comic nicknames—it all sounds like the recreation of an apolitical late adolescent; but the actions had a political edge, since the fighting was between the students from Trier and those from Prussia's eastern provinces. In a period of political repression, brawling with such individuals was how many Rhinelanders, not just university students, expressed their discontent with Prussian rule. Marx was elected one of the leaders of the group of Trier students, and his role in the physical disputes culminated, during the summer of 1836, in his participation in a duel with sabers—an old German university tradition, still occasionally practiced today—defending the honor of the middle-class Rhinelanders against the eastern aristocrats.[5]

Karl's bad behavior evoked his father's disapproval for the way he was veering off course. Heinrich had sarcastic words about the dueling; he repeated warnings about excessive frequentation of taverns; he reminded Karl of the family's expectations for him, "the hope that you might, one day, be a support for your brothers and sisters." He also criticized Karl's way with the family's money—not, as many accounts suggest, that Karl was spending too much of it, but that his manner of accounting for it was chaotic and disorganized:

> Your accounts, dear Karl, are à la Carl, disjointed and without result. Briefer and more consequential, just put the figures regularly into columns, and the operation would have been very simple. One demands order of a scholar, especially of a practical jurist.[6]

Heinrich's conclusion was that a change of university was necessary. As he wrote at the end of the 1835–36 academic year, making the statement official, "I do not just grant my son Carl Marx permission to do so, but it is my will that he enroll at the University of Berlin to continue his studies of law and public administration that he has begun in Bonn."[7] Moving to Berlin would mark a major change in Karl's life. He would be much further off from his family, a four-day trip by stagecoach, since there were no rail connections between the Prussian capital and its western provinces until the end of the 1840s. Berlin, with its 300,000 inhabitants, about twenty times that of Bonn, was a different world from the little Rhenish university town. Residing in Berlin was Marx's first experience in big city living that would become the rule rather than the exception for the rest of his life.

Berlin was not quite yet the center of industry, commerce, and finance it would become within a few decades. Steam-powered factories and an industrial workforce, to the extent that they existed, were overshadowed by the many artisans, toiling in small craft workshops, and the ubiquitous *Eckensteher*, day laborers licensed by the government to stand on street corners and wait for work. Above all, the city was a royal residence and the seat of government of one of Europe's great powers. It possessed a lively cultural and artistic life: theaters, operas, and ballet beckoned; art enthusiasts could visit its excellent new art museum; music lovers could attend concerts at the *Singakadamie*, the city's renowned choral society, or hear the virtuoso pianist Franz Liszt perform. Sarcastic musical and theatrical critics, and a growing group of sardonic humorists, dissected the artistic aspirations and flayed the pretensions of their creators and consumers. The city's intellectual life was varied and diverse, but centered on its university. Like Bonn University, the University of Berlin was an eminently Prussian institution, but it was known for its intellectual quality and for its sober, serious, and scholarly atmosphere. These attracted curious students from all over Europe, including Jakob Burckhardt and Søren Kierkegaard. It was the presence of the court and the state bureaucracy that made such an intellectual and cultural efflorescence possible, but that also created a distinct tension between a largely authoritarian regime and a group of artists and thinkers who had their own distinct ideas.

Heinrich Marx, in sending his son to the university in the Prussian capital, was banking on the sober and serious side of the university's and the city's intellectual life. Once there, Karl could put his wild year behind him, and resume a systematic and orderly path toward his goal. Of course, the distance from his family and many features of big city life could combine to thwart Heinrich's aspirations for his son, by creating a very different kind of distraction than the drinking, brawling, dueling, and disorderly finances in Bonn.

Detours in and obstacles to the young Karl Marx's path from *Gymnasium* pupil to successful jurist, from adolescence to manhood, lurked everywhere—even unexpectedly in Trier itself, from Marx family friends, the Westphalens. Johann Ludwig von Westphalen was a senior Prussian state bureaucrat, a councilor of the Trier district government. He and Heinrich Marx knew each other; they shared similar, liberal, constitutional monarchist yet pro-Prussian political views, and Enlightened Protestant religious ones; they frequented the same social circles—both were members of Trier's Casino—and probably had professional relations as well, since Johann Ludwig was the official of the district in charge of prisons and Heinrich an attorney whose practice included criminal defense. Their children were playmates: Johann Ludwig's daughter Jenny with Karl's older sister Sophie, and Johann Ludwig's son Edgar with Karl. As the boys grew up, they attended the *Gymnasium* together.

At some point in Karl's adolescence, his attentions turned to his playmate's sister, and he began to court her. The transition from family friend to lover was far from smooth or simple. Karl was the passionate, importuning suitor, and Jenny the reluctant object of his attentions. She responded to his declarations of love by stating that she was fond of him—in German, a play on words, "I'm fond of you," expressed *Ich habe dich lieb*, as opposed to "I love you," or *Ich liebe dich*. Jenny later conceded that Karl's impetuous bearing and his stormy declarations of love frightened her. She feared giving in to him, admitting to herself that her feelings were reciprocal, becoming lost in her love for him, and then seeing his passions cool in the course of a relationship, leaving her loving a man who was "cold and withdrawn."[8] Yet by the summer of 1836, when Karl at eighteen was at home from Bonn before leaving for Berlin, she yielded to his importuning and the two became engaged.

This engagement, the beginning of a lifelong mutual commitment, has been repeatedly portrayed as a fairy-tale romance, linking a beautiful young woman, "the prettiest girl in Trier," the "queen of the ball," an "enchanted princess," daughter of a high Prussian official, from a distinguished aristocratic family, with a hairy, swarthy commoner, of suspiciously Semitic antecedents—a remarkable triumph of love and affection over prejudice and social differences. Such an account was beginning to make the rounds in Marx's own lifetime. On his wife's death in 1881, an obituary of her, written by Marx's son-in-law Charles Longuet in the French newspaper *Justice*, stated: "We might guess that her marriage with Karl Marx, son of a Trier attorney, was not made without difficulty. There were many prejudices to vanquish, most of all that of race. We know that the illustrious socialist is of Israelite origins." Sending the notice on to his and Jenny's daughter, Marx snorted, "The entire story is simply made up; there were no prejudices to vanquish," and added some cutting remarks about what a nitwit his son-in-law was.[9]

Marx's sarcastic observation deserves attention. The social differences between the Westphalen and Marx families were less than might appear at first glance, and Jenny's acceptance of Karl's proposal is more understandable when we take her own prospects into account. There were aspects of the relationship between Karl and Jenny that were unusual, even downright subversive in their rebellion against accepted ideas of manhood and of proper relations between men and women. These led to skepticism and opposition to the engagement in both families, but were grounded less in Karl's Semitic past than in his uncertain future.

Johann Ludwig von Westphalen, was a senior Prussian bureaucrat and also a governmentally recognized aristocrat, having secured his registration in the official list of noblemen living in Prussia's Rhenish possessions. Yet, examined more closely, this picture of a Prussian aristocrat and high government official begins to blur and dissolve.[10]

In the initial decades of the nineteenth century, as the society of orders began to be abolished in Germany, the nobility, enjoying the most special privileges and rights in this society, responded to changes threatening its position with a regrouping and reorientation. The most blue-blooded aristocrats, those who could trace their genealogy back across centuries, began to refer to themselves as the "primeval nobility" (in German, *Uradel*), rejecting any association with and sometimes personally insulting the "nobility of letters patent" (in German, *Briefadel*) or the "nobility of [state] service" (in German, *Dienstadel*), whose nobility was of more recent vintage and bureaucratic origin.[11] Johann Ludwig von Westphalen was precisely such a second-rank nobleman, his father having received a title of nobility in 1764, six years before Johann Ludwig's birth, for his services as privy secretary to the Duke of Braunschweig.

Not only was Westphalen's noble status suspiciously second rate, his personal past was suspiciously Napoleonic. He began his bureaucratic career, like his father, in the Duchy of Braunschweig, but when that duchy, along with a big chunk of Prussian territory, was incorporated into the Kingdom of Westphalia—a German state Napoleon had created in 1807, and handed over to his brother Jérôme to rule—Westphalen became a French-style bureaucrat, from 1809 to 1813 sub-prefect in the town of Salzwedel. Following the collapse of Napoleon's rule in central Europe, like other Napoleonic officials he was taken over into Prussian state service, first in Salzwedel itself and then in Trier, where he never advanced beyond the rank of councilor in the Prussian district administration. There were many reasons for this truncated career, but one was certainly his political position: like many survivals of the Napoleonic era, including Heinrich Marx, Johann Ludwig was sympathetic to liberal political doctrines, including the idea of a constitutional monarchy—an attitude that did not help his bureaucratic career prospects.

Finally, Johann Ludwig von Westphalen was married twice, to two very different women. His first wife, Lisette von Veltheim, from an old Prussian noble family of the sort beginning to call themselves the primeval nobility, died as a result of complications from childbirth in 1807. Five years later, Ludwig married Caroline Heubel, from a middle-class family, whose father was a retired Prussian military horse-care expert, a "master of the stalls." The children of the first marriage, growing

up under the influence of Ludwig's devout mother and his aristocratic
in-laws, all became adherents of the Awakening, and politically conservative; while Caroline's children, Jenny and her younger brother
Edgar, following their parents, were religious rationalists and politically to the left. The distinction between the children was greatest in
Lisette von Veltheim's oldest son, Ferdinand, who combined the religious inclinations of his relatives with a distinct animosity toward his
stepmother. In the decade of the 1850s, following the suppression of the
Revolution of 1848–49, Jenny would be living with Karl and their children as political refugees in London, while her half brother Ferdinand
was the Prussian minister of the interior, known as the strongman of
the government ministry in the age of reaction.

In view of these features of Johann Ludwig von Westphalen's
life, friendly relations between his family and that of Heinrich Marx
during the 1820s and 1830s do not seem quite so unusual, although
the descriptions of their actual nature come not from contemporary
accounts but from Karl Marx's brief reminiscences, told in old age, to
his faithful daughter Eleanor. (Eleanor ensured that there would be
few contemporary accounts by burning most of her parents' love letters after their death; just a few fragments survive.) Karl frequently
related how Johann Ludwig had taken him under his wing as a boy
and teenager, strolling together, and introducing him to the works of
Shakespeare, the beginning of a lifelong passion. This admiration for
his future father-in-law is often mentioned; less frequently noted is
that Jenny von Westphalen knew, liked, and admired Heinrich Marx.
Indeed, one of the more interesting emotional contours of Karl and
Jenny's relationship was their respect and affection for each other's
fathers. As in many other aspects of Karl's emotional life, his mother
was left out. Heinrich's awkward and foreign wife Henriette did not
get along with the Westphalens, and they did not care for her either.[12]

In spite of the developing feelings between him and Jenny, throughout the engagement Karl remained the anxious, insecure lover, voic-

ing repeated doubts about Jenny's fidelity, almost getting into a duel over aspersions cast on it, and complaining that she did not write to him. The writing was important because in the five years following their engagement, from the summer of 1836, before Karl went off to the University of Berlin, to the summer of 1841, when he returned to the Rhineland after receiving his doctorate, the young lovers were physically together in the same city exactly once—and during that meeting they had a terrible fight and nearly broke up. Their relationship was almost entirely epistolary, and at times not even that, existing only in their imaginations.[13]

Yet Jenny stuck with Karl throughout the entire seven years of their engagement. It is commonly asserted that her devotion to a questionable individual in spite of her widely recognized desirability—five years before Karl's proposal, she had even been briefly engaged to a Prussian lieutenant—can only be attributable to true love. This, too, is part of the fairy-tale story, and is about as accurate as that of the Westphalens' social superiority to the Marxes. The assertions that Jenny was the prettiest girl in the city and queen of the ball, to say nothing of an enchanted princess, came from her husband, thirty years after the fact, when he was trying to cheer her up after a scary episode of smallpox that had brought her close to death and left her face scarred. Jenny was certainly an attractive young woman, known for her vivacity and social graces, although in Karl's company she tended to fall into an awkward silence.[14]

One feature of Jenny's situation is usually overlooked in most accounts of her relationship to Karl; it is documented in a single line of her father's state confidential personnel dossier, maintained on him, as on all Prussian state officials: "[He has] no fortune." Johann Ludwig von Westphalen had run through his entire share of his family's money in the first decade of the nineteenth century, trying, unsuccessfully, to be an estate owner, gentleman farmer, and real estate speculator. After that debacle, he and his family were entirely dependent on his salary as a state official, and following his retirement in 1834 on a modest pension—a sum only three quarters of Heinrich Marx's yearly earnings. Jenny would not have had a substantial dowry and so would not have been able to make a brilliant match. Out of the question was a young man even from the elite, such as it was, of Trier—a city she despised as petty, backward, and clerical, the "site of complaint, the old nest of those rotten priests, with its miniature humanity." There was the option of her previous fiancé, from the very lowest rank of the officer corps, and apparently also rather a bore.[15]

Karl Marx was a questionable choice, with problematic future prospects, but he did have an exciting side, one that pointed to adventurous prospects beyond narrow and provincial Trier, and so might not have looked so bad compared to other possibilities. Such a calculating attitude might seem incompatible with the strong romantic feelings the young lovers articulated, but Jenny herself, "entirely a person of reason and understanding" as she was, "frequently remind[ed] you [Karl] of external things, of life in reality, instead . . . of forgetting all else in the world of love and finding consolation and blessedness in it."[16]

These practical matters were very much on the minds of the two lovers' parents, and their reactions point to the truly unusual, strongly rebellious feature of the young couple's relationship. Karl was just eighteen at the time. He had no means of supporting his future bride—and would be facing a good decade without any income before he might even begin to be in a position to do so. Contemporaries strongly believed that young men from middle-class families should not even think of getting married until they had a position enabling them to support a family. There was nothing peculiar about women from backgrounds similar to Jenny's getting married at a young age, but they were expected to marry an older man, with better and more settled prospects. Karl's and Jenny's parents certainly fit that pattern, as Heinrich Marx and Johann Ludwig von Westphalen each had a good decade on their spouses. A man marrying a woman older than him—Karl was four years younger than Jenny—was scandalous; it violated accepted norms of masculinity and of relations between the sexes. Long before he formulated his communist theories, or absorbed the radical, atheist ideas of the Young Hegelians, Karl Marx's marriage proposal was his first rebellion against nineteenth century bourgeois society.[17]

Like many rebellions, this one had its moments of hesitation. Karl himself was painfully aware of the unusual difference in ages; his insecurity in the relationship and fears of Jenny's infidelity stemmed from the suspicion that Jenny, using the reason and understanding she eminently possessed, would perceive his unsuitability—in spite of the romantic storm of feelings he could express, and, on good days, conjure up in her. The ever practical Jenny understood the difficulties Karl's prospects posed for their engagement. A letter from her reminding him of this, unfortunately not preserved, made a strong impression on Karl, leaving him close to a nervous breakdown.

At first, only Karl's parents knew of the engagement. Heinrich was supportive of the young couple, even acting as a go-between while his son was in Berlin. Henriette, if not actually opposing the relationship, seems to have been more skeptical. These attitudes were, perhaps, a reflection of their own practical, arranged marriage, with Heinrich regretting the absence, in his own life, of his son's youthful impetuousness and romantic attitude, and Henriette rather less impressed, especially as they involved a connection to a family that did not much care for her. Jenny was reluctant to let her parents in on the news, but that reluctance was uncalled for. Once informed, they were delighted; her father, in particular, was very enthusiastic about her choice of his protégé, claiming he was "unspeakably happy" over her engagement to "such an excellent, noble and extraordinary" young man.

For all his enthusiasm, Johann Heinrich saw Karl's marriage with Jenny as taking place years in the future, when his prospective son-in-law had acquired a steady position and could support his daughter in the style to which she had become accustomed. He made all these observations about Marx in a letter to Jenny's half brother Ferdinand, who, along with other relatives of her father's first wife, was far from unspeakably happy about her unconventional choice of a younger man with at best unclear career prospects. It is often speculated that Karl's Jewish background played a role in this skepticism, but conservative German Evangelicals were by no means opposed to Jews who, like Karl, had converted to Christianity. One of their main leaders, Friedrich Julius Stahl, was just such a converted Jew. But the relatives' continuous opposition would make Jenny's life difficult throughout the course of the engagement.[18]

WHEN KARL BEGAN HIS studies at the University of Berlin in the fall of 1836, his engagement only intensified the difficulties already inherent in his choice of a career. If he really were to marry Jenny, he would need a secure position as soon as possible. His father did not let him forget the circumstances, reminding him that "for the man [there is] no more sacred duty than the one he has taken up toward the weaker sex," that "The certainty must proceed out from you that in spite of your youth, you are a man who deserves the esteem of the world, who will conquer that esteem by charging ahead. . . ." Heinrich's letters to his son always posed the dilemmas raised by Karl and Jenny's engagement as a question of Karl's manhood.[19]

Karl's actions, though, showed little in the way of manly charging ahead, or even proceeding at a plodding pace toward a legal career. While the carousing and brawling that filled much of his year in Bonn were gone, as his father had hoped, Marx found other diversions from the juridical straight and narrow. Distracted by Berlin's lively cultural scene, he developed strong literary interests, spending a substantial portion of his first semester at the university writing a "Book of Love," a collection of romantic poetry, which he sent off to Jenny. He attempted to write a play and a satirical novel, then theatrical criticism, and made some—not very successful—efforts to start the publication of a yearbook on that topic. Of these youthful writings, at least the ones that have been preserved (Karl burned a number of them in well-justified dissatisfaction), the less said the better. One useful point could be made: that the poems dedicated to Jenny were not just romantic but Romantic—characterized by strong individualized expressions of longing and passion, and a deep communion with nature. For most of his life, Marx despised Romanticism, both for political and aesthetic reasons. He would later write off his Romantic poetry as a youthful embarrassment, but it does show how much his love for Jenny had affected his view of the world.[20]

The greatest diversion from the path to a legal career was Marx's encounter with the ideas of the philosopher Georg Wilhelm Friedrich Hegel—in its own way as intoxicating as the beer Marx consumed in Bonn and as emotionally stimulating as his love for Jenny von Westphalen. Hegel's ideas are notoriously complex and convoluted; an adequate account would require (at least) a whole book, so readers will forgive the summary sketch that follows, picking up on those aspects of the philosopher's thought that would set the stage for Marx's own ideas.[21]

The starting point for Hegel's philosophy was his criticism of and expansion on the ideas of the eighteenth-century German philosopher Immanuel Kant. These two greatest figures of German idealism were both lifelong bachelors, married as it were to the ethereal world of philosophy. They were personally quite different, Kant withdrawn and austere, Hegel active and sociable. Hegel had difficulty in 1806 concluding his *Phenomenology of Spirit* because of the impending birth of an illegitimate child he had fathered on a barmaid. Intellectually as well, Kant's austere and stringent reasoning contrasted with Hegel's complex and baroque philosophical formulations.

Enormously impressed with the Enlightenment epistemology of empiricism, the intellectual understanding that valid knowledge about the world can only be obtained through sense perception, Kant wondered what guarantee there was that our sensory perceptions offered a valid knowledge of the objects of these perceptions, the "things in themselves," as he said. He concluded that there was no guarantee, that we could not know things in themselves, but that we could investigate the nature and shaping of our perceptual apparatus and thus obtain a certain form of knowledge about it, separate from perceptions, the celebrated synthetic a priori judgments.

Hegel certainly agreed with Kant's observations on the limits of empiricism, but felt that they did not go far enough. Why assume that there was only one, static form of perceptual shaping, and that such a shaping was independent of the object of our perceptions? Rather, Hegel understood the shaping of perceptions and the object of perceptions as interactive or "dialectical"—a word Marx himself would employ to characterize his own views, although less frequently than his followers did. In Hegel's way of thinking, the perceiving subject would interact with the object of perception so as eventually to undermine the shape and frame of the subject's perceptions, usually because the interaction would lead to a self-contradiction in the framework of perception. This self-contradiction would bring forth a new frame, and then this interactive process would repeat all over again, resulting in yet another perceptual framework. The result of this process of repeated interaction between a thinking subject's frame of perceptions and object of perceptions, Hegel asserted, was that the subject would eventually come to recognize the object of its perceptions, which had formerly been seen as alien and other—as "externalized" or "alienated" from itself (Hegelian concepts that would play a large role in Marx's thinking)—as a part of, in fact, a product of itself. A subject's consciousness of objects outside itself would ultimately be transformed into an expanded version of self-consciousness. Another, integrally related result of this process was that the individual perceiving subject would come to understand its self-consciousness as part of a cosmic, collective subject, developing throughout human history, and also coming to self-consciousness, which Hegel called Absolute Spirit or Mind.

There are two ramifications of this philosophical theory relevant to understanding its use by Hegel's successors, including Marx. One is that Hegel saw philosophy as an imperialist branch of knowledge, incorporating all others, its methods and conclusions being reproduced in these other forms of knowledge and also affirming them. The intellectual process of the development of forms of perception, from initial, unreflective perceptions to Absolute Knowledge, the self-knowledge of the Absolute Spirit, occurred within human history. Forms of logical development were paralleled in a similar way in the physics of the natural world, or in the understanding of law, politics, and government. Wherever Hegel looked at a systematic, organized body of knowledge, what the Germans call *Wissenschaft*, he saw his philosophical theory. In this understanding, he was remarkably successful and influential. In the period of Hegel's greatest influence, the second quarter of the nineteenth century, a substantial proportion of German scholarship—not just in philosophy but in history, legal and political theory, art history, linguistics, Orientalism, and, perhaps especially, theology—used Hegelian forms of reasoning.

A second point, following from the previous one, was Hegel's understanding of his philosophical system as self-proving. If Hegel could represent his philosophy as the culmination of the systematic development throughout history of the highest forms of human intellect in philosophical reasoning, then this proved that his philosophy was the culmination of all previous philosophical reasoning. Self-consciousness became the highest form of proof for Hegel and his followers.

Although this whole line of reasoning may seem today arcane, vague, and terribly abstract, to contemporaries it packed a powerful punch. Not only guidelines for academic research and writing, Hegel's ideas became almost a religious cult. Young men from a rationalist background in particular, for whom the doctrines of organized religion had lost their emotional impact, were strongly attracted to Hegel's ideas, undergoing a conversion experience, almost ecstatically rejoicing in their self-understanding as part of Absolute Spirit. One of Hegel's students, Wilhelm Vatke, wrote to his brother about his embrace of Hegel's ideas: "You will think I am insane when I tell you that I see God face to face, but it is true. The transcendent has become immanent, man himself is a point of light in the infinite light and like recognizes like. . . . Oh, if I could only describe to you how blessed I am."[22]

Such effusions were not Marx's style, but the letter he wrote his father in November 1837, the only one preserved from his time at the University of Berlin, shows him as another worshipper of the cult of Hegel.[23] It began with a blast of Hegelian rhetoric:

> There are moments in life placed like boundary markers in front of an era that has run out, but simultaneously point definitively in a new direction.
>
> In such a transitional point, we feel ourselves compelled to observe the past and present with the eagle eye of thought and so to obtain consciousness of our genuine position. Indeed, world history itself loves such retrospectives and perceives itself, which often stamps it with the semblance of retrogression and stagnation, while it is actually just throwing itself into an armchair to comprehend itself, to work through and encompass spiritually its own deed, the deed of Spirit.

Already, in this introduction, Marx, in good Hegelian fashion, identified himself with the world-historical deed of Spirit achieving consciousness of itself. More practically, he informed his father of his intellectual development, during his first year at the University of Berlin, and of his efforts to write a philosophy of law based on the ideas of Kant. But, Marx explained, reiterating Hegel's critique of Kant, his efforts failed, because they assumed that perception and analysis were independent of the object, "where the subject runs around the object . . . [posing] arbitrary categorizations," whereas, as Hegel would find appropriate, "the reason of the thing itself must as self-contradictory move onwards and find its unity in itself." Marx then described his introduction to Hegelianism: "A curtain had fallen, my most sacred [*sic*] had been torn apart, and new gods had to be inserted. . . ." Becoming acquainted with Hegel "from beginning to end . . . ever more firmly, I chained myself to the current world philosophy. . . ." After receiving this inspiration, Marx "ran like mad in the garden on the filthy water of the Spree . . . ran to Berlin and wanted to embrace every day laborer standing on street corners." He ended his letter, in exalted literary fashion, by explaining that he had been writing for hours, it was 4 a.m., and his candle had burnt down to the end.

Having bared his soul to his father, Karl was probably not expecting the savage and hostile response he received to this letter, which initiated a period of crisis in his life. Heinrich was in no mood when he sat down on December 9, to let his son know what he thought of his new Hegelian beliefs. What angered him was not his son's interest in philosophy or literature in place of jurisprudence, or the hints that a scholarly rather than a juridical career might be in the offing. Karl, in his long letter to his father, had been careful to preserve his options, and remained, for all his years at the University of Berlin, formally enrolled in the faculty of law. Nor was Heinrich averse to a possible change in his son's career. He had welcomed Karl's literary interests, wondering if they might enable him to advance more quickly than other aspiring jurists (as he would need to, in view of his engagement to Jenny), suggesting that Karl write an ode in honor of Prussia for the anniversary of the Battle of Waterloo. Heinrich had even been open to the idea of his son aspiring to an academic position.[24]

Rather, it was the touchy issue of his son's lack of progress toward an appropriate manhood that put his father into a rage. Karl had "taken on an obligation possibly beyond his years, but for that reason all the more sacred to sacrifice himself for the well-being of a girl who . . . had made a great sacrifice . . . of her prospects . . . chained herself to the destiny of a younger man." Yet what had he done? In Bonn, he had been the "wild ringleader of wild lads," but his record in Berlin was worse. "Disorderliness, dull floating around in all areas of knowledge, dull meditation in front of a darkling oil lamp; running wild in the scholars' night-gown and with uncombed hair, instead of running wild with glasses of beer. . . . And here, in this workshop of senseless and purposeless learnedness, this is where the crop will ripen, that will nourish you and your beloved, the harvest will be gathered that will serve to fulfill your sacred obligations?"

In this letter, for the first time, Heinrich sharply criticized Karl's financial acumen, condemning him not just for poor bookkeeping but for excessive spending. Yet even here, the criticism was not so much for Karl's wasting money as for his lack of order and progress:

> As if we were little men made of gold, the Herr son, against all agreements, against all custom, disposes of 700 talers in one year, while the richest cannot even spend 500. And why? I'll be fair; he's no wastrel, no spendthrift. But how can a man who every week or two invents new [philosophical] systems, and must tear up the old, laboriously created works, how can he descend to petty matters? How can he subordinate himself to petty order? Everyone has his hand in his pocket, and everyone cheats him . . . but a new money order is once again soon written.

Finally, Heinrich formulated his indictment: his son was squandering his talents, deploying his intellect in useless ways rather than forwarding his career. "My clever, talented Karl" was busy spending sleepless nights in his room, inventing and rejecting philosophical theories, "hunt[ing] up the shadow of learnedness." He was not attending

lectures or sitting for exams. Nor was he following his father's advice
to pay visits to influential, well-connected individuals who would help
him in his career. In short, Karl was wasting the family's commitment
to him, wasting its resources, failing to take the proper path to manhood. Heinrich concluded by ordering his son to come home for the
Easter vacation in 1838, in effect demanding that he would then have
to put matters in order. Heinrich had admitted at the start of his letter
that his bad mood was in part the product of a constant and unshak-
able cough, with which he had been plagued for nearly a year. That
summer he had been to Bad Ems, to take the waters, but they brought
him no relief. Neither Heinrich nor his doctors, who thought his cough
came from gout, knew it, but the tuberculosis that would kill him had
reached its final stages. A month after writing this letter, he had to take
to his bed, which he would never leave.[25]

Karl did travel to Trier during the Easter recess in 1838, the one
time in his four years at the University of Berlin that he returned home.
While deeply Catholic Trier was celebrating Christ's tormented death
and glorious resurrection, the Marx family was stuck in the phase of
torment. The visit must have been very difficult for Karl, verging on
the nightmarish. The father whom he loved and respected, for all their
differing views, lay on his deathbed. Meeting Jenny, after a year and a
half of separation brought no relief, but instead made Karl's emotional
situation worse. Under the pressure, Karl and Jenny had an angry
fight, in the course of which he called her a "crude, common girl," and
threatened to denounce her to her brother Edgar, then Karl's fellow
student in Berlin. Realizing that he was about to destroy the ties to the
woman he loved, and whose emotional support he needed even more
now, Karl apologized in time to avoid the worst. But his angry outburst
nourished Jenny's fears of what might happen if his passionate attachment to her were to grow cold, and left the future of their relationship
in doubt. After this disastrous visit, Karl left Trier on May 7, 1838;

his father died three days later. Only after Karl was back in Berlin did he receive the news of his father's death, which affected him deeply, as Edgar von Westphalen reported in a letter to Henriette Marx.[26]

A number of Marx's biographers have suggested that Marx himself was ill with tuberculosis at the time, citing the result of an 1841 draft physical that found him unfit for military service because of "repeated spitting of blood." [27] If this were so, he would not have lived another four decades. The spitting of blood might have been the result of a bad case of pneumonia or bronchitis—or might not have existed at all. Both Heinrich and Henriette had arranged for a private physician's report for the Prussian military authorities, for the purpose of emphasizing their son's physical ailments. This desire to shield a son from the army was not at all uncommon among the German upper middle class of the time; the newer ideal of serving as a young man's patriotic duty was still making slow headway, particularly among the reluctant Rhenish subjects of Prussia's monarchy. Writing an ode in honor of Prussia's military glory, as Heinrich suggested Karl do, was one thing; actually contributing to it was rather another.[28]

If Karl's physical health was not affected by his father's death, his future plans and aspirations certainly were. All of the careers he envisaged presupposed a healthy father with a substantial income, a good portion of which he could expend supporting his son for years. Now the possibility of that support was gone. The Marx family still enjoyed a reasonable affluence from the property it owned, primarily from Henriette's dowry and inheritance. A decade after her husband's death, and after outfitting three daughters with dowries, Henriette still received the eminently respectable income of 1,200 talers a year.[29] But this sum would not support Henriette and her other children and simultaneously keep Karl in the fashion to which he had become accustomed. As a result, Karl's thoughts turned toward his inheritance, his share in his father's estate.

Karl was still a minor when his father died, but the Napoleonic

Code (to the considerable anger of later nineteenth-century feminists) did not recognize widows as the guardians of their own children. So Karl received a court-appointed guardian, one of Heinrich Marx's colleagues, the Trier attorney Johann Heinrich Schlink. He had the difficult task of mediating between the son, pressing for his inheritance, and the widow, reluctant to make expenditures. Schlink was an admirable guardian, even traveling to Berlin to meet Karl personally and hear his complaints. It was very likely Schlink's mediation that brought about an interim settlement. Karl received from Henriette 160 talers in 1838, supposedly to cover the costs of his obtaining his doctorate, and she lent him a further 950 talers against his share of his father's estate and as an advance against his share of her estate, upon her eventual death.[30]

There was nothing particularly unusual about disagreements between widows and their children over an estate, or about the interim settlement Henriette reached with Karl. Both were features of nineteenth-century family property arrangements under the Napoleonic Code. But in this particular case, the circumstances of Marx's engagement and the relationship between the Marx and Westphalen families brought an additional element of emotion and rancor into the situation. As an argument for the interim settlement, Karl let his mother know, via his guardian, that without the necessary funds he would be unable to finish his studies, and Jenny would have no choice but to reject him. Lending money to her son meant that Henriette had to continue her connection with the Westphalens, who had quite pointedly snubbed her after her husband's death, refusing to pay a condolence call, and not receiving Karl Marx's brother Hermann, when he came to pay a call on them: ". . . you will never make the moral sacrifice for my family as we have all made for you . . . you can never replace what we have all tolerated and suffered for you," Henriette told Karl.[31]

Karl did succeed in obtaining enough money to pay for the rest of his Berlin studies, albeit at the cost of increasing tension with his mother. Although his circumstances were more straitened after his father's death, his previous disorganized and careless life continued. On several different occasions between 1838 and 1840, he ran up a tab with a tailor, a dry-goods merchant, and a book dealer, and was unable or unwilling to settle. The frustrated creditors were still trying to collect via the university's student disciplinary system after Marx had left Berlin.[32]

All these measures were interim solutions to his financial problems, predicated on the assumption that he would eventually have a secure, well-paying position. Partly as a result of general economic trends, but mostly because of Marx's intellectual and political radicalism, this position would never materialize, so that the interim measures of the years 1838 to 1841 became the rule over the following quarter century. He would continue to try to make up for his lack of income by borrowing money from his mother or her family; he quarreled with them over his inheritance; he filled in the gaps with an irregular income from writing, and miscellaneous funds from anyone who would lend him the money, or give it to him outright.

Naturally, in 1838 Karl could not foresee these long-term consequences. In the shorter term, though, he went through a period of personal realignment and drift, as he came to terms with the emotional and economic impact of his father's death. He stopped attending lectures in the faculty of law and gradually gave up plans for a juridical career. For at least part of 1839, he was preoccupied with defending his and Jenny's honor, preparing for a duel with a Berlin acquaintance, possibly Werner von Weltheim, Jenny's stepcousin, who had taunted Karl about Jenny's brief first engagement. It took the combined efforts of Jenny, her brother Edgar, and Eduard von Krosigk, the cousin of Weltheim's fiancée, to call it off before the two young men met with pistols at twenty paces.[33]

Gradually, Marx managed to place his life on a new footing. Thinking of an academic career, he started to work, at first in somewhat desultory fashion, on preparing a doctoral dissertation that would apply Hegel's methods to the study of ancient philosophy. As he immersed himself in the writings of ancient Greek philosophers, the ecstatic and awe-inspiring feelings that the system of Hegel's thought had imbued in him began to fade against the much more difficult task of choosing a dissertation topic and applying to scattered texts Hegel's concepts of philosophical development. Strongly influencing these efforts were the individuals who introduced him to Hegelian philosophy.

Unlike some of his slightly older contemporaries, Marx could not experience Hegel personally, because the philosopher had died in the cholera epidemic of 1831. But in the thirteen years before his death when he taught at the University of Berlin, Hegel had founded a school and recruited a body of disciples, particularly numerous in Berlin itself, but in other parts of Germany as well. It was these disciples who initiated Marx into the mysteries of the master's ideas.

One important, and generally somewhat underrated, influence on Marx was a Berlin professor of legal history, Eduard Gans. With a personal background containing similarities to Heinrich Marx— he had converted from Judaism to Protestantism to be eligible for a professorship—Gans was a riveting public speaker, who filled the university lecture halls not just with students but with educated members of the general public. He reinterpreted Hegel's views of legal and political developments a bit to the left, openly espousing constitutionally guaranteed civil liberties and parliamentary government, points about which the master himself had been studiedly vague. Unlike most central European intellectuals, Gans had good personal and intellectual connections in France, including a friendship with Alexis de Tocqueville, the celebrated liberal intellectual, best known today for his penetrating analysis of the practice of democracy in the young North American Republic. Gans was also one of the first Germans to take note of the Saint-Simonians, the early French socialists, who developed the ideas of collective instead of private ownership of industry and economic planning in place of the free market. He shared their concerns about the conditions of artisans and the nascent working class, although he rejected both their socialist ideas and Hegel's notions about reviving the guild system, advocating instead workers' production cooperatives.

Marx attended Gans's lectures, and the professor noted the industriousness with which he did so. The ideas expressed there clearly made an impression on the young Marx, and a number of passages in the *Communist Manifesto* would be taken, almost verbatim, from Gans's writing. Gans was a mentor and adviser in the making; had he not died of a stroke in 1839 at the age of forty-two, Marx's life might have taken a quite different path.[34]

Instead, the major intellectual influence on Marx as well as the personal connections that would shape his post-university plans came from a loosely knit group of philosophers, theologians, and freelance intellectuals, contemporaries called the Young Hegelians.[35] In part connected to the university, but also a substantial element of the broader cultural scene in Berlin, these Young Hegelians combined deeply earnest intellectual speculation with a raucous and bohemian lifestyle, in a way that proved very attractive to Marx, and one that would draw him into a radical political stance. The youth of these Young Hegelians was at least as much a political and ideological reference as a chronological one. The term "Young" came into the European political vocabulary following the French Revolution of 1830, and it referred to a generational transition, as political radicalism and the individuals who supported it went from nostalgic reminiscences of the great days of the French Revolution of 1789 to forward-looking aspirations for change. The pioneering example of this transition was the secret society "Young Italy," founded by the Italian revolutionary Giuseppe Mazzini, the most prominent leader of democratic and republican radicalism, not just on the Italian Peninsula but across the entire Continent. Closer to home in central Europe was the literary movement "Young Germany," whose best-known member was the poet Heinrich Heine (both Heine and Mazzini would play roles in Marx's life), and whose socially critical literature was officially prohibited in 1835 by the new German Confederation. This central European league of states was created by the Congress of Vienna in 1815, ending the wars of Napoleon, and destroyed in 1866 as a result of the wars of German unification, ultimately resulting in a Prussian-dominated German Empire.[36]

The radicalism of the Young Hegelians emerged from Hegel's program of applying the methods and conclusions of his philosophy to every *Wissenschaft*, when they did so for a *Wissenschaft* central to German academic life: Protestant theology. Hegel had begun this enterprise, but with ambivalent results. Hegelian theology could be seen as a version of religious orthodoxy. The stage of development in which spirit perceived the object as its other could be related to the Old Testament God separate and distinct from humanity, while spirit perceiving its object as a form of self-consciousness and itself as part of Absolute Spirit would correspond to the Christian idea of the Trinity. There were other aspects of Hegel's thought that were rather more heterodox. His assertion that humanity's consciousness of God was God's self-consciousness, or his contention that God was nothing without His creation, sounded suspiciously pantheistic, going against the understanding, particularly important to Germany's born-again Protestants, of a personal God. Hegel's integration of theology into philosophy also raised Pietists' suspicions, when Hegel stated that philosophy asserted the conceptually grasped truth of what in religion was belief and representation. For Christians, to whom a personally felt belief was central to their faith, and certainly more important than human reason, this was another potentially subversive idea.

The Young Hegelians actualized the subversive potential of Hegelian theology by synthesizing rationalist ideas that had been developing among German Protestants since the eighteenth century, particularly the scholarly investigations today called the Higher Criticism of the

Bible: the investigation of the Old and New Testaments as historical documents, and the attempt to ascertain in them which is an empirically correct representation of events and lives in ancient Palestine, and which is a later accretion or mythological account. The first Young Hegelian to make theological waves was David Friedrich Strauss, from the University of Tübingen, a onetime Protestant pastor, who had gone to Berlin to further his theological studies by taking classes from Hegel and his students. Strauss's *Life of Jesus Theologically Examined* (1835) asserted that the Gospel stories of Jesus's life and death were not empirical accounts but mythical projections of the hopes, beliefs, and expectations of Jews in Roman Palestine, an externalization and alienation of their group self-consciousness. This academic tome went off like the proverbial bombshell in the life of the educated public, provoking angry denunciations from the orthodox, and fervent accolades from its enthusiasts.[37]

Strauss's initial insights were, in eminently Hegelian fashion, developed further and also contradicted by a University of Berlin lecturer in theology, Bruno Bauer. In his *Critique of the Gospel of St. John* (1840) and his *Critique of the Synoptic Gospels* (1841), Bauer asserted that Strauss's description of Christian scriptures as the externalization, in mythical form, of group consciousness overlooked the importance of religious self-consciousness. The authors of the Gospel accounts took up and transformed myth into an expression of human self-consciousness. The final Young Hegelian salvo came from the Bavarian philosopher and theologian Ludwig Feuerbach, whose *Essence of Christianity* (1841) generalized Strauss's and Bauer's insights. For Feuerbach, all religions, and Christianity in particular, were expressions of the alienated human self-consciousness of itself as a species. The characteristics of a transcendent Divinity, His infinite love, justice, and mercy, for instance, were, according to Feuerbach, the best elements of humanity as a species, attributed—in Hegelian terms externalized and alienated—to a mythical supreme being.

In the space of less than a decade, from the mid-1830s to the mid-1840s, the Young Hegelians were swept along by a wave of intellectual speculation, theological controversy, and political contention that turned them from insiders to outsiders, moderates to radicals, believers to atheists. Marx was just one of many of the Young Hegelian intellectuals caught up in this wave, and it shaped his thought, his actions, and his personal life.

As they began their studies of religion, the Young Hegelians, like the theologians who first developed Higher Criticism, were trying to reinforce and purify their belief, in good Protestant fashion sorting out the originally and authentically Christian text in the biblical message from later additions. The unintended result of their scholarship and its literary expression was to undermine faith altogether, so that by the early 1840s many of the Young Hegelians had become outright and explicit atheists. Yet their atheism usually had a religious edge, since it involved transferring the sense of the transcendent from God to humanity. Ludwig Feuerbach's description of his ideals as "anthropotheism," or his statement that "My religion is no religion," exemplify the piety of the Young Hegelians' godlessness.[38]

The Young Hegelians' political path paralleled their religious one. Not only did they originally see their ideas as reinforcing Protestant piety, but also, at least for the Prussians among them, as supporting the monarchy, and articulating its best traditions and ideals. Arnold Ruge, a University of Halle lecturer in education, who was the organizational mastermind of the Young Hegelians and editor of their journal, the *Halle Yearbooks*, stated that "Prussia is the Protestant state and its principle is light and scholarship."[39]

This connection between Prussia, Protestantism, religious rationalism, and the Enlightenment is reminiscent of the intellectual nexus surrounding Heinrich Marx's conversion to Protestantism, and the spirit in which the young Karl Marx was raised. Like Heinrich, the Young Hegelians had good reasons for affirming the connection. While assertions that Hegelianism was the official philosophy of the Prussian state are rather exaggerated, it is true that Prussia's longtime minister of religious and educational affairs, Karl von Altenstein, was impressed with Hegelian ideas and a bureaucratic patron of those who asserted them. In many ways a hangover from the era of liberal reforms in Prussia at the beginning of the nineteenth century, Altenstein's influence had been waning in the 1830s, and any protection he could offer the Young Hegelians ceased with his death in 1840. That was also the year that the new monarch, Friedrich Wilhelm IV, a strong supporter of the Awakening, came to the throne. As a result, the Prussian government's educational and cultural policies turned steadily against the ideas of Hegel and their proponents. The Young Hegelians responded by moving to the left, collaborating with the liberal opposition in Prussia, and increasingly advocating democratic and republican ideas.[40]

Both political and religious developments converged in changing, much for the worse, the prospects of the Young Hegelians. They aspired to professorships at German universities, and a number of them—including Ruge, Bauer, and Feuerbach—had taken the first step on the academic ladder, obtaining positions as lecturers. The concurrent radicalization of their thinking and the increasing conservatism of government policy doomed their aspirations: there was no place in mid-nineteenth-century German universities for atheists or democrats. Not a single Young Hegelian would obtain a university position; they would be forced into careers as freelance writers, journalists, and other financially uncertain occupations. Some found their way into artistic and bohemian circles; others became left-wing political activists, and, following the failure of the 1848 Revolution, spent the rest of their lives in exile. The Young Hegelians, and Marx in his own unique way among them, became a lost generation of German intellectual life.[41]

The Young Hegelian usually seen as the most important influence on Karl Marx is Ludwig Feuerbach. Even people with only the vaguest knowledge of Marx's life and ideas have heard of his "Theses on

Feuerbach," especially the celebrated eleventh and final thesis: "Philosophers have hitherto only interpreted the world; the point is to change it." These theses were part of the enormous mass of notes and comments that Marx made on his many different readings. During his lifetime, he never attempted to publish the theses, or make them known to a wider public. They only appeared in print after his death, when Friedrich Engels, acting as Marx's literary executor, found them among his very extensive papers. Although Marx certainly had read and appreciated the writings of Feuerbach, the two men never met personally or collaborated on any intellectual or political projects. Indeed, Feuerbach explicitly rejected Marx's efforts to initiate a collaboration.[42]

A more important but often neglected influence on Marx was another of the Young Hegelians, Bruno Bauer. This is not completely surprising because, in contrast to the saintly Feuerbach, Bauer was an unsavory character. Contemporaries saw him as an intellectual opportunist. He began his intellectual and scholarly career as a conservative Hegelian, a vehement critic of David Friedrich Strauss and the author of a book on the Old Testament asserting the reconciliation of Hegelian philosophy and religious orthodoxy. Within a few years, Bauer had swung far to the left, turning into the most radical of the Young Hegelians, an open atheist and advocate of republicanism. Bauer also had the reputation of being a nasty individual—Strauss never forgave his initial, very hostile polemics, even after Bauer had come around to his point of view—and arrogant and self-centered to boot. His intellectual and political development after the end of the Hegelian era has done little to enhance his reputation: in the 1850s and 1860s, he became a conservative and an increasingly vehement anti-Semite, one of the founders of racial anti-Semitism in central Europe.[43]

There is a lot of dispute about the exact extent of Bauer's intellectual influence on Marx, but the close personal relations between the two, and Bauer's role in bringing Marx into the social network of the Young Hegelians, is beyond doubt. Marx first encountered the Young

Hegelians during the summer of 1837, when he became a member of the Doctors' Club, a group of Berlin Hegelians whose leading member was, as Marx informed his father, the "lecturer Dr. Bauer." Marx's partner in his proposed yearbook of theatrical criticism was Bauer's brother-in-law, Adolf Rutenberg. At social events of the group, Marx and Bauer were often seen off to one side, discussing philosophical questions. Marx was a frequent visitor at the home of Bauer and his brother Edgar, another member of the group of Berlin Young Hegelians; and one of only two classes Marx took at the University of Berlin after he gave up his legal studies was a course Bauer offered on the Hebrew prophet Isaiah.

One of the last official acts in favor of the Young Hegelians by the friendly minister of religious and educational affairs von Altenstein was to offer Bauer in 1839 a position as lecturer in Protestant theology at the University of Bonn, an institution where Bauer's prospects for a professorship seemed better than in Berlin. After Bauer left for Bonn, he and Marx engaged in an extended correspondence. (Unfortunately, Marx's side of the correspondence has not survived.) Bauer began making plans for Marx to come and join him in Bonn, encouraging him to finish his dissertation, informing him of the Bonn University regulations concerning eligibility for a lectureship, even suggesting some classes that Marx could teach. Contemporaries saw Marx as Bauer's protégé, which he was.[44]

But before Marx could join Bauer in Bonn, he would have to conclude work on his doctoral dissertation. The thesis he wrote—placed in today's academic cubbyholes, it would belong to the history of philosophy—was a comparison of the theories of nature found in the writings of the Greek philosophers Democritus and Epicurus.[45] Without going into a lengthy exposition of the dissertation, we can see in it the state of Marx's personal and intellectual development at the end of his university studies.

One aspect of the thesis was decidedly academic. Marx's dissertation was revisionist; in it, he attempted to develop a new and different interpretation, and to overturn long-established scholarly opinions, certainly the attitude expected from an iconoclastic Young Hegelian. Scholarly opinion had argued that the post-Aristotelian Greek philosophers were epigones, disciples with little of significance to say, and that the atomistic theories of Epicurus were just an inferior restatement of the original ideas of the earlier philosopher Democritus. Marx set out to prove the opposite, to show that Epicurus' atomism was original, and more significant and profound than the initial work of Democritus.

His procedure was eminently Hegelian. Arguing that the ideas of Epicurus represented an advance in the process of human intellectual development and human self-consciousness, Marx concluded:

> For Epicurus, atomism is thus, with all its contradictions, the natural science of a self-consciousness that, in the form of abstract individuality, is absolute principle. This science is implemented and perfected to its highest consequence, which is its dissolution and conscious contrast to the universal. For Democritus, by contrast, the atom is only the universal objective expression of empirical research into nature. The atom remains for him thus a pure and abstract category, a hypothesis that is the result of experience and not an energetic principle, and so thus both remains without realization and does not further determine the course of empirical natural research.[46]

The Hegelian point Marx was making (the unclear and awkward language, apparent in the original German, is Hegelian too) involved perceiving the philosophical form of the dialectical development of human self-consciousness in past intellectual trends. Epicurus' ideas, for Marx, were a higher stage of thought, since they were closer to the Hegelian understanding of a dialectical movement of self-consciousness, leading to its own contradiction, against Democritus' undialectical conceptions, in which the concepts of the thinking and perceiving subject were used to categorize the object of its perception but had no intrinsic connection to it. This contrast between the two ancient Greek thinkers was not unlike Hegel's critique of Kant, Marx showing himself to be a dutiful pupil of the Hegelian master. More precisely, Marx showed himself to be a true Young Hegelian, a pupil of Hegel as reinterpreted by Marx's teacher and mentor Bruno Bauer, since what evolved in Marx's conclusion was not spirit, as Hegel would have asserted, but human self-consciousness, as Bruno Bauer suggested. It was Bauer, as well, who had described the Greek philosophers of the Hellenistic era as a high point in the dialectical progress of self-consciousness.[47]

Quite another aspect of Marx's situation comes to light in the dedication of the thesis to Marx's "dear paternal friend, Ludwig von Westphalen." This dedication contained a number of flattering passages: "to give you [Westphalen] a small proof of my love"; "to admire an elderly man who possesses the strength of youth"; "a living *argumentum ad oculus* that idealism is no illusion but a truth." It is hard to know what in those remarks was aimed at reinforcing Westphalen's agreement to let Marx marry his daughter, and what reflected Marx's strong admiration for his boyhood mentor—although there is no reason to think that the two motives were in conflict.

The dedication also contained a political and religious/philosophical polemic. Following in the footsteps of Bruno Bauer, Marx praised the way Westphalen "greets every progress of the age with the enthusiasm and sobriety of the truth . . . never draws back from the threatening shadows of the retrograde ghosts, from the often dark and clouded heaven of the times. . . ." "Progress" and "dark" (in German, *finster*; it has the connotation of sinister as well) were code words used by Germany's freethinkers to describe their ideals and the attitudes of their devout enemies. By employing them, Marx was proclaiming his adherence to the freethinkers' ranks, as the Young Hegelians in general did.

In the preface to his thesis, Marx carried his support of freethinking further, articulating it in sharper and more drastic fashion. He asserted that the "confession of philosophy" is the "confession of Prometheus." He cited Prometheus' statement in the original Greek (which, of course, would have been no bar to any educated German's understanding of it), but its translation is "with a word, I hate each and every god." This confession, he reiterated, is also philosophy's, "its own saying against all heavenly and earthly gods, that do not recognize human self-consciousness as the highest divinity. There shall be no god besides it."[48] Here as well, Marx was following Bauer to an increasing radicalization of Young Hegelian thought, from an attempt to purify and justify Protestant theology to a parody of it, as the ironic reference to the Ten Commandments' assertion of monotheism makes clear, from freethinking to atheism.

Having completed his dissertation, Marx needed to submit it. After the death of Eduard Gans and the departure of Bruno Bauer, the University of Berlin had become steadily more hostile to Hegelian thought, especially its freethinking and atheistic Young Hegelian variant. In any event, by the time Marx finished his thesis, he was no longer a student at Berlin: his studies had exceeded the statutory maximum of four years, and he had not applied for an extension, so he was dropped from the university's rolls. Marx chose instead to submit his dissertation to the University of Jena; it was the only German university that required neither a residence period nor a formal defense at which the degree candidate appeared in person, for the acceptance and approval of a dissertation. For those reasons, its fees for granting a doctorate were the lowest.[49] Hostile commentators have sometimes described Marx's doctorate as a mail-order diploma, but this seems rather unfair. Jena was a reputable university, not a diploma mill, to use modern parlance, and the doctoral dissertation that its faculty approved was a work of considerable erudition and scholarship, written by someone with serious aspirations to an academic career. The University of Jena formally granted Marx his doctorate on April 15, 1841.

Doctorate in hand, Marx returned to the Rhineland in June 1841. He had personal business in Germany's western fringes, his long-term engagement to Jenny; family business, the final settlement of Heinrich Marx's estate; and professional and occupational business as well: following Bruno Bauer to the University of Bonn, where he was planning to start his career, once again in Bauer's footsteps, as a philosopher/theologian, or, more precisely, a philosopher/anti-theologian. It would take just a few months of residence in Trier and Bonn for all these plans to be disrupted. Marx's life would take an unexpected turn, leading him forever out of the arena of scholarship and esoteric intellectual inquiry and into a quite different world of polemical journalism and political controversy.

3

The Editor

·◦)▯(◦·

MARX'S RETURN TO HIS native region in 1841, at the age of twenty-three, marked the beginning of his adult life. Personal circumstances and political trends converged in a combination of aspirations denied and hopes fulfilled to make that beginning difficult and precarious. Right after his return, the prospect of an inheritance dissolved, leaving him without assets or income. Just as Marx was trying to gain a toehold in academia, the connection between Hegelian philosophy and the Prussian state was coming to an end, a termination signaled by the dismissal of Bruno Bauer, Marx's mentor, political ally, and close friend, from his post as lecturer at the University of Bonn in March 1842—terminating not just Bauer's academic career but his protégé's as well. Meanwhile, the renewal of personal contact between Marx and his fiancée, after a three-year absence, took a quite propitious turn, only Karl's lack of assets and gainful employment made it difficult to see how he and Jenny could ever get married. Marx did find a way out of this difficult situation: by moving, as most Young Hegelians were, from philosophy to political action, from aspirations for a state-sponsored career to aspirations toward subversion of the Prussian state.

. . .

MEMBERS OF THE FAMILY met with a notary in Trier, on June 23, 1841, to draw up a division of Heinrich Marx's estate, an act spelling the end of Karl's expectations of an inheritance. After carefully totaling up Heinrich's assets, subtracting from them Henriette's dowry and inheritances from her family, and dividing what remained, the "marital community of property" between the widow and her children, each of the surviving children was entitled to a grand sum of 362 talers. Since Marx had already borrowed over 950 talers from his mother, he was not entitled to anything from his father's estate—even assuming that the other costs of his university education were not to be deducted from his share of the inheritance.[1]

Marx described this division of the family's property in bitter terms. "My family, in spite of its affluence, poses difficulties for me, which expose me to the most wretched conditions," he wrote to one fellow Young Hegelian, Arnold Ruge. He would not explain more precisely what these "private crude and disgusting actions" were, but in a subsequent letter to Ruge, he stated that "I have had . . . a falling out with my family, and, as long as my mother lives, I have no right to my fortune."[2] Legally speaking, Marx's grievances had no foundation, and since he had taken a class in inheritance law at the University of Berlin, he would have known that. The division of Heinrich Marx's estate between his widow and their children followed very carefully the provisions of the Napoleonic Code, and Karl's debts outweighed his share of the inheritance. Karl continued to suspect his mother of hiding assets from him, but his sense of grievance, as the second letter to Ruge suggests, was mostly due to his mother's refusal to offer him an advance on the inheritance he would receive after her death. Karl's suspicions and grievances, paired with his mother's determination to hold fast to her dowry and inheritances, and to dole them out to her children in what she saw as equitable fashion, would permanently poison his relations with his mother and his surviving siblings.[3] In 1841, the initial result of the division of Heinrich Marx's estate was that Karl would continue to be dependent on his mother's largesse for support until he could obtain gainful employment.

The path to employment seemed to run through Bruno Bauer and the University of Bonn, and for most of the year following Marx's return to the Rhineland, he lived in that university town and worked on his academic career, preparing his habilitation, the postdoctoral dissertation, required as a prerequisite to a professorship, and designing a lecture course on logic. Bauer was planning to start a new philosophical journal, an *Archives of Atheism*, with Marx as co-editor. Plans were well advanced, contacts with potential publishers initiated, and Young Hegelian circles abuzz with the news of this audacious project. The journal never did get off the ground, but another of Bauer's projects did, a satirical pamphlet entitled *The Trumpet Blast of the Last Judgment Against Hegel the Atheist and Anti-Christ*. Adopting the pose of a born-again Christian, Bauer denounced the great philosopher himself as the source of the Young Hegelians' subversive, godless ideas. Marx was suspected, incorrectly, of being the co-author of the pamphlet. He did work on a sequel Bauer was planning to publish, concerning Hegel and Christian art, a work probably designed as an attack on German Romanticism, which was suffused with admiration for the pious Middle Ages.[4]

This aggressive godlessness was calculated to create a scandal, a favorite intellectual and political tactic of the Young Hegelians.[5] One does have to wonder, as contemporaries did, whether Marx and Bauer's provocations were entirely compatible with their scholarly career plans, whether editing an *Archives of Atheism* was quite the right course of action for an aspiring professor of Protestant theology.[6] Well aware of these issues, Bauer counseled Marx to take a cautious stand. When Marx was still in Berlin finishing his thesis, Bauer told his young supporter to call on top Prussian government officials to plead his case. He warned Marx that he should be careful whom he spoke to in private in Bonn and what he said. Finally, he advised Marx to formulate his dissertation in exclusively scholarly terms, leaving out the aggressively atheistic preface, for it would just give "weapons [to those] who would like to keep you from a professorship for a long time. . . . Just not now! Later, when you have a chair . . . you can say what you want in whatever form you want."[7]

Bauer, though, proved unwilling to heed his own advice. Even as Marx was returning to the Rhineland to work with him at the university, he was burning the bridges connecting him to the Prussian government. Behind Bauer's decision was the change in state policy resulting from the deaths of the long-term minister of education and religious affairs Karl von Altenstein and the monarch, Friedrich Wilhelm III, in 1840. The old king had been willing to tolerate Hegelians at Prussian universities and in Prussian state service, but he had been deeply conservative and authoritarian. At first, the attitudes of his successor, Friedrich Wilhelm IV, were unclear to the public. It seemed possible that he might be more liberal than his predecessor; even the cynical Bauer was willing to suspend judgment. Soon enough, it became clear that Prussia's new ruler was an adherent of the Awakening, a supporter of Romantic cultural ideals, and an enthusiast for the pre-1789 society of orders; none of these attitudes would do followers of Hegel any good. The new minister of religious and educational affairs, Johann Eichhorn, loyally implemented the ideas of his royal master.[8]

This rightward and anti-Hegelian turn of official policy only encouraged Bauer to ratchet up his provocations. He rejected the compromise solutions Eichhorn proposed, such as returning to Berlin to do research in ecclesiastical history on a state stipend, accepting a transfer from the faculty of theology to the philosophical faculty, or even applying for a position as professor of ecclesiastical history. Instead, he sent the minister his history of the Synoptic Gospels with the request that he be appointed a professor of theology. As he wrote to Arnold Ruge, he would only be satisfied "when I have been authorized, as a professor, to preach the system of atheism publicly." Bauer was seeking martyrdom, albeit of an atheistic nature, which he received from the Prussian government when it finally dismissed him from his lectureship in March 1842, although not until the competing bureaucratic and academic memoranda on his case had been leaked to the press, creating an enormous scandal among Germany's educated classes.[9] As a parting shot, Bauer enlisted Marx for a public, atheist provocation. Right around Easter time in 1842, the two went to the nearby village of Godesberg, a favorite excursion site from Bonn, rented donkeys, and galloped through the village on them parodying Jesus's entry into Jerusalem—an incident spread by word of mouth in the vicinity of Bonn, and emphasized a few years later in a book Bauer published about his personal and political struggles.[10]

Bauer then returned to Berlin to press an appeal in his case. His chances of prevailing were slim indeed, but he still seemed to think that he had a legitimate claim on a university position, a viewpoint the authorities found immensely annoying, as Marx was told by Ferdinand von Westphalen, now well launched on his bureaucratic career.[11] The whole long, difficult, and problematic relationship between the Prussian monarchy and Enlightened ideas—a relationship central to Heinrich Marx's career and to his son's aspirations—had come to an end. A radicalized, Young Hegelian, atheistic version of Enlightenment and a Prussian state controlled by devout conservatives with a hankering for the society of orders could not exist harmoniously, but only as sworn enemies.

With Bauer's dismissal and departure for Berlin, Marx was left alone and friendless in Bonn. Finding life there unbearable, he planned a move to nearby Cologne, the Rhineland's largest city, but gave up his plans, ostensibly "because life there is too noisy for me, and one does not get to better philosophy for all the good friends."[12] Yet Marx had spent four and a half years in Berlin, which was four times as large as

Cologne, without noise or good friends being a problem. Other motives were probably at play: the higher cost of living in Cologne and Marx's very limited funds. His private dilemmas and broader political trends had converged in an unpleasant fashion.

AFTER FIVE YEARS OF an epistolary relationship during which Karl and Jenny existed for each other largely in their respective imaginations, the two lovers were reunited in person during 1841–42. They were by no means always together, since most of the time after his return from Berlin Karl was living in Bonn, a two-day journey by steamboat from Trier. Still, he was present for the first six weeks of his return from Berlin and again for six weeks in the winter and spring of 1842, when Jenny's father was dying, as well as for a brief visit that summer. The two had also met earlier in the summer of 1841, when Jenny herself made the trip down the Rhine to visit family friends in Neuß, to the north of Cologne. In a letter Jenny wrote to Karl at the time, she told him that her mother had forbidden her to see him unless she was chaperoned by her brother Edgar, "to preserve outward and inward propriety":

Oh, my little heart, how that fell heavily on my soul, like a hundred-weight! Outward and inward propriety!!—oh, my Karl, my sweet only Karl!

And yet, Karl, I can, I feel no regret, I shut my eyes, firmly, firmly and I see then your blessedly laughing eye—you see, Karl, then, in that thought, I am blessed—to have been everything to you and now nothing more to others. Oh, Karl, I know very well what I have done, and how I would be despised before all the world, I know that all and yet I am joyful and blessed and would not give up the memory of those hours for any treasure in the world. That is the most precious to me, and shall remain so forever. It is only when

I think that I must still live separately from you for so long, once again so totally surrounded by wretchedness and misery, then I shake uncontrollably.[13]

It may be churlish for the historian to wish to uncover a maiden's secrets, but it is difficult to read this passage as anything other than as a description—modest, reticent, full of euphemisms, written, like Karl's poetry, in the Romantic cultural idiom—of the young couple having engaged in sexual relations. There are no details on time and place, and we may suspect that it was a onetime event, or at best repeated very infrequently, since the couple did not have many unchaperoned moments, and Jenny did not become pregnant.

It was still a remarkable step for her to take. Premarital sexual relations were far from unusual in early nineteenth-century Germany, and, in fact, probably on the increase, as the demographic evidence of rising illegitimacy rates and ever more frequent bridal pregnancies implies. But these practices were characteristic of the working class and the rural population, and perhaps in very rarified circles of bohemian artists and intellectuals (some Young Hegelians among them) in Berlin. It was virtually inconceivable behavior for the very proper daughter of a high Prussian state official from a straitlaced provincial city.[14]

If Jenny did violate every canon of respectable female chastity—"despised before all the world"—she surely did so as a sign of her love for and commitment to Karl—"everything to you and now nothing more to others"—after all the long years of their distant, almost virtual engagement. Had Karl been a cad of nineteenth-century melodrama, or, more prosaically, like defendants in nineteenth-century paternity suits, he would have walked away from Jenny, perhaps with a few choice words about how he could no longer associate with an unchaste woman. Karl, though, was already committed to Jenny, and had been since their engagement. Physical intimacy would not change that commitment but reinforced his dilemma of not having a job enabling him to marry the woman he so loved. As Jenny pointed out in her revealing letter, it was torment for her to have to "still live separately from you for so long," but the pair could only be together once Karl had found gainful employment. With Bruno Bauer's dismissal and the end of Karl's own academic prospects, that separation seemed to stretch indefinitely into the future.

MARX'S SOLUTION WAS THE one other Young Hegelians were pursuing at the time: renouncing a career as an academic in the service of the Prussian state, he would become a freelance writer in opposition to that very state. During the first half of 1842, he proposed a number of articles to Arnold Ruge, in part based on the work Marx had been doing with Bruno Bauer in the previous six months. Ruge, whose *Halle Yearbooks* had been suppressed by the Prussian authorities, had set up shop under the new title of the *German Yearbooks* in Dresden, in the Kingdom of Saxony, not under Prussian jurisdiction. In what would become an uncomfortably familiar pattern in Marx's life, only one of the promised articles actually arrived, and it was quite late in doing so. Ruge, whose entire publishing schedule was disrupted by Marx's dilatoriness, was strikingly tolerant with him, his patience a sign of recognition of Marx's talents and abilities as somebody whose writing was worth waiting for. Marx excused himself, pleading family difficulties, but also admitted that his time had been absorbed by another, closer outlet for his writing, a recently founded newspaper in Cologne, the *Rhineland News*.[15]

Marx's involvement with this newspaper was a nodal point in his intellectual, personal, and political development, a bridge between his past life and his future endeavors. His affiliation with the journal transformed him from a scholar into an activist—or, more precisely, from a scholar with an activist bent into an activist with a scholarly tendency. It brought him into contact with communist ideas and set the framework for his self-designation as a communist. Marx's work with the *Rhineland News*, particularly the four stormy months when he served as its informal editor, from mid-October 1842 to mid-February 1843, was a period of intense and productive effort that would make him known, in impressive fashion, to three very different audiences. The first was the Young Hegelians, and, more broadly, radical intellectuals throughout central Europe. To them, Marx would cease to be just the protégé of Bruno Bauer, and become an author and polemicist in his own right. A second audience was the Prussian authorities, for whom Marx would become a subversive troublemaker and appropriate subject for persecution and oppression. Marx and the Prussian kingdom became mutual enemies, and remained so until his death. Finally, Marx would gain a strong recognition among the influential inhabitants of Cologne, the Rhenish metropolis—not just the city's nascent communists or its radical republicans, but its moderate liberals as well, and not just its marginalized, bohemian intellectuals, but its professionals, merchants, bankers, and members of the chamber of commerce.

All this recognition, even the negative, hostile kind, was powerfully affirmative for Marx, after years of difficulties making his way in the world. He visibly enjoyed being a polemical journalist and a crusading newspaper editor. For the following two decades, both his efforts at earning a living and his plans for political engagement centered on journalistic projects. Avocation, occupation, aspiration to improve the public welfare—journalism fulfilled the preconditions for choosing a career that Marx had articulated in his *Abitur* essay of 1835, albeit in a more bitter and contentious way than he had described in the Kantian idealism borrowed from his father and his teachers.

THE *RHINELAND NEWS* CAME into existence as the result of several opportunities. First was the journalistic one, opposition to the newspaper monopoly in the Rhineland's largest city of the *Cologne News*, a position it had gained in 1837 by purchasing its chief competitor. Attempts in 1840 to start a competing newspaper, the *Rhineland General News*, although granted a license to publish by the Prussian authorities, had gone poorly. The potential competitor was dull, limited, and, above all, underfinanced. Its editors, reaching the end of their funds, wanted a new, better-financed try, and they proposed to do so by using a new business institution, raising money for their project by the sale of stock shares.[16]

In mid-1841, they approached a young Cologne jurist from an affluent family, Robert Jung, with their plan. A supporter of the Young Hegelians, Jung elicited the assistance of another youthful radical intellectual, the son of an affluent Jewish merchant and sugar refiner, Moses Hess. Like Jung, Hess found this idea of a newspaper funded with shares of stock intriguing; it also fit his personal interest in a journalistic career. Hess, a critic of the anti-clerical and godless attitudes of the Young Hegelians, was a socialist or communist (contemporaries frequently used the two words interchangeably), one of the first Germans to become an adherent of the ideas of the French followers of Henri de Saint-Simon and Charles Fourier, who envisaged a society in which private property had been abolished and replaced by collective ownership. It may seem odd today for a communist to be an opponent of atheism, but early communism was suffused with a religious aura—albeit generally in the form of an unconventional spirituality. This was certainly true of Hess, who had rejected the dour Orthodox Judaism of his father, and developed an appreciation for Christian doctrines without actually converting to Christianity. Communists involved with corporations may seem even odder, but in the 1840s it was not at all unusual for socialists to perceive this form of business enterprise as a step away from individual and family ownership toward collectivism.[17]

Jung and Hess eagerly seized on the proposal and went about the business of gathering investors. There were legal difficulties in establishing a corporation, so they settled on a related business form, a *Komman-ditgesellschaft*, similar to a Common Law limited partnership, in which the liability of most investors was limited to their investment, while a few general partners had a broader exposure to risk. The three general partners were Jung; the Cologne banker Dagobert Oppenheim; and the newspaper's publisher, the book dealer Engelbert Renard.[18]

The identity of the investors reflects the second consideration behind the founding of the newspaper: differences within Cologne's elite. Many of the investors were affluent outsiders in Cologne, migrants to the city, entrepreneurial innovators who were shaking up the established ways of the Rhenish metropolis. These investors tended to view the *Cologne News* as the voice of Cologne's insiders, a group they saw as a clique with questionable and self-interested connections to the municipal government. There was even a special word in the Cologne dialect for this group, *Klüngel*, a term still in use today. A number of the outsiders, such as the industrialist's son Gustav Mevissen, or the banker and chamber of commerce president Ludolf Camphausen, were Protestants, and so outsiders in another way, in one of Germany's most Catholic major cities. This confessional dynamic helped shape the attitudes of the Prussian government toward the emerging *Rhineland News*. The authorities were not at all unhappy about a potential competitor undermining the *Cologne News*, because it had the reputation of being sympathetic to pro-Catholic and anti-Prussian viewpoints. The Prussian district governor of Cologne was actually one of the initial investors in the new project.[19]

Finally, there were the politics of the proposed newspaper. The capitalists behind the *Rhineland News* were political liberals, who wanted an end to the legally unrestrained, authoritarian rule of the Prussian monarch and his state bureaucracy. Also in their sights were the special privileges of the nobility, a remnant of the pre-1789 society of orders. In place of these, they envisaged a constitutional monarchy, whose fundamental document would guarantee basic civil liberties, proclaim equal rights under the law, and establish a legislature elected by (male) property owners. The early 1840s were a period in which liberals throughout the Prussian kingdom—but especially in the Rhineland, one of their strongholds—intensified their campaign for a constitution. Such liberal capitalists were not at all interested in seeing the newspaper that would be a vehicle for their political views promote the abolition of private property, so they rejected Hess's aspirations to be its editor. Hess's personal eccentricities—he was given to having visions and was notoriously querulous to boot—did not improve his prospects. Instead, the stockholders turned to one of Germany's most eminent economists, and a prominent liberal political figure, Friedrich List; but he was recovering from a broken leg and unable to take up the offer. Instead, the position went to an economically versed journalist, one Gustav Höfken.

Höfken proved to be an inept editor, but the problems he had went beyond his modest journalistic skills to the mismatch of his ideology with that of the newspaper's backers. Cologne was a financial center and a river port, a commercial city whose economy centered on its position as a midpoint between products coming from Germany and those from the Atlantic world. In contrast to other parts of western Germany, it had relatively little industry. Free trade was considerably more popular to the city's businessmen than were the protectionist ideas that List espoused and that his protégé Höfken wanted to make the center of editorial policy. In doing so, he put himself at odds with both the stockholders and the general partners, so that he lasted as editor just a few weeks from the start of publication in January 1842.[20]

The issue over which Höfken announced his resignation was his unwillingness to accept an article written by Bruno Bauer. His departure paved the way for the Young Hegelians, led by the general partner Robert Jung, to take over the paper. Höfken's successor as editor was Adolf Rutenberg, the Berlin Young Hegelian who was Bruno Bauer's brother-in-law. Bauer, whom Jung described as "our most admirable co-worker," was tremendously excited by the change in editorial policy, and hoped that the paper would be a vehicle for his atheistic ideas. Arnold Ruge, as well as other supporters of radical Hegelian views, also began to write for the newspaper, including a number of members of the Doctors' Club who had introduced Marx to Hegelianism as a student in Berlin.[21]

IT WAS THESE CLOSE connections that enabled Marx to write for the *Rhineland News*. Two long essays of his appeared in the spring and summer of 1842, Marx's first foray into the public sphere. They showed the influence of his classical education at the *Gymnasium* and the Hegelian reasoning he had learned at the university in Berlin. At least as impressive as the content of these essays was their style— angry, sarcastic, and polemical, not features of Marx's previous writings. This change reflected the influence of the Young Hegelians in general, and Bauer in particular, as they came into increasing conflict with the Prussian monarchy. Marx gave the Young Hegelian style his own distinct personal twist, characterized by the use of nastily amusing analogies and a practical, anti-idealistic, almost cynical take on politics, two characteristics that would become a permanent feature of his political writing.

The first, and longer, of the two essays, and the one that made the greatest impression, dealt with freedom of the press. Marx blasted its enemies, linking their arguments to an archaic society of orders, to an authoritarian Prussian state trying to prop up this society, and to intellectual trends defending it. Unlike some of the Young Hegelians, particularly Bauer, who reveled in criticism and negativity, Marx's piece was also affirmative, praising freedom of the press as part of a broader encomium of freedom, articulated in opposition to the nature of the

Prussian monarchy.[22] Not just Marx's criticisms but his affirmations as well were posed in anti-Prussian terms: once again typical of the Young Hegelians, but also reflecting his upbringing in the city of Trier.

Marx began by blasting the Prussian government, portraying the arguments of the official newspaper, the *Prussian State News*, as representing childish intellectual capacities—counting, smelling, and believing in ghosts. (The passage about ghosts is significant because it would appear, in somewhat altered form, in the *Communist Manifesto*). Having disposed of the Prussian authorities, Marx turned his attention to the debates on freedom of the press in the recently concluded Rhenish Provincial Diet, the main topic of his essay. The very nature of the Diet provided additional ammunition for Marx. Powerless, provincial pseudo-legislatures created by the Prussian government in the 1820s, the Diets were elected, deliberated, and voted along the lines of the society of orders, with deputies representing the province's higher nobility, its lower nobility, its town burghers, and its peasants. This arrangement was quite unpopular in the Rhineland, where two decades of French rule between 1794 and 1814 had eliminated legal distinctions between different social groups. Until the 1840s, the Diets deliberated in secret, which vitiated their representative character, since the voters quite literally did not know what the deputies they elected had said in debates or how they had voted on questions under discussion. The very existence of the Diets was a parody of the liberals' aspirations to a constitutional parliament.[23]

Marx brought together liberal aspirations for an effective legislature, and for a constitution guaranteeing basic rights, such as freedom of the press, and liberal hostility to the society of orders, in discussing a speaker representing the lower nobility who had asserted that the question of publication of proceedings had been placed by the government in the "hands of the Diet." According to Marx, this was taking a basic right—freedom of the press—and transforming it into a privilege of a constituted body of the society of orders, the Provincial Diet.

"The citizen does not want to perceive his rights as a privilege. Can he regard it as right to add new privileged groups to old ones?" Following up on this, he added sarcastically, "According to the speaker . . . the province should regard the prerogatives of the provincial diet as its own rights; why not also the prerogatives of some class of state officials, of the nobility or the priests?"[24] Here, Marx was defining freedom of the press as one of the universal human rights articulated in the French Revolution, and denouncing its opponents as lackeys of the Prussian state and advocates of an obsolete society of orders.

Marx then placed the ideas of opposition to the press in an intellectual context, presenting these ideas as examples of political thought influenced by artistic Romanticism, and its nostalgia for the Middle Ages:

> When our speaker from the order of the knights with almost comic seriousness, with almost melancholy dignity and nearly religious pathos, developed the postulate of the high wisdom of the Provincial Diet and of its medieval freedom and independence, the uninitiated will be surprised to see him take a different position on the question of freedom of the press. There, he sinks from the high wisdom of the Diet to the thorough lack of wisdom of the human race, from the independence and freedom of the privileged orders he recommends above to the principled unfreedom and dependence of human nature. We are not surprised to encounter one of the many forms apparent today of the Christian knightly, modern feudal, in short, of the Romantic principle.[25]

Continuing in a Hegelian vein, he denounced Romantic thinkers for their perception of freedom as a particular privilege of individual social orders, rather than being "tied to the essence of humanity, to reason, thus common to all individuals." This was a version of the universal human rights of the French Revolution inflected by Hegel's philosophy.

Marx also used this assertion of freedom of the press as a universal human right to criticize the supporters of press freedom in the Rhenish Diet, in particular its chief proponent, the Cologne banker Heinrich Merkens. Merkens had defended freedom of the press by describing it as a byproduct of freedom of occupation—the freedom to start a newspaper being like the freedom to open a tailor's workshop, in spite of guild restrictions. Marx praised the practical nature of Merkens's ideas, contrasting them favorably with the impractical projects of many German intellectuals that produced changes in the realm of ideas but none in social and political reality. This self-consciously hardheaded stance would be central to Marx's future writing; but his invidious comparisons between the practical banker and the impractical intellectuals was no endorsement of Merkens's assertions.

Quite the opposite. Marx had a sarcastic retort to them, perhaps an observation left over from his unfinished work on Christian art: "Rembrandt painted the Mother of God as a Dutch peasant, why shouldn't our speaker paint freedom in a form that is known and familiar to him?"[26] Freedom of occupation and freedom of the press, Marx went on, were all examples of a broader generic freedom; but "is it not totally erroneous, in this unity to forget diversity and even to make a species into a norm, into the sphere of the other species? It is intolerance on the part of one species of freedom, which is only willing to tolerate others, when they fall away from themselves and declare themselves that species' vassals."[27] More generally, Marx concluded, the defenders of freedom of the press at the Provincial Diet, in this respect like the opponents of freedom of the press, did not understand that freedom of the press was one example of broader universal human rights, and could only see it in a limited, narrow context.

Having strongly criticized limitations on freedom of the press, Marx accentuated the positive, combining Hegelian argumentation, colorful analogies, and ironic asides to offer an encomium of a free press:

The free press is the everywhere-open eye of the people's spirit, the embodied confidence of a people in itself, the speaking ribbon that connects the individual with the state and the world, culture made corporeal, which transforms material struggles into spiritual ones and idealizes their crude material form. It is the uninhibited confession of a people to itself and, as is well known, the strength of confession leads to redemption. It is the spiritual mirror in which a people contemplates itself, and self-contemplation is the first precondition of knowledge. It is the spirit of the state that can be sold by peddlers in every cottage, more cheaply than material gas. It is all-sided, omnipresent, omniscient. It is the ideal world that is constantly spilling out of the actual one, and, as an ever-richer spirit, newly animating, flowing back into it.[28]

The argument described, in Hegelian fashion, a free press as the objectification of the people's spirit—and not an objectification alienated from its spirit, but one that knew itself as such. The radicalized version of Hegel's ideas was also deployed in Marx's ironic yet serious description of a free press as all-sided, omnipresent and omniscient, attributes of divinity, or of Hegel's philosophical version of divinity, Absolute Spirit. And since the free press was the objectified spirit of the people, Marx was placing the people in the same transcendent position Hegel reserved for Absolute Spirit: Marx's encomium of the press became a praise of democracy, the rule of the people, and an even stronger attack on a very authoritarian Prussian state.[29]

It is no surprise that the article was well received by fellow Young Hegelians such as Jung and Ruge, but it attracted a wider following. Ludolf Camphausen received a letter from his brother, Otto, then at the beginning of a distinguished career in the Prussian state service, inquiring, "Who is the author of the admirable article on the proceedings [concerning freedom of the press] of the Rhenish Provincial Diet?

What do the deputies from Cologne say about it?" The Prussian minister of the interior was also impressed, albeit in a negative way, condemning the piece as a subversive attack on the state.[30]

The second, rather shorter essay Marx wrote for the *Rhineland News*
was couched in a more defensive tone, and dealt with the touchy issue
of the atheism of the Young Hegelians.[31] The occasion was a lead article
in the *Cologne News* that had denounced its competitor for publishing
such material and had called on the censors to prohibit these offenses to
religious sensibility. Cleverly, the *Cologne News* presented its advocacy of
censorship as a defense of freedom of the press, asserting that the anti-
religious excesses of the Young Hegelians were discrediting the cause
of press freedom. This assertion made a reply trickier than in the essay
on freedom of the press. Marx could not just attack a Prussian government unpopular among Cologne's and the Rhineland's Catholics; he
also had to mollify those Catholics' religious sensibilities. He himself
was keenly aware of this problem. Right after finishing his article, he
wrote to Arnold Ruge, "On the Rhine, the religious element is the most
dangerous. The opposition has in recent times become too accustomed
to carrying out its opposition in the church."[32]

Marx asserted that "hatred of Protestant theology against philosophers" was the reason Prussian authorities opposed Strauss and
Feuerbach for daring to "regard Catholic dogmas as Christian ones." In
other words, not atheism, but a pro-Catholic attitude was the problem
the Prussian government and its theological spokesmen had with the
Young Hegelians. After appealing to St. Augustine, and pointing out
that the Pope had refused to join the Holy Alliance, the counterrevolutionary league of European states emerging following the defeat of
Napoleon—and so suggesting that Catholics were by no means required
to support conservative governments for religious reasons—Marx
went on to describe the "Christian state," a favorite phrase of conservatives in Germany, as one favoring a particular Christian confession,
like in Ireland. He was portraying the Catholics of the Rhineland as

being oppressed by a Protestant Prussian government, just as the Irish Catholics were oppressed by the Protestant government of England, a popular analogy among Rhenish Catholics of the time. As soon as a state granted different religious confessions equal rights, Marx suggested, it was no longer Christian but philosophical, a "realization of reasoned freedom . . . a work that philosophy completes."[33]

Marx was attempting to rework and redefine his political and philosophical principles to appeal to a potentially hostile audience. Downplaying the atheism of the Young Hegelians, he emphasized instead their opposition to a conservative—and also Protestant—Prussia for his audience of Rhenish Catholics, and impugned the motives of the Young Hegelians' opponents for that audience as well. It was an eminently political performance implying a change of course for the Young Hegelian radicals. Another way to put it would be that the essay reflected the thinking of someone in charge of a larger political enterprise—a newspaper editor, for example.

IT WAS BECOMING INCREASINGLY clear by the summer of 1842 that the *Rhineland News* was going to need a better editor. The venture in oppositional publishing was running into steadily mounting hostility from the Prussian government. The news that Rutenberg, a notorious Young Hegelian already under police surveillance in Berlin, was to become the new editor, infuriated the minister of the interior, and he insisted that under no circumstances could Rutenberg be allowed to work for the paper. So, officially, the editor remained the newspaper's publisher, but Rutenberg worked informally. By May 1842, the interior minister was demanding the immediate suppression of the *Rhineland News* for "propagating French-liberal ideas" and for being a "decisive organ of Young Hegelian propaganda . . . [that] professes the non-belief of the *Halle Yearbooks* and the opinion that contemporary philosophy will replace Christianity." The Cologne district governor and the Rhenish provincial governor both spoke out against such a drastic measure, fearing it would make a bad impression on the educated public, even those members who did not share the paper's views. They suggested that the affluent investors would moderate the editorial policy, or perhaps grow tired of funding the deficit and let the *Rhineland News* go out of existence. Eventually, the Prussian central government agreed to wait until December to see if the editorial tone would change or if the newspaper would cease altogether.[34]

These official calculations were not without justification. Readership of the *Rhineland News* had been growing steadily since its appearance; postal subscriptions, the chief way to purchase the newspaper, almost quadrupled from 264 in the first quarter of 1842 to 1,027 by the end of the third quarter. This was a respectable record, but badly overshadowed by the *Cologne News*, whose press run of 8,500 far exceeded its upstart competitor; the difference was particularly noticeable in Cologne itself, where most of the investors resided. They were beginning to wonder about their money, since within six months of the founding of the *Rhineland News* about three quarters of their investment had been spent, but the newspaper was still far from a breakeven point of 2,500 subscriptions.[35]

The usual account of the situation puts the blame on Adolf Rutenberg, described as an incompetent alcoholic. Most of these negative opinions came from Marx himself, who, as Rutenberg's successor, was not an entirely objective witness.[36] Rutenberg did have a reputation as a heavy drinker and was said to have lost a position as geography teacher at the Royal Prussian Military Academy as a result. But he had his accomplishments. Circulation was rising; Rutenberg was going about the business of recruiting correspondents, and was an able copyeditor. What he did not provide, though, was strong intellectual guidance to the newspaper. He never wrote a single article himself, and editorial policy was set primarily by Robert Jung and Moses Hess, who had dropped his legal action and returned to the newspaper following the resignation of Höfken.[37]

Both Hess and Jung were proponents of Marx. Hess's opinion of Marx was high indeed. The two men became acquainted in Bonn in the summer of 1841, after Marx's return to the Rhineland. After their meeting, Hess described Marx as "my idol . . . he combines the deepest philosophical seriousness with the most cutting wit; imagine Rousseau, Voltaire, Holbach, Lessing, Heine and Hegel united in one person . . . then you have Dr. Marx." Jung's praise was less rhapsodic— how could it not be—but he passed on to Marx his endorsement of a letter he had received from Eduard Meyen, one of the Berlin Young Hegelians, encouraging Marx to work for the *Rhineland News*: "Will not Marx soon come forth and show what he really has in him?"[38]

It seems likely that Hess and Jung were behind Marx's hiring by the *Rhineland News* in mid-October 1842. Marx did not replace Rutenberg as the editor, as biographies often assert. While he did receive an employment contract—which must have been personally very welcome, in view of his need to find work in order to marry Jenny—Engelbert Renard remained the official editor, and Rutenberg continued to work for the paper as copyeditor and translator of articles from the French press. Hess and Jung brought Marx on board to reinforce their editorial role; he would use the talents he had shown in his articles on freedom of the press to present a more vigorous and active editorial policy, to help continue the circulation increase and to convince the investors to refinance the newspaper.

Marx certainly did take energetic action when he joined the editorial staff, but not what Jung or especially Hess, had in mind. His editorial plans were already expressed in a letter, reading very much like a job application, sent to Dagobert Oppenheim in August or September 1842. Marx planned to tone down the newspaper. Young Hegelian "general theoretical considerations on the constitution of the state" would be eliminated, since Young Hegelian political radicalism, and the atheistic ideas to which it was integrally linked, were alienating "the largest portion of free-thinking practical men, who have undertaken the laborious task of fighting for freedom step by step, within constitutional limits"—in other words, Cologne's and the Rhineland's bourgeois liberals who were financing the newspaper, and whose further support would be needed to keep it in business. A moderation of tone would be necessary for the Prussian authorities as well, to avoid the danger of "a tightening of the censorship or even the suppression of the newspaper," a fate, Marx noted, that had befallen earlier radical opposition journals. To enforce these tasks, a strong editorial hand would be needed that would direct the journalists working for the newspaper, and not leave the tone of articles up to their authors.[39]

Once appointed to the editorial staff, Marx moved to implement his plan. He assiduously courted liberal members of the bourgeoisie, getting chamber of commerce president Ludolf Camphausen to produce articles criticizing the Prussian government's handling of the financing of railroad construction, and the physician Heinrich Claessen, a prominent Cologne liberal, to write a series on the reform of municipal government. Marx worked closely with one of the journalists Rutenberg had recruited, Karl Heinrich Brüggemann, a onetime student radical, who was tending toward more moderate politics. In collaboration with Marx, Brüggemann wrote a number of pieces strongly advocating free trade and denouncing protectionism, producing a clear position for the *Rhineland News* on this point in contrast to the vacillation and temporization that had characterized its past stances. This support for free trade was the most important social and economic cause that the *Rhineland News* advocated while Marx was involved in its editorial work, and it left a strong impression on Marx.[40] Even after he became a communist, he would continue to be an adherent of free trade.

Marx's efforts to tone down the Young Hegelianism of the *Rhine-*

land News led to a clash with his university friends and his patron Bruno Bauer over the existence—or reputed existence—in Berlin of a "Society of Free Men," a Young Hegelian group advocating atheism and calling on supporters to leave the Christian churches. The group's attitudes, and their practice of demonstrating them in alcoholic fashion in Berlin's taverns, had already been an embarrassment for the *Rhineland News* in the summer of 1842, and in November of that year the Young Hegelians' chief organizer, Arnold Ruge, accused the Free Men of being dilettantes and lacking the moral seriousness needed to bring about political change in Germany. Marx, who thoroughly agreed, proceeded to publish a letter attacking, in similar vein, the Berlin Young Hegelians' "revolutionary romanticism, their addiction to their own genius, their dubious seeking of fame. . . ."[41] Both Marx and Ruge had hoped that their criticisms would spare Bruno Bauer, whom they regarded as too sensible to take part in such antics; but Bauer identified with the Free Men and wrote a sharp and offended reply to Marx. Future attempts by Marx and Ruge to work with Bauer proved ultimately unsuccessful, and less than two years after the blowup, Marx would refer to Bauer as "my long-term friend, who is now estranged. . . ."[42]

Certainly, issues of individual personalities were involved in this break: Bauer, Ruge, and Marx were all touchy and easily offended. But controversy over the Free Men pointed to a broader, fundamental difference of opinion within the ranks of the Young Hegelians over the question of what it meant to be a radical. For the Free Men, radicalism was about lifestyles and the rejection of social conventions, both exemplified by their public avowal of atheism. For Marx and Ruge, on the other hand, radicalism was about political change; and without denying the Young Hegelians' criticism of religious orthodoxy, they sought to downplay it in public, and to move toward a criticism of the social and political circumstances that encouraged and enforced this orthodoxy. The differences were not insurmountable and it was clearly possible to move between the two camps—Marx's future friend and collaborator Friedrich Engels was one of the Free Men—but the development of two separate and distinct paths of radicalism was clear.[43]

The trickiest editorial task for Marx, at which he was least successful, was dealing with the Prussian government. Even the moderate course he was trying to take offended the authorities. As part of the new pro–free trade editorial policy, the newspaper published an attack on Russia's economic protectionism, pointing out how it harmed Prussian interests. The government perceived the articles as an attack on the czar, the king of Prussia's friend and ally.[44] This official unwillingness to meet the *Rhineland News* halfway only encouraged Marx's tendency not to restrain himself. His two articles on the debates in the Provincial Diet concerning a law against wood theft were so hostile to the institution of the Diet that the infuriated provincial governor demanded the subversive editor be fired; only, unaware of Marx's new editorial position, he blamed Rutenberg, who duly lost his job.[45]

Marx also made it a practice to bait the official Prussian censors, often midlevel bureaucrats without a university education, who had a hard time understanding the articles in the *Rhineland News*. They would strike quite innocent pieces and allow more subversive ones to appear in print, putting the government in the odd position of denouncing the newspaper for publishing material that had passed its own censorship. Well aware of this problem, Marx worked captiously to emphasize it. With feigned innocence he asked the resident censor at the paper, Police Councilor Laurenz Dolleschall, a man whose intellectual capacities were not remotely in Marx's league, who could conceivably have written the article attacking the Provincial Diet—a snarky remark that was quickly retailed around in Cologne. In a more public move, he refused to submit the page proofs to Dolleschall one day, forcing the latter to leave the Provincial Governor's Ball late in the evening and come to Marx's apartment asking for them. Marx bellowed out the window that there were no proofs, because the newspaper was not publishing the next day, publicly humiliating the censor.[46]

Marx continued this baiting at a higher level, taking on the provincial governor. Writing in the name of Renard, the official editor of the *Rhineland News*, he responded to the governor's condemnation of the newspaper's new policy by presenting it as a pro-Prussian enterprise, "help[ing] to pave the path to progress on which Prussia is leading the rest of Germany. . . ." Far from spreading pro-French ideas, the newspaper was bringing forth a "German liberalism that can certainly not be unpleasant to the government of Friedrich Wilhelm the Fourth." Indeed, Marx continued, his newspaper was the first "to bring the north German spirit, the Protestant spirit, into the Rhineland and southern Germany. . . ." Rather than being irreligious, the *Rhineland News* was following in the footsteps of Martin Luther in opposing "church dogmas." These remarks drew on ideas the Young Hegelians had espoused in the mid-1830s about the progressive role of the Prussian state and its close connections to Hegelian philosophy. By the following decade, when the born-again new monarch had denounced both progress and Hegel, and the Young Hegelians had become republicans and atheists, the remarks were a provocation—as contemporaries understood very well.[47]

The new editorial policy Marx implemented proved eminently successful. The upward trend in circulation accelerated, reaching 3,300 subscribers by early 1843, well past the breakeven point. Encouraged by the good news on circulation and attracted by the new content of the paper, the investors proved willing to put in additional funds.[48] Whether Marx's sarcastic and provocative attitude would mollify the Prussian authorities—a central element of his plans for the newspaper—was another matter.

· · ·

BY MARX'S OWN TESTIMONY, it was during his editorial tenure at the *Rhineland News* that he first came into contact with the "social question," the debate of the condition of the lower classes, that led to the genesis of his communist ideas.[49] In some ways, it is hard to argue with Marx's own reminiscences on that point. While Marx had some earlier exposure to the theories of Henri de Saint-Simon from Eduard Gans, and even Johann Ludwig von Westphalen, he first studied socialist ideas intensively when he was living in Cologne in the fall of 1842. It was there that he published his first observations on socialism and communism. In his two article series on the debates in the Rhineland Provincial Diet concerning a new law about wood theft and on the difficult economic conditions in his native Moselle Valley, Marx dealt publicly with economic and social issues for the first time. Drawing a straight line between these early investigations and writings and Marx's later communist theories, though, would be quite misleading.

While this point is lost in most biographies, Marx also mentioned in his reminiscences that the debates about free trade and protectionism were an important impetus for his growing concern about economics. The pro–free market stance he took on this debate as editor of the *Rhineland News* also colored his discussion of the travails of the Moselle Valley winegrowers and other members of the rural lower classes in western Germany. Marx largely placed the blame for their condition on the policies of the Prussian government and the actions of its officials — not on capitalists or the market economy. His initial public pronouncements on the topic of communism were hardly favorable; if anything, they were distinctly anti-communist. Indeed, the version of communism that Marx would adopt was shaped by his opposition to many of the aspects of it that he learned about in 1842.

Moses Hess had been running a weekly discussion circle and reading group in Cologne on communism and the social question since the summer of that year. Its members were an oddly mixed bunch. There were Young Hegelians, such as Robert Jung, and future communist

activists, including the physician Karl d'Ester and the Prussian artillery officer Friedrich (Fritz) Anneke, both of whom would work with
Marx during the 1848 Revolution. But other participants were not so
far to the left: the industrialist's son and future liberal political leader
Gustav Mevissen, a friend of Jung's at the time, also courting Jung's
sister; the pro–free trade journalist Karl Heinrich Brüggemann (who
would become editor of the *Cologne News* in 1845, when it switched to a
liberal political stance); or the attorney Gustav Compes, another future
Cologne liberal politician. Chamber of commerce president Ludolf
Camphausen may have been an occasional participant.[50] When Marx
moved to Cologne in October 1842 to take up his editorial position on
the *Rhineland News*, he joined the discussion group. Their precise readings are unknown, but they may have included some of the contemporary French socialists, such as Victor Considérant, Pierre Leroux, and
Pierre-Joseph Proudhon.[51]

Marx's first detailed encounter with communist ideas left a decidedly negative impression. He perceived advocacy of communism as
part of the Berlin Young Hegelians' lifestyle-based radicalism that he
rejected. Marx's acid description of the articles they published in the
Rhineland News before he became editor makes the point: "beer suds
pregnant with global upheaval but empty of thought in a slovenly style,
permeated with some atheism and communism (which the gentlemen
have never studied). . . ." Once he became editor, he made it clear that
he would no longer accept such pieces:

> I declared [to the Berlin Young Hegelians] that I regarded the
> smuggling of communist and socialist dogmas, a new world view,
> into occasional pieces of theatrical criticism as inappropriate, even
> as immoral and demanded a completely different and more thorough
> discussion of communism, if it has to be discussed. I desired then
> that religion be criticized more in the criticism of political conditions
> than political conditions be criticized in religion . . . that when phi-

losophy was discussed there be less peddling of products produced by the firm of "atheism" . . . than that the content of philosophy be brought to the people.[52]

This skeptical attitude, a rebuke to Marx's ally Moses Hess, who had also been trying to smuggle communist ideas into the newspaper, characterized Marx's initial public appraisal of these ideas in an article in the *Rhineland News* of October 16, 1842. It was his very first piece to appear after taking his editorial position.[53] The piece was a polemic, denouncing the *Augsburg General News*, Germany's leading newspaper, which had accused the *Rhineland News* of publishing two articles advocating communism. One of those articles dealt with the poverty of workers living in large apartment houses (still an unusual feature in the 1840s social landscape) in Berlin, and called for an end to private property as a way to deal with their plight. The other reported on a scholarly conference in Strasbourg, at which one speaker had asserted: "Today the middle class is where the nobility was in 1789; then the middle class laid claim to the privileges of the nobility and obtained them; today the social order that possesses nothing demands to participate in the riches of the middle class, which is now at the helm."

The themes of both these pieces—that the workers' condition could only be improved by abolishing private property and that a workers' revolution against the bourgeoisie would be a logical successor to the bourgeois revolution against the nobility—were central to Marx's future theories. At the time, he had a different response, or more precisely, a triple response, all of which reveals a certain embarrassment in having to defend the results of a past editorial policy he was in the process of revising. One response was to focus on the conditions revealed in the two articles, and to drop any discussion of their remedies. Marx pointed out that the middle class was in charge in most Western European countries, as even Prussian conservatives admitted, and that workers in England and France were making demands on that middle

class. He also noted that economic conditions in Germany were difficult, although the examples used to make that point—"that Germany is
poor in people who are economically independent, that ⁹/₁₀ of educated
young men must beg the state for bread for their future, that our rivers
are neglected, that shipping is in wretched condition, that our once blos-
soming commercial cities are no longer flourishing . . . that the surplus
of our population helplessly wanders around, going under as Germans
in foreign nationalities"—were from the arsenal of liberal criticism of
conditions in Germany during the 1840s, rather than expressing communist or radical ideas.

A second response was to turn the accusations back on the accuser.
The *Augsburg General News*'s Paris correspondent, Marx asserted, had
proposed socialist ideas. Reactionaries—unfairly comparing the moderate Bavarian newspaper to the extreme right—supported the restoration of the guilds, a communistic notion. They also opposed the
division of landed property, endorsing the ideas of the French communist Charles Fourier. This *tu quoque* argument seems by far the least
convincing of Marx's assertions.

Most interesting and unexpected is the third argument. The *Rhineland News*, Marx argued, would not concede communism any "theoretical reality," much less any effort at "practical realization." He found the
theory much more ominous than the practice. The "intellectual implementation" of communist ideas would be the "genuine danger," for such
ideas could "defeat our intelligence, conquer our sentiments. . . ." To
meet that danger, he proposed a careful study of the works of prominent
communists, for the purpose of engaging in a "fundamental criticism"
of their ideas. By contrast, "practical attempts [to introduce commu-
nism], even attempts en masse, can be answered with cannons. . . ."
The man who would write the *Communist Manifesto* just five years later
was advocating the use of the army to suppress a communist workers'
uprising!

Marx's 1842 rejection of communism emerges into clearer focus when we consider the approach he took to social and economic questions at the time: a Hegelian diagnosis of the problems coupled with an anti-Prussian prescription of the solution. Marx's diagnosis appeared, above all, in the two articles he wrote on the Rhenish Provincial Diet's debate on a new law directed against wood theft.[54]

Concerns about the theft of wood, and the appropriation of forest products by non-owners of forest lands, were very widespread in Germany during the 1840s. One, more conservative response to the situation was to understand it as a crime wave, an indication of the moral decay of the lower classes and their increasingly criminal tendencies. Another, less common but distinctly more left-wing response was to blame the problem on the cruel and inhumane attitude of the state forest administration. Ludwig Simon, a fellow student of Marx's at the Trier *Gymnasium*, by the mid-1840s a practicing attorney in Trier, made a name for himself and launched a dramatic political career by fervently advancing this line of argument in court, defending violators of the forest laws.[55]

Marx's take was different, and reflected his personal experiences and intellectual influences. Following closely in the footsteps of his Berlin teacher, Eduard Gans, he understood the theft of wood as a result of the transformation of the legal nature of property. In the era of the society of orders, the privileged orders had their particular written rights, but the poor exercised their unwritten "customary right" to gather certain kinds of wood, particularly windfall—branches and limbs that had fallen from trees and were lying in the forest. This was possible because in that society property had a "vacillating character," partly private, partly communal, partly governed by civil laws, partly by public law, "as we encounter in all institutions of the middle ages." The French Revolution had changed the nature of law. It was now written, codified, and universally applicable. Individuals' property rights were therefore unitary and fully guaranteed. But unwritten, customary rights, such as the right of the poor to gather windfall on other people's forest property, were no longer valid. This understanding of changes in property rights probably also reflected Marx's knowledge of his father's legal efforts. Among Heinrich Marx's clients were the villagers of Thalfang, near Trier, whom he represented in an unsuccessful attempt to retain their customary usage rights.[56]

Marx portrayed these changes through Hegel's representation of human history as the progressive realization of reason. The old regime's law was based on "understanding," a conceptually inferior form of categorization, stemming from the empirical perception of individual objects, conceived in isolation from each other. By contrast, the new legal system was based on "reason," Hegel's totalizing system of cognition. "Rights no longer depend on the coincidence of custom being according to reason, but custom itself is now based on reason, because rights are based on the [written and codified] law, because custom has become the custom of the state."[57]

But such a positive development left the poor out in the cold (literally, since the wood gathered was often used for winter heating). Marx offered a useful analogy, pointing out that in the process of the revolution the property of the monasteries had been seized and sold off, transformed into private property—and the revolutionaries "were right to do so." The monks received compensation for the loss of their property; but the poor, who had the customary right to receive charity from the monks, received no such compensation. "A new boundary line was drawn up and they were cut off from their old rights."[58]

How were the poor to be helped in this situation? Marx's essay actually provided no clear answer. He waxed sarcastic about suggestions in the Diet to turn this unauthorized gathering of windfall into a felony, and had scathing remarks about how forest owners were becoming "monopolists," who would prohibit poor children from gathering and selling berries. His proposal that the owners of forest lands could sue the peasants gathering wood on their property was only slightly less sarcastic, since, as he admitted, the wood gatherers were very poor, and would not be able to pay any civil judgment. Marx's Hegelian analysis of the plight of the poor was separated from any solution to their problems.

Insofar as Marx had an answer to the question of poverty during the time he was editing the *Rhineland News*, it appeared in the article series he wrote at the beginning of 1843 on the poverty of the winegrowers in the Moselle Valley. This was Marx's native region, where his family owned a small vineyard, so he was personally well informed about the topic. The winegrowers were facing a very steep decline in the price of their wines, a result that both contemporaries and later historians attribute to Prussia's creation of the *Zollverein*, or all-German tariff union of 1834, which opened the Prussian wine market to competition from vintners in southern Germany.[59]

Marx in his first article certainly accepted this view, but he noted how differently the government and the population presented the causes. For the government, it was the result of the winegrowers enjoying a pre-1834 protected market, where unprecedentedly high prices had made it possible for them to live in a "luxury they had never known before." With declining wine prices, there would have to a market shakeout, and the poorer vintners would lose their previous luxury as well as their land. By contrast, the Association for the Encouragement of Viticulture along the Moselle and Saar rivers, whose members were mostly Trier notables, presented the situation as the result of the energy and initiative of the winegrowers, who had invested in their lands and increased their output, only to be done in by the policies of the Prussian government that exposed them to foreign competition and did not decrease the high tax burden weighing on them when market conditions became less favorable. It was not just the small vintners who were suffering, the association's members asserted, but all growers of wine, large and small.

Marx's commentary on this situation was to note that government officials saw themselves as representing the general good, the common interest of the inhabitants of the Prussian state. They rejected the contrary opinions of the winegrowers, because the latter were just asserting their special, private interests. Marx was following Hegel here, in the latter's observation that state officials were the "universal order," the group that understood the needs of all of society. Marx did not entirely disagree with this viewpoint, but he did modify it by observing that the officials identified themselves with the public good they claimed to represent. Criticism of their judgments about the public good became personal criticism. The official "believes the question of whether his area is in good condition, is a question of whether he is administering it well." Not only would officials react with considerable hostility to criticism; they would see their critics as being in the wrong: their administrative measures were correct, and the problem lay with the inhabitants of the region, who were unable to change. In these observations lay the seeds of Marx's future concept of ideology: that social conditions shaped individuals' ideas so as to further the interest of the social group to which they belonged.

His account of the Prussian bureaucracy's worldview was also a criticism of it as only seeming to represent the general good, but being unable to do so, because of its group self-interest. What measures Marx himself would have proposed to deal with the growing impoverishment of the vintners is unknown, since his proposals were reserved for the last of a five-part series, and the Prussian authorities prohibited the series after the first two articles. The second article did explain how a solution could appear: via a free press. This, according to Marx, would be the third element between the bureaucracy and special interests, "political without being governmental and official . . . civic and bourgeois without being mixed up in private interests and their needs. . . . In the area of the press, the [state] administration and the administered can in equal measure criticize their basic assumptions and their demands . . . in equal validity as citizens, no longer as persons but as intellectual powers."[60]

Although certainly Hegelian in nature, this argument about the power of the press against a self-assured bureaucracy resistant to public criticism also came from the arsenal of 1840s liberal criticism of central European conditions. In particular, Marx cited the writings of David Hansemann, a wool wholesaler from the Rhenish city of Aachen, a prominent Rhineland liberal and a close associate of the liberal Ludolf Camphausen.[61] In this respect, as in most others, Marx's initial forays into the social question show someone skeptical of communist notions, and still thinking about social and economic questions along the lines of a pro-capitalist and pro–free market nineteenth-century liberalism, if perhaps with more sympathies for the poor than many free market liberals. There is no mistaking the animosity toward authoritarian Prussian rule that colored his accounts of social and economic issues.

MARX'S OBSERVATION THAT PRUSSIAN bureaucrats took criticism of them personally was all too prescient. The provincial governor of the Rhineland, Justus von Schaper, the one government official willing to tolerate the *Rhineland News*, had previously been the district governor in Trier. He was outraged by Marx's suggestion in his article on the Moselle winegrowers that Prussian officials were responsible for their plight. His alienation meant that there was no one left to fend off the demands that the newspaper be prohibited. In a decree published on January 21, 1843, the Prussian authorities announced that the *Rhineland News* would cease publication at the beginning of April.[62]

Its supporters were not willing to let it go without a fight; they gathered a petition with 1,000 signatures, mostly from the upper classes of Cologne, calling on the authorities to reverse their decree. Admittedly, members of the *Klüngel*, the well-connected local insiders, withheld their names, as did Cologne's most devout Catholics, unimpressed by Marx's attempts to conciliate their religious feelings. But the substan-

tial support from most of Cologne's elite was a sign of their endorsement of Marx's policies of opposition to authoritarian Prussian rule.[63]

Feelings ran high at an extraordinary stockholders' meeting held
on February 12, 1843, at which the investors debated how to proceed.
Debates centered on Marx himself and the opposition to Prussia he
represented. The general partners, Jung and Oppenheim, supported
by a few other speakers, pressed for endorsing Marx's course: better
to let the newspaper go under than to moderate its tone in the hope
of conciliating the Prussian government. Most investors reluctantly
followed the opposite path: dismiss the controversial editor and hope
this would get the government to change its mind. Ironically, this was
a strategy Marx himself had already tried, when he banished atheism and communism from the pages of the *Rhineland News* and sacri-
ficed Adolf Rutenberg to the authorities. But this reiteration of Marx's
strategy was even less successful than the original effort. Neither the
promised change of editors, the large petition from Cologne, a special
petition of the stockholders to the king directly, nor a delegation sent
by the stockholders to Berlin, had any effect, and the newspaper came
to an end.[64]

Marx was present at the stockholders' meeting, but had little to say
in his own defense. This meeting was the first occasion at which one of
his personal weaknesses would be revealed: he was no great orator. In
intimate personal conversations, he could make a powerful and positive impression—and not just on close adherents, like Jung and Hess.
Saint Paul, the intellectually sophisticated last Prussian censor of the
Rhineland News, was every bit as impressed with Marx's ideas and personality. Speaking with a lisp and in a pronounced Rhineland accent,
Marx could not generate the same favorable impressions in front of a
large audience.[65]

The loss of his editorial position was yet another frustration in his
career and his personal life since Marx finished his studies at the Uni-

versity of Berlin. The Prussian government had suppressed his news-paper; his supporters among the investors in the *Rhineland News* had abandoned him; and he was once again, frustratingly for his relations with Jenny, unemployed. But Marx's brief and stormy tenure as de facto editor of the *Rhineland News* had revealed both journalistic and editorial skills—his polemical talents, inspiring his friends and infuri-ating his enemies, and his capability at recruiting an impressive group of co-workers.

To a good deal of the wider public, these abilities remained unknown, due to the peculiar legal nature of the editorial arrangements of the newspaper. The Prussian officials who decided to suppress the *Rhine-land News* attributed its subversive nature to the Young Hegelians in general, and Adolf Rutenberg in particular. Ironically, only by reading newspaper reports of their decision did they learn that Marx had been behind the acid attacks on the Prussian authorities.[66] Among Cologne's notables, though, Marx had made a big impression. They chipped in to offer him financial support in the difficult years following the sup-pression of the *Rhineland News*. Wilhelm Weitling, a tailor and future rival of Marx for leadership of the nascent communist movement in Germany, would later derisively say of him, "He owes his influence to other people. Rich men made him a newspaper editor, that's all."[67] We could strip Weitling's observation of its sting and observe that it was correct: although not all precisely rich, the members of Cologne's middle and upper classes—in short, that bourgeois stratum of society Marx would later attack—impressed by his vivid and vigorous jour-nalism and his forthright political stance, would continue to endorse his actions throughout the decade of the 1840s.

They decisively demonstrated this opinion five years later, dur-ing the Revolution of 1848, the political maelstrom of mid-nineteenth-century Europe. In April of that year, Ludolf Camphausen was appointed by the king as Prussia's first—and last—liberal prime min-ister. He promptly offered a position on his staff to the vigorous young man he had met as editor of the *Rhineland News*.[68] By that time, Marx had broken with the liberalism he had endorsed in his first major foray into journalism. In support of far more radical goals, he began a second, much larger journalistic venture, the *New Rhineland News*, whose financial backing came from those Cologne notables who had seen Marx at work in the metropolis half a decade earlier.

The years 1842–52 were Marx's Cologne decade. From his appointment to an editorial position on the *Rhineland News* at the start to the arrest, indictment, and conviction of his followers in the Cologne Communist Trial at its end, the city remained a source of support and potential base of operations for him. With the exception of about six months in 1842–43 and fifteen months during the revolutionary period in 1848–49, Marx did not live in Cologne itself, in the Rhineland, in Prussia, or even in one of the states of the German Confederation. He lived abroad, an émigré and an exile. In those years of banishment, both self-imposed and ordered by the authorities, his intellectual horizons would expand, his political, social, and economic views would be steadily radicalized, and the social milieux of his personal and political associates would be drastically transformed. But in the course of all this, Marx never lost touch with Cologne and continued to move further along the path that he first began there.

4

The Émigré

·:ɔ⫴ɕ·:

THE LESSON MARX DREW from his experiences at the *Rhineland News* was that moderation would not work with the Prussian monarchy. Efforts to placate the authorities just led to frustration. He wrote to Arnold Ruge, "It is bad to perform a servant's duties, even for the cause of freedom, and to fight with one hand tied behind your back. I have gotten tired of the hypocrisy, the stupidity of crude authority, and our flattering, bending, turning our backs and searching for just the right words."[1] Marx wanted to say what he thought, to express the radical, democratic, and republican ideas common among the Young Hegelians. As was always the case with him, expressions of radicalism meant study and analysis of the causes of radicalism and of its consequences—a process that would lead to still more radical formulations. This was impossible in Prussia and, more broadly, within the boundaries of the German Confederation.

Following the example of many left-wing contemporaries, Marx resolved to be an émigré, to move where he could say what he thought without fear of the censor or the censorious reader. As his tenure at the *Rhineland News* was coming to an end, he began inquiring about a position in a foreign country. An initial possibility in Zurich did not work out, but in January 1843, Arnold Ruge's *German Yearbooks* were prohibited by the Kingdom of Saxony, acting under pressure from the Prussian government. Ruge proposed to move his publication abroad, and to employ Marx as a co-editor. After negotiations running through the spring of 1843, Ruge, with Marx's enthusiastic support, decided on a somewhat different enterprise, the founding of the *Franco-German Yearbooks*, a journal that would promote a collaboration of French- and German-speaking radicals. Marx wanted the journal to appear in Strasbourg, but Ruge insisted on Paris. The magazine would be published and distributed from Zurich by a German émigré radical, Julius Fröbel, a prominent mid-nineteenth-century figure, today best known for his uncle Friedrich, the inventor of the kindergarten. Marx would receive a respectable if not luxurious salary of 550 talers a year, plus honoraria for any articles he wrote.[2]

What this meant personally for Marx is evident from another letter he sent to Ruge in March 1843, as the two were negotiating the publishing venture. "As soon as we have concluded a contract, I will travel to Kreuznach and get married. . . ." The issue that had been haunting the engagement for seven long years had finally been resolved. Marx had a position with which he could support his bride. The new job was not an unalloyed blessing: Jenny, in particular, was reluctant to leave the country, but for her as well, the chance to get married was worth all the potential difficulties.[3]

In his letter to Ruge, Marx indicated that he would not be traveling to Trier for his wedding, but to the spa town of Kreuznach, at the junction of the Nahe and Rhine rivers, to the northeast of Trier, where Jenny and her mother had been living since the death of her father. A week before the nuptials, Karl and Jenny signed a notarized marriage contract, a brief one-page document containing three clauses. The first, establishing a marital community of property, reiterated the standard arrangements of the Napoleonic Code. By contrast, the second clause modified these arrangements, stating that future inheritances would become part of the marital community of property, instead of remaining the separate property of the inheriting spouse. This was a concession to Jenny, since Karl had the expectation of an inheritance from his mother, while Jenny could not look forward to any such future bequests. The final clause stated that debts contracted by either of the two future spouses before their marriage were their separate responsibility and would not become debits charged against the marital community of property. This was another concession of Karl's, as he had been accumulating debts ever since his father died five years earlier. Jenny, while presumably head over heels in love with Karl, was clearly also thinking soberly and practically about their future life together— as she had done since the beginning of the engagement. With property relations clarified in advance, as was typically the case in bourgeois marriages, the wedding could take place: on June 19, 1843, there was first a civil ceremony, as required by the Napoleonic Code, and then a religious one, in the Protestant church in Kreuznach.[4]

The newly married couple departed for a brief honeymoon, up the Rhine River to the far southwestern end of the German states and Switzerland. In two weeks, they ran through all their cash, a present from Jenny's mother, that was intended to last until Karl began his new job. Supposedly they left the money out in their hotel rooms, allowing friends and acquaintances to take it and not pay it back. This story, reiterated by biographers, is based on a third-hand account told thirty years after the fact by Karl and Jenny's oldest daughter to Karl's friend, the gynecologist Dr. Ludwig Kugelmann, who passed it on to his daughter Franziska, who wrote it down. In the retelling, the story has become an ominous portent of future money troubles that would continuously plague the marriage as a result of the couple's lax attitudes toward their finances. Stripping the account of the accretions it gained over the years in its continued retelling reveals something rather different: the inability of Jenny's mother to provide her daughter with an appropriate dowry, a substantial capital that would yield a continuous income to the young couple, as would be expected of any respectable marriage at the time. Jenny did receive the household furnishings a respectable bride normally brought into her marriage—linens, furniture, table silver—but most of the silver was poor quality, outdated or simply worn out.[5]

After the honeymoon, the couple returned to Kreuznach, lodging with Jenny's mother and brother Edgar, until their departure for Paris in mid-October. The close proximity to family members did not prevent the newlyweds from conceiving their first child. Jenny was pregnant by early August 1843. The initial months of the marriage also gave Marx the leisure to do some intellectual work he had been preparing since he moved to Bonn from Berlin. One aspect of this work would become a feature of Marx's way of absorbing information: reading texts and making elaborate excerpts. Of course, in the days before scanners, photocopiers, microfilm, much less typewriters, extensive excerpting was the only way to procure and store information; but Marx always took unusually extensive notes, generally much more than was necessary for the project at hand. The spa town of Kreuznach had a surprisingly good municipal library, created by the city fathers for the use of the many affluent and well-educated visitors who came to take the waters. Marx made good use of these facilities, taking notes on the histories of the major European countries and the United States, as well as going over some classics of political theory, including works by Montesquieu, Machiavelli, and Rousseau.[6]

Besides reading, Marx was also writing, preparing an essay for the *Franco-German Yearbooks*, a critique of Hegel's *Philosophy of Law*. For well over a year, Marx had been considering writing a criticism of the master's main work on politics.[7] The manuscript, although ultimately never finished like so many of Marx's larger intellectual efforts, was his first theoretical venture, showing the state of his thought after editing the *Rhineland News* but before his departure for Paris and intellectual and political encounters in continental Europe's great metropolis.

The *Critique of Hegel's Philosophy of Law* consisted primarily of Hegelian reflections, particularly influenced by the philosopher Ludwig Feuerbach, on the political issues Marx had discussed when editing the *Rhineland News*.

Feuerbach was one of the Young Hegelian philosopher-theologians, along with David Friedrich Strauss and Bruno Bauer, who had argued that human understandings of divinity involved the projection—by a process of externalization, emptying out, and alienation—of collective human characteristics onto an imaginary supreme being. Both Feuerbach and Bauer had extended this critique of religion to Hegel's ideas themselves, understanding Hegel's concept of an Absolute Spirit that was the motive force of nature and human history as precisely the same kind of projection of collective human characteristics onto an imaginary entity the Young Hegelians had perceived in religion. Where Feuerbach differed from Bauer and the other Young Hegelians was in his conception of what was being alienated in both religious ideas of a deity and Hegel's concept of Absolute Spirit: not exclusively consciousness or self-consciousness, but the human race or species in its natural, material—or, as Feuerbach liked to say, "sensuous"—existence. Feuerbach, in other words, was a materialist, who propounded a distinctly biological version of materialism, since he saw human species existence as constituted above all in sexual relations.[8]

Marx, even at the height of his enthusiasm for Feuerbach, was skeptical of this naturalist materialism, stating that Feuerbach "references nature too much and politics too little."[9] But he found Feuerbach's criticism of Hegel's ontology a promising way to criticize Hegel's politics. Feuerbach asserted that Hegel had confused subject and predicate: Absolute Spirit as subject of history had characteristics or predicates of humanity as a species, while it was really humanity as a species that was providing the characteristics of Absolute Spirit. Marx's critique made a parallel point: Hegel described the Absolute Idea as the subject and state and society as its predicates, while in reality the determinations were reversed.

This line of reasoning may seem both abstruse and abstract, but Marx was using his philosophical argument to make a political point. He showed how Hegel's derivation of the forms and functions of government from the development of the Idea exalted the powers of the monarch, enhanced the social and political position of the landed nobility, and reinforced the authority of state officials. Marx had sarcastic words for the way Hegel made "the governing power [into] the emanation of the prince," because the prince represented the bodily existence of the "subject of the Absolute Idea," rather than the prince being the constitutionally designated head of the executive, the governing power. He went on at some length about how Hegel derived, from the "natural principle of the family," the nobility's entailed estates, and their right to special parliamentary representation in a House of Lords. There was similar sarcasm for Hegel's philosophical derivation of the privileged position of the state bureaucracy.[10]

Such arguments were intellectually more elaborate versions of the polemics Marx had written while editing the *Rhineland News*, and demonstrated, by the choice of political targets, his republican and democratic sympathies. The absence, though, of the major topics of his future thought is certainly striking. The *Critique of Hegel's Philosophy of Law* had nothing in it about political economy, the working class, or socialism.

There was only the faintest hint of Marx's future views in a lengthy passage in which he discussed the nature of democracy. Such a regime of popular sovereignty would exist as a republic, but a republic, as opposed to a monarchy, was just "the abstract form of the state." Rather, Marx stated, democracy was a form of government whose "existence, whose reality, in its genuine basis, can always be traced back to the authentic man to the authentic people and is posited as the product of that people." Establishing a democratic government would not just be a matter of the proper constitution but also of the relationship of state and society. In both the monarchy and the republic, he observed, there was a contrast between individuals as private parties, concerned with their own interests—"property, contract, marriage, civil society"—and the state. The latter was the "organizing form" of these private lives, propagating universally valid laws regulating them, but lacking the same content these private lives had, and establishing a contrast between the particular, private interests of individuals' lives and the abstract, universal law-giving of the state. A genuine democracy would be the "true unity of the universal and particular," where the state would be a "particular form of the people's existence." Recent French writers had suggested that in such a regime, the state—as a form standing for the universal, common interest against private particular interests—would "perish." This perishing was not a literal disappearance, in the mode of anarchism, but the creation of circumstances in which the state "no longer count[s] as the totality," that is, was no longer opposed to the private interests of civil society.

Marx was unclear as to what social changes would be needed to produce such a democratic state, although there was a hint in one comment he made: "Property, etc., in short the entire content of law and the state is, with few modifications, the same in North America as in Prussia."[11] Bringing this comparison into conjunction with Marx's remark that a republic was the abstract form of the state and lacked the necessary content of democracy, it appears that his vision of democracy required some modification—albeit as yet quite unspecified—of existing property arrangements.

There were at least three rather different intellectual impulses behind this very particular invocation of democracy. One was clearly Hegelian; the unification of the universal and the particular was integral to the concept of Absolute Spirit. But it was a version of Hegel as modified by the Young Hegelians' critique of religion. Just as, Marx argued, politicizing Feuerbach, that divinity was the externalized and alienated representation of the essence of humanity, so government was the alienated and externalized form of humanity. Feuerbach's atheist religion called for re-inscribing humanity with its characteristics previously ascribed to a deity. Similarly, in Marx's version of democracy, public interest, the universal common good, would no longer be the exclusive property of a state standing against and opposed to society. Instead, there would be a regime in which the particular, private concerns of civil society would simultaneously articulate the universal common good, since both would be manifestations of the people, the basis of democracy.

Marx attributed this regime, in which the state would "perish," to "recent Frenchmen," possibly making an oblique reference to the French socialists he had been studying in Cologne.[12] There was probably another French source of Marx's ideas, the eighteenth-century thinker Jean-Jacques Rousseau. Thick black lines in the margin of Marx's excerpts from Rousseau's *Social Contract* emphasized the latter's description of the union of private interests in the general will.[13] Marx's idea of the unity of the particular with the universal, of the private interests of civil society with the general interests of the state in a democratic regime, were not dissimilar to Rousseau's concepts, if expressed in Hegelian form.

Most of the *Critique of Hegel's Philosophy of Law* consisted of a reiteration, in more intellectual language and philosophical form, of themes Marx had already expressed in his articles for the *Rhineland News*. Those few passages in the manuscript that went further, toward a new arrangement of state and society for which Marx had as yet no new designation and simply called "democracy," drew on an eclectic group of intellectual sources. The combination of Jean-Jacques Rousseau, Ludwig Feuerbach, and perhaps the 1840s French socialist Victor Considérant certainly deserves to be called eclectic, and it remained vague and imprecise, lacking content, detail, or any idea of how the new social and political order would come into existence. All of this would only emerge during the year and a half that Marx would spend in Paris.

Arnold Ruge, accompanied by Moses Hess, went on to Paris in August 1843, two months ahead of Marx, to take the initial steps in organizing their periodical. Ruge's later description of the hopes he placed in his move elucidates the magnetic attraction of the French capital for émigré German radicals: "At the end of our journey, we find the great valley of Paris, the cradle of the new Europe, the broad magic kettle in which world history is steaming, and out of which it ever and again bubbles forth anew." Marx might not have used such exalted language, but he too would have felt the attraction and challenge of the Continent's great metropolis.

The city was enormous. Ruge recalled standing at its highest point, at the top of Montmartre, and seeing before him an infinite urban panorama: "We could not encompass it in one view, the extent of the city ran around us, it made a semi-circle, whose end, on both sides was beyond our view. . . . What we have before us, as far as the eye can see is all Paris. . . ."[14] Its population surging toward the million mark, Paris was a couple of orders of magnitude larger than provincial German cities such as Trier or Cologne, and well above the 300,000 inhabitants Berlin had counted during Marx's student days.

Beyond just the absolute number of inhabitants, no central European city could compete with the richness and diversity of the cultural and intellectual life in the great French metropolis. Every kind of literature abounded, from the classics portrayed by the Comédie Française, to the Romantic writings of Victor Hugo or Jules Michelet, to the realism of Honoré de Balzac, whom Marx admired greatly, to the popular forms of literature in the boulevard theaters and the enormously successful works of the sentimental novelist Eugène Sue, whom Marx deeply despised. The art world was no less varied, from the old masters at the Louvre to the avant-garde realists, such as Courbet, to the intensely politicized satirical cartoons and lampoons of Daumier.

Daumier's work pointed to the major reason for Marx and Ruge's relocation to Paris: the city's role as the capital of what was, in spite of its defeats in the Napoleonic Wars, still the Continent's wealthiest, most powerful, and most influential country. The so-called July Monarchy, installed in France after the revolutionary Parisian street fighting of July 1830, was a liberal constitutional regime, containing the sorts of guarantees of basic civil liberties that Marx, in the *Rhineland News*, had advocated in vain for Prussia. Although by the 1840s the French government was following a somewhat more conservative course and had placed some restrictions on the free expression of political ideas, even this more limited setting for political debate was a sharp change from the censorship and authoritarian bureaucracy in Prussia. The entire left-right political spectrum—not to mention groups claiming to be in another political dimension altogether—was vigorously present in Paris, from conservatives to pro- and anti-government liberals, to radical democrats and republicans, to pacifist Fourierist socialists, to revolutionary communists. Supporters of all these views articulated their opinions forthrightly in the periodical press, parliamentary debates, legal and clandestine associations, public and private gatherings. Not only were the vigor and forums of political debate in Paris greater than in Prussia, so were the social circles in which it was expressed. Marx had previously been involved with a small group of Young Hegelian intellectuals, and then, while editing the *Rhineland News*, with the more numerous but eminently bourgeois notables of Cologne. In Paris he met working-class political activists, and spent time in taverns both with artisans belonging to illegal, secret societies and with members of legal mutual benefit associations.

Paris was the capital of the entire Continent. Political exiles from across Europe flocked to the city, where they could express their ideas freely and even hope to influence public policy in ways that would reverberate back home. Leftists and liberals from the Iberian Peninsula and Italy, Poland and Russia, even the Danubian principalities of

Moldavia and Wallachia, core of the future Romania, were all a part of the Parisian political scene. Marx's contacts with the Russians, in particular, are well documented.[15]

Living in Paris brought Marx into close proximity with radicals from other countries, but becoming an émigré meant new and often quite different contacts with Germans. They were the largest group of foreigners in Paris, some 60,000 strong by the mid-1840s, or about one Parisian in seventeen. Many dissident German intellectuals were living in the French capital, including Young Hegelians and other radicals Marx had met in Berlin and Cologne, but also a host of new acquaintances. Two well-known examples were the celebrated poet and man of letters Heinrich Heine, whose political attitudes vacillated between liberal and more radical perspectives; and August Ludwig von Rochau, onetime student radical and later unconventional liberal, who would coin the famous term *Realpolitik*. Paris's German intellectuals included some historically more obscure figures, veteran leftists who had been active for years in radical secret societies, such as Jacob Venedey, German Mäurer, and August Hermann Ewerbeck.[16] Marx would move in their circles as well.

These long-term leftists did socialize with their fellow intellectuals, even of other political persuasions, but they also shared a social scene with members of a quite different milieu: the substantial majority of Paris's German inhabitants, who were journeymen artisans come to France because they were unable to find work in central Europe. About one third of the tailors, shoemakers, and cabinetmakers—the three most numerous but also worst paid crafts—in Paris at the time were Germans.[17] These artisans made up the bulk of the membership in the secret societies led by intellectuals such as Ewerbeck or Venedey; like their fellow craftsmen all across the Continent, they joined mutual benefit societies to guard against the dangers of their proletarian existence, particularly unemployment-generating illness. And like their French counterparts, they were experimenting, in eclectic and unsystematic fashion, with socialist and communist ideas, mixing vaguely understood notions about collective workshops, often drawn from memories of the guild system, with biblically based, if theologically dubious, understandings of justice and equity.[18]

The elements of Marx's intellectual evolution between the fall of 1843 and the end of the following year—in particular, his redefinition of the future ideal regime as communist; his investigation of the works of the major economists of the day and incorporation of their findings into his new worldview; his identification of the working class as the vehicle for political transformation; and his restatement of Feuerbach's version of Young Hegelianism, to put an emphasis on the labor process—were all conceptually distinct from his personal experiences in Europe's leading metropolis. Marx by no means accepted everything or everyone he met in Paris. Older and more experienced, with more responsibilities than when he was a young and enthusiastic student in Berlin, Marx was far more discerning in assessing the new intellectual and political currents he encountered in Paris, and deciding which he preferred to reject, than he had been in 1837 when he embraced the doctrines of the Young Hegelians. Yet it is hard to avoid the impression that life in Paris played a major role in shaping Marx's future.

KARL AND JENNY ARRIVED on October 11 or 12, 1843. During their sixteen-month stay, they resided at several different addresses on the rue Vanneau, in the fashionable Faubourg Saint-Germain.[19] At first, they lodged with Arnold Ruge, the radical poet Georg Herwegh, and their spouses. Some writers have, rather naively, seen this living arrangement as a socialist commune, misled by Ruge's ironic description of it as "a bit of communism." Ruge's plans, which included a cook and housekeeper for the common apartment, and delivery of all foodstuffs, thus making shopping unnecessary, were designed primarily to enable the émigrés "to live more cheaply," no small point in such an expensive city. Disagreements among the wives brought the common household to a quick end, and the Marxes moved out, but just to another apartment down the block.[20]

Shortly after the Marxes' arrival, Ruge fell ill, so Marx had to take over responsibility for editing the *Franco-German Yearbooks*. He threw himself into the task with the same energy he had shown in editing the *Rhineland News*, but with much less success. The French part of the *Yearbooks* fell away, because Ruge and Marx were unable to get any French contributors, in spite of making rounds of the many left-wing circles in Paris. Although they, like all educated Europeans of the time, could read French with some facility, their spoken French was poor and they had trouble making themselves understood.

Language problems were not the only issue, since they had the help of Moses Hess, who spoke better French from a previous stay in Paris, as a translator. There were also political and intellectual differences that made cooperation difficult. Most of the French socialists the German editors met rejected political action as a means to bring about their new society, counting instead on the voluntary formation of communes, without the need for subversive activities or revolutionary struggles. These socialists also understood their social and economic plans in religious terms: communism was the authentic realization of the ideals of Christianity. The radical, atheist German intellectuals, subversives in trouble with the Prussian authorities, were not at all congenial to these French socialists. Realizing some of these difficulties, the editors shifted their attention to the leaders of the non-socialist radical opposition to the July Monarchy, men like the poet Alphonse Lamartine, or the attorney Alexandre Ledru-Rollin, both of whom would play leading roles during the Revolution of 1848. But they had no more success in eliciting their cooperation. There was a group on the French left that probably would have been sympathetic to the émigré radicals: the overt revolutionaries, who combined an appeal to the heritage of Jacobinism, including its anti-clericalism, with a growing interest in socialist doctrines. Only these men, such as Armand Barbès, or Louis-Auguste Blanqui, France's leading revolutionary conspirator, were in jail for their attempts to foment uprisings, and so unavailable for collaboration.[21]

If efforts to recruit French authors for the *Yearbooks* failed, Marx was able to pull together enough German contributors to bring out a double issue at the end of February 1844. It was the first and last issue. Ruge had hoped, following the example of the *Rhineland News*, to create a corporation to publish the magazine, but found no investors. The *Franco-German Yearbooks*, financially a partnership between Ruge and Fröbel (Marx was asked to join, but had no funds to put into the venture), was seriously undercapitalized.[22] One setback would destroy the enterprise, and when the Prussian authorities confiscated copies as they came into Germany, Julius Fröbel gave up on the magazine, and Marx and Ruge were unable to find anyone to replace him. As the publishing venture failed, quarrels among its leading figures broke out. Ruge and Hess got into a vicious fight over a small sum the former had given the latter as an advance on an article never delivered. Ruge paid Marx, at least in part, not in cash but with copies of the *Yearbooks*—an object lesson in economics, which Marx did not fail to comprehend. Marx and Ruge then quarreled bitterly, and broke off relations with each other. Ostensibly, the issue between them was the extramarital affairs of Georg Herwegh, another member of the *Yearbooks'* inner circle (he was consorting with Franz Liszt's ex-mistress), Ruge denouncing Herwegh's immorality, Marx contending that Herwegh's questionable personal life should not impede political collaboration with him.[23]

This turn of affairs was particularly painful to Marx, since it occurred as the number of his dependents was growing. Jenny gave birth to a daughter on May 1, 1844. Her parents named the child Jenny, and she quickly came to be known in the family as *Jennychen*, "little Jenny." Jenny took the infant, at the age of six weeks, to visit her mother, who had moved back to Trier from Kreuznach. When mother and daughter arrived in Trier, the little girl was half-dead, probably because she was not nursing but receiving some dreadful gruel, a prime source of infant mortality at the time. The family physician decided the baby needed a wet-nurse, so the daughter of an old family retainer was hired. Jenny would bring the wet-nurse, who could do double duty as household help and even spoke a little French, back with her to Paris.

Dressed in the latest Parisian fashions, "for once more elegant than everybody" in Trier, showing off her daughter, Jenny was a big success and was soon receiving regular visits from all her past acquaintances. She herself took the "difficult walk" and went to see her mother-in-law. But the meeting with Henriette Marx, to her surprise, went extremely well. Pleased at the news of her son's position, Henriette was accepting and loving to her daughter-in-law, a noticeable change from past experiences. Jenny remarked in a letter to Karl on "What success does, or, for us, rather the semblance of success that I have been able to maintain with the finest tactics."[24]

Much to her and Karl's delight, they were rescued by Karl's supporters in Cologne, who raised the substantial sum of 1,000 talers and sent it to him, "personally to compensate you for the sacrifices you have made for our common cause." Heinrich Claessen, the Cologne liberal who directed the efforts, compared Marx to Daniel O'Connell, the celebrated Irish nationalist leader, whose followers collected a "national subscription" for him so that he could devote himself full time to politics. So Marx's studies, leading him toward communism, were financed by Cologne's bourgeoisie, yet more evidence of the powerful impression Marx had made when editing the *Rhineland News*, and of the local celebrity that he had achieved.[25]

IF THE *FRANCO-GERMAN YEARBOOKS* failed both as a business venture and a political intervention, the two articles Marx wrote for the double issue represented important steps in the development of his worldview. One of these articles, "Introduction to the Critique of Hegel's Philosophy of Law," argued that the Young Hegelians' critique of religion should not be an end in itself, but lead toward a criticism of social and political conditions. In doing so, Marx, for the first time, began to develop a theory of how the political and social changes he envisaged would come to pass. The second article, "On the Jewish Question," formulated as a review of Bruno Bauer's book by the same name, was both a critique of the Young Hegelians and the first public formulation of Marx's communist ideals.[26] Marx's connection of economic criticism to his discussion of the legal and social standing of the Jews in that piece has led to persistent charges that he was an anti-Semite—charges involving an anachronistic conception of both anti-Semitism and Jews.

The "Introduction to the Critique of Hegel's Philosophy of Law" began by confirming the Young Hegelians' idea of religion as an alienated expression of collective humanity. But humanity, Marx went on, was "the human world, state, society. This state, this society produces religion, an upside-down consciousness of the world, because the world itself is upside down." Religion, as the expression of an alienated human existence, was simultaneously a protest against this existence and consolation for it, in Marx's famous phrase—borrowed from Bruno Bauer—the "opium of the people."[27] Consequently, Marx asserted, the philosophical criticism of religion, or the attempts of the Free Men in Berlin to develop an atheist lifestyle, did not suffice; needed was a criticism of the social and political circumstances that were articulated in alienated form by religion. If philosophy had previously "exposed the holy form of human self-alienation," it was now necessary "to expose self-alienation in its unholy form. The critique of heaven is thus transformed into a critique of the earth, the criticism of religion into a criticism of law, the criticism of theology into a criticism of politics."

Such criticism would perceive current conditions in Germany—the

absolutist state, the society of orders, the Romantic intellectuals and
enthusiasts for the ancient Germanic tribes or the Middle Ages, and the
jurists of the Historical School of Law, who justified these conditions—
as similar to those in France before the Revolution of 1789. Since then,
France, England, and other countries of Western Europe had become
constitutional monarchies, characterized by basic civil rights, equality
under the law, and a strong elected parliament, so the further continuation of pre-1789 circumstances in the German states was an archaic
and anachronistic parody of its predecessor. When editing the *Rhineland News*, Marx had envisaged peaceful and gradual ways to change
these circumstances; now he concluded that their removal, as had been
the case in France, would require a revolution, or as Marx put it, in one
of the many pithy phrases he used in the essay, "the weapon of criticism
cannot replace the criticism of weapons."

A rerun of 1789 in Germany, Marx continued, would only result in
circumstances like those in the post-revolutionary France of the 1840s.
Ever since his arrival in Paris, Marx had been intellectually and personally in contact with enemies of this post-revolutionary order, who
had pointed out its many social, economic, and political defects. A German revolution, he suggested, would have to go further, not just to raise
Germany "to the official level of the modern nations, but to the human
heights, which are the near future of these nations." This need to exceed
past revolutions, in effect to have Germany take the lead in nineteenth-
century revolutions, as France had done in the previous century, does
sound like a moral imperative, intermingled with a bit of national pride.
But the final turn in Marx's argument, dealing with how this German
revolution was to come about, eliminated the moral imperative and
also underscored the vanguard position of Germany, paradoxically by
emphasizing its retrograde character.

Marx asserted that a "radical revolution," leading to "universal
human emancipation," was not a "utopian dream" for Germany; rather,
it was the more modest alternative of a "political revolution," that is,

one modeled on the French revolutions of 1789 and 1830. The reason
for this assertion was the first public example of Marx's theory of social
classes. In Marx's view, a political revolution required a class of civil
society to identify its particular emancipation with the universal emancipation of civil society. For the French Revolution of 1789, he ascribed
this revolutionary role to the bourgeoisie—an ascription derived from
the French socialist authors he had been reading—but denied that its
contemporary German counterpart could carry out the same role. The
German bourgeoisie refused to represent the universal interests of
civil society, but was just one of a large number of social and political
groups, including the state bureaucracy, the nobility, and the monarchy, all of whom were competing with each other to advance their own
particular interests. This was criticism strongly reminiscent of Marx's
article for the *Rhineland News* concerning the debates on freedom of the
press, when he denounced the different groups in the Rhenish Diet for
seeing press freedom as a particular interest, rather than one example
of a universal articulation of civil liberties.

In his articles on wood theft in the *Rhineland News*, Marx had not
been able to identify any revolutionary class. Now he derived its chief
criterion: a class whose burdens were so great, whose conditions were
so difficult, whose possibilities for action within the existing socioeconomic and political system were so restricted, that it could only achieve
its emancipation by a total reversal of all existing conditions. This
would occur through

> The formation of a class with radical chains, a class of civil society
> which . . . possesses a universal character through its universal suf-
> fering and raises no claims to a particular right, because no par-
> ticular injustice but injustice pure and simple is done to it . . . which
> does not stand in a one-sided antagonism to the consequences of the
> German state system, but in an all-sided antagonism to its presup-
> positions, a sphere, finally, which cannot emancipate itself without

emancipating all other spheres of society, which, in a word, is the complete loss of man, thus can only regain itself through the complete regaining of man. This dissolution of society as a particular [social] order is the proletariat.[28]

In this paragraph, the working class appears as the moving force behind, and the subject of, history. It is the successor to Hegel's Absolute Spirit, Bauer's human self-consciousness, and Feuerbach's human species essence. Marx, one could say, invented the working class for political reasons: to realize the aspirations emerging from his frustrating encounters with authoritarian Prussian rule. His political reasons were shaped by the Young Hegelians' philosophical efforts to find a human and material version of Hegel's cosmic unity of the development of Absolute Spirit, and by French radicals' and socialists' criticism of the post-revolutionary order in their country. Marx's personal acquaintance with the actual working class, with its own suffering, actions, aspirations, and ideas, was barely beginning when he placed his revolutionary hopes in it.

The essay concluded with an express articulation of Marx's portrayal of the link between his philosophical-political aspirations and the working class: "The emancipation of the German is the emancipation of man. The head of this emancipation is philosophy, its heart is the proletariat. Philosophy cannot realize itself without the abolition of the proletariat and the proletariat cannot abolish itself without the realization of philosophy." The final word was an articulation of the project of the *Franco-German Yearbooks*: "the day of the Germans' resurrection will be announced by the crowing of the Gallic rooster." A forthcoming radical revolution in France would lead to an insurrection in Germany; or perhaps, as one might imagine from a native of Trier, a new revolutionary war by a revolutionary French government, along the lines of the one in the 1790s, would bring revolutionary changes to Germany.

The goal of this even more radical revolution, the "universal human emancipation" it would bring in its wake, remained vague. The other essay of Marx's published in the *Franco-German Yearbooks*, "On the Jewish Question," began to elucidate this point, articulating for the first time Marx's understanding of human emancipation as involving an end to capitalism. In doing so, he identified capitalism with the Jews, in derogatory fashion, so that his critics frequently charge him with being an anti-Semite. The charges have been awkward for Marx's defenders, who have tiptoed around the essay in embarrassed fashion.[29] The problem with the whole debate on the essay is the almost irresistible temptation to read it in the light of twentieth-century German history, and the Nazis' "Final Solution to the Jewish Question." Understanding what Marx had in mind when writing the piece means removing it from the twentieth century's totalitarian regimes, mass murders, and racial anti-Semitism, and putting it back into its original context of the 1840s—in particular, the debate over the "emancipation" or granting of legal equality to the Jews, and the linked ideas of liberal Protestant theologians and Young Hegelian philosophers on the topic.

The essay Marx wrote was a critical review of, and commentary on, two works by Bruno Bauer, both written in 1843, in which he had opposed the emancipation of the Jews. These had stirred up a large controversy, and Marx's comments were one small piece of a much wider debate, which Marx himself followed closely.[30] Bauer's own position, at least at first glance, seemed out of place in the question of Jewish emancipation. Much of the opposition to this emancipation in central Europe had come from political and religious conservatives, who saw both the individual German states and a broader German nationality as deeply permeated with the divinely revealed principles of Christianity, making it impossible for Jews, who rejected such principles, to be citizens or subjects with rights equal to those of Christians, or even to belong to the German nation at all. One might have expected the Young Hegelians, who perceived both divine Christian revelation and

the Christian divinity it revealed as the alienated expression of humanity's self-consciousness, to support Jewish emancipation.

Bauer, though, employing his Hegelian interpretation of religion,
took the opposite position. Christianity, he asserted, demonstrated
human self-alienation in its highest form, since its divinity, its externalized and alienated human species self-consciousness, was Jesus
Christ, a human being. Theological reflection on the fact that Christianity understood "man, a consciousness, as the essence of all things"
led ultimately to the Enlightenment, and to the emancipatory, Hegelian
critique of human self-alienation in religion. By contrast, Bauer continued, in religion the Jew "was much too concerned" with "satisfaction
of natural needs . . . washings, purifications, his religious selection and
purification of daily foods, that he could even think about what man
is, altogether." Jews were a particular, self-absorbed group. Their Sab-
bath observance was solely for them, and they found nothing wrong
with letting "Christian servants or neighbors" do their work on the Sab-
bath, or Christian employees perform business deals. Bauer worked
himself into a rage on this point, describing Jewish religious attitudes
as "the mere cleverness of sensual egoism," as "crude and repulsive," as
"hypocrisy."[31]

This particularist, self-centered religious attitude, Bauer contended,
made Jews unfit for potential citizenship. Even actions by Jews demonstrating a different perspective—and Bauer referred explicitly to the
argument of Gabriel Riesser that Jews had participated in the German
nationalist uprising against Napoleonic rule—did not serve to qualify
them, since these actions involved an arbitrary dispensation from the
Jewish laws of ritual purity, and were therefore in themselves hypocritical. As Bauer put it, the Jew "is and remains a Jew, in spite of
his being a citizen and living in universal human relations: his Jewish and limited essence always wins out over his human and political
obligations."[32]

For Bauer, Christianity, even if it was an expression of human self-alienation, was at least a step on the road to human emancipation. Judaism, on the other hand, was a historical dead end, not even potentially compatible with human emancipation. This conclusion was the Hegelianized and radicalized version of an argument against emancipation frequently articulated by liberal Protestant theologians, the intellectual milieu from which the Young Hegelians had emerged. Such liberal theologians could not argue that Judaism was an inferior religion because Jews did not accept the divinity of Jesus, since these liberal theologians did not accept the divinity of Jesus either. Rather, they described Judaism as ethically inferior to Christianity. It was particularist, limited to a Chosen People, instead of being universally available. It was focused on the performance of ritual practices rather than on the examination of conscience and moral decision making. Germany's liberal Protestant theologians would repeat this invidious comparison well into the twentieth century. During the mid-nineteenth-century debate on Jewish emancipation, their theological position was politicized. It was used to condemn Jewish economic practices as self-interested, immoral, and exploitative, and to assert that individuals tied to a self-centered and particularist faith could not act as citizens of a wider polity, along with people not sharing their religion. Both criteria led to a liberal opposition to Jewish emancipation.[33] This attitude was one response to the question with which Heinrich Marx had wrestled for a substantial portion of his life: what would be the place of the Jews, a "nation" of the society of orders, after that society had come to an end?

While this was a difficult question for Heinrich, his son, who had learned liberal Protestant theology both in its original form and in its secularized Young Hegelian version, had no difficulty in accepting its perception of Judaism as a historically backward and ethically inferior religion. He wrote to Arnold Ruge in 1843, specifically in reference to Bauer's attitudes, that the "Israelite faith is repulsive to me." But the political consequences Marx drew from this view were the opposite of the attitudes of Bauer and liberal opponents of emancipation, namely, an explicit endorsement of equal rights for Jews.[34] In his essay on the Jewish Question, Marx suggested that the very same reasoning granting Jews equal rights led to the demand that society be transformed in a communist direction. This may seem like a puzzling conclusion, but it was a result of the combination of Marx's study of contemporary history and society done in Kreuznach, his attitude toward religion expressed in his other essay in the *Franco-German Yearbooks*, and his efforts to envisage a future social and political order in a space beyond the world created by the French Revolution.

To make his point about Jewish emancipation, Marx turned to an unexpected source, the writings of Alexis de Tocqueville about the United States.[35] In that country, as the French traveler had observed, a multitude of religions flourished, all of which were separated from a secular state. This "emancipation of the state from Judaism from Christianity, from religion altogether," Marx asserted, was the "political emancipation of the Jew, the Christian, of the religious person in general." In contrast to Bauer, who understood emancipation in terms of religions' similarity to modern, Enlightened, public-spirited, atheist ideals, Marx saw the realization of atheism in the secularization of the government. By making it possible for adherents of all religious confessions to be citizens, Marx asserted, the government was annulling religion in regard to politics and public life, just as (again explicitly referencing the United States) by introducing universal manhood suffrage, it was annulling the role of property in politics.[36]

Marx was not, of course, asserting that the United States of the 1840s was a communist country, any more than it was an atheist one. Just the opposite, he noted, faithfully following Tocqueville, in private life both religion and property had a very vigorous existence. His point was to contrast the particular existences of civil society—different religions, different social classes, with different amounts and kinds of property—to the universal position of a democratic state, where all citizens were equal under the law, and all had the right to vote. If Marx had stopped there, arguing that emancipation of the Jews was part of the creation of a democratic state, and an important step in the direction of such a state, no one could have accused him of anti-Semitism. Marx, though, was not content with the contrast between a state, even a democratic and republican one, representing the universal public interest, and a civil society, where different individuals and groups, including social classes with very different amounts of property and personal possibilities, pursued their own particular interests. Rather, such circumstances, as Marx had explained in his published and unpublished accounts of Hegel's philosophy of law, were a form of human alienation he was seeking to overcome.

This was where Marx introduced the distinction between "political emancipation" and "human emancipation." The latter form, abolishing human self-alienation within civil society, going beyond even the radical ideas of the French Revolution, was the "emancipation of humanity from Judaism." Using Feuerbach's language, Marx stated that he was concerned not so much with Judaism as a religion but with the "genuine Jew" in his practical life. Reiterating Bauer's hostile opinions, Marx described the "worldly basis" of the Jews as "practical need, self-interest." The "worldly cult" of the Jew was "haggling and bargaining," the "worldly God" was money. "The emancipation from haggling and from money, thus from the practical, real Jewry would be the self-emancipation of our time."

Having identified Jews with capitalism, Marx conversely identified capitalism with the Jews. If egoism and practical need were principles of Judaism, they were also principles of civil society. These principles were articulated as money, "which is the essence of man's labor and his being that has been alienated from him. That alienated being dominates him and he worships it." This alienated world of the Jews "reaches its high point with the completion and perfection of civil society, but civil society is first perfected in the Christian world. . . . It is thus not only in the Pentateuch or the Talmud that we find the essence of today's Jew but in contemporary society . . . not only as the narrow, limited existence of the Jew, but as the Jewish narrow, limited existence of society." The end to this state of affairs, Marx suggested, would occur when society succeeded in abolishing "the empirical essence of Jewry, haggling and its presuppositions," when the "conflict of individual-sensual existence with the species existence of humanity is abolished." The very last sentence of the piece reads: "The societal emancipation of the Jew is the emancipation of society from Jewry."[37]

In this essay, Marx explicitly endorsed the view of Judaism as an ethically inferior religion, and the practical consequences of this religion for everyday life articulated by liberal Protestant theologians and their Young Hegelian interpreters. Unlike them, he did not see these ostensible moral failures as a reason to deny Jews civic rights. Instead, Marx understood the emancipation of the Jews as the implementation of universal human rights developed in the eighteenth-century French and American revolutions, interpreting these rights, as he interpreted most aspects of politics, society, and economics, in Hegelian terms.

Marx did use this negative picture of the Jews as a way to attack capitalism. He did not, as would be the case with most anti-Semites, identify capitalism or the worst aspects of capitalism with the Jews; but he did perceive capitalism as arising out of Jewish economic practices. This perception appeared in other writings of his from the time, including his first essays on economics, the so-called Paris manuscripts. There, Marx denounced capitalists for constantly seeking to invent new products in order to get money from their customers. For the capitalist, he wrote, "every product is a bait to lure the essence of the other, his money . . . every genuine or possible need is a weakness which leads flies to the flypaper." The capitalist "incites pathological desires [in his customer], ferrets out every weakness in him," in order to receive money for the sale of his products. While today we might think of this condemnation in terms of advertising and consumer capitalism, in mid-nineteenth-century central Europe, well before the consumer era, such attacks were frequently levied against Jewish peddlers and moneylenders, who were accused of exploiting their peasant customers in just this way, by "outfitting them . . . with every possible, superfluous, useless and defective need. . . ."[38]

This view of capitalism as a Jewish creation, but one not limited to Jews, reaching its high point when Christians took over "Jewish" capitalist attitudes, was common to a number of Marx's contemporaries. Moses Hess had submitted an essay on money to the *Franco-German Yearbooks*, making points about Jews, money, and capitalism very similar to those Marx used in his piece. Hess's work was not published in the *Yearbooks*, but Marx had read it before writing his essay on the Jewish Question. Hess had also told Arnold Ruge that following the abolition of capitalism and the creation of a new communist society, it would be necessary to guillotine "just a few . . . property owners, stubborn bankers, Jews, capitalists, landowners and landlords"—a drastic identification of Jews with a capitalist social order. Another of Marx's Parisian acquaintances, Heinrich Heine, had described Hamburg, Germany's preeminent commercial center, as a "city of hagglers" inhabited by "baptized and un-baptized Jews (I call all Hamburg's inhabitants Jews). . . ."[39]

Marx, Hess, and Heine all came from a Jewish background, although they had all distanced themselves from the Jewish religion. Marx is often described as a self-hating Jew, but it would be difficult to say the same of Hess or Heine, since the latter had an ironic, detached attitude toward Jewishness, and the former became a proponent of a proto-Zionism.[40] It would be more appropriate to say that in the 1840s all three were living in an era when being Jewish was understood primarily in terms of religious affiliation or as membership in a "nation" of the society of orders. Later on in the century, with the rise of Darwinist ideas, conceptions of Jews as a biologically distinct group of common descent, a "race," whose membership was involuntary, would become the rule; but it would be incorrect to apply the intellectual paradigms of the 1880s and 1890s to the period four or five decades earlier. By mid-nineteenth-century standards of Jewishness, Marx was the least Jewish of the three. He had been baptized as a child, and received a Protestant religious education. Heine, by contrast, was not baptized until adulthood, and Hess, although breaking with his family's Orthodox Judaism, never became a Christian.

Marx's identification of Jews with capitalism certainly provided ammunition for later anti-Semitic attitudes within the labor and socialist movement, but there is another aspect of his thought, more important for Marx's own political aspirations, that the essay on the Jewish Question reveals. Marx believed that Jews should have equality of rights as citizens. Their emancipation was a goal worth fighting for, and an important indicator of a democratic political order. He also believed that the movement from a democratic and republican order to a communist one would involve eliminating from society those obnoxious Jewish characteristics that enemies of Jewish emancipation were using to disqualify Jews from citizenship in the first place. There was a certain disjunction between Marx's initial, democratic and republican political goals and his further communist ones. The disjunction was not limited to the Jewish Question, but would run through Marx's political aspirations as articulated in the *Communist Manifesto*, and would dog his efforts at political change, from the Revolution of 1848 to the Paris Commune of 1871.

FOLLOWING HIS BREAK WITH Arnold Ruge, Marx was politically on his own in Paris. A few months later, he was personally on his own as well, when his wife, taking little Jenny with her, went to Trier for an extended visit to her mother. Jenny had some anxieties about leaving her husband alone in a city that had a well-developed reputation for sexual licentiousness, but there was no need for her to worry.[41] In her absence Karl continued his political activities, read economists voraciously, and developed his communist ideas. His one important personal encounter was not with a chorus girl but with Friedrich Engels.

Marx moved in the same circles after the collapse of the *Yearbooks* that he had before. He continued to associate with German intellectuals in Paris, having some success in getting them, especially their leading figure Heine, on his side in his feud with Ruge.[42] Marx also pursued contacts with both French socialists and radical émigrés from other countries. It was at this time that he first encountered the Russian anarchist Mikhail Bakunin. Some decades later, the two would become bitter enemies, a hostility perhaps encouraged by memories of their earlier friendship.

Marx also intensified his connections to the secret societies of German artisans. He reported to Ludwig Feuerbach in August 1844 that the leaders of these groups had been reading out loud to their followers excerpts from Feuerbach's *Essence of Christianity* twice a week, during the summer. Although Marx would certainly have endorsed spreading atheist notions among the radical artisans, it is not clear if the initiative to do so came from him, since Hermann Ewerbeck, one of the secret society leaders, was a great Feuerbach enthusiast, who eventually published a French translation of the *Essence of Christianity*. Nonetheless, Marx's knowledge of the secret meetings of secret societies suggests a growing involvement with them.[43]

At the beginning of 1844, a biweekly German-language journal, *Forwards!*, began publication in Paris. The original founders were a dubious duo, an eccentric theatrical director and a Prussian police spy; but in the spring of 1844, secret society leaders and other leftist intellectuals, including Marx, gained greater influence on its editorial policy. Hoping that the small publication could, at least in part, replace the *Franco-German Yearbooks*, Marx pushed for it to adopt a socialist editorial policy. To that end, he published an essay in *Forwards!* on the uprising of the Silesian weavers, the first example of a working-class insurgency in central Europe, using the occasion to reiterate his views on the proletariat as the vehicle for political change.[44]

It was a couple of weeks after Marx's essay on the Silesian weavers appeared, on August 23, 1844, that Karl Marx and Friedrich Engels met in person for the first time. Out of this meeting would come a life-long political and personal collaboration, seeming in retrospect so close that the two men are invariably described together: Marx & Engels™, so to speak. In part, this representation points to the odd closeness of two such dissimilar people: one tall and fair, the other short and dark; one practical, businesslike, and good at earning money, the other moving in a realm of abstract ideas and chronically having trouble making ends meet; son of a businessman and son of a lawyer; one of Protestant, the other of Jewish background, or, as emphasized in a past era of racial thinking, one of Nordic and one of Semitic descent. The way these differences, these contradictory personal characteristics, could be overcome in a common cause was, one might say, almost dialectical. The common cause was cemented by an intimate friendship, making them the Damon and Pythias of communism.[45]

Like so many well-known features of Marx's life, this portrayal of the two men's lifelong ties as inevitable from the first meeting is a half-truth, ironing out personal and political differences, and projecting the relationship of later years onto the early period of their acquaintance. The information about Marx and Engels's initial encounter is on the scanty side—just three paragraph-long retrospectives by the protagonists, perhaps surprising for the significance of the event, although neither of the two was much given to writing memoirs. Other evidence has been suppressed: after Marx's death, his daughters Eleanor and Laura destroyed letters he wrote critical of Engels. Still other letters were kept hidden for decades, and only published at the end of the twentieth century in the new *MEGA*.[46] Looking more closely, it does seem that the initial meeting of the two men launched a period of intellectual and political cooperation, but one that did not always go smoothly. In the years after their first encounter, the two went their separate ways for longer periods of time, and contemporaries saw Marx's closest collaborators in his friends in Cologne.[47] The relationship between Marx and Engels only became truly unbreakable in the early 1850s, when they were both political refugees in England. It was also then that certain of their contrasting personal characteristics became fully developed, particularly Engels as the practical moneymaker and Marx as the impecunious theorist. So, rather than understanding this first meeting as the almost miraculous unity of opposites leading inevitably to a permanent collaboration, it might be more helpful to see what impulses brought the two men together.

The initiative for the meeting lay with Engels. Born in 1820 in the city of Barmen in the Wupper Valley about thirty-five miles to the east of Cologne, across the Rhine River, he was the son of Friedrich Engels, Sr., a prominent textile manufacturer in a region that was a central European pioneer of industrialization.[48] Then as today, the Wupper Valley was home to several varieties of particularly intense Protestantism, and Engels's father was a prominent lay proponent of the Awakening, the German version of revivalism, directed against both the Enlightened, rationalist religion Marx was taught and also the Calvinist orthodoxy prevalent in the area. Sent as a young man, after his years at the *Gymnasium*, to be a commercial apprentice in the North German port city of Bremen, Engels had a crisis of faith, intensified by reading the works of the Young Hegelians. The many notes he took on David Friedrich Strauss's *Life of Jesus*, complete with sarcastic observations about biblical literalism and German revivalists, have been preserved and testify to his movement from piety to non-belief.[49] In contrast to Marx, for whom the transition from a rationalist, Enlightened religion to Young Hegelian atheism may have been intellectually stormy but was personally smooth, for Engels it meant a painful break with his family background, especially his father.

Engels's conservative and pious family had none of the reservations of the Marxes about their son serving in the Prussian army, and Engels did his military service in 1842, as an officer candidate in the artillery, stationed in Berlin. Being a soldier agreed with him, and he was a lifelong armchair strategist. In later years, his nickname in Marx's circle would be "The General." While in Berlin, Engels was a regular member of the Free Men, and wrote several pieces for the *Rhineland News*, continuing the practice of occasional freelance journalism that he had begun while living in Bremen.[50] After the end of his one-year army service, he returned to the Wupper Valley and, on a visit to Cologne, met Moses Hess, who convinced him of the virtues of communism.

Engels's father sent him to England for further commercial training with the family's business partners in Manchester, and also to keep him away from his subversive and atheistic German friends. The paternal plan backfired badly: the stay in Manchester only reinforced the young Engels's radical and communist sympathies. Manchester was, as contemporaries said, "Cottonopolis," the global symbol and global center of the industrial revolution. As many people lived in this English provincial manufacturing town as in the Prussian capital, but in place of Berlin's intellectual and cultural attractions—the royal palace, the university and Academy of Sciences, the Opera House and the *Singakademie*—Manchester featured hundreds of steam-powered textile mills, whose emissions blanketed the city in a dense cloud of smoke and coal dust. This vast manufacturing establishment generated enormous amounts of wealth, but also massive misery. The contrast between the suburban villas of the manufacturers, bankers, and cotton wholesalers and the factory workers' slum neighborhoods—narrow streets, filthy, permeated with raw sewage, and shrouded in a perpetual gloom of pollution—made it clear just which groups received the wealth and which the misery. Manchester was as much the city of working-class struggle as of working-class suffering, where the English radicals, the Chartists, denounced the plutocratic government and demanded universal manhood suffrage. Trade unionists strove, in everyday effort, to improve wages and working conditions; socialists proposed sweeping changes to all of society. A year before Engels's arrival, in the Plug Riots—a combination general strike, insurrection, and outburst of rage at working-class existence—the city's factory proletariat had risen up and only been suppressed with a large deployment of armed force.

Associating after business hours with the city's many political opponents of the existing order, Engels also found an informal entrée into working-class life through his mistress and future companion, an Irish immigrant named Mary Burns, a factory worker and domestic servant. He decided to write a book about his experiences, emphasizing the contrast between rich and poor, outlining the misery and exploitation of the industrial workers who produced the capitalists' wealth: *The Condition of the Working Class in England* (published in German in 1845). While in Manchester, Engels continued to send in pieces to the *Rhineland News*. As a result of this connection, he wrote an article on political economy for the *Franco-German Yearbooks*.[51] On his way home from Manchester, he stopped in Paris to meet the editor of the newspaper and magazine that had published his writing.

The meeting went far more successfully than expected. Engels stayed with Marx for ten days. They laid plans to co-author a book criticizing Bruno Bauer and his lifestyle-oriented radicalism. But their collaboration was not purely intellectual. Engels, the bachelor, and Marx, leading a bachelor existence while his wife and daughter were in Trier, went out each night to a café on the Quai Voltaire. The entertainment had a political edge, since they met with émigré radicals from Germany and other European countries. One of the participants in the get-togethers was Mikhail Bakunin, who took Engels to a meeting of a secret society of French communist workers.[52]

Marx and Engels got along so well because of issues and conditions specific to each of them. For Marx, Engels was a quite different kind of collaborator from his previous ones. Up to that point, Marx, who had started his university studies at a very youthful age, had largely worked with older, more experienced men, including Gans, Bauer, Hess, Jung, Claessen, Camphausen, and Heine, who provided him with intellectual and professional opportunities. The most recent example of such a patron, Arnold Ruge, made no secret of the fact that he regarded Marx as his protégé. Following their personal and political conflict, Ruge also made no secret of his disappointment and, increasingly, disgust at what he saw as his former protégé's ungrateful behavior.[53]

With Engels, the relationship was reversed. He was two years younger than Marx, less experienced and less well connected, and had sought out the notorious editor of the *Rhineland News* by letter and in person—another example of the impact Marx had made during the few months he held that position. Engels became Marx's protégé and Marx enjoyed the new opportunity to be a mentor, a role that would expand over the following years. Another of Marx's long-term political associates, Wilhelm Liebknecht, 1848 revolutionary and one of the founders of the German labor movement, remembered how, in London exile during the 1850s, Marx, "in possession of his advantage of 5 or 6 years over us 'young lads' was conscious of the entire superiority of his mature manhood. . . ."[54]

The collaboration with Marx gave Engels the chance to escape from an escalating existential dilemma: a communist in training to be an eminently capitalist textile merchant and manufacturer, an atheist living in a household of born-again Christians. His letters to Marx from Barmen after their initial meeting are eloquent testimony to this dilemma. There were triumphant reports of the progress of communism in the Wupper Valley and in Cologne. But Engels's own personal life was wretched. After a few days working "in the factory of my old man . . . it is just too dreadful not only to remain a bourgeois, but, still more, to be a manufacturer, a bourgeois actively opposing the proletariat." Engels's pro-communist attitudes had "reawakened all the religious fanaticism of my old man." Engels Senior and all of the relatives went around with a "divinely blessed face of misery" in response to the insubordinate young man's radical ideas. "You have no clue," Engels wrote Marx, "of the malice of this Christian hunt, complete with its beaters, on my soul."[55] The personal and the political converged in the young Friedrich Engels's life, as his communist and atheist allegiances exacerbated the difficult relationship with his authoritarian father, and the prospect of pursuing these allegiances with the assistance of the older and more experienced Marx offered a way out of increasingly intolerable domestic circumstances.

A VERY CONSIDERABLE PORTION of Marx's efforts and energy during the nine to ten months between the failure of the *Franco-German Yearbooks* and his expulsion from France was devoted to writings on economic and philosophical questions. These "Paris manuscripts," or "Economic and Philosophical Manuscripts of 1844," remained unpublished in Marx's lifetime and, in fact, for fifty years after his death. After the Second World War, when excerpts were widely translated, they became the center of an extensive scholarly dispute. One camp saw the manuscripts as examples of a "young Marx," concerned with broad existential and philosophical issues, contrasted to a more dogmatic and positivist older Marx, for whom these initial interests had been overlaid or replaced with more narrowly economic questions and the advocacy of an unflinching class struggle. Others did not disagree with this chronology, but saw the older Marx as the genuine Marx, whose theoretical insights marked a break with his fuzzier, excessively Hegelian and existentialist earlier thinking.[56]

In retrospect, this whole debate, fueled by strongly differing opinions about the (ostensibly) communist regimes of the Eastern bloc, and by 1960s-era searches for alternative lifestyles, is not very enlightening for Marx's own ideas. Creating distinctions between a young and an old Marx overlooks the persistence of Hegelian concepts in his intellectual efforts. The idea that the Paris manuscripts were concerned with an existentially understood alienation can only be supported by a very partial reading of these manuscripts, ignoring their extensive discussions of economic questions—admittedly, parts that were generally left out of the published excerpts so popular in the 1960s. Rather, a comprehensive consideration of the manuscripts demonstrates Marx's incorporation of his readings of prominent economists of the late eighteenth and early nineteenth centuries into his critiques of civil society, and his advocacy of its communist transformation.

The manuscripts dealt with a rich variety of topics, not always closely connected, including materialist speculations on the creation of the human race, a discussion of Shakespeare's ideas about money, and a lengthy materialist-Feuerbachian critique of Hegel's philosophical writings.[57] The heart of the manuscripts, though, stemmed from Marx's reading in Paris, for the first time, of the classics of political economy by Adam Smith, James Mill, David Ricardo, and Jean-Baptiste Say (the Englishmen in French translations). Although Marx did look at the works of a few early socialist critics of economic orthodoxy, such as Eugène Buret, the vast majority of his notes, and of the corresponding citations in his manuscripts, came from mainstream, pro-capitalist economists.[58] The conclusions Marx drew from them were deeply pessimistic for the condition of the proletariat.

Comparing the classical economists' three sources of income—wages of labor, profit of capital, and rent of land—Marx concluded that wages were the least likely to increase, and would usually be reduced to subsistence level. He explained this development in a number of different ways: in terms of the tendency of food prices to change with

wages, keeping their purchasing power constant; in capitalists shift-
ing their investments to the greatest source of profits, while workers
were generally stuck in one particular occupation and threatened with
unemployment; and in the capitalists' ability to place the burden of net
payments to the agricultural sector on the workers. Marx followed up
this static analysis with a dynamic one, quoting Adam Smith that when
"the wealth of society is in decline . . . no one suffers more cruelly from
its decline than the workers."[59] Marx admitted that when social wealth
was increasing, and capitalists were competing for workers, wages
could rise, but hours of labor would increase, wearing out the workers
and shortening their lives. He also noted that social wealth increased
via mechanization and the rise of factory employment, a growing division of labor, and a concentration of capital, so that the number of
capitalists would shrink, while former capitalists would themselves
become workers, all of which would reverse the favorable effects for the
workers of, as we might say today, a growing gross domestic product.
Once more quoting Adam Smith, Marx noted that economic growth
would eventually come to an end in a stationary state, when wages
and profits were low, most income flowed to landowners, workers
would be reduced to a subsistence minimum, and an excess population
would die off. "Thus in a declining condition of society progressive
misery of the worker, in progressing condition, complicated misery, in
completed final condition, stationary misery."[60]

The prognoses Marx drew from the work of the leading political
economists of his day did involve an emphasis on the negative side
of their findings, but they were not fundamentally different from the
conclusions reached by Smith or Ricardo themselves. Unlike many
of today's perennially optimistic economists, who so often envisage a
future of economic growth and rising prosperity (at least, if no one
interferes in the operation of free markets), political economy of the
early and mid-nineteenth century was the "dismal science" that foresaw
a declining, or, at best, a stationary future—especially for the lower

classes—which the maximum productivity and efficiency generated by free markets could delay but not avert. In these respects, Marx, with his pessimistic views about the decline of wages to subsistence levels, the increasing concentration of capital combined with declining profits and rates of interest, and the increasing claims of landowners on national income, was no dissident from the political economy of his day, but expressed the dominant, orthodox viewpoint.[61]

Marx's pessimistic prognosis appears in his attitudes toward a less orthodox contemporary, whose writings helped shape his view of industrialization. This was the German radical Wilhelm Schulz, a friend of Ruge and Fröbel, whose *Movement of Production*—even the title sounds like Marx's version of economics—published in 1843, was quite influential in the Paris manuscripts, arguably more so than Engels's essay on economics that appeared in the *Franco-German Yearbooks*. Decades later, in writing *Capital*, Marx would continue to praise Schulz's work.[62] Schulz explained, in powerful and evocative detail, how the progress of manufacturing in Great Britain, and the parallel expansion of national production, went along with the impoverishment and even physical deformation of the working class as a result of factory labor, condemning as sophists those who attempted to prove statistically that the workers were becoming better off. He asserted (with considerable impact on Marx) that even if workers' real wages were rising, their relative poverty was increasing; that is, the workers' share of national income was declining.[63]

Where Marx did not follow Schulz, though, was in the latter's contention that mechanization was decreasing the amount of difficult physical labor workers would have to perform. Nor did he consider Schulz's suggestion that founding workers' cooperatives might help mitigate their condition. Marx certainly did not agree with Schulz's attacks on the Young Hegelians' atheism and his call for religiously inspired social and political reforms.[64] In his selective reading of Schulz's book, singling out the darkest passages that made up a relatively small part of the work, Marx was demonstrating his fundamental agreement with the views of mainstream political economists—both their skepticism of reforms that interfered with the operations of the free market and their dark portrait of the ultimate end of free market economic activity.

Marx criticized mainstream economists for having devised "laws" of economic development, but not "conceptualiz[ing] these laws, i.e., they did not follow out how they proceeded from the essence of private property." Both conceptualizing and proceeding from an essence were fundamental to the Hegelian project of understanding intellectual disciplines as part of a philosophical system. This is what Marx undertook, albeit using his own version of Feuerbach's materialist reformulation of Hegel, in the philosophical part of his economic and philosophical manuscripts.

Marx observed that political economy had shown that "The worker becomes all the poorer, the more wealth he produces, the more his production increases in extent and strength. . . . With the valuation of the world of things, the devaluation of the world of man increases in direct proportion. Labor does not just produce commodities; it produces itself and the worker as a commodity. . . ."[65] Marx interpreted philosophically this interrelated process of society's enrichment and the proletariat's impoverishment as a threefold alienation.

One form of alienation was the emptying out (*Entäusserung*) of workers into the product of their labor, commodities and capital, which became alien to workers and possessed power over them. This process in economics was "just as in religion," Marx noted, reiterating the Young Hegelians' critique of religion as humanity alienating its essence in an imaginary divinity and subjecting itself to that divinity: "the more objects the worker produces, the less he can possess and the more he comes under the domination of his product, of capital."

Workers were not just alienated from the product of their labor; the process of labor itself had become alienated. There is a distinct twentieth- and twenty-first-century tendency to understand this "alienated labor" as referring to mechanical, repetitive, monotonous work, of the sort performed on assembly lines. Of course, there were no assembly lines in the 1840s, and Marx had no personal acquaintance with earlier forms of repetitive labor, such as textile workers tending a mule jenny, since the workers with whom he associated in Paris were skilled craftsmen, who toiled in small workshops lacking steam-powered machinery.[66] Rather, Marx asserted that the process of labor was alienated and externalized because its product was alienated and externalized: labor was the "activity of externalization." He continued: "The activity of the worker is not his self-activity. It belongs to another, it is the loss of his self." Marx even criticized Charles Fourier for his denunciation of "leveled out, parcelized and thus unfree labor" as just a rejection of a "particular form" rather than of all forms of labor in a capitalist society. Fourier's concept seems similar to a contemporary understanding of alienated labor as boring, unskilled, repetitive work, but Marx specifically rejected this concept as an inadequate understanding of the alienation of the labor process.[67]

The third version of alienation Marx diagnosed from the conclusions of political economy was the alienation of human "species being" or "species essence" (in German, *Gattungswesen*). This was a rather more mysterious notion than the alienation of the product of labor or the alienation of the labor process. It was, as so often in Marx's work in this period, a concept stemming from the Young Hegelian critique of religion, Ludwig Feuerbach's idea of what was being alienated and externalized both in terms of human notions of a divinity and Hegel's concept of Absolute Spirit. Marx reinterpreted Feuerbach's concept, writing Feuerbach in August 1844, as the work on the Paris manuscripts was well advanced, to say that Feuerbach's work provided the "philosophical basis of socialism" and that the "concept of the human species . . . is the concept of society."[68]

"Alienated labor," Marx stated, "alienates man from the species; it makes his species life into the means of his individual life . . . life activity, productive life appears only as a means for the satisfaction of needs, the need for the preservation of physical existence."[69] This was the further development of a point Marx had made a year earlier, when he had contrasted, in his critique of Hegel's philosophy of law, the particular purposes of individuals and families in civil society with the universal purposes of the state. In a capitalist system, individual labor was alienated from the interests of human species understood as society; it did not express these human species interests. Alienated labor, Marx continued, alienated "man from man"; it was labor separated from human society.

In drawing this revised distinction between the particular and the universal, Marx was also revising Feuerbach's conception of human species essence or species being as incorporated in physical, reproductive love, to one in which species essence consisted of productive labor: "It is precisely in the manipulation and transformation of the objective world that man proves himself to be genuinely a species being. This production is his working species existence." As Marx put it at a later point in the manuscript, "We see how the history of industry and the objective existence of the development of industry is the open book of human essential powers. . . ." Marx developed the idea that the basis of human existence in society was collective and cooperative labor, transforming products of nature from notions put forth by Moses Hess as reinterpreted in the light of the works of classical political economy. First articulated in the Paris manuscripts, this concept would remain central to his philosophical, historical, and economic analysis for the rest of his life.[70]

Communism, as Marx understood it in the Paris manuscripts, was the abolition of the threefold alienation of labor stemming from private property. In discussing the consequences of the abolition of private property, Marx was careful to distance himself from "crude communism" and the "animalistic form" of communism, the community of women. (The accusation that communists wanted to make women into men's collective property was a common form of conservative attack on communism, in the 1840s and later.) Rather, his communism had more Hegelian, philosophical elements:

> positive abolition of private property as human self alienation and thus as the genuine appropriation of human essence by and for man. . . . This communism is . . . the true dissolution of the clash between man and nature, and between man and man, the true dissolution of the clash between existence and essence, between objectification and self-confirmation, between freedom and necessity, between individual and species. It is the solution to the riddle of history and knows itself as this solution.[71]

Marx's communism was the materialist form of Hegel's Absolute Spirit. It was also the new version, inflected by Marx's reading of political economy, of the "democratic" state he had described as a political ideal in his critique of Hegel. Marx had even referred to this democratic state as the "solution to the riddle of all constitutions," just as he described communism as the solution to the riddle of history. In communism, as in the earlier description of a democratic ideal, the distinction between particular private activities and universal human activities would be abolished.

Marx's understanding of society and social existence had been influenced by his experiences with radicalized Parisian workers. In a telling passage, he described how meetings of communist workers presaged a future communist society:

> When communist artisans unite, at first doctrine, propaganda, etc. is the purpose of their meetings. But as they meet, they appropriate a new need, the need for society, and what appeared as a means now becomes an end. One can observe this practical movement in its most shining results, when one sees a meeting of socialist French

workers. Smoking, drinking, eating, etc. are no longer there as means of connection and as connecting means. Society, the association, the conversation, which, in turn, has society as its goal, suffices for them. The brotherhood of man is no phrase, but a truth to them and the nobility of humanity shines out at us from figures hardened by labor.[72]

This distinctly romanticized description of the meeting of a secret society marked a new stage in Marx's invention of the working class. Not just the necessary instrument of revolutionary political change, as he described the workers in the "Introduction to the Critique of Hegel's Philosophy of Law," they were now the group whose social practices were articulations of the future social and political order Marx envisaged. Both these steps in his evolving perception of the nature and historical significance of the proletariat reflected his Parisian experiences: his encounters with socialist workers and his intense reading of political economists.

THE PROCESS OF WRITING the economic and philosophical manuscripts clarified Marx's ideas and gave him an intellectual agenda. In an introduction to the manuscripts composed toward the end of his reflections, rather than at the beginning, he announced his intention of writing a series of short pieces, criticizing in Feuerbach's version of Hegelian philosophy "justice, morality, politics, etc." He would begin this critical series with a short work on political economy. In early 1845, Marx signed a contract with the left-wing Darmstadt publisher Karl Julius Leske, to write such a book, *A Critique of Politics and Economics*. There was considerable interest among Marx's Cologne acquaintances, and among German-speaking socialists throughout Europe, in the proposed work.[73]

This plan to publish critiques of different aspects of the bourgeois and capitalist society in mid-nineteenth-century Europe, beginning with economics, remained a project Marx would pursue for the rest of his life. It was a difficult task for an author who had trouble completing any work he began, and who was frequently distracted from his long-term goals. Marx never got beyond the initial critique of political economy. His research and writing on economics of the 1850s and 1860s culminated in the enormous and ultimately unfinished *Capital*, whose subtitle was "A Critique of Political Economy," which represented the first stage of the original critical project.

If the project got off to a slow start in 1845, it was not just Marx's work habits that were to blame. Rather, it was the long arm of the Prussian monarchy, reaching out to harass its enemies, outside of Prussian jurisdiction. The Prussians threatened Marx's publisher (who resided in Hessen outside Prussian territory) and forced him to insist that Marx tone down the political implications of his book, and ultimately to cancel the contract altogether. This action was directed against Marx personally; much more difficult was the result of an action by Count Arnim, the Prussian ambassador in Paris, aimed at German radicals there more generally. Arnim wanted the French government to expel a group of them who had published anti-Prussian writings. François Guizot, the moderate-liberal French prime minister, may not have wanted to give in to the demands of a conservative government and endorse its attitude about freedom of the press, but as an enemy of the French radicals and socialists, he was not altogether happy about having foreigners of similar opinions circulating in the capital. After lengthy negotiations, he agreed to issue expulsion orders for five Germans: the founders and current editor of *Forwards!* as well as Marx and Ruge, editors of the defunct but distinctly anti-Prussian *Franco-German Yearbooks*. The French Ministry of the Interior did not actually know where Marx resided to serve him with the expulsion order, so Marx voluntarily turned himself in to the police after hearing about the orders from the other dissidents. Well ensconced in Paris, pursuing his studies of history and political economy, working on the left-wing German-language newspaper, and trusting that the French liberal government would hardly give in to its reactionary Prussian counterpart, Marx did not take the expulsion order seriously. Then, to his dismay, he found that he had one week to leave the country.[74]

At the end of January 1845, Marx left France for Belgium, accompanied by one of his Cologne admirers, Heinrich Bürgers, who had been visiting Marx in Paris. As the two rode the postal coach through northern France, Bürgers thought it necessary to start singing, "in order to dispel the thoughtful and depressed mood" that Marx "sought in vain to master."[75] If Karl was depressed at his expulsion, his wife, left behind to wind up the family business in Paris, was stressed and infuriated. Just at the beginning of her second pregnancy, with little Jenny in tow, Jenny dashed around the city, trying in vain to get back the deposit on their rented apartment, hoping, apparently with equally little success, to arrange auctioning off the family's furniture. "These are the wonderful consequences of this governmental, guizotian infamy," she complained to Karl.[76]

Jenny's anger, like Karl's depression, is easy to understand, but the targeting of her husband by the Prussian government was evidence of his increased political stature. Unlike the suppression of the *Rhineland News*, when the Prussian authorities were not quite clear who was responsible for the editorial policy of the newspaper, they now had Marx in their sights as an enemy of the state. There were standing orders to arrest him, should he set foot on Prussian territory.[77] Not content with that, the Prussian government, as the demands of its ambassador in Paris show, was determined to harass and undermine Marx's position, even if he was outside its immediate grasp.

Marx could no longer live peacefully as an émigré. If he wished to remain on the Continent and continue his intellectual and political activities, he would have to fight back against the Prussian government, aiming at its overthrow. How such an anti-Prussian commitment would accompany the pro-communist one he had developed during his sixteen months in Paris was a question that would dominate the four and a half years of Marx's life that followed his expulsion from France, the period of his most direct and intense revolutionary activity.

5

The Revolutionary

THE LIVELY NIGHTTIME ENTERTAINMENT Marx and Engels had enjoyed after their meeting in Paris was not to be had in Brussels. Contemporary observers noted how the Belgian capital became "quiet, very early in the evening."[1] Entertainment aside, the enforced move from Paris to Brussels seemed to have thrust Marx into the margins, from the political and intellectual center of the Continent to the capital of a small, newly founded country, whose continued independence was chronically in doubt. But Brussels offered more possibilities than appeared at first glance. The Belgian capital became Marx's home for three years, his longest continued period of residence in any one place between leaving the University of Berlin in 1842 and his arrival as a refugee in London in 1849. The time in Brussels was Marx's revolutionary apprenticeship, preparing him organizationally, intellectually, and politically for his role in the turbulent politics of the Revolution of 1848–49. Like all apprenticeships, this one had its share of false steps, difficult lessons, and wrong turnings. But as Marx learned his revolutionary craft and political circumstances turned more favorable, the value of the apprenticeship would become clear.

. . .

IF NOT QUITE ON Paris's scale, the quarter million inhabitants of Brussels during the 1840s created an urban world that was nothing less than substantial. Rather like the French capital, there was a German colony, consisting of some émigré intellectuals and a larger group of craftsmen. Also like Paris, radical and liberal political refugees from across the Continent had found their way to Brussels. The excellent royal library was convenient for Marx's studies of philosophy and political economy. Brussels's location, with easy access to Cologne, Paris, and London, the three foci of Marx's political activity, was a decided advantage. Admittedly, the Parisian socialist scene was lacking. As one contemporary noted, "one has to search for socialists with a lantern" in Brussels.[2] But in Belgium, whose independence in 1830 from the Netherlands had come simultaneously with the drafting of a constitution fully guaranteeing civil liberties, Catholic conservatives, liberals, and radicals all publicly and energetically propagated their views.[3]

In Brussels, Marx continued and expanded the activities he had begun in Paris. One theme was to enhance ties with a radical secret society of German artisans. Marx also worked persistently on publishing projects designed to recreate an émigré political journal along the lines of the *Franco-German Yearbooks*. His intellectual efforts, including the projected work on political economy, and the unfinished political and philosophical commentaries on trends in German radicalism coauthored with Engels and Moses Hess, which has come to be known as *The German Ideology*, were closely connected to these publishing ventures. Marx would also meet and associate with political radicals from other countries, both refugees and Belgians, leading to the high point of his pre-revolutionary activity, his involvement in the Brussels Democratic Association, formed toward the end of 1847.

Although similar to his previous efforts in Paris, Marx's activities in Brussels proved more intense and conflict-laden. As he endeavored to shape the political program and revolutionary orientation of the chief German émigré secret society, he clashed with other prospective leaders of the nascent labor movement. Marx's theoretical development emerged out of his angry and sarcastic critiques of Young Hegelian and socialist intellectuals. When these criticisms became public, they heightened personal and political antagonisms, arousing controversy, and creating both more loyal followers and more embittered enemies. These growing controversies intersected with Marx's family life, particularly in the ever sensitive area of his finances, so that it became even harder to raise money and to make ends meet. His persistent financial difficulties, sharpened by the economic crisis Europe experienced in the years 1845–47, increased Marx's personal irascibility, heightening the polemical in his political and intellectual endeavors, which in turn created yet more problems for him. By 1847, both the broader European political situation and Marx's personal circumstances were in crisis mode.

IN THE SUMMER OF 1845, Marx, along with Engels, who had joined him in Brussels, took a trip to England, while Jenny, pregnant with a second child, visited her mother in Trier.⁴ The journey was primarily to do research for the planned critique of political economy, and most of it was spent in Manchester. Which aspects of the bourgeois dreams and capitalist nightmares of the city Engels showed his friend is unknown. What we do know is that both men sat together in Manchester's public libraries, studying the works of English political economists. Marx's wide reading included seventeenth-century pioneers of political economy, William Petty and Charles Davenant, but also his own contemporaries, such as John Stuart Mill, whose assertions about international trade Marx described in his notes as "beautiful nonsense."⁵

On the way back to Brussels, the two men stopped for a couple of weeks in London, where Engels introduced Marx to English and German radicals he had met during the year he was working in Manchester. The Germans were members of the League of the Just, the main exile German secret society, composed of several hundred radical journeymen artisans and a few more intellectual leaders. The members, both working-class and more educated, veered between a Jacobin radicalism akin to the ideals of Robespierre and variations on the socialism prevalent in Paris. Marx had associated with this group while he was in Paris, but its most resolute leaders and activists had been implicated in the attempted French republican uprising of 1839 and had fled the country, settling in London, where they enjoyed the very liberal British policy on granting political asylum. In London, the radical leaders organized a new branch of the secret society, which by the mid-1840s had become its largest and most active, and harbored the group's European-wide central committee. They also created, to facilitate its activities and recruit new members, a German Workers' Educational Association. In contrast to the secret society, the association was an open public group, a flourishing enterprise that had seven hundred members at its peak, offering them opportunities for socializing, recreation, adult education, and a mutual benefits fund to help support them during periods of ill health or unemployment.[6]

These artisan associations were run by a troika of German leaders. Two were themselves craftsmen, the shoemaker Heinrich Bauer and the watchmaker Joseph Moll, a Cologne native. The third, dominant figure among them was Karl Schapper, an example of a quite different social type that had come into existence in Europe during the first half of the nineteenth century: the professional revolutionary. First involved in radical politics as a student at the University of Giessen at the beginning of the 1830s, Schapper participated in three different failed conspiracies and revolutionary putsches in Germany, Switzerland, and France between 1833 and 1839, the last of which brought him into London exile. Tall and powerfully built, with a prominent dark mustache, Schapper looked the part of a man of action. He lived for his political agitation, spending hours in pubs with artisans calling for revolution, and, when legally possible, using his accomplished oratory in public meetings to demand the same.[7]

Countless twentieth-century Marxist activists, including Lenin, eagerly adopted the hallmarks of the professional revolutionary, continuous single-minded conspiracy and agitation, but Marx never did. Neither Marx's professorial demeanor, nor his scholarly interests, nor his family commitments and the financial demands they made upon him fit these requirements. His encounter with such a revolutionary, though, would provide him with a crucial link to the social group he had designated as central to his political aspirations.

Schapper's political connections went well beyond the ranks of German artisans. He had ties to Giuseppe Mazzini, Europe's leading democratic radical and tireless organizer of clandestine subversive groups. Schapper also worked closely with émigré French radicals. The membership of the Workers' Educational Association he led, while mostly German, had a scattering of other nationalities, including Scandinavians, Dutch, Swiss, Italians, and a "genuine Turk," a Muslim from one of the Bulgarian provinces of the Ottoman Empire. Perhaps the most important connections were with English radicals, the Chartists, who combined the demand for a democratic government in Britain, to be guaranteed by a "people's charter," with labor agitation containing at least some socialist elements. Either directly through Schapper, or via Engels, Marx met a number of these radicals in London, including Ernest Jones, who would become a long-term political ally.

The English radicals were interested in uniting the leftists of different European countries, or at least the émigré leftists from different countries residing in London, an idea Karl Schapper strongly endorsed. During their stay in London, Marx and Engels were part of the preliminary preparations, although the actual founding of the "Fraternal Democrats" only occurred in September 1845, after they had returned

to Belgium. Marx's political activities would focus on the German radicals of the League of the Just and the English radicals leading the
Fraternal Democrats in the two years after his trip to England.[8]

SOMETIME EARLY IN 1846, Marx and Engels decided to create a network of communists across Europe, by founding a Communist Committee of Correspondence. From the group's central office in
Brussels, they would send out circulars and reports on communist theory and political economy, while their correspondents in the German
states and elsewhere on the Continent would send them information
about activities in their localities. If their network contained primarily
German-speaking communists, they also made efforts to international-
ize it, calling on their English connections and attempting to recruit
Pierre-Joseph Proudhon, one of Paris's most prominent socialist
thinkers, and a personal acquaintance of Marx.

The whole endeavor was for the purpose of preparing a congress, at
which delegates could meet and devise a political program. Sometimes
the proposed congress was described as a communist one, and at other
times as democratic—not necessarily a distinction, since Engels publicly proclaimed communism to be the contemporary form of democracy. It was not entirely clear if the congress participants would be just
Germans, or if it would include representatives from different European nations. As the Fraternal Democrats were drawn into the plan
and began to provide its organizational backbone, which was certainly
the case by 1847, the congress became more explicitly international and
democratic in orientation.[9]

The organizing attempts of the Committee of Correspondence were
unsuccessful; its efforts never reached beyond the circle of Marx's
personal acquaintances. There was occasional correspondence with
communists in Germany, but the general tenor of their reports was discouraging: supporters were scarce; they lacked money to support the

enterprise; and they found it poorly designed and badly implemented. As for the circulars to be issued from Brussels dealing with theoretical and economic questions, only one ever appeared: an attack on Hermann Kriege, an émigré German communist living in New York. The tone of denunciation in the circular was so vehement that Marx and Engels's correspondents, who agreed with the political point they were making, found their way of doing so positively offputting in its extreme hostility.[10]

For all the problems with Marx and Engel's organizing efforts, interest in socialism and communism was growing in Germany, particularly in the western provinces of the Prussian monarchy, where a number of periodicals devoted to communist ideas appeared in the mid-1840s: in their native Rhine Province, the *Mirror of Society* and the *Rhenish Yearbooks of Social Reform*; in the neighboring province of Westphalia, the more colorfully named *Westphalian Steamboat*. Both Marx and Engels wrote occasional pieces for these journals, but they aspired to have their own, under their individual control, and, like the *Franco-German Yearbooks*, published abroad, outside the reach of press censorship. They envisaged this journal as just one product of a publishing company that would also bring out a library of German translations of the works of French and English socialists.[11]

These plans were not solely the work of Marx and Engels. Behind them was a third, Moses Hess, who had moved to Brussels in the fall of 1845 with his female companion, and lodged next door to the Marxes. Each of the trio had associations with the other two directly. Engels, for instance, had met Hess a good year before his encounter with Marx in Paris; the *Mirror of Society* had begun as a collaboration between Engels and Hess, without Marx's involvement. "The triumvirate, Marx, Hess and Engels," as the anti-communist German democrat Karl Heinzen described them, formed a working group of three equal partners. Letters from German radicals such as Hermann Ewerbeck and Karl Ludwig Bernays in Paris, or Wilhelm Weitling and Georg Weerth in England, were addressed to them jointly, perceiving them as part of a common enterprise. Ewerbeck noted in one letter that "I always write for all of you."[12]

Hess was crucial to the publishing plans because he was quite accomplished at getting journals started and works published. Both Rhenish socialist periodicals were originally his doing. It was Hess who negotiated with two pro-communist Westphalian capitalists, Julius Meyer, owner of an iron forge, and Rudolph Rempel, a linen wholesaler, both of whom had supported the *Westphalian Steamboat*, about financing the proposed new publications. An agreement seemed to have been reached, but the whole enterprise collapsed in June 1846. It is hard to know exactly what happened, but Hess's own account noted that the crucial agreements between him and Meyer and Rempel were purely verbal, so it is likely that all the parties were hearing what they wanted—and, given Hess's tendency to conflate his aspirations with reality, the outcome was no surprise.[13]

Marx could not contain his anger when the project collapsed. His Cologne friends attributed what was probably a severe case of bronchitis to his agitation and frustration. Rising from his sickbed, Marx wrote an outraged letter to Meyer and Rempel, denouncing them for violating their contractual obligations—taking at face value Hess's assertions. The two Westphalians replied in equally angry terms, and the story of the falling out, which quickly became known in leftist circles, reflected poorly on Marx, alienating some of his friends and associates. Explaining the attitudes of German radicals in Paris, Hermann Ewerbeck informed Marx: "The 'party' is kaput in the esteem of the people."[14]

Marx continued to look for a publisher, but the printers he approached were either afraid of the Prussian authorities or skeptical of the series as a business venture, two often related issues. By 1847, he was pursuing another project: a journal of political economy, to be funded by selling shares of stock, along the lines of the *Rhineland News*.

Marx was still courting potential investors when the outbreak of the 1848 Revolution gave him the opportunity for more direct forms of political action.[15]

In view of the effort Marx put into these publishing projects, and the anger he showed when they were thwarted, he must have attached a good deal of importance to them. These potential publications, quite unlike his association with the radical émigré artisans of the League of the Just, were directed toward an educated and affluent audience. Even before he moved to Brussels, Marx had perceived the proletariat as the social group that would be the key to his increasingly revolutionary aspirations. The centrality of the working class and its importance for his theories would only increase and be more elaborately justified during his time in Brussels. Yet for all his commitment to the working class, he continued to pursue his associations with the bourgeoisie. Both of these trends would be very apparent in the major theoretical works Marx authored or co-authored in the years 1845–47.

THREE SUBSTANTIAL WORKS OF philosophy and social and economic theory are associated with Marx's time in Brussels: *The Holy Family*, *The German Ideology*, and *The Poverty of Philosophy*. Commentaries on them tend to portray a straight path, leading directly from Marx's initial and tentative attempts at articulating communist ideas in Paris to the Brussels works and on to the well-formulated and trenchantly expressed positions of the *Communist Manifesto*. A straight line certainly can be drawn through Marx's Brussels writings, but only by neglecting a substantial majority of their actual content, which encompassed a meandering mass of polemics, denouncing with a wide variety of sharp arguments ranging from trenchant to dubious the Young Hegelian intellectuals and other communist thinkers. All too often, the polemics became an end in themselves; at other points, they were a form of veiled self-criticism, in which Marx furthered his own theoretical development by denouncing other people's expressions of ideas that he himself had previously held.

The first of the three works was in fact written in Paris, and in the hands of the publisher by December 1844, but appeared in print shortly after Marx's arrival in Brussels. Officially jointly authored with Engels, Marx had written all but the first few chapters.[16] The book's witty yet ponderous title, *The Holy Family. Or, the Critique of Critical Criticism: Against Bruno Bauer and His Associates*, indicated its main thrust against those Young Hegelians who supported a lifestyle-based radicalism, emphasizing the criticism of revealed religion. The work took the form of hostile commentaries on articles appearing in the *General Literary News*, a journal Bauer and his supporters had established in Berlin that lasted about a year until its suppression by the Prussian authorities.

Marx and Engels certainly found a lot to criticize in the articles, making derisive remarks about the authors' inability to translate English or French phrases into German correctly, their excessive use of modifiers, their misunderstandings of the eighteenth-century French materialists or the political dynamics of the French Revolution. The widely varied polemics went on at some length, with Marx, to take just one example, denouncing Bauer's writings on the Jewish Question three different times, without saying substantially more than he had in his own article on the topic in the *Franco-German Yearbooks*. The impression of scattershot criticism and excessive, at times obsessive, detail was one that Marx's own friends had on reading the work.[17]

The book was widely reviewed in German literary journals; the reviewers agreed that the authors were followers of Ludwig Feuerbach. They generally did not pick up on the nuances: that Marx was projecting his politicized, labor-oriented version of Feuerbach's ideas. *The Holy Family* contained a few passages on labor in capitalism as an example of human self-alienation that summed up, very briefly, themes discussed at great length in the unpublished Paris manuscripts. Marx, describing himself as an advocate of Feuerbach's "real humanism," denounced Bauer's "speculative idealism," his understanding of political, social, or economic conditions, as representing the development of the idea, or human self-consciousness, rather than seeing human material conditions expressed in political struggles and social and economic structures. After making this point in referring to the French Revolution and socialism, Marx expanded it. Following Feuerbach's critique of Hegel's Absolute Spirit as a version of religious self-alienation, Marx described Bauer's attribution of the driving force in human history to self-consciousness as a version of religion—or, as he sarcastically remarked, "The religious savior of the world is finally realized in the critical savior of the world, Herr Bauer."[18]

This was meant to sting, since Bauer was proud of his atheism. Marx heightened the criticism by denouncing Bauer's ideas as "Christian-Germanic," putting Bauer in the same camp as the born-again Christian conservatives of Prussia's Friedrich Wilhelm IV and his followers—the very people who had torpedoed Bauer's academic career. To describe Bauer's ideas as fundamentally similar to theirs was an unfair criticism, made with the intent of tarring someone politically on the left—albeit in ways with which Marx strongly, and not unjustifiably, disagreed—with doctrines of conservatism. In his polemics of the period, Marx repeatedly made use of this tactic.

The Holy Family, reflecting its Parisian origins, was strikingly francophile. The portrayal of the French Revolution as a triumph of the bourgeoisie over the nobility and the onset of a capitalist social and economic system—an idea that French socialists and radicals and even liberals and moderates had repeatedly brought forward—was central to Marx's view of politics and to his criticism of the Young Hegelians. Marx's invidious comparison of the Young Hegelians' speculative juggling of economic concepts with the French socialists' investigations of the nature of property, value, and wage labor pointed to his preference for French theorizing. Marx even described Pierre-Joseph Proudhon's *What Is Property?*, with its celebrated assertion that "Property is theft," as the contemporary equivalent of the abbé Sièyes's *What Is the Third Estate?*, one of the seminal documents of the French Revolution of 1789.[19] This comparison was an early version of one of Marx's fundamental political concepts: the parallels between a future socialist revolution, in which workers would overthrow the reign of the bourgeoisie, and the French Revolution, when the bourgeoisie ended the rule of the feudal nobility.

Marx's second major theoretical effort during his time in Brussels is commonly known as *The German Ideology*, although, as the researchers on the new *MEGA* have painstakingly demonstrated, such a work does not and never did exist.[20] *The German Ideology* as book title appears only once in a letter to the editor Marx wrote in 1847 announcing that one volume of a two-volume work would not be appearing in print. In the surviving manuscripts, the line "Ideology in General, and the German Ideology in Particular" designates a chapter.

This dissection of a title may seem picky and pedantic. But it is important, because the manuscripts of what is known as *The German Ideology* were not one intellectually consistent enterprise. They evolved in erratic fashion, acquiring and shedding co-authors, and differing in argument and proposed method of publication, between their origination in late 1845–early 1846 and their final abandonment by mid-1847. The work began as a collaboration between Marx, Engels, and Hess; it was to contain critiques of the Young Hegelian radicals along the lines of *The Holy Family* that were to appear as a series of articles to be published in the proposed revival of the *Franco-German Yearbooks*. Parts of this original emphasis continued throughout the project; in particular, criticism of one of the Young Hegelians reached enormous length.

As the manuscript expanded, Marx began to think of it as a book, and, increasingly, a two-volume work. The first volume would be a biting critique of the Young Hegelians; the second, an equally savage attack on the "True Socialists," a group of German intellectuals professing socialist ideas. Moses Hess was, in many ways, the intellectual leader of the True Socialists, so that a project beginning as a collaboration among Marx, Engels, and Hess ended up as an assault on Hess's own ideas. Since Hess had introduced Marx to socialism, and strongly influenced his initial concepts of it, the denunciation of the True Socialists was a form of veiled self-criticism. A manuscript of the two proposed volumes circulated in 1846 and 1847, but Marx was unable to find a publisher for it. A small excerpt from the second volume, an attack on the True Socialist Karl Grün, published in the *Westphalian Steamboat* in 1847, was the only portion of the work to appear in print during Marx's lifetime.

The initial stages of the book, composed in the fall of 1845, were a continuation of the materialist, Feuerbachian polemics of *The Holy Family*, describing a church meeting, the "Council of Leipzig," at which "Saint Bruno" (i.e., Bruno Bauer) denounced the schismatic Ludwig Feuerbach, the heretical authors of *The Holy Family*, and their fellow heretic Moses Hess. The chapter title was an inside joke: there really had been a church council in Leipzig in 1845, a meeting of dissident, mostly Unitarian, German Protestants of generally leftist political sympathies.[21] As this example suggests, *The German Ideology* began as a work written for a small circle of intellectuals, well acquainted with each other and in the know, underscoring Marx's commitment to this group even after he established connections with Karl Schapper and the communist German artisans in London.

The work then took an odd turn, in late 1845 and the first part of 1846. Marx and Engels focused ever more on the ideas of a member of Bauer's circle, one Johann Schmidt—generally known by his pen name, Max Stirner—who had made a reputation for himself as a particularly acerbic critic of religion and a proponent of a lifestyle-oriented radicalism. His marriage ceremony to the feminist Marie Dähnhardt had been deliberately designed as a scandalous spectacle rejecting the connection between marriage and religion. The ceremony was held in

Stirner's Berlin apartment rather than a church, and the officiating
clergyman was confounded by the guests, who acted as if they were at
a tea party, or paid no attention to the proceedings. Stirner followed
up his provocative marriage with an equally provocative book, *The
Unique Individual and His Property*, generally known in English by the
looser translation, *The Ego and Its Own*. Infuriating communists as well
as the more politically oriented Young Hegelians, the author asserted
that egoism should be the highest ethical principle; that individuals'
intellectual and physical capabilities were equivalent to property ownership; and that revolution was useless, because true social and political change was only possible through the transformation of individual
consciousness.[22]

Marx and Engels became obsessed with Stirner, and the portion
of the book devoted to him, originally just a small part of the "Council
of Leipzig," got completely out of hand. They blasted his ignorance,
denounced his capitalist sympathies, and made fun of his speaking in
Berlin dialect, but at increasingly bizarre length. Most of the extant
manuscript of *The German Ideology* deals with Stirner—about 65 percent
of the 517 pages in the German-language collected works, an obsessive attention paid to a distinctly minor figure who died soon afterward in obscurity. Published editions of *The German Ideology* tend to
omit the criticism of Stirner almost entirely, and the judgment of Franz
Mehring, Marx's first major biographer, that these writings were a
"super-polemic . . . [that] . . . soon degenerates into hair splitting and
quibbling, some of it of a rather puerile character," has been widely
shared ever since.[23]

One feature of Stirner's work that did reverberate strongly, if
briefly, among the Young Hegelians was his criticism of Feuerbach's
concept of human species essence. If Feuerbach had asserted that
divinity was the projection of species essence onto an imaginary being,
Stirner retorted that Feuerbach's species essence, and the concept of

humanity in general, was the projection of human individuals onto another imaginary being. Marx and Engels rejected Stirner's assertions, but even as they criticized them, they realized that there were weaknesses in Feuerbach's concepts. Increasingly, the chapter on Stirner came to include long passages criticizing Feuerbach. Finally, in the spring of 1846, Marx and Engels decided that the material on Feuerbach should become a separate chapter, with the subtitle "The German Ideology," which has become the public face of their unpublished work. It was in this chapter that Marx made the distinctions between his ideas and Feuerbach's (which had previously been briefly and vaguely articulated) clear and apparent.[24]

Marx and Engels described the essential characteristic of humanity in terms of economic activity: "One can distinguish humans from animals by consciousness, religion, or in any way you want. Humans themselves begin to distinguish themselves from animals, as soon as they begin to *produce* their means of subsistence. . . . By producing their means of subsistence, humans produce, indirectly, their material life."[25] The idea that what made human beings human was their collective production, their working together to procure their subsistence from nature, had already appeared in the Paris manuscripts. Marx and Engels now fleshed it out by emphasizing three elements of production: productive forces, that is, technology and economic organization; the division of labor; and forms of property. Combined, these three elements of production generated social classes.

This material production, according to Marx and Engels, determined ideas, culture, forms of law, and politics—all united under the concept of ideology. Their explication followed along the lines of previous criticisms of the Young Hegelians for making ideas, rather than economic conditions, the moving force in history. But, as was the case with the notion of humans as producers, it was formulated more specifically and with much greater clarity:

> The production of ideas, representations of consciousness, is, as a
> first point, immediately woven up with the material activity and
> the material intercourse of humans, the speech of genuine life. . . .
> The same is true of intellectual production, as it is represented in the
> language of politics of the laws, of morality, of religion, metaphysics,
> etc., of a people. . . . Morality, religion, metaphysics and other ideol-
> ogy and the corresponding forms of consciousness thus no longer
> retain a semblance of independence. . . . It is not consciousness that
> determines life, but life that determines consciousness.[26]

Economic activity, the "production of the material conditions of life,"
was the descendant of Hegel's Absolute Idea, Bauer's infinite self-
consciousness, and Feuerbach's human species essence as the moving
force in history, from which all other aspects of history appeared in
alienated and disguised form.

A good portion of the chapter was a recounting of human history—
mostly European history, from classical antiquity through the Middle
Ages and the early modern era, then the French Revolution and on to
the mid-nineteenth century—in terms of the changes in the productive
forces, the division of labor, and property. Marx and Engels concluded
that the course of history led to situations in which productive forces
had developed to such an extent that further development "just produces perdition." The very same historical development also produced
a social class "that must bear all the burdens of society," which as a
result of its social position developed a consciousness of the necessity
of revolution, and eventually rose up against the dominant class and
overthrew it.[27]

Marx and Engels saw this process as happening in their own time,
leading to the creation of a communist society. Communism, they
insisted, was not an ideology: "Communism is for us not a condition
that can be created, an ideal, to which reality will have to conform. We
call communism the genuine movement that abolishes the existing state

of affairs."[28] In terms of the three elements of production, communism would, of course, involve the replacement of private property with communal ownership. In this chapter, Marx and Engels also introduced the idea, stemming from French socialist thinkers such as Saint-Simon, and articulated by Moses Hess (very likely the source of Marx's own thinking on this point), that a communist society was only possible following the growth of industrialization and of a capitalist world market. Communism, in other words, had not been an option throughout human history (an idea popular with a number of Marx's contemporaries) but emerged out of the progress of the productive forces.[29]

A particularly striking aspect of Marx and Engels's outline of communist society was their assertion that communism would involve the abolition of the division of labor. In a celebrated passage, they made this point in vigorous and witty language:

As soon as labor begins to be divided then each person has a determined exclusive sphere of activity that is forced upon him, from which he cannot depart; he is a hunter, a fisherman, a shepherd or a critical critic and must remain so, if he does not wish to lose the means to maintain his subsistence. In a communist society, on the other hand, where each person does not have an exclusive circle of activity, but can learn and be trained in any branch he pleases, where society regulates general production and in that way makes it possible for me to do one thing today, another tomorrow, to hunt in the morning, to fish in the afternoon, to herd cattle in the evening, and, after dinner, to criticize, just as I please, without ever becoming hunter, fisher, herdsman or critic.[30]

This assertion, probably taken from Charles Fourier, who envisaged a society in which individuals would enjoy their labor and would work on tasks that most appealed to them, has frequently drawn skeptical commentary. It seems difficult to reconcile with the specialization required in an industrial society, and contains evident internal difficulties as well: might not society's regulation of general production be at odds with individuals' wishes to do as they please? Marx and Engels themselves introduced an element of irony in their assertions, given that their future communist included among his occupations being a critical critic, an activity they repeatedly described in their manuscript as producing worthless nonsense.

The discussion of the division of labor in the chapter on Feuerbach was complicated and multifaceted, a reflection of the incomplete nature of the surviving manuscripts. In some passages, Marx and Engels linked the division of labor to class differences between workers and capitalists, so that the abolition of the division of labor would correspond to the creation of a communist society without social classes. At another point, the authors noted that the division of labor led to a product of labor standing independent from and against those who created it. The contrast between particular individuals and their joint product led to the desire for a common interest, in the form of the state, an "illusory commonality," hiding the existence of different and conflicting class interests.[31] This assertion was a continuation of a train of thought begun with the new social and political order described in Marx's *Critique of Hegel's Philosophy of Law*, where the particular interests of individuals in civil society and the general interest as represented by the state would coincide. Abolishing the division of labor and, with it, different social classes and private property, was Marx's new iteration of this aspiration, informed by his study of political economy and by the controversy over Max Stirner's attacks on Feuerbach's conception of humanity.

In this Feuerbach chapter, Marx and Engels certainly criticized Feuerbach's conception of an ahistorical human species essence; but their development of a positive alternative to it outweighed their criticism, which lacked the vehemence, anger, and sarcasm of their other forays against the Young Hegelians. As their manuscript evolved, a new critical target emerged, the True Socialists, the group of pro-communist German intellectuals, part of a more explicitly political turn to the project that included a section (not preserved) criticizing liberalism in Germany.[32]

Marx and Engels's denunciation of the True Socialists ran in parallel with their attacks on the Young Hegelians: that both groups placed intellectual movements rather than the political struggles resulting from social and economic conditions at the center of the historical process, rendering their ideas, for Marx and Engels, yet another example of ideology.[33] Their chief target, Karl Grün, was accused of regarding religion and politics as the "essence of man," and of being ignorant of "genuine production"—that is, the structures of the economy and of production. Grün and other True Socialists were denounced for seeing the goal of the socialist movement as the liberation of "man," and the redemption of "men" from their alienated condition, following in the footsteps of Feuerbach's theories of religion as human alienation.[34]

What provoked the greatest ire for Marx and Engels was the True Socialists' insistence that German *Wissenschaft* was required to transform the doctrines of communism and socialism expounded in France and England into philosophically authentic and correct theories. This appeared to them as downright perverse, taking the English and French criticisms of economy and society and their proposed political remedies and transforming them into questions of conceptual development. True Socialism was "nothing but the distortion of proletarian communism and the more or less related parties and sects of France and England into the heaven of the German spirit and . . . German sentimentality."[35]

Following the invidious comparisons of the Young German authors between dreamy Teutons and the vigorous practicality of Germany's neighbors, Marx and Engels quoted Heine on how Britannia ruled the waves, Russia and France held the land, but Germany had undisputed dominion over the "airy realm of dreams." Not surprisingly, Marx and

Engels linked this German tendency toward impractical philosophy with economic, social, and political backwardness, with a country lacking modern industry, modern political institutions, well-developed social classes, and sharper class antagonisms. German society was not yet divided into bourgeois and proletarians, as was the case in England or France; most Germans were *Kleinbürger*, petit bourgeois. The use of this phrase in the discussion of the True Socialists marked the beginning of its long career as a Marxist political epithet.[36]

Yet Marx's own previous thought was strikingly similar to the ideas condemned in *The German Ideology* as petit bourgeois. In the Paris manuscripts, Marx had described communism as the recovery of human essence from its alienated existence. In "The Introduction to the Critique of Hegel's Philosophy of Law," he had stated that the heart of the future communist revolution was the proletariat, but its head was philosophy, and he had also spoken about the advantages of German philosophy for the development of communism. In *The Holy Family*, Marx and Engels had designated their standpoint as "real humanism," a Feuerbachian phrase the True Socialists employed.[37]

The biting criticisms of the True Socialists were a form of externalization and objectification not unlike the processes of alienation explained in Hegelian philosophy. Marx took his own previous ideas and projected them onto other thinkers, where he could then reject them without having to criticize himself. He would repeat this process in future works, particularly *The Eighteenth Brumaire of Louis Bonaparte*. It was the only form of self-criticism that his personality would allow, and one that enabled him to maintain his position as the person articulating the direction of human history.

Composing these lengthy manuscripts criticizing the Young Hegelians and True Socialists required Marx to put off his planned critique of political economy. As he told his long-suffering publisher, Karl Leske, "it seemed to me very important to send out in advance of my positive development a polemical piece against German philosophy and against German socialism as it has hitherto existed . . . to prepare the public . . . for . . . my economics. . . ."[38] At the beginning of 1847, Marx returned to economics, once again in the form of a critical attack on a contemporary, in this case Pierre-Joseph Proudhon, in *The Poverty of Philosophy*.

One of the leading French socialist theorists of the 1840s (today, Proudhon is generally regarded as an anarchist, but contemporaries placed him along with other socialists), Proudhon's famous assertion that "Property is theft" had made him a figure known, admired, and hated throughout Europe. Moving from bon mots to a system, Proudhon's magnum opus, *The System of Economic Contradictions, Or: The Philosophy of Poverty*, applied Hegel's philosophy to the principles of political economy in order to demonstrate the latter's internal contradictions. Marx's response, ironically retitling Proudhon's work, was to ridicule these findings of contradictions, to show that Proudhon had not understood political economy, particularly as propounded by David Ricardo—Adam's Smith's chief disciple, and the leading figure of pro-capitalist economics—and also to assert that the Frenchman had not understood Hegel either.

Proudhon, for instance, had maintained that there was a contradiction between the use of a commodity and its market value: the larger the harvest, the more food there was, the more useful for humanity, but the lower the price of food would be. Marx's sharp retort was to point out that Proudhon's contradiction was really no contradiction at all, since price was formed by the working of supply and demand, and Proudhon had just discussed supply but had nothing to say about demand. If demand increased sharply, then prices could go up, in spite of a rise in supply.[39] Marx proceeded to analyze other basic concepts, thrashing Proudhon's account of the paradoxes in the labor theory of value, the division of labor and the use of machinery, the rise of ground rent, as opposed to the decline of interest, or the potentially inflationary effects of union organizing and strikes. In each of these instances, Marx care-

fully demonstrated his mastery of basic Ricardian concepts—the determination of goods' value by the amount of labor expended in producing
them, or rent on land as the difference in return between the most and
the least fertile property.[40]

If Marx had little patience with his target's understanding of
Ricardo, his patience with Proudhon's understanding of Hegel was
even shorter. In a derisive passage, Marx caricatured Proudhon's philosophical development of economic concepts:

> . . . impersonal reason . . . is forced . . . to pose, oppose and com-
> pose itself—position, opposition, composition. To speak Greek, we
> have thesis, antithesis, synthesis . . . Hegel's . . . sacramental for-
> mula: affirmation, negation, negation of the negation. . . . Apply this
> method to the categories of political economy, and . . . you will have
> translated economic categories, known by everyone, into a little
> known language, in which they look as though they had emerged,
> newly formed, from a head of pure reason. . . . [41]

It is one of the more peculiar features of the history of Marxism that
thesis, antithesis, synthesis—the phrase Marx used to mock Proudhon's misunderstanding of Hegel—would come to be regarded as the
quintessence of Marx's methodology.

Rather, this assertion of Proudhon's misunderstanding of Hegel
brought up the central theme of the entire work. Marx, employing the
ideas he and Engels had worked out in their manuscript about Feuerbach but never published, accused Proudhon of granting abstract
philosophical concepts priority in understanding economics over the
actual material conditions of production. Proudhon's work was in "the
old Hegelian manner . . . not a profane history, a history of men . . . a
sacred history, a history of ideas . . . man is nothing but an instrument,
which the idea or eternal reason exploits in order to develop itself. . . . If
you pull the curtain of this mystical language, it comes to be said that

M. Proudhon gives you the order in which economic categories are arranged in his head."[42] Admittedly, Marx thought that Proudhon did a much poorer job of arranging these mental categories than Hegel ever had, but disdain for Proudhon's mental untidiness was subordinate to criticism of his placing abstract concepts ahead of concrete material production in understanding economics.

As with Marx's assertions in *The German Ideology*, the criticism of Proudhon was an externalized form of self-criticism. Marx had persistently described himself as an admirer of Proudhon's ideas from his time as editor of the *Rhineland News* through the publication of *The Holy Family*, and had tried to recruit Proudhon to his communist committee of correspondence. Proudhon's project of providing a Hegelian critique of political economy was very similar to what Marx was trying to do in the Paris manuscripts.

Although *The Poverty of Philosophy* was not the critique of political economy that Marx had been promising since 1845, it was the first time that basic concepts of Marxist economics, such as use value, exchange value, and modes of production, made their appearance. Just as *The Holy Family* provided short, published summaries of Marx's longer and more complex theorizing in the unpublished Paris manuscripts, *The Poverty of Philosophy* included briefer, published versions of a number of ideas in the unpublished chapter on Feuerbach in *The Germany Ideology*.

One aspect of *The Poverty of Philosophy* distinguished it from all of Marx's previous works: Marx wrote the book in French. He saw the intellectual significance of the circles of Parisian socialists and radicals he had encountered before his expulsion from the French capital as so great that he needed to intervene directly in it, writing a book in French (while all German intellectuals could read French, the opposite was not the case), soliciting assistance in perfecting his French style, and paying the costs of publication himself. Marx's aim was never fulfilled, because the book never reached its intended destinations; the publishers took Marx's money but did not send any free publicity copies to Parisian socialist leaders as he requested. A few copies circulated hand to hand among German émigré intellectuals in Paris.[43]

Marx had revised and expanded the materialist critique of Hegel and the post-Hegelian vision of a communist society he had developed in the years in Kreuznach and Paris. He had replaced Feuerbach's human species essence with a conception of humans as collective producers, working in distinct forms of social and economic organization with associated levels of technology. In turn, these features interacted to produce a society partitioned by the division of labor into different and antagonistic social classes. A communist future and a working class that would bring it about in revolutionary fashion had been tied much more closely to the history of the French Revolution of 1789 and to the doctrines of political economy—and not so much to the socialist critics of these doctrines as to their orthodox defenders, particularly the English economist David Ricardo. Marx had reached these results through a series of increasingly bitter criticisms of his contemporaries, criticisms that were implicitly directed at his own, earlier views, suggesting they were not tough-minded and practical enough. Yet his efforts to bring his increasing theoretical clarity to the attention of a public consisting primarily of radical German intellectuals and their French counterparts had been largely unsuccessful, partly as a result of the difficulties in publishing, but also a consequence of his own problems in formulating consistent accounts of his ideas, and of his penchant for launching vehement polemics—witty and cutting, but also lengthy and obsessed—that could become an end in itself. This polemical edge would also appear in the personal and political conflicts in which he became involved over the course of 1846.

MARX'S EFFORTS TO RALLY support through his projected communist committee of correspondence and his connections with the London communists also led to breaking off contacts with former political associates. Favorable observers have described these breaks as necessary steps toward theoretical clarity and unity of action; more hostile ones attribute them to Marx's dictatorial tendencies and his desire to turn allies into subordinates. There were certainly elements of both motives, but they primarily reflected Marx's attempt to carve out a position for himself among émigré German radicals who were on their own in foreign countries, generally in difficult personal and financial circumstances, all the while facing the constant pressure of hostile Prussian and Austrian governments. Since these émigré radicals were, at best, very loosely organized, political action occurred in informal personal relations, so that political conflicts were invariably personalized. Three substantial clashes accompanied Marx's political course in 1846 and 1847: with Friedrich Engels and Moses Hess, with Wilhelm Weitling, and finally, with Karl Grün.

The first of these, a little-known episode that took place around the beginning of 1846, began with a personal slight, Jenny von Westphalen's disparaging remarks about Engels's mistress, the Manchester factory girl Mary Burns. Jenny's hostility toward Burns, whom she described to Karl as an "intriguing, ambitious woman, a Lady Macbeth," was pronounced; two years later, well after Marx and Engels had reconciled, she insisted on sitting on the opposite side of the room from Mary at public events. By contrast, Jenny was quite friendly with Hess's female companion, Sybille Pesch, also from a working-class background, who spent a lot of time with the family during the months that she and Moses lived in Brussels. Among other things, she helped to take care of the Marx children. But Pesch was a figure with a dubious past; the rumor was that Hess had met her when he was a customer at a brothel in Cologne where she worked. Hess, well aware of these issues in view of his own companion's background and the stories told about her, saw Jenny's attitude toward Mary Burns as upper-class contempt for a worker who did not know her proper place. Both Hess and Engels blamed Marx for the situation, asserting that Karl was not acting like a proper male head of the household, but was letting his wife's prejudices determine his opinions.

The conflict quickly developed political ramifications. Marx let his friends in Cologne know that Engels lacked the intellectual ability to carry out the necessary theoretical work and philosophical criticism in which they were engaged. This judgment was accompanied by sarcastic remarks about Engels as the "friend of the proletarians," his mistress in particular, and a "tall lad." This last was a sarcastic denunciation of Engels as a Prussian, since the "tall lads" were the six-foot-tall soldiers that the eighteenth-century Prussian king Friedrich Wilhelm I had recruited for his army. Marx had nothing better to say about Hess, whom he described as a "sponge," a dreamer and spiritualist incapable of practical political activity. It was Marx's Cologne friends Heinrich Bürgers and Roland Daniels who asserted that Hess "carries around the ballast of so much nonsense in his head," and that he aspired to be the "high priest" of communism; but their comments were undoubtedly reflections of Marx's own attitudes.[44]

Marx and Engels were able to reconcile, probably by working on the enormously lengthy chapter on Max Stirner for *The German Ideology*. By criticizing "Saint Max," Engels could break with his own past—both his own friendship with Stirner, as fellow members of the Free Men, and his previous enthusiasm for Stirner's work that Engels had perceived (somewhat oddly) as providing a theoretical basis for communism—and prove his philosophical capabilities to Marx's satisfaction.[45] The chapter on Stirner, enormously out of scale when compared to the rest of the manuscripts comprising *The German Ideology*, makes more sense if it served the purpose of restoring the two men's friendship.

Hess, by contrast, was not reconciled with Marx. He prepared to leave Brussels, which he did at the end of March 1846, to devote himself to socialist periodicals in the Rhineland, soon to be prohibited by the Prussian government. The break with Hess was by no means total.

Hess's behavior for the next few months—and, indeed, for the rest of his life—would oscillate between cooperation and being appalled by Marx. But the close working connection that marked the relationship in late 1845 and early 1846 was irrevocably gone, and the brief time in which the triumvirate of Marx, Hess, and Engels had held sway was permanently over.

Marx's second major clash, with the working-class socialist Wilhelm Weitling, is better known. A journeyman tailor, Weitling was one of the German artisans living abroad, belonging to radical secret societies, who had developed vaguely socialist ideas of unorthodox Christian inspiration. Unlike most of his fellow artisans, Weitling put his thoughts down on paper, writing two books—*Guarantees of Freedom and Harmony* and *The Gospel of a Poor Sinner*—that made him a well-known and influential figure among German émigrés. His imprisonment in Switzerland for advocating socialist ideas added a nimbus of martyrdom to his reputation.

After being active with the League of the Just in Paris and London, Weitling came to Brussels in 1846 to work with Marx, who had previously written warmly about him. Their collaboration quickly collapsed, during one of the very first meetings of the Communist Committee of Correspondence, at the end of March 1846. Pavel Annenkov, a Russian émigré who was present, described how Marx, sitting at the head of the table, began to question Weitling sharply, and in steadily more critical fashion, about how he could justify his ideas. Weitling defended himself, insisting that his agitation was giving the workers hope in their misery and oppression. But Marx cut Weitling off and retorted that spreading confused ideas and dubious hopes among the workers, promoting concepts lacking in *Wissenschaft*, was "an empty and unconscionable toying with preaching sermons," which would just lead to the ruination of the oppressed. The two men argued and Marx, growing steadily angrier, pounded on the table with his fist, stood up, and shouted, "Ignorance has never yet helped anyone!"[46]

This episode is often reported as an example of Marx's contempt for the workers he supposedly wanted to liberate and his anti-democratic, dictatorial tendencies. These accusations were first raised by Weitling himself, who let everyone know that Marx was planning to eliminate workers from the leadership of the communist movement and replace them with bourgeois intellectuals, because the workers were untrustworthy. Moses Hess, who was not present at the meeting, but received a letter about it from Weitling, described Marx's treatment of Weitling as "nauseating," and announced he would have nothing more to do politically with Marx. Characteristically, he changed his mind within a few months and began attempting a political reconciliation.[47]

What does not appear in Annenkov's reminiscence is why Weitling and Marx were shouting at each other in the first place. Weitling, in his letter to Hess, explained their differences: Marx had insisted that "at the moment there can be no talk of the realization of communism; the bourgeoisie must first take control." This was an issue that Marx was considering in his theoretical writings at the time, linking the onset of communism to the development of capitalist industry, in contrast to Weitling's idea that communism had always been possible throughout human history. It was also an issue that had been debated among the London communists, who had roundly renounced Weitling's view. Weitling's trip to Brussels to work with Marx and Engels was designed to find a new field for his political activity, since his former supporters in the League of the Just had rejected his ideas and claims to leadership.[48]

Weitling himself was in a difficult position at the time. He was broke, had sought to borrow money from Marx and was dependent on him for his meals. Even after the confrontation at the Committee of Correspondence, Weitling stayed in Brussels and continued to try to work with Marx and Engels. When this proved impossible, he needed money from them to leave. The funds were procured by Moses Hess from Marx's friends in Cologne.[49]

The dispute between Marx and Weitling reflected the insecure position of émigrés, lacking material support and an organized following, while striving for a dominant position in a radical political movement. Hess's motives were quite similar. While he claimed to be appalled by Marx's insistence on creating an approved doctrine and rejecting other points of view, just a few months earlier when he and Marx had been getting along quite well, he was very enthusiastic about the idea of establishing a definitive communist political program.[50]

Such striving for a dominant position in the nascent communist movement was most apparent in the third of these confrontations, with the True Socialist Karl Grün. Although relatively neglected by historians, it was the most extensive, the most public, and the most controversial of Marx's clashes at the time. Personal antipathy, political and intellectual differences, and personal rivalry were mixed together. While there was a strong element of petty nastiness in the confrontation, the issues raised would recur in major ways during the turbulent politics of the 1848 Revolution.[51]

The controversy began shortly after Marx moved to Brussels, when he read a copy of Grün's book on the socialist and communist movement in France and Belgium, designed as an introduction for educated German readers. Marx began making dismissive remarks about Grün, describing him as a dilettante and a hack writer rather than a serious author. Hess, who actually tended to agree with Marx on this point, nonetheless told Grün about these negative opinions. Marx was not content with merely muttering; he prepared a written attack on Grün that was integrated into the section on the True Socialists in *The German Ideology*, and ultimately became the only portion of the work to appear in print.

The confrontation with Grün was woven deeply into the fabric of the additional communist committees of correspondence Marx was trying to set up. The letter to Proudhon in May 1846, inviting him to be Marx's Paris correspondent, contained a postscript denouncing

Grün as a "knight of the literary industry, a kind of charlatan who makes a business of dealing in modern ideas. . . . Watch out for this parasite."[52] Following up on this initiative, Engels was dispatched to Paris in August 1846, ostensibly to set up the Paris bureau of the Communist Correspondence Committee, in fact to do battle with Grün among the German artisans in the secret societies there.

Grün, though, was not hapless like Weitling or dreamy and indecisive like Hess. He was an able writer and supple politician, ready and willing to fight back. Present in Paris, not exiled to Brussels, he was able to win the contest for access to Proudhon, in part by rank personal flattery. Proudhon roundly rejected Marx's warnings about Grün, and let Marx know he would only cooperate with him in his proposed communist network if Marx would help Grün bring out a German translation of Proudhon's *Philosophy of Poverty*.[53] Rather than agree to Proudhon's terms, Marx attacked him as well by writing *The Poverty of Philosophy*, a decision that naturally angered the French socialist. He annotated his personal copy of Marx's book with the words: "a tissue of vulgarity, of calumny of falsification and of plagiarism," and moved closer to Grün, who steadily developed his reputation as Proudhon's adviser and interpreter for the German-speaking world. Grün moved to fortify his position with the radical German artisans in Paris by, among other things, taking them on tours of the Louvre. Engels's repeated assertions of his success in driving out Grün's influence and his supporters were followed by frustrated observations of their recurrence. Engels's heavy-handed manner, which included at one point a fistfight with a politically opposed artisan, cannot have helped his and Marx's cause any.[54]

Grün went over to the offensive in the pages of the *Trier News*, a German newspaper propounding socialist doctrines, and in Marx's old adversary, the *Cologne News*. He denounced Marx as an "intellectual customs agent and border guard, appointed on his own authority," who would only let socialist ideas pass if he approved them, and would otherwise try to confiscate them and keep them out of circulation.[55] Responding to Marx's charges that his work on French socialism was superficial and popularizing, Grün scornfully noted that he at least had published a book, and a widely read one at that, while Marx had been unable to finish any major work. In a short story in the *Cologne News*, Grün described a simultaneously sinister and pathetic "Dr. Ludwig" (a thinly disguised Marx) as an unkempt, ungroomed fanatic unable to support his family, and whose revolutionary dogmas led honest German artisans to perdition.

What, exactly, did Marx have against Grün politically? The essay published in the *Westphalian Steamboat* treated Grün's ideas as one of a piece with the Young Hegelians and the True Socialists, whose politics were based on idealized conceptions of humanity rather than concrete conditions of material production. Another political theme gradually emerged, articulated by both Marx and Engels in public writings and private correspondence. This was the idea that Proudhon and Grün sought to introduce socialism without a revolution that would abolish capitalism, by creating workers' cooperatives funded by a state bank. Grün himself sometimes posed the controversy similarly, contrasting his and Proudhon's plans for peaceful reform with Marx's demands for violent revolution.[56] Whether Proudhon's and Grün's plans to abolish a market economy via state-supported producers' cooperatives fit under the heading of reform is another matter, but their idea was not without similarities to the Young Hegelians' understanding of radicalism as a change in lifestyle: both involved dramatic change outside the political arena, a possibility Marx regarded as problematic at best.

Ideological differences do not entirely explain the vigor of Marx's attacks on Grün, since there was a lot in Grün's work on French and Belgian socialism that was congenial to Marx. Grün denounced the liberal regime in Belgium as facilitating capitalist exploitation of the workers, under the guise of protecting civil rights; he spoke of the concentration of capital and the impoverishment of the proletariat; he was critical of the efforts of Fourier and his followers to get wealthy individuals to finance his socialist schemes. Grün called for the abolition of wage labor, and for the proletariat to assume political power; he expressly associated his socialism with atheism.[57] There was certainly much else in the book Marx rejected, but Marx had no trouble adopting and praising the ideas of Wilhelm Schulz, whose concept of Christian social reform was considerably further from Marx's ideas than Grün's Feuerbachian socialism. Marx could also cooperate with other men politically in spite of ideological differences, as he was doing with Hermann Ewerbeck in Paris and Karl Schapper in London at the very same time that he was leading his campaign against Grün.

It is hard to avoid noticing the strong element of personal antipathy in Marx's attitude, which was considerably more pronounced than in his relations with other rivals of the time. Marx meant literally his condemnation of Grün as a fraud and opportunist. The chief point of his published attack on Grün's book was to denounce him as a plagiarist. After he broke with the two Westphalian capitalists Meyer and Rempel, following the collapse of the publishing project, Marx angrily returned the money they had collected on his behalf with the remark that he was no Karl Grün—implying that Grün was a self-interested opportunist who used funds collected for political purposes to his personal advantage. Marx was not alone in feeling this way; several of his correspondents reported similar stories, and it seems that Grün, at least in some circles, had a reputation for less than scrupulous use of money.[58]

There is a further element that defined their tempestuous relationship: their very considerable similarities. Friends when they had attended the University of Bonn, they had both later moved from Bonn to Berlin. Like Marx, Grün was an academic manqué, although his interests ran to art history rather than philosophy. Marx had attempted to hire Grün when he was editing the *Rhineland News*. The newspaper had been suppressed before this was possible, but Grün then made a name for himself editing the *Mannheim Evening News*, another prominent left-wing newspaper. Like Marx, he had been dismissed from his position due to government pressure. Following Marx's path, Grün became an émigré in Paris, where the two men had moved, amiably, in the same circles, so that Grün was later astonished to hear that Marx was attacking him. Grün's idea of writing a book that would introduce French socialist ideas to the German educated public overlapped substantially with the project that Marx, Hess, and Engels were pursuing at the same time, that of editing German translations of French socialist authors. The similarities hardly stopped there. Like Marx, Grün was not particularly neat, clean, or fastidious; also like Marx, he had difficulties supporting a family. The conflict between the two men arose precisely because they were so similar, because they were both seeking to occupy the same niche in the German socialist movement: that of the theorist who could provide the missing link between French ideas and German social conditions. Contemporaries, even Marx's supporters, understood that personal differences were integrally linked with the political disputes in which Marx had become involved. Marx's personal circumstances in Brussels also were becoming increasingly difficult; all this certainly encouraged the irascible side of his personality, and his tendency to create sharp alternatives and then insist on one to the exclusion of the other.

HAVING BEEN EXPELLED FROM Paris at the urging of the Prussian government, Marx was by no means secure in Brussels. He gave the Belgian authorities written assurances that he would not engage in any political activity, offering the Prussians no pretext to demand his extradition. But the report that the Prussian government was planning to do just that led Marx, six months after he arrived in Brussels, to renounce his Prussian citizenship and to inform the Prussian authorities that he was planning to emigrate to the United States. His hope was that the authorities would be only too happy to see him go and would not trouble themselves about him further.[59]

Marx did not leave for the States, as he had no plans to. The possibility of a new extradition request continued to hang over his head for the rest of his residence in Brussels. Yet these threats, severe as they may have been, took a backseat to his steadily increasing economic difficulties. While in Brussels, his family responsibilities continued to grow. Marx and Jenny's second daughter, Laura, was born on October 26, 1845; their son, the ill-fated Edgar, on February 2, 1847. In order to economize, Marx gave up his apartment in May 1846 and moved his family into a hotel with furnished rooms, which meant employing fewer servants. Then, and through the rest of his life, Marx's poverty would always be a genteel poverty; except on one disastrous occasion, he never proposed that Jenny keep house for him, and her frequent pregnancies and bouts of ill health would have made that a difficult prospect. Karl and Jenny were very fortunate in regard to their household help. The young woman from Trier who had accompanied Jenny to Paris did not make the move to Brussels, so Jenny's mother found a replacement from another one of the Westphalen family retainers, Helene (Lenchen) Demuth, who would remain with the couple for the rest of their lives.[60]

Nonetheless, Lenchen was yet another mouth to feed. The failure of the potato crop in 1845 and the dire grain harvest the next year had doubled food prices, increasing the cost of everything else—not a small problem when Marx's income was far from keeping pace.[61] There was an additional and perhaps unexpected source of expenses for Marx: his role as aspiring political leader. Potential and current followers and associates expected financial support. Marx funded Weitling even while shouting at him, and received requests for money from Karl Ludwig Bernays and Hermann Ewerbeck in Paris. Visits from new adherents, such as the former artillery officer Joseph Weydemeyer or the

Silesian Wilhelm Wolff, were encouraging signs and generally led to carousing, but Marx had to put up his guests.[62]

As Marx's expenses grew, his income shrank inversely. At the beginning of his stay in Brussels, his friends and supporters in Cologne and the vicinity continued to send him money, as they had done when he was living in Paris. But Marx's increasing turn toward a militantly anti-bourgeois communism made him ever more reluctant to depend on them for funds. As he wrote to Joseph Weydemeyer, "There still exist in Cologne several bourgeois who would probably advance me money for a fixed term. Only these people have for some time turned to a direction opposed in principle [to mine], so I would just as soon not be obligated to them in any way."[63] Like many radical intellectuals of the era, Marx tried to support himself as a freelance author, but press censorship in Germany made it almost impossible for him to get published. What little he earned that way was more than consumed by the expense of self-publishing *The Poverty of Philosophy*. Marx did receive some money from his mother, and he continued to press, unsuccessfully, for an advance against his share of her estate.[64]

His circumstances became increasingly straitened. In May 1846, he had pawned the last of the family's gold and silver, and most of the linens, yet another reason to move into furnished rooms. The following winter, he received a visit from the journeyman typesetter Stephan Born, one of the radical German artisans living abroad, who would be an important labor leader during the Revolution of 1848. Many years later, Born remembered seeing Marx's "highly modest little apartment, furnished, one can well say, in impoverished fashion, in a [working-class] suburb of Brussels." About the time of this visit, Marx was trying to keep his head above water by writing some very dubious IOUs. Engels, Marx's future savior in financial matters, was in equally difficult circumstances, dependent on a monthly check from his father. When it did not arrive, Engels too had recourse to the pawnshop, or to sending Marx COD letters from Paris. Marx's other leftist associates were doing no better. He wrote Weydemeyer, "You see poverty and misery all around! At the moment, I do not know what to do to help myself out."[65]

Although Marx himself denied it, it is hard to believe that his "private misery," as Moses Hess put it in regard to the break with Weitling, was not directly tied to the political "party strife."[66] Certainly, Marx's friends and supporters rebuked him for his antagonistic attitudes, and his tendency to personalize political differences. Joseph Weydemeyer was appalled by Marx's treatment of the two Westphalian capitalists after they refused to support his publishing project, accusing him of wanting "to make out of these conflicts a question of party, conflicts that are quite personal and have no connection with questions of principles. . . ." Weydemeyer went on to emphasize the background of Marx's personal economic difficulties, noting that Marx had rejected the money the capitalists sent him, refusing to engage in "begging," as he said. Instead, Weydemeyer pointed out, the money was support for "party authors who have gotten into financial difficulties" because political censorship prevented them from earning a living with their pens. Hermann Ewerbeck was no less critical of "this break with the bourgeois, who at least have a noble will and money" needed for the crucial "publication of your writings."[67]

The severity of the clash with Karl Grün seemed even less comprehensible. Hermann Ewerbeck rebuked Marx's "grudge against and hatred of Grün," seeing this personal basis for political antagonism as unworthy of someone he regarded as the "Aristotle of the nineteenth century." Heinrich Lüning, editor of the *Westphalian Steamboat*, was unhappy with the "too bitter and offensive tone" of the attacks on Grün. Admitting that both Grün's ideas and his personality were dubious, Lüning pointed out that he was nonetheless on the same side as other socialists: "what's the purpose of beating someone with a club, when they are working at least halfway in the same direction?"[68]

Marx's friends tended to place the blame for the many personal conflicts in which he was involved on Engels's "dictatorial demands and
his overbearing tone," his "arrogance and vanity."[69] It was true that
Engels's interventions often did make matters worse, and his letters
to Marx were filled with contemptuous and condescending remarks
about other political activists. But Engels did not cause Marx's conflicts so much as he reinforced Marx's inclination to bring together the
personal and the political, an inclination exacerbated by the difficult
condition of the family finances and Marx's politically precarious position as an émigré and apprentice revolutionary.

Drawing a balance of Marx's activities toward the end of 1846 after
almost two years in Brussels, the negatives would rather outweigh the
positives. Trying to rally and organize the German-speaking communists across Europe had produced just a handful of followers and a
lot of personal antagonisms. The publishing plans and the attempts to
bring Marx's theoretical insights to the left-wing German-speaking
intellectuals had largely been foiled. Ties to the workers, in whose
name he spoke, were generally made through other intellectual leaders
with whom Marx did not always see eye-to-eye.

Engels himself articulated these discouraging perspectives in a
letter he wrote to Marx from Paris in November or December 1846.
He recounted his frustrations with the supporters of Grün among the
German artisans in Paris. There was still no "organ," no publication
with which Marx could articulate his ideas to the public, so that he
and Engels remained dependent on the London communists, who had
let Marx's communist correspondence "go to sleep in the Lord." After
relating differences with the communist German artisans in London,
Engels noted that openly asserting them would be useless. "These lads
would declare themselves to be the 'people' the 'proletariat' against us,
and we could only appeal to a communist proletariat that in Germany
has yet to be formed."[70]

Such experiences were typical of the frustrations radical émigrés felt across all of Europe. Trying to be a revolutionary in a situation where the authorities were firmly in command was hard enough, and trying to do so from a foreign country was even harder. Energies were dissipated in fruitless quarrels, and personal antagonisms would embitter political controversies and divert them into largely useless channels. The situation would change rapidly in 1847, as the pillars of political order began to shake and totter. New opportunities for political action would open up for Marx, and he would gain the chance to formulate and circulate his ideas in a number of different public forums. The outbreak of revolution at the beginning of 1848 would increase all these possibilities exponentially and make clear that the painful revolutionary apprenticeship in Brussels, for all its difficulties, had been a worthwhile period of preparation.

PART II

Struggle

6

The Insurgent

BEFORE THE STORM ARRIVES, the wind picks up and the skies darken. Animals seek shelter and people sense, uneasily, the declining air pressure. The year 1847 was filled with signs of an approaching revolutionary storm—not just apparent in retrospect, but evident to contemporaries. A commercial, financial, and industrial crisis—today, we would say a severe recession—following on the harvest failures of the two previous years, drastically shook public confidence in the existing systems of government. As trust in the political status quo of Europe waned, its many and varied opponents, what contemporaries called the "party of movement," accelerated and redoubled their oppositional activity. Paris, the Continental center, was the scene of political mass meetings, lightly disguised, for legal reasons, as enormous banquets. In this "banquet campaign," leaders of the opposition spoke in favor of a democratic franchise.

The form of meetings spread throughout urban France, and speeches calling for reform were increasingly mixed with invocations of the heroic revolutionary days of 1789 and 1793. In Southern and Eastern Europe, where absolutist governments still reigned, it was a radical step to call for the very same constitutional monarchy that the French opposition was criticizing. The Prussian king, Friedrich Wilhelm IV, summoned his Provincial Diets to meet together in Berlin, only to discover that this "United Diet" was dominated by liberals, who demanded that he grant a constitution. Similar widely known, public confrontations between an absolutist monarch and some form of representative institution controlled by a liberal opposition were features of 1847 in Rome, where the Consultative Assembly of the Papal States called for a constitution, and in Budapest, where the Hungarian Diet squared off against the Austrian Empire. These and many other portents of imminent political change acted as galvanizing shocks, prompting organizing efforts and the formulation of political platforms. In the German states, the radicals articulated theirs in Offenburg and the liberals in Heppenheim, in September and October 1847, respectively.

For Marx, this surge of political activity was a welcome reprieve from the doldrums in which his efforts had been stranded by late 1846. He became deeply involved in two different organizing efforts: the transformation of the London-based League of the Just into the Communist League; and the creation of an international democratic association in Brussels. Both these new organizations offered him the opportunity to articulate to a broader public the theories he had been developing: for the Brussels democrats, Marx's thoughts on free trade and its relation to the development of capitalism and of a revolutionary proletariat; for the Communist League, his famous manifesto.

All of Marx's efforts were directed toward the planned international democratic congress, whose realization was ever more likely in the climate of rapid political change. But the change came even more rapidly and drastically than Marx expected. The initial sign was in Switzerland, today the very epitome of conservatism and tranquility, but in the mid-nineteenth century a turbulent and troubled land, also Europe's most left-wing country. The victory of the radicals in the Swiss Civil War of 1847, a result of the inability of the great powers, especially the Austrian Empire, to intervene on behalf of the outnumbered Swiss conservatives, was the first portent of looming revolution in Europe. There followed uprisings in southern Italy at the beginning of 1848 and then the decisive stroke: the overthrow of the monarchy in France and the proclamation of the republic in Paris at the end of February. Waves of insurrection rolled out of Paris across the Continent, reaching the German states in mid-March.

Using his influential position within the newly reorganized Communist League and his long-term contacts in Cologne, Marx took scant time to join the revolutionary fray. For a little over a year, from the spring of 1848 through the spring of 1849, Marx was, for the first and last time in his life, an insurgent revolutionary: editing in brash, subversive style the *New Rhineland News*; becoming a leader of the radical democrats of the city of Cologne and of the Prussian Rhineland; trying to organize the working class in Cologne and across Germany; and repeatedly encouraging and fomenting insurrection. In all of these activities, Marx persistently promoted the revolutionary strategy he had first envisaged in his essay on the Jewish Question, and would present in scintillating language in the *Communist Manifesto*. He pressed for a democratic revolution to destroy the authoritarian Prussian monarchy. At the same time he aspired to organize the working class to carry out a communist uprising against a capitalist regime he expected such a democratic revolution to establish. In effect, Marx was proposing a double recurrence of the French Revolution: a repetition of its 1789–94 phase in mid-nineteenth-century Prussia, and also a workers' seizure of power at the end of the 1840s modeled on the bourgeois seizure of power at the end of the 1780s. These two efforts, as Marx would discover in his interactions with the workers, democratic radicals, and True Socialists of Cologne, would prove noticeably more difficult to implement simultaneously in practice than in theory.

. . .

IN FEBRUARY 1847, THE London communists dispatched Joseph Moll to Brussels, to negotiate with Marx and Engels about a reorganization of the League of the Just. The latter agreed to support these plans, and, at a congress held in London in June of that year, the group was renamed the Communist League. Marx himself did not attend; his interests were represented by Engels, as delegate of the Paris branch, and Wilhelm Wolff, his Silesian supporter, as the Brussels delegate. Marx claimed that he was too short of funds to go himself. Since he had found the money for other projects at that time, such as the publication of *The Poverty of Philosophy*, Marx may have assigned a lower priority to developing a closer connection with the London communists, or was waiting to see how the planned reorganization turned out.[1]

Despite his absence, he approved the results. The League's emphasis was shifted from revolutionary conspiracy to open propaganda; the organization prepared to bring out its own journal. The former slogan, "All Men are Brothers," was replaced with a new one, devised by Karl Schapper: "Proletarians of all countries [or "Workers of the world," as it is usually translated into English] unite!"—a sentence that has become indissolubly linked to Marx. New statutes announced the community of goods as the organization's aim. A "Communist Confession of Faith," written by Engels, a very distant first draft of the *Communist Manifesto*, became the group's political program. The League even took Marx's side in his dispute with Karl Grün, denouncing the latter as "a literary knight of industry and exploiter of the workers."[2]

Marx formally joined the League, probably after the congress, and became president of the Brussels "Congregation," as the new statutes called the League's local affiliates. Following the practice of the London communists, their Brussels counterparts founded a Workers' Educational Association, which enrolled roughly seventy to one hundred German artisans in the Belgian capital by the fall of 1847. At about the same time as Marx was firming up his associations with the London communists, he was obtaining a publishing outlet for his views. This was a small German-language newspaper, the *German-Brussels News*, much like the Parisian *Forwards!* and in fact published by Adalbert von Bornstedt, one of the publishers of *Forwards!* Bornstedt was a controversial choice, since he had previously been a Prussian spy, as was well known in émigré and radical circles. But Marx felt the opportunity of access—finally—to an uncensored German-language newspaper outweighed any reservations radicals had about Bornstedt's past. As he wrote to Georg Herwegh, "The opposition in all its nuances found it more pleasant to take offense at Bornstedt's name. . . . Will these people ever lack for excuses not to do anything?" It is hard to miss the desire for action in that statement.[3]

Neither Bornstedt nor the newspaper he published were completely on Marx's side. The anti-communist German democrat Karl Heinzen, for instance, denounced Marx and Engels in the pages of the *German-Brussels News*. Their responses would flow into the *Communist Manifesto*. At the end of September, Bornstedt and other German radicals living in Brussels joined with Belgian democrats and émigrés to plan a public meeting that would found an international democratic society, along the lines of the London Fraternal Democrats. When the meeting was announced, Marx was out of town, negotiating with his mother's Dutch relatives about the possibility of receiving an advance on his inheritance. Engels, holding the fort in his absence, was convinced that the entire plan was a plot by Bornstedt and his sympathizers to undermine Marx's leadership of the German Workers' Educational Association.

Given his chronic hostility toward fellow leftists, Engels may have been exaggerating the planners' motives, but the success of his response to political dangers, real and imagined, showed the effectiveness of the Brussels branch of the Communist League and its affiliated Workers' Educational Association. With only twenty-four hours notice, he and other leaders of the group mobilized thirty members of the workers' association to attend the meeting. As agreed beforehand, they proposed that Engels should be one of the vice presidents of the newly founded democratic association—an honor Engels had at first rejected, "because I look so dreadfully young," but finally agreed to accept. On Marx's return to Brussels, Engels, moving back to Paris to continue his campaign against Karl Grün, resigned his position in favor of Marx.[4]

The newly founded organization's ponderous name, "Democratic Association Having as Goal the Union and Fraternity of All Peoples," belied its suppleness and energy. With at least two hundred members, the association sponsored large, regular public meetings, both on domestic themes, such as the need for a more democratic franchise in Belgium, and on international ones, like the recreation of an independent Poland. By late 1847 and early 1848, as political tensions in Europe ratcheted steadily higher, these meetings attracted as many as 1,000 attendees. Marx was the principal speaker at a meeting in January 1848 devoted to free trade and protectionism. His hour-long talk, in French, was greeted (as the minutes record) with "lively applause," and with the decision to fund its publication as a pamphlet, which appeared a few weeks later.[5]

Marx's dual position in Brussels, presiding over the German Workers' Educational Association, and as vice president of the international Democratic Assocation, proved advantageous in his dealing with the German communists and English radicals in London. The London-based Central Authority of the new Communist League, not entirely happy about the echo of its reorganizational congress among its European affiliates, decided to hold a second congress in November 1847. The German communists in Brussels, the one Continental congregation to support unreservedly the new course of the League, were crucial to the plans, and the League's leadership insisted that Marx personally attend this meeting. He made the trip, although his finances were more desperate than ever. Jenny and the children, left behind in Brussels, were all ill; Jenny was "truly harassed by creditors and finds herself in a totally wretched financial embarrassment." Marx's attempt to deal with the situation revealed his own embarrassment. From London, he sent a letter asking his Russian acquaintance Pavel Annenkov for a loan of 200 francs to help out his family. Annenkov should send the money to Jenny without informing her of Marx's involvement, and Marx would pay the loan back when he received the advance on his inheritance.

The political situation in London and Brussels had developed noticeably more favorably than the family finances since the First Congress of the League the previous June. Marx seized the opportunity, and the outcome of the League's Second Congress marked another step in his growing influence over its program and policy. Newly adopted statutes redefined the League's purposes as the overthrow of the bourgeoisie; the rule of the proletariat; and the end to class society and to private property—explicitly communist goals articulated in Marx's own terms. The congress commissioned Marx to write a programmatic document for the League, which would become the *Communist Manifesto*. While in London, Marx, in his capacity as representative of the Brussels Democratic Association, negotiated with the Fraternal Democrats about the planned international left-wing congress. Definitive arrangements were made to summon such a congress to Brussels at the end of September 1848, with a follow-up meeting scheduled for London in 1849.[6]

In contrast to the previous year, 1847 had proven very successful for Marx's political activity. He had overcome his previous isolation and failures, and was now affiliated with groups that offered multiple possibilities for political action, and in which he held key positions. Brussels and London were well covered, between the Central Authority of the Communist League, the Fraternal Democrats, and the Brussels Democratic Association and German Workers' Association. In Paris, Engels was a leading figure in the local Communist League, and in Cologne two congregations of the League existed, one led by Marx's long-term confidants Roland Daniels and Heinrich Bürgers, the other by friends and associates of Moses Hess, who was now reaffiliated with Marx. The *German-Brussels News* provided an outlet for Marx's writings; plans for a journal of political economy were moving ahead; and the Communist League itself was planning to bring out its own journal, starting at the beginning of 1848 with Wilhelm Wolff as its editor.[7]

The International Democratic Congress, well on its way to fruition, would be the culmination of all these political efforts, and set the stage for future, revolutionary political actions, just as the initiatives of the "party of movement" were shaking the European political order. These multifaceted affiliations offered Marx the opportunity to set down in print the ideas on economic development, social conflict, and political strategies he had been developing since he moved to Brussels, and the entrancing prospects of revolutionary action provided the context in which he formulated these ideas.

In February 1848, as the revolutionary wave in Europe was gathering force but still far from its peak, two pamphlets written by Marx appeared in print, published by the Brussels Democratic Association and the Communist League, respectively. Both reflected his years of study and the formulation and reformulation of his ideas, but also the imperative demands of a rapidly radicalizing political situation. One of the pamphlets, the printed version of his speech on free trade, is quite obscure; the other, the *Communist Manifesto*, has become the most renowned of Marx's writings. A consideration of their content reveals Marx's thinking and planning on the eve of a continentwide revolution in which he would be a determined participant.

On September 16–18, 1847, an international congress of economists met in Brussels, at which leaders of the English Anti–Corn Law League, fresh from their victory in repealing tariffs on imported grain, joined their Continental counterparts to call for global free trade. Their views prevailed over the few adherents of protectionism who attended the congress. Marx was a registered participant, but was unable to gain the floor to give his prepared speech, which then formed the basis of his remarks in January 1848 to the Brussels Democratic Association. The speech was a striking example of Marx's transformation of free market economic orthodoxy into a call for communist revolution.[8]

Proponents of the 1846 Corn Law had argued that its abolition of tariffs on imported grain would lower food prices, thus improving the workers' standard of living. Marx responded by citing David Ricardo, "the apostle of English free-traders, the most distinguished economist of our century," that over the course of the business cycle such a reduction in food prices would lead to cuts in wages, wiping out any gains in purchasing power. Proponents of free trade also argued that declines in food prices would stimulate consumption and increase demand, resulting in expanded production, more employment, and higher wages. Marx retorted that industry would grow by accumulating capital, that is, by introducing machinery and extending the division of labor—which would tend to lower employment and reduce wages. This had occurred, he pointed out, over the previous quarter century in Manchester. The number of textile workers had decreased, and their wages had declined, but they produced much more cotton. Mechanized English competition had destroyed handloom weaving and spinning in India: "the muslin of Dacca, renowned in all the world for its beauty and firmness of texture, is equally eclipsed by the competition of English machines."

Arguing that free trade impoverishes the working class and entire underdeveloped countries, while enriching a small group of capitalists, hardly makes the policy sound very attractive. Yet Marx denounced free trade's opposite, protectionism, as "conservative," as a feature of the "old regime," and praised free trade as "destructive." "It dissolves the old nationalities and pushes to the extreme the antagonism between the bourgeoisie and the proletariat. In a word, the system of commercial liberty hastens the social revolution. It is solely in that revolutionary sense, gentlemen, that I vote in favor of free trade." One can only imagine what an uproar this speech would have caused had Marx gained the floor at the economists' congress.

It is easy to imagine a socialist supporting protectionism as a rejection of the primacy of the capitalist free market. Karl Grün, for instance, had described protective tariffs as "socialism in the midst of politics."[9] Marx himself was not opposed to interference in free markets per se. He strongly supported trade unions and strikes, denouncing Proudhon for his rejection of them. Marx, though, remained loyal to free trade, a doctrine he had strongly endorsed in his pre-communist days as editor of the *Rhineland News* in 1842–43. Five years later his support of free trade continued, but as the path to an imminent communist, or—as Marx put it for the Brussels democrats—"social" revolution. The imminence of such a revolution was the main theme of the *Communist Manifesto*.

In 1847, a number of different proposals for a new program for the Communist League were in circulation. Moses Hess, residing at the time in Paris, had submitted his own draft program, but Engels, as he wrote delightedly to Marx, "played a devilish trick on Mosi" by getting Hess's draft discussed without the latter's knowledge, and Engels's revision was sent on to London with the endorsement of the Parisian communists. "Naturally, no devil may know of this, or we'll all be kicked out and there will be a huge scandal."[10]

Engels entitled his own new draft "Fundamentals of Communism." Like the first version, it was written as a catechism. Making use of religious forms for political agitation was a common practice at the time for documents designed to appeal to a wider audience; the Lord's Prayer or the Apostle's Creed were also popular for this purpose. Engels's document had twenty-five questions, each with its distinctive answer, but already by question four the answers were very lengthy, and not at all catechismlike. As he worked on the program, Engels became dissatisfied and told Marx on the eve of their departure for the congress in

London, "I think that we would do best if we abandoned the catechism form and entitled the thing Communist *Manifesto*."[11]

The November 1847 League Congress then assigned Marx the task of writing the organization's revised political platform. As was so often the case, he had trouble meeting his deadlines, and the League's Central Authority had to send him a threatening letter at the end of January 1848 insisting on delivery of the document within a week.[12] It was just as well that Marx took his time, for the result was a literary masterpiece: compact, pithy, elegant, powerful, and sarcastically amusing all at once. Employing the structure and arguments of Engels's "Fundamentals of Communism," Marx reworked it in light of his own life history. The resulting manifesto, although purporting to speak in the name of an objective historical process, relentlessly leading to its revolutionary conclusion, was a deeply personal expression of Marx's own experiences and intellectual development.[13]

The piece began with the famed assertion of the specter of communism haunting Europe, and the consequent need for communists to explain their ideas. The next step was not, as one might expect, a description of communist ideas, but a sketch of human history based on the division of society into classes and the struggles between these classes. Dealing primarily with recent history, the development of capitalism and the rise of a capitalist bourgeoisie, the account turned to the economic, social, political, and cultural consequences of this development, described in memorable language: "the idiocy of rural life," the disdain for the "lumpenproletariat . . . bribed tool of reactionary intrigue," or the assertion that the bourgeoisie "produces above all its own gravedigger. Its decline and the victory of the proletariat are both equally inevitable." That last pronouncement provided a climactic conclusion. An increasingly crisis-ridden capitalism had created an ever larger, ever more impoverished proletariat, whose class struggles pushed it in the direction of a revolutionary overthrow of capitalist society, just as the bourgeoisie had previously overthrown the old regime society of orders. This entire section was a representation in dramatic and polished form of the ideas first developed in the chapter on Feuerbach in *The German Ideology*.

Only after this historical review did Marx proceed to a section about communism, but it said little about a future communist society. Instead, this section was an exposition of the Feuerbach chapter's account of ideology. Attacks on communism as contradicting justice or morality were met with the sharp retort that "the ruling ideas of an age are the ideas of its ruling class." Moral values were ideological, based on existing systems of production, so that communism was not an offense against justice and morality, but just against capitalist justice and morality. Also following the Feuerbach chapter, Marx insisted that the advocacy of communism was not itself ideological, but the "universal expressions of the actual relationships of an existing class struggle. . . ."

The analysis of history under the sign of class struggle and attacks on the denunciation of communism formed the familiar, often-cited portions of the *Communist Manifesto*. Although based on Marx's understanding of the socioeconomic and political circumstances of the 1840s, they read and have been read as universal historical and sociopolitical commentary. The remaining 35 percent of the pamphlet was much more specific to the time and place, and so less often considered. But it is crucial to understanding Marx's actions in the Revolution of 1848 and for seeing the development of his political polemics. The section on communism concluded with a ten-point program for a future communist government. There followed an analysis of other theorists of socialism and communism, giving Marx another opportunity to attack the True Socialists and to emphasize the differences in his understanding of socialism compared to his contemporaries. A very brief concluding segment offered an overview of political conditions in Europe and North America, highlighting the communists' relationship to the "party of movement." The work ended on a celebrated note of revolutionary bravado: "May the ruling classes tremble at the thought of a communist revolution. The proletarians have nothing to lose in that revolution but their chains. They have a world to win"; and then, appearing in public, printed form for the first time, Karl Schapper's motto: "Proletarians of all countries, unite!" A detailed commentary on the *Manifesto* would entail a book in itself, so I will just try to show some of the ways that Marx poured his own past experiences and intellectual development into a political program.

The trumpet blast of the introductory paragraph announced the "specter [or ghost] of communism" haunting Europe, invidiously comparing this childish "fairy tale" of ghosts with the reality of communist ideas. Marx had used precisely this comparison in his May 1842 article on freedom of the press in the *Rhineland News*. Then, it was the conservative Prussian government that had a childish belief in ghosts, seeing the demand for freedom of the press as a "French specter." Marx had posed the comparison philosophically, contrasting the Prussian government's naive and childlike belief in unreflected sensory perception with human rights as developed in the philosophically more advanced and mature Hegelian political spirit. In the *Manifesto*, the same contrast emerged in political terms, as the "powers of old Europe" perceived the specter of communism naively and in childish form. Contrasted to this childish understanding, this "fairy tale of a specter of communism," were the actual "viewpoints, goals and tendencies" of the communists themselves that the *Manifesto* would provide.[14]

In this dramatic introduction, Marx asserted that conservative European governments denounced political opposition as communistic —a fair enough observation. But he went on to make another, stranger suggestion, that radical political oppositionists denounced their conservative opponents as communistic. That was hardly typical of radical opposition in 1840s Europe, but it was something Marx himself had done. As editor of the *Rhineland News*, he had responded to the *Augsburg*

General News's condemnation of his editorial policies as communistic by denouncing conservative thinkers, ostensibly supported by the Augsburg newspapers, as the real communists.[15]

A particular target of Marx's ire as a Young Hegelian and editor of the *Rhineland News* was the government of Friedrich Wilhelm IV of Prussia, and its Romantic, born-again Christian conservative supporters, with their strong sympathies for the pre-1789 society of orders. One feature of the *Manifesto*'s discussion of the consequences of capitalism that is important but invariably overlooked was an assertion of the anachronistic and doomed nature of the Prussian government and its proponents. As observers have often noted, the *Manifesto* included an encomium for the bourgeoisie. Praising its "highly revolutionary role," Marx admired the brutal energy of the bourgeoisie in tearing down existing social, economic, and intellectual systems to build its own, characterized by ceaseless change. The encomium culminated in a celebrated sentence; to quote the standard translation: "All that is solid melts into air, all that is holy is profaned and man is at last compelled to face, with sober senses, his real conditions of life, and his relations with his kind."[16] An entire literature of cultural criticism has been built around this assertion of ceaseless, kaleidoscopic change, relating it to the modernist and post-modernist cultural scene, and to the seemingly endless, ever more accelerated innovations of late-twentieth and early twenty-first-century capitalism. This interpretation has helped preserve Marx's reputation as a prophet, when some of his other predictions, such as the impoverishment of the working masses, have not quite worked out as planned.[17]

But such an interpretation is based on a mistranslation of the original German. The famed sentence, beginning in the original "*Das stehende und das ständische verdampft*," would be more accurately, if not quite so elegantly, rendered in English: "Everything that firmly exists and all the elements of the society of orders evaporate, everything sacred is deconsecrated and men are finally compelled to regard their position in life and their mutual relations with sober eyes." The bourgeoisie, in other words, would defeat the Prussian conservatives Marx had battled while editing the *Rhineland News*. Economic power deriving from the capitalists' steam engines ("to evaporate" in German is *verdampfen*, containing within it *Dampf* or "steam") would terminate the anachronistic society of orders that Friedrich Wilhelm IV and his supporters idealized. Following Marx's theory of ideology, the intellectual and artistic correlates of that society, particularly Romantic glorification of the devout Middle Ages, would also end. Its place would be taken by the secularized worldview and the cool, detached perceptions of artistic realism, already circulating among the authors of Young Germany, most prominently Marx's Paris friend Heinrich Heine.

Marx's confrontation with Prussian conservatives was included in another of the *Manifesto*'s observations about the cultural characteristics of capitalism: the imminent end of nations and nationalism. "National distinctiveness and conflicts between nations disappear more and more with the development of the bourgeoisie, with free trade, the world market, the uniformity of industrial production and the relations of life corresponding to them."[18] This passage was one of Marx's least successful predictions, in view of the ever greater importance of nationalism in pre-1914 Europe, beginning with the revolutionary outbursts of 1848, and reaching a tortured, nightmarish climax during the First World War. Yet if we remember Marx's own organizational efforts and experiences in the months immediately before writing the *Manifesto*—attending the International Congress of free trade economists in Brussels, or working with the London Fraternal Democrats and the Brussels Democratic Association, both of which were based on the cooperation of radicals of different nationalities—then we can see how such an argument might have originated.

In this respect, Marx's attitude would have been hardly atypical for radicals in 1840s Europe, who imagined different nationalist movements cooperating against undemocratic, monarchical rule. Marx though, and Engels as well, had a noticeably negative view of some versions of 1840s German nationalism. They poured scorn on nationalists who derived national qualities from the ancient Teutonic forests, or the Germanic Middle Ages, and talked about a "Christian-Germanic" nation. Friedrich Wilhelm IV and his conservative supporters sometimes liked to patronize this kind of German nationalism and oppose it to a godless and revolutionary France. Such nationalism, tied to conservatives with a hankering for the society of orders, was for Marx yet another past relic that capitalism was eliminating.[19]

In these passages, Marx was recycling the earlier arguments he had devised as a Young Hegelian newspaper editor and democratic opponent of authoritarian Prussian rule for communist revolutionary purposes. He was also reinterpreting his own Young Hegelian past, making the causes he espoused examples of the brutal yet triumphant forward progress of a capitalist bourgeoisie in central Europe. Reaching even further back into his life, he pressed into service the ideas of his Berlin teacher, Eduard Gans, to evoke human history as the history of class struggles. Comparing Gans's memoirs with the *Manifesto* highlights Marx's use of his teacher's text.

Hegelian themes were also present in two aspects of Marx's very scanty discussion of communism. Marx used Hegelian reasoning to escape a self-reflexive theoretical dilemma: how could he and Engels, good bourgeois both, possibly be communists, since their theories tied ideas and political allegiances to class standing and tied communism to

> Free man and slave, patrician and plebian, baron and serf, guild-master and journeyman, in short oppressor and oppressed, stand in constant conflict to one another. . . . In ancient Rome, we have patricians, kings, plebians, slaves; in the Middle Ages, feudal lords, vassals, guild masters, journeymen and serfs. . . . [In] Our epoch, the epoch of the bourgeoisie. . . . The entire society divides ever more into two great hostile camps, in two great classes, standing directly against each other: bourgeoisie and proletariat.
>
> (Marx and Engels, *Communist Manifesto*)

the opposition of the proletariat to the bourgeoisie? The answer Marx gave was by an analogy to the origins of the French Revolution, when some nobles had joined the cause of the bourgeoisie. He was referring to the revolutionary episode at the meeting of the Estates General in June 1789, at which some of the noble and clerical deputies of the first two Estates joined with the Third Estate, to create the National Assembly. Evidence of an impending proletarian revolution, analogous to the bourgeois French Revolution, was that some bourgeois had gone over to the proletariat: "a part of the bourgeois ideologues who have worked their way up to a theoretical understanding of the entire historical movement." This was, of course, a reference to Marx and Engels themselves. It was also a tribute to Hegel's philosophical notion of self-consciousness as the highest form of proof, and that to understand a process was to transcend it and leave it behind. Because they could understand their relationship to their social class and to the place of that class in history, Marx and Engels could go beyond the bourgeois forms of thought to which their theories of ideology would otherwise consign them and affiliate with the proletariat: a distinctly Hegelian and idealist element in a self-consciously materialist theory of socioeconomic and political conflict.

> Just as once, master and slave, later patrician and plebian, then feudal lord and vassal stood against each other, so now the idle man and the worker. If one visits the factories of England, one will find hundreds of men and women, hungry and impoverished, in the service of just one individual sacrificing their health, their enjoyment of life, just for their continued impoverished existence. (Gans, *Memoirs*)[20]

The sole description of a communist society in the *Manifesto* was the assertion that it would be "an association in which the free development of each is the condition for the free development of all." This was the latest version of the ideal of a social organization reconciling the particular interests of individuals and the general interests of state and society, first evoked in Marx's unfinished 1843 essay on Hegel's

Philosophy of Law. There described in explicitly Hegelian terms as the reconciliation of the universal and the particular, this ideal persisted through Marx's affiliation with Feuerbach's materialist humanism, his initial, Feuerbachian version of communism, into the more hard-edged, agitational, rhetorically distinctly un-Hegelian *Communist Manifesto*.

If the *Manifesto* had little to say about the future communist order, it was quite explicit on how such an order would be reached, presenting a ten-point program for a future communist government, taken almost verbatim from Engels's draft program of the Communist League. The measures proposed included ideas common to the radical left of the 1840s, and by no means exclusively communist, such as a progressive income tax, as well as others proposed by the French socialists, like abolition of inheritance or the creation of a state bank, with a monopoly on credit.

The state bank was a signature idea of Proudhon, whom Marx had fiercely attacked. It might seem unfair of Marx to denounce Proudhon while adopting his ideas, but for Marx the crucial feature of socialist measures was their political context. Proudhon had envisaged such a bank as coming into existence within a legally, constitutionally, and economically regularly functioning capitalist society, rather than as part of a revolutionary upheaval. The ten-point program in the *Manifesto* was designed specifically for a revolutionary government, one modeled on the radical, Jacobin phrase of the French Revolution of 1789.

This was evident in the program's fourth point, the "confiscation of the property of emigrants and rebels," a measure the Jacobins had practiced with considerable success. The model of the French Revolution was still more apparent in Engels's draft, which called for the expropriation of the property of large landowners, industrialists, and owners of railroads and shipyards, offering them compensation in *assignats*, the paper currency of the French Revolution.[21] Even more to the point was the assumption that there would be emigrants and rebels in the first place. The action program of the *Manifesto* was a plan for revolution and civil war, based on the previous experiences of the Reign of Terror, the most radical phase of the French Revolution in the years 1793–94. Marx had studied this period extensively when he was in Paris, at one point even planning to write a history of the Convention, the revolutionary parliament of the period. Here too, Marx was reflecting a common radical perception of the 1840s that perceived future revolutions in terms of the great past model of revolutionary action.

The transition from capitalism to communism was to occur through just such a revolutionary upheaval. Before listing the ten-point program, the *Manifesto* explained its basic idea: "despotic impositions into property rights and into bourgeois relations of production, through measures that appear economically insufficient and unsupportable but in the course of the movement go on beyond themselves. . . ." Seen in the light of the history of the radical phase of the French Revolution, Marx and Engels were proposing to take measures such as seizing some capitalists' property. This would lead to unrest—those "emigrants and rebels"—but also to other capitalists refusing to cooperate with the communist government, creating an economic crisis, which in turn would allow the government to take still more drastic measures— precisely how things worked in France between 1792 and 1794.

This version of communism, in which the emphasis was placed on the violent, revolutionary process of creating a communist regime, rather than on the post-capitalist society itself, was one that Marx and Engels sharply differentiated from competing forms of socialism. They denounced "reactionary" socialism, by which they meant conservative critiques of capitalism. A few of these were circulating in Prussia at the time, particularly in the *Rhenish Observer*, a government-supported newspaper in Cologne that Marx had vigorously attacked in the pages of the *German-Brussels News*.[22] Marx and Engels made short shrift of "bourgeois" socialism—what we would today call social reform—the amelioration of the condition of the working class within the existing capitalist society. There was also a discussion of "critical-utopian" socialism, practiced by the followers of Charles Fourier in France and Robert Owen in England, who proposed to start communist experiments within a capitalist society. Marx's and Engels's skepticism of the possible success of such measures was widely shared by contemporaries; even their bête noire, Karl Grün, had strong doubts about the viability of these schemes.[23]

These critiques of other versions of socialism were taken from Engels's "Fundamentals of Communism," but Marx inserted an additional version not in Engels's draft. This was True Socialism, the only socialism or communism known in Germany on the eve of the 1848 Revolution. Marx continued his previous attacks on the True Socialists for replacing French socialist criticisms of the capitalist economy with Hegelian language, such as "the externalization and emptying out of human essence," concepts Marx himself had used in his True Socialist phase. The True Socialists were also denounced as philistine German petit bourgeois, another familiar motif. But the *Manifesto* introduced a new reason to attack this group, namely, as tacit or open supporters of the absolutist German governments.

Marx asserted that the problem with the True Socialists' attack on capitalism was that it extended to the political aspects of capitalist society: the rule of law, a constitutional and representative government, and guarantees of civil liberties. It was fine to denounce these as adjuncts to capitalist exploitation of the workers in countries like France and England that already had liberal political institutions. In the German states, such as Prussia, where the liberal opposition was vigorously demanding a constitution by 1847, attacks on liberal institutions just "served the German absolutist governments, with their retinue of rotten priests, school teachers, backwoods noble landlords and bureaucrats, as a welcome scarecrow against the threatening upward aspirations of the bourgeoisie." This scathing invective was taken from a similar, if less colorful description, in Engels's draft, but there it was used to describe the beneficiaries of governmental, conservative socialism.[24]

Denouncing the True Socialists as lackeys of Germany's conservative governments was a new theme in Marx's contest with other central European communist intellectuals that had not appeared previously in his published or unpublished writings. The accusation had first been raised by the anti-communist democrat Karl Heinzen. He had applied it to all of Germany's communists, including Marx and Engels, whose differences with other communists were only known to a small group of insiders. Both Marx and Engels, outraged by Heinzen's comments, had responded vigorously in the fall of 1847 in the pages of the *German-Brussels News*.[25] While Marx evidently felt that Heinzen's contentions did not apply to him, he was willing to make use of them against the other German socialists, once again demonstrating the anti-communist roots of his communism, or at least the way that Marx appropriated anti-communist themes to attack other versions of communism.

As Marx's first biographer, Franz Mehring, pointed out a century ago, this accusation was profoundly unfair: the True Socialists were not counterrevolutionary supporters of the Prussian government, and during the Revolution of 1848 they were strong proponents of a democratic Germany.[26] The *Communist Manifesto*'s newly invented reason to condemn the True Socialists reveals Marx's political stance on the eve of the 1848 Revolution. Following the reasoning he had first propounded in his essay on the Jewish Question, Marx wanted to have both an anti-Prussian and a communist revolution, a double recurrence, as it were, of the French Revolution of 1789. The result of the anti-Prussian revolution was to be a liberal constitutional state, with the full panoply of civil liberties and the rule of law.

This was, as Marx had made clear in the *Manifesto*, precisely the sort of capitalist regime whose pernicious character he was exposing and whose overthrow he was advocating. Why bother, then, fighting for such a regime—or, to pose the question in terms of political strategy—was the organization of a nascent working class in central Europe for a communist future compatible with the organization of an anti-Prussian, democratic revolution? At the time he was writing the *Manifesto*, Marx saw the forthcoming revolution as occurring in a close but not immediate future. First, there would be an international democratic congress to bring together radicals from Europe and North America, to draft a political program and outline a political strategy, all of which would have helped to deal with this question. Instead, no sooner had the *Communist Manifesto* left the printers, in February 1848, than Marx found the revolution he had foreseen breaking out all around him.

IT IS DIFFICULT TO appreciate today the electrifying impact of the barricade fighting that gripped Paris for three days at the end of February 1848, ending with the overthrow of the monarchy and the proclamation of the republic. Republics are the default form of governmental organization at the beginning of the twenty-first century; in the United States, the conservative political party even calls itself Republican. But in the middle of the nineteenth century, republics were new and daring kinds of government; in Europe, at least, the political aspiration of adherents of the extreme left. The last time a French Republic had been proclaimed in Paris was in 1792: the results were the Reign of Terror and a decades-long, European-wide war. Whether there would be a new revolutionary war, or a wave of revolutionary repercussions across Europe, was unclear, but the proclamation of the republic made all previous political plans obsolete, and for the adherents of radical revolution, such as Marx, the result was an enormous acceleration of political activity.

It is possible that Marx dashed off to London to discuss the new situation with the leaders of the Communist League. Arguing in favor of such a trip was the decision of the League's Central Authority to move its seat from London to Brussels. League leaders in London, including the troika of Schapper, Bauer, and Moll, prepared to head for the Continent where the revolutionary action was taking place; in the meantime, the central direction of the League was placed in Marx's hands. But neither Marx nor the League leadership could remain in Brussels.

The proclamation of the republic in Paris was perceived as a threat to the status quo in Belgium, bringing up the prospect of an invasion by a French revolutionary army, an uprising by Belgian radicals imitating their French counterparts, or both at once. The Belgian government viewed with extreme suspicion the rapidly growing Brussels Democratic Association, which had already created a large and active affiliated group in Ghent, and was threatening to become the nucleus of a republican insurrection. As a vice president of the association, a politically active foreigner who would provide a good scapegoat for unrest, Marx was already in the authorities' sights. His mother's unpolitical decision at this point to grant him an advance on his inheritance in the amount of 6,000 French francs (about 1,250 Prussian talers) only magnified the authorities' suspicions. The money arrived in Brussels just at the end of February, and the Belgian police were convinced that it was actually sent for the purpose of purchasing weapons for an insurrection.[27]

As a result, Marx was summarily instructed on March 3, 1848, that he had twenty-four hours to leave the country. Not bothering to wait for the deadline to expire, the police burst into his apartment that afternoon, and carried him off to jail. When a visibly distraught Jenny, in the company of the leading Belgian members of the Brussels Democratic Association, went to speak to her husband, she was arrested as well, "locked up," as an angered Karl explained, "in a dark room with common streetwalkers." Both Jenny and Karl were released the next day, but they had to leave Belgium with their children immediately, abandoning all their furnishings and possessions. Their belongings, packed into six crates weighing a total of 405 kilos, only caught up with them eight months later, after a lengthy bureaucratic odyssey.[28]

While personally very disruptive, the expulsion was a political opportunity for Marx to return to Paris, now more than ever the seat of a European-wide revolutionary movement. The provisional government of the French Republic was dominated by the former radical opposition, whose leaders Marx and Engels had assiduously cultivated. A few days before Marx's expulsion, as storm clouds were gathering around him, Ferdinand Flocon, minister in the provisional government and a particular object of Engels's attention in 1847, issued an invitation to "brave and loyal Marx" to return to the French Republic, the "field of asylum for all friends of liberty." Marx was only too pleased to accept. By mid-March, almost all the leading figures of the Communist League were in Paris, and the Central Authority could reconstitute itself there.[29] Just a week later, the revolution reached the two German great powers. Following fighting on the barricades in Berlin and Vienna, the chastened monarchs were forced to appoint liberal governments, making it possible for exiled German radicals to return to the political fray in their home country.

A large group of the Parisian German exiles, led by Adalbert von Bornstedt, the publisher of the *German-Brussels News*, and Georg Herwegh, proposed to arm the German artisans residing in Paris, most of them unemployed as a result of the economic crisis in 1846–47, and march them back into Germany as a revolutionary legion, to fight for a German republic. Demonstrating a sober view of the political situation that he would maintain throughout the midcentury revolution, Marx denounced this proposal as foolish adventurism, which would culminate in disaster. He was quite right about the outcome of the march of the German Legion, whose largely unarmed and badly provisioned members barely staggered to the Franco-German border. After crossing the Rhine, they were promptly dispersed, arrested, or forced back into exile. Marx succeeded in getting the Communist League to oppose the proposal and most members of the League to stay clear of the dubious adventure.[30]

In line with previous League considerations, and of one mind on this topic with Schapper, Marx proposed that the artisan members of the League should peacefully return to Germany. Marx's friends in the provisional government of the French Republic would help with their travel expenses. Marx wanted League members, once back in Germany, to found workers' associations in different cities, now that the new, liberal governments of the German states had guaranteed the freedom of association. Ultimately, he was aiming at a national network of such groups. The city of Mainz, second largest on the Rhine after Cologne, and home to a number of the more active artisan members of the Communist League, would be the node of the organizing efforts. League members there would proclaim themselves a provisional central committee of German workers' associations.

For himself and his closest political associates, including Engels, Schapper, Wilhelm Wolff, and other top members of the Communist League, Marx had something different in mind. They would all return to Cologne, the city in which he still had many sympathizers, and establish a radical newspaper, the *New Rhineland News*, a continuation of the journal Marx had edited with such verve in 1842–43. Once again, Marx would be what he longed to be, a crusading newspaper editor. This time, following the establishment of freedom of the press in Prussia, he could express his views openly and with all the invective he had previously tried to hold in check. By mid-April, Marx and most of his associates were in Cologne ready to put his plans into action. Marx's ideas followed the outline he had sketched in the *Communist Manifesto*. The newspaper would call for the creation of a revolutionary German republic, a German version of France in 1792–94, the "bourgeois revolution," in Marx's terminology. The nationwide network of workers' associations would support such a revolutionary initiative, but it would also prepare for the next stage in politics, the communist workers' revolution.[31]

Cologne in the spring of 1848 was deep in the whirlwind of revolution. Everywhere in the Rhenish metropolis, the previously prohibited black-red-gold German national flags were flying, even from Prussian government buildings. The Café Royal, gathering center of the city's left-wing intellectuals, had hastily dropped its monarchical self-designation and renamed itself Stollwerck's German Coffeehouse. The few pro-Prussian conservatives in this Catholic Rhineland city, whose inhabitants were now free to express their hatred of Prussian colonial rule, kept out of sight. But liberal supporters of a constitutional monarchy, pro-republican democrats, and anti-Prussian Catholic conservatives were all vigorously present in public life. This was a political scene, much like other large German cities at the height of revolutionary enthusiasm, in the "springtime of the peoples." But Cologne had one distinct difference: the presence of a large and active communist movement. Members of the city's Communist League Congregation had mobilized thousands of the city's artisans and laborers to invade City Hall (leading terrified city councilmen to dive out of windows to evade them) and demand jobs for the unemployed, lower taxes for the workers, and lawmaking in the hands of the people.

In Cologne and its vicinity, workers, artisans, and laborers, inspired by the outbreak of revolution, were busy taking action on their own without any specific communist direction. They were holding public meetings, formulating their grievances and demands. More angrily, they were mobbing and threatening their employers, calling for better wages and more favorable terms of employment. Occasionally, these demands spilled over into violent uprisings. One widely reported riot had seen the skilled metalworking artisans of nearby Solingen attack and demolish a large industrial foundry, whose cheap products were competing with their expensive craft goods.

Everything in and around Cologne seemed to be moving in the direction that Marx's political strategy demanded: the recurrence of the French Revolution directed against the Prussian monarchy and the recurrence of the French Revolution by the workers directed against the bourgeoisie were both underway. But just a few weeks after Marx's arrival, it became clear that things were not working out quite as he had hoped. The members of the Communist League in Mainz were not up to their assigned task of creating a national network of workers' associations. A League emissary reported back to Cologne: "In Mainz I found the League at the onset of complete anarchy; Wallau was in Wiesbaden; Neubeck was in a café playing dominoes while a meeting was scheduled; Metternich [not Franz von Metternich, the deposed, reactionary Austrian chancellor, but the republican revolutionary Germain Metternich], who, admittedly has a lot to do, regards the cause with the greatest indifference. . . ."[32] The planned national federation of workers' associations, led by members of the Communist League in Mainz, never came into existence.

By the second half of 1848, Marx had severed his ties with the Communist League. Several years later, a League member, cigarmaker Peter Roeser, interrogated by Prussian police, would tell them that Marx had dissolved the League altogether in the spring of 1848. Historians have hotly debated whether or not this dissolution actually took place, and there are good arguments against the assumption of a formal dissolution.[33] It is striking, though, that there is no mention of the League in Marx's public pronouncements or his surviving private papers during the period of his peak revolutionary activity from June 1848 until his arrival as a political refugee in London in the fall of 1849.

Marx's difficulties with the Communist League and with the organization of the working class for his dual revolutionary goals were painfully evident in Cologne itself. The Cologne communists, under the leadership of the municipal charity physician Andreas Gottschalk, a committed activist and enthralling public speaker, had been, in contrast to their Mainz counterparts, very active. Not only had they led a mass demonstration that stormed City Hall, but, almost to the date of Marx's arrival, they founded an enormously popular Cologne Workers' Association. At its peak in June 1848, it counted 8,000 members, about one third of Cologne's adult men.[34]

Gottschalk's group was seemingly exactly what Marx wanted, but his workers' organization presented more problems than benefits. There was the matter of personal rivalry: Gottschalk, who was every bit as jealous of potential rivals as Marx, wanted such rivals far away from the largest city in western Germany. He thought that Marx should return from exile to his native Trier and Engels to his native Wupper Valley, where they could stand for election to the newly summoned German National Assembly. The arrival in Cologne of Marx and his close associates, who made up the Central Authority of the Communist League, was precisely what Gottschalk did not want to see happen. In May 1848, he resigned from the League, making it clear that he would not take directions from Marx.[35]

Closely related to the personal problem was a political one: Gottschalk was a True Socialist, a friend, pupil, and close confidant of Moses Hess.[36] His mentor had evaded a confrontation with Marx by leaving Cologne and going to Paris shortly after Marx's arrival, but Gottschalk, as the influential leader of the Workers' Association, was in a position to carry out Hess's policies. Marx's assertion in the *Communist Manifesto* that the True Socialists were working for the Prussian conservatives by attacking the liberal opposition now met its test in real life. Gottschalk's refusal to support the campaigns against the Prussian monarchy led by Cologne's democrats did fit that picture. Mostly, Gottschalk's opposition to the liberals and the democrats came from the left, denouncing them as not radical or revolutionary enough. He refused to cooperate with the democrats in the elections to the German National Assembly in Frankfurt, and the Prussian Constituent Assembly in Berlin, both held on the same day in May 1848. The enormously popular Gottschalk would not even stand as a communist candidate in these elections, instead denouncing them as a bourgeois farce and appealing to members of the Workers' Association to boycott them. The main beneficiary of his successful appeal was Cologne's devout and generally conservative pro-Austrian Catholics (a group Marx had seen as the chief threat to the leftists in the Rhineland), who were dominant at the polls, choosing the city's archbishop to represent them in Berlin.

In June 1848, Gottschalk escalated his radicalism, calling for the establishment of a workers' republic in Germany. However, he also insisted that any action taken to bring such a republic about would be counterproductive. Most Germans, he asserted, favored such a regime and it would appear in the near future largely without the need for much effort. These were ideas of his mentor Moses Hess. As early as 1843, Hess had told Arnold Ruge that the vast majority of the population was for communism, and that a communist society would largely emerge of its own accord.[37] Marx, who saw communism as the outcome of a long process of organization, agitation, and political struggle, culminating in insurrection, civil war, and international warfare, regarded such visions of the peaceful and effortless onset of a communist regime as nothing short of delusional.

Marx had much more success in founding a radical political newspaper than in organizing the working class. The idea of reviving the *Rhineland News* had been circulating in Cologne as soon as a liberal government in Prussia abolished press censorship, and it was Moses Hess who moved first to do it. By early April 1848, Hess was negotiating with potential financial backers, publishers, and foreign correspondents, but after a decisive organizational meeting held on April 12, the day after Marx's arrival in Cologne, Marx and his supporters were in charge of the enterprise. Hess left shortly thereafter for Paris, and played little part in the politics of the 1848 Revolution. (Marx's defeat of his mentor cannot have helped Andreas Gottschalk's relationship with him.) It seems likely that Marx's followers packed the meeting, but the outcome also reflected Marx's position in the city, in particular the memories of his very energetic role as editor of the *Rhineland News* five years earlier.

The plan was to fund the newspaper, like the *Rhineland News*, by selling shares of stock. Over the next six weeks, Marx and his associates worked frantically to gather funds to get the enterprise underway. They hoped to receive a big piece of the funding from Engels's wealthy father. But the devout and conservative Friedrich Engels, Sr., as his son told Marx, "rather than giving us a thousand talers, would like to fire a thousand rounds of grapeshot at us." In the end, the money was raised: 13,000 talers. Marx contributed part of the advance on his inheritance he had received from his mother. Engels added a smaller sum, what must have been a substantial portion of his very modest personal assets. Most of the funds came from Marx's fans in Cologne and the vicinity—a number of well-off smaller businessmen and professionals, by no means all of them radical leftists, impressed by the vigorous editor of the *Rhineland News*, and willing to give him another try. The first issue of the *New Rhineland News* duly appeared at the beginning of June.[38]

The newspaper would be Marx's chief venue for political action during the 1848 Revolution; he and his followers were often known to contemporaries as the "party of the *New Rhineland News*." Supplementing his journalism, at the beginning of July, Marx began attending the meetings of the Democratic Society, Cologne's radical political club, which Gottschalk had denounced as bourgeois. Marx and his associates quickly came to dominate the meetings in the summer and fall, and played an important role in setting its policy; Marx's long-term Cologne supporter Heinrich Bürgers, a member of the editorial board of the *New Rhineland News*, was elected the club's vice president. Like their fellow radicals across central Europe, Cologne's democrats sought to strengthen their movement by creating regional and national federations of political clubs. Marx and Engels were leading figures at a congress of democratic clubs from the Prussian Rhineland and Westphalia, held in Cologne in August 1848. After some contention with potential rivals, particularly the Bonn professor Gottfried Kinkel (at one point verging on fisticuffs), the delegates to the congress chose Marx and his associates for a majority of the positions on the directory of the district federation of democratic political clubs.[39]

By the fall of 1848, Marx was an influential revolutionary, editing a newspaper with a rapidly growing circulation, and playing a significant role in local and provincial radical politics. He aspired to be a national political figure, and the *New Rhineland News* increasingly obtained a national readership, as can be seen from the letters to its editors, which poured in from the Bavarian provinces in the southeast, from Greifswald in Pomerania in the north, on to Königsberg in the far northeast of Prussia, and from all central European points in between. The correspondents reported on political struggles in their hometowns, asked Marx for political advice, and requested work or job recommendations. The actress wife of the newspaper's Vienna correspondent even asked Marx to arrange a position for her in the repertory company of a German theater.[40] In spite of the growing reach of his newspaper, Marx remained primarily a provincial figure, a revolutionary leader of the second rank, not quite at the level of the most prominent and influential politicians, the front-benchers in the German National Assembly meeting in Frankfurt (among whom were Marx's onetime classmate Ludwig Simon from Trier, and his former patron Arnold Ruge) and the Prussian Constituent Assembly in Berlin. Although incapable of directly shaping events at the national level, the dynamics of the revolution ensured that Marx had ample opportunity to carry out his insurrectionary aspirations.

In fact, the *New Rhineland News* was very much Marx's newspaper. He was employed as "editor-in-chief," with a three-year contract guaranteeing him editorial autonomy and a yearly salary of 1,500 talers— the most lucrative post he ever held, although it is unclear if he was ever paid in full, due to the newspaper's financial difficulties. Besides his editorial contract Marx was also a powerful stockholder, so that he had created a secure and autonomous position for himself, quite unlike his unacknowledged, precarious status at the newspaper's predecessor, at the mercy of its investors.[41] The editorial offices of the *New Rhineland News*, one flight up at No. 17 Unter Hutmacher in the maze of narrow streets of Cologne's old city (typesetting and printing were on the ground floor), became Marx's political headquarters. From there, he would pursue a policy of attacking the same enemies and pursuing many of the same goals he had in 1842–43, only doing so this time in more open, vehement, and radical form.

The *New Rhineland News* fired off one salvo after another denouncing the Prussian royal house, its officials and soldiers. As the Cologne police commissioner put it, Marx "allows himself each and every libel of our constitution, our king, and our highest state officials in his ever more widely read newspaper." Just to give one example of what was inflaming the good policeman, consider a lead article from the August 9, 1848, issue. Almost parenthetically, in writing about the need for cooperation between Polish and German nationalists, Marx took on Prussian officialdom: "Where is the Rhinelander, who has not had business with a freshly imported Old Prussian state official, who has not had the opportunity to admire this incomparable, pretentious know-it-all attitude, this union of narrowness and infallibility, this crudeness that tolerates no contradiction! Among us, of course, these Old Prussian gentlemen have no . . . stick at their disposal to beat us, and, from the lack of the latter, some have died of sorrow."[42]

The 1848 Revolution was supposed to have brought Germany's authoritarian monarchies under parliamentary control, by the Prussian Constituent Assembly in Berlin and the German National Assembly in Frankfurt. Much of the invective of the *New Rhineland News* focused on these revolutionary parliaments: for not being revolutionary, for not exercising popular sovereignty and bringing the pre-revolutionary authorities to heel. The Prussian Assembly, whose liberal majority declared that its purpose was "reaching agreement" with the king on a constitution, as opposed to the radical demand for writing a constitution on its own authority, was constantly mocked as the "reaching agreement assembly" or the "agreement reachers." As for the Frankfurt Assembly, Marx wrote in November 1848, "The strictest verdict has already been issued on it—the ignoring of its decisions and—its being forgotten." This denunciation was written at a moment of revolutionary crisis in Prussia, but in the more peaceful atmosphere of June 1848, less than two weeks after the newspaper had started publishing, Marx had already written a lead article denouncing both assemblies as *Inkompetent*—the German phrase meaning both incompetent but also lacking in authority and jurisdiction. Marx had nothing better to say about the new liberal governments of the individual German states, including the Prussian prime minister, Marx's former patron, Ludolf Camphausen.[43]

In place of this timorous political moderation, Marx insisted, in one of his very first articles, that the ultimate goal of the democrats would have to be the "German republic, one and indivisible," a telling phrase from the slogan of the Jacobins during the Reign of Terror in the French Revolution. The *Feuilleton* (the part of European newspapers devoted to serializing novels or dealing with literary and cultural matters) of the June 19, 21–22, and 26 issues of the *New Rhineland News* entertained its readers with a German translation of the trial of Louis XVI before the Convention: a trial ending, notoriously, in the guillotining of the monarch. Marx denounced the moderate democrats of the Frankfurt National Assembly for desiring a "republic of provincial philistines, far from all atrocities and crimes that soiled the first French Republic, free of blood and despising the red flag . . . [where] each honest burgher could lead a quiet and peaceful life in all blessedness and honorableness." The sarcasm only underscores Marx's own aspirations toward a rerun of 1790s revolutionary Jacobinism in 1840s Germany.[44]

Marx explained that an indivisible German republic would emerge as much from "domestic conflicts as a war with the East. . . ." The war with the East, that is, with the czar, whose autocratic realm was seen by all radicals—and Marx was quite typical in this respect—as the pillar of reaction and counterrevolution in Europe, was the central element in Marx's revolutionary strategy. Revolutionary war had made radical revolution possible in the 1790s; Marx saw a new revolutionary war as leading to the same goal. Reminiscing about the newspaper decades later after Marx's death, Engels asserted that war with Russia and the creation of a united German republic were its two main themes. War with Russia was a constant preoccupation, from the paper's earliest issues to its final one in May 1849, which contained a vision of an international revolutionary army marching into Eastern Europe to challenge the czar.[45]

The reader might note that something seems to be missing in this account of the editorial policy of the *New Rhineland News*: communism. Although it was an open secret at the time that the editors were all communists, the newspaper published few denunciations of capitalists, and its lack of coverage of the nascent labor movement was striking. The language of the paper, intellectual and academic, full of foreign words and literary and historical references, made it difficult for a literate but poorly educated member of the lower classes to understand. To be sure, during the 1848 Revolution newspapers were often read out loud to a crowd by someone with a better education who could explain difficult points, but the demanding style of the *New Rhineland News* made even that a considerable task. Unlike other left-wing newspapers in Cologne, which were designed for a popular readership, Marx's intellectualized product aimed primarily at an educated audience.[46]

It was not just lack of trying that prevented the class struggle from appearing in the *New Rhineland News*, as became very evident in the summer of 1848. The season began with the June Days, the fierce barricade fighting in Paris between forces of the republican government and the working-class population of the eastern part of the city. While most leftists in Germany treated the events as a tragedy, pitting a republican government against people who should have been its strongest supporters, Marx and Engels openly glorified the insurgents. They praised their failed uprising as the first step toward a future communist revolution, directed against a republican regime that was still very far from existing in Germany.

Cologne democrats rejected Marx's interpretation of the June Days, and after repeated criticisms from them, Marx repudiated his own writing. At the August 4, 1848, meeting of the Cologne Democratic Society, Marx gave a speech asserting that it was only through "the use of intellectual weapons" that the "interests of the individual classes" could find "a mutually agreeable compromise. . . ." Instead of class harmony, "the denial of mutual concessions, as well as perverted concepts of the relationship between the classes of the population," had led in Paris "to a bloody outcome." Marx went on to denounce the idea of a revolutionary dictatorship in the name of a "single class," which his old rival Weitling had proposed in Cologne a few weeks previously, as "nonsense." Rather, a revolutionary government would have to be made up of "heterogeneous elements" that would "reach agreement about the most appropriate form of administration through the exchange of ideas."[47]

This renunciation, even condemnation, of the class struggle, coming from the man who had just written the *Communist Manifesto* six months earlier, sounds, well, downright un-Marxist. The Marxist-Leninist compilers of the admirable collection of documents about the Communist League refused to believe in the authenticity of the speech, and concluded that Marx must have been misquoted.[48] If he had, Marx made no attempt to correct the misapprehension. Rather, his speech fit very well with the ceaselessly anti-Prussian editorial policy of the *New Rhineland News*, and the newspaper's attempts to rally all inhabitants of the Rhineland behind a policy of destroying authoritarian Prussian rule.

Provoking or exploiting hostility between different social classes would only weaken such a coalition.

This idea of temporarily renouncing anti-capitalism for anti-Prussian purposes was a point on which Marx and his True Socialist rival, Andreas Gottschalk, strongly disagreed. At the beginning of July 1848, the Prussian authorities arrested Gottschalk, on blatantly trumped-up charges, and kept him in prison until his trial and eventual acquittal in December. While Gottschalk was in jail, Marx and his followers, especially the London communists Joseph Moll and Karl Schapper, moved to take over the Cologne Workers' Association and turn it into a vehicle for the mobilization of the workers to support such an anti-Prussian revolution. They used the meetings to educate the members on economic and political topics. How Schapper, Marx's point man for the association, went about this can be seen from an account written by an embittered adherent of Gottschalk: "At this point citizen Schapper gave a long speech about current affairs, with historical and statistical remarks, which just about took up all the remaining time in the meeting, and added, at the conclusion, the promise, to give in the future a statistical overview of all the countries, peoples and tribes of Europe."[49]

This hostile and amusing description, which does correspond to Schapper's oratorical style, pointed out the problem with trying to use the Workers' Association as an educational auxiliary to the democrats. The workers themselves were not interested; under the direction of Marx and his associates, membership in the Cologne Workers' Association dropped by over 90 percent from the level it had reached under Gottschalk's leadership.[50] Either prong of Marx's strategy of a double recurrence of the French Revolution—a democratic revolution against Prussia, or a workers' revolution against the bourgeoisie—had its possibilities. Combining the two proved impossible. Attacking Prussian rule meant neglecting class antagonisms; cultivating the workers' hostility of the bourgeoisie meant ceasing to work with other democrats in

Cologne and the Rhineland. The revolutionary crises of September and November 1848 offered Marx an opportunity to implement the anti-Prussian side of his revolutionary plans. By the time of the third and final crisis of the revolution, in May 1849, he had increasingly abandoned these attempts and returned to the organization of the working class that he had neglected for much of the previous year, a decision that tended to limit his insurrectionary enthusiasm.

The crisis of September 1848 involved, as did so many other aspects of the mid-nineteenth-century revolutions, a nationalist issue: the uprising of the German inhabitants of the two northern duchies of Schleswig and Holstein against Danish rule, in which they demanded the duchies' accession to a united German nation-state. The liberal government of Prussia had supported the insurrection with its troops; but under heavy pressure from the czar, and ignoring the protests of the German National Assembly, the Prussian government concluded an armistice with the Danes in September 1848, and dropped the cause of the insurgents. This was an issue tailor-made for Germany's leftists, combining nationalist sentiments, opposition to the czar, and hostility to a return of the conservatives to power in Prussia. What made this situation particularly explosive in Cologne was that it coincided with a drunken brawl between civilians and soldiers of the Prussian garrison, in which the soldiers had gotten out of hand and marched through the streets assaulting passersby and smashing shop windows. Prussian soldiers would not fight the nation's enemies but would attack their monarch's Rhenish subjects.

Marx, back from a combined fund-raising and agitation trip to Berlin and Vienna, moved quickly to exploit the situation. He and his friends in the Democratic Society summoned a public mass meeting to create a Committee of Public Safety in Cologne, the very name a reference to the revolutionary experience in France during the rule of the Jacobins in the 1790s. They followed up this urban meeting with one held on Fühlingen Heath in the village of Worringen, to the north of the city, where a large crowd of 7,000 to 10,000 rustics heard speakers, including Friedrich Engels (Marx, the poor public speaker, was not present), call for a Red Republic and demand that the peasants hurry to the city, when the moment came for a showdown with the Prussian soldiers.

The moment did finally come on September 25, when the police tried to arrest a number of the radicals in Cologne, including Engels and Joseph Moll, then president of the Workers' Association, resulting in rioting and the building of barricades. The city was briefly in a state of insurrection, but by that evening the barricades had been abandoned and the Prussian authorities instituted martial law. The Democratic Society and the Workers' Association were shut down, and the *New Rhineland News* suppressed for twelve days. It had been a genuinely revolutionary moment, coinciding with uprisings in southern Germany. The strongly anti-Prussian and anti-Russian tome of events certainly fit Marx's plans, although the nationalist undertones hardly corresponded to the contention in the *Communist Manifesto* that nationalism was on the way out.[51]

As a result of this confrontation, both Moll and Engels had to flee the country to avoid arrest. Engels spent the subsequent months wandering through France and Switzerland, largely out of touch with Marx, definitely out of money, and at times questioning his own future. Engels's parents bombarded their absent son with letters telling him that Marx and his fellow godless communists had dropped him, and no longer cared for him. These missives, carefully crafted by Friedrich's mother Elise, with whom he was on far better terms than his father, were not without effect. Nor were they entirely untrue. Both the newspaper's investors and several of Marx's left-wing associates, including Hermann Ewerbeck and the Cologne communist physician Karl d'Ester, wanted Marx to break with Engels, because Engels's difficult personality had led to constant conflicts with the editorial staff. Marx went out of his way to assure his colleague that whatever other leftists may have thought, "That I could have left you in the lurch even for a minute is pure fantasy. You always remain my *intimus*, as I am, hopefully yours." As for the accusations from Engels's family, Marx ascribed them to Engels's father, a *Schweinehund*. Marx even sent Engels money to support him, a reminder that the future flow of funds in their relationship, in the opposite direction, was by no means preordained.[52]

Martial law in Cologne was lifted on October 3; the Democratic Society and the Workers' Association resumed meeting and the *New Rhineland News* began publishing again a week later. If he was lacking two of his close associates, Marx nonetheless had the institutional resources to meet the next major political crisis in November, when Friedrich Wilhelm IV sent the army to dissolve the Prussian Constituent Assembly in Berlin. Before the soldiers could carry out his royal will, the deputies voted to call on Prussian citizens to boycott paying taxes, until their elected representatives could freely carry out their deliberations.

With the Constituent Assembly finally acting in revolutionary fashion, Marx threw himself wholeheartedly into the fight. Every day, the masthead of the *New Rhineland News* proclaimed: "No more taxes!" In contrast to the events in September, which were largely limited to Cologne and its vicinity, Marx used his position on the directory of the provincial federation of democratic clubs in November to organize both a tax boycott and then armed resistance to the Prussian government across the length and breadth of the Rhine Province, with wide support from the region's democrats and broad public approval.[53] The struggle was a bitter one. It took the authorities much longer than in September to restore order; but in the end, by December 1848, this resistance too had been beaten down. Marx fully expected to be executed for his insurgent deeds; he was merely indicted for incitement to rebellion and for resistance against the government authorities.[54]

· · ·

ALMOST HALF A YEAR lay between the revolutionary crises of November 1848 and May 1849, and in that time Marx had had to confront a number of difficult situations. In some ways, the indictment was the least of his problems. His trial, in February 1849, turned into an enormous triumph. In his speech defending himself to the jurors, he held up a copy of the Napoleonic Code and praised it as the legal system of a "modern bourgeois society," contrasting it to the society of orders, with its absolutist monarchy, and its supporters among noble landlords and government bureaucrats. The Prussian Constituent Assembly, Marx went on, in its decision to call for a tax boycott represented precisely this modern legal order, against the monarch's arbitrary decree of dissolution, so in defending the Assembly he was acting legally.

In this speech, Marx took ideas from the *Communist Manifesto* concerning the relationship between socioeconomic systems and the law and applied them to contemporary politics. Oddly, this one major example of Marx publicly using ideas from the *Manifesto* during the 1848 Revolution came before a very bourgeois audience, since jurors were selected from the ranks of the highest taxpayers. The praise of the Napoleonic Code was doubtless designed to appeal to them, as it was very popular in the Rhineland, but this praise also reflected Marx's memories of his father, a very Napoleonic jurist, and his own legal studies in Bonn and Berlin. It certainly appealed to the jurors, who voted unanimously to acquit Marx—which, admittedly, was what happened at most political trials in the Rhineland during and after the midcentury revolution.[55]

Two Prussian non-commissioned officers claimed that after the trial Marx boasted to them, "the courts can't touch me now."[56] Marx denied their assertions, but in the winter and spring of 1849 financial problems rather than government persecution posed a greater threat to the *New Rhineland News*. The newspaper, whose press run had reached the quite respectable level of 6,000 copies, was very short of funds. The original investors were reluctant to put any more money into the enterprise. Marx's previous fund-raising trip, in August and September, had brought in 2,000 talers from Polish nationalists, who appreciated his anti-Russian and anti-Prussian stance. But that money was soon spent, and the period of martial law, when the newspaper could not appear, was yet another severe financial blow. Short-term notes were issued to close the gap in finances, although the purchasers of these notes were making a political statement rather than a lucrative investment. By early 1849, as Marx wrote, "all the correspondents and creditors of the newspaper were letting loose against me." He fell into arrears on the typesetters' wages. The proletarians could not subsist on revolutionary rhetoric. They threatened to strike and hung up in the composition room a large banner reading: "When it's a question of money, good-natured feelings are at an end," a well-known remark that the liberal opposition leader David Hansemann had used to denounce the king of Prussia. Marx was on the road, once again seeking funds for the newspaper, in the second half of April and the first ten days of May 1849, this time in northern Germany, but with very little success. As a result, he was absent from his political headquarters in Cologne when the final revolutionary crisis broke out.[57]

In the January 1849 elections to the Prussian parliament, Marx had continued his anti-Prussian strategy one last time, working closely with the Cologne democrats. He strongly opposed the proposal of Andreas Gottschalk, who had been freed from jail and was back in action after his trial and acquittal the previous month, for separate workers' candidates. Gottschalk's followers (Gottschalk himself was in Paris, with his mentor Moses Hess) fought bitterly with Marx in the Workers' Association on that point, and lost. Their leader got in a parting shot, denouncing Marx for wanting to have the workers "escape the hell of the Middle Ages, by voluntarily plunging into the purgatory of a decrepit rule of capital"—in other words, through a revolution against Prussia, leading to a liberal-democratic, capitalist regime, that the workers would then have to oppose.[58]

Following the elections, which proved to be a victory for the democrats and Marx's strategy, Marx reversed course. Endorsing his rival's
strategy, he announced in April 1849 that he and his followers were
leaving the provincial democratic committee and calling for the creation of a new federation of revolutionary workers' associations. His
newspaper, for the first time, began to deal with social issues, including printing a lecture on "Wage Labor and Capital" in which Marx
related the results of his economic studies. Marx seemed to be on the
verge of abandoning his strategy of a broad-based democratic revolution against the Prussian monarchy, and putting his efforts exclusively
into the organization of the working class.[59]

This realignment occurred precisely as the final crisis of the 1848
Revolution in Germany was breaking out. It began with a most unrev-
olutionary action, the creation of a constitution by the German National
Assembly in Frankfurt that named the king of Prussia the emperor of
Germany. This collaboration with the pre-revolutionary authorities—
and a particularly reactionary pre-revolutionary authority at that—
was exactly why Marx had condemned the National Assembly in the
first place. He, like other radical democrats in Cologne and across Germany, treated the decision with the greatest contempt.

Rather the opposite of Marx's expectations, it was Friedrich Wilhelm IV who rejected the Assembly's decision and the German public
who supported it. Mass meetings throughout central Europe, attended
by armed members of the militia and great crowds of citizens, endorsed
the constitution, and took oaths vowing to fight and die for it. This was
the insurrectionary moment Marx had been expecting ever since he
began publishing the *New Rhineland News*. Only the radical-democratic
revolution he had been seeking happened just as he had broken with
the democrats and called for a separate, socialist and working-class
political organization.

In the climactic days of May 1849, tensions mounted rapidly in
western Germany. The Prussian army kept a tight rein on Cologne.

The soldiers of the garrison turned the artillery mounted on the walls inward toward the city. So there was no insurrection in the Rhenish metropolis, but there was a groundswell of political protest. Four different meetings of representatives of political clubs from across the province took place there, as did an even larger gathering of mayors and city councilmen. The tone of most of the meetings was harsh: support for the National Assembly and its constitution, attacks on their Prussian overlords, even calls for secession from the Prussian monarchy. Close to Cologne itself, insurrections broke out to the south in the university town of Bonn, and to the north in Düsseldorf, as well as farther north, in the lower Rhine weaving districts and to the east of the province among the metalworkers of Solingen and Remscheid and the textile workers in the Wupper Valley. Largely working-class insurgents erected barricades; militiamen battled with Prussian troops. These struggles were part of a wider insurrection that reached in a broad arc through central, western, and southwestern Germany.

In this atmosphere of revolutionary upheaval, the *New Rhineland News*, far from promoting an uprising, preached caution and skepticism of the "bourgeois" political movement. The new provincial federation of workers' associations—most of whose groups came from agricultural villages along the Rhine River—refused to be drawn into insurrectionary plans. Engels, who had returned from his exile to Cologne in January 1849 to stand trial and be acquitted, could not resist joining the insurgency, especially as it had broken out in his native Wupper Valley. His presence was not a success—often attributed to political differences between him and the insurgents there, but mostly a result of his less than tactful personality. Engels loudly boasted that the insurgents had taken hostage a reactionary and especially religious banker; should the Prussians attack, he would have the man shot. Appointed "inspector of the barricades," he replaced all the black-red-gold German national flags with red ones, after which the insurgent leadership insisted that he leave town.[60]

It is hard to know which was worse for the revolutionary movement, Marx's reluctance to take action or Engels's excessive willingness to do so. Neither of these problems hampered the Prussian
authorities. Frustrated by the refusal of the jurors to convict Marx of
press offenses, they looked in the spring of 1849 for other measures
to silence his radical newspaper. Spies and agents provocateurs could
prove nothing. But in the crisis of May 1849, the Ministry of the Interior received a report that Marx was deeply involved in a planned
insurrection—although Marx was carefully keeping his distance from
the uprisings spreading throughout much of Germany. It was the
excuse the government needed. Marx, who had renounced his Prussian
citizenship and had never regained it, was expelled from the country as
an undesirable alien.[61]

With the expulsion of its editor-in-chief, the *New Rhineland News*
came to an abrupt end. The swan song issue, dated May 19, 1849, was
printed in revolutionary red. Enormously popular, it had to be reprinted
repeatedly, eventually selling 20,000 copies. Calling for the emancipation of the working class, while predicting a future of revolutionary
terrorism and war with the czar, it was a final act of insurgent defiance.
On the same day that the last issue appeared, Marx, accompanied by
his family, Engels, and other political associates, left Cologne, traveling south up the Rhine River, probably by steamboat, on his way out
of Prussian territory.[62] Although he certainly was not expecting his
departure to be permanent or even long-lasting, exile would be Marx's
fate for the rest of his life.

7

The Exile

·•⊰❙❙❘❙⊱•·

MARX LEFT COLOGNE JUST a couple of days after Prussian troops had suppressed the insurrections in the kingdom's western provinces. In retrospect, their actions showed that the mid-nineteenth-century revolutions were reaching their end; but to contemporaries, the revolutionary struggles were still very much underway, reaching a high point of military confrontation whose outcome was profoundly uncertain. In Baden and the Palatinate, the far southwest of Germany along the Rhine River, radicals had seized power, and were striving to form a revolutionary army to fight for their cause. Hungarian soldiers, now the forces of an independent republic severing all its ties with the Austrian Empire, had reconquered Budapest from Habsburg troops, and were marching along the Danube on Vienna. Radicals controlled much of central Italy, including the Papal States. Seizing power in Rome, they had proclaimed a republic there and forced the Pope to flee. After Pius IX departed, the revolutionary leader Giuseppe Mazzini arrived, along with his military expert, Giuseppe Garibaldi, who was organizing yet another revolutionary army.

As all the insurgents understood, the ultimate fate of the revolution across the entire Continent would depend on the outcome of political struggles in France. Democrats and socialists there were negotiating an alliance, seeking new supporters, and striving to win back the ground they had lost in the second half of 1848. Were they to regain power, then the political and military weight of continental Europe's most powerful nation could be thrown onto the scales in behalf of the insurgents. The struggles of the spring of 1849 would then become the initial phases of a new revolutionary upheaval.

Most immediately in the second half of May 1849, but over the following three and a half years, Marx would try to ride this revolutionary wave, seeking to bring the communist strategy he had initiated in April 1849 into an existing or renewed insurrectionary outbreak. In a painful and difficult process, beginning with his expulsion from Cologne in May 1849 and ending with the conclusion of the Cologne Communist Trial in November 1852, Marx would watch his hopes for a new revolution expire. His intransigent political strategy would expand the ranks of his enemies and deplete those of his friends. Losing his last base of support in Germany, he would be driven from one provisional refuge to another, all the while becoming steadily more impoverished and experiencing ever greater difficulties in his personal and family life. Out of these series of defeats would emerge a new theory of the preconditions for revolution, and a literary masterpiece, *The Eighteenth Brumaire of Louis Bonaparte*. In that work, Marx would offer a veiled self-criticism of his own actions during the 1848 Revolution, but also find a way to extend the hopes of that year into a dismal future.

MARX'S WHEREABOUTS IN THE second half of May 1849 remain a bit of a mystery. Contemporary evidence is very scanty, and biographical accounts usually take at face value Friedrich Engels's self-justifying memoir.[1] Retracing Marx's and Engels's steps in light of their previous positions, especially their break with the democrats in April 1849, nonetheless illuminates an obscure sequence of events.

Although expelled from Prussia, Marx could still legally stay in other German states, and he spent the two following weeks doing so. According to Engels's account, he and Marx journeyed to Frankfurt, where they hoped to convince the National Assembly to take decisive revolutionary action in supporting the insurrections in southwestern Germany. Foiled by the cowardice of the petit-bourgeois democrats, the two men traveled on to the insurrectionary regimes themselves, but found the same petit-bourgeois lack of revolutionary decisiveness.

How much of this actually happened, or at least happened as Engels claimed it did? One has to wonder just how well the democrats received Marx's proposals for insurrection, given that he had just been denouncing their insurrectionary efforts. A decade later, Karl Emmermann, who had commanded a sharpshooters' battalion in the army of the revolutionary southwest German regimes, recalled the attitudes and actions of Marx and Marx's left-wing rival Karl Vogt in the spring of 1849: "To be sure, they will always drive forward, whip and sting— that is a necessity to them—however, always just up to the moment of the deed; then they will again wind things down, because it is either still too early, or already too late, or not political. . . ." A contemporary newspaper report had Marx telling the revolutionary government of the Palatinate just that. Engels, who eventually did join the revolutionary army, maintained that his participation was a good thing, for otherwise "the whole band of democratic bums" would have claimed that Marx and his followers were "too cowardly to fight"—an accusation that dogged Marx during his London exile in the early 1850s.[2]

Following their tour of the insurgent centers, Marx and Engels, along with Marx's family and other confidants, made their way to Bingen, in the Grand Duchy of Hessen. There, they were arrested by Hessian troops and brought to Frankfurt, but then released. They returned to Bingen and remained in the city for a few days, until the beginning of June. What exactly was the Marx team doing in this obscure Rhine River town? Bingen was on the border of the Grand Duchy of Hessen with Prussia; it was also home to Julius Hentze, a radical former Prussian army officer from whom Marx was trying to raise money. Combining these two facts leads to the suggestion that Marx was hoping to restart the *New Rhineland News* just outside Prussian territory. One of the few documents preserved from this period is a press release issued in Bingen on May 31, 1849, and signed by the entire editorial board of the *New Rhineland News*. It asserted that the *West German News*, a newspaper begun by the very energetic Cologne democrat Hermann Becker after Marx's departure, was not, as Becker claimed, the successor to the *New Rhineland News*. "When and where the *New Rhineland News* will reappear, the undersigned editorial board reserves for a more detailed statement." Such a declaration rather suggests that Marx and his friends were hoping to resume publishing their newspaper.[3]

These plans never came to fruition, probably because Marx could not find the necessary funds, and at the beginning of June, the group that had held together for the previous two weeks suddenly dissolved. Jenny took the children and went to her mother in Trier. Engels returned to the Palatinate, where he mocked the insurgents as petit-bourgeois dilettantes and made fun of their preparations to fight the approaching Prussian army to such an extent that a group of them arrested him as a Prussian spy. Several years later, after the Prussians had restored order for them, the Bavarian authorities held a show trial of the revolutionaries and issued a propaganda piece, proving that the latter had unleashed a reign of terror in the Palatinate—arresting, for instance, an innocent Prussian newspaper editor. The Bavarian officials were unaware that their innocent victim of revolutionary terror was none other than the notorious communist Friedrich Engels!

Bavarian misapprehensions aside, the incident was the third time in six months that Engels's tactless remarks and excessive behavior had alienated fellow leftists. Recognized by one of the officials of the revolutionary government, the Cologne communist physician Karl d'Ester, Engels was released and joined the armed volunteer corps commanded by August Willich, another radical ex-Prussian army officer. While most of the soldiers in the revolutionary armies were reluctant, very badly armed draftees, who ran away rather than confront the invading Prussians, Willich's corps fought bravely. After battles in the Palatinate and in Baden, Engels ended up with Willich and most of his men as a refugee in Switzerland. From early June until late July 1849, he and Marx, as well as the other members of the editorial board of the *New Rhineland News*, were out of touch, had little idea of the others' whereabouts, and frequently feared the worst.[4]

Marx made for Paris, not as a refugee or political exile, as he publicly insisted, but as a representative of the central committee of German democratic clubs—the same group from whose provincial directory he had resigned in April 1849.[5] Conditions in the French capital were very different from Marx's last stay the previous April. Following the defeat of the Parisian working-class insurgents in June 1848, and especially after the election of Louis Napoleon Bonaparte, nephew of the great Napoleon, as president of the republic in December, the pendulum of French politics had swung far to the right. Speculations about a restoration of the monarchy were rife. Marx's French friends, who had staffed the provisional government and welcomed him in the spring of 1848, were now banished to the opposition.

Meeting up with past acquaintances, Marx found that they were making plans to return to power—a move Marx saw as crucial to reanimating the revolution, not just in France but across Europe. The conservative French government offered the opposition its opportunity by sending French troops to Italy, to overthrow the Roman Republic and restore the Pope. On June 13, 1849, Parisian leftists led tens of thousands of demonstrators into the streets to protest this move. The organizers were divided as to whether it was to be a demonstration—

a peaceful sign of opposition to the government's policies, still rather unusual in the mid-nineteenth century—or an armed attempt to overthrow that government. Most participants were unarmed, but instead of perceiving this as a gesture of goodwill, the conservative government responded with a massive show of force, dispersing the demonstrators and arresting the leftist leaders.

A number of German radicals, including the representatives of the insurgent governments with whom Marx was in close contact, were prominently involved in the demonstration. One has to wonder if Marx himself took part. There is no definitive evidence, but a brief piece Marx wrote for a German newspaper, with its description of desperate demonstrators throwing chairs into the street to hold up cavalry charging at them, does sound like an eyewitness account.[6]

His initial hopes for a new wave of revolution dispelled, Marx made plans to settle in Paris for a longer stay. He sent for Jenny and the children, even though a cholera epidemic was raging in the French capital and the family finances were increasingly difficult. Jenny pawned the last of her jewelry just to keep them going. Marx's response to his personal and political challenges was a reprise of his previous experience in Paris, "a literary and mercantile enterprise," as he wrote to Engels—in other words, German-language publications to circulate in Germany, but edited outside the repressive apparatus of the German states. An anthology of the best articles from the *New Rhineland News* was one possibility; an expanded version of "Wage Labor and Capital" another. Continuing this emphasis on economics, already a focus of Marx's publishing efforts on the eve of the 1848 Revolution, was a proposal for a monthly periodical on political economy. As in 1847, such plans would require financial support from within Germany; Marx and his associates were busy in July 1849 trying to raise the necessary funds.[7]

The French government, as part of its policy of isolating subversive political refugees, had no intention of letting Marx carry out these plans. The authorities announced that he would be permitted to remain in France only if he transferred his residence to the Department of Morbihan, a remote and deeply conservative coastal district in Britanny. Residing there, Marx would have had no political contacts and no way to support his family, even assuming he survived the move. Roland Daniels, the communist physician living in Cologne, warned him that the department was "the unhealthiest stretch of France, damp, muddy and exuding fevers, the Pontine Marshes of Brittany." Coming down with malaria would be the inevitable result of living there.[8]

When Jenny joined Karl in Paris, they had discussed their options for moving on, and the original plan had been to head for Geneva. But Marx was increasingly suspicious of Switzerland: the government of that small country, susceptible to the pressure of the counterrevolutionary great powers, was already beginning to treat foreign political refugees harshly—a trend that would be reinforced in the course of 1849 and 1850. Along with many other persecuted leaders and activists of the 1848 Revolution, he decided to move to London, capital of an island great power, with a liberal policy on political refugees. Leaving behind the children and a very pregnant Jenny in Paris for a few weeks, Marx reached London, via Boulogne, on August 27 or 28, 1849.[9]

At the time, he was thirty-two years old, halfway through his life. As an adolescent and young man he had moved frequently, between 1835 and 1849 residing in Trier, Bonn (twice), Berlin, Cologne (twice), Brussels and Paris (three times). Previously, the Rhineland had been at the center of his wanderings, anchored at either end by Paris and Berlin, the capitals of the two great powers that had shaped the region and held the keys to its destiny. Moving to London meant breaking out of this path and heading toward a different future. Like most of the political refugees flooding into London, Marx did not see things that way; he still had expectations of an imminent return to the Continent following a renewed revolutionary upheaval. As late as 1861, he was making plans to return to Germany. None of these expectations would come to pass. Marx would remain an exile in London until his death.

. . .

RESIDING IN LONDON WAS the culmination of the trend in
Marx's life toward big city living. London was enormous; with 2.4
million inhabitants in 1850, the world's most populous city. About
20,000–30,000 of them were German immigrants: as in Paris, mostly
craftsmen, with an admixture of émigré intellectuals and also a smaller
group of businessmen and bankers. Marx would spend time in the
working-class neighborhoods of the East End, with its many immigrant German artisans; he would look for funds and business deals in
the City. His family would live in sets of rooms in Soho—immigrant,
bohemian, and slummy—in central London; and later move to the newly
built, suburban neighborhoods of North London. In all these different
areas, Marx would have to confront a feature of the metropolis: the
crushingly high cost of living.

Not quite the same center of ideas and creative art as Paris, or even
Berlin, London was a metropolis of science. The library of the British Museum was an unmatched storehouse of knowledge. Its rotunda,
the round Reading Room (today a museum exhibit in which tourists
are pointed to Marx's favorite seat), was soon to become Marx's home
away from home. New developments in physics, chemistry, and biology, whether generated in the colleges and research institutes of the
city, or arriving from elsewhere, were the subjects of publication, public
lecture, and private discussion. Administrative and political capital of
the one major overseas colonial empire existing in the world during
the first three quarters of the nineteenth century, London was also the
nerve center of global capitalism. The decisions of the Bank of England
and the movement of the prices of financial instruments on the London
Stock Exchange reverberated around the world. News and information constantly poured into London, and came out, organized in print:
as business publications like *The Economist*, up-market newspapers like
The Times, and popular publications like the *Daily Telegraph*. Major

newspapers all had to have a London representative, a fact that would prove Marx's financial salvation in the 1850s.

In September 1849, the most salient characteristic of London was that it was fast becoming the capital of exiles from the Revolution of 1848, an offshore haven of liberal politics and tolerant policies toward political refugees from a Continent where the forces of counterrevolution were increasingly gaining control. Marx threw himself into political activity on his arrival in London, beginning with the creation of a refugee committee, to raise money for these political exiles stranded on an alien island. He followed that up by reactivating the Communist League as a vehicle for his increasingly radicalized political strategy. Another facet of his political engagement was to create a journal, edited abroad but published and circulated in Germany, a plan initiated in Paris and brought to fruition in London. *The New Rhineland News: Review of Political Economy* was announced in January 1850.

The title underscored Marx's increasing emphasis on economics, but it reminded readers of his revolutionary role in the recent past. Crucial to Marx's new political efforts was the assistance of his former associates at the *New Rhineland News.* As he was poised to leave Paris, Marx had urgently requested that Engels join him in London. His friend was unsafe in Switzerland, Marx reminded him, in danger of falling into the hands of the Prussians who would "shoot him twice," for his role in the insurrections in the Wupper Valley and the German southwest. Even if he were safe, in Switzerland "you can do nothing," while in London "we will do business."[10] The French government, however, refused to allow the subversive Engels to cross its territory. Instead, he had to make a giant detour. Traveling south from Lausanne to Genoa, Engels took a slow boat to London, passing his time during the five-week trip making sketches of the Spanish and Portuguese coast, finally arriving on November 12, 1849.[11]

Over the next year and a half, almost all of Marx's closest political collaborators fled the Continent for the British Isles, to the point that

Engels could write in May 1851, "It appears the entire *New Rhineland News* will be sitting together in London by this summer. . . ."[12] Joining Ernst Dronke, Ferdinand Freiligrath, Wilhelm Wolff, and Karl Schapper (Joseph Moll had fallen in battle with the Prussians) were other communists, such as the former Prussian officers Joseph Weydemeyer and August Willich, and a trio of young radical intellectuals: Wilhelm Pieper, Peter Immandt, and Wilhelm Liebknecht, political refugees of the 1848 Revolution, who moved toward communism while in London exile. It was potentially a very good team, provided Marx could keep all the members together under demanding and difficult conditions.

Marx's work commenced with a meeting held on September 18, 1849, just three weeks after his arrival in London. It resulted in the creation of a Committee to Support German Political Refugees, which issued an appeal for funds that circulated in England, Germany, and the United States. Joining Marx on the committee's directory were two radical émigrés, as well as two German craftsmen, Heinrich Bauer and Karl Pfänder, members of the German Workers' Educational Association in London, the group that had been closely intertwined with the Communist League. The meeting itself was held in the Educational Association's headquarters on Great Windmill Street.[13]

The group was renamed the Social Democratic Refugees Committee in November. During its first two months of existence, it gathered the respectable sum of £36, and issued support to fifteen different refugees. The pace of assistance picked up as donations increased, and the committee provided over four hundred support payments between November 1849 and April 1850. The individual amounts were small but badly needed, since German political refugees were having a hard time in London—unemployed, with very precarious lodging, and sometimes no choice but to sleep in the parks or on the street. It was unselfish assistance, but there was a political point as well. Marx kept a list of all the recipients of the committee's benevolence, in the hope that they might swell the ranks of his supporters in a future revolutionary moment.[14]

The work on the refugee committee brought Marx back into close contact with the artisans of the Workers' Educational Association, the onetime chief supporters of the Communist League that Marx had dropped in the first flush of evolutionary enthusiasm during the spring of 1848. Members of the League remaining in London, often fans of the conspiratorial style of the Communist League's predecessor, the League of the Just, had not been entirely happy about this decision. They had made attempts to revive the League as a clandestine group and contact adherents on the Continent at the beginning of 1849.[15] Now Marx decided to endorse and support these efforts, a significant turnabout from his previous advocacy of open, public, political organizations. But as the revolutionary movements in continental Europe were defeated one by one in the summer of 1849, and political repression increased, working in secret became the radicals' main option. Marx's plan was to create a widespread clandestine group that could emerge from secrecy, following a new revolutionary outbreak that he was expecting in the near future.

The exact circumstances of the reconstitution of the League and of Marx's resumption of his position in its Central Authority have remained one of the secret society's secrets, but the fall of 1849 seems like a plausible date, and the work of the refugee committee a probable first move. The initial evidence of a revived Communist League comes from the beginning of 1850, in some circuitous mentions in letters by Marx and Willich. Several years later, the Prussian police interrogated Peter Roeser, the Cologne cigarmaker and communist activist, who told them that Marx had written him in early 1850, suggesting he start a new League Congregation in that city. The reconstituted London Central Authority made its presence known only in the "March Address" of 1850, a statement of political principles and prospects for future revolutions drawn up by Marx and Engels and sent to the Continent via a secret emissary, the same Heinrich Bauer who was a leading figure on the refugee committee.[16]

As he had done in Brussels, Marx combined his engagement in the Communist League during 1849–50 with work on a journal of political economy. *The New Rhineland News: Review of Political Economy* was designed, like its predecessor, to be a corporation; but lacking access to his long-term Cologne supporters, Marx found investors few and far between. Publication began on a shoestring.[17] Georg Schuberth, the magazine's Hamburg publisher, "enjoyed in the booksellers' world"— as Marx's friend, the poet and experienced author Ferdinand Freiligrath, informed him—"a most dubious reputation." Sure enough, Schuberth demanded extra funds from Marx to proceed to printing, which occurred late; his distribution of issues was chaotic and delayed. Against his contractual obligations, Schuberth insisted on cash in advance from book dealers; Marx's representative in Hamburg even considered taking Schuberth to court.[18]

The journal's retail sales were also problematic. It was unclear if the local agents were supposed to deal directly with Marx or with the publisher Schuberth. In Cologne, where good sales were expected, there was a conflict between two different local agents, which ended up making it difficult for subscribers even to get their copies.[19] The first issue was supposed to appear in January 1850, but it was still at the printers the following month, and subscribers had not received their copies in March. The initial three monthly issues finally appeared by May 1850, but as Marx's agent in Hamburg informed him, "It is now the end of June and still no manuscript [of any additional issues]. People are furious. . . ."[20] The original plan for the review had been to ramp up production from a monthly to a weekly, and when political circumstances were right, to a daily newspaper. Instead, because of the problems with printing and distribution, the frequency of publication declined. Four issues had appeared by June 1850, followed by a long pause over the summer, and then a last double issue in December of that year. Marx was hoping to resume publishing in 1851 as a quarterly, but in vain.[21]

Behind this tragicomedy was a depressing political reality, the growing strength of repression and counterrevolution in central Europe. The review was published in Hamburg, then an independent municipal republic, where liberal ideas were stronger and the pressure of the Prussian government weaker than in most of central Europe. But even there, there was considerable reluctance to publish Marx's radical writings. A potential alternative to the problematic Schuberth was one Herr Koehler, but he would only publish the review "if the tone of the monthly is not very passionate." Similar problems appeared in gathering subscribers. In the radical city of Düsseldorf, tavern keepers refused to let Marx's friends put out sign-up lists for subscription, fearing the authorities would revoke their licenses.[22] Marx was saving his most subversive ideas for his clandestine writings, but even the milder forms of political radicalism published in the journal were difficult to advocate publicly in post-revolutionary central Europe.

MARX'S CLANDESTINE STATEMENTS AT this time were indeed extreme, as demonstrated by the March Address of 1850, in which he described his new revolutionary strategy for the members of the revived Communist League.[23] The document began with the assumption of an imminent European-wide revolutionary upheaval, "through a new independent uprising of the French proletariat or through an invasion of the Holy Alliance against the revolutionary Babel." This new revolution would bring to power the "petit-bourgeois democrats," that is, the 1848 radicals of the Prussian and German National Assemblies and the activists of the democratic clubs. These individuals, Marx and Engels noted, were calling themselves "reds" and "republicans," but the workers should not be deceived; they were their main enemy.

The democrats' radical-sounding political and socioeconomic program would just make the workers' lives temporarily more bearable. It would not lead to the abolition of private property and the eradication of social classes. Nor would it result in the conquest of state power by the workers and a dominant position for the "association of proletarians, not just in one country, but in all the dominant countries of the world." To achieve these ends, the workers would need to "make the revolution permanent."

In the forthcoming revolution, the workers would have to be organized independently of the democrats—hence the need to revive the Communist League. And not just organized, but armed "with flintlocks, muskets, artillery and munitions." Thus prepared, they would have three main tasks. One was to expand and deepen revolutionary violence:

> The workers must, above all, during the conflict and immediately after the struggle, counteract, as much as possible, bourgeois efforts to calm things down and force the democrats to carry out their current terrorist phrases. They must work towards ensuring [that] the immediate revolutionary excitement not be suppressed right after the victory of the revolution. Just the opposite, they must attempt to keep it up. Far from opposing so-called excesses, examples of the people's revenge on hated individuals or public buildings connected with hateful memories, they must not just tolerate such excesses but take over the leadership of them.

The second task would be to outbid the democrats: in place of the progressive income tax they endorsed, communists should demand a tax on upper incomes so great "that big capital perishes." Communists should respond to calls for provincial and local self-government, a standard part of the democratic political agenda, with the demand for revolutionary centralization, "like in France in 1793," during the reign of the Jacobins.

The third point examined the political implementation of such policies. Marx and Engels asserted that the workers had to be politically independent and put up "workers' candidates," against "bourgeois democratic ones," in elections. The workers:

> must not let themselves be bribed by the slogans of the democrats, such as "in doing this you are splitting the democratic party and giving reactionaries the possibility for victory." All such phrases are ultimately about swindling and cheating the workers. . . . If the democrats act from the very beginning in decisive and terroristic fashion against the reactionaries, then their influence at the elections will, in any event, be annihilated in advance.

This drastic political program reflected Marx's implicit self-criticism. The policies he denounced in the March Address—opposing individual and chaotic violent actions, cooperating with the democrats while avoiding independent workers' politics, and seeking a compromise left-wing political program—were all central features of his own activities during most of 1848–49 as editor of the *New Rhineland News* and member of the Cologne Democratic Society and the Rhenish democratic provincial directory. It was Marx's left-wing rivals, Andreas Gottschalk and Gottschalk's mentor Moses Hess, who had proposed the policies he now espoused. The very phrase with which the March Address concluded, "The revolution in permanent session!" was coined by Gottschalk, in an article he wrote in January 1849 denouncing Marx for opposing Gottschalk's plans to put up workers' candidates against the democrats in the elections to the Prussian parliament. In April 1849, when Marx withdrew from the provincial democratic directory and began to advocate a workers' political movement, he was adopting his rivals' policies. The unexpected uprisings of May 1849 had interrupted this political change of course, but in exile it reached its conclusion.

In contrast to Marx's realism, Moses Hess's ideas about politics had always contained strong elements of fantasy. The March Address, with its rejection of any cooperation with the non-communist democrats and its vision of an imminent, more radical, more violent, and more terroristic revolution in the face of the growing strength of reaction on the Continent, seems rather fantastic. One might wonder, as some biographers have suggested, whether this revolutionary vision, so different from his previous political realism, was intended to inspire disheartened followers, or to win over artisan adherents of conspiratorial politics in the Workers' Educational Association. Yet Marx's public and private statements from the time both suggest that he genuinely endorsed these extreme points of view. Writing to Joseph Weydemeyer in December 1849, Marx stated that he expected no more than "three perhaps even two monthly issues" of the review to appear before the revolution broke out again in full force, or, as Marx put it, "the great global fire intervenes."[24]

The review itself adopted a more moderate language than the March Address, but beneath its more measured expressions the same intransigence lurked. Marx's essay on "Class Struggles in France, 1848 to 1850," which appeared in the first three issues, was a brilliant, scintillating history of the defeat of the revolutionary forces in France. Rather than despairing, the essay asserted that such defeats were the precursor to a forthcoming proletarian revolution—one that would declare itself "in permanent session," creating a "class dictatorship of the proletariat" and the "abolition of class differences," but would also go to war with the counterrevolutionary European powers: "the new proletarian uprising in France that will immediately coincide with a world war."[25]

Attacks on non-communist radicals were another feature of the review. The fourth issue included an article denouncing one of Germany's most prominent democrats, Gottfried Kinkel, Marx's rival for control of the democratic Rhenish provincial directory during 1848. In the spring of 1849, Kinkel had fought with the insurgents in southwest Germany and had been captured by Prussian troops. Tried by a Prussian court-martial, he attempted to save his own life by appealing to the nationalist sentiments of his German military judges. Marx denounced him for not provoking them to put him in front of a firing squad.[26]

In taking these extreme positions and making intransigent demands, Marx was swimming in a broader current of European exile politics. From safe havens in Switzerland or Great Britain, leftist political refugees were looking forward to a new revolution and revolutionary war, while advancing ever more radical political schemes.[27] They could not believe that the hopes of 1848 and the struggles of 1849 had been in vain, or that the victory of their enemies was complete. They turned to the vision of an even more drastic revolution in the offing, one that would sweep them triumphantly back into power.

Apocalyptic dreams of a revolutionary future were one way for exiles to bear the wretched conditions of their daily lives. Marx's own circumstances, in terms of his skills, education, and opportunities, put him among those most severely affected by the condition of exile. The move from relatively well paid editor-in-chief of the *New Rhineland News* to penniless political refugee marked the beginning of a six-year period of wearing and soul-destroying poverty. It would engender personal and family crisis, as well as profound parental tragedy.

The extremity of Marx's financial miseries began immediately before his expulsion from Cologne. He had expended all his available funds, including the last of the advance on his mother's inheritance, paying the debts of the *New Rhineland News*. Marx, who claimed to have spent 7,000 talers doing this, presented his actions as a personal sacrifice, as paying a debt of honor. Jenny identified with, and fiercely defended, her husband's actions. She presented them to Joseph Weydemeyer as the courageous, self-sacrificing decisions of a man of honor: "To save the political honor of the newspaper, and the civic honor of the Cologne acquaintances, he let all the burdens be placed on him, he gave up his machine [the newspaper's new printing press], he gave up all his income, on leaving he even borrowed 300 talers to pay the rent on the newly rented office, to pay the back wages of the editors and so on—and he was driven out by force."[28]

Marx's claim to have expended 7,000 talers on the newspaper seems greatly exaggerated. Even if he included in that sum all three years of his 1,500 talers annual salary as chief editor, he never had anywhere near so much money. He did put all his assets into liquidating the *New Rhineland News*, and it was a considerable and lasting burden to him; but preserving honor was only part of his motivation. By paying debts Marx could avoid legal bankruptcy proceedings by the newspaper corporation, which would have exposed the paper's financial dealings and its backers, thereby opening them up to political persecution and making any possible revival all the more difficult. The business manager of the *New Rhineland News*, Stephan Naut, continued winding up its affairs, paying off creditors and seeking payments from debtors, for a good year after Marx's expulsion from Cologne.[29]

If the eminently bourgeois action of paying off his enterprise's debts was but a small step on the way to a communist revolution, it left Marx without money to meet his current living expenses. Lying ill in London at the beginning of September, he wrote to Ferdinand Freiligrath: "I am truly in a difficult condition. My wife is in an advanced state of pregnancy; on the fifteenth of this month she must be gone from Paris and I do not know how I can get the money together needed for her to journey from Paris and settle here."[30] Somehow, Marx did find the funds for his wife and children to join him in London; but he then had to face the problem of supporting his growing family. Karl and Jenny's son Heinrich Guido was born on November 5, 1849, and their daughter Franziska not long afterward, on March 28, 1851. The family

settled in Soho, a slum district in inner London where many émigrés
resided, but their miserable surroundings were no bargain. "Conditions
here," Jenny Marx wrote, "are completely different from Germany. All
six of us live in one room, with a little study attached, and pay more
each week than for the largest house in Germany [in one month]."[31]

The family's problems with expenses paled before their lack of
incoming monies. Exiles with easily marketable skills, such as physicians and engineers, or those with business experience, had the best
chances of getting a job. Craftsmen and laborers might find work at
lower wages, but writers, lawyers, or refugees with broad humanist
backgrounds had the greatest difficulties. A fortunate few could give
public lectures, or tutor curious Britons in German, but such occupations quickly became overcrowded, and Marx, whose English-
language skills at the time were still very rudimentary, could not have
done these in any event. As late as 1856, seven years after his arrival
in London, Marx feared that his English would not suffice for a din-
nertime conversation.[32]

Part of the idea behind the review was to provide both Marx and
Engels with an income, but its poor sales and the questionable financial
and managerial practices of their German associates brought Marx
just 130 talers from the first three issues. Jenny was reduced to writing
begging letters behind her husband's back, telling Joseph Weydemeyer
in Frankfurt that the family desperately needed every last taler and
asking him to send her any sales monies he might have received, rather
than passing them through the distributor in Cologne and the publisher
in Hamburg.[33] Marx had hopes of getting a publisher's advance for a
book on political economy, but in an increasingly counterrevolutionary atmosphere his work was political poison. Even his offer to write
entries on politics and political economy in Great Britain for Brock-
haus Publishers, then as today Germany's leading producer of diction-
aries, handbooks, and encyclopedias, was rejected.[34]

A number of prominent political refugees were the beneficiaries of fund-raisers conducted on their behalf; but Marx, although he certainly worked hard at raising money and distributing it to his fellow refugees, was too proud to take any for himself. Reiterating a position he had held very strongly during his time in Brussels, he refused to countenance such support, and even rebuked one of his German supporters, Ferdinand Lassalle, when the latter circulated an appeal for funds to support Marx in exile. At one particularly desperate moment, when both his landlady and the actual owner of the building were coming after him, seizing the family effects in the process, Marx borrowed £30 from the refugee committee—a move he kept very secret—but, so he claimed, he paid the money back "to the last farthing."[35]

The family's expenses were large and unrelenting; its income was, at best, small and erratic. Reconciling these two meant taking on new debt. Marx began issuing bills of exchange, IOUs repayable from individuals who supposedly owed him money. Creditors were reluctant to accept these IOUs, and bankers to discount them. If Marx could find someone to take the notes, there were embarrassing scenes when they came due, as Marx and his friends scrambled to find the money to cover them. At one particularly difficult moment, Marx wrote his mother, in March 1851, telling her that if she did not cover his IOU, he would return to Prussia and let the police arrest him. Henriette was unimpressed, evidently understanding that her son's threat was just a bluff.[36] In less sophisticated financial transactions, Karl and Jenny began running up tabs—with shopkeepers, at the pub where Marx drank, with their landlady, and with everyone else who would extend them credit. Those too came due, and Marx would issue still more IOUs, or find himself spending whole days, even weeks, "running around" all over London, seeking funds to make a partial payment. Family members were pressed into service; six-year-old Edgar knew enough to tell his father's creditors, with a cockney accent, "No he an't upstairs!"[37]

Edgar's antics sound amusing, but for Marx and his family there was nothing comic about their condition. This is how Jenny described one of the periodic financial disasters to Karl when he was out of town in June 1852:

> I had firmly decided not to torment you constantly with money problems, and now here I am again. But truly Karl, I no longer have any good course. Marengo [the landlady] came and will not wait any longer, she has really put me in a state of terror. She has already had our belongings auctioned off. And, in addition, baker, governess, tea grocer, grocer, and the terrible man, the butcher. I am in a state, Karl, I no longer know what to do. For all these people, I am exposed as a liar, I must have some advice . . . Karl I cannot hold out here any longer. And where shall I go? If I were to run off [to evade the creditors], then we would be lost.[38]

What comes through in this desperate appeal is the crushing burden of repeated borrowing, and Jenny's fear of losing the family's very last refuge. The emotions were particularly pronounced for her here as a woman alone, with her husband and protector temporarily absent, but Karl himself expressed similar fears of losing his home and being crushed by debt.[39]

Jenny's letter reflected a strong element of genteel poverty. She feared not just debt but financial dishonor, having given her word that she would pay and then could not. Although there was no money for food, the children had a governess, in addition to the maid Lenchen Demuth. As was typically the case with genteel poverty, this condition marked a coming down in the world, from the revolutionary year in Cologne when the Marxes had been relatively affluent, even lending money to members of their circle.[40] The political defeat of the 1848 revolutionaries and the expulsion of their leaders was simultaneously a personal defeat for Karl and Jenny. It made their impoverished life in London particularly bitter and fueled increasingly fantastic hopes of a renewed revolutionary upheaval.

Marx's friends and political associates knew very well the precarious state of his finances and wondered how much longer he would be able to hold out in a crushingly expensive London with little or no income.[41] In the summer of 1850, Marx and Engels pursued a drastic solution to these financial difficulties, the idea of moving to New York City. There were political motives in this decision, but financial concerns were a powerful force. Engels too was broke, cut off from the regular allowance his parents had been sending him since 1844. His revolutionary actions in Elberfeld and Baden had been the last straw. Even his long-suffering mother wrote that "since you are pursuing a path, that we, to put it mildly, cannot endorse, so you cannot expect that we will support you in it, especially as you are of an age and possess the capabilities to earn your own living."[42]

Odd as it may sound, New York was then the world's third largest German city, after Berlin and Vienna. The substantial German immigrant community there, and in other American cities, included radical political refugees and labor activists, among whom Marx and Engels hoped to find supporters and purchasers of their writing.[43] In the early 1850s, a fair amount of Marx and Engels's political activity took place in the United States. Marx's chief American adherent was a young draftsman and architect named Adolf Cluss, who had been a member of the Communist League in the Rhineland city of Mainz. Then a bachelor, with a secure, good-paying job as a mechanical draftsman at the Navy Yard in Washington, D.C., Cluss vigorously advocated for Marx among German immigrants in the United States, even more vigorously attacked Marx's enemies, and regularly reported back on his activities, and on American politics more generally. Jenny wrote to Cluss, "Your letters incite the greatest joy. My husband always says, 'if we had many lads like Cluss, then we could really accomplish something.'" Eventually drifting away from communism, Cluss would join the Republicans—under Lincoln a radical if eminently pro-capitalist political party—and become a prominent Washington architect.

Among the buildings he designed is one that today houses part of the Smithsonian Institution.[44]

The fate of Marx's supporter is perhaps an indication of what would have happened to Marx and Engels themselves had they carried out their plans to move to America. For other nineteenth-century German radicals, the trip across the Atlantic was a one-way political journey; none of them ever played a role in European politics again. The fact that Marx did not move to New York would prove to be a major turning point in his life, comparable only to the unexpected death of his potential mentor, Eduard Gans, in 1839.

The American plans came to nothing because neither Marx nor Engels could raise the money for the transatlantic passage. Engels told his family that he had broken with Marx and the communists, and wished to move to America to go into the cotton wholesaling business. But his mother, fearing that close proximity to German radicals in New York would only encourage a relapse into his old bad habits, proposed instead to send him to Calcutta, to work for a German merchant named Heilgers. Family members casually brushed aside Engels's fears of fevers in tropical Bengal, insisting that his "healthy, strong stomach and body" would protect him.[45]

Marx approached his mother's Dutch relatives, sending Jenny to his uncle Lion Philips in Kaltbommel, in August 1850. After a very stormy crossing of the English Channel, Jenny arrived at her in-laws during a steady rain, soaking wet, and at first unrecognizable. In spite of her claims that Karl had been offered a professorship in New York, the uncle was unwilling to offer any money—presumably, another advance on Karl's future claims to his mother's estate. Weaving "little Jewish-Christian marginal comments on communism" into the conversation, Karl's uncle made it clear that Marx's family was no more willing to support godless radicalism than Engels's was.[46]

The attempt to relocate to New York affected a decision Marx and Engels made a few months later, this one in the fall of 1850. Engels, playing on his previous claim to have broken with the communists and devoted himself to business, proposed to live in Manchester and to act as his father's representative. Although Engels's family apparently had their doubts about the genuineness of Friedrich's conversion to capitalism, they accepted his offer. Arriving in Manchester, Engels went through the books and found that his father's business partners, the Ermen brothers, were cheating him. His inside information quickly made him indispensable to his father and guaranteed him a position with a potentially lucrative income.[47]

Engels would be, as Jenny wrote, "a great Cotton lord" while remaining "the same old Fritz."[48] In view of his deep political and personal objections to being a capitalist, it was a considerable sacrifice, but it guaranteed his own future, and helped Marx and his family survive their debts and expenses in London. Engels's move to Manchester implied a division of labor between the two men. Marx, living in the global metropolis, would be the chief theorist and activist; Engels, earning money in the provincial industrial city, would offer advice and provide the financial support helping Marx to maintain himself and his family at the expensive center of intellectual and political life. This arrangement cemented a political and personal partnership; from that point on, to themselves and their contemporaries, they would be "Marx and Engels." Remittances from Manchester—prosaically as postal money orders, more colorfully in the form of bank notes cut in half and sent in two separate envelopes—allowed Karl and Jenny to make partial payments to their creditors and sometimes to keep them at bay. In the early years of Engels's employment, when he was just establishing himself, he could only offer modest support, moving the Marx family's financial situation from impossible to merely desperate.[49]

THE POVERTY AND LONELINESS of exile was profoundly magnified by personal tragedy: Heinrich Guido and Franziska Marx each lived for little over a year. Heinrich Guido's death, on November 19, 1850, was a shock. He died "Suddenly, by one of the cramps he had often had. A few minutes before, he still laughed and was having fun." It is hard to diagnose the baby's death posthumously—meningitis or even crib death might be possibilities; his mother's memoirs described it as pneumonia. Whatever the cause, the death of her son was a great blow to Jenny. A few days afterwards, Marx wrote to Engels that Jenny, whose pregnancy with Franziska was already advanced at this time, "is in a truly dangerous condition of being worked up and upset. She had nursed the child herself and had purchased his existence with the greatest sacrifices in the most difficult of circumstances. In addition, the thought that the poor child has been a victim of our wretched conditions, although he did not lack for any care."[50]

A profound sense of having come down in the world pervades these remarks—Jenny nursing the child instead of paying a wet-nurse, the suspicion that the poverty of their surroundings played a role in Heinrich Guido's fatal illness. These feelings became even more pronounced a year and a half later, when Franziska died at 1:15 a.m. on April 14, 1852. Her death, the result of a respiratory ailment (possibly whooping cough), unlike her brother's, was not a surprise, since she had been ill for much of her short life. But after two infant deaths in the space of fourteen months, Engels, in his consolation letter, expressed Karl and Jenny's own apprehensions: "I have seen to my regret that my fears about your little girl have been all too quickly confirmed. If there were only some way that you and your family could move into a healthier area and a more spacious apartment!"[51] Whether or not the slum neighborhood and the cramped rooms contributed to the deaths, it was the case that three of the four children born in London died at birth or in infancy, while two of the three born in Brussels survived to adulthood. The family's poverty certainly cast its shadow on Franziska's death, since Marx had to spend the day of his daughter's funeral running around, seeking money to pay the undertaker.[52]

Almost as upsetting as these infant deaths was a birth in the household. The family servant, Lenchen Demuth, bore a son, Henry Frederick (Freddy), on June 23, 1851. The space in the birth certificate for the name of the father was left blank, and Engels stepped forward to claim paternity. Decades later, on his deathbed, he admitted that he had done so at Marx's request, to save Marx's marriage, and that Marx was actually the father of the child. Two of Marx's daughters, Laura and Eleanor, horrified at what they had learned about their father, suppressed the information, and the truth about the paternity did not become public until the 1960s. Even today, there are skeptics who refuse to believe that Karl fathered a child on his maid, or, rather more bizarrely, maintain that the letter setting forth Engels's deathbed confession was a Fascist forgery. If the letter was forged by the Fascists, then they must have known a lot of unpublicized details of Marx's private life.

In fact, there is a good deal of corroborating evidence: Jenny Marx's cryptic remarks in her reminiscences, written fifteen years later, about a crisis in her marriage; correspondence between Marx and Engels referring indirectly to the situation; and the fact that Lenchen's son had quite a dark complexion, like Marx, and very much unlike the fair Engels. Clinching proof comes from new documents that surfaced in the 1990s, letters originally collected by David Rjazanov in conjunction with his preparations for a complete edition of Marx's and Engels's works. Following the editor's arrest in the great purges, the documents were hidden in Stalin's secret archives for six decades, until the end of communism in the USSR. They show that the adult Freddy Demuth was aware of the truth about his own paternity and that Engel's deathbed confession was well known to the leaders of the German Social Democratic Party. They had no doubts about its authenticity and no hesitations about covering it up.[53]

In view of the family's being crowded into one and a half rooms in their Soho apartment, one does have to wonder when and how the conception occurred. It might have been during Jenny's absence in the Netherlands, when she was trying to raise money for a move to New York from Karl's relatives; but an August 1850 date seems improbable for a late June 1851 birth. Possibly, it was at some unobserved moment, late at night, or during the day when Jenny was taking the children for a walk. The emotional circumstances of the conception—a onetime occurrence, or part of a longer affair; some kind of coercion, physical or otherwise, on Karl's part, or Lenchen as willing partner—are all completely unknown.

The baby was put out to foster parents, a typical fate of illegitimate children of household servants in the nineteenth century, and all too often a death sentence. But Freddy Demuth survived and returned on occasion to visit his birth mother. Karl's daughters always wondered about the visitor. One can only imagine how Jenny's suspicions of her husband must have grown as she watched the progress of Lenchen's pregnancy in the tiny apartment but heard from her servant no word about the man responsible. Engels's avowal of paternity made it possible for Jenny to repress her doubts and save her marriage. The best way to put it was that the paternity of Freddy Demuth was one of those open family secrets, which everyone knows but no one will acknowledge, even to themselves. In the end, Freddy outlived all Karl's legitimate children, dying without descendants in 1929.

AS IF UNCEASING FINANCIAL pressures, the deaths of two children, and the near unraveling of his marriage were not enough, Marx's early years in London exile were also a period of political and personal isolation. After breaking with the non-communist democrats in the German political refugee community, and then with the communists, Marx had few followers left: Weydemeyer and Cluss off in America, Engels a bit closer in Manchester, along with two communist circles, each consisting of ten to twenty members, in Cologne and London.

Ideological differences certainly played a role in these disputes, but as with Marx's troubled relations with Karl Grün some five years earlier, personal and political motives were closely intertwined.

The break between Marx and the democrats occurred at the end of 1849 and the beginning of 1850 over the question of support for the refugees. Invited to attend a meeting to create a unified refugee support committee, Marx responded by denouncing the entire enterprise for failing to include among the invitees two of his supporters, Conrad Schramm and Ferdinand Wolff, or any of the workers "who have, for years, been at the head of the London German democrats." Bewildered leftists did not understand why Marx and his friends had not attended the meeting anyway, and asked that further individuals be co-opted onto the committee.[54]

Behind these procedural issues lay a broader question of political orientation. Prominent German exiles were working toward the unification of all the émigré radicals in London, an ambition shared by refugees from other European countries, leading to the creation of a European Democratic Central Committee in 1851.[55] Before the 1848 Revolution, Marx had supported just such a policy in the London Fraternal Democrats and the Brussels Democratic Association; the *Communist Manifesto* announced that communists "labor everywhere for the union and agreement of the democratic parties of all countries." Marx's turn toward an exclusively communist radicalism, to be built on a working-class following, now led him in the opposite direction: against cooperation with the "petit-bourgeois" democrats, and toward treating them as a political enemy.

Picking a fight with refugee democrats in London was hardly an ideal move. Most of the exiled leftists supported the democrats against the communists. The democrats even founded their own workers' association, which quickly drew adherents away from the communists of Great Windmill Street. As one German traveling from London to

Switzerland in early March 1850 reported, perhaps somewhat exaggeratedly, just three months after the clash over the refugee committee, "Engels and Marx . . . are excluded from all groups of the emigration and from the German workers' associations." The same report went on to describe August Willich as the "head of the [German] communists" in London.[56]

In the spring and summer of 1850, tensions mounted swiftly among the leadership of the Communist League, pitting Marx and Engels against August Willich and Karl Schapper. At a climactic meeting of the League Central Authority on September 15, 1850—during which adherents of both sides asserted, in emotionally overwrought fashion, their expectation of dying in revolutionary action—Marx and Engels engineered the Authority's transfer to Cologne, where their own followers were in charge. Willich and Schapper, who had the support of a substantial majority of the German communist artisans in London, then constituted their own Communist League and declared Marx and Engels expelled from it. The two leaders' supporters in Cologne responded by expelling Willich and Schapper from the original Communist League.[57]

Following the split in the League and Engels's move to Manchester, the pro-Marx Communist League in London consisted of about a dozen individuals, who met informally on Wednesday evenings in the Rose & Crown on Cross Street in Soho. The communists in Cologne, now the League's official leaders, were a group of the same size, although politically more active—but only as long as they could keep their existence hidden from the Prussian police. Marx himself increasingly renounced political activism. Using the admissions card to the great library of the British Museum he had acquired in June 1850, he spent his days there from nine in the morning until seven in the evening, studying the works of political economists such as John Stuart Mill, and Samuel Lloyd, an expert on monetary questions. Wilhelm Pieper reported to

Engels in January 1851 that "Marx lives very withdrawn. . . . When one comes to Marx, one is greeted, not with compliments, but with economic categories."[58]

For Marx and Engels, their isolation from the other German émigrés was the result of adherence to political principle, a viewpoint faithfully endorsed by Marxist and Leninist historians ever since. Since the spring of 1849, Marx had regarded the "petit-bourgeois" democrats as not revolutionary enough; only a working-class-based movement could be authentically revolutionary. Not being revolutionary or proletarian enough was hardly a reproach that could have been leveled at Willich or Schapper, or the substantial majority of German communist artisans in London who supported them.

Marx's political motivation for this break veered in the opposite direction: Willich and his supporters were *too* revolutionary, planning to introduce communism by violent—and, if necessary, military— means in the next revolution, which they saw as imminent. Marx, who was equally convinced of the imminence of the revolution, perceived it as only the first step in a long process of reaching a communist state and society. He distinguished his viewpoint very clearly from Willich's at the meeting of the Central Authority of the Communist League that led to the split in the organization: "While we say to the workers: you have 15, 20, 50 years of civil war to go through, to change conditions, to make yourselves capable of exercising power, instead of that is said [by Willich and Schapper]: We must come to power immediately, or we can go to sleep."[59]

As clear as these ideological distinctions may have seemed to Marx, they were in practice more than a little blurred. To anyone outside the orbit of the left, all the plans for a new, radical revolution, by democrats and communists alike, seemed equally extreme, as the entire German-speaking world learned when the Prussian police arrested Marx's Cologne supporters and put them on trial in 1852. Rank-and-file leftists did not entirely distinguish between the two communist factions.

Searching the homes of radical workers in Germany, police found written material from both Marx's group and Willich and Schapper's. When Marx explained the difference between himself and Willich to his Cologne adherents, he asserted that the next revolution would bring the petit bourgeoisie to power, but would be followed by a "social republic," a "social-communist" regime, and finally, a "purely communist" one. In this explanation, distinctions between his view and that of Willich seemed to be more of degree than kind.[60]

Whatever ideological clarity might have been apparent at the time of the break between Marx and Engels and Willich and Schapper faded within a few months. In November 1850, Gottfried Kinkel came to England, after his liberation from a Prussian prison in a daring jail break, a move that made him the hero of German émigré radicals in Europe and North America. Kinkel, who had already clashed with Marx during the 1848 Revolution, was appalled by the attack on him published in Marx's review. He and Willich began a close collaboration in exile politics, so close that Marx and Engels's correspondence became replete with references to "Kinkel-Willich," treating as one entity the insufficiently revolutionary petit-bourgeois leftist and the excessively revolutionary communist extremist.[61]

Contemporaries had another explanation for the many political disputes and splits in which Marx became involved. They blamed such skirmishes and schisms on his personality. It was "not because of their doctrines, but because of their personal incompatibility and constant drive toward domination," as one political exile reported in Switzerland, that Marx and Engels had been excluded by all the other German democrats in London. Willich and Schapper described the reasons for their break with Marx and Engels in the same way. It was not about "principles" but "purely personalities." They accused both men of "persecut[ing] in every imaginable fashion" anyone "who was not dependent enough, unconditionally to blow into the horn of these people."[62]

Marx's political opponents certainly respected his intellect. Armand Goegg, a prominent democratic exile, asked Marx to contribute a piece for a magazine he was editing, which would contain the opinions of the "25 most esteemed members of the advanced democratic party in Germany." Even August Willich, in his inimitable Prussian-military-communist fashion, had a high opinion of Marx. His post-revolutionary plans included this command: "Citizen Karl Marx is called upon to present himself in Cologne within 48 hours and to take over the direction of finances and social reform. . . . Disobedience of this order, any resistance or effort to argue, as well as inappropriate jokes, will be punished by death."[63]

The controversy between Marx and Engels on the one hand, and the exiled German democrats and the Willich-Schapper communists on the other, was carried out almost entirely by means of personal insults. Marx's opponents denounced his intellectual arrogance and tyrannical leanings. The story of how he and Engels had attended a meeting of the Workers' Educational Association while drunk, and had to flee to avoid a beating at the hands of the outraged proletarians, resentful of intellectuals' condescension, made the rounds in London and was retold as far off as Cincinnati, a city filled with German immigrants. There were repeated accusations, ventilated both in the German press and in German-language newspapers in the United States, that Marx was taking money for himself from the refugee committee—probably based on rumors about the time when he had borrowed £30 from it. Unlike the attacks on his arrogance and condescension or his unpopularity with the workers, which Marx laughed off, these accusations genuinely angered him, since he had for years made it a point of honor to refuse to accept such donations from others, even when they were offered to him. His one moment of weakness only increased his indignation.[64]

Marx shot back in similar fashion. Kinkel and Willich, along with most of the exiled German democrats, tried to float a "revolutionary loan" among the Germans in America, with the proceeds to be used for political agitation in Germany, and the loan to be repaid by a future revolutionary government. This plan, for all its fantastic elements, did actually succeed in raising money, and Marx immediately accused his opponents of putting these funds in their own pockets. Besides such embezzlement, Karl Schapper was also accused of running off with the fiancée of one member of the Communist League and making her his wife.[65] But it was August Willich, above all, who drew Marx's ire:

> Willich, in spite of his philistine-noble . . . NCO's moral hypocrisy is just a common . . . swindler and . . . so I am informed by a respectable Philistine, card cheat. The lad hangs around in the pub all day . . . where he can consume for free, and pay by bringing in customers, whom he entertains with his stereotypical phrases of passion for the future revolution . . . in which he no longer believes. . . . The guy is a lazy, greedy bum [the German word, much pithier than the English, is *Schmarotzer*] of the worst kind. . . . [66]

This condemnation of communist leaders as lazy cheats, living off the workers, has been a classic of anti-communism from the mid-nineteenth century to the present. Marx's use of such vivid rhetoric to denounce his rival was of a piece with his other deployments of anti-communism for communist purposes.

These factional conflicts also included legal actions that had a certain farcical quality. Willich and Schapper sued Marx's followers for control of £16 from the Workers' Educational Association, only to have the court reject their claims. The two convinced Karl Göhringer, an innkeeper and Communist League member whose London pub was a favorite watering hole of German exile radicals, to let one of Willich's followers take Marx to court over the £5 tab Marx had run up. But the feud had its darker, more violent side as well. Conrad Schramm, one of Marx's adherents, challenged Willich to a duel. Fought in Belgium to evade English legal disapproval, the encounter at twenty paces ended

with Schramm bleeding on the ground. He was lucky to survive the
exchange of shots with a soldier and experienced marksman. Recovering from his wounds, Schramm, along with Pieper, attended a London banquet in February 1851, sponsored by British and Continental
exile radicals. Willich and Schapper's working-class adherents, who
were present at the banquet, spotted Marx's followers. They chased
them out into the winter night, beating and kicking them, to screams
of "Spy, spy," and "Haynau, Haynau" (a reactionary Austrian general,
who had been beaten up by workers when touring a London brew-
ery), and angry recriminations about the funds of the Workers' Association. Pieper turned up at Marx's apartment at midnight, disheveled
and bleeding.[67]

This internecine conflict became an obsession for Marx and Engels.
It pervaded their correspondence and increasingly outweighed their
hostility toward the reactionary governments actually in power in
post-revolutionary Europe. The exile radicals were "thieving scum,"
Marx told Engels, adding, "I prefer the existing governments to the
provisional ones [proclaimed by the London radical exiles] in every
respect. . . ." Marx successfully placed a spy on the committee administering the revolutionary loan, one of his new young followers, Peter
Immandt, who provided him with compromising details. Gathering all
sorts of hostile accounts from his adherents, Marx was busy preparing
a polemical pamphlet to be directed against his enemies. "The Great
Men of Exile," a collection of scurrilous stories and nasty anecdotes,
focused particularly on Gottfried Kinkel. Both he and Engels were
aware that such a publication would provide aid and comfort to conservatives, but they planned to go ahead anyway.[68]

The projected pamphlet was a last-ditch attempt to win the battle
for public opinion among the German political refugee community in
Europe and North America, but attacking its two most popular leaders, Kinkel and Willich, was a losing proposition. By the summer of
1851, a story circulated in London's refugee circles that following a

renewed political upheaval in Germany, the first act of any new revolutionary government would be to have put Marx up against the wall and shot. "Miasmas of the pestilent democratic sewer," Marx called this and similar tales. He was appalled that visitors incautiously repeated them in front of Jenny, still reeling from the death of her son, the recent birth of her daughter, and constant harassment by the family's creditors. "The tactlessness of some people," Marx wrote Weydemeyer, "is in this respect often colossal."[69]

It is hard to miss a strong element of pettiness and exaggerated egos in these controversies. This frequently leads historians to reject the spats as trivial and unimportant compared to Marx's writing and ideas, while others see them as examples of his arrogance and intolerance of different points of view. There is something to that, although the accusation arguably fits Engels more closely than his friend. Yet Marx's personality did not prevent him from working with leftists of different viewpoints in 1848, in the *New Rhineland News*, the Cologne Democratic Society, and the democratic provincial directory. Rather, personal clashes developed in the difficult circumstances of political exile and as a result of the evolution of Marx's views on revolution.

Marx was not alone in factional pettiness. The hothouse atmosphere pervading the émigré world in London contributed to political clashes resulting from personal hypersensitivity. The united German democrats, whom Marx opposed, did not remain united very long. Two mutually hostile factions—one led by Kinkel, the other by Arnold Ruge—emerged in the course of 1851–52, and they fought each other bitterly with hyperbolic denunciations.[70]

The factional differences within the Communist League followed from another element of refugee life. The leaders of the anti–Marx and Engels majority, Schapper, and especially Willich, were examples of the social type of professional revolutionary. Marx's sarcastic remarks about Willich hanging around pubs all day, talking politics, underscore the latter's commitment to constant agitation. Such agitation was a twenty-four-hour matter, since Willich, generally wearing a red sash instead of a belt, resided in collective housing with German artisans in London, in a barrackslike paramilitary atmosphere, befitting the former Prussian officer's conception of a budding revolutionary army. He was a political bachelor, announcing that he would only marry and have a family following the victory of a communist revolution.[71]

Reconciling his political convictions with his physical desires proved difficult for Willich. He shared his bed in the barracks with a succession of strapping, blond journeymen artisans. His homosexuality was an open secret, but no one objected or tried to exploit it politically. When Willich misinterpreted the friendly gestures of a London salon hostess, the Baroness von Brüningk, as a sexual advance, and was bodily thrown out of her house by the servants, this heterosexual transgression became the talk of the German exiles. Willich sent an emissary to Marx, begging him not to mention the indiscretion in his pamphlet on exile scandals, rather a far cry from planning to shoot Marx should he make jokes about Willich's communist revolution.[72]

This incident proved that the Spartan Prussian revolutionary was human, too. It also highlighted the difference between the two groups. Although both were led by intellectuals of affluent backgrounds, Schapper and Willich shared a common lifestyle with the artisans who made up a substantial majority of the Communist League, and the German émigrés in London more generally. Their representation of themselves as men of the people proved politically much more appealing to the large majority of German artisans in London than Marx and Engels's as bourgeois Hegelian intellectuals; and their attacks on Marx and Engels for being arrogant and condescending to the workers, for being "literati and semi-scholars," struck home.[73]

Marx and Engels would not have denied Willich's attacks on them. Even before the 1848 Revolution, they had made a distinction between the German artisans—politically immature, socially and economically underdeveloped—and the future working class in whose name they claimed to speak. Broader popularity was something they specifically rejected. Gustav Adolf Techow, a former Prussian army officer they attempted to recruit into the Communist League as a counterweight to Willich, remembered a conversation he had with them:

> I said to them, I recognized what they said about forming a political group was correct, but . . . the personal poison, that they put into these attacks, the base motives which they always assumed [in others] when as a rule, it was just errors or weakness—all this must . . . increase the ranks of their deadly enemies, let their group appear to the public purely under the aspect of personal struggles and weaken within the group itself the necessary trust in the selflessness of its leaders. . . . [Since the *New Rhineland News*] they had emancipated themselves from the boring, stupid, good-natured German phrase-making and chosen French sharpness and clarity for their form of expression. . . . They had never striven for cheap popularity, quite the opposite![74]

Marx and Engels were making a virtue of their inability to gain supporters. Yet their failure to do so rankled. At that same meeting, Marx told Techow that he and Engels were headed for America, "and it was a matter of indifference, if this miserable Europe perishes."[75] As a result of their alienation, the two friends clung to each other even more firmly. The first contemporary observations of Marx and Engels as a political duo appear in descriptions of their complete isolation from the other German political exiles in London during the early 1850s.[76]

If the isolation of the early 1850s sealed their partnership, it also transformed Marx's thinking about the onset of revolution. Belief in an imminent revolutionary upheaval, one in which he could play an influential role, was increasingly difficult to maintain, given the ever greater strength of political reaction in continental Europe and Marx's beleaguered position among the political exiles. It was then that Marx developed the idea that a revolution would occur in the wake of a cyclical capitalist economic crisis. Since this idea has appeared throughout the twentieth century and into the twenty-first as the quintessence of Marxism, it may be surprising to realize that Marx himself had not always advanced it. The *Communist Manifesto*, for instance, discussed economic crises and the workers' revolution, but did not assert that one was the origin and precondition of the other. Marx's plans for reviving the 1848 Revolution, as counterrevolutionary forces gained the upper hand, turned on a new working-class uprising in France and the revolutionary government emerging from it becoming involved in a great war against the counterrevolutionary powers. As late as the spring of 1850, he was continuing to think along those lines.[77]

In the last issue of *The New Rhineland News: Review of Political Economy*, written after Marx's political and personal isolation had become complete, he first developed an explicit connection between economic crisis and revolutionary upheaval. A revolution would only be possible "when both factors, the modern forces of production and the bourgeois form of production come into contradiction with each other." Until this happened, "the manifold petty strife of the different elements of the continental party of order," as well as the "moral outrage and the enthusiastic proclamations of the democrats," would have no effect. "A new revolution is only possibly in the wake of a new crisis. The former, however, is just as certain as the latter." Written about the time Engels moved to Manchester to work in his father's business, this passage initiated a central theme of the two friends' correspondence over the following years: speculation about the outbreak of the next economic crisis and the revolution it would bring about in its wake.[78] This belief in waiting for the crisis became so central to the thought of Marx's followers that its origin in the politics and exigencies of the early years of Marx's exile has quite vanished from view.

. . .

AT THE PUBLIC BANQUETS and private meetings of the London exiles' political committees, or in their overheated pub conversations, secret agents of the Prussian and Austrian government were present, constantly listening in. The clandestine contacts of exiles with their followers back in continental Europe were not at all clandestine to the political police of the German states. These agents were not just passively eavesdropping; they were actively engaged in shaping the exiles' political positions, manipulating them to fight with each other and to take positions favorable to the counterrevolutionary governments. London political refugees were vaguely aware of the presence of police spies; Marx himself received several warnings. But the exiles' constant practice of denouncing their factional rivals as police spies desensitized them to the very real presence of such people in their midst. These agents' ability to infiltrate exile groups, and to manipulate them and their conflicts, turned out to be far greater than the exiles imagined.[79]

One of the denizens of Willich's barracks was a certain Charles Fleury—real name Carl Krause—a Prussian agent who introduced Willich to two other spies in the guise of radical refugees, Cherval—real name Joseph Crämer—and Wilhelm Hirsch. By 1852, it was evident to Willich himself that these men were spies, but he kept up relations with them, hoping to employ them as double agents, and part of their role as police spies involved convincing Willich that they really were double agents. A more distant associate of Marx, Julius Hentze, had been recruited by the Prussians, but in contrast to his communist rival, Marx himself was primarily the object of agents of the other central European great power. Two of these Austrian agents, Hermann Ebner and Jànos Bangya, had close ties to Marx, and were able to steer him in directions politically amenable to their government.

Ebner was a Frankfurt literary agent, a relative of Ferdinand Freiligrath, who introduced Marx to him. Claiming that he could find a publisher for Marx's planned book on political economy, Ebner implored Marx, in flattering language, to send him "little stories" about the "conditions of the emigration in London," perhaps "something spicy" about Lajos Kossuth, the exiled leader of the Hungarian nationalists. A publisher never emerged; but Marx, his ego already stroked, and trusting Ebner, did send him hostile accounts of the émigrés in London, early versions of his planned pamphlet, which the agent duly sent on to his masters in Vienna. In a particularly charming piece of historical irony, the government of the Austrian Republic made a present of the report to the government of the USSR in 1955, after the Soviets agreed to end their occupation of Austria and to recognize its neutrality during the Cold War.[80]

Bangya, a colonel in Kossuth's revolutionary Hungarian army who was forced to flee to Western Europe following its defeat by Austrian and Russian forces in 1849, was a much more active and influential Austrian government agent. Rather entrepreneurial in his espionage, he also reported to the Prussians, and had connections with French monarchists as well. Charming and amiable, on his return to London from Paris at the beginning of 1852 he contacted Marx and quickly gained his confidence. Bangya never expressed anything but the highest regard for Marx, praising him as the "sole capable German man." Marx responded by offering to induct Bangya into the Communist League. A friendly face to the family in their isolated London life, Bangya invited Karl and Jenny to dinner and paid calls on Jenny when Karl was in Manchester with Engels. Bangya's promise to provide some funds to help with the family debts was one of the few glimmers of hope for Jenny in the depths of her financial despair.[81]

Presenting himself as a militant revolutionary, Bangya collaborated with Marx politically, feeding him derogatory inside information about exile democrats such as Kossuth and Kinkel, which Marx was always willing to believe. The colonel exploited differences between the communist factions, telling Marx, quite untruthfully, that the Willich-Schapper group had sent an emissary to Magdeburg to attack Marx's views among the radical workers there. Bangya promised to raise money for Marx and to find a publisher for "The Great Men of Exile." Neither materialized, and suspicions about Bangya grew among Marx's circle in the fall of 1852. Both Ernst Dronke and Wilhelm Wolff became convinced that Bangya was a police spy; even Jenny had her doubts. But Marx remained loyal, infuriating his closest friends. "Marx won't hear of anything" against Bangya, Dronke informed Engels, and "recently made a big scene, because of my lack of belief in Bangya." Wilhelm Wolff, agreeing with Dronke, told Engels that "The Moor is struck with blindness and acts positively insulted that I, Dronke, etc. [think] differently and express our opinions."[82]

It was Bangya's promise to procure a publisher that did him in. His excuses for not doing so became less and less convincing, and when he supposedly found one in Berlin for whom there was no entry in a publishers' directory—a nice piece of detective work by Dronke, duly reported to Engels—his falsehoods caught up with him. Even so, it took months before Marx ceased believing Bangya's efforts to lie his way out of the situation and recognized him as a police spy. The incident was a lesson in Marx's personality: the same supreme self-assurance that made it possible for him to continue on his path in spite of everything alienated most of his peers and isolated him, making him vulnerable to the clever spy's flattery.[83]

The Austrian government cultivated Marx because he despised the "petit-bourgeois" democrats of the exile European Democratic Central Committee in London. The leading figures in this pan-European radical group were the radical Italian nationalist Giuseppe Mazzini and the Hungarian nationalist Lajos Kossuth, both of whom wanted to break up the Austrian Empire by excising its Italian and Hungarian territories for respective nation-states. Contemporaries were quite well aware of the convergence of Marx's and the Austrians' opponents; accusations that Marx was a paid agent of the Austrians dogged him through the 1860s, and have been repeated recently by historians.[84] Ironically, the point is that Marx was not a paid agent. Austrian spies promised him benefits in the form of book contracts and publishers' advances, but were unable to deliver. Had the Austrian authorities been a little less cheap, and willing to fund the publication of Marx's collection of scandals about the democratic émigrés, they could have produced disarray among their enemies and gained Marx's closer collaboration. That a militant revolutionary, a lifelong opponent of authoritarian rule, came so close to working for one of the most reactionary of the post-1850 European governments was a lesson in how the unbearable circumstances of life in exile exacerbated the most difficult elements in both Marx's personality and his political orientation.

MARX'S TRANSFER OF THE Communist League's Central Authority to Cologne in 1850 was not an entirely happy decision. Earlier the same year he had been quite critical of the passivity and inaction of the Cologne communists, to their considerable annoyance. But Cologne was Marx's last bastion, the one place he still commanded an admiring following. His adherents there rebuffed Willich and Schapper's emissaries, telling them they trusted Marx, yet another example of how the conflict between the two factions of the Communist League was carried out in personal terms.[85]

The Cologne communists did become more active in the fall of 1850 and the winter of 1851, primarily because of a new adherent, Hermann Becker, a radical Cologne democrat. Nicknamed "Red Becker" (a reference to both his hair color and his politics), he was a popular and dynamic speaker and political agitator who had been distant from Marx during the 1848 Revolution. Marx, in turn, had rejected Becker's claims that his newspaper, the *West German News*, was the successor to *The New Rhineland News*. But Becker's successful newspaper, the only democratic voice in western Germany during a period of growing reaction, provided favorable coverage of Marx and the communists. The plans of Heinrich Bürgers, Marx's veteran Cologne supporter, to join the newspaper's editorial board were thwarted by the Prussian authorities, who suppressed the publication in July 1850. After that, the Cologne communists were Becker's chief opportunity to engage in radical politics.

Although he and Marx agreed to keep his affiliation with the communists secret, "not to spoil the things with the petit-bourgeois customers," Becker joined the Communist League in the fall of 1850 and quickly came to play an important role. He led a League delegation to Braunschweig in May 1851 to confer with North German democrats, and prepared to hold a secret communist congress. Becker's new ties to Marx were not just conspiratorial. At the beginning of 1851, Marx arranged with Becker to publish the *New Rhineland News: Review of Political Economy*, and the two made plans to bring out a multivolume edition of Marx's collected essays. The Prussian government's intimidation of printers terminated these efforts, although not before the initial installment of the first volume of essays appeared in print.[86]

Small scale when compared to the revolutionary events of 1848–49, these actions were impressive set against the backdrop of Marx's isolation and impoverishment in London. They came to a sudden and abrupt end in May 1851, when Peter Nothjung, a League member and Cologne tailor, was arrested at the railroad station in Leipzig while carrying clandestine documents of the Communist League, enabling the authorities to arrest the last vestiges of stalwart Cologne communists over the next few weeks. They were held in jail for the next sixteen months, and finally brought to trial in October 1852 on charges of conspiracy to overthrow the government.[87]

The prisoners were kept in solitary confinement, in dark narrow cells, with few opportunities for exercise or fresh air. They were cut off from most visitors, including their attorneys. Particularly outrageous to contemporaries, even those unsympathetic to the communists, was that the wife of one of the prisoners, Roland Daniels, the Cologne physician, was only permitted to talk with her husband in the presence of a gendarme. By the standards of twentieth-century totalitarian regimes—and, one might add, of some twenty-first-century democratic ones—this treatment of ostensibly dangerous subversives seems rather mild. It is a tribute to the old-fashioned, gentlemanly attitudes of nineteenth-century observers that they did not see it that way.

The prisoners' treatment and the decision to make their arrest into a major political affair came directly from none other than Friedrich Wilhelm IV. He wanted a show trial, in which the entire 1848 Revolution would be blamed on a secret subversive conspiracy. As part of his counterrevolutionary policy, Friedrich Wilhelm had reluctantly issued a constitution for his realm, but his preparations for the trial were designed to evade his role as a constitutional monarch. Rather than coordinate actions with his council of ministers, as was constitutionally required, the monarch worked with fellow Evangelicals lacking any official position, most prominently the principal of a deaf-and-dumb school in Berlin. The monarch had his own personal secret agent, Wilhelm Stieber, a former police detective, whose decades-long career was dogged by persistent accusations of illegal actions, blackmail, and a wide variety of abuses of power—a man who also had a personal grudge against Marx, dating from the 1848 Revolution.[88] Stieber was ordered to provide evidence of a giant revolutionary conspiracy by whatever means necessary, but to do so without his royal master seeming to be involved. These efforts were underway even before Nothjung was arrested, and the subsequent exposure of the secret Communist League provided just the opportunity Prussia's ruler wanted.

Unaware of these machinations at the highest levels of the Prussian kingdom, Marx saw the arrest of his followers and their trial primarily in terms of his differences with his fellow London exiles. He blamed the arrest on the ultra-revolutionary proclamations of Schapper and Willich, whose shrill statements, he felt, had alerted the police. It was hard for Marx to convey to his supporters his political strategy for the

trial, since the Prussian police were lurking in wait for his letters, ready
to arrest their recipients, as they ultimately did, on a tip from Jànos
Bangya. Marx's advice, parts of which did reach Cologne, was that
the defendants should describe Schapper and Willich as revolutionary conspirators, planning a violent communist uprising. By contrast,
Marx and his adherents were not opposing the Prussian government,
but just waiting for a revolution against it to happen as the result of an
economic crisis. Only then would they form a communist opposition to
the radical government in power.[89]

The Cologne Communist Trial, which finally began on October
4, 1852, was front-page news throughout central Europe. In Cologne
itself, large crowds gathered in the courthouse square, cheering the
defendants and threatening the gendarmes and soldiers escorting them
from jail. To make its case, the prosecution presented the defendants
as dangerous subversives, who wanted to destroy religion—a sensitive
issue in Catholic Cologne. The state's prosecutor also emphasized that
the communists wished to confiscate capitalists' property, an effective
move for a jury that included a leading sugar beet manufacturer, as well
as prominent merchants and members of the chamber of commerce.
Revisiting all the revolutionary events in Cologne during 1848–49, the
prosecution, much as its royal master wished, attributed them to the
secret schemes of communist conspirators. To underscore the dangers
posed by the accused, the chief state's attorney melodramatically placed
a dagger before him on his desk during the first week of the trial.[90]

Undoubtedly the star of the crown's case was the king's secret
agent, who often seemed more in charge of the prosecution than the
state's prosecutors. Stieber proudly flaunted a cache of secret communist documents he had acquired in London, stolen by one of his spies
from the offices of the Willich-Schapper group. After relating hair-
raising details of the planned insurrection, Stieber described how he
had helped the French police in Paris arrest the conspirators and told
a dramatic tale of how Cherval—in reality his agent provocateur—had

attacked Stieber in his Paris apartment and wounded Stieber's wife in the ensuing hand-to-hand combat.[91]

The eleven defendants responded with a number of strategies. One employed by Dr. Roland Daniels, as well as the other professionals and intellectuals among the accused (their ranks included a pediatrician and a chemist), was to deny any political connections. Daniels's interest in communism, and his extensive correspondence with Marx, he insisted, was purely scientific and scholarly in nature. Three defendants—Nothjung, Heinrich Bürgers, and Peter Roeser, who had confessed to belonging to a secret organization—followed Marx's lead, presenting their group, in contrast to Willich and Schapper's followers, as opponents of a future revolutionary government rather than enemies of the existing Prussian monarchy. The prosecution's retort was to point to revolutionary documents Marx wrote, such as the March Address (Marx admitted, privately, that it was quite compromising), and to assert that the differences between the two communist factions were purely personal. Stieber himself said that "the actual difference between the party Marx-Engels and Willich-Schapper consisted of the question of whether, after the next successful revolution, Herr Marx or Herr Willich would be the dictator. . . ."[92]

Of all the accused, it was "Red Becker" who put up the most overtly political defense. Never denying his association with Marx, he rejected the idea that he belonged to a secret group led by the latter. Instead, he insisted on his independent actions, and portrayed himself as a consistent defender of the people's freedom against Prussian oppression. Becker's strategy was similar to the one Marx used when he was in the dock in 1849. Both Marx and Engels, however, were unhappy with this strategy in view of Becker's repudiation of the Communist League, although they had agreed that his affiliation with the League would be kept secret.[93]

Following the initial excitement, public interest in the trial waned, as the evidence showed that the defendants were a small group with lit-

tle subversive effect, hardly Friedrich Wilhelm IV's imagined ubiquitous conspirators with a continentwide influence. Speculation about an
acquittal increased as both sides concluded their cases. Then, Stieber
suddenly appeared in court asking to be heard, announcing that his
agents had just acquired a secret minute book of the meetings of Marx's
followers in London, proving that they were indeed revolutionary conspirators. This assertion galvanized Marx into action. He gathered up
notarized affidavits denying the material in the minute book, providing evidence contradicting its assertions—for instance, the minutes had
the wrong day of the week for the regular meetings of Marx's London
associates—and, above all, a copy of Wilhelm Liebknecht's handwriting, showing that it differed considerably from the "Liebknecht" who
had supposedly written up the minutes. Spending every last shilling he
had, plus additional funds from Engels (Marx's friend Peter Immandt
tried to raise money from one of Stieber's operatives), Marx worked
"all day and deep into the night" to gather the material and send it,
via secret intermediaries (one of them, unbeknownst to Marx, was the
Austrian spy Hermann Ebner) to the defense attorneys in Cologne.
Jenny wrote to Adolf Cluss: "A whole office has been established in
our home. There are two or three scribes, others run errands, still others gather the pennies together so that the scribes can continue to exist
and bring forth proofs of the most outrageous scandals of the old official world. In the middle of all this my three faithful children sing and
whistle and are often almost knocked down by their papa as he dashes
around. It is a whirlwind of action."[94]

Becker's defense attorney, Karl Schneider II, who had been president of the Cologne Democratic Society during the 1848 Revolution,
already had a sample of Liebknecht's handwriting, and was able submit it to the court as he cross-examined Stieber. The secret policeman,
warned in advance, deftly evaded the evidence, claiming that it was not
Wilhelm Liebknecht who had written the minutes but another man,
one "H. Liebknecht." The existence of this H. Liebknecht was every

bit as real as the rest of the secret minutes: they had been forged by Stieber's spies, Hirsch and Cherval, who were also Willich's confidants. Marx's rival, it turned out, had known all about the forgeries, but had not said anything about them, part of his strategy of deploying the Prussian spies as double agents. When he learned of their role in the Cologne Communist Trial, he rushed off with Hirsch to a London magistrate and they swore out an account of what had actually happened—frustrating Marx, who had hoped that he could get a warrant issued for Hirsch's arrest. Although sent off to Cologne, Willich's affidavit never reached the court. Supposedly, Hirsch himself traveled to Cologne, but Schneider II refused to see him, although it is unclear whether Hirsch's journey (assuming this actually happened) was on Willich's or Stieber's behalf.[95]

Marx and Engels were jubilant, and confidently expected, as Engels wrote, that "the matter can end not with the conviction of the Cologne defendants, but with the arrest of Herr Stieber for perjury and other Prussian crimes against the godless French criminal code."[96] Ironically, the two communists, who asserted in their *Manifesto* that justice and law were merely an instrument of class interests, believed that the truth would win out in court and justice would triumph. It was the deeply devout, moralizing monarch and his agents who had cynically exploited the legal system, caring nothing for guilt or innocence according to the law, making use of theft, forgery, and perjury to further their political ends.

The verdict was announced on November 12, 1852, while soldiers guarded the courthouse from an angry, hostile crowd of spectators. The jury's decision was a crushing blow to Marx and Engels's expectations. Seven of the eleven defendants were found guilty, and sentenced to three to six years imprisonment in a fortress; they would have to serve every single day. The three working-class defendants, Roeser, Nothjung and Friedrich Lessner, a tailor, all would remain active in the labor movement after their release. Roland Daniels, although acquitted, died a few years later from tuberculosis contracted in jail. His fellow doctor, Abraham Jacobi, also acquitted, emigrated to the United States, and became a professor of medicine at Columbia University. Both Heinrich Bürgers and Hermann Becker, after serving out their sentences, joined the liberal and democratic opposition to the Prussian government. In 1878, two decades after his release from the fortress, Red Becker was elected mayor of Cologne—a belated act of revenge on the Prussians. He proved to be a very successful municipal administrator; during his term of office, the city threw down its medieval walls, replacing them with broad boulevards, which still shape its urban space today.

The ramifications of the Cologne trial were palpable among the London radical exiles. Willich's popularity among the German artisans there, already in decline, collapsed when evidence of his long and close connection with Prussian spies was revealed. The Willich-Schapper Communist League was dissolved, and Willich thought it prudent to move to the United States, where German émigré radicals greeted him with great enthusiasm. Like many of these radicals, Willich threw himself into the fight against slavery. A brave and skillful military man, he served in the Union Army during the Civil War, eventually promoted to major general—the first and last communist to hold such high rank in the American armed forces. Marx and Engels amassed their evidence about Stieber's forgery, which they explained in a pamphlet, *Uncovering the Scandals of the Cologne Communist Trial.* Some copies were printed in the United States and never reached Europe; thousands printed in Switzerland were confiscated, probably following a tip to the police from Bangya, as the publisher tried to smuggle them over the border into the German states. The pamphlet, which had many similarities to "The Great Men of Exile," was once again a rearguard struggle in a difficult situation. On the Wednesday after the announcement of the verdict, Marx at his weekly pub meeting with his London followers proposed that they dissolve the Communist League. Their agreement brought the group to an end. Marx explained his decision in a letter to

Engels: with the arrest and conviction of his followers in Cologne, all prospects of effective political action had vanished.[97]

THE *COUP D'ÉTAT* OF Louis Napoleon Bonaparte, on December 2, 1851, by which he turned himself from president of the French Republic into First Consul, and shortly thereafter into Emperor Napoleon III, was a severe blow to the radical exiles in London. Their hopes of a renewed revolutionary upheaval centered on France had suddenly been extinguished, and they were facing a future of unchallenged reaction and counterrevolution. Marx was somewhat less affected by the coup than his fellow exiles, in view of his new theory of economic crisis and revolution; even for him, however, France remained the center of revolutionary expectations, and within a few weeks of the coup he had begun writing an analysis of it. He had a lot of material at his disposal: his own insider's knowledge of French politics, reports sent to him by friends on the scene, and the detailed coverage in the London press. Originally planned as a series of installments, the account was published in the United States by Marx's supporters, Weydemeyer and Cluss, as a pamphlet entitled *The Eighteenth Brumaire of Louis Bonaparte.*[98]

Marx took a defeat of the revolutionary cause and turned it into a literary masterpiece. In *The Eighteenth Brumaire*, his writing was at its best: keeping his sarcasm under control, and not losing himself in endless denunciations of his opponents, Marx cloaked his profound insights in a sharp sarcastic wit and clever turns of phrase. Profound Marxist apothegm emerged from the pamphlet, such as "first time as tragedy, second as farce" (based on a remark by Engels), "the tradition of past generations weighs like the Alps on the brains of the living," "well grubbed old mole," and many, many others.[99]

The basic analysis of the pamphlet followed *The Class Struggles in France*, composed two years earlier, by identifying political movements with social classes. Marx described the socialists and communists as the representative of the workers, the non-communist democrats as the exponents of the petit bourgeoisie, the moderate republicans and monarchists as representing different elements of the capitalist class, and the conservatives as being for the large landowners. In contrast to his previous work, which had treated Louis Napoleon with contempt (as did most contemporaries), Marx had to reckon with the future emperor. He described him as leader of his own distinct political grouping, which Marx associated with a particular social class, France's smallholding peasants.

More than anything, the work became a profound postmortem on the 1848 Revolution, a dissection of its failure at the very center of European-wide revolutionary aspirations. Marx criticized French leftists for seeing 1848 as a rerun of 1789. This was the main theme of the celebrated opening of *The Eighteenth Brumaire*, in which Marx explained how previous revolutionary movements evoked past ideals, pointing out how Martin Luther had portrayed himself as the Apostle Paul and the French revolutionaries of 1789–93 had tried to recreate the ancient Roman Republic. The same action in 1848, evoking the Revolution of 1789, had just led to a pitiful and farcical outcome. What Marx did not mention, however, was that the French radical politicians he mocked were the same people he had been cultivating for years before the outbreak of the Revolution. Their support had enabled him and his associates to move from Brussels to Cologne in the spring of 1848. His hopes for the revival of a European-wide revolutionary movement, from December 1848 to June 1849, had rested on them. Marx's own political strategy as editor of the *New Rhineland News* and in the German democratic movement had centered precisely on evoking the 1789 Revolution. He had called for a German republic one and indivisible, for a revolutionary war against Russia, and had glorified and endorsed the radical and terrorist actions of the Jacobins. In this respect, *The Eighteenth Brumaire* was a particularly drastic example of Marx's practice of engaging in self-criticism through the criticism of others.

In *The Class Struggles in France*, Marx's vision of a renewed revolution was based on the events of the 1790s—a workers' uprising, followed by a war between a revolutionary France and the European powers—a possibility now precluded by Marx's criticism of the idea of repeating past revolutions. A new revolution would have to break with the past rather than continue its traditions: "The social revolution of the nineteenth century cannot draw its poetry from the past but from the future. It cannot begin with itself, before it has shrugged off all superstitions from the past."[100] Marx's refusal to offer explicit visions of a future communist society expanded to include the revolutionary transition to that future.

If Marx was unwilling to speculate about the nature of a future communist revolution, he did seem to know where it would begin. In a passage toward the end of the work, he described how Louis Napoleon had destroyed the French legislature and the constitutional division of powers, concentrating all power of the bureaucratic French state on a dictatorial executive. Marx presented this process in Hegelian terms, as the internal logic of historical development, through which a future revolution needed only to target this one center of state power. When that revolution occurred, "all Europe will jump up from its seat and jubilantly cry out: Well grubbed old mole!"[101] The phrase was from *Hamlet*—more precisely, from the standard German translation of *Hamlet* that Marx had learned as a teenager from Johann Ludwig von Westphalen. It was also an implicit invocation of Mirabeau, one of the great orators of the Revolution of 1789, whose fiery speeches caused contemporaries to exclaim, "Well roared lion!"—an observation that Marx had previously quoted in his 1842 articles on freedom of the press in the *Rhineland News*.[102] The contrast between the powerful roar of the mighty king of the jungle and the quiet, patient preparation of the tiny mole was Marx's way of underscoring how future revolutions would differ from previous expectations of revolution, including his own.

The place where French state power was concentrated, and where a revolution would be so dramatic that all of Europe would be forced to jump up and take notice, was of course Paris. For all Marx's evocation of a fundamentally different future revolution, this passage suggests that he still expected it to begin in Paris, following a pattern that had emerged in 1789, 1830, and 1848. Well into the 1860s, he continued to look to Paris for a decisive revolutionary outbreak. By the end of the decade, his doubts about the Parisian epicenter of the world revolution were emerging. When revolution finally did strike Paris in 1870–71, with the overthrow of Napoleon III and the creation, struggles, and destruction of the Paris Commune, it confirmed Marx's developing doubts that a Parisian revolution would have continent- and worldwide galvanizing effects.

Marx wrote *The Eighteenth Brumaire* as his personal and political fortunes were reaching their nadir: the 1848 revolutions had been suppressed and hopes for their resuscitation were increasingly dismal. He was isolated and broke in the midst of quarreling political refugees in London. The pamphlet expressed his hopes for a transition from a reactionary and counterrevolutionary present to a revolutionary future. It presented a failed revolution as the necessary precursor to a successful one. The unfulfilled expectations of 1850 would not be realized; instead, there would be a (mostly) new and different revolution. The current situation was dismal on the surface, but beneath that seemingly solid surface of counterrevolutionary military dictatorship, a little mole was burrowing away.

In the long run, the piece was one of Marx's most influential and successful works, and not just among his followers. The renowned anthropologist and philosopher Claude Lévi-Strauss, hardly an heir or disciple of Marx, admitted that "I rarely broach a new sociological problem without first stimulating my thought by reading a few pages of *The 18th Brumaire*. . . ."[103] As a contemporary message of revolutionary hope and inspiration, the pamphlet did not get very far. Printed in

New York, it sold poorly among German-Americans; few copies ever reached Europe, and Marx's efforts to have an edition printed there were unsuccessful. The handful of readers of *The Eighteenth Brumaire* were profoundly impressed with Marx's analysis, but its message never had much of an audience.[104] Marx's isolation in exile and the arrest and imprisonment of his followers in Cologne marked the end of a ten-year phase of political activism. Until the year 1859, Marx would be shut out of political activity. From a revolutionary actively intervening in events, even causing them to happen, he would be reduced to an observer, commenting incisively on current conditions, and seeking any last piece of evidence that would indicate a change for the better.

8

The Observer

FOR MARX, THE PERIOD between the mid-1840s and the early 1850s was characterized by extensive organizing, inflammatory journalism, and insurrectionary aspirations, shot through with bitter polemics, envenomed recriminations, and personal and political rivalries. In generating a whirlwind of contentious politics, Marx reflected the broader flow of European history. Nothing dominated the era more than the continentwide revolutions of 1848, preceded by years of rising confrontation and succeeded by a phase of apocalyptic visions anticipating even more violent, drastic, and far-reaching revolution.

The subsequent seven years that came in the wake of the revolution's fury, the period between 1852 and 1859, proved altogether different. Authoritarian regimes, most prominently in France with the accession of Louis Napoleon Bonaparte, who now called himself Emperor Napoleon III, came as a virulent response to the rebellions that had convulsed continental Europe. Open political opposition was marginalized while radical versions of it were completely suppressed. This was, as contemporaries and later historians said, an "age of reaction." Marx's personal priorities followed broader historical trends in this era as well. Sheltered from repression in England, a liberal offshore haven in a reactionary era, disheartened by the results of the Cologne Communist Trial, and disgusted with exile strife, Marx withdrew from active political life. He wrote to Engels in October 1853, "At the next opportunity I intend to issue a public declaration that I have nothing to do with any party. I am no longer inclined, under the pretext of party, to allow myself to be insulted by every party jackass." Although Marx never did issue such a declaration, he certainly lived out its principles, giving up any engagement with the German artisans and European political refugees in London—whose activities were definitely at a low ebb during this era, although not fully extinguished.[1]

Marx himself was at a low ebb for most of the 1850s, his time and energy taken up with supporting his family while battling poor health and personal tragedy. His social contacts declined steadily as he retreated away from politics into private and family life. In December 1857, he wrote that "Except for the family circle, I am now quite isolated here. The few acquaintances are seldom seen, and, in general, one doesn't lose much for it."[2]

Marx justified his political passivity by his 1850 thesis that the next revolution would only break out after an economic crisis. In the interregnum between revolutions, when political action would accomplish little, he would finally write the book on political economy he had been planning for years, and so arm himself intellectually for the next insurgent outbreak.[3] But the demands of earning a living and his frequently depressed and downcast emotional state meant that he made little progress on this task. Rather, Marx's intellectual efforts went into his steadily expanding work as a freelance journalist. At least temporarily unable to change the world, as he aspired to do in his theses on Feuerbach, he had to settle for interpreting it. In his very extensive journalism, Marx provided incisive commentary on the politics of reaction-era Europe, observed closely commercial and financial conditions, and evaluated new business developments, all the while looking for any evidence of the hoped-for economic crisis. His journalistic observations were the one time in his life when he paid close attention to conditions in Asia and thought on a global scale.

THROUGH THE 1850s, DEATH continued to stalk the family. Jenny was forty-three when she gave birth for the last time, in July 1857, following a difficult and painful pregnancy. The child was stillborn—a powerful blow to the mother, but one that also inspired strong feelings in Karl. Just what "circumstances immediately connected" with the birth made a "dreadful impression on my imagination," or whatever leading to the stillbirth was a "torture" for him to remember, remains mysterious; even his close friend Engels did not understand the references.[4]

Perhaps these painful memories stemmed from a much greater tragedy—not that of a child born dead, but the unexpected death of Edgar, a lively, deeply loved child, who died at the age of eight on April 6, 1855. The conditions of his illness—lasting about a month, with stomach pains, a fever, temporary improvements followed by setbacks—all suggest a ruptured appendix, although tuberculosis of the stomach cannot be ruled out. As the condition of their beloved "Musch" ("the fly") worsened, the mood of his parents became steadily more somber. His death early in the morning, in his father's arms, was an intolerable blow. His mother, his sisters, and Lenchen Demuth all sobbed inconsolably. Jenny could not bear to stay in the dreary Dean Street rooms in Soho; she had to get away from the site of the tragedy, but even that did not help. Months later, the least reminder of her son's death would cause her to break out in tears. Her husband, barely able to master his emotions, felt no better:

> The house is naturally completely deserted and empty after the death of the dear child who was its enlivening soul. It is indescribable how much we miss the child, everywhere we turn. I have gone

through all manner of trouble but now I know for the first time what genuine misfortune is. I feel broken down. Fortunately, since the day of the burial, I have had such severe headaches that thinking, hearing and seeing have passed me by.[5]

The death of this son was the greatest tragedy in Marx's life. At Edgar's funeral, his friend and political associate Wilhelm Liebknecht attempted to console him, reminding him of his wife, daughter, and friends, but Marx, close to losing control, just groaned in reply: "All of you cannot give me my boy back." Edgar's death left Marx depressed and dispirited for the next two and a half years. If he did not give in completely to despair, it was only, as he told Engels, because of the "thought of you and your friendship . . . and the hope that together we can still do something sensible in the world."[6]

In this bleak family picture, there was one small ray of light: the birth of a daughter, Eleanor, on January 17, 1855. The first months of the little girl's life were difficult and it seemed that she might go the way of Heinrich Guido and Franziska. But Eleanor, a precocious and energetic child, survived, the only one of the children born in London who did so. Her two sisters, a good decade older, doted on her; her parents were amused and proud. But Eleanor's flourishing, for all the joy it brought to her family, could not compensate for Edgar's death.[7]

BY THE EARLY 1850s, Marx was an experienced journalist, who had written regularly for four newspapers and two magazines. In the years 1853–62, he put this journalistic experience to good use, writing for six different newspapers, in England, the United States, Prussia, Austria, and even South Africa. Unlike previous circumstances, this work was undertaken at the behest of newspapers neither under Marx's control or influence nor designed for his political purposes. Marx's editors gave him quite a bit of latitude; he could make political

points, and work out theoretical issues in in his articles, but his journalism was no longer a form of political agitation.

The bulk of Marx's journalism appeared in the *New York Tribune*,
then the leading newspaper in the United States, best known today
for its opposition to slavery and for its chief editor, the pundit and
Republican politician Horace Greeley. His associate, Charles Anderson Dana, had met Marx in Cologne in November 1848, at the very
peak of a revolutionary crisis. Impressed and charmed by Marx, Dana
kept in touch, and in 1851 he offered the political exile the opportunity
to write a series of articles about the midcentury revolution in central
Europe. Busy with polemics against his fellow refugees, and his book
on political economy, still very unsure of his English, Marx turned
the writing over to Engels. The latter's ghostwritten articles have frequently been reprinted as a book under the title *Germany: Revolution and
Counter-Revolution.*[8]

The series was a big success, and Dana requested that Marx, the
ostensible author, write regular pieces for the *Tribune.* Starting in the
second half of 1852, Marx began writing the articles himself. At first
his knowledge of English was insufficient, and he needed the editorial assistance of Wilhelm Pieper; but with some practice, he became
comfortable writing in English, although his prose remained distinctly
Teutonic all his life. Marx would dash articles off in his scrawled
handwriting. Jenny would then write out a fair copy, which would be
dispatched by steamer to New York. (The correspondence took place
before the laying of an effective transatlantic telegraph cable in 1866.)
Over the course of a decade, Marx was paid for 487 pieces, many
appearing in the *Tribune* as lead articles. About a quarter of them were
actually ghostwritten by Engels, who pitched in when Marx's health
problems made it hard for him to write, but Engels also wrote articles
on military matters, which were "The General's" specialty.[9]

Marx found other outlets for his work, placing a few items in left-
wing and oppositional English newspapers, some of which would be

reprinted and obtain a much wider audience. He wrote briefly for a Dutch-language South African newspaper, but could not agree with its editor on payment. For nine months in 1855, he was the London correspondent of the *New Oder News* in Breslau, until the Prussian government forced the oppositional journal out of business. Its editor founded a Viennese newspaper, *The Press* (predecessor to *The New Free Press*, one of the great liberal newspapers of pre-1914 Europe), for which Marx wrote, more sporadically, in the early 1860s.[10]

Considerable work went into these articles. To get material, Marx regularly read the major English newspapers, a large portion of the French and German press, and some selected articles from Italian and Spanish papers as well. He pored over Blue Books, the reports of the British parliamentary investigative committees, and went through volumes of *Hansard*, the record of parliamentary debates. Marx did do some occasional personal reporting, attending debates in the House of Commons as well as riotous demonstrations in Hyde Park, but his journalism was more like that of today's columnist than a reporter. His substantial essays (which occupy five to ten pages when reprinted in the collections of his works) contained extensive commentary, shot through with typical ironic and satirical invective. The sheer volume of his newspaper work is impressive. Although the journalism is sparsely examined in most biographies, the extent of the newspaper articles written by Marx between 1853 and 1862 was greater than everything else he published during his lifetime put together. In the eulogy summing up the life of his friend, Engels emphasized—quite rightly—the intellectual and political significance of Marx's journalism.[11]

IF THE JOURNALISM OF the 1850s was by far the largest part of Marx's published writings, it was equally the most lucrative. The need to support his family and pay off the debts he had accumulated was a major factor. Creditors continued to harass the family into 1852–53, as Marx began his work as a correspondent. The pawnshop remained a frequent recourse, and Engels sent Marx money as best he could. Jenny reported back to him: "Karl was enormously happy when he heard the fateful double knock of the mailman: Voilà, Frederick, £2, saved! he cried out." However, Engels, who had financial problems of his own, could not always come through, so Marx was forced to scour the German community for loans. This was no easy task since most of its members were well aware of his bad credit record.[12]

As the newspaper work continued and expanded, financial conditions began to improve. Feeling more optimistic about his prospects by the end of 1853, Marx wrote to Engels to say he regretted not having started his journalism earlier: "If we both—you and I—had only got this English correspondent business going at the right time in London, you wouldn't be sitting in Manchester, tormented in the counting house and I wouldn't be tormented by my debts."[13] With more money coming in, little signs of comfort began to reappear in the family. Unlike with Heinrich Guido, Jenny was able to hire a wet-nurse for Eleanor. Starting in 1853, the family enjoyed big German Christmas celebrations, with a cornucopia of gifts for the children. Wilhelm Liebknecht, in his reminiscences of Marx, described the Sunday family picnics of the mid-1850s. In mild weather, Karl, Jenny, the children, the servant, and various guests would march for over an hour from Dean Street north and west to Hampstead Heath, with Lenchen carrying in her basket a large veal roast and fruit. On the Heath, the picnickers purchased bread and cheese, shrimps, snails and beer, consumed a substantial midday dinner, and then sat and chatted or read the Sunday papers while the children played. Trudging back, they sang folksongs, or Karl and Jenny would declaim from Shakespeare and Goethe's *Faust*. It was an idyllic scene, and testament to a modest rebound from the depths of exile poverty.[14]

In the fall of 1856, the family was able to move to a new home: 9 Grafton Terrace, in Kentish Town. The rent at £36 per year was relatively reasonable, although this was because the subdivision was unfinished and streets were unpaved, so the whole area became a muddy morass when it rained. Still, it was a house, much bigger than the furnished rooms in Soho. The money needed to furnish it came mostly from a small inheritance Jenny had received from an uncle who had recently died. It was the first time in over seven years that the Marxes had their own furniture, a break with the rootless existence they had been leading. The new location, a long, three-mile walk from the refugee German intellectuals in Soho or the bankers in the City, and even further from the German artisans living in the East End, was another indication of Marx's withdrawal from exile politics and from the social life associated with it.[15]

The move might be seen as culminating a transition in his life, from penniless political exile to middle-class, settled paterfamilias. And it might be seen that way, were it not for the persistent financial crises. Hardly had the family moved into the new house than Marx was forced to issue a desperate appeal to Engels for funds. Eventually, Engels agreed to send the family £5 each month, but that did not suffice. Marx continued to look for new sources of credit to pay his bills, a very difficult task considering that his previous creditors were threatening to seize his assets. In July 1858, he sent Engels another desperate appeal, including a list of the family's expenses and debts which Jenny had drawn up. Marx had hoped to consolidate the debts via a new credit from a savings and loan association; but after paying a £2 application fee, he was turned down as not creditworthy. In the end it was Engels who took out the loan to help Marx with his finances.[16]

By the mid-1850s, Marx was earning a good income from his journalism, having reached an agreement in 1856 with the *New York Tribune* by which he would receive £200 per year as a European correspondent—quite an upper-middle-class income for the time. Taking into account exchange rates (about 6⅔ Prussian talers per English pound), his income was close to what his father had earned in the

1830s, although the cost of living in England's burgeoning capital was far higher than in a German provincial town. In view of Marx's quite respectable earnings, his most recent biographers have rejected the older story of the family's continuous desperate poverty throughout the decade of the 1850s, and have seen the root of their fiscal problems in Karl's extravagance and poor money management.[17] There is certainly something to this argument; by the late 1850s, the Marxes were no longer desperately poor, as they had been at the beginning of the decade. A closer look, though, at their debits and credits shows both the limitations on their income and the expansion of the outlay faced by Karl and by Jenny, who ran the household's finances, as a respectably married woman would.

Being one of the *New York Tribune*'s European correspondents was not quite so lucrative as the salary might suggest. Arranging transatlantic payments was tedious and expensive. Marx had to write an invoice or bill of exchange on Dana and give it to a London banker, who would send it to his correspondent bank in New York. The latter would present it to the *Tribune* for payment, and the payment would then make its way back to London and into Marx's hands—once a substantial fee had been deducted. The first time Marx tried it, the whole process took over two months, and he discovered that bankers did not handle small amounts right away, but waited until they had a number of such small bills together before they sent them. After that experience, he began waiting until he had written a number of articles, and accumulated a larger sum on account, but that meant taking out new debts to meet his household expenses in the interval. Ferdinand Freiligrath, the poet and former member of the editorial board of *The New Rhineland News*, by far the best known of Marx's associates, had fled Prussia and was working as a banker in London. He directed Marx to financiers who would discount his bills and give him cash right away, but that meant accepting less than face value.[18]

The yearly £200 payments themselves hardly endured. Begun in

1856, they were cut in half by November of the following year as a result of the paper's economic difficulties stemming from the 1857 recession. Both Karl and Jenny understood the irony: the long-awaited economic crisis that was to lead to the new outbreak of revolution was undermining their family finances. Charles Dana, who comes across in the correspondence as very friendly and sympathetic, did his best to soften the blow and accepted as much of Marx's work as possible. Before the cutback he had offered Marx additional funds from another of his publishing ventures, writing articles for a planned American encyclopedia. With Engels's very considerable assistance, Marx took on the offer, but it was tedious hackwork, and did not entirely make up for the lost journalistic income.[19]

If Marx's income was not quite so extensive as might at first appear, his expenses were also higher than they might have seemed. By far the most significant contribution was the continuing burden of debt Marx had contracted between 1849 and 1853, when he had no regular income but mounting expenses for political activities. Even when optimistic about his future financial prospects, this load continued to bedevil him. With enormous efforts he claimed, rather optimistically, to have reduced his total debts from £80 to £50 between January and September 1854, but by 1858, the figure had swelled to well over £100. Old debts recurred. Continuing recourse to the pawnshop meant equally continuous interest payments; the need to run up a tab for groceries was another problem. Even after moving to Grafton Terrace, Marx still owed money to shopkeepers in Soho. There were also new debts, particularly for the doctor, stemming from Jenny's pregnancies, the children's illnesses, expensive to treat whether they had fatal or happier outcomes, and Marx's own chronic health problems. (At the time, hemorrhoids, liver, and gallbladder complaints and rotten teeth topped the list.) Marx spent the better part of the second half of 1856 in northern England—in the summer with his family in the Yorkshire village of Camberwell, in the fall with Engels in Manchester—hiding out

Johann Ludwig von Westphalen, Marx's childhood mentor and father of his future bride.

(BUNDESARCHIV BERLIN-LICHTERFELDE)

Jenny von Westphalen, Marx's future bride, in the early 1830s, about the time of her abortive engagement to a Prussian lieutenant.

(INTERNATIONAL INSTITUTE OF SOCIAL HISTORY, AMSTERDAM)

Marx as a student at the University of Bonn in 1836. Note that he is wearing the uniform of the German student fraternities.

It was at the University of Berlin, shown here in the 1820s, that Marx became acquainted with the theories of Hegel, which would inform his thought for the rest of his life.
(BPK, BERLIN / ART RESOURCE, NY)

G. W. F. Hegel (1770–1831). The great philosopher's ideas had distinctly radical religious and political implications, which he very carefully ignored.
(BPK, BERLIN / ART RESOURCE, NY)

Eduard Gans (1797–1839). The University of Berlin professor of legal history, perhaps Hegel's leading disciple, and a considerable intellectual influence on Marx, might well have become the latter's mentor, had Gans not died of a stroke at a young age.

(BPK, BERLIN / ART RESOURCE, NY)

Friedrich Engels in the early 1840s. "I look so dreadfully young," was his own opinion of his appearance then.

(INTERNATIONAL INSTITUTE OF SOCIAL HISTORY, AMSTERDAM)

Bruno Bauer (1809–1882). Bauer, a difficult person and controversial figure, even among the radical Young Hegelians, was Marx's mentor, until the two came to disagree about the political implications of their interpretations of Hegel.

Ludwig Feuerbach (1804–1872). Feuerbach did develop Hegel's theories in a materialist direction, but his intellectual influence on Marx has often been exaggerated.

The Rhenish city of Cologne, shown in this 1845 print as a bustling commercial metropolis, was the center of Marx's political activity during the decade 1842–52.

October 1848, barricades with the Cologne Cathedral in the background. Marx's revolutionary efforts in 1848–49 attacking Prussian rule in Cologne and the Rhineland rather overshadowed his attempts at working-class organization or advocacy of communism.

Trier in 1822: lots of Roman ruins and medieval buildings but little urban substance.
(STADTMUSEUM SIMEONSTIFT TRIER)

At the Cologne Communist Trial of 1852, almost all Marx's remaining supporters in Germany were either convicted and imprisoned or forced out of politics. Among the defendants, in the box on the left-hand side of the picture, the physician Roland Daniels is standing at the back, next to the gendarme, and Hermann "Red" Becker is standing in the front row, speaking.
(RHEINISCHES BILDARCHIV DER STADT KÖLN)

Moses Hess (1812–1875). An important source of Marx's ideas, Hess aspired to be a communist political and intellectual leader, but his dreamy and ineffectual personality made him no rival to the more energetic and determined Marx.

(ARCHIV DER SOZIALEN DEMOKRATIE DER FRIEDRICH-EBERT-STIFTUNG)

Karl Grün (1817–1887). The leading communist in the German-speaking world during the 1840s, Grün replied sharply and effectively to Marx's attacks on him.

(ADOLF HINRICHSEN, ED., *DAS DEUTSCHE SCHRIFTSTELLER-ALBUM* [BERLIN: VERLAG VON WILHELM FRIEDRICH ASCH, 1885])

August Willich (1810–1878). The Prussian army officer turned communist, shown here in his Union Army uniform of the U.S. Civil War, posed as a radical man of action, contrasting himself to Marx, the theoretical intellectual.

(ARCHIV DER SOZIALEN DEMOKRATIE DER FRIEDRICH-EBERT-STIFTUNG)

Wilhelm Liebknecht (1826–1900). Marx's chief advocate in Germany from the 1860s onward, Liebknecht was often regarded (and denounced) as just carrying out Marx's orders. In fact, he had a mind of his own and disagreed with his mentor about important political decisions, which often frustrated and angered Marx.

Ferdinand Lassalle (1825–1864), seen in this photograph as both agitator and dandy.

David Urquhart (1805–1877). The eccentric, pro-Moslem British politician was an important influence on Marx, who shared his vehemently anti-Russian sentiments and his suspicions of the British prime minister Lord Palmerston.

(GERTRUDE ROBINSON AND DAVID URQUHART, *SOME CHAPTERS IN THE LIFE OF A VICTORIAN KNIGHT-ERRANT OF JUSTICE AND LIBERTY* [OXFORD: BLACKWELL, 1920])

Friedrich Engels in 1857, the respectable and affluent businessman.

(ARCHIV DER SOZIALEN DEMOKRATIE DER FRIEDRICH-EBERT-STIFTUNG)

Adolf Cluss (1825–1905). Marx had a very high opinion of Cluss, his main adherent in the United States during the 1850s. Cluss later renounced communism, joined the Republican Party, and became, after the U.S. Civil War, a leading Washington, DC, architect.

(MATTHEW BRADY, COURTESY ADOLF CLUSS PROJECT)

Marx in 1861, at the prime of life: financial setbacks, increasingly severe health problems, and intellectual and political labors would soon age him substantially.

(BUNDESARCHIV BERLIN-LICHTERFELDE)

Coming up in the world: 41 Maitland Park Road in North London, where Marx lived from 1874 until his death in 1883.

(INTERNATIONAL INSTITUTE OF SOCIAL HISTORY, AMSTERDAM)

The miseries of exile: the Marx family lived in a small apartment in this house on Dean Street, in Soho, for much of the 1850s.

(BUNDESARCHIV BERLIN-LICHTERFELDE)

Jenny Marx in 1869. Her father's daughter, she was both Marx's secretary and a left-wing journalist in her own right. The cross she is wearing was not a sign of religious affiliation but the symbol of the Polish uprising of 1863.

The Marxes' second daughter, Laura. Although she shared her older sister's views, she was not quite so intellectually or politically engaged as Jenny was.
(INTERNATIONAL INSTITUTE OF SOCIAL HISTORY, AMSTERDAM)

The Marx family servant, Helena (Lenchen) Demuth. Marx's paternity of her illegitimate son, Freddy, was, for decades, a closely guarded secret.
(BUNDESARCHIV BERLIN-LICHTERFELDE)

The Marxes' youngest daughter, Eleanor, as a precocious twelve year old in 1867.
(INTERNATIONAL INSTITUTE OF SOCIAL HISTORY, AMSTERDAM)

L'INTERNATIONALE A LA HAYE. — Le départ des délégués après la dernière séance du Congrès.

Delegates leaving the 1872 Hague Congress of the International Workingmen's Association, watched by curious spectators. This congress marked the high point of Marx's influence over the IWMA, which he used to terminate the organization altogether.

(INTERNATIONAL INSTITUTE OF SOCIAL HISTORY, AMSTERDAM)

The 1875 Gotha Congress, uniting the pro- and anti-Prussian wings of the German socialist movement, is presented here as the personal reconciliation of Lassalle and Marx—definitely not a viewpoint that Marx himself endorsed.

(ARCHIV DER SOZIALEN DEMOKRATIE DER FRIED- RICH-EBERT-STIFTUNG)

In this picture of Marx, from the early 1870s, he looks aging, ill, and emaciated:
more a mortal man than an icon.

The elderly Jenny von Westphalen in the 1870s. (INTERNATIONAL INSTITUTE OF SOCIAL HISTORY, AMSTERDAM)

Marx toward the end of the 1860s. The future iconic image is already apparent. (BPK, BERLIN / ART RESOURCE, NY)

Not quite yet an icon: the grave of Karl Marx and Jenny von Westphalen in Highgate Cemetery, as it originally was, before the erection of the giant Marx bust in 1956.

(WILHELM LIEBKNECHT, *KARL MARX ZUM GEDÄCHTNISS. EIN LEBENSABRISS UND ERINNERUNGEN* [NUREMBERG: WÖRLEIN & COMP., 1896]) from the family physician, Dr. Jonas Freund. The latter was demanding payment in a particularly energetic way, since he was in serious financial trouble himself and would have to file for bankruptcy two years later.[20]

If there was an element of excess in these expenditures, it arose from Karl's concern for Jenny and his daughters. The maids (Lenchen Demuth was joined for a few years in the late 1850s and early 1860s by her younger sister Marianne) would spare his wife, worn out by pregnancies at an advanced age and concern about her children's health, the physical work of running a household. The stress of managing the budget and fending off creditors was already too much for her. A larger residence in a better neighborhood, far from cholera-ridden Soho, removed Jenny from the constant reminders of Edgar's death. Public schools did not exist, just church-sponsored charity schools for the poor, so the older daughters, little Jenny and Laura, attended a private school for proper young ladies. Karl and Jenny intended to bring up their daughters as such, which meant additional expenses for lessons in Italian and French, drawing and music.[21] Karl's protestations to Engels, as he shamefully confessed, in July 1858 that all his additional journalistic income had not been able to keep his debts from increasing, contained an element of self-justification. Yet they also revealed the intersection of his finances and his devotion to family:

> If I wished to move in the direction of the most extreme reduction of expenses—i.e., take the children out of school, get a purely proletarian apartment, abolish the maids, live on potatoes—then the auctioning off of our effects would not suffice to satisfy just the creditors in the vicinity and so make possible the withdrawal into some hole-and-corner refuge. The show of respectability, which up to now has been maintained, was the only means to avoid a collapse. For my part, I would ask the devil to live in Whitechapel [an East London slum neighborhood], if I could finally have a peaceful hour

again, and go about my work. For my wife, in her current condition, such a metamorphosis would be connected with very dangerous consequences, and for the girls, who are growing up, it would
scarcely be appropriate.[22]

In the end, the income Marx obtained from his journalism—sometimes
respectable, always erratic—did not enable his family members to escape
from the genteel poverty in which they had lived for so many years.
Rather, it just raised the condition of genteel poverty to a higher level.

MARX'S JOURNALISM IN THE years 1853–58 encompassed
an enormous variety of subjects, from the 1854 revolution in Spain
to the particularities of Lady Bulwer-Lytton, who was committed to
an insane asylum on what she and her defenders claimed were false
diagnoses of insanity. Three major topics dominated his writing: the
Crimean War of 1853–56, and its implications for the foreign policies
of the great powers and the domestic politics of Great Britain; the conditions and conflicts of the British Empire in Asia, including the Second Opium War with China in 1856–60, along with the massive Indian
uprising against British imperial rule in 1857, and the implications of
these conflicts for global capitalism; and the causes and consequences
of the worldwide recession of 1857, including what Marx hoped would
be a new wave of revolutions in Europe. His treatment of each of these
topics reveals how he fleshed out his economic and political theories
and tested them against the intractable reality of the age of reaction.

It was his reportage on the Crimean War of 1853–56 that transformed Marx into a prominent journalist, admittedly with a little
help from Engels, whose ghostwritten articles on military tactics and
strategy during the siege of Sevastopol were particularly noteworthy.
American audiences were enthralled by the accounts of the conflict
and disappointed by dispatches on calmer matters when the hostilities

ended.[23] The fascination with this war is hard to understand today. If recalled at all, it is remembered for Tennyson's "Charge of the Light Brigade," or Florence Nightingale's nursing of sick and wounded soldiers, while the actual military confrontation, fought over the mysterious "Eastern Question" on the margins of the European world, and ending without much in the way of results, seems both dubious and irrelevant.

Contemporaries would have disagreed. The war was the first clash between the great powers of Europe in almost forty years, in fact, since the final defeat of Napoleon in 1815. The Napoleonic Wars had been full-out, all-encompassing conflicts, and it was widely suspected that the new war would not remain a limited engagement, merely pitting Russia against France and England on the shores of the Black Sea, but would expand into a continentwide conflict, involving all the powers. Marx heard these concerns personally from his mother-in-law. Her stepson and Jenny's half brother, Ferdinand von Westphalen, minister of the interior in a Prussian government precariously clinging to neutrality, had informed her that she should prepare herself for a return to an era of warfare on a Napoleonic scale.[24]

For the exiled revolutionaries, the war had a special significance. As early as the 1830s, the leader of the Polish political refugees, Count Adam Jerzy Czartoryski, had hoped for a war between the liberal powers, England and France, and the conservative power, Russia, over the Ottoman Empire, whose current and future status made up the so-called Eastern Question. Such a war, he thought, would lead to the liberation of Poland from czarist oppression.[25] Marx's own political contacts were with radical democratic émigrés from Poland, not the aristocratic and politically moderate Czartoryski. Nonetheless, Marx shared the count's hopes about the political potential of a war with czarist Russia.

In 1848–49, Marx had persistently called for a revolutionary war with Russia. He conceived of the war largely as a rerun of the French

Revolution, pitting a revolutionary France, with the assistance of insurgents in other European countries, against all the other great powers, joined in a counterrevolutionary union. Around the time of his arrival in England, Marx had become increasingly hopeful that a future war with Russia would follow Count Czartoryski's lines, with the British government adopting an anti-Russian foreign policy. Marx expected the impetus for reorientation to come from England's capitalists, who would renounce non-intervention in continental European affairs in order to create a European and global mercantile hegemony.[26]

In view of these expansive hopes, the Crimean War could not help but be a major disappointment. It was not fought by a revolutionary government but by the authoritarian regime of Napoleon III, and by an English coalition ministry composed of Whig aristocrats and Tory moderates. Such governments would not engage in all-out conflict, to say nothing of a revolutionary war. Marx's coverage of the Crimean War attacked their failure to act decisively. As the diplomatic tensions rose between the czarist realm and the Western powers in early 1853, he asserted that the British and French governments would never press their position to the point of going to war. When the war did begin in October, he criticized the British and French for not actually fighting but seeking a peace involving Austrian mediation, that would largely grant all of Russia's demands and leave their Turkish ally to its fate at the hands of the czar. The invasion of the Crimea appeared to Marx a halfhearted and militarily inept effort. He and Engels constantly asserted that if the Western powers did not expand the conflict beyond a limited war in the Black Sea, the superior forces of the czar would inflict a humiliating defeat. As late as the summer of 1855, when the British and French armies besieging Sevastopol had already seized part of the outer ring of fortifications, Marx and Engels continued to insist on Russia's better position and future prospects for victory.[27]

Little disappointed Marx more than the craven attitudes of the English capitalists. Far from calling for the more vigorous prosecution of the conflict, or just supporting the government's plans for a limited war, the two most prominent Radical parliamentary representatives of England's manufacturers, Richard Cobden and John Bright, took a strong anti-war stance. They asserted that there was no economic necessity for the war and no economic benefit from prosecuting it. In extreme frustration, Marx denounced the "Peacemongering Bourgeoisie," a phrase diametrically opposed to the epithet of "warmongers" his twentieth-century disciples would hurl at capitalist politicians.[28]

In some ways, Marx's dispatches floated in a broader tide of British public opinion. Politicians and journalists denounced the government's indecisive policies. The very inept showing of the British Expeditionary Force in the Crimea triggered a parliamentary commission of inquiry and the resignation of the government. Its successor, led by the veteran Whig politician Henry Temple, Viscount Palmerston, promised a more effective prosecution of the war. Palmerston was true to his word. Besieged Sevastopol fell in October 1855, and the Russians sued for peace the following year.[29]

At this point, Marx parted company with most of British public opinion. He became increasingly convinced that behind the ploys and feints of the foreign policies of Her Majesty's government was one obscene fact: that the Whig leader and prime minister Lord Palmerston was actually a paid agent of the czar. Marx maintained this assertion both in his public journalism for the *New York Tribune* and in his private correspondence with Engels and other political allies, and continued to do so well into the 1860s.[30] After extensive study of parliamentary papers, Marx decided that Palmerston's activities as a Russian agent extended back at least a quarter century, and that his policies during previous tenures as government minister had been aimed at betraying the interests of opponents of Russia across the world, from Poland to Afghanistan. Marx's reading of old pamphlets at the British Museum led him to the conclusion that Palmerston was hardly the first traitor in high places, that Russian bribery of Whig politicians was a practice that had been going on for well over a hundred years. He outlined these accusations in a twelve-part series he wrote for newspapers in Sheffield and London, both named *The Free Press*, in 1856–57. After his death, the articles, themselves just a fragment of an unfinished longer work, were gathered by his daughter Eleanor and reprinted as *The Secret Diplomatic History of the Eighteenth Century.*[31]

The newspapers in which Marx published his views were controlled by a British politician, David Urquhart, a strange and perversely fascinating figure. Urquhart was what today would be called an "Orientalist," someone who believed that the society and culture of the peoples of the Islamic world were very different from those of the West and alien to it. But, unlike most nineteenth-century European Orientalists, who regarded that Eastern "other" as inferior to Europe, Urquhart saw it as distinctly superior. He advocated the replacement of the handshake with Turkish salutations, lauded Turkish baths and Turkish clothing, and was a tremendous admirer of Islamic monotheism. Urquhart's views on domestic policy were every bit as peculiar as his opinions of the Near East. His core belief about English politics, the need to purge centuries of Norman innovations and to return the United Kingdom to its ancient Anglo-Saxon institutions, represented a seventeenth-century radicalism that seemed quaintly archaic after the French Revolution. Urquhart's position on the Crimean War was of a piece with the rest of his eccentric opinions. He opposed the war, but not out of pacifist or pro-Russian and anti-Turkish attitudes. Rather, he believed that the entire war effort was a sham, whose real purpose was to coerce the Turks, eminently capable of defending themselves against the Russians, into conceding to Russian demands. Behind such a policy, according to Urquhart, stood the treasonous attitudes of— who else?—Lord Palmerston.[32]

After reading Marx's condemnation of Palmerston in the *New York Tribune*, Urquhart sought Marx out and came from Sheffield to London for a personal meeting with him. The anti-war rallies in the industrial areas of the Midlands, which Urquhart and his followers launched, sent addresses to Marx praising him for his trenchant observations. Marx began to write occasional pieces for Urquhart's newspapers; one of Urquhart's supporters reprinted Marx's articles as pamphlets that sold over 15,000 copies. Quarrels over proper compensation (Marx was never paid for those pamphlets reprinting his articles) limited the cooperation, but it was still considerable—the largest political commitment Marx made in a period when he was generally avoiding such activity.[33]

If there was ever any proof of the adage that politics makes strange bedfellows, it was the collaboration of Marx and Urquhart. Their many differences were manifest. Urquhart rejected the demand for universal manhood suffrage raised by the more modern English Radicals, the Chartists, Marx's main connection to English politics since the 1840s. Urquhart's belief that the revolutions of 1848 were fomented by agents of the czar was rather too much for Marx, who had been an 1848 revolutionary himself, and a vehemently anti-Russian one— as he made a point of telling Urquhart in their private conversation. Marx and Engels were reluctant to become close to Urquhart. They regarded him, as did most of the British political class, as a crackpot— or as Marx's American disciple Adolf Cluss put it in an article Marx inspired, a modern-day Don Quixote, whose initial, praiseworthy anti-Russian attitudes had hardened into a monomaniacal obsession.[34]

If Marx, for all his hesitations and his recognition of Urquhart's peculiarities, nonetheless worked with him, it was because he agreed with two of Urquhart's core positions: his Russophobia and his profound suspicions of Lord Palmerston. Marx had his own distinct reasons for endorsing these beliefs; examining them offers insights into his political orientation in a frustratingly reactionary era.

The anti-Russian stance had been central to Marx's position before and during the 1848 Revolution, and in this respect he was no differ-

ent from most radicals in mid-nineteenth-century Europe. As Count
Czartoryski's policies show, war against Russia was a preferred option
for those seeking to upset the political status quo, and the Crimean
War seemed the ideal opportunity, bringing political radicals onto the
anti-Russian bandwagon. In Marx's political calculation, opposition to
Russia took on an ever higher value during the 1850s. Ghostwriting
for Marx, Engels made the point to American readers in April 1853, as
the tensions over the Eastern Question were mounting steadily. Engels
asserted that since 1789

> there have been in reality but two powers on the continent of
> Europe—Russia and Absolutism, the Revolution and Democracy.
> . . . But let Russia get possession of Turkey, and her strength
> is increased nearly half, and she becomes superior to all the rest
> of Europe put together. Such an event would be an unspeakable
> calamity to the revolutionary cause. The maintenance of the Otto-
> man Empire, the arrest of the Russian scheme of annexation, is a
> matter of the highest moment. In this instance the interests of revo-
> lutionary Democracy and of England go hand in hand.[35]

This aim of thwarting Russia by preserving the Ottoman Empire
was paramount for Marx, even overshadowing his sympathy for revolution. When the Greek-speaking inhabitants of Aetolia and Epirus
rose against Turkish rule early in 1854, Marx dismissed the insurgents
as "robbers of the mountains," whose insurrection was the result of
"Russian intrigues," led by "Muscovite emissaries," quite a statement
for the author of a *Manifesto* which proclaimed that communists would
support every revolutionary movement. Marx dismissed English liberal proposals for the reform of the Ottoman Empire, including equality between Christians and Muslims, or the establishment of a secular
state, as fanciful and impractical calls for a "perfect social revolution."
Like many former 1848 revolutionaries, Marx was developing a more

realistic and power-oriented position, one dubbed by an old Paris émigré acquaintance, August Ludwig von Rochau, as *Realpolitik*.[36]

Marx's hostility to Russia was part of a broader attitude adopted by both English politicians and Continental political refugees. The belief he shared with Urquhart that Lord Palmerston was a czarist agent was more uncommon and peculiar. To be sure, Palmerston, an elderly veteran of English politics, who had first held office in 1807, had accumulated more than his share of enemies over the decades. Catty critics remarked, for example, that his inability to give a rousing speech was caused by his fear that his false teeth would fall out. Whatever most of his enemies would say about Palmerston, his being a traitor to England and a Russian agent was the last thing they would assert. Indeed, Palmerston's reputation for patriotism was universal, his designation as "the most English minister" a common sobriquet by the 1850s. As was characteristic of the era, this patriotic stance went along with support for liberal and constitutional governments in continental Europe and a strong commitment to limit Russian power. Of all the cabinet ministers during the Crimean War, Palmerston was the one most inclined to advocate firm measures, even considering expanding the war as Marx himself wanted.[37]

In view of Palmerston's position, contemporaries found David Urquhart's accusations that he was a traitor the stuff of conspiracy theories. Marx's endorsement of Urquhart's charges, independently developed, was not well received either. Engels maintained a discreet silence, but Ferdinand Lassalle, Marx's one political associate who had remained in Prussia and not been indicted in the Cologne Communist Trial, was openly skeptical. After seeing Marx's evidence that Palmerston was a Russian agent, Lassalle astutely pointed out to his political mentor that the Whig statesman was an aggressive supporter of the war party in England, and that most of Marx's proofs of Palmerston's ostensible pro-Russian policies actually demonstrated an anti-Russian stance. Lassalle continued, drawing on personal experience:

It is not without significance that diplomats I know personally, who over a period of 10–15 years have had relations with him [Palmerston] and who are themselves so corrupt that they are up to their necks in corruption, have not the least suspicion that he has been bribed but regard him as genuinely anti-Russian. And, to be sure, diplomats who are especially initiated into the secrets of Russia.[38]

How did Marx reach the strange conclusion that England's most vehement anti-Russian politician was actually a Russian agent? Unlike David Urquhart, Marx was not given to conspiracy theories, yet he endorsed this one wholeheartedly. He had certainly done extensive reading in Blue Books and parliamentary debates, current issues of *The Times* and yellowing eighteenth-century political pamphlets he found in the Reading Room of the British Museum. What led him to the conclusion was his interpretation of this reading in the light of his theories of social class and political power and of the circumstances of the age of reaction.

Although Marx perceived the United Kingdom as the quintessentially capitalist country, he found its bourgeoisie unwilling to take on the task of governing, turning it over instead to the landed classes. He saw the latter as divided into two factions: the enlightened, great landowners, whom he identified with the Whigs, and the small, provincial gentry, the basis of the Tories. Marx was unquestionably more sympathetic to the Tories, because he perceived them as a party "always run by parvenus, Pitt, Addington, Perceval, Canning, Peel and Disraeli." Marx praised the ironic, witty, and articulate Benjamin Disraeli, the leading figure of the parliamentary opposition during the Crimean War, as the "ablest member of the present parliament."[39]

For the Whig aristocrats, Marx had nothing but contempt. They were hypocrites, who pretended to be friends of the people while passing reactionary legislation: since 1688, "all laws directed against the people are initiated by the Whigs." They were unprincipled, abandoning their basic ideas for political advantage, as Palmerston did, when he supported the Great Reform Bill of 1832, largely for the purpose of limiting political reform. Lord John Russell, another major Whig figure who was both an ally and a rival of Palmerston, did the same, according to Marx, when he dropped his endorsement of the Corn Laws under the pressure of the industrial bourgeoisie.

A more friendly observer might see these actions as examples of political flexibility and of the ability to compromise; but for Marx they were just "all the shams that form the essence of Whigism." Whigs demonstrated the same hypocrisy and lack of principle in foreign affairs. According to Marx,

> Yielding to foreign influence in fact [Palmerston] opposes it in words. . . . He knows how to conciliate a large phraseology with narrow views, how to clothe the policy of a peace-mongering middle-class in the haughty language of England's aristocratic past, how to appear an aggressor where he yields, and a defender where he betrays. . . . If the oppressors were always sure of his active support, the oppressed never lacked a great ostentation of his rhetorical generosity. [40]

For Marx, hypocrisy, lies, and corruption made up the essence of England's ruling political faction—and necessarily so, given their position as great aristocratic landlords administering a bourgeois-capitalist society. Marx saw the leader of this group as a hypocritical traitor, a man celebrated for his English patriotism yet actually taking directions from the czar.

Marx's own personal experiences reinforced this willingness to see the ostensible English patriot as a Russian spy. In the very recent past, Marx had tied himself closely to a purported revolutionary, who had turned out, to his considerable embarrassment, to be a secret agent of the Austrian and Prussian governments; he had watched a Prussian

policeman weave a web of forgery and perjury that had put his friends
and supporters in jail. Justifying his opinion of Palmerston to an evidently unconvinced Engels, Marx wrote in November 1853, just a
year after the conclusion of the Cologne Communist Trial and after he
had finally admitted that Jànos Bangya was a police spy:

> Curious as this may appear to you, by my precise retracing of the
> footsteps of the noble Viscount over the last 20 years, I have come to
> the same conclusion as the monomaniac Urquhart—that Palmerston
> has been sold to Russia for the last several decades. . . . We have
> neglected this point altogether too much and one must know with
> whom one has to deal. All of diplomacy reproduces on a large scale
> Stieber Ban[g]ya and Co.[41]

FOR MARX, A CRUCIAL, distinguishing feature of capitalism as
an economic system was its global scope. The *Communist Manifesto* had
celebrated the global reach of the bourgeoisie. Marx's outlines of his
planned work on political economy during the 1850s always had as a
concluding chapter an analysis of the world market.[42] Yet for all this
evocation of what would later be called globalization, Marx's own historical and political analysis remained distinctly Eurocentric. He did
pay close attention to developments in the United States, but regarded
the North American republic as an overseas outpost of European
culture and society. British parliamentary debates over the proper
government of India and the imperial conflicts of the 1850s, all duly
covered by Marx as a *New York Tribune* European correspondent, gave
him the one opportunity in his life to analyze non-European societies
and European imperial rule. His reflections showed many of the features of mid-nineteenth-century social and political thought, but very
little of twentieth-century Marxist interpretations of imperialism and
capitalism on a global scale.

Marx's interest in the Orient began, as was invariably the case among nineteenth-century German intellectuals, with the Bible. Engels wrote him in May 1853 about a book he had been reading by Charles Forster, an English Bible critic, who described the Old Testament genealogies of Noah as a listing of Bedouin tribes. Following Forster, Engels discussed the ancient Orient—from the Assyrians to the rise of Islam—as the product of Bedouin invasions. Marx, most interested in Engels's observations, noted that the key question for him was "Why does the history of the Orient appear as the history of religion?" His answer was that in the "East," which included for Marx Persia, India, and the Ottoman Empire, there was no private property in land. "This is the real key, even to the oriental heaven."[43]

In further correspondence, Engels suggested that the chief reason for the lack of private property was the dry climate, which made a state-run irrigation system a necessity for civilization. Marx agreed with him, but added that the Eastern empires consisted primarily of a myriad of small villages, each with some form of collective agricultural property, generally accompanied by small-scale craft production. With this exchange of letters, Marx's basic theory of government, society, and economy in Asia was formed; future discussions, mostly in his unpublished drafts on political economy, would not change it much.[44]

The chief opportunity for Marx to apply these theories came in his articles on British colonial rule in India, which appeared in the *New York Tribune* just a few days after this correspondence and drew directly on the ideas developed in it.[45] Both economically and politically the most important part of the British Empire following the loss of most of its North American possessions and the abolition of slavery in the Caribbean colonies, India was not yet the jewel in the crown of the later Victorian era. It was still ruled by the British East India Company, a state-sponsored but private corporation, an increasingly archaic remnant of the eighteenth century that was equal parts colonial authority, trading and economic development firm, and band of thieves.

Marx's portrayals of British India emphasized at different times these different features of the East India Company's rule. In 1853, he portrayed the British as the latest in a long line of conquerors, who ruthlessly exploited and looted "Hindostan." But the "misery inflicted by the British on Hindostan is of an essentially differently and infinitely more intensive kind than all Hindostan had to suffer before." British rule was a capitalist social revolution, introducing private property in land, and dismantling the state-run irrigation system. "British steam and science uprooted, over the whole surface of Hindostan, the union between agricultural and manufacturing industry . . . separate[ing] Hindostan, ruled by Britain, from all its ancient traditions, and from the whole of its past history."

Yet this condemnation of British imperial rule turned into a defense of its legitimacy. Marx explained to the readers of the *New York Tribune* in his noticeably Teutonic English that the separation of India from its past had its positive features:

> Now, sickening as it must be to human feeling to witness those myriads of industrious patriarchal and inoffensive social organizations disorganized and dissolved . . . and their individual members losing at the same time their ancient form of civilization, and their hereditary means of subsistence, we must not forget that these idyllic village-communities, inoffensive though they may appear, had always been the solid foundation of Oriental despotism, that they restrained the human mind within the smallest possible compass, making it the unresisting tool of superstition. . . . We must not forget that these little communities were contaminated by distinctions of caste and by slavery, that they subjugated man to external circumstances instead of elevating man [to] the sovereign of circumstances, that they transformed a self-developing social state into never changing natural destiny.

Since such a civilization was easy prey to foreign aggression, "The question, therefore, is not whether the English had a right to conquer India, but whether we are to prefer India conquered by the Turk, by the Persian, by the Russian, to India conquered by the British."

What made the British perversely more desirable as conquerors was precisely the extreme disruption they brought to a static Indian society, which would be followed by the creation of more dynamic social and political order. Although this "work of regeneration hardly transpires through a heap of ruins," it was already underway. Private ownership of land would lead to economic development; railroad construction would bring the onset of modern industry. Between the introduction of a free press, and the implementation of a European system of higher education, a class of state administrators and scientists was just beginning to emerge. The British were also creating a future state for them: the political unity, telegraph network, and an all-Indian army resulting from British colonialism would be the "sine qua non of Indian self-emancipation, and of India ceasing to be the prey of the first foreign intruder."

Marx's take on imperialism had little in common with the views of his twentieth-century adherents, who have emphasized the negative, socially and economically retarding effect of capitalist, colonial rule while generally holding a more favorable opinion of pre-colonial society. Instead, his view emerged from the debates of mid-nineteenth-century European, but above all British, practitioners of a nascent social science. Like Marx, the sociologist Herbert Spencer, the legal historian Henry Maine, and the anthropologist Edward Tylor each understood Asian societies as static and incapable of the progress Europe had achieved. Only the adaptation of Western institutions would enable Asian societies to change. But they tended to be skeptical of the extent to which such institutions could be transferred to Asian countries. Even Tylor, the most optimistic among them, saw the need for a constant infusion of Western ideas.[46]

Marx certainly agreed with his contemporaries that Asian societies were static and incapable of change—a notion asserted by Hegel in the early nineteenth century, as much as by later social scientists. But he also thought that once the proper, capitalist institutions were present, Asians would advance quite vigorously. He quoted a British observer "that the great mass of the Indian people possesses a great industrial energy, is well fitted to accumulate capital and remarkable for a mathematical clearness of head and talent for figures and exact sciences." The course of progress, though, as had been the case in capitalist Europe, would be neither smooth nor pleasant. "Has the bourgeoisie," Marx asked, "ever effected progress without dragging individuals and people through blood and dirt, through misery and degradation?"

Marx's defense of British colonialism in India was very much like his 1847 advocacy of free trade for its destructive effects, advancing capitalism and, through it, a future revolution. Imperial rule, Marx informed his readers, was an integral part of the capitalist system, with its global project of "the centralization of capital . . . universal intercourse founded upon the mutual dependency of mankind . . . and . . . the development of the productive powers of man and the transformation of material production into a scientific domination of natural agencies." But only, Marx continued, "When a great social revolution shall have mastered the results of the bourgeois-epoch, the market of the world and the modern powers of production, and subjected them to the common control of the most advanced peoples, then only will human progress cease to resemble that hideous pagan idol, who would not drink the nectar but from the skulls of the slain."

That last powerful, richly symbolic sentence, which in many ways sums up Marx's entire understanding of the historical process, was also a call for an improved, enlightened, and socialist colonial policy: note its description of a future in which the world market would be under control of the "most advanced," that is, European, "peoples." Marx did see the prospect of an eventual Indian revolution for national independence, led by the new class of capitalists and professionals British rule was gradually creating. In his reporting on the 1857 Indian rebellion against this rule, such an Indian bourgeoisie was not in evidence. Instead, Marx emphasized the more parasitic features of the East India Company.

The uprising, which for a while seemed as if it might drive the British out of India altogether, was an enormous shock to contemporaries, prompting a wide-ranging debate about its nature and origins. Marx's own reporting reflected a number of the themes of this public debate, such as Islamic hostility to the rule of a Christian power, or the insurrection as result of an anti-British conspiracy of the native rulers. For all his criticism of the insurgents, Marx attributed responsibility for the uprising to British colonial policy, which he denounced in no uncertain terms.[47]

In 1857, Marx concentrated on the burden of taxation; he denounced the seizure of property, directly by British troops and indirectly by government policy. The British, he said, were "foreign conquerors who have . . . abused their subjects"—portraying them in this sense as very similar to previous conquerors. These British exactions, Marx suggested, went largely to the benefit of politically connected insiders—the officers of the East India Company and senior civil servants—appointed "nominally by seniority and merit, but really to a great extent by favor." Joining this corrupt group were the politically connected businessmen, stockholders of the East India Company, and a handful of British merchants who controlled the "foreign trade of India." It was only "individual British subjects" who benefited from imperial rule, while the British taxpayers shared with the Indian subjects its expense, "and it may well be doubted whether, on the whole, this dominion does not threaten to cost quite as much as it can ever be expected to come to."[48]

This analysis of British colonialism does not seem "Marxist" at all, but more like an older (Marx undoubtedly would have said petit-bourgeois) strain of radicalism that denounced the British government for its high taxes, spent on lavish sinecures for undeserving aristocrats and corrupt officeholders. As a critique of the British Empire, it had previously been articulated by Cobden and Bright, those two "Peace-mongering" representatives of English industrial capitalism Marx disliked so much during the Crimean War.[49] The analysis also downplayed precisely what Marx regarded as the feature distinguishing British rule in India from that of previous conquerors, its socially revolutionary consequences.

Benjamin Disraeli, the Tory leader whose political acumen and intellectual acuity Marx so admired, placed these revolutionary consequences at the very center of his analysis of the Indian uprising. Yet Marx was deeply disappointed with Disraeli's three-hour oration in the House of Commons in which he expounded his views. The problem for Marx was that the consequences of British rule Disraeli outlined—namely, abolishing the feudal and seigneurial privileges of Indian noble landlords, cutting British subsidies to native princes, and seizing control of their territories outright—were features of this rule that Marx supported, as steps toward the destruction of a static Asian society.[50] Rebellion against this rule was reactionary, opposing the triumph of a capitalist world market that would lead to socialism. Marx definitely disagreed with English radicals who saw the Indian insurgents as nationalist freedom fighters. Jenny wrote scornfully to Engels about Ernest Jones, who "turns all the Indians into Kossuths and celebrates the Indian patriots."[51]

When Marx turned to other conflicts of the British Empire in Asia, he had even less to say about capitalism as a global economic system. He discussed the British war with Persia in 1856 in terms of the balance of power in Europe, condemning Britain's anti-Persian policy for increasing Russian influence in the region.[52] The Second Opium War of 1856–59 was about both capitalism and colonialism, stemming from the illegal British export of opium from its Indian colony to China in order to balance its trade deficit with the Chinese Empire, and to avoid the drain of British silver reserves. Marx was very familiar with the balance of payments question, which he discussed at some length in his articles on economics.[53] But in covering this war he emphasized its diplomatic consequences, once again perceiving British military action as leading to an increase in Russian power. Insofar as the war had economic results, Marx saw them as bad for British capitalism, cutting off British access to Chinese markets and encouraging the Chinese to sell their tea and silk to the Russians. This emphasis on the pro-Russian results of British policy was connected to Marx's coverage of the Crimean War, since the architect of the Chinese and Persian policies was the same prime minister, Lord Palmerston, whom Marx had denounced as a secret agent of the czar.[54]

For all Marx's evocation of capitalism as a worldwide economic system, his intense interest in the consequences of British colonial policy was strikingly Eurocentric, focused on English domestic politics and on the European balance of power. In part, this attitude was a reflection of the nature of imperialism in the middle decades of the nineteenth century, when Great Britain was the only power to possess an extensive colonial empire. The building of competing European overseas empires only began in the 1880s, at the very end of Marx's life. But Marx's political focus also reflected his opinion of the primacy of Europe and North America in global affairs. Writing to Engels at the end of 1858, when Marx was more optimistic about the prospects for revolution than he had been in years, he explicitly discussed the connection between global capitalism and communist revolution in Europe in a way he had never done for events in Asia:

> The inherent task of bourgeois society is the creation of the world market . . . and of production on its basis. Because the world is round, it seems that this process has been brought to its conclusion with the colonization of California and Australia and the opening of China and Japan. The difficult question for us is this: on the [Euro-

pean] continent, the revolution is imminent and will immediately take on a socialist character. Will it not necessarily be crushed in this little corner, because on the much larger terrain the movement of bourgeois society is still in the ascendant?[55]

This speculative statement was the only time when Marx wondered whether a socialist revolution in continental Europe could be overwhelmed by a globally dominant Anglo-American capitalism. Such a revolution, in spite of Marx's expectations, never occurred in his lifetime. Rather, it was twentieth-century communist revolutionaries in Russia, China, or Cuba who had to grapple with the question Marx briefly posed in 1858.

A RENEWED REVOLUTION, MARX had proclaimed in 1850, would begin with a new economic crisis. No sooner had he made this proclamation then he began to search for glimmers of an emergent crisis, finding them in harvest failures, a rise in interest rates, or declines in the stock market. Marx was not chary of alerting readers of the *New York Tribune* of the "approaching economic disasters and social convulsions"; he informed them that British industrial production's "movement of expansion is becoming accelerated at the very moment when markets are contracting," asserting in 1855 that "a few months more and the crisis will be at a height which it has not reached in England since 1846." He queried Engels about business conditions and market outlets in the Manchester textile industry, seeking signs of an economic crisis, which his friend was quick to provide. As Wilhelm Liebknecht remembered, Marx's constant expectation of an economic crisis became a standing joke among his London friends and associates.[56]

The long-awaited crisis finally did occur in 1857, beginning in the United States and spreading across the globe. It was a substantial downturn, generally regarded as the first worldwide recession.

Exulting in the viral expansion of economic distress, Marx wrote to Conrad Schramm, his old ally from the Communist League, about the "earthquake-like effects of the general crisis, which every connoisseur must savor. . . ." Jenny added an observation about how the onset of an economic crisis had dispelled the long period of gloom and depression in which Karl had been mired since the death of his son:

> Although the American crisis has been very perceptible in our money-bag, since Karl only writes once weekly for the Tribune instead of twice . . . you can very well imagine how high up the Moor is. His entire previous ability to work and his ease of mind and manner has returned, as well as the vigor and cheerfulness of spirit, that had been broken for years, since the great sorrow, the loss of our dear child of the heart, for whom my heart will always mourn.[57]

With his optimism newly restored, Marx plunged into renewed activity. Busy during the day with his newspaper correspondence, he worked through the night to complete his treatise on economics before the imminent outbreak of revolution. His correspondence with Engels during 1857 and 1858 turned to future revolutionary prospects, including possible relations between German insurgents and a revolutionary France (both men continued to believe a European-wide upheaval would commence in Paris), and ironic observations about how the looming economic and political crisis would upset the domestic stability their lives had recently achieved after years of upheaval.[58] In a well-known passage, Engels told Marx that he was concentrating on riding and shooting, in preparation for forthcoming revolutionary warfare. Marx, who was rather more skeptical about horsemanship (although Engels did make repeated efforts to introduce him to the sport, and actually got Marx into the saddle for two hours one day), tried to calm him down, pointing out that there would "soon come more important opportunities to risk your neck. . . . I do not believe that cavalry is the specialty in which you are most needed for Germany."[59]

Marx analyzed the origins and nature of the 1857 economic crisis both in his journalism and in his correspondence with Engels. Two central features of this analysis, the role of credit and of international financial transactions, are of particular interest because Marx never developed a full discussion of either in *Capital*.[60]

Marx's thinking about capitalism during the 1850s was influenced by the growth of a new kind of financial institution, the *Crédit Mobilier*: the world's first corporate bank, whose capital was raised through the sale of stock shares rather than coming from bankers' own assets. It was a daring innovation of the Pereire brothers, onetime Saint-Simonian socialists themselves. Most financiers of the day were deeply suspicious of this new kind of finance, seeing it as an elaborate form of fraud. At times, Marx was inclined to agree. "Swindle" became a favorite term of his to describe the bank. Its close connections to Napoleon III—whose regime Marx, like many contemporaries, perceived as fraudulent— only contributed to his suspicions.[61]

In other moments, Marx found the bank's operations legitimate, a good example of capitalism hurtling toward crisis. This was the opinion that came to the fore in 1857. The bank invested primarily in industrial and railroad corporations, either underwriting initial public offerings or purchasing the stock of existing firms listed on the Paris Bourse. What intrigued Marx about these financial operations was, as we would say today, the bank's leverage. Its statutes allowed it to borrow up to ten times the value of its capital. Almost giddily fascinated, Marx thought this borrowing set the stage for crisis. The bank's leveraged investments greatly increased the productive capacity of French industry, beyond the market's ability to purchase all its products. In addition, the bank invested its borrowed funds in stock shares that could drastically fall in value during an economic crisis brought on by the very overproduction the leveraged investments had created, leaving it unable to meet the demands of its creditors.[62]

Engels offered his own version of the connection between leverage and overproduction, based on his observations of English textile manufacturing, where businesses were mostly family-owned or private partnerships rather than corporations. These firms, Engels noted, issued bills of exchange, secured by their stores of raw materials or manufactured goods. With the funds generated by these credits, a "mercantile community," Engels calculated, could increase its capital and thus its production by 50 percent. The bills of exchange were short-term credits, but they were rolled over when they came due, until the economic crisis created by overproduction stemming from the credit-based expansion of output led the firms' creditors to call in their loans.[63] The empirical basis for this interpretation of excessive leverage as the origin of an economic crisis came from the experiences of Marx and Engels in bourgeois occupations. It was not so much the philosophical ideas of Hegel or the economic theories of Ricardo that informed their insights as it was their work as business columnist and cotton wholesaler, respectively.

The second element of Marx's take on the 1857 recession also stemmed from his work as a journalist, namely, his analysis of the international propagation of the crisis following the balance of payments. The crisis would spread from creditor countries to their debtors, as the former would call in their loans from the latter. The debtors would have to call in loans from their debtors in turn, or their central banks would have to raise interest rates to keep money in the country. When the Bank of England raised the discount rate to 9 percent, Marx became especially excited, seeing this move as evidence that the crisis had reached the heart of world capitalism and a new revolution could not be far off. Although he looked primarily at trade and credit relations between European countries, as well as the United States, his analysis did contain a global note. Marx analyzed the persistent balance of payments deficit European countries ran with China, which led to silver leaving Britain and the Continent, driving up the price of silver relative to gold. The rise in silver prices affected the exchange rates of the major European currencies, which had different ratios of gold to silver in their backing, and helped to shape the spread of the economic crisis via the balance of payments.[64]

A large part of Marx and Engels's jubilant mood came from following the progress of the crisis from one country to the next. Marx wrote Engels in October 1857: "The American crisis . . . is beautiful. The setback to French industry was immediate. . . . The complaints of the English money-article writers that their English trade is sound but their clients abroad unhealthy is original and lively. How are things with the Manchester manufacturers?"

Engels replied: "The effect back on England seems now to have commenced. . . . All the better. Commerce is now once again worthless for 3–4 years. Now we have some good fortune." A month later, he turned to Germany: "In Hamburg, things look terrific. . . . There has never been a panic so complete and classical as in Hamburg. Everything is worthless, absolutely worthless, except for silver and gold . . . for the moment, Hamburg is commercially annihilated. The German industrialists . . . will once again suffer heavy blows."

"So much as I myself am in financial distress, following this outbreak I have not felt so cozy since 1849," Marx summed up for his friend.[65] Contributing to these expectations was early evidence that the age of reaction in Europe was coming to an end. In 1858, Friedrich Wilhelm IV of Prussia became mentally incapacitated and had to turn the reins of state over to his brother, Prince Wilhelm, who promptly dismissed from office the reaction-era government ministers.[66]

Such political developments helped keep Marx's hopes up even as signs of economic recovery became increasingly apparent in the course of 1858.[67] The long-awaited economic crisis had not led to a new wave of revolutions. But it had energized Marx, bringing him out of the torpor and depression that had plagued him since the death of his son. At the end of the 1850s, just as at the decade's beginning, Marx's private mood and broader trends of European politics seemed to coincide. The age of reaction waned, and the position of the great powers became unsettled. After a long period of hibernation, movements of political opposition began to stir in 1858–59, and Marx was prepared to end his role as a detached observer and become, once more, a political activist.

9

The Activist

THE DREARY STASIS OF the age of reaction and its authoritarian regimes was succeeded by twelve years of reforming governments,
lively public debates, and intensifying political struggles between 1859
and 1871. Crucial issues that had ignited the revolutions of 1848—
national unity, constitutional and democratic government, the "social
question"—returned to centerstage. At the same time, veterans of the
midcentury revolution, Marx most certainly among them, gradually
accompanied by a new generation of activists, pondered how their previous causes could be revived and what forms of political action would
be needed to do so. This new burst of political contention in the years
after 1859 accompanied and influenced the hegemonic struggles of the
great powers begun in the Crimean War of 1853–56. They continued
and intensified, reaching their climactic conclusion in the existential
clash between Prussia and France in 1870–71.

These two trends, the return of possibilities for political action
and the continuation of the conflicts of the great powers, formed the
backdrop to Marx's own political orientation. His fundamental objec-
tives remained unchanged: organizing the workers for a class struggle
leading toward socialism, opposing authoritarian rule in Prussia, and

advocating revolutionary war against the czar. But new great power initiatives posed by Napoleon III and Otto von Bismarck, and the nationalist passions they summoned up, complicated the once clear connections between war and revolution. Marx's political means became as complicated as his ends. Should he retain his residence and focus of political action in England, or should he return to Germany? Would his political activity center on journalism, as it had in the past, or would it shift to the nascent institutions of the labor movement? Besides such strategic perspectives, Marx's personal circumstances—his mother's death, his wife's illness, the maturing of his daughters, the deterioration of his health, and the disastrous effect of the American Civil War on his already shaky finances—would strongly influence his choices.

IF THE CRIMEAN WAR only evokes the faintest of memories today, the equally significant Northern Italian War of 1859 is completely forgotten. In April of that year, armies of Napoleon III invaded the Austrian provinces of northern Italy, joined by the emperor's ally, the small northwest Kingdom of Piedmont-Savoy. The allied armies' defeat of Habsburg troops at the bloody Battle of Solferino on June 24 was the decisive sign of the end of the age of reaction and the onset of a new era of movement in European politics, beginning with a heated dispute over the war itself.

Leftists in general, and German radicals in particular, from the French Revolution through the Crimean War, had understood great power warfare in ideological terms, pitting the forces of change against those of the status quo. This new conflict posed a question: which was the revolutionary and which the counterrevolutionary side? One argument perceived the war as a step in the direction of Italian national unity and the liberation of Italian territory from foreign rule—a precursor to and signal for similar movements on the part of the Hungarians, the Poles, and of course the Germans. The war was a blow against a reactionary Austria and its supporters among the German states, who represented, according to the radical émigré Ludwig Bamberger, "disunity and partition into petty states, darkness, Jesuitism, reaction and the whorish way of doing things of the patriarchal rule of the police." But it was equally possible to understand the war as an act of imperialist aggression by the French emperor, and just the beginning of his conquests. Imitating his uncle, he would follow his march into Italy with one into Germany, so that an intervention in the war on Austria's side would be a revolutionary step against foreign invasion and toward German national unity. As Jacob Venedey, another radical émigré, put it: "Fight, bleed and prevail for a united Germany and you will bring the united German parliament home from the battlefield."[1] The debate over how to interpret the war raged furiously during the first half of 1859, among both the radical exiles and their counterparts at home, finally able to articulate their views openly as the era of reaction waned. German nationalists took both sides in the debate, but their common nationalism carried them in opposite political directions.

Marx and especially Engels had a very clear position in this controversy: they were ferociously anti-Napoleonic and called, in nationalist fashion, for a military intervention of the other German states on Austria's side. Engels articulated these ideas in a pamphlet, entitled *Po and Rhine*, written with Marx's endorsement, and published anonymously in Berlin. The pamphlet argued that the western regions of Germany, along the Rhine River, were the future object of Napoleonic aggression. Their best defense would be to defeat the emperor in northern Italy, on the Po River, before he even marched on the Rhine. Taking the Austrian side in the Northern Italian War meant opposing the national unification of Italy and endorsing the Habsburgs' oppressive rule over the northern end of the Italian peninsula, a painful position for Marx and Engels, who had vigorously supported the cause of Italian national unity during the 1848 Revolution. Engels, like other pro-Austrian and anti-French leftists, argued that support for Habsburg rule was just temporary; a future German revolutionary regime would liberate Italian national territory. Most of his pamphlet was taken up with the assertion that possession of territory in northern Italy was not necessary for German military security.[2]

This convoluted argument awkwardly aligned the revolutionary communists with the generally pro-Austrian conservatives and moderate liberals they despised. Marx's political spin on the situation was to assert that Napoleon III was acting as a tool of the czar. Revolutionaries demanding the dissolution of the Austrian Empire were just doing the Muscovites' bidding, since the latter would pick up the pieces of the former Habsburg realm and incorporate it into a Pan-Slavic empire.[3] As a result of the 1859 war, Marx intensified his own long-term hostility to Russia. He increased his collaboration with David Urquhart, appearing on the platform of anti-Russian meetings in London that Urquhart's followers organized. Marx even declared that he was part of "a war that we, together with the Urquhartites are fighting against Russia, Palmerston and Bonaparte, in which people of all parties and all walks of life are participating, in all the capitals of Europe, as far off as Constantinople. . . ."[4] Marx's hostility against Russia was a significant feature of all the forms of political action in which he was engaged, from 1859 until 1871, and in every single political position he took on the issues of the day.

STRONG OPINIONS HAD LITTLE value if they could not be heard, and the rapidly changing political situation in Europe made it urgent to be heard. "Germany's fate is hanging in the balance," Marx wrote to Engels in May 1859. "A moment may come, and very soon, when it will be of decisive importance that not only our enemies, but we ourselves, can express our opinions . . . in print."[5] In the three ensuing years, Marx made three separate attempts to bring his opinions before a wider German-language public. Each of these attempts was, ultimately, a failure, but in each case Marx recruited new allies and explored new options, which would come to fruition in the second half of the 1860s.

Just as Marx was sharing with Engels his opinions about the importance of getting their views in print, he was pursuing an opportunity to do so among the Germans living in London. In contrast to London's German businessmen, as well as Marx's old enemy Gottfried Kinkel, who took a pro-Prussian and anti-Austrian stance in 1859, the communist artisans of the Workers' Educational Association supported a newly founded left-wing weekly, *Das Volk*, in English, *The People*. Associated with this newspaper were a motley crew of exile intellectuals, including the anti-Prussian South German democrat Karl Blind, a onetime member of the Communist League; Bruno Bauer's younger brother Edgar, who doubled as a Danish police spy; and the leading member of Marx's circle of younger adherents, Wilhelm Liebknecht.

Liebknecht brought Marx the news in May 1859 that the newspaper was in financial difficulties, so that Marx could bring it under his control. Between May and August 1859, Marx threw himself into that effort. He and Engels published a series of articles in the paper. They all dealt with the war of 1859: the heroism of the Austrian forces, betrayed by their incompetent generals, the dangers to Germany posed by Napoleon III and the czar, and the inadequately nationalist policies of the Prussian government. Using his considerable journalistic and publishing experience, Marx set out to make *The People* a viable and successful enterprise, increasing its subscriptions, expanding its advertising, and straightening out its chaotic bookkeeping and general administration. There were new subscribers from more affluent circles, attracted by the articles on diplomacy and able to understand Marx's difficult literary style. The costs of improving the paper well outweighed additional subscription revenues, and unlike Marx's past journalistic ventures, no affluent stockholders or private assets (just some small sums Engels could contribute) made up for the initial losses, so that by the end of August 1859, *The People* had run out of money and had to cease publication.[6]

As much as the paper had been an abortive publishing venture, it did bring Marx back in touch with the German artisans in London and their Workers' Educational Association, for the first time since the controversies of the Communist League in the early 1850s. By the fall of 1859, Marx was giving lectures on economics and other topics in the association, a practice he continued through the 1860s.[7] These renewed contacts with the London German artisans would prove quite useful, especially after the founding of the International Working Men's Association in 1864.

THE MOST PROMINENT AND the harshest voice against Austria in the debate among German radical exiles belonged to Karl Vogt. A leading intellectual and scientific figure, professor of zoology at the University of Geneva, and soon to be one of the pioneering Darwinians of central Europe, Vogt had been a leader of the left in the German National Assembly during the 1848 Revolution. At the climax of the revolutionary confrontations in the spring of 1849, the radical rump of the Assembly, shortly before its dissolution, had appointed Vogt one of the "Regents of the Realm," making him member of a kind of revolutionary German national government-in-exile. In 1859, Vogt tacitly endorsed Napoleon III's aggressive war, and called on Prussia to act in Germany as Piedmont had in Italy. This drastic proposal, from a prominent revolutionary veteran, was enormously controversial, motivating both passionate supporters and angry opponents.[8]

Vogt's views were anathema to Marx, an extreme example of what he opposed and what he was trying to counter in *The People*. It was one of the authors connected with *The People*, Karl Blind, who informed Marx that Vogt was in the pay of the French emperor. These assertions then appeared in *The People*, and in an anonymous pamphlet, presumably written by Blind. Marx also informed Wilhelm Liebknecht about them, who repeated them in an article he wrote for the *Augsburg General News*.[9]

Marx was not prepared for Vogt's response. Besides disagreeing with Marx politically, Vogt disliked the man personally—a legacy of the 1848 Revolution, when Marx had repeatedly attacked him and his politics in the *New Rhineland News*, and Marx's associate, Wilhelm Wolff, had insulted Vogt and challenged him to a duel. Vogt sued the Augsburg newspaper for libel and defamation of character, and followed up his legal action with a pamphlet in which he set out to turn the tables on his accusers, focusing his fire on Marx. Rehashing controversies among the radical London exiles at the beginning of the 1850s, he accused Marx of being in the pay of the Austrian government, and of having betrayed radicals to the German political police. Going further, he claimed that Marx was the head of two secret societies, the *Bürsten-heimer*, the Brush House Crowd, and the *Schwefelbande*, or Brimstone Gang, that engaged in counterfeiting and extorted money from democratic exiles by threatening to turn them over to the police.

While the court dismissed Vogt's legal actions on a technicality, the first edition of his pamphlet sold out almost immediately. His charges were reprinted, among many other places, in Berlin's *National News*, and in London's leading mass-circulation newspaper, the *Daily Telegraph*. A parody of the Brimstone Gang even made an appearance as a float in the 1860 Breslau Mardi Gras parade. The radical German exiles in London promptly disavowed Marx. Blind denied having ever told Marx his suspicions about Vogt or having written the pamphlet against him. Much more painfully, the poet Ferdinand Freiligrath, by far the best known member of Marx's circle, refused to support Marx either publicly or privately. In a personal meeting, Marx lost his temper and shouted at his onetime colleague. Although a modicum of politeness was restored in their relations, their friendship and political collaboration was at an end.[10]

In this increasingly difficult situation, Marx resolved to take the offensive by imitating his enemy's tactics, writing a pamphlet denouncing Vogt as an agent of the French emperor and suing the *National News* in Berlin for libel and defamation of character. Most of Marx's time in 1860 was taken up gathering evidence and preparing for legal action. Spinning out an enormous web of correspondence, he devoted hours of writing to produce his counterblast, the pamphlet entitled *Herr Vogt*, which appeared in print in November 1860.[11]

Marx biographers, impatient with their hero to finish *Capital*, tend to regard the whole concentration on Vogt as at best a bizarre, largely pointless obsession, and at worst an example of a tendency to blow up minor personal slights into major points of political principle.[12] Marx was touchy about his personal honor—although that was the rule rather than the exception among the middle and upper classes of nineteenth-century Europe—but such an interpretation ignores his own personal history and the political surroundings that influenced his decisions.

Vogt's accusations seemed to return Marx to the abyss of the early 1850s, when the vast majority of German political refugees in London despised him and circulated hateful stories about him. Marx tried to keep the whole matter hidden from Jenny, fearing the effect of recalling that time of extreme poverty, political and social isolation, and the death of their children. She proved, however, to be more resilient than her husband thought. When she found out about the charges brought against Karl, she responded with outrage rather than dismay, denouncing the "baseness, common crudity and cowardliness" of her husband's enemies, and of his friends who would not stand up for him.[13]

Besides past traumas, current political controversies were also motivating Marx. The attack on Vogt was an intervention in the political debate raging among German leftists over the appropriate relationship of a revived nationalist movement to the military and diplomatic initiatives of Napoleon III. Karl Blind had informed Marx of his suspicions about Vogt, while both Blind and Marx were sitting on the platform at a meeting of David Urquhart's followers devoted to denouncing the Northern Italian War of 1859 as a result of Russian machinations. In attacking Vogt, Marx was aiming at the German radicals who proposed to join in or get a free ride off a Franco-Russian alliance against Austria.[14]

Marx was also envisaging a future of political upheaval in continental Europe, in which he hoped to play an important role, all impossible if he was personally compromised by Vogt's attacks. His decision to elevate his differences with Vogt into a public feud was only taken after consultations with Engels and Wilhelm Wolff. At first, they told Marx to ignore Vogt and concentrate on political economy, but then both men agreed with Marx that the strife with Vogt had become a "party matter" rather than a personal one. Leaving the charges unanswered would make future socialist political initiatives impossible.[15]

Marx's campaign against Vogt was less than successful. His legal actions were doomed from the start. As his Berlin political contact informed him, Prussian judges were not concerned with the personal honor of a radical subversive: the courts refused to allow Marx to open proceedings against Vogt, a decision confirmed after repeated appeals.[16] The anti-Vogt pamphlet did appear, and it is one of the distinctly non-canonical works of Marx. Rather like *The Secret Diplomatic History of the Eighteenth Century*, it is passed over in silence, or gets at best a brief embarrassed mention.

Herr Vogt is certainly not a great theoretical work. It suffers from two of Marx's chronic literary problems: his distinctly academic tendency to go on at length, gathering material and not writing it up (both Engels and Jenny were painfully aware of this), and his inability to restrain himself when engaging in political polemics.[17] The fury of the personal attacks in the pamphlet is reminiscent of the unpublished "Great Men of Exile" from the early 1850s. Yet *Herr Vogt* is quite revealing of Marx's position at a critical period of nineteenth-century European history.

Based on a mass of evidence he had collected from his correspondence, Marx vigorously refuted Vogt's charges. The Brush House Crowd, he pointed out, was the name of a group of left-wing German artisans living in Switzerland, who had taken Willich and Schapper's side in their fight with Marx and Engels for control of the Communist League. The Brimstone Gang was a group of mostly student radical refugees from the 1848 Revolution, also based in Switzerland. Their name was an ironic reference to their future in hell as a result of the atheistic views they expressed in the taverns they frequented. Their actual connections to Marx were tenuous: Wilhelm Liebknecht had been a member, but before he met Marx. Engels, living in 1849 as a refugee in Switzerland, occasionally joined the group's gatherings. He was a welcome guest, since he paid for the drinks.[18]

After clearing up these and related charges, Marx turned to more recent politics, lighting into Vogt's plans for a European revolutionary alliance that would join German nationalists, Prussia, France, and Russia against the Austrian Empire. After denouncing the idea of revolutionaries cooperating with Russia, Marx emphasized Vogt's perception of Louis Napoleon Bonaparte as an ally of German nationalists. He pointed out that Napoleon III would insist on annexing German territory on the left bank of the Rhine River as compensation for supporting ostensibly nationalist pro-Prussian and anti-Austrian initiatives. Vogt's unwillingness to accept the obvious consequence of his ideas was, according to Marx, evidence that Vogt was a paid agent of Napoleon III.

This argument, that a united German nation-state under Prussian leadership was only possible through the cession of territories to France and Russia, was a typical polemical point of pro-Austrian authors in the debate on the Northern Italian War. Where Marx differed was by placing his polemic in a broader global context, which is most apparent in the key chapter of the book, obscurely titled "Dâ-Dâ Vogt." The original Dâ-Dâ was an Algerian author, a supporter of French colonial rule, because Napoleon III would sponsor the creation of a united Arab nation-state. Vogt's proposals, Marx argued, were basically the same, with the Germans in the place of the Arabs. In this comparison, Marx, unlike his later followers, did not perceive imperialism as an economically driven relationship between capitalist European countries and pre-capitalist Asian or African ones. Instead, he described both the African Dâ-Dâ and the German Vogt as tools of a French imperialism that preyed alike on pre-capitalist North Africa and the capitalist and industrialized Rhineland.[19]

Herr Vogt might well be compared to Marx's other anti-Napoleonic polemic, *The Eighteenth Brumaire*. The latter's long-term influence was much greater; it has become a canonical text of Marxism, while the former has languished in obscurity. Yet at the time of their publication, it was *Herr Vogt* that was the more influential and better read work. To be sure, in the battle for public opinion between the living Herr Vogt and the pamphlet *Herr Vogt*, the former was the clear winner. But Marx's polemics were something of a secret tip, known to readers who shared the suspicion—which circulated fairly widely in left-wing circles—that Vogt was in Louis Napoleon's pay. And Vogt indeed was. After the overthrow of the emperor in 1870, the new republican government in France published his secret correspondence and accounts, which included a hefty payment of 50,000 francs to Vogt in 1859. Marx took a good deal of pleasure in seeing his suspicions confirmed.[20]

Marx's efforts against Vogt—not so much the pamphlet itself as the extensive correspondence he conducted in preparation for it—brought him new political allies. A major supporter was the veteran German revolutionary Johann Philipp Becker, who had been attempting to overthrow the established central European order since 1830. Another adherent was Viktor Schily, a democratic émigré in Paris, and, like Marx, a native Rhinelander. Marx also recruited Sigismund Borkheim, a London merchant, and former member of the Brimstone Gang. All three shared Marx's suspicions of Vogt as well as Marx's hostility against Napoleon and Russia, and his disdain for the Prussian king-dom.[21] The ties forged in Marx's campaign against Vogt would remain after 1864 and the founding of the International Working Men's Asso-ciation, when these men became important supporters of Marx's efforts to increase the group's influence on the labor movement in Europe.

IN THE COLUMNS OF *The People* and the pages of *Herr Vogt*, Marx's voice was strident but its resonance was weak. As Engels pointed out to his friend at the beginning of the Vogt affair: "we have seen more than once that an émigré newspaper or a German brochure printed in London can only conquer a public presence in Germany, if the mat-ter can be kept going for at least a year. It is impossible to be directly present in Germany, in political or polemical terms on behalf of our party." Quite aware of this problem, Marx had toyed with some des-perate solutions, including sending, under a pseudonym, articles to the *New Prussian News*—the voice of the extreme right-wing, Evangelical conservatives in Prussia—denouncing the pro-Vogt refugee democrats in London.[22]

Marx balked at remaining the perpetual spectator, especially as conditions in Prussia were changing rapidly, making radical political activity once again possible. Speculations about a political amnesty were circulating, and it was announced almost immediately after the death of Prussia's mentally incapacitated Friedrich Wilhelm IV in January 1861.[23] Refugees could now contemplate returning to a Prus-sia very different from the authoritarian kingdom of the reaction era. The former regent, on the death of his royal brother Wilhelm I, had appointed moderately liberal government ministers. Democrats and more militant liberals from the Revolution of 1848 joined together to form a new political party, the "Party of Progress." Closely tied to the Party of Progress was the National Association, a league of liberals and democrats across central Europe that called for the union of the

German states under Prussian leadership—a proposal Marx despised, but one whose public articulation had previously been prohibited. The Party of Progress did well in elections to the Prussian parliament in 1861 and 1862—a little too well perhaps, because its parliamentary representatives soon clashed with the monarch and his top generals, leading to a four-year-long period of political upheaval known as the Conflict Era. Ultimately, this confrontation between the monarch and his parliament would make the fortune of Otto von Bismarck, appointed Prussia's prime minister in 1862; but at times the kingdom seemed on the brink of revolution. Only how was Marx to become involved? His political base in Cologne that had served him so well for a decade was gone, dispelled by the Cologne Communist Trial. His supporters were scattered or had joined the Party of Progress.[24]

Marx's remaining options in Germany were closely linked with Ferdinand Lassalle. Born to a middle-class Jewish family in Breslau in 1825, the always controversial Lassalle had been a fiery leftist agitator in the Rhenish city of Düsseldorf during the 1848 Revolution. He was part of the circle of Marx supporters—the "party of the *New Rhineland News*," as contemporaries said—and correspondent for the newspaper, which also reported in detail on his agitation and many clashes with the Prussian authorities. Following the suppression of the revolutionary movement in 1849, Lassalle neither emigrated nor went to jail, unlike Marx's other political associates, but remained an isolated outpost of radicalism on the Rhine River—"the only one left," as he wrote to Marx in 1855—trying to hold the fort in an increasingly repressive environment.[25]

That same year, he moved to Berlin, a daring and confrontational step, because it was unclear if the police would let such a known subversive reside there. After a protracted struggle, he was able to gain a residence permit, thanks to his personal connections with Alexander von Humboldt, the famous naturalist and philosopher, an elderly savant who was both a sympathizer with left-wing ideas and a friend of the reactionary Friedrich Wilhelm IV. Lassalle used his stay in Berlin to publish a lengthy study of the ancient Greek philosopher Heraclitus, a work that appeared to considerable scholarly acclaim, and made him a well-known figure in the intellectual and avant-garde circles of the Prussian capital.

It was Lassalle who arranged for Marx to be a correspondent for the *New Oder News* in Breslau, and later *The Press* in Vienna, both journals edited by Lassalle's cousin. Lassalle found a Berlin publisher for Marx's *Toward a Critique of Political Economy*, the first result of Marx's decades-long studies in economics, and for Engels's *Po and Rhine*. Marx consulted Lassalle closely on political issues in Prussia, and on his lawsuit against Karl Vogt. Lassalle raised much of the funds needed for the publication of *Herr Vogt*. He even lent Marx money when the latter found himself characteristically short and Engels was unable to help.[26]

By the beginning of the 1860s, it was clear that Marx's main artery to renewed German political activity ran through Lassalle. But this route had its own distinct problems. Unlike most of Marx's associates, Lassalle would not defer to Marx's intellectual authority. He wanted to be an independent thinker and radical theorist: a philosopher producing his own interpretation of Hegel, an economist, and a political strategist. During the early 1850s, when Marx's followers in Cologne asked for guidance on the future shape of European politics and the possibilities of a new revolutionary upheaval, Lassalle had proferred his own opinions instead of requesting advice.[27]

The political divergence of the two men was particularly evident at the time of the Northern Italian War. Lassalle's opinions put him in the Karl Vogt camp: he saw Austria as the main opponent of revolutionary movements in Europe. His own pamphlet, *The Italian War and the Task of Prussia*, rejected the rescue of Austria in northern Italy in the name of German nationalism. Instead, Lassalle wanted the Prussians to prove their nationalist credentials by imitating Napoleon III. Lassalle advocated sending the Prussian army north to seize from Denmark the duchies of Schleswig and Holstein, with their mostly ethnically German population, a major issue of national unity left over from the Revolution of 1848. In a lengthy correspondence with Marx, he rejected the latter's analysis and vigorously defended his own position, including a belief in Karl Vogt's bona fides, as well as a skepticism about seeing the hand of the czar behind diplomatic and military confrontations.[28]

Two truly prophetic letters, written at the time of the Battle of Solferino, appeared in this correspondence. Lassalle informed Marx and Engels about the perverse effects of their call for a national war against France. Berlin newspapers, he asserted, were promoting "rotten hatred of France." They were injecting their "passion, through the nationalist veins into the heart of the lowest class of the population and among democrats." The press's attacks were only ostensibly aimed at Louis Napoleon; their real target was the "revolutionary development of France." As refugees, Marx and Engels were out of touch with public opinion and unaware of "how little de-monarchized our people is." Most Prussians, Lassalle thought, rejected radical republican ideas in favor of loyalty to the ruling dynasty. A national war with France would only tie the Hohenzollerns' subjects more closely to their royal masters. Lassalle's vision would come frighteningly true in 1870. Eleven years earlier, it marked out profound differences between him and Marx and Engels. All three men were supporters of German nationalism, and all sought to link German nationalism to a revolutionary cause; but the way they did so was almost diametrically opposite—a disagreement on crucial issues of the time that made political cooperation difficult.[29]

Beyond policy differences there was the matter of Lassalle's personality and private life. Flamboyant, egocentric, and self-dramatizing, he was a profoundly polarizing figure. The Cologne communists did not trust him and refused to admit him to the secret Communist League in 1850. They rebuked his self-centeredness—"big-mouth and egotist," was one comment about him—and feared that he was a police spy. The fact that he was not indicted in the Cologne Communist Trial, unlike all of Marx's other friends and associates, only increased these suspicions. Stories of how Lassalle showed off his silk dressing gown and lavish apartment to the workers reached Marx during the reaction era. Marx's informants were motivated by jealousy of Lassalle and personal hostility to him, but that did not make their stories false.[30]

The most polarizing aspect of Lassalle's life was his relationship with women, especially with Sophie Countess von Hatzfeldt, who had been trapped into marriage to an abusive husband. During the 1840s, Lassalle had come to her rescue, residing with her, managing her divorce trial, systematically mobilizing public support against her husband, and even arranging to steal incriminating documents from him. His assistance had brought her into left-wing circles, where she was known simply as "the Countess," for there were no other pro-communist aristocratic women with whom she could be confused. During the 1848 Revolution, Marx had lent her money; he and Lassalle had protected her son Paul, years later one of Bismarck's top diplomats, from his father's wrath and claims to custody. Heinrich Bürgers, another Cologne communist, was the teenage boy's private tutor. In 1853, the Countess won her divorce case. She received a very large settlement, and provided Lassalle with a generous portion of it. It was enough for him to have all the silk dressing gowns and beautifully furnished apartments he might wish, and to pursue his intellectual and political career without having to worry about money, a fortunate condition Marx could only aspire to in his dreams. A good part of the hostility Lassalle invoked stemmed from his unconventional private life. It was unclear what was worse—that he was a gigolo, living off the assets of an affluent older woman, or that (his actual relationship with the Countess) he was not a gigolo, that he lived with and off an affluent older woman without providing her any sexual favors.[31]

In March 1860, Lassalle invited Marx to come to Berlin, as soon as an amnesty was issued, to discuss with him founding a radical newspaper, a continuation in new political circumstances of the *New Rhineland*

News; and he renewed the offer ten months later, with the proclamation of the amnesty.[32] Marx was profoundly torn by this opportunity to rejoin the fray, to raise his voice and have it heard in a critical situation, once more to have the opportunity to engage in the form of political activity he knew best, that of the crusading newspaper editor. It would require, though, close cooperation with Lassalle—a person with whom Marx had crucial disagreements, and whom Marx, like most leftists, did not entirely trust. Marx's personal attitude toward Lassalle emerges in his correspondence with Engels. The two used a fantastic array of anti-Semitic invectives to describe the controversial activist. He was "the little Yid Braun," "Itzig," "Jacob the Weasel," "Isidor Berlin Blue Dye." The letters have a particularly ugly ring, but also suggest how Marx and Engels saw Lassalle's personal faults in terms of anti-Semitic stereotypes: the vulgar, pushy parvenu parading in his silk dressing gowns, his vanity, impudence, and tactlessness on display.[33]

For all his personal antipathy to Lassalle, Marx could not reject his offer out of hand; it was the only apparent opening for his return to political activism. But future plans were interrupted by a grave family crisis. In November 1860, Jenny came down with smallpox. The three daughters were hustled out of the house, sent to stay with Wilhelm Liebknecht's family, and hastily revaccinated. Karl and Lenchen cared for the gravely ill Jenny around the clock, until Engels sent £10 so Karl could hire a nurse to relieve them. Although his letters to Engels about Jenny's illness are Stoic and laconic, as befitted his classical education, even the slightest reading between the lines suggests that Karl was beside himself at the thought of losing his wife, and unable to contemplate a future without her after their quarter century together. He tried desperately to take his mind off the horrible prospect by reading Darwin's *On the Origin of Species* and taking up the study of calculus. By New Years Eve 1861, it was clear that Jenny would survive, although facial scars from the illness remained visible for years.[34]

With his wife's health improved and his daughters back in the house, Marx returned to the idea of a voyage to Berlin. He had an additional incentive to explore becoming a German newspaper editor again: in February 1861, the publishers of the *New York Tribune*, consumed by the impending Civil War on native soil, suspended the services of their European correspondents.[35] Marx was now without his chief source of income; the modest sums he received as correspondent of the Viennese newspaper could not compensate. Becoming a Prussian newspaper editor was a prospect that was both politically and personally engaging.

MARX LEFT LONDON ON the last day of February 1861. He journeyed first to the Netherlands, to speak with his Dutch relatives about yet another advance on his mother's inheritance. Following almost three weeks of negotiations, he received £160 to help settle his debts. Traveling on to Berlin, there were no problems crossing the Prussian border. (Marx feared he might be arrested, in spite of the amnesty.) After an all-night train trip, pleasant enough "save for a 6½ hours delay at Oberhausen, a tedious little place," he arrived in the Prussian capital at 7 a.m. on March 18, the thirteenth anniversary of the barricade fighting of 1848.

Lassalle rolled out the red carpet for his guest. There were elaborate dinners, with prominent guests, including the elderly General von Pfuel, who as prime minister during the 1848 Revolution had defied the king's orders to carry out a *coup d'état*. Marx found the eighty-two-year-old soldier still intellectually vigorous, radicalized in his old age, and regarded by the court as an atheist and a Jacobin. Lassalle engaged in a little provocation of that court by taking Marx to the opera and seating the notorious subversive right next to the royal loge. Marx found the performance, a three-hour ballet, extremely tedious, but was very impressed with the scenery—"everything being represented with photographical truth." Lassalle's publicity-seeking made its mark, and the official government newspaper, the *Prussian News*, reported on the "return to the fatherland" of the onetime revolutionary. What the newspaper did not report was that the onetime revolutionary, in investigating political circumstances, especially the likelihood of a clash between the liberal bourgeoisie and the monarch, and between civilians and the army, perceived good preconditions for a future revolution. Marx bargained hard in Berlin with Lassalle and the Countess about the conditions for starting a radical newspaper.[36]

But the trip was not all business. He left Berlin for the Rhineland, saw old friends in Cologne, newer ones in the Wupper Valley, and then traveled on to Trier, visiting his mother for the first time in about fifteen years. During most of the 1850s, the two had only communicated via the Dutch relatives, and then only about Karl's demands for an advance on his inheritance. Marx's sister Emilie, the one sibling remaining at home with Henriette, had married in 1859, at a quite advanced age, just short of her thirty-seventh birthday. Marx derisively called her husband, Johann Jacob Conradi, the "Prussian NCO." He was actually a Prussian government official, an engineer, specializing in flood control and river navigation. Henriette had moved in with Emilie and her husband. Karl had written to his mother to say that he suspected the couple of having designs on her estate, after which she refused to consider any more possibilities of an advance on the inheritance and, for a while, broke off all contact with her son.

These were not the best circumstances for a visit, but it all went off surprisingly well. Tactfully renouncing any discussion of property, Karl spent his two days in Trier catching up on family matters. He seems to have enjoyed the company of his brother-in-law (at least to judge by the friendly letters Conradi later wrote him) and found his mother little changed in her basic attitudes, but elderly and enfeebled. His comment to Lassalle about the visit, that what "interested me in the old lady was her very fine spirit and the unshakeable consistency of her character," was rather a backhanded compliment, but at least lacking the hostility with which he had referred to his mother for decades. Helping to mellow Marx's feelings was that Henriette "took the intiative" in financial matters, without his prompting, and tore up the IOUs he had written to her for advances on his inheritance, thus increasing his future claims on her estate.[37]

Personal and political business successfully accomplished, Marx returned to England in May 1861, with a proposal for a Berlin newspaper to begin publishing that fall. Engels came down to London toward the end of May; he and Marx spent three days discussing the proposal but ultimately rejecting the idea. There were personal considerations—not so much for Marx himself, but for the people around him. His daughters were extremely unwilling to move. "The thought of leaving the land of their Shakespeare," their mother wrote to Engels, "is terrible to them; they have become English through and through. . . ." Jenny herself had "little yearning for the fatherland, the 'precious,' beloved faithful Germany," as she wrote sarcastically. Sarcasm aside, she did not want her two older daughters, now young women of sixteen and seventeen years of age, anywhere near the libertine circles in which Lassalle and the Countess moved. And Engels, without whom Marx would not undertake the journalistic enterprise, did not wish to leave his commercial position and place his own hard-won financial security at risk.[38]

Another major issue was Marx's lost Prussian citizenship. Without it, he could be expelled from the country at any time, as had already happened in 1849. While in Berlin, he started renaturalization proceedings. Lassalle, who continued these negotiations for Marx after the latter's return to London, grew increasingly frustrated with the authorities' stalling; he repeatedly barged into the offices of the Berlin police commissioner and the Prussian minister of the interior demanding explanations, but never got a straight answer to his inquiries. Count von Zedlitz, the police commissioner, did tell Lassalle that insofar as he had anything to do with the matter, no one of republican opinions like Marx could ever become a Prussian citizen.[39]

These were all weighty difficulties, but they paled before the issue of working with Lassalle. He insisted that he and Marx act as co-editors-in-chief of the prospective newspaper, with an equal voice in editorial policy. When Marx asked about Engels's position, Lassalle replied that if he wanted to have three editors-in-chief, that was fine, but Marx and Engels together could only have one vote, so that Lassalle could not be outvoted by them. This exchange underscored the problem: the newspaper would be Lassalle's enterprise, with money raised from his Berlin friends and acquaintances, or received from the Countess. Marx would not be in charge and would all too likely end up playing second fiddle.[40]

The discussions contined in July 1862, when Lassalle paid Marx a visit in London, staying for three weeks. There were pleasant moments, such as an excursion to Windsor Castle and the ensuing picnic, with Lassalle, Marx's family, and Lothar Bucher—another democratic refugee, soon to become a secret agent of Bismarck—but the visit was largely a personal and political disaster. Lassalle flaunted his money, spending £1 per day on cigars and cab fare, grating to Marx, who smoked foul-smelling cheap stogies and went everywhere on foot. Lassalle's proposal to help the Marxes out financially by taking Jenny to Berlin as a companion to the Countess may have been well meaning but it infuriated Jenny's parents, who feared for their daughter's virtue if she were anywhere near the Countess and her friends, much less living with her. Almost two decades later, long after Lassalle's death, the women of the Marx family were still furious with him. After Lassalle consumed, all by himself, a roast that Lenchen had been planning to serve to the whole family, the maid informed her master that the visitor was a "vain, dishonest lad," not to be trusted. In a political discussion, probably relating to Napoleon III, Lassalle shouted so loud that the neighbors came by to ask if everything was all right.[41]

The decision not to pursue the idea of a Berlin newspaper was a renunciation of Marx's belief, held since the beginning of his exile in 1849, that he would one day return to Germany and resume his radical political activity. Exile in England had become comfortable and familiar, too much so for a risky new venture in central Europe. The question was whether this refusal to return was a broader rejection of political activism. Marx continued to work intensively on his treatise on political economy, but the question remained: would he be content with the role of a radical scholar, or would he seek out some other venue of political activism?

FOLLOWING THE FINAL COLLAPSE of the Berlin newspaper project, Marx had no clear path to any of his political goals. He could only watch and grumble privately to Engels as others took the initiative, while persistent financial difficulties and mounting health problems increasingly dominated his life. Marx's experiences between the summer of 1862 and the summer of 1864 were painfully reminiscent of his earliest years in exile.

The new financial problems stemmed from a very simple source: he had no regular income. A brief re-engagement for the *New York Tribune* ended in late 1861, followed shortly thereafter by the departure of Marx's patron, Charles Anderson Dana, from the newspaper. The arrangements with *The Press* in Vienna, never very lucrative, survived the *Tribune*'s termination of Marx's services by just eight months.[42] Even when he had a regular income, it only sufficed to service his debts, and once that income disappeared, his situation deteriorated very quickly. He wrote to Engels on June 18, 1862:

> It is very revolting to me to discuss with you once more my poverty, but what can be done? My wife says to me every day, she wishes that she and the children lay in the grave and I really cannot hold

it against her, because the humiliations, tortures and terrors that are to be borne in this situation are, in fact, indescribable. . . . As you know from your own experience, there are the existing running expenses that must be paid in cash. That occurred by re-consigning items to the pawnshop at the end of April. But this source has been so exhausted that a week ago my wife made the vain attempt to take some of my books. I am so sorry for the poor children, as this is all occurring in the exhibition [1862 London World Exhibition] season, when their acquaintances are having a good time, and they have to go through terrors, so that no one visits them and sees through our filthy circumstances.[43]

It all seemed like a cruel reprise of the early 1850s. Jenny suffered new humiliations when she tried to put off creditors. Unable to keep up appearances, the family could not see any visitors. One of the most painful debts was for a piano that had been purchased on installments for their daughters. Economizing by canceling their piano lessons paradoxically made matters worse. The piano teacher had not yet been paid, and terminating his services meant receiving and paying his bill. Of course, alongside these debts were ones for more basic items: rent, gas, and the "baker, tea grocer, greengrocer as all those devil's things are called."[44]

So serious were these setbacks that by the fall of 1862 the philosopher and political agitator for the first time in his life sought a position in business. The job appears to have been arranged by Marx's Dutch cousin August Philips, who had commercial and personal ties with the director of a London-based railway. While visiting England on business in the summer of 1862, Philips had mentioned Marx to his business friend and encouraged his cousin to apply for the job. Supposedly, Marx was turned down for his bad handwriting—which was execrable—although there might well have been more to the story. (The episode is poorly documented.) The attempted assistance was one of many examples of the concern of the Philips family, quite successful capitalists, for their errant communist relative.[45]

Marx was once again forced to borrow from friends and acquaintances. Engels, his chief source of funds, had to borrow money himself, a result of the crisis in the textile industry stemming from the Civil War and the loss of the chief supply of cotton. As Marx pressed his friend continuously for money, the latter grew steadily more irritated. The situation came to a boil in January 1863, when Marx, who would have been starting at the railroad then, had his employment plans worked out, responded to a letter from Engels reporting the death of his mistress Mary Burns with a renewed request for money. Engels was furious, and the friendship between the two men reached a nadir, not seen since their disputes in Brussels in 1845. Both retreated from the brink and apologized, but Marx's finances remained untenable.[46]

In the end, he was temporarily saved by two inheritances. One, long awaited, was from his mother, who died on November 30, 1863. Seriously ill with the skin disease that plagued him at the time, Marx rose from his sickbed, and, taking two gigantic bottles of medicine with him, journeyed to Trier. He spent ten days there but accomplished little, because the estate was in probate, so he gave his brother-in-law a power of attorney, another sign that Marx had renounced his former suspicions of his sister's husband. Henriette's death did not fundamentally change her son's attitude toward her. His letter to Jenny from Trier was quite sentimental, but only in reminiscing about their adolescence and young love. Mentions of his mother in that letter, and in others to Engels, were all about business—mostly derogatory references to his mother's carelessness with the paperwork connected to her testaments, and the drunken incompetence of the notary who had advised her. There was just one odd remark: the observation that Henriette had died exactly forty-nine years, to the day and hour, after her marriage to Heinrich Marx, "as she had foreseen." It was not the way a rationalist, a man of *Wissenschaft*, would view the world. This reference to Henriette's psychic abilities, which lacks the scorn with which Marx usually treated his mother's foibles, was just the faintest sign that the reconciliation between the property-obsessed mother and her errant son, begun with his visit in 1861, had made some progress. Thanks to Henriette's destruction of his IOUs, when the will was finally probated and the Dutch relatives paid out Marx's share of her estate, he received 7,000 Dutch gulden, or about £580.

Unlike the long-awaited inheritance from his mother, the second was quite unexpected. Marx's close friend and political ally Wilhelm Wolff passed away in his Manchester exile on May 9, 1864, leaving Marx some £700, the bulk of his assets. The influx of funds enabled Marx to pay off his debts and the family to move into a new, larger, and more luxurious house (each of the daughters had her own room) at 1 Modena Villas, on Maitland Park Road in North London. Biographers wag their fingers at this aggressive spending when the financial future was so insecure, but even a more careful husbanding of the two windfalls would not have resolved the basic problem of the lack of a steady income. Further financial difficulties, at least, were put off for a few years.[47]

Even worse than Marx's financial problems was the sudden and dramatic detorioration of his health. Toward the end of October 1863, a growth had developed on his back, eventually reaching the size of a fist, so that he could no longer stand upright but had to move around all bent over. After a month of home remedies to avoid the expense of a doctor's visit, the family physician was finally summoned. He told Jenny to leave the room, and, with Lenchen holding Karl down, took out his scalpel and cut through the growth, releasing a flood of blood and pus.[48]

This was the beginning of the period (there may have been one brief earlier episode in the 1850s) when Marx had to deal with his notorious carbuncles—repeated growths on his back, thighs, buttocks, and genitals that plagued him for the rest of his life. The latest medical opinion is that the illness was *Hidradenitis suppurativa*, an autoimmune disorder, whose effects are similar to acne, but on a much larger scale—fist-sized growths, not small pimples, destruction of the outer layer of skin, not just redness and scarring. The disease is painful, disfiguring, and even today very difficult to treat. In Marx's time, there was nothing helpful that could be done. The chief remedy he used, strongly promoted by Engels and his physician, was to take arsenic, a Victorian-era "wonder drug." Its only effect was to poison him. At one point, frustrated by the inability of doctors to cure him, Marx took a straight razor and cut through one of the growths himself; it was a minor miracle that he did not get infected and die.

Stress generally worsens the effects of disease, and Marx surely had more than enough stress. After years of seeing the recurring growths, Jenny came to the conclusion, supported by Engels, that overwork, late hours, and inadequate exercise were aggravating her husband's condition. Their preferred remedy was for him to take more time off and not work so hard, but that made it even less likely that he could play an active political role.[49]

This was doubly frustrating because upheavals in European and world politics between 1862 and 1864 called for revolutionary intervention. To Marx and Engels, the most important, albeit the most distant, was the American Civil War. Their sympathies were fully with the North and the anti-slavery cause, although Engels, powerfully impressed by the military capabilities of southern generals—he saw Stonewall Jackson as "by far the best guy in America"—despaired, at times, of the Union's chances. Marx found his friend's opinions "determined a little too much by the military aspect of the thing," and not taking into account the long-run significance of the North's economic and demographic superiority. These would need to be brought to bear, Marx thought, by a revolutionary war—and the campaigns of the Union Army came closer to Marx's ideal of a revolutionary war than any armed conflict in his lifetime.[50]

Nearer to home was the 1863 Polish uprising against Russian rule, which enjoyed very widespread left-wing sympathies. Marx and Engels joined in the chorus for Poland and Marx began writing an essay on the insurrection, whose potential victory he described as the "annihilation of today's Russia," or at least the termination of its "candidacy for world domination." Only the malevolent power of the czar defeated the insurgents, with some assistance from the Prussian government—yet another proof, for Marx, of its reactionary policies, and its hostility to Polish and German nationalism. Both Marx and Engels blamed the defeat of the uprising on the refusal of its aristocratic leaders to adopt measures of revolutionary war, in this respect not up to the standards of Lincoln, Grant, and Sherman. Instead of mobilizing the Polish peasants, they pinned their hopes on the dubious prospect of intervention by Napoleon III.[51]

Still closer to Marx were the conflicts and controversies in Germany. The struggle between the Party of Progress deputies in the Prussian parliament and the government led by Bismarck became steadily more virulent, as the parliamentarians refused to approve the budget, leading Bismarck to order the illegal collection of taxes and attempt to suppress opposition newspapers and to arrest opposition leaders. In his most optimistic moments, Marx thought a revolution in Prussia was in the offing, an armed conflict between the liberal bourgeoisie and the authoritarian government.

Shaping this judgment was Marx's opinion of Bismarck. Like most contemporaries, he saw the Prussian prime minister as an ultra-reactionary, born-again Christian conservative, who shared the former Friedrich Wilhelm IV's endorsement of the society of orders and anti-constitutional, monarchical rule. Bismarck had in fact begun his political career in that way. During the Revolution of 1848, he expressed his extreme reactionary opinions in such a provocative fashion that even the king, who never shied away from public provocation, was a little appalled. But the burly, balding Prussian statesman had changed his views during the era of reaction. He had come to understand that repression was not enough, that he would have to win over public opinion by endorsing German nationalism. Bismarck did so by taking up a radical and nationalist cause dating back to the Revolution of 1848. In 1864, he launched a war pitting all the German states, including the great powers Prussia and Austria, against Denmark over the northern duchies of Schleswig and Holstein. Marx and Engels saw the quick victory of the German states' forces over a badly outnumbered Danish army, followed by an international peace conference to decide the status of the disputed territory, largely in terms of the counterrevolutionary connection of the Prussian government to Russia. They were sarcastic about the idea that a Prussian government could represent German nationalism. Their cynicism was not shared by much of central European public opinion.[52]

Most striking to Marx were the actions of Ferdinand Lassalle. In mid-1863, Lassalle founded a labor party, the General German Workers' Association. During the following year, he traveled all across central Europe in an enormous campaign of agitation and association, organizing local branches of the group, and promoting his platform of the introduction of democratic suffrage, to be followed by state credit for workers' production cooperatives. The self-glorifying activist put himself at the center of these campaigns, making dramatic entrances into cities where he spoke. On one famous occasion, he even allowed the workers to unhitch the horses from his carriage and pull it in themselves.

Lassalle was establishing an independent workers' political voice; in doing so, he was withering in his condemnation of the Party of Progress as cowardly and inactive bourgeois democrats. Both aspects of his agitation were very congenial to Marx and Engels, corresponding to political goals they had been following since 1849. On the other hand, the self-dramatization and self-glorification of Lassalle's activities seemed to magnify the worst features of his personality; Marx promoted Lassalle in his disdain from "Itzig" to "Baron Itzig." The attacks on the Party of Progress for its inability to deal with Bismarck increasingly shaded into praise for the latter, as Lassalle weighed the possibility of rejecting the long-term affiliation of the labor movement with democratic and republican ideas in favor of support of the Prussian monarchy. Rumors flew—later proven true—that the labor agitator was secretly meeting with the conservative prime minister, offering to combine forces against the Party of Progress. Here, once again, was the awkward choice Marx had confronted in 1848–49, between opposing an authoritarian Prussian government, which meant organizing across class boundaries, and organizing an independent working-class movement, which would not necessarily be hostile to Prussia.

Marx was well acquainted with Lassalle's activities, and the political issues they raised, receiving reports from Wilhelm Liebknecht, who had returned from exile to Berlin in 1862. Engels especially, and other associates as well, wanted Marx to come out with a forthright statement condemning Lassalle for having gotten far too close to the Prussian authorities. In private, Marx was scathing about Lassalle, yet he refused to make any public statements about him and his labor party. Marx might have learned the lesson of his past disputes with rivals, from Karl Grün to Karl Vogt, and decided that polemical exchanges with fellow socialists and radicals were a losing affair. Or perhaps, in view of his financial difficulties and worsening health, Marx was in no position to challenge Lassalle's leadership, and so, once again, found himself condemned to political passivity.[53]

THE TWO-YEAR PERIOD of political passivity and involvement with personal problems came to an abrupt end in September 1864 because of two largely accidental events. One was the result of Ferdinand Lassalle's final act of self-dramatization. He fell in love with the daughter of a high Bavarian state official, and following a frustrated courtship, challenged her fiancé to a duel; he was shot to death in Switzerland on the last day of August 1864. It all strongly resembled a soap opera, but as a result the General German Workers' Association was lacking a president. The Countess and others in Germany turned to Marx. Marx refused, pointing out that he was not a Prussian citizen and so could easily be expelled from the country. But he remained involved in the affairs of the group and its planned newspaper—the first daily socialist paper in Germany, the *Social Democrat*, which started appearing in Berlin at the beginning of 1865.[54]

Although Marx's involvement with the German labor movement thus began accidentally, it was a logical consequence of his past as a radical revolutionary, the chief surviving leader of the Communist League, and Lassalle's mentor and theoretical inspiration. Marx's second political initiative in September 1864, eventually rendering him an internationally known figure, was even more fortuitous. It emerged from a public meeting at St. Martin's Hall in London on September 28, 1864, sponsored by British trade unions and French workers' associations, held for the purpose of supporting the cause of Polish independence from Russian rule.

One of the French organizers, "a certain Le Lubez," approached Marx and asked him if he could find a German worker in London to speak at the meeting. Marx suggested Johann Georg Eccarius, a tailor and a member of the German Workers' Educational Association, who had taken Marx's side in the past factional battles of the Communist League. Marx himself sat on the platform at the meeting, without speaking, as he had done at similar anti-Russian meetings organized by David Urquhart. It has never been entirely clear why Victor Le Lubez approached Marx, since Le Lubez was a follower of Proudhon, with whom Marx had clashed vigorously in the past. Perhaps it was Marx's own long political history of anti-Russian and pro-Polish attitudes that made him an appropriate contact; or possibly it was his action a few years earlier in organizing financial assistance, with the help of the Countess, for the veteran French revolutionary Louis-Auguste Blanqui.[55]

Whatever the reason for the invitation, it had far-reaching consequences, since at the meeting participants decided to found an organization, the International Working Men's Association, that would sponsor an international labor congress in Brussels the following year. The organizing committee appointed a subcommittee to draw up statutes that co-opted Marx as a member. He attended meetings sporadically because of health problems, until Eccarius let him know that the proceedings were dominated by followers of Giuseppe Mazzini, the democratic but very anti-communist Italian nationalist, whom Marx regarded with contempt. The feeling was mutual.

Marx invited committee members to his new house to work on the statutes. The meeting on Maitland Park Road went on until 1 a.m., and adjourned in exhaustion. Marx then drafted his own version of the statutes and an "Address to the Working Class," later known as the "Inaugural Address," a manifesto for the new organization—measures which the organizing committee approved unanimously on November 1, 1864.[56]

By the end of that year, Marx had found the focus for political activism he had been seeking since 1859. It did mean a departure from his previous activity as a newspaper editor, a change of which Marx was very much aware. Writing to Joseph Weydemeyer, his old friend now living in St. Louis, he remarked, "Although I have systematically refused, for years to participate in all 'organizations,' this time I accepted, because it involves a matter where it is possible to have an important effect."[57] The center of the "International Association" was in London, so that Marx could guide the group's development in person and seek to put its provisional organization on a permanent and secure footing. At the same time, he would try to get his friends and supporters in Germany to affiliate the nascent labor movement there with the association. This was a task buffeted by personal rivalries, factional quarrels, strong differences of political opinion, and, especially, by the rising tide of nationalism and great power warfare. With all its difficulties, it would absorb Marx's energies and satisfy his desire for activism until the Franco-Prussian War of 1870–71 and the Paris Commune of 1871 brought the entire post-1859 period of European history to an end.

THE INTERNATIONAL WORKING MEN'S ASSOCIATION (IWMA for short) is generally known as the "First International," a retrospective designation after the founding of the "Second" or Socialist International of 1889, which still exists today, and the "Third" or Communist International of 1919, officially dissolved in 1943. But understanding the IWMA in light of future developments obscures its contemporary context and especially Marx's role in the organization. Unlike the two later groups, which were international leagues of Socialist or Communist parties, the IWMA was a loose federation of affiliated workers' societies. Twenty-three English trade unions, with upward of 25,000 members, were the backbone of the group. On the Continent, trade unions were either illegal or barely organized; Continental affiliates were primarily workers' mutual benefit and educational societies, as well as ill-defined, often semi-conspiratorial groups. The Continental affiliated societies, to the extent legally possible, were grouped together into national sections that would correspond with a central office in London, known as the General Council.[58]

Unlike its two successors, the IWMA did not have an "internationalist" political orientation as opposed to a "nationalist" one. Quite the opposite, it was formed at a meeting in support of a popular nationalist cause, Polish independence from Russia. Marx himself did not understand the International Association as an anti-nationalist group. He specifically rejected the idea of turning the IWMA into a "central government . . . of the European working class," a plan he attributed to his despised rival Mazzini. When some French members of the General Council proclaimed that nations no longer existed, Marx replied ironically, and to the considerable delight of the Englishmen in attendance, "that our friend Lafargue etc., who has abolished nationalities, spoke to us in French, i.e., a language that ⁹⁄₁₀ [of] the auditorium did not understand."[59]

Marx's plans for the association appeared in his agenda for the First Congress of the IWMA, held in Geneva in the summer of 1866, after the Belgian government blocked the original plans for a congress in its country. The items for action included the advocacy of social reform—a shorter workday, limitations on women and children's labor, the replacement of indirect with direct taxation, an international inquiry into workplace conditions—and the endorsement of producers' cooperatives and trade unions. There were just two expressly political points, both taken from the arsenal of nineteenth-century radicalism: the replacement of standing armies with militias; and "the necessity of annihilating the Muscovite influence on Europe . . . [via] the reconstitution of Poland on a social and democratic basis."[60]

The most effective actions of the IWMA, with the greatest public resonance and working-class support, centered on labor disputes. The International raised funds from unionists across Europe to support the strike of Berlin printers and typesetters in 1865, Paris bronze workers in 1867, and Geneva construction workers in 1868. In a particularly well known action, its members convinced German artisans not to be recruited as strikebreakers during the London tailors' strike of 1866. This intervention to prevent workers of one nationality from breaking strikes in another country was repeated on a large number of occasions and may well have been the most popular of the IWMA's actions, and the chief source of its working-class support.[61] Marx personally emphasized the effectiveness of union action against skeptics who advocated the formation of producers' cooperatives, and asserted that unions could not succeed in increasing workers' wages. His essay

"Value, Price and Profit," a popular exposition of economic ideas he was preparing for publication in *Capital*, was read to the General Council in June 1865, precisely in order to refute these socialist but anti-union positions.[62]

Unions, or any other kind of working-class organization, could only succeed in a favorable political environment, all too often lacking in 1860s Europe. Marx vigorously endorsed campaigns for a more democratic franchise, in the hopes of increasing workers' parliamentary representation. He was particularly proud of the prominent role of the English leaders of the IWMA in the newly founded Reform League that advocated universal manhood suffrage for Great Britain. The League's agitation and the general turmoil and upheaval in British political life of the mid-1860s were enormously encouraging to Marx, who at times saw the emergence of a revolutionary situation. The actual upshot of this political contention, the expansion of the franchise in the Second Reform Bill of 1867, was rather a disappointment, but he still hoped for the outbreak of a revolution, perhaps beginning in Ireland.[63]

For all Marx's revolutionary aspirations, the chief political opposition in the IWMA came precisely from revolutionaries within its ranks, members of secret societies, who saw infiltrating the IWMA as a step toward fomenting European-wide insurrections. French secret society revolutionaries repeatedly denounced the working-class activists who had helped create the International Association as paid agents of Napoleon III, or, at least, as being unwilling to challenge the emperor's authoritarian rule and openly advocate a republic. Marx's efforts to mediate between the two groups, via his friend Viktor Schily, the German political émigré living in Paris, were rejected by both sides. When the two French factions argued their differences before the General Council, its English members concluded that the French really needed an authoritarian ruler like Napoleon III to keep them in line! Ultimately, most of the secret society members left the IWMA, although they maintained a foothold in an affiliated society of French émigrés in

London, repeatedly attacking Marx and his political positions. They presented themselves as internationalists, and denounced Marx's support of anti-Russian and Polish nationalism as reactionary and containing a suspicious hint of German nationalism.[64]

By contrast, Marx's chief supporters and loyal allies in the IWMA were the English trade unionists, who were in no sense revolutionaries or socialists. In view of this alliance, one must wonder whether Marx was guiding the International in the direction of revolution or reform. Marx felt that supporting union organization, and pressing for more democratic governments and greater social reforms, would spur on the clash between workers and capitalists, leading, as the *Communist Manifesto* suggested, to a revolutionary outcome. This connection between reform and revolution came into question in the socialist movement at the very end of the nineteenth century. Adherents of reform of capitalism as an end in itself clashed bitterly with proponents of revolutionary action leading to a socialist regime. The reformists were dubbed "revisionists," people who were revising Marx's doctrines of revolution. But the question of reform versus revolution was inherent in Marx's own political strategy of the 1860s; the IWMA and the political situation of the era did not last long enough to bring this dilemma to the fore.

Marx himself had a modest role in the IWMA. He was one of twenty to twenty-five members of the General Council and the corresponding secretary for Germany. When offered the presidency of the General Council in 1866, he rejected it, stating that the position should be filled by a worker. Shortly thereafter he proposed, successfully, to abolish the office of president of the General Council altogether. Yet for all Marx's reticence, he was, as he himself asserted, "in fact the head of the whole business."[65] He preferred to exert his "influence behind the curtains," drafting documents, making proposals at sessions of the General Council, and holding formal and informal meetings in his London house.[66] It was through such meetings that Marx's second daughter Laura met and became engaged to a member of the General

Council, Paul Lafargue (the same Lafargue whom Marx had rebuked for believing nationalities did not exist), a French student activist who had to flee the country for his opposition to Napoleon III's rule.[67]

Since Marx was at his best in small groups, working behind the scenes was the most effective way to exert his influence. It was also compatible with the weeks and months when repeated outbreaks of his skin disease kept him out of action altogether. The primary problem Marx saw during his guidance of the IWMA was the organization's annual general congresses: Geneva in 1866, Lausanne in 1867, Brussels in 1868, and Basel in 1869. Given the informal procedures for affiliation with the IWMA, pretty much anyone could show up; since the congresses were held on the Continent, Marx's English supporters often did not attend, as was the case with Marx himself, who only attended one general congress in 1872. Voting arrangements for the delegates were ad hoc and decided at the individual congresses. Outcomes were unpredictable, and Marx tended to fear the worst. He always heaved a sigh of relief when the congresses were over.[68]

TRYING TO GUIDE A post-Lassalle German labor movement from a remote location proved considerably more difficult than guiding the policies of the IWMA. The problems began with the legacy of Lassalle himself. In public, Marx was very generous to the memory of his friend. He wrote the Countess that Lassalle had "died young in triumph, like Achilles," a remark she promptly publicized. Marx also issued public statements attacking anti-communist democrats—"these petit-bourgeois canaille" and the "cowardly impudence of the bourgeois newspapers"—who were denouncing Lassalle as overly pro-Prussian. Even in private, both Marx and Engels praised Lassalle as one of their old comrades from 1848, who had the courage to act on behalf of the working class.[69]

No verbal blandishment, however fulsome, could suppress the legacy of Lassalle's passion for Prussia. After his death, reports surfaced that Lassalle had been planning a bizarre political coup. He intended to travel to Hamburg to proclaim the duchies of Schleswig and Holstein annexed to Prussia in the name of the labor movement, once more aligning himself with the policies of Prime Minister Bismarck. To the extent that Lassalle's successors continued and endorsed his policies in favor of Prussia, Marx would find it hard to work with them.[70]

The sticking point was the refusal of the competing leaders of the General German Workers' Association to affiliate with the International. This difficulty is often interpreted as a conflict between nationalism and internationalism. The philosopher Isaiah Berlin, in an often-cited but not very accurate biography of Marx, even described Lassalle as a precursor of the Fascists.[71] Such a description of the difficulties that Marx had with Lassalle is a fundamental misrepresentation of the situation in the 1860s. Marx himself was not totally opposed to German nationalism. Rather, his particular version of nationalism was, as it had been since the 1840s, strongly anti-Prussian. The Prussian monarchy, for Marx, was a lackey of the czar, an ally of the French emperor Napoleon III, and an enemy of the creation of a united German nation-state.

As late as 1869, Marx let the French revolutionary Louis-Auguste Blanqui know that German national unity "could only be achieved by a German revolution that would sweep away the Prussian dynasty, which was a servant of the Muscovite, still is and always will be."[72] This version of nationalism contrasted with the one endorsed by Lassalle and his followers, who perceived the Prussian monarchy as the vehicle for German national unity—a difference of opinion that had been debated in Germany at least since the Northern Italian War of 1859. In the end, when the German nation-state was created under Bismarck's guidance by the Prussian monarchy, the anti-Prussian version of German nationalism became obsolete; but in the mid-1860s such an outcome was by no means a foregone conclusion.

It was these differences of opinion and the related question of whether to work with Bismarck's conservative Prussian government against the liberal and bourgeois opposition that made cooperation between Marx and the German labor party so difficult. "Red Becker," Marx's old Cologne ally and rival, by the 1860s a member of the Party of Progress, posed the point openly in the press: how could Marx and Engels, two men known for their anti-Prussian revolutionary past, continue to support a group that was so solicitous of Bismarck's authoritarian regime? Mixed in with these political differences were personal antagonisms. The contenders for the role of Lassalle's successor—including the Countess; Johann Baptist von Schweitzer, editor of the Berlin socialist newspaper; and Bernhard Becker, Lassalle's former assistant and Lassalle's own choice—suspected that Marx was trying to use affiliation with the IWMA to gain control of the General German Workers' Association. Such suspicions were encouraged by old rivals of Marx, like Moses Hess, who had been a follower of Lassalle. As Paris correspondent for the *Social Democrat*, Hess sent in anti-Marx articles, or at least pieces Marx interpreted as attacks on him. Bernhard Becker, during a speech given in Hamburg in March 1865, asserted that Marx's party consisted of all of three people: the "Master," Marx; his "secretary," Engels; and his "agent," Wilhelm Liebknecht.[73] The contrast between someone leading an organization with thousands of members and an exiled theorist with dubious claims to political leadership was evident in this insult.

In view of these cross-currents, it is remarkable that Marx even briefly agreed to cooperate with Schweitzer, who was, in Marx's perceptive estimate, the most intelligent and best qualified of Lassalle's potential successors. Marx and Engels wrote a few articles for the *Social Democrat*, and Schweitzer, who had a high opinion of Marx, repeatedly attempted to mollify him about articles in the newspaper that Marx found objectionable. Schweitzer's efforts, running from the end of 1864 through February 1865, seem to have paid off, and Marx continued to agree to work with him. It was not Marx who broke off the connection, but his political representative on the spot in Berlin, Wilhelm Liebknecht, who did so, denouncing Schweitzer to Marx as just a tool of Bismarck.[74]

By the end of February 1865, far from getting the labor movement in Germany to affiliate with the International, Marx had terminated his ties with it, leaving him with two alternatives. One was his associate Liebknecht, expelled from Berlin by the Prussian authorities for encouraging the labor movement to oppose Bismarck's conservative government. Liebknecht moved to Leipzig, in the Kingdom of Saxony, where officials of the conservative but pro-Austrian Saxon government welcomed him, and granted him a residence permit. Liebknecht set out to organize an anti-Prussian labor movement. Marx could also rely on one of the friends he had gained in his campaign against Karl Vogt, the veteran revolutionary Johann Philipp Becker. A thorough enthusiast for the IWMA, Becker, from his residence in Geneva, organized a section of German-speaking Swiss; workers' associations in the German states could affiliate with the International through his Swiss group. Initiated into left-wing politics in the age of secret societies, Becker never lost his enthusiasm for revolutionary conspiracy, which made him an awkward ally for Marx, given the latter's opposition to conspiratorial groups in the IWMA. Still, Becker and his organization were, for the next three years, the only way for German workers' societies to affiliate with the International, giving Marx, as the corresponding secretary for Germany, someone with whom he could correspond.[75]

ALL THESE ORGANIZATIONAL ARRANGEMENTS Marx had painfully devised were for him ultimately the means to revolutionary upheaval. The five turbulent years of 1866–71 were an age of upheaval, the climax of the era of European history begun with the Northern Italian War of 1859. Mass politics and political confrontations took on a dimension they had not reached since the Revolution of 1848. Even in the relatively peaceful United Kingdom, enormous demonstrations for a more democratic franchise in England led to the Second Reform Act, while anti-English nationalist agitation in Ireland mounted steadily. Things were still more turbulent on the Continent: a rising tide of anti-Napoleonic, pro-republican meetings and demonstrations in France, a coup and new nationalist government in Romania, a revolution in Spain, uprisings in southern Italy, nationalist mass meetings in the Austrian Empire. A wave of strikes across the Continent accompanied this political turmoil, creating an atmosphere in which the International could advance its cause. The period was also marked by two shattering wars, between Prussia and Austria in 1866, and between Prussia and France four years later. These wars unleashed nationalist furies; revolutionized, in a peculiarly Bismarckian way, the German states; upended the balance of power; and led to the proclamation of a republic in France and a short-lived revolutionary regime in Paris. Navigating these waters proved far more treacherous for the International, eventually calling into question the underlying basis of Marx's activism.

The upheaval began with Bismarck, who launched a diplomatic campaign in the spring of 1866 that led to a war between Prussia and Austria in June of that year. Bismarck demanded the abolition of the German Confederation, the league of central European states created by the Congress of Vienna. In its place, he wanted a united German nation-state, including a German parliament elected by universal manhood suffrage. Contemporaries found it hard to believe that the conservative prime minister would make such demands, since they were an endorsement of the radical, nationalist program of the revolutionaries of 1848. They feared that a war between Prussia and Austria arising from Bismarck's initiative would enable Napoleon III to seize German territory on the Rhine. Almost all the smaller German states took Austria's side in the diplomatic confrontations and ensuing war. Marx and Engels shared their contemporaries' doubts and fears, mocked

Bismarck's nationalist credentials, and saw his policy as dictated by Russia in allegiance with Louis Napoleon's France. They expected a Prussian defeat in the war and hoped that it might lead to a revolutionary situation—although both were doubtful that the Berliners would have the courage to rise up against Prussian rule.

In a military campaign that astonished Europe, Prussia's outnumbered but better armed and led troops scored a decisive victory over Austria and its allies in just six weeks, so quickly that Louis Napoleon had no time to mobilize his army. Even Engels, Marx's military expert, was profoundly impressed. No less astonishing, Bismarck carried out his revolutionary proposals. He abolished the German Confederation, annexed into Prussia a number of German states that had fought on Austria's side, and united this expanded Prussia with the smaller states of northern Germany into a new North German Confederation (in spite of its name more a federal state than a Confederation) with a *Reichstag*, or parliament, elected by universal manhood suffrage. Nationalists and former revolutionaries of 1848, along with members of the Party of Progress and the National Association, rallied to the Prussian statesman who had carried out their ideas as they themselves could not.[76]

There was an effort to bring Marx into these ranks. Already in the fall of 1865, one of Bismarck's agents, Lothar Bucher, another 1848 revolutionary involved in the revival of the labor movement (Lassalle had named him executor of his will), offered Marx employment as a financial columnist for the official Prussian gazette, the *State-Advertiser*. Marx, informed by Wilhelm Liebknecht of Bucher's change of political allegiance, rejected the proposal. In April 1867, when Marx was visiting his German friend Dr. Kugelmann in Hanover after bringing the manuscript of the first volume of *Capital* to his publisher in Hamburg, the pro-governmental forces tried again, inviting Marx to a meeting with Rudolf von Bennigsen, the head of the National Association, one of the most prominent liberal nationalists to go over to Bismarck.

The meeting was arranged by Bennigsen's close associate Johannes Miquel, a onetime member of the clandestine Communist League, whom Marx had regarded as one of his most promising followers. It is unclear whether Marx actually met with Bennigsen, but he certainly was not prepared to follow Lassalle in endorsing Prussian policies in the name of German nationalism.[77]

While Marx and Engels were unwilling to join the crowd of revolutionaries entering the camp of the Prussian prime minister, they recognized a fait accompli when they saw one: "one must take the garbage as it is," Marx wrote. Rather than denouncing Germany's new political circumstances, they thought the labor movement should exploit them, particularly the democratic franchise in elections to its Reichstag.[78] Wilhelm Liebknecht certainly saw things in this way. Teaming up with a young woodworker named August Bebel, then at the beginning of a political career that would transform him into the patriarchal head of the German labor movement by 1900, Liebknecht turned to the federation of German workers' educational societies, and wrested the leadership of this group away from the liberals who had founded it. Liebknecht and Bebel both ran for the North German Reichstag, and both were elected by constituencies in Saxony. Marx was quite impressed with the way these two leftists could get things done in parliament even though they were so outvoted. He was particularly impressed by Liebknecht's amendment to the law abolishing the guilds and instituting freedom of movement. It stated that nothing in the law overruled previously existing Prussian legislation limiting children's working hours, and secured almost unanimous support from the distinctly non-socialist deputies.[79]

But there was a problem with Liebknecht, as far as Marx was concerned, particularly his combination of labor agitation and radical politics. Liebknecht had been elected to the Reichstag on the ticket of the People's Party, a South German, democratic (Marx and Engels said "petit-bourgeois"), anti-Prussian political movement, not as a workers' candidate. In his public speeches and in the *Democratic Weekly*, the People's Party newspaper he edited, he stated that labor concerns would have to take a backseat to political issues, the struggle for democracy and against authoritarian Prussian rule. Liebknecht even supported the cause of the monarchs, the king of Hanover and the prince of Hessen, deposed by the Prussians after the 1866 war. Such rulers, in Marx's view, were just outdated reactionaries, whose departure from the scene was hardly regrettable.[80]

The Lassalleans, on the other hand, had no hesitations about denouncing bourgeois and petit-bourgeois democrats while proclaiming the organization of the working class as their prime political task. Johann Baptist von Schweitzer, after writing to Marx to praise him as the "head of the European labor movement," printed in 1869 a twelve-part series in the *Social Democrat* about Marx's newly published *Capital*, the most publicity the work had ever received. But Marx's earlier differences with the policies of the General German Workers' Association, particularly the group's tacit support for authoritarian Prussisan rule, did not vanish in the new political environment.[81]

Marx and Engels viewed the competition between the two labor movements in terms of the personal failings of their leaders. Schweitzer, the chief Lassallean, was very "clever," but also a "scoundrel." Marx thought that Schweitzer did have one thing right: Wilhelm Liebknecht's "incompetence." "Little Wilhelm," as Marx and Engels liked to call him, "is getting stupider every day."[82] In making such derisive judgments, Marx was personalizing a dilemma of his long-term political strategy, evident since the 1840s: uniting anti-Prussian and anti-capitalist movements. In 1848–49, he had not been able to bring the two diverging forms of opposition together; twenty years later, they had become independent political parties. Marx blamed the personal shortcomings of their leaders for their inability to pursue jointly these divergent goals.

In his official capacity as IWMA corresponding secretary for Germany, Marx refused to take sides between the two German labor movements, to the considerable annoyance of Liebknecht, who kept calling on Marx to denounce the Lassalleans publicly. But for all Marx's refusal to take a public stand, for all the nasty remarks he made about Liebknecht in letters to Engels, and for all the positive comments he had about Schweitzer and the Lassalleans, there can be no doubt that Marx saw Liebknecht, Bebel, and their followers as the future of the German labor movement. The problems with them would be resolved, Marx thought, by their coming to see things his way; the solution he saw to the problems of the General German Workers' Association was that group's dissolution.[83]

Marx's hopes by the end of the 1860s did in fact seem on their way to realization. At a congress held in the Thuringian city of Eisenach in August 1869, Liebknecht's and Bebel's federated labor associations reorganized themselves as the Social Democratic Labor Party, and affiliated with the International Working Men's Association, thus breaking with members of the People's Party who could not accept the new group's socialist goals. Marx's critical comments to and about Liebknecht by no means came to an end, but in his evaluations of the progress of the labor movement across all of Europe he became increasingly positive about developments in Germany. He and Engels began to wonder if the priority they had always assigned to the workers of Paris was still valid, or if the Germans had now taken over a leading position in continental Europe.[84]

NOTHING IN THE NEW European circumstances following the war of 1866 changed Marx's commitment to the IWMA, and his extended efforts on its behalf. At times, though, repeatedly tormented by his skin disease and overwhelmed by recurring financial difficulties, he seems to have been weighing an escape from his commitments. Marx's proposal to move the General Council of the International

Association from London to Geneva, thus taking the group's operations out of his hands—an idea he floated to Engels in August 1868,
and repeated in a similar way a year later—certainly sounds like that.
In the end, his commitments to the International continued unbroken.[85]
At the very least, a major reversal of his family's finances at the end of
the decade helped to make this decision easier.

By 1866–67, Marx had run through the inheritances he had received
a few years earlier; the recurring family financial crises, complete with
debts, medical expenses, disputes with his wife, and increasingly desperate pleas to Engels, had come to the fore again. Following a couple
of years of the usual temporary expedients, a new inheritance, received
not by Marx but by Engels, finally provided a permanent resolution.
When Friedrich Engels, Sr., passed away in 1861, Friedrich Engels's
siblings, deeply suspicious of their communist brother, decided his portion of their father's estate would not include any share of the family
textile manufacturing business in Germany. Instead, the family money
invested in the firm of Ermen & Engels in Manchester, for which Engels
had worked as a clerk since 1850, would be used to secure Friedrich a
partnership in the business.[86]

Engels feared that he was being cut out of the family's property
and pawned off with the dubious promise of a partnership, but he did
become a partner in Ermen & Engels in 1864. Five years later, he sold
his interest in the firm to the Ermen brothers, taking out the value of
the partnership, plus an additional sum for signing a non-competition
agreement, although the communist businessman had no intention of
opening a competing enterprise; he wanted to retire and devote himself
to the politics of the labor movement. The settlement he received meant
that even after paying off his family, not only could he live from the
interest but he also had enough money to settle Marx's debts. In addition, he was able to increase his largesse by paying Marx an annual
income of £350. Marx was "quite knocked down by your too great

generosity," which brought to an end three decades of chronic financial difficulties beginning with his father's death in 1838.[87]

At the time his money worries were put aside, Marx had two major concerns about the policies of the IWMA. One centered on the politics of Great Britain, the world's leading capitalist nation. The actual results of the expansion of the franchise in the Second Reform Act of 1867 had proven a disappointment: labor candidates, standing for office before a more democratic, more working-class electorate, had been trounced at the polls by moderate liberals or even Tories. Following closely Engels's reports on the elections in Manchester, Marx concluded that a major reason for this political debacle had been the hostility between English and Irish workers. The English despised and looked down on the Irish for what they saw as their alien religion and inferior colonial status. The solution to the problem, he thought, lay in an Irish revolution—a prospect enhanced by the rapid growth in the late 1860s of Irish nationalist agitation, after almost two decades in abeyance. An independent or at least autonomous Ireland would, Marx hoped, change the whole dynamics of working-class politics in England and throughout the entire world. He wrote in 1870: "After dealing for years with the Irish question, I have come to the conclusion that the decisive blow against the ruling classes in England (and this is decisive for the labor movement all over the world) can be dealt not in England but in Ireland." What Marx had in mind was an agrarian upheaval, in which Irish tenant farmers, keenly remembering the horrors of the Great Famine of 1846–51, would confiscate the property of the great landlords, who were members of the English aristocracy. Such a blow to the English aristocracy in Ireland would be a major step toward an English revolution. "I have always been convinced, that the social revolution must seriously begin from the ground up, that is from property in land."[88]

The central role of a socialist workers' uprising in Paris, key to

Marx's revolutionary expectations for the previous quarter century, was giving way to an emphasis on the radical potential of Irish nationalism and the organizational strengths of the German labor movement. Both new expectations raised questions about future dilemmas of the labor movement that would not become entirely evident until some decades after Marx's death. Unlike Engels with two Irish mistresses, or the Marx family's enthusiastic endorsement of Irish nationalism (little Jenny and the adolescent Eleanor were particularly passionate partisans), English workers competing with the Irish for jobs were less ebullient. The devoutly Catholic Irish workers were similarly less than enthralled with the political goals endorsed by Marx and his left-wing English allies, such as the campaigns of the Italian revolutionary Garibaldi to seize the territory of the Pope for a united Italian nation-state.[89] Marx's endorsement of Irish nationalism to revolutionize the English working class pointed to a future long-term problem of the labor movement: the obstacles that religious, national, and ethnic differences presented to working-class solidarity.

The other major issue faced by the International in the late 1860s was the relationship between Marx and the Russian anarchist Mikhail Bakunin. The struggle between the two men, which grew particularly embittered in the following decade and led to the demise of the International, has become part of the anarchists' political creed, pitting their ostensibly libertarian, decentralized, and anti-statist views against the authoritarian and state-centered perspective of the Marxists. This contrast, forged in the political confrontations between anarchists, socialists, and communists of the late nineteenth and early twentieth centuries, was not particularly evident in the 1860s. Marx's own views on a communist future, soon to be revealed in his writings on the Paris Commune, looked to a federalist and decentralized regime; Bakunin's insistence that his followers owed him unquestioning obedience does not seem entirely anti-authoritarian.

If there was an inevitable conflict between communists and anarchists, it certainly was not apparent in the relationship between Marx and Bakunin. The two had been friends as political émigrés in Paris during the 1840s, and had been on the same insurgent side during the Revolution of 1848. Following Bakunin's escape from Siberia and his return to Europe in the 1860s, he and Marx had renewed their acquaintance. Marx was quite impressed, writing to Engels in 1864 that Bakunin was "one of the few people who after 18 years has not gone backwards but has developed further." When Bakunin took up residence in Italy, Marx regarded him as a political ally, who would counteract the anti-communist ideas of Giuseppe Mazzini in the IWMA's Italian affiliates. Marx's favorable attitude toward Bakunin was particularly impressive in view of his long record of hostility and suspicion of Russia and all Russians.[90]

What caused the breach between the two was the question of secret societies. Bakunin, always a fan of such groups, had been attempting since 1864 to gather European socialist revolutionaries in a secret organization. In 1868 he tried again, with the creation of an International Alliance of Socialist Democracy, whose members included many Swiss activists in the IWMA, among them Marx's close ally Johann Philipp Becker, a long-term secret society enthusiast. It was Becker, not Bakunin, who proposed that the Alliance should join the IWMA as an affiliated society. But both Marx and Engels believed that Becker was only acting as Bakunin's puppet, the tool of Russian and Pan-Slavist intrigues. Marx quickly convinced the General Council of the IWMA to reject the idea of affiliation with another international organization, especially one organized on a clandestine basis. Bakunin agreed to the dissolution of his group and the entrance into the International of its national branches as ordinary affiliated sections, which duly occurred in 1869.[91]

Although the dispute seemed to have been amiably resolved, the differences in political orientation were not so easily put aside. Marx's opposition to the politics of secret societies and his determination to keep the IWMA clear of these organizations, previously focused on French radicals, now found a new source of enmity in Bakunin. The Russian émigré and his supporters were particularly active in Spain and southern Italy, parts of Europe where unions and workers' associations were few and far between, and the politics of secret societies were prevalent. Increasingly, Bakunin's followers became the IWMA in those countries. An initial clash between pro-Bakunin supporters of secret societies and anti-Bakunin proponents of the political line Marx endorsed in the General Council rocked the French Swiss affiliate of the IWMA in the spring of 1870. Amid accusations of manipulating mandates and packing meetings, each group expelled the other from the International. When Russian émigrés told Marx of Bakunin's close ties to Sergei Nechayev, the Russian secret society leader who had had a member of his group murdered to gain control of his assets—an incident famously portrayed in Dostoevsky's *The Possessed*—Marx became even more convinced of Bakunin's pernicious influence.[92]

The 1870 Congress of the IWMA seemed likely to bring a major clash with Bakunin and his followers, so Marx arranged to hold the meeting in Mainz, where Bakunin had little influence.[93] But the congress was never held, overtaken by the military confrontation between Prussia and France that had been widely expected ever since Prussia's victory over Austria in 1866. Marx and Engels had observed closely the rumors and expectations of war, as they did military and diplomatic matters more generally, and their speculations followed familiar channels: positively, the way that war might lead to revolution; negatively, the way it would increase the czar's power. By 1868–69, though, they decided that a war between France and Prussia was not in the offing.[94]

As a result, the actual outbreak of war in July 1870 was both unexpected and deplorable. Marx's daughter Jenny, writing to Dr. Kugelmann, described the family's "surprise and indignation at the turn affairs have taken. . . . The revival of chauvinism in the 19th century is indeed a hideous farce!"[95] As Jenny's comment suggests, she, like her father, saw the war as a case of French aggression. This viewpoint was common at the time, for contemporaries were unaware of the wily Bismarck's diplomatic strategies for pushing France into declaring war so that Prussia could fight it on the most favorable terms.

Bismarck hoped that Napoleon III's declaration of war would be met by a wave of nationalist indignation in Germany, rallying the entire nation behind the Prussian monarchy. His expectations were fully justified: in demonstrations, parades, sermons, newspaper editorials; in bars and taverns, on the streets, in the fields, and just about everywhere else, Germans rallied to Prussia's cause, even those defeated and occupied by Prussia a few years earlier. In a sign of just how well Bismarck had calculated, Marx and Engels joined the German nationalist ranks. "The French need a thrashing," Marx wrote to Engels at the outbreak of the war. Note it was the French who needed a thrashing, not just their emperor. Jenny von Westphalen, expressing her husband's views in starker and less sophisticated form, stated: "How they all deserve the Prussians' thrashing; for all the French, even the tiny little clump of the better ones, still have chauvinism stuck to the most distant corner of their hearts. Now, for once, it will be beaten out of them."

If Karl and Jenny's sentiments were expressed in private correspondence, Engels went public with his nationalist views. He took the lead in establishing a patriotic committee of Germans in Manchester that would raise funds to provide aid for wounded soldiers and became its secretary-treasurer. In his keynote address at the founding meeting, he proclaimed, in front of four hundred Manchester Germans, that the conflict was "in France a war of the government, in Germany a war of the people." It was not, he continued, "the first time that Germany had fought against her will for the sake of honour and independence." The *Elberfeld News* published a report on the unexpected patriotism of its subversive native son, to the utter astonishment and dismay of Wilhelm Liebknecht, who was trying to lead the Social Democratic Labor Party to condemn both the Prussians and the French as aggressors—that is, to take the viewpoint Marx and Engels had always adopted, until they were swept away in the wave of nationalism.[96]

Engels persisted in this view for weeks. His appreciation of the brilliant military strategy of Helmut von Moltke, the chief of the Prussian General Staff, or the daring of German soldiers—"prize lads"—in their bayonet charges against entrenched French positions, only reinforced his nationalism. Marx, though, was already beginning to have second thoughts. The nationalist war of 1870, he thought, like the nationalist uprising against Napoleon's rule in 1813, was taking on a distinctly reactionary political tone:

> "Jesus My Certainty" sung by Wilhelm I, with Bismarck on his right hand and Stieber [Marx's nemesis from the Cologne Communist Trial was chief of German military intelligence] on his left is the German Marseillaise! Just like 1812 and afterwards. The German Philistine seems to be positively enchanted by the chance to ventilate his inherent servility without embarrassment. Who would have imagined it possible that 22 years after 1848 a national war in German would possess such a theoretical expression![97]

FERDINAND LASSALLE'S WARNING LETTERS from 1859 about the pernicious political effects of a war against France had long been forgotten, and were lying somewhere in a pile of papers in Marx's cluttered study.

The statement of the IWMA on the war, written by Marx himself, shows something of this altered mood. It condemned Napoleon III for beginning the conflict, and described it as a defensive war on the part of the Germans, a point Marx insisted that Liebknecht, Bebel, and their followers endorse. But the statement also denounced the idea of a German war of conquest, pointed out that the Prussian government had cooperated closely with Louis Napoleon Bonaparte in the past, and warned, as might be expected from Marx, of the intrigues of the czar, lurking in the background.[98] These qualifications were only borne out by the further progress of the war.

The battles were one disaster after another until the defeat of the main French army at Sedan in September 1870, and the capture of the French emperor—making it crystal clear that he was no Napoleon, as his uncle had been. The sole alternative in France to despair was revolution: the republic was proclaimed in Paris, and the new government of national defense began a revolutionary war. Its leaders fled besieged Paris for the South of France to raise new armies; among those involved in the effort was Marx's son-in-law, Paul Lafargue, who settled, along with Laura and their child, in Bordeaux, to the evident relief of Laura's parents. As the French government became politically more acceptable to Marx, Bismarck adopted precisely the policy Marx had condemned, demanding the cession of Alsace and Lorraine.[99]

That same September, the retired Engels moved to London to join his friend, bringing to an end the extensive correspondence the two had maintained for the previous twenty years. Without the evidence of their letters, the change in their opinions toward the war is harder to track. At first, the proclamation of the republic made little difference: Marx suggested that the French members of the IWMA should remain passive and wait for a peace treaty before resuming political and social action. He denounced as "nonsense" the idea advocated by his French secret society opponents of proclaiming a revolutionary government or "Commune" in Paris. But even as early as mid-September, Marx and Engels were becoming uneasy about the war, provoked by the news that the Prussian government had arrested the leaders of the Social Democratic Labor Party. By the end of the year, they had renounced their previous nationalism and become partisans of the French Republic, asserting that if its new armies could only hold out long enough, British and Russian pressure would force the Prussians to conclude a compromise peace.[100]

This was also the calculation of the French government, but neither military successes nor the intervention of the other great powers (officially neutral, but sympathetic to the Prussians) was forthcoming, so it agreed to an armistice in January 1871. There remained the peculiar matter of a permanent peace treaty. With whom would Bismarck sign such a treaty? Neither the emperor, now a prisoner of war, nor the provisional government of the French Republic could claim the political legitimacy to do so. On Bismarck's insistence, during the armistice, elections were held for a French National Assembly that would have the sovereign authority to end the war. Duly held in February 1871, the elections resulted in a victory for the conservative monarchists, who favored making peace, even a peace of defeat. It was above all in Paris that pro-war radicals were victorious.

A majority of the inhabitants of the French capital were opposed to the newly elected National Assembly, even before it began meeting nearby in Versailles. On March 18, 1871, radicals proclaimed a new, revolutionary government in Paris, a "Commune," whose supporters were a broad political mixture of Jacobins in the mold of Robespierre, social democrats of the Revolution of 1848, socialists of various sorts, including activists of the IWMA, as well as a large group of patriots and supporters of the republic. Facing a hostile national government, surrounded by German troops, the Paris Commune, from the moment of its inception, was in a precarious position. It looked for allies where it could find them, including repeated appeals for support to the International Working Men's Association.[101]

Marx was personally in touch with the leaders of the Commune, mostly via a German merchant who made periodic business trips from London to Paris. The existing correspondence is sparse: just two letters, one of which is largely taken up with denouncing Marx's enemies in the IWMA, the secret society revolutionaries of the "French section" in London, who had rushed to Paris to participate in the revolution. In the other, written in mid-May 1871, toward the end of the Commune's existence as the national government in Versailles was getting ready to invade Paris, Marx suggested that his Parisian supporters send crucial documents to a "secure place," that is, London.

None of this implies a powerful commitment to the insurgent regime. In letters to Liebknecht and Kugelmann of April 1871, and retrospective ones to the English member of the General Council Edward Beesley in June 1871, and to Ferdinand Domela Nieuwenhius, a Dutch socialist, a decade later, Marx asserted that the Commune's leadership had, from the very beginning, missed the opportunity to take vigorous action. The Commune could have seized the assets of the Banque de France, sent the Paris National Guard to march on Versailles, or at least fortified the heights of Montmartre against an incursion of troops loyal to the national government. Such actions would have changed the balance of power between the Parisian insurgents and the national government, and promoted a negotiated settlement between them.[102]

Marx's cautious attitude toward the revolutionary regime in Paris also reflected differences within the IWMA itself. A number of the British trade unionists on the General Council, as was true with most left-wing opinion in England more generally, supported the government of the new French Republic, not the insurgent Commune in Paris. Ten days after the proclamation of the Commune, Marx volunteered in the General Council meeting to write an address on the topic for the IWMA; but he had nothing ready for the next two and a half months.

In the interval, while Marx was hesitating, the Commune's enemies were increasingly identifying it with the International in general and with Marx in particular. The Versailles government attributed the Commune to the subversive machinations of the International and its *chef*, Marx. Crudely forged documents, ostensibly demonstrating Marx's and the IWMA's role, were produced. Odd rumors, such as the claim that Marx was Bismarck's private secretary and was secretly manipulating the Commune in the interests of Prussia, were widely circulated in the French press, and made their way across the Channel. The denunciation of Marx and the IWMA reached a high point in June 1871, when the Versailles government sent troops to Paris to destroy its revolutionary opponent. Public opinion in England and the entire Western world was horrified by the actions of the beleaguered insurgents: sending armed women into battle against the French army, shooting the archbishop of Paris as a hostage, and burning buildings as a measure of military defense. All of these actions were attributed to communism, to the IWMA, and to Marx, "head of a vast conspiracy," according to the *Pall Mall Gazette*. Marx and Engels fired off letter after letter to the press, mostly to English and French newspapers, but also Italian, Austrian, and American ones, denouncing their coverage. Marx even threatened the editor of the *Pall Mall Gazette* with a duel if he did not retract his charges. In spite of this indignation, Marx enjoyed his notoriety, writing to Dr. Kugelmann that he was "the best calumniated and the most menaced man of London," and adding, "it truly does one good after a boring twenty-year-long swamp idyll."[103]

It was in this spirit that Marx finally produced his statement on the Commune for the IWMA, *The Civil War in France*. The piece is one of Marx's classic political polemics, beginning with a savage personal denunciation of the Versailles government: its head, the veteran liberal politician Adolphe Thiers, was "that monstrous gnome"; its foreign minister, Jules Favre, was "living in concubinage with the wife of a drunken resident in Algiers." It was not just the personal and moral failings of the Versailles government Marx denounced, but the combination of corruption and lack of patriotism: its members had acted in the fall of 1870 to sabotage the continued war against the Germans and later schemed to get a commission on the loan floated to pay the German war indemnity, but their commission could only be paid after the revolutionary government in Paris was suppressed.

Marx contrasted this corrupt government, combining bourgeois liberals like Thiers and reactionary, aristocratic, royalist backbenchers, with the revolutionary Paris Commune. A "majority" of its

members "were naturally working men . . . acknowledged representatives of the working class"; their government was dedicated to the
"Emancipation of Labour," to "the expropriation of the expropriators,"
to "Communism." Breaking with his long-term reluctance to speculate
on a communist future, Marx described the regime as "the glorious
harbinger of a new society." The entire centralized state administration
that had characterized France—with its bureaucracy, gendarmerie,
standing army, judiciary, and established church—would be abolished.
Sounding a lot like his anarchist rival Bakunin, Marx described a
communist future of decentralization and direct democracy. Public life
would be run by locally elected communes, federated across the territory of the nation. Elected officials would be bound by their voters' will,
and subject to immediate recall if their actions displeased their con-
stituents. Members of the Commune would only receive a workman's
wages, so that government would be cheap and taxes low—a proposal
of an older, pre-communist radicalism. In the first draft, Marx even
used the phrase "economical government" to describe the Commune, a
slogan of pro–free market English liberals and radicals. Separation of
church and state would be a feature of the new communist regime, as
would secular public education—two additional pre-communist radical
ideas, and aspects of the Commune strongly emphasized by its non-
communist English defenders.[104] With this government, the workers
could carry out the communist aim of "united co-operative societies . . .
regulat[ing] national production upon a common plan. . . ."

This representation of a communist future differed from Marx's
previous plans for communists to take over the existing state apparatus
and deploy it for revolutionary purposes. Engels had once even speculated on staffing the revolutionary government with commercial clerks,
who could do a more efficient job of governing than the legally educated state officials typical of the German bureaucracy.[105] The polemic
was certainly a break with attitudes Marx had held less than a year
previously at the outbreak of the Franco-Prussian War, when he had

called for a French defeat and explicitly denounced revolutionary action by French socialists, even calling the idea of a Paris Commune "nonsense." From the mid-1840s onward, Marx had seen a socialist uprising in Paris as the initial shot of a European and perhaps worldwide revolution, but by the late 1860s he no longer perceived Paris as the vanguard of socialism and the labor movement. His private skepticism about the Paris Commune seems more in line with the new attitude he had adopted than his public praise for the insurgent municipality.

Marx knew quite well at the time what most historians have since discovered, that the Paris Commune was no socialist government. The unpublished first draft of *The Civil War in France* went over the measures of the Commune systematically, finding just one that perhaps could be considered socialist, and noting that measures for the benefit of the middle class were at least as frequent and significant as those reserved for the workers.[106] It was the attacks on the Commune as a subversive communist regime, with the IWMA and Marx personally in the background pulling the strings, attacks begun by the Versailles government and spread by the press in England, across the Continent, and in the United States, that propelled Marx to identify the Commune with his communist future.

Praising the Paris Commune as the forerunner of a future communist society terminated Marx's patient seven-year-long effort at building up the IWMA. It meant breaking with the English trade unionists, Marx's allies and the basis of his authority in the General Council—allies Marx badly needed in his struggle against Bakunin and his followers, who had supported the republican national French government and rejected revolutionary insurrection. At best, Marx's political future was uncertain; at worst, his dramatic association with the Parisian insurgents would bring his period of political activism to an end. And one has to wonder if Marx's patience with his role in the International was wearing thin, if the pain and physical disability of his untreatable skin disease were making political action increasingly difficult for him. If so, the whole point of *The Civil War in France* was to preserve a glorious vision of communist revolution for a future in which he would no longer play a role. In that sense, the address on the Commune marked the beginning of the end of Marx's activism, of his attempts, as a veteran of the 1848 Revolution, to play a role in European politics during the period of war and upheaval begun in 1859.

PART III

Legacy

10

The Theorist

IN THE TWO DECADES between 1850 and 1870, Marx developed
the mature version of his philosophical, social, and economic theories.
When we think of such theories, we imagine a bearded scholar poring
for hours over tomes in the British Museum; but usually Marx's theoretical pursuits had to be crammed in beside far more time-consuming
activities: émigré politics, journalism, the IWMA, evading creditors,
and the serious or fatal illnesses that plagued his children and his wife,
and, after the onset of his skin disease in 1863, Marx himself. All too
often Marx's theoretical labors were interrupted for months at a time
or reserved for odd hours late at night.

Even without these detours, Marx always tended to work slowly
and revise constantly. He had difficulty getting the final version of his
thoughts down on paper, so it is no surprise that he never developed the
critiques of society and intellectual disciplines first planned in 1845.
The results of his theoretical deliberations are frustrating to interpret,
albeit for opposing reasons in different branches of knowledge. Marx's
writings after 1850 on philosophy, society, and history were fragmentary: snippets of journalism or suggestions from correspondence, relevant passages in political polemics, or economics treatises. In spite of

occasionally mentioned plans, he never produced an extensive theoretical work, which has led commentators and interpreters to focus their attention on his 1840s manuscripts—incomplete, but at least substantial. By contrast, the problem with the writings on economics is that there was too much. Two books were published in Marx's lifetime: *On the Critique of Political Economy* of 1859, and *Capital*, Volume One, of 1867. The latter, as anyone who has ever picked it up knows, is lengthy and dense. Besides the material that appeared in print, Marx left behind an enormous array of manuscripts on economics that Engels sorted through and edited into Volumes Two and Three of *Capital*. Further manuscripts on the history of political economy were later published as *Theories of Surplus Value*. But reducing the mass of handwritten manuscripts even to three thick books meant leaving out a large volume of unpublished writings, to say nothing of Marx's extensive notes on economics and the many discussions of economic questions in his correspondence.

For this intellectual labyrinth, simultaneously fragmentary and overwhelming, a useful guide is Ferdinand Lassalle's pithy description, written in 1851, of Marx as a thinker: "Ricardo become a socialist; Hegel become an economist."[1] At the very beginning of a two-decade period of theoretical contemplation and development, Marx's perceptive disciple had focused on two key themes. He was undisputedly a follower of Hegel, but what did it mean to be a Hegelian after 1850, when a new and distinctly non-Hegelian philosophy—that of positivism— was in the ascendant? This new development posed a problem not just for philosophy per se but for an understanding of human history and human society. The other point of Lassalle's remark was that Marx's understanding of economics was shaped by the ideas of David Ricardo, the great English political economist and chief disciple of Adam Smith. In the two decades after 1850, if not beyond, Marx would attempt to elaborate his version of Ricardo's deeply pessimistic view of the future of capitalist development. He would create from it a system of political economy demonstrating how a capitalist economy would, as a result of its own inner workings, give way to a socialist one. This was a difficult task in itself, but even more challenging because it took place in a very different time: not the crisis-ridden era of the early nineteenth century when industry came to England, but the twenty-five-year period of prosperity and accelerated economic growth following 1850. Marx's efforts to affirm his own version of the Hegelian legacy while incorporating the positivist intellectual trends of the time is the subject of this chapter; the creation of a communist version of Ricardo's political economy in a rather different era from that in which Ricardo lived and worked is the topic of the next.

POSITIVISM INITIALLY APPEARED AT the beginning of the nineteenth century, but it quickly advanced to a leading status in European intellectual and cultural life only after 1850. Positivists, and many contemporaries who did not use that term, saw human knowledge emerging from empirical perception of the world. Unlike the eighteenth-century empiricists, whose ideas were heavily criticized by Kant and Hegel, positivists understood empirical knowledge as a result of scientific procedures—experiment, organized data gathering, and mathematical analysis—rather than simple sense perception. At first, the physical sciences provided the model for positivist epistemology, but after Charles Darwin's *On the Origin of Species* appeared in 1859, evolutionary biology became a steadily more important template for the acquisition of knowledge. Contemporaries took these scientific models and applied them to every imaginable intellectual discipline, from anthropology and sociology to literary criticism; perceptions of human history were recast in terms of evolutionary stages of the advance of science.[2]

This development represented a particular problem for Marx. His socialism was *wissenschaftlich*, but the *Wissenschaft* he had in mind in making these claims was the Hegelian scholarship that he had joined at the University of Berlin and that was still intellectually dominant in the 1840s. The rise of positivism by the 1850s and 1860s was producing a very different form of *Wissenschaft*. Marx, who along with Engels followed scientific developments closely, was very much aware of this intellectual transformation. Could his theories continue to be *wissenschaftlich* while still being Hegelian, or would he jump on the positivist bandwagon as well?

For Marx's onetime comrades the Young Hegelians, the new intellectual trends were painfully apparent. Marx had little sympathy with their complaints. When Bruno Bauer visited Marx in London at the end of 1855, he observed, as Marx wrote with amusement to Engels, that "In Germany— horrible indeed!—nothing more is purchased and read than miserable compilations from the field of the natural sciences." A couple of years later, Arnold Ruge announced that he was planning a new version of the *German Yearbooks*. According to Marx, "Its main task is to be a struggle against materialism, in industry and the natural sciences, also against comparative linguistics, which is sprouting up everywhere, in short, against everything for which

---

COMMUNIST MANIFESTO (1848)

In proportion as the bourgeoisie, i.e., capital, is developed, in the same proportion is the proletariat, the modern working class, developed—a class of laborers, who only live as long as they find work, and only find work as long as their labor increases capital. These laborers, who sell themselves by the piece, are a commodity, like every other article of commerce, and are consequently exposed to all the vicissitudes of competition, to all the fluctuations of the market. . . . In proportion as the repulsiveness of the work increases, the wage therefore decreases. Nay more in proportion as the use of machinery and division of labor increases, in the same proportion the burden of toil also increases . . .

exact knowledge is necessary."[3] These remarks sound distinctly positivist, the attitudes of a man abandoning his own previous allegiance to Hegelian thought for a new worldview, based on the empirical findings of the sciences.

In his public pronouncements after 1850, Marx sounded a distinctly positivist note. If we juxtapose his description of the impoverishment of the working class in the *Communist Manifesto* with a similar examination sixteen years later in the Inaugural Address to the International Working Men's Association, we can clearly see the increasing positivism.

The *Manifesto* described a dialectical process in which

> ## INAUGURAL ADDRESS (1864)
>
> Dr. Smith, the medical deputy, ascertained that 28,000 grains of carbon and 1,330 grains of nitrogen were the weekly allowance that would keep an average adult . . . just over the level of starvation diseases, and he found furthermore that quantity pretty nearly to agree with the scanty nourishment to which the pressure of extreme distress had actually reduced the cotton operatives. . . . The result of his researches . . . the silk weavers, the needle women, the kid glovers, the stocking weavers, and so forth, received on the average, not even the amount of carbon and nitrogen "just sufficient to avert diseases . . . of the agricultural population . . . more than a fifth were with less than the estimated sufficiency of the carbonaceous food . . . more than one third were with less than the sufficiency of the nitrogenous food. . . ."[4]

labor is transformed into its opposite, capital, and the workers' labor impoverishes them as it is externalized in the capital it creates. Sixteen years later, dialectics was gone. In its place was a scientific definition of malnutrition, complete with the requisite number of grains of nitrogen, and the results of survey research. The transition from Hegelian to positivist forms of representation leaps off the page.

Many still influential older works of scholarship, often written without considering the Hegelian-inflected texts of the 1840s, simply treat Marx as a positivist.[5] But looking more closely at his responses to developments in the natural and physical sciences after 1850, a more complex picture emerges, in which he both accepted and criticized new scientific advances. He accommodated his philosophical presuppositions to them, but also held fast to his philosophical basics, while articulating them in a form more acceptable to a positivist era.

One of Marx's first encounters with science after 1850 came from a close friend and political associate, Roland Daniels. In 1851, before the Cologne physician was arrested and indicted in the Cologne Communist Trial, he wrote to Marx about a theoretical work he was preparing, *Microcosm: Draft of a Physiological Anthropology*. Daniels's starting point was the same as Marx's had been in the 1840s, Ludwig Feuerbach's notion of sensuous humanity as the basis of knowledge and historical development. But for Daniels, the sensuous human being of Feuerbach's theories was a physiological human being: "the human organism is and remains my measure." History and society were physiological, the reflex responses of human organisms to stimuli from their environment. Following in Feuerbach's footsteps, Daniels wanted to create a physiological philosophy—a scientific, materialist, and practical atheism—sharply differing from the philosophical and idealist atheism of the Young Hegelians. Daniels understood socialism in physiological terms: "Interest [on loans] is a matter of indifference to me, but not the purity of my food." A socialist society would aim to improve scientifically determined public and individual health, to their maximum extent. Daniels suggested that socialist demands could be summed up in one sentence: "Production according to strict scientific criteria solely with regard for the human organism."

Unfortunately, only Daniels's side of the correspondence has been preserved, but Daniels's comments on Marx's replies are informative. Marx apparently told Daniels that his whole approach was "sometimes too mechanical, sometimes too anatomical," that he was unable to integrate human consciousness into his explanation of history or to explain how society, if constituted by physiological laws, could ever be changed. Marx even asserted that he found Bruno Bauer more *wis-*

senschaftlich than Feuerbach—perhaps surprising given Feuerbach's materialism and Bauer's idealism.[6] But this attitude certainly fit with a rejection of positivism. Feuerbach's own later writings moved in a positivist direction, criticizing Hegel for stating that truth has to be found in a dialectical historical process rather than simply being available to perception. Marx showed considerable interest in Daniels's ideas—he filled Daniels's letters with underlinings and marginal emphases—but his rejection of explanations of human history and society, of the foundations of philosophy and the arguments in favor of socialism in terms of scientific physiology, suggest a skeptical attitude toward positivism.

Perhaps he needed something more convincing than his friend's physiological philosophy to move him. A logical place to look for such an impetus would be the greatest intellectual event of the positivist era, and the most significant scientific event of the entire nineteenth century. The publication of *On the Origin of Species* not only revolutionized science; it evoked emulation and repulsion in virtually all aspects of European cultural and intellectual life. As everyone knows, or thinks they know, Marx offered to dedicate *Capital* to Darwin, and repeatedly claimed that Darwin's findings on nature confirmed his own on human society. Yet while Marx accepted the scientific validity of Darwin's theories and endorsed them, in positivist fashion, for their support of atheism and ideas of progress, he also advanced a Hegelian criticism of Darwin's concepts and showed skepticism about their application to the study of human history and society.

Marx's introduction to Darwin came from Engels, who had acquired a copy of *On the Origin of Species* within two weeks of its publication in November 1859. He read rapidly and enthusiastically and reported to his friend that the book was "just terrific . . . up to now there has never been such a wonderful attempt made to prove historical development in nature, at least not with such success."[7] It took Marx a year to follow Engels's recommendation and actually read the book himself, which he did while nursing his wife through her bout with smallpox. "Although developed in a crude English way, this is the book that contains the basis for our views in natural history," he told Engels. In January 1861, he wrote Ferdinand Lassalle that "Darwin's writing is very important and suits me as the basis in natural history for the historical class struggle. . . ." Once awakened, Marx's interest in Darwin's ideas continued for years. He repeatedly discussed evolutionary theory with his friends and associates in London, attended lectures and studied the writings of Darwin's chief popularizer, Thomas Henry Huxley, and avidly read authors who claimed to have developed improved versions of the idea of natural selection.[8]

From this, it would be easy to conclude that Darwin's writings had converted Marx to the positivist idea of natural science as the basis for knowledge. But there was a more skeptical side to Marx's attitudes about the great biologist. After rereading *On the Origin of Species*, he wrote to Engels in June 1862 that

> with Darwin's work, which I have looked at again, it amuses me that he says he is also applying the "Malthusian" theory to plants and animals, as if the whole point with Herr Malthus were not that his theory is not applied to plants and animals, but to humans— with geometric progression—in contrast to plants and animals. It is remarkable how Darwin recognizes among beasts and plants his English society with its division of labor, competition, opening of new markets, "inventions" and Malthusian "struggle for existence." It is . . . reminiscent of Hegel, in the "Phenomenology," where bourgeois society appears as the "spiritual animal kingdom," while in Darwin the animal kingdom appears as bourgeois.[9]

This summary of Darwin's work was the very opposite of positivism, in which the natural sciences provided a model for the understanding of the world. Instead, it took the Hegelian position that philosophy—or, in Marx's version, a philosophically inflected political economy—could evaluate and criticize the conceptual basis of other branches of knowledge, including the sciences. As Marx considered the matter further, he became more skeptical about claims that Darwin's theories provided a guide to economy and society. After his son-in-law Paul Lafargue met with Clémence Royer, Darwin's French translator in 1869, and was disappointed at her capitalist (if otherwise left-wing and anti-clerical) credentials, Marx told him it was no surprise that she was "bourgeois." Darwin had transposed the struggle for existence in English laissez-faire capitalism into the natural world, so Darwinists naturally saw this as reason "for human society never to emancipate itself from its bestiality."[10]

Marx came to see Darwinism as part of a positivist trend that was undermining the position of Hegelian ideas. In a well-known after-word to the second edition of *Capital*, he denounced contemporary German thinkers who saw Hegel as a "dead dog," and insisted on the validity of his dialectical methods, which he had applied in his critique of political economy. Marx left those German thinkers so critical of Hegel anonymous in print, but in a letter to Engels he suggested that the problem began with Feuerbach, "who has a lot on his conscience in that respect." In another letter to his friend Dr. Kugelmann, he called out the critics by name. Two were the economist Eugen Dühring, and the famous physiologist and experimental psychologist Gustav Fechner, whose experiments with stimuli and mathematical formulations about them were reminiscent of Roland Daniels's proposals. Two more were prominent German Darwinians: Ludwig Büchner and Friedrich Albert Lange.[11] Both of these men were leftists, and Lange was even a partisan of the labor movement, which he hoped to justify along Darwinian and Malthusian lines. But their rejection of Hegel's dialectic in favor of a positivist view of the world, in which the biological sciences would be the model for cognition and social action, strongly aroused Marx's ire.

If this were Marx's view of Darwinians, why would he offer to dedicate *Capital* to Darwin? The answer is quite simple: the story that Marx tried to dedicate *Capital* to Darwin is a myth that has been repeatedly refuted but seems virtually ineradicable. It was Edward Aveling, the lover of Eleanor, Marx's youngest daughter, who asked Darwin's permission to dedicate to him a popularization of Darwin's theories that he had written. Darwin's negative response got mixed up with Marx's papers when Eleanor sorted them out after her father's death.[12]

Marx did have a favorable opinion about some implications of Darwin's theories. He saw them as yet another intellectual blow struck in favor of materialism and atheism, a point on which contemporary supporters and opponents of Darwin tended to agree. Marx was quite disappointed when Thomas Huxley, Darwin's fierce polemicist, "opened a back door" to religious belief in a speech given in Edinburgh in 1868, and refused to admit the materialist implications of the ideas he was defending. Following with considerable interest the researches of German scientific followers of Darwin, such as the zoologists Gustav Jäger and Ernst Haeckel, Marx noted that in their work "the cell as primal form is given up" in favor of "clumps of protein" found in the fossil record. "This primal form must naturally be followed down to the point where it can be chemically manufactured. And they seem close to it."[13] This chemical analysis of living organisms was amenable to someone who in his 1844 Paris manuscripts had already speculated about materialist theories of human origin.

Similarly, Marx was impressed with Darwin's theories in their role as scientific proof for the existence of progress. In 1866, he read the work of an obscure French geologist, Pierre Trémaux, *Origin and Transformation of Man and Other Beings*. It purported to explain human and animal evolution as a result of geological influences. Marx regarded Trémaux's work "as a very important improvement on Darwin," above all because "Progress, which in Darwin is purely accidental, is here necessary on the basis of the periods of development of the body of the earth." Engels's harsh criticism of Trémaux as someone who did not understand Darwin, and whose "ridiculous items of evidence . . . are ⁹⁄₁₀ based on false or distorted facts," did not deter his friend's admiration.[14]

When Engels was planning to plant reviews of *Capital* in the German press, to stir up interest in his friend's treatise on economics, Marx proposed that Engels describe his work as proving that "current society, economically regarded, is pregnant with a new, higher form," and that "socially, [it] is the same gradual process of upheaval that Darwin has proven in natural history." Marx suggested that Engels describe both developments as being encompassed by the "liberal doctrine of 'progress.'" Engels's review, using Marx's suggestions, duly appeared in *The Observer*, a left-wing (Marx would have said bourgeois-democratic) Stuttgart newspaper, in December 1867.[15]

Marx's remarks about Darwin and progress were an astute observation concerning the relationship between the theory of natural selection and the idea of progress. Darwin himself knew that his explanation of how organisms adapt to their changing environment said nothing about progress or improvement, and once noted, sarcastically, that by bees' criteria they were an improvement on people. Most contemporary Darwinians, though, felt their hero had demonstrated progress in nature and justified the existence of progress in human history and society, a crucial idea for positivists. Marx, if endorsing his own distinct version of the idea of progress, also understood that Darwin's theories did not in fact justify it. In a bow to positivist conceptions of science, he was attracted to Trémaux's dubious notions because they provided a justification for progress. Attempting to sell the ideas of his economics to a democratic and liberal public, fervent believers in progress, he suggested that Engels link his work to a popular misunderstanding of Darwin's theories, centered on the ideas of progress.

In this regard Marx appears as an ambivalent observer of post-1850 positivism. Unlike Bauer and Ruge, Marx was not waving the Hegelian banner, openly resisting the positivist trend. He paid considerable attention to scientific advances and wanted to appropriate the growing authority of the natural sciences for his political program and economic theories, under the heading of progress. But he was also not willing to renounce Hegel's insistence on the critique of scientific concepts or the Hegelian notion that truth was not empirically evident, but emerged in a process involving historical development and conceptual reformulation. Exactly how Marx would have combined Hegelian modes of thought with the positivist priority of the sciences is not entirely clear. Likely, such a combination would have involved an emphasis on an atheist and materialist view of the world. Neither atheism nor materialism were necessary features of positivist thought, and they were certainly not part of Hegel's elaborate philosophy, but they might have provided a vehicle for bringing together Hegel's dialectics and the positivist embrace of the natural sciences.[16] In the afterword to the second edition of *Capital*, Marx asserted that in Hegel, dialectics was standing on its head and needed to be put on its feet—that is, transformed from idealist to materialist. This assertion, one of the better known of Marx's theoretical statements, pointed in the direction of such a reconciliation. Marx toyed with the idea of writing a treatise on dialectics, a late version of his 1840s plans to write critiques of different branches of knowledge. This treatise was intended to "shake off" the "mystical form" in Hegel's version, and might have addressed the question of the compatibility of Hegelian thought with the positivist intellectual priority for the natural sciences. It would be composed, he wrote in 1868 to one of his admirers, a German artisan named Joseph Dietzgen, when he finished his critique of political economy. The latter was never completed, so that the philosophical treatise was never written, and Marx never precisely formulated his mature views on the topic.[17]

POSITIVISM WAS AS MUCH a social theory as a philosophical program. Its viewpoints intersected with the social theory Marx had developed during the 1840s. Three major issues emerged from this intersection. Positivists had a picture of human history as a progression through stages, leading from lower to higher forms of civilization, as the French positivist guru Auguste Comte put it, from civilizations characterized by superstitious to religious to scientific forms of thought. (Admittedly, Comte thought the scientific era needed a new form of religion, and he was prepared to be its high priest.) Marx's view of the conflictual development of human civilization through different modes of production, ultimately emerging in communism, had distinct similarities to such positivist formulations.

Social action was of considerable interest to positivists, particularly to Herbert Spencer, the prominent nineteenth-century English positivist, and one of the founders of the modern discipline of sociology. In *The Eighteenth Brumaire*, Marx had sketched out a theory of social action, emphasizing the links between social classes, whose existence was rooted in the mode of production and the division of labor, on the one hand, and political movements and their intellectual expression, on the other. Just exactly how Marx himself envisaged these linkages is an important issue for understanding his social theory.

The positivist evocation of the biological sciences as the model for the acquisition of knowledge had produced a new category of social understanding, that of "race," of biologically distinct divisions in humanity. Marx's chief category of social understanding was social classes derived from the division of labor. But race was by no means unknown to him and to Engels; the growing interest in race, often inflected by Darwinian or pseudo-Darwinian ideas about natural selection and the "survival of the fittest," was another challenge for Marx in adapting his theories to a new intellectual age.

MARX ARTICULATED HIS OPINIONS on the stages of human history in the introduction to *On the Critique of Political Economy*, published in 1859. There, the ideas that Marx and Engels had developed in their writings of the late 1840s, but only articulated in fragmentary and polemical form, were synthesized and presented as a compact doctrinal statement:

> In the social production of their life, people enter into specific, necessary relations of production . . . correspond[ing] to a specific stage of development of their material forces of production. The totality of these relations of production forms the economic structure of society, the factually existing base, on which a juridical and political superstructure is raised. . . . The mode of production of material life determines the social, political and intellectual process of life in general. It is not the consciousness of men that determines their being, but, just the opposite, their social being determines their consciousness. At a certain stage of development the material forces of production in society come into conflict with the existing relations of production, or with the relations of property (the latter being just a legal expression of the former). . . . From being forms of development of the forces of production, these relations are transformed into their shackles. An era of social revolution begins . . . one must always differentiate between the material upheaval in the economic determinants of production, which can be observed exactly by means of the natural sciences, and the juridical, political, religious, artistic, or philosophical, in short, ideological forms, in which men become conscious of this conflict and in which they fight it out. . . . In a rough outline, Asiatic, ancient, feudal and modern bourgeois modes of production can be described as progressive epochs of economic formation of society. The bourgeois relations of production are the last antagonistic form of the social process of production . . . but the productive forces developing in the womb of bourgeois society are simultaneously creating the material conditions for the resolution of this antagonism. With this social formation, the pre-history of human society is concluded.[18]

This passage contained not just one but many forms of stages of history. The most obvious one, usually attracting interpreters' attention, was the different modes of production. Marx described them as "progressive epochs"; their succession is a story of the steady improvement in the ability of human beings to produce.

Marx had devised the "Asiatic" mode of production in his *New York Tribune* articles on India during the 1850s, but his use of the concept was not geographically specific, nor was it linked to a particular era of human history. He found the Asiatic mode of production among the ancient Germanic tribes, in the highlands of the Hunsrück to the south of Trier in Marx's youth, and contemporaneously in nineteenth-century India and parts of the czarist empire.[19] Different historical stages could co-exist; progress occurred in different parts of the world at different times and at a different pace. Marx, like his contemporaries, saw economic progress—or, as he would have said, the productive forces realized in the bourgeois mode of production—as being most pronounced in Britain, Western European countries, and North America.

Herbert Spencer characterized two broad stages of human society, the "militant" and the "industrial," with the former designating the entire pre-industrial, pre-scientific past, and the latter marking a new epoch in the history of the world. Marx also described an emergent new epoch: the end to the prehistory of human society, occurring when the antagonisms of bourgeois society were resolved. Since Marx had noted just a few sentences previously that social antagonisms were resolved by means of social revolution, the concluding sentence of the passage was a not particularly hidden reference to the forthcoming social revolution that would end bourgeois society and bring about a communist regime. Although Marx could have described communism as another stage in the progress of modes of production, he instead designated it as a fundamental break with all past human society, a new epoch for which everything preceding was just a "pre-history."

Spencer, admittedly, was a libertarian, who ranted against almost any form of government action: his new epoch of world history was an idealized version of the pro–free-market policies of Victorian-era capitalism. Marx's new era of human history would only occur when the social world Spencer so admired was overthrown. Yet for all their very considerable disagreements on when the new stage of human history would appear, and how its society would be shaped, both men agreed that it would be a new scientific era, one fundamentally different from the human past.

Marx was well acquainted with the works of the positivists, and was less than impressed with them. Not surprisingly, he evaluated Herbert Spencer's writings as "economic trivia . . . spiced with pseudo-philosophical or pseudo-scientific slang." He thought a little better of Comte, admitting that the Frenchman was good at synthesis, but calling his synthesis "wretched compared to Hegel," and denouncing Comte's philosophical system as "positivist shit." There were a number of English positivists on the General Council of the IWMA—the "whole Comteist clique," as Marx called them. Marx got along well with their leader, Edward Spencer Beesley, professor of history at the University of London, praising him as "a capable and daring man," and greatly admiring his defense of the Paris Commune. Marx also thought that Beesley was at his best when he was not following positivist doctrines.[20] Yet for all the distance Marx kept from these doctrines, his own image of progress through distinct stages of historical development and a twofold division of human history into an earlier, irrational era and a later, industrial and scientific one, contained distinctly positivist elements. Today, a visitor to Highgate Cemetery in North London can see the graves of Karl Marx and Herbert Spencer standing face to face—for all the intellectual differences between the two men, not an entirely inappropriate juxtaposition.

· · ·

ONE OF THE BEST known aspects of Marx's social theory are the comments in the introduction to *On the Critique of Political Economy* about the relationship between an economic base and a political and ideological superstructure. Those comments were a reformulation in more prosaic and positivist terms of a celebrated, poetic passage from *The Eighteenth Brumaire*, in which Marx explained the differences between the liberal parliamentary supporters of the Orléans dynasty in France and the conservative adherents of the Bourbons:

> Under the Bourbons, large landed property had ruled, with its priests and lackeys, under the Orléans, high finance, big industry, large commerce, i.e., capital, with its retinue of lawyers, professors and elegant public speakers. . . . What thus kept these two caucuses apart . . . was the material conditions of their existence . . . the rivalry between capital and landed property. That simultaneously old memories, personal enmities, fears and hopes, prejudices and illusions, sympathies and antipathies, convictions, articles of faith and principles tied them to one or the other royal house—who would deny it? Arising from the different forms of property, from the social determinants of existence is an entire superstructure of uniquely shaped sensations, illusions, modes of thought and fundamental views of life. The entire class shapes and forms them from their material foundations and from the social relationships that correspond to them. The isolated individuals, to whom these flow through tradition and upbringing, can imagine that they are the actual motives and starting point of their action.[21]

Whether formulated poetically or prosaically, the evocation of base and superstructure was a powerful and effective metaphor, but also one that did not explain the connection between social structures and economic interests on the one hand, and ideas and political movements on the other. Elucidating this connection was a concern of Marx's followers, beginning with Engels, who explained the passage in 1891 as meaning that, "in the last analysis," economic structures were dominant in the determination of social and political action.[22] Engel's explanation simply substituted one metaphor for another. Twentieth- and twenty-first-century Marxists and neo-Marxists, living in an age when the superstructure, in the form of political mass movements and mass media, has become complex and labyrinthine, have focused on this issue at great length. The diversity and intellectual wealth of Marxist approaches to the connection between base and superstructure owes a good deal to the fact that Marx himself never made any definitive statements on the topic. But his descriptions of social and political action, in journalism or political polemics, do suggest some ways that he perceived the connection, and cast further light on Marx's response to the positivist atmosphere of the decades after 1850.

When Marx himself talked about the connection, he frequently employed the words "secret" or "mystery," both translations of the German *Geheimnis*. Secrets were at the root of revolutions. In a speech given in 1856, Marx proclaimed: "the emancipation of the proletarian, that is the secret of the 19th century, and of the revolution of that century." But secrets were also at the root of opposition to revolution. The working class in England was "divided into two hostile camps," he wrote to American correspondents in 1870, "English proletarians and Irish proletarians. . . . This antagonism is the secret of the powerlessness of the English working class, in spite of its organization. It is the secret of the preservation of the power of the capitalist class."[23]

In a mordant account of British political life, Marx told the readers of the *New York Tribune* in 1854 that "the secret of these blue-book dodges is the very secret of the alternate Whig and Tory succession in government, each party having a greater interest to maintain the capability of its opponent for succession, than by ruining their mutual political 'honor' to compromise the government of the ruling classes altogether." Marx used the latest news on the Spanish Revolution of 1854–56 to assert that Europe's capitalist middle class, formerly an enemy of "military despotism," had become a supporter of it when the workers began to challenge bourgeois domination. "This," he continued, "is the secret of the standing armies of Europe, which otherwise will be incomprehensible to the future historian."[24] Secrets, in all these passages, were at the root of big structures and large-scale trends, but Marx found secrets in individual, smaller-scale events as well, the results of parliamentary elections, for instance, or Louis Napoleon's *coup d'état*.[25]

The "secret" in each of these instances was the inner logic of the collective self-interest of social classes, and its effects on political and ideological movements. It was not always clear from Marx's presentation of this inner logic whether the members of the class concerned were aware of it, whether they were in on the secret. Sometimes, they clearly were: Marx thought that the "ruling classes" in England consciously pitted English against Irish workers "through the press, the pulpit, humor publications, in short all the means standing at the disposition of the ruling classes." On the other hand, in the descriptions of the rise of Bonapartism and military despotic rule, of the social revolutions of the nineteenth century, and especially in the initial formulation of *The Eighteenth Brumaire*, the inner logic of collective class self-interest was not consciously present among individual members of the class.

What made the secret something secret? Secrecy, in discussions of politics, often has the connotations of conspiracy, of something consciously hidden from public view. Marx used that meaning in his pamphlet on the Cologne Communist Trial, which was an exposé of a conspiracy to frame the Cologne communists. The German word *Enthüllungen* in the pamphlet's title literally means an exposure or unveiling (usually translated, a bit inaccurately, as "revelations"): a making public of the secret conspiracy of the Prussian government.

Marx's 1850s polemics against Lord Palmerston employed that version of "secret" in a long listing of secret treaties, secret actions, and Palmerston's own ostensible role as being secretly in the pay of the czar.

This was a meaning in opposition to the understanding of "secret" as representing the inner logic of a class's self-interest. The two contrasting meanings were very visible in Marx's pamphlet on eighteenth-century British foreign relations, an odd work commentators often pass over in embarrassed silence. The title under which it is known today, *The Secret History of Eighteenth Century Diplomacy*, was given to a reprint after Marx's death by his daughter Eleanor. But Marx's own title, *Revelations of the Diplomatic History of the Eighteenth Century*, made a similar point. In the pamphlet, Marx argued, in very Teutonic English, that from the early eighteenth century onward, the statesmen in charge of British foreign policy had been bribed tools of the czar. To uphold that position, they had to resort to a conspiratorial secrecy.

> In perusing these documents, there is something that startles us even more than their contents—viz., their form. All these letters are "confidential," "private," "secret," "most secret"; but in spite of secrecy, privacy, and confidence the English statesmen converse among each other about Russia and her rulers in a tone of awful reserve, abject servility, and cynical submission, which would strike us even in the public despatches of Russian statesmen. To conceal intrigues against foreign nations secrecy is recurred to [*sic*] by Russian diplomatists. The same method is adopted by English diplomatists freely to express their devotion to a foreign court.

Marx believed that the supposed pro-Russian foreign policy was the result of bribery and political manipulation because it did not express the inner logic of the collective interest of the English ruling classes. Commerce with Russia, Marx pointed out, made up just 2 to 3 percent of British foreign trade in the eighteenth century. The explicit justifications of the policy made in economic terms, which Marx (in line with his understanding of the linkage between base and superstructure) would ordinarily regard as the "secret" of British policy, were a fraud to hide the conspiratorial secret of Russian bribery and illicit influence:

> At the time, then, there developed on the Cabinet, at least, the onus of inventing mercantile pretexts, however futile, for their measures of foreign policy. In our own epoch, British Ministers have thrown this burden on foreign nations, leaving to the French, the Germans, etc., the irksome task of discovering the secret and hidden mercantile springs of their actions. Lord Palmerston, for instance, takes a step apparently the most damaging to the material interests of Great Britain. Up starts a State philosopher, on the other side of the Atlantic, or of the Channel, or in the heart of Germany, who puts his head to the rack to dog out the mysteries of the mercantile Machiavellism of "perfide Albion," of which Palmerston is supposed the unscrupulous and unflinching executor.[26]

It is easy enough to understand what is secret about conspiratorial secrecy; but the secrecy that Marx attributed to the inner logic of collective class interests is not quite so self-evident. Its secrecy consisted of the fact that it was not immediately empirically obvious, but was obtained through a theoretical understanding of the world in terms of the centrality of social classes emerging from the mode of production and the division of labor. This understanding, Marx thought, offered a superior interpretation of empirically evident conditions to a simple perception of these conditions, or a positivist evaluation of them in terms of the natural sciences. The priority of theoretical understanding for the interpretation of empirically gained evidence was a Hegelian heritage, but it was more broadly characteristic of the epistemological program of German idealism. Its starting point was Kant's assertion in the introduction to *The Critique of Pure Reason* that the scientific revolution began when Copernicus rejected the empirically obvious fact that the sun revolved around the earth.

One example of Marx's critique of forms of positivist understanding of his contemporaries was his attitude toward the Belgian mathematician Adolphe Quételet. One of the most impressive social scientists of the nineteenth century, and a founder of the modern discipline of statistics, Quételet had created, in good positivist fashion, what he called a "social physics," which emphasized the existence of statistical regularities in society and economy. Marx admired Quételet's work tremendously, but also noted that although he had proven "how even the seeming accidents of social life through their periodic recurrence and their periodic averages possess an inner necessity," he had "never succeeded in interpreting this inner necessity."[27] Positivists might dispose of scientifically obtained and mathematically arranged data, but the interpretation of its "inner necessity" required a theoretical analysis.

Marx's study of economics, as will be seen in the next chapter, was filled with the exposure of secrets and mysteries, showing how things looked different when viewed in the light of the inner logic of the capitalist system than when they were empirically perceived in the system's operation. Marx regarded the exposure of these secret connections of inner logic as essential to creating a *Wissenschaft*, an organized body of knowledge. In 1868 he wrote to Dr. Kugelmann about this topic, denouncing the "vulgar economists," a group Marx identified with the pro-capitalist followers of David Ricardo, whom he saw as intellectually far more superficial than their master:

> The vulgar economist has not the slightest suspicion that the genuine daily relationships of exchange and the extent of [commodities'] value cannot be immediately identical. . . . And then the vulgar economist believes he has made a great discovery, when in response

to the unveiling of the inner connection, he insists that things look different in their appearance. In fact, he insists on holding fast to semblance and regards that semblance as the ultimate. In that case, why bother with a *Wissenschaft*?[28]

This eminently Hegelian passage, a version of which also appeared in the third volume of *Capital*, unpublished in Marx's lifetime, even used Hegel's term, "semblance," to denounce the insufficiency of empirical perception for obtaining of knowledge. In this passage, Marx was presenting an intellectual program quite different from the positivist conception of knowledge as empirically obtained through scientific procedures. If Marx's outline of historical stages showed him at his most positivist, his account of the nature of *Wissenschaft* involved an affirmation of the Hegelian intellectual legacy and a skepticism toward the positivism that replaced it as a dominant mode of thought. The secret, one might say, of Marx's account of social and political action in terms of base and superstructure was the continued and even renewed presence of Hegel's ideas.[29]

THEORIES OF RACE AND historical accounts devised in terms of racial difference became increasingly common in Europe after 1850. Darwin's theories, but also the growth of historical linguistics (contemporaries said "philology"), with its figure of the Aryan, encouraged the development of racial theories in an age when science appeared as a model for the acquisition of knowledge.[30] The first major formulation of racist ideas came in 1853 with a treatise by the French author Joseph Arthur, comte de Gobineau, the *Essay on the Inequality of the Human Races*. Two individuals who had been important sources of Marx's ideas, Bruno Bauer and Moses Hess, abandoned the previous Hegelian idealism and turned to concepts of race. Under the influence of the Crimean War, Bauer became convinced that the future of Europe lay in a struggle between the inferior Slavic and the superior Germanic race; to these ideas he added the notion that Jews were racially alien to Germans and so could never be equal citizens in a Germanic state. Hess shared Bauer's belief in Jewish racial distinctiveness, but used it to argue that the Jews should have their own nation-state in Palestine, making him one of the very first proponents of Zionism.[31]

Marx was well acquainted with theories of racial superiority and had a low opinion of them. He read Gobineau's book with some care and remarked that "to such people it is always a source of satisfaction to have somebody whom they think themselves entitled to despise."[32] Marx practiced what he preached, since the letter was written to his son-in-law Paul Lafargue, who was partly of African descent. Quite aware of Lafargue's racial background, Marx described him in letters as "the Negrillo" and "our Negro." He had no problem with his daughter marrying a man of mixed race—at least, the problem he had was with Lafargue's lack of a steady income, not his origins. Writing to his son-in-law's father, François Lafargue, about Reconstruction policy in the United States after the Civil War, Marx remarked in a celebrated (in retrospect, overly optimistic) observation, which he repeated in *Capital*: "The workers of the North have finally completely understood that labor, in so far it is branded in black skin will never be emancipated in white skin." Marx was less sanguine about the southern states, noting that there, "the poor whites relate to the niggers" just as English workers related to the Irish. In other words, their feelings of superiority, strongly encouraged by the ruling class, diverted them from class solidarity—a conclusion it would be hard to dispute.[33]

One might wonder if such racial speculations would have included Jews, in view of the increasing perception of them as a race by Bauer and Hess. Marx, like most Europeans of the mid-nineteenth century, seemed generally to have viewed Jews in religious and cultural terms; the many caustic comments about Jews in his letters certainly went in that direction. The one time when Marx used racial language to characterize a Jew was in a letter to Engels in 1862, at the end of Ferdinand Lassalle's unhappy visit with the Marxes in London. Marx, given to endless anti-Semitic observations about Lassalle, wrote in the language of racial denigration:

> It is now completely clear to me, that, as proven by the shape of his head and the growth of his hair, he [Lassalle] stems from the Negroes who joined the march of Moses out of Egypt (if his mother or grandmother on his father's side did not mate with a nigger). Now this combination of Jewry and Germanism with the negroid basic substance must bring forth a peculiar product. The pushiness of this lad is also nigger-like.[34]

This was an ugly outburst, even by the standards of the nineteenth century. It also demonstrated Marx's non-racial understanding of Jews. The "combination of Jewry and Germanism" that Marx saw in Lassalle was cultural and political—the efforts of a man from a religious Jewish family in Silesia to become a prominent German literary and philosophical figure and a leader of German nationalism. The biological deprecation referred to Lassalle's ostensible African ancestry, and this letter shows Marx adopting quite a different attitude toward African descent than he took with his own son-in-law's family, or in his discussion of the corrosive effects of racism on working-class solidarity. Marx wrote this letter to Engels at the same time he was deeply concerned about the prospects of the Union and the anti-slavery cause in the Civil War. It shows an inconsistency between his public advocacy of anti-racist policies and his private ventilation of racial stereotypes; or perhaps it was just that the hostility in the letter was more directed toward Lassalle than toward Africans.

Most of the time when Marx and Engels thought about racial differences, it was not Jews or Africans they had in mind, but Europeans, Russians in particular. In September 1863, at the time of the Polish uprising against Russian rule, Marx met a Polish émigré in London and described him to Engels:

> The most interesting acquaintance that I have made here is that of Colonel Lapínski. He is undoubtedly the most intelligent and creative Pole that I have met to date—and simultaneously a man of action. His sympathies are all on the German side, although in manners and speech he is French. Instead of the struggle of nationalities, he knows only the struggle of races. He hates all Orientals, and counts equally in their ranks Russians, Turks, Greeks, Armenians etc.[35]

Marx certainly seems to have been intrigued by the Polish colonel, but it is unclear if he agreed with him about race, or what Marx meant by "race" altogether. Was a race, in Marx's usage, a distinct biological group, a sort of generic grouping of nationalities, similar to the way philologists of the time created families of languages, or was it just a description of the inhabitants of a region? When Engels wrote to Marx a year before, calling Gottfried Kinkel a "model Rhinelander, with all the prejudices and small-mindedness of the race," the word was evidently not a reference to Kinkel's inherent biological characteristics.[36]

A clue to Marx's thought comes from his opinions on Russia. According to a book on the Polish question written by a French author, Elias Regnault, Marx reported to Engels that the original Russians were "Mongols or Finns. . . . They are not Slavs; do not belong in any way to the Indo-Germanic race. . . . Panslavism in the Russian sense a government invention." Marx changed his mind after reading Pierre Trémaux, whose innovations on Darwin's evolutionary theory he appreciated, even if no one else did. Another of the advantages of Trémaux's work was that "In historical and political application" it was "much more important and much richer than Darwin. For certain questions, such as nationality etc., here alone the natural basis found." As part of his theory of the influence of geology on biological descent, Trémaux asserted that the Russians were in fact Slavs, not Mongols, but as a result of their residence on "the dominant ground formations in Russia the Slav is tartarized and mongolized." Trémaux, Marx noted, had applied the same theory to Africa to prove that "the common Negro type is only the degenerate form of a much higher one."[37]

With these comments, Marx seemed to be moving in the direction of a biological or geological explanation of differences in nationality— in any event, one connecting nationality to descent, explained in terms of natural science. The form was idiosyncratic, but it was certainly within the bounds of European racial thinking at the time, and another example of the influence on Marx of positivist ideas about the intellectual priority of the natural sciences. The point of all these different racial categorizations of Russians was political: to show that Russians were different from and alien to other Slavs. Science would delegitimize "Pan-Slavism," Russian aspirations to leadership of the Slavic world, and provide additional support for the Polish demand for liberation from tyrannical Russian rule.

Marx was considering these ideas about race at the same time that he was devising a theory of historical stages shaped by different modes of production. One has to wonder about the relationship between the two. As is so often the case with Marx's thinking on philosophical, historical, and sociological questions in this period, there are no written traces of a systematic confrontation with the problem, but there are some interesting clues. These lie in a series of articles on Pan-Slavism that Engels wrote for the *New York Tribune* toward the end of the Crimean War, under Marx's name and with Marx's encouragement and editorial suggestions. Rejected by the *Tribune*, the manuscripts themselves have not survived, but Engels's detailed prospectus for the series has been preserved.[38]

The prospectus began: "General Introduction. Romans, Teutons and Slavs. 2000 year long struggle of the first 2, eliminated by civilization, revolution & impossibility of the lasting rule of one tribe over another. Entrance of the Slavs as the third great race, demand, however, not just equal status, but domination of Europe." If these rough notes of Engels's correspond in any way to Marx's ideas, then they suggest that the two men saw racial differences primarily as a feature of pre-capitalist societies. The continuing significance of race in Russia would just be another proof of the socioeconomic backwardness of the realm of the czar. This idea that the growth of bourgeois civilization was making racial differences less important seems very much like the prediction in the *Communist Manifesto* that national differences were on the wane in view of the growth of the capitalist world market—and about as accurate.

Marx's ideas about race were part of his broader confrontation with new scientific developments, and the increasing intellectual hegemony of a form of philosophical and social theorizing based on these developments. Certainly not rejecting new intellectual trends, Marx sought to use them to advocate and defend his own conceptions, of the philosophical bases of perception, the stages of historical development, the nature of a capitalist economy, or the relationship between economic structures and social action. In part, he began to articulate his ideas in the language of these intellectual trends, and even to identify his own ideas with them. But Marx was not just an adherent of positivism; he was a critic of it as well. The understanding of *Wissenschaft* he had absorbed in his study of Hegel during his youth never left him. Marx insisted that true knowledge emerged from understanding the hidden inner logic of empirically observable phenomena, rather than simply from empirical observations themselves, even when those observations were carried out using the methods of the natural sciences. This was another reaffirmation of the intellectual heritage of Hegel and of German idealism, and a rejction of positivist conceptions of knowledge.

• • •

AFTER MARX'S DEATH, ENGELS became his chief interpreter, and ideas of Marxism in the late nineteenth and early twentieth century spread primarily via Engels's writings. There have been many strongly clashing investigations of just how accurately Engels represented Marx's views. Authors who stress intellectual differences between the two men tend to do so by comparing the Hegelian-inflected young Marx of the 1840s with the positivist elderly Engels, some four or five decades later. While these were the periods when both men produced their most complete statements, such a comparison downplays Marx's own intellectual development after the middle of the century. Proponents of an opposing interpretation, intent on establishing the fundamental agreement between Marx and Engels, emphasize the positivist passages in Marx's later works, omitting or downplaying his ambivalence toward positivism.[39]

It would be fair to say that Engels was always a positivist. In the very first letter he wrote to Marx in October 1844, he described the circumstances in his native Wupper Valley, to which he had returned after his year in Manchester and his visit with Marx in Paris. Engels talked of how his homeland "has made greater progress in every respect than over the last 50 years." He praised the more civilized tone of society, the growth of political opposition to the Prussian government, and noted that "Industry has made rapid progress . . . whole forests are extirpated and the whole thing stands now rather above than below the level of German civilization. . . ." Part of this progressive development was the growth of the proletariat in the Wupper Valley. If the workers developed "according to the same laws as their English counterparts," they would soon become communists.[40] Communism as the logical outcome of the progress of industry and civilization, occurring through stages of history, as represented by natural laws—in this letter, the young Engels was presenting a distinctly positivist view of society. The only part of the positivist program missing was the normative character of the natural sciences for other forms of human understanding. This would be explicitly formulated fifteen years later, when Engels read Darwin.

The path to Engels's reception of Darwin was paved by his increasing fascination with the progress of science. In a positively dithyrambic letter of July 14, 1858, Engels informed Marx that "people have, incidentally, no idea about the enormous progress made in the natural sciences over the last thirty years." Both the "gigantic development of organic chemistry" and the improved use of the microscope had "revolutionized physiology. . . . Everything [living] is cell." Physics had progressed equally rapidly, in particular the "correlation of forces," the transformation of kinetic energy into heat, heat into light, or electricity into magnetism.

Engels did understand accurately two of the important trends of mid-nineteenth-century science: "cell doctrine," the idea that living organisms are composed of cells; and the physical study of force and energy, moving away from the Newtonian focus on the mechanics of moving particles. In this same letter, Engels proceeded to identify these scientific discoveries with Hegel's philosophical ideas: "The cell is the Hegelian thing in itself and in its development goes precisely through the Hegelian process, until finally the 'idea,' the respective complete organism develops out of it." "Old man Hegel," Engels went on, "would have enjoyed" learning about the new results of physics, the transformation of one kind of force into another. For the results of comparative physiology, "The Hegelian business about the qualitative leap in the quantitative row is also very nice here."[41]

Engels wrote in 1865 to the German Darwinian and Malthusian socialist Friedrich Albert Lange, "I am naturally no longer a Hegelian but still have a great piety and attachment to the colossal old boy." He conceded the "nonsense in the detail of the philosophy of nature," but contended that "The modern scientific doctrine of the mutual interac-

tion of the natural forces . . . is just another expression or rather positive proof of the Hegelian development of cause and effect, mutual
interaction, force etc."[42] Engels was identifying Hegel with positivism,
turning the latter's methods of intellectual inquiry into the results of
investigations in the natural sciences. Although Marx sometimes took
a similar point of view, he was more inclined to contrast Hegel's methods to the positivist ones.

If Engels saw dialectical philosophy, in good positivist fashion, as
the expression of the natural sciences, he also could reverse the procedure, rejecting scientific findings when they did not fit his philosophical views. Denouncing the Second Law of Thermodynamics, he wrote
to Marx: "You cannot imagine anything stupider." The idea of gradual equalization of temperatures, or, as it would later be formulated,
increasing entropy, led to a world "that begins in nonsense and ends in
nonsense." Although the second law was seen as "the finest and highest perfection of materialism," it envisaged a progressive cooling of the
universe. Such a development implied "the original hot condition, from
which things cooled off, absolutely inexplicable, even absurd, thus pre-
supposes a God."[43] Since, for Engels, philosophy included atheism and
materialism, and that philosophy was based on the natural sciences, a
science that led to a questioning of atheism and materialism could not
be science.

We might imagine nineteenth-century (especially German) philosophical and social theory as placed along a line, at one end of which
were Hegel's ideas: the intellectually hegemonic position of philosophy,
and the distrust of empirical evidence that had not been subject to philosophical investigation and criticism. At the other end would be the
positivists, with their priority on scientific method and a scientific form
of empiricism. The mature version of Marx's theories, as well as can
be gathered from their fragmentary expressions, seems to have been
about halfway along the line, although in some instances he was much
nearer the positivist end, at other times the Hegelian one. Marx, of

course, reformulated Hegel's idealism in materialist terms and replaced Hegel's dialectical philosophy with a philosophically inflected political economy. Engels, by contrast, was far over at the positivist end of the line. In spite of his references to Hegel, the *Wissenschaft* he proposed as the basis for socialism was derived from the intellectual model of the natural sciences in its nineteenth-century positivist mode.

11

The Economist

IN THE WAKE OF the global recession of 1857, Marx began writing his long-planned treatise on political economy. The idea of such a treatise had initially been conceived when he first studied the major political economists in Paris during the mid-1840s. In the following decade, exploiting the storehouse of knowledge in the British Museum, he had deepened his knowledge of economic theories and explored empirical evidence of the development of capitalism, writing up some results of his researches in his commentaries on business and finance for the *New York Tribune*. Influencing his interpretations were the theoretical reflections he had devised under and against the influence of positivism.

Marx's plans for his treatise were expansive and ambitious. He would subject the ideas of the leading political economists of the day— particularly Adam Smith and his chief disciple, David Ricardo, but also Thomas Malthus, Jean-Baptiste Say, James and John Stuart Mill, to say nothing of many other, lesser figures—to Hegelian conceptual criticism. For all Marx's disagreements with these theorists, he endorsed a number of their chief ideas, such as the determination of goods' value by the labor required to produce them, the tendency in a capitalist society for the rate of profit to fall over time, and the relationship between the rent of land and differences in agricultural output. His Hegelian critique would not so much refute the proposals of these economists as it would reformulate their fundamental notions with greater theoretical precision and greater empirical accuracy. Finally, Marx would connect the tendencies of economic development that Smith and Ricardo had discerned with his theories of the stages of human history into a broad panorama of the violent rise, antagonistic flourishing, crisis-ridden decline, and revolutionary disappearance of capitalism.

It was a lot to do, and Marx's initial efforts at the end of the 1850s turned into a quarter-century-long theoretical, empirical, and mathematical odyssey. Unlike Homer's wily hero, Marx never reached an Ithaca of political economy, but continued to wander around an intellectual Mediterranean, with a few stops, of shorter and longer duration, at islands of publication. While he was on his journey, both the economic landscape of nineteenth-century capitalism and the intellectual landscape of economic thought were changing around him. The intellectual voyage was only finished after his death. In the following decade, painstakingly deciphering Marx's scrawled script and laboriously reconciling his different draft manuscripts and extensive notes, Engels compiled and published the rest of Marx's treatise. By the time it appeared, most economists lived in a different intellectual universe from that of Smith and Ricardo; Marx's efforts to reaffirm the economic orthodoxy of the mid-nineteenth century appeared as a dissenting and unorthodox economics four decades later.

Marx's initial unpublished draft of 1857–58 is known as the *Grundrisse* (German for "construction sketch" or "blueprint"), a name given it by the Russian editors who first published the manuscript in 1939. This preliminary attempt, 800 pages strong, was a variegated work, mixing carefully structured arguments with isolated comments, well-connected passages with random insights, and issues from the Paris manuscripts of 1844 with observations from Marx's journalism of the 1850s. For all the fragmentary, non-linear nature of the manuscript, it contained basic themes of Marx's economics that he would pursue for the rest of his life. A few excerpts from the *Grundrisse* appeared in the slender *On the Critique of Political Economy*, published in Berlin in 1859, a work that was the proverbial tip of the iceberg. The pamphlet dealt primarily with money and economists' monetary theories, revealing little of the thematic wealth of its unprinted predecessor.

Marx worked on his economics treatise with heightened intensity in the first half of the 1860s, producing a better-structured draft of the entire work in 1861–62, which included a history of economic thought not found in later manuscripts, and eventually published separately as *Theories of Surplus Value*. A third, and by far the best organized and clearest version of the treatise, was written in 1864–65. It had grown too long to be published all at once, so Marx excerpted the initial 40 percent and revised it extensively for publication. This became Volume One of *Capital*, which was published in Hamburg in 1867. In the 1870s, Marx made a number of changes and corrections to this work for the second German-language edition of 1873, and the French-language edition, published two years later. An English-language version, in spite of Marx's efforts to procure a translation and publisher, only appeared in 1887, after his death.

All these printed versions left the majority of Marx's planned treatise still unpublished. Marx hoped to have the remainder of the work done shortly after the first volume appeared, and he continued to work on the book until the last year of his life. But his efforts after 1867 remained scattered and fragmentary; when Engels collected, organized, and transcribed Marx's writings posthumously, he had to have recourse to the manuscripts from the 1860s. Although Volumes Two and Three of *Capital*, as edited by Engels, were published in 1885 and 1894 respectively, in most respects Volume One was written after Volumes Two and Three and on many important topics contained Marx's latest thinking and formulations.[1]

Summarizing, criticizing, and placing in historical context this giant mass of published and unpublished material would demand a book—many books!—in itself. Readers, I hope, will be content with a briefer account, beginning with the Hegelian conceptions of Marx's work, outlining Marx's main economic concepts, and showing how these were developed into a diagnosis of nineteenth-century capitalism and a prognosis of its ultimate demise. Three crucial features of Marx's economic theory—the tendency of the rate of profit to fall; the so-called transformation problem, the transformation of values into prices across an entire capitalist economy; and the determination of farm prices and ground rent—remained unpublished during his lifetime. Marx's struggles with the problems inherent in these features illuminate the relationship between his ideas and those of his predecessors and contemporaries. In the last third of the nineteenth century, growing discontent with existing theories of political economy led to the development of two new and strongly opposed versions of economics: the "Historical School" and neoclassical marginal utility theory. The reception of Marx's ideas and the criticisms by adherents of these newer trends demonstrates how Marx's ideas were shaped by his predecessors and by the socioeconomic environment in which they lived. In contrast, there was much less in Marx's work relevant to trends either in the economy or the economic theory of the late nineteenth and twentieth centuries.

CAPITAL BEGAN WITH THE simple perception of the capitalist economic system as an immense number of useful goods produced and exchanged. (The German *Ware*, goods for exchange or sale, is usually rendered in English as "commodities," a bit misleading, since Marx did not have in mind the contemporary meaning of commodities as raw materials, but goods and services more generally.) If goods, having incommensurable uses—cloth on the one hand and grain on the other—were to be exchanged, they needed some common measure of value, so their exchange implied the existence of a currency, transforming bartering goods into selling them, trading them for money. Trading goods to increase one's store of money, rather than to exchange one good for another, Marx continued, was what made money into capital. This kind of exchange, increasing wealth and value, he argued, was only possible through the exchange of money with a specific kind of commodity, human labor power.

The rest of Volume One of *Capital* then explained the implications of that exchange: its relationship to the workday, its differentiation of kinds of capital, and its role in creating surplus value, the increase in wealth enjoyed by capitalists as a result of their exchange with workers. Marx elaborated the production of surplus value, including a detailed investigation of the factory system, the changes in the working day, changes in employment and in the structure of capital, and long-term trends in the distribution of the income resulting from the growth of a capitalist economy. The development of these concepts and their empirical investigation took up most of the first volume of *Capital*.

While surplus value had been extracted by the exchange between capitalists and workers, it still had to be realized—that is, the goods workers produced had to be sold in the market, for capitalists to make a profit. If Volume One of *Capital* was about distribution, Volume Two became an investigation of circulation, of the process of buying and selling in the market. Volume Three then returned to the process of production in light of the results on circulation. This work dealt with the transformation of value (whose extraction was considered in Volume One) through sale (Volume Two) into price and relationship of this transformation to the falling rate of profit—both processes considered in regard to the whole economy, and not just individual firms. Volume Three also considered specialized issues emerging from the intersection of production and circulation, such as currency, credit, and finance, and then specific forms of capitalism, including agriculture, mining, and urban real estate. The volume and the work ended—or was designed to end, because Marx never completed even a rough draft of this final section—with an explanation of the differences between Marx's analysis of capitalism and that of Smith and Ricardo, and an invocation of the capitalist economic system's structuring of a class society.

This form of proceeding was fundamentally Hegelian. Authors have compared Marx's economic treatise with Hegel's *Logic*.[2] A more appropriate comparison might be to another of Hegel's works, the *Phenomenology of Spirit*, which began with simple, immediate sense perception, and moved up a conceptual ladder of increasing complexity, each rung in the ladder generated by the ultimate inadequacy of the previous one, as it was more carefully elaborated. *Capital* began with the simplest forms of economic activity, the production and exchange of goods, and developed a theoretical structure of increasing complexity, each step emerging out of the inadequacy of the previous one: money needed to explain how objects with incommensurate uses could be exchanged, the nature of labor power to explain how equal exchanges could produce profits, the analysis of circulation to explain how extracted surplus value could be realized, to give just a few examples. At the end of the analysis was a complex class society, containing all its inequalities and tendencies toward self-destruction.

A crucial part of Hegel's process of conceptual and historical development was the movement of self-externalization and self-estrangement, in a word, alienation, and the recovery of the capacity and material that had been alienated. As early as the Paris manuscripts of 1844, Marx had transformed Hegel's insights into an explanation of political economy, in his discussion of the alienation of labor under capitalism. Whole passages in the *Grundrisse* were just repetitions of these viewpoints, first written down fifteen years previously. In *Capital*, Marx did not use the language of alienation and self-estrangement, but he did talk about the "fetishism of commodities," the way capitalism turned the process of the actualization of human labor into a thing, a commodity, or good for sale, distinct from the workers who had produced the commodity and holding power over their lives.[3]

If Marx's use in *Capital* of the concept of commodity fetishism is evidence of a link to ideas from the 1840s, his opposition of secrets to semblances, and his description of inner connection and inner logic as the truth in his economic work, reflected his methodology after 1850 and his ambivalent feelings about the increasingly dominant positivist understanding of knowledge. In describing the fetishism of commodities, Marx stated that "The mysterious character of the commodity form thus simply consists of the fact that it reflects back to men the societal character of their own labor as the objective characteristics of the labor product itself. . . . thus also reflects the social relationship of producers to their total labor as a social relationship of objects existing outside themselves."[4] This passage, reminiscent of the philosophical analysis of the Paris manuscripts, pointed out the difference between appearance and inner logic. Goods appear in the marketplace, are sold at market prices that appear independent of individual control; but this appearance veils the inner logic of the labor process, the production of those goods by workers, who have lost control of the products of their own social labor.

This evocation of secrets as the inner logic of an empirically perceived semblance was most noticeable in the unfinished third volume, in which Marx planned to bring his entire system together as a totality and to compare it with the ideas of the classical political economists. At the beginning of Volume Three, he insisted that surplus value was the hidden form of profit, that the rate of profit and idea of value emerging from credit were both a "semblance," while the rate of surplus value was "the invisible, but the essential to be discovered." Marx felt that in distinguishing between the rate of profit and the rate of surplus value, he had "for the first time uncovered this inner connection." He insisted that supply and demand, which bourgeois economists asserted determined prices, was just a semblance, rather than the reality of value determined by labor time, which could only be found by investigation of the inner connections of value.[5]

Getting to the conclusion of this volume and his entire work, Marx discussed the idea first formulated by Adam Smith, and endorsed by his followers, that the sales price of a commodity was made up of the incomes of those who had produced it, and that those incomes could be divided into rent on land, profit (or interest) on capital, and wages of labor. Marx described this idea as "the Trinitarian form, which encompasses all the secrets of the social process of production." The secrets that Marx had uncovered in his investigation were that these forms of income were not independent but were, ultimately, the products of labor in the capitalist system of production. The best classical economists, Marx asserted, had penetrated the semblance of the three forms of income, but remained, as a result of their advocacy of the capitalist system of production, "imprisoned in the world of semblance they themselves had critically dissolved."[6] It was only by engaging in the Hegelian labor of conceptual development that Marx was able to show how the semblance of the system depended on the connected logic of its inner workings.

Marx's methodology might be compared with two other common forms of social science investigations of empirical reality. In one, stemming from the nineteenth-century positivists, social scientists posit the various terms of their model (today, in a more mathematical mode, they say their "independent variables") and use it to explain empirical findings. In *Capital*, Marx certainly developed a model of a capitalist economy, a model that, even by the end of the first volume, to say nothing of all three, had many terms and concepts. But these were all developed out of the initial conditions of goods produced and exchanged. Each step of the development followed from the inadequacy of the previous one to explain different, empirically evident aspects of capitalism. That procedure would reveal the inner logic of the system, as more positivist forms of modeling, beginning with a large number of terms, would not.[7]

A second version of modeling is one used by economists, both in Marx's time and today. This version employs a reduced number of terms to produce a deliberately simplified model of economic reality, in that way revealing the effects of what the economists regard as crucial factors. In a further step, economists are supposed to bring back in the neglected factors, but they have been known not to do so, and to apply their simplified model directly in making policy recommendations. This is not unlike Marx's procedure, only the terms Marx brought back in were not so much modifications of his initial premises as consequences of their conceptual development, a distinctly dialectical aspect of Marx's mode of investigation.

MARX'S ECONOMIC THEORY WAS framed by five conceptual distinctions: between use value and exchange value; between the use of money to exchange commodities and the use of money to accumulate capital; between labor and labor power; between constant and variable capital; and between the rate of surplus value and the rate of profit. Only after making these distinctions, which, as might be expected from Marx's methods, emerged from one another, could Marx develop his analysis of capitalism and his diagnosis of capitalism's future, and distinguish these from the versions offered by contemporary political economists.[8]

The distinction between use value and exchange value was conceptually straightforward. Use value was the subjective benefit an individual received from the consumption of a good or service; exchange value the price paid for that good or service in the market. Exchange required a common measure of value, or money. The producer of a commodity sold it, turning its use value over to the purchaser, received the good's exchange value in the form of money, and then purchasing another commodity with that money. Marx used the example of a farmer who sold the wheat he had grown and employed the proceeds to buy linen cloth from a handloom weaver, while the weaver used the money he received from the sale of the cloth to buy a Bible. The mention of the purchase of the Bible and the spiritual use value it possessed was meant ironically, but the point was to illustrate the relationship between exchange and the division of labor.[9]

This simple exchange, for Marx, was not capitalism. Rather, capitalism involved a different version of the process of exchange. In this version, money was used to purchase a commodity, and then that commodity was sold at a profit, so that more money existed at the end of the chain of transactions than at the beginning. This use of money to increase value, Marx asserted, turned money into capital. But, as he noted, how could this happen if goods sold for their exchange value? Where did the extra value—the "surplus value," as Marx said—come from?

The answer to this question involved Marx's intervention in a long-running debate among political economists concerning the labor theory of value. First advanced by Adam Smith, elaborately formulated by David Ricardo, and endorsed in the standard economics text of Marx's time, John Stuart Mill's *Principles of Political Economy* (1848), this theory stated that the value of a good was given by the amount of labor needed to produce it.[10] "Socially necessary labor time" was the phrase Marx used. The problem, as Ricardo's critics pointed out (and Marx, unusually well read on political economy, was well aware of this problem), was that using such a measure of value failed when applied to the value of labor itself. It was conceptually unclear how labor could be both valued and the measure of value. If one tried to overcome this objection by stating that the value of labor was labor itself, then both the value of the good produced and the value of the labor needed to produce it were the same. Such an equality of value implied that capitalists could not make any money, unless—as some socialists, including Marx's old rival Proudhon, suggested—they were systematically cheating the workers, and paying them less than the value of their labor. Marx rejected this idea, and in his 1859 pamphlet explained that future publications would provide the solution to this fundamental problem of the labor theory of value.[11]

In the *Grundrisse*, Marx went over the problem a number of times, before formulating the solution he would adopt in his economic writings. Workers, he asserted, did not sell capitalists their labor; rather, they sold them what Marx first called "ability to labor" and "capacity to labor," before settling on the phrase "labor power." The exchange value of the labor power was the labor time needed to produce that labor power—that is, to keep workers and their families alive and working, maintaining their standard of living. The use value of the labor power, on the other hand, was the labor itself, which had the unique property of increasing value. Formulated in terms of labor time, the standard contemporary measure of value, Marx's argument was that workers in a textile mill, to take a typical industrial establishment of the 1860s, worked a twelve-hour day transforming raw cotton into cotton yarn. The yarn the workers produced in six hours, half the workday, when sold, sufficed to pay their wages, to compensate them for their labor power, as well as half the other costs of their employer for raw cotton, fuel for the machinery, heat and light for the factory building, and depreciation of the productive facilities. But they continued to work the remaining six hours, and the product of that time, when sold, both replaced the other half of the material costs of their employer and added a surplus value, the profit of the capitalists.

In a famous passage, laden with sarcasm, yet also expressing his historical philosophy, Marx described this sale of labor power as "liberty, equality, property and Bentham."[12] Capitalists and workers, two freely contracting parties, made an equal trade, the workers receiving the fair exchange value of their labor power, in return for which the capitalists got to consume the use value of this labor power. Each side was trading what it had to sell, the workers their labor power, the capitalists their money for wages, and each, as the utilitarian philosopher Jeremy Bentham proposed, was acting in self-interest.

Marx added one final feature to his basic concepts: the distinction between different kinds of capital. Contemporary economists distinguished between "fixed" and "circulating" capital, the former including structures and production facilities, the latter raw materials and finished goods. Marx endorsed that distinction and discussed it at some length in the posthumously published Volume Two, but also lumped together fixed and circulating capital under the heading of "constant capital." Against this constant capital, he counterposed "variable capital," the cost of workers' wages, an idea developed in the *Grundrisse* from a concept of Ricardo's political economy, the "wages fund": the proportion of national income available to pay workers' wages. Marx gave the concept a Hegelian twist, defining wages as capital, uniting seemingly opposite conceptions, and also pointing to the central role of labor in creating capital.[13]

Marx's counterposing of constant and variable capital served another crucial purpose of his economic theory, particularly relevant to the central proposition of the falling rate of profit. He asserted that the constant capital contained in any given good for sale did not increase its value; the price of raw materials, machinery, structures, fuel, etc., was just passed on in the finished goods. Only variable capital, human labor power, could increase the value of commodities.[14] Marx distinguished between the rate of surplus value, the ratio of capitalists' profit to their labor costs, and the rate of profit, the ratio of capitalists' profit to their costs for both labor and materials and machinery, or for living and dead labor, as he sometimes described these two forms of capital. Although the rate of profit corresponded to the way capitalists themselves calculated returns on their investments, it was a semblance, for it was the rate of surplus value that determined capitalists' profit.

With these conceptual distinctions in place, Marx was ready to begin articulating his theory. Capitalists, driven by competition in the market, were fighting to increase or at least maintain their profits; and given the origin of profit in surplus value, Marx perceived two ways they could do so. One he called "the extraction of absolute surplus value," by which he meant the lengthening of the working day, so that workers would devote a greater proportion of their labor time to producing profits for their capitalist employer and a lesser proportion to producing goods that, when sold, would pay their wages. In this discussion of the extraction of surplus value, which began about a third of the way into Volume One, Marx dropped the form of abstract reasoning he had used previously, and began to cite empirical material. Using as his chief source the Blue Books, reports of British parliamentary commissions of inquiries, Marx painted a dark picture of misery and exploitation, of exhausted and ill workers, even young children, laboring day and night. He told the story of the washerwoman Mary Anne Walkley in London, who, while toiling on cleaning the dresses for ladies preparing for the ball of the Princess of Wales in 1863, was literally worked to death.[15]

At the same time, this capitalist exploitation generated working-class resistance, in the form of campaigns for a legally guaranteed shorter working day, and in the demands of trade unions for shorter hours.[16] Marx's theory of surplus value helps explain his support of the International Working Men's Association and the trade unionism it sponsored. Unions' advocacy of shorter working hours was central to the class struggle, for it involved the workers seizing back from the capitalists a portion of the value they created, decreasing the capitalists' surplus value and hence their profit. It was a reformist action, but one that struck at the root of the source of capitalists' profits, and led toward the end of the capitalist system.

Marx understood that extending the working day, even if there were no working-class opposition, ran into physical limitations, unless all the workers were going to join Mary Anne Walkley in the grave. The greater part of his analysis was focused on the extraction of what he called "relative surplus value," generated by making labor more productive. Even if such more productive workers devoted the same proportion of their working day to replacing the capitalists' equipment and raw materials costs and generating a profit for them, they would produce more goods during those hours and so generate more profits. Marx thought it was "the immanent drive and constant tendency of capital to raise the productive power of labor. . . ."[17] Capitalism was all about producing more and producing more productively.

The increase in labor productivity was the result of the expanded use of machinery. Marx's many illustrations of this point came from England in the first two thirds of the nineteenth century, the land of steam engines, mule jennies, and power looms. As Marx saw it, this trend was not just ongoing but intensifying. Machinery, the fuel needed to run it, and the raw materials processed by it made up a steadily increasing proportion of capitalists' expenditures, as compared to the money they spent on workers' wages. To use Marx's phrase, the "organic composition of capital," the ratio of constant to variable capital, was steadily rising.[18]

The consequences of this trend were both varied and far-reaching. The greater expenses needed for ever more machinery put smaller firms out of business and encouraged the formation of steadily larger capitalist enterprises. Larger firms and greater output required larger markets—an entire world market. Craft producers, such as the Indian handloom weavers, were driven out of business, and their countries turned into sources of raw materials. Emigrants from industrial countries settled in Australia or North America, and created still more markets for industrial goods and still more sources of raw materials.[19]

Yet the very same process leading to the production of ever greater societal wealth was producing ever greater immiseration. As production became steadily more mechanized, capitalists' demand for labor decreased, driving down wages for regularly employed workers, and creating a growing number of workers who were irregularly employed or completely unemployed. If they did not join the waves of emigrants, they became, in Marx's celebrated phrase, members of an "industrial reserve army." In this way, capitalism created a constant condition of overpopulation for the working class. But the introduction of steadily more expensive machinery required that it be run for longer hours to amortize its costs, so that the expansion of mechanization produced simultaneously unemployment and a longer workday for those workers who were still employed.[20]

Marx also suggested that the fluctuations in the size of this reserve army were the cause of the business cycle and of regularly recurring commercial crises. The causation on this point was not entirely clear, and it seems more logical to turn cause and effect around, to see the business cycle as determining the size of the industrial reserve army: in boom times, the unemployed would have been more likely to find jobs, and the size of the industrial reserve army would have declined, while in recessions, with growing unemployment, its ranks would have increased. In any event, Volume One of *Capital* lacked an explicit theory of business cycles and commercial crises. There was more on the topic in the posthumously published Volume Three, which noticeably differed from the assertions in Volume One. After the disappointment of his hopes of revolution to follow in the wake of the global recession of 1857, Marx rather downplayed the importance of crises for the end of capitalism.[21]

What he did see as leading to the end of capitalism was the contrast between the wealth created by the growing productivity of labor, resulting from the increasing organic composition of capital, and the misery these same trends caused for the workers. In a chapter entitled "The Universal Law of Capitalist Accumulation," Marx summed up, in angry tones, the general direction of the process driven by the increasing organic composition of capital:

The law, which . . . constantly keeps relative overpopulation or the industrial reserve army in equilibrium with the extent and energy of accumulation, binds the worker more firmly to capital than the fetters of Hephaestus bound Prometheus to the rocks. The law determines an accumulation of misery corresponding to the accumulation of capital. The accumulation of wealth at one pole is thus simultaneously the accumulation of poverty, tormented labor, slavery, ignorance, brutalization and moral degradation at the opposite pole, i.e., on the side of the class that produces its own product as capital.[22]

Following this drastic statement, Marx set out to offer empirical evidence of it, using (as with almost all the material in his book) developments in Great Britain from the mid-1840s to the mid-1860s. He related the enormous expansion of exports, from £58.8 million in 1847 to £188.9 million in 1866, the steady increase in high incomes according to the income-tax statistics, and the growth of production in coal and iron. This evidence of increasing capitalist production and accumulation was familiar to Marx, as he had been reporting on it for the *New York Tribune* since the early 1850s, and had made it a practice to carry around notebooks in which he wrote down economic statistics.[23]

Against this backdrop of increasing bourgeois affluence, Marx deployed a wealth of evidence about the misery and poverty of the working class. The Blue Books he cited revealed badly undernourished shoemakers or Londoners who could not afford the high rents of the metropolis and were thrown out on the street. They reported on over-filled poorhouses, on farm workers who toiled in labor gangs in which women and children kept down adult male workers' wages, but paid for it with frequent teenage pregnancies. The diet of those abused farm laborers was worse than that of prisoners in jail.

Marx's accounts were disturbing documents of exploitation, oppression, and poverty; they make for uncomfortable reading even today. But they were, quite in contrast to the discussion of the growing industrial output and wealth of the upper classes, static, snapshots of the 1860s, with no indication of whether conditions then were worse or better than in past years. Marx knew that circumstances had changed in England since the early years of the industrial revolution at the beginning of the nineteenth century. Writing about the initial phases of industrialization in Russia during the 1860s, he stated that in the czar's empire, "so fruitful in all infamies, the old atrocities from the childhood period of English factories stand in full bloom."[24] This denunciation of Russia was a tacit admission that such atrocities were no longer occurring in England, that conditions had improved over the previous forty to sixty years.

Besides not taking change over time into account, Marx's portrayal of working-class misery was also selective. He buttressed his position with accounts of the poorest and most defenseless of the lower classes in the United Kingdom. In the International Working Men's Association, Marx had met British trade unionists, representatives of better-off workers, and had seen those workers in the rallies he had attended in Hyde Park and on the platform of meetings called by David Urquhart or the IWMA; but such workers were not included in his descriptions of the conditions of the English working class in the 1860s.

In the concluding chapters of Volume One, Marx set his picture of working-class impoverishment into a broader panorama of the history of capitalism. It began with "primal" or "original accumulation" (both those phrases are better renderings of the German *ursprüngliche Akkumulation* than the standard English translation, "primitive accumulation"), the appropriation of surplus value by the pre-industrial capitalists of the sixteenth through the eighteenth centuries. Before machinery increased the productive power of labor, capitalists extracted surplus value by scarcely legitimated theft: seizing the farmers' common lands and forcing sturdy yeoman into misery as landless laborers, exploiting slaves, looting colonial subjects. With these observations, Marx integrated into his communist economic theories the criticism of British rule in India as a system of organized theft and corruption he had taken from pre-socialist British radicals and published in the *New York Tribune*. Following the onset of the industrial revolution, this open theft was replaced with the extraction of surplus value from the workers by means of industrial employment.

Peering into the future, Marx reiterated the predictions he and Engels had first made twenty years earlier in the *Communist Manifesto*. Capital would accumulate in fewer and fewer hands, as the financial demands of the increasing organic composition of capital drove smaller firms out of business. Production would be increasingly centralized and mechanized, designed for maximum efficiency. Productivity would grow, as would the global connections of the capitalist market economy. All these developments would be features of a future socialist economic system, already developing under the aegis of capitalism. At the same time, the general law of capitalist accumulation dictated that alongside the increase in capital, there would arise

> the mass of misery, oppression, servitude, degeneration, exploitation, but also the outrage of the steadily growing united and organized working class, schooled by the mechanism of the capitalist process of production itself. The monopoly of capital becomes a fetter on the means of production that have previously blossomed with capitalism and under it. The centralization of the means of production and the societal character of labor reach a point where they become irreconcilable with their capitalist shell. It is exploded. The hour of capitalist private property strikes. The expropriators are expropriated.[25]

This powerful and oft-cited passage was not the end of Volume One of *Capital*. The book continued for a few more pages with another aspect of the capitalist future: an account of how the growing population of England's settler colonies was gradually transforming them from islands of cheap land and working-class prosperity into centers of capitalist misery and exploitation like their mother country. While adding on this very final segment was rather an anticlimax after the powerful evocation of the end of capitalism, the discussion of colonization was both part of Marx's understanding of capitalism as a global system and also of his consistent use of the development of capitalism in Great Britain as a global model. Following the stages theory of history he had outlined in *On the Critique of Political Economy*, he perceived the British experience as the initial example of a universal process of capitalist development that other countries would have to emulate. At the very start of the book, in the preface to the first edition of Volume One, Marx cautioned his German readers about his use of English examples: "Should the German reader, shrug his shoulders, like a Pharisee, at the conditions of the English industrial and agricultural workers, or optimistically calm himself by thinking, that in Germany things are by far not yet so bad, then I must call out to him: De te fabula narratur!"[26] Breaking into Latin to emphasize, "It is your story being told!" Marx was asserting that the English examples employed in his narrative of capitalist expansion, exploitation, oppression, and ultimate self-destruction were no peculiarity of the island kingdom but universal directions of human history.

THE DEVIL, AS THE saying goes, is in the details, and the broad picture of the origins, nature, and destiny of a global capitalist economy in Volume One of *Capital* left a number of crucial issues for future publications. In a letter to Engels in April 1868, outlining his plans for the development of his work, Marx emphasized the "tendency of the rate of profit to fall in the progress of society," the appearance of surplus value to capitalists as profit, and the "transformation of surplus profit into ground rent."[27] Of these three points, the falling rate of profit was the key, helping to explain the other two, and also demonstrating Marx's relationship with the classical political economists of the early nineteenth century.

Elucidating the long-term direction of the rate of profit was a constant theoretical and empirical concern for Marx, from the first draft of his economics treatise until the eve of his death. In the *Grundrisse*, he described the law of the tendency of the rate of profit to fall as "in every respect the most important law of modern political economy . . . in spite of its simplicity, it has, up to now, never been intellectually grasped. . . ." The point was made in a different way in Volume Three of *Capital*, where Marx described the tendency of the rate of profit to fall as "an expression specific to the capitalist mode for production for the increasing development of the societal productive power of labor."[28] Since increasing labor productivity was central to his explanation of the extraction of relative surplus value in Volume One, and that extraction to his theory of the ultimate self-destruction of capitalism, his analysis of the falling rate of profit stood at the very heart of Marx's understanding of the life and death of the capitalist mode of production.

In both the *Grundrisse* and *Capital*, Marx did not claim to have invented the law of the tendency of the rate of profit to fall. Quite the opposite: he felt that his analysis explained correctly, for the first time, a characteristic observation of the political economy of his day. It was Adam Smith who had first asserted this tendency. David Ricardo had reformulated it in a different and more rigorous form, and it was once again endorsed in John Stuart Mill's standard work. For the latter two, the tendency had ended in a "stationary state," where the economy stopped growing, because the rate of profit had fallen so low that new investments were no longer profitable—a final ending that was Ricardo's nightmare, but an almost utopian prospect to Mill.[29] Both men perceived the falling rate of profit as culminating in some form of the end of capitalism. Marx thoroughly concurred, although his version of capitalism's end, a workers' uprising leading to a communist regime, was hardly one that the pro-capitalist political economists would have endorsed.

In his letter to Engels laying out the plans for work on the economics treatise after Volume One, Marx explained that the falling rate of profit "results from the idea already developed in Book One of the change in the composition of capital with the development of the social force of production. This is one of the greatest triumphs over . . . all previous economics." Marx's basic analysis, developed in Volume Three, was that competition among capitalists led them to become more productive by introducing ever more machinery, so that the value of the means of production—machinery, structures, fuel, raw materials—steadily rose compared to the value of labor; or, as Marx said, the ratio of constant to variable capital, the organic composition of capital, increased. Since according to the labor theory of value only labor could increase value or create surplus value, the price of the means of production just being passed on in the cost of the goods produced, then with the growing organic composition of capital, the rate of profit, the ratio of surplus value to capital invested, had to fall.[30]

Marx developed this initial insight in a wealth of elaborations, qualifications, and formulations. Quite a few of these formulations were explicitly algebraic, some even reflecting his study of calculus. There is one formula, not actually used by Marx—it did appear in his unpublished manuscripts, although incorrectly, due to a mistake in calculations—but much simpler than his, which shows the point of Marx's assertions and also reveals the problems with his assumption. First proposed by Samuel Moore, the English translator of Volume One of *Capital*, whom Engels consulted in editing the more mathematical sections of Marx's manuscripts, the formula has since been used frequently by commentators on Marx's economics.[31] The rate of profit is the return on investment, or, in Marx's language, the ratio of the surplus value (s) to the sum of the constant capital, the machines, structures, raw materials, etc. (c), and wages, or variable capital (v). This makes the rate of profit $\frac{s}{c+v}$. Moore proposed to divide numerator and denominator by v, giving $\frac{\frac{s}{v}}{1+\frac{c}{v}}$. The numerator of this new fraction is the rate of surplus value, and the denominator 1 plus the organic composition of capital.

What Marx was saying is that if the organic composition of capital, $\frac{c}{v}$, increased as more and more expensive machinery was used in production, costing steadily more than the workers' wages, the denominator increased, so that the entire fraction, the rate of profit, would tend toward zero. This is true, but only on the assumption that the numerator, $\frac{s}{v}$, the rate of surplus value, stays the same, or increases at a slower rate than $\frac{c}{v}$ does. If the increase in the organic composition of capital meant that capitalists were simply using more machinery, more raw materials, more fuel, and building more factory buildings, this assumption would be correct; but not if this new machinery were more productive than the machines or the unpowered artisanal labor it replaced. Increased productivity would mean that the workers could produce the goods whose sale was needed to pay their wages in a shorter part of the working day, leaving a greater proportion of the working day for the production of surplus value for the capitalists, thus increasing the rate of surplus value. This increasing productivity of labor across the entire capitalist economy was a central feature of Marx's analysis.

Even through his clumsier and more complicated formulations, Marx was aware of this problem, and he sought to resolve it: in the manuscripts making up Volume Three of *Capital*; in other, mostly algebraic manuscript studies of the falling rate of profit; in his correspondence with Engels; and, implicitly, in his discussion of the relative rate of surplus value in Volume One of *Capital*. He returned to the problem over and over again, writing down equations for the last time in 1882, a year before his death, and offering many explanations and solutions, none of which appeared to him entirely satisfactory.

One possibility was to assume that the rate of surplus value remained constant over time and across different economic sectors with varying ratios of constant to variable capital. Marx sometimes made that assumption, but he knew it was not accurate, for when he compared economically more advanced countries, such as the United Kingdom, with economically less advanced ones, like Austria, he took it for granted that the rate of surplus value would be higher in the former. A related possibility was that, considering the entire economy, the rate of surplus value might increase over time, but more slowly than the organic composition of capital. This, too, was an assumption made without any supporting reasoning or evidence.[32]

Marx found such solutions ultimately unsatisfying, as can be seen from his systematic consideration, in Volume Three, and in unpublished manuscripts, of the differing consequences for the rate of profit from different tendencies in the development of the rate of surplus value and the organic composition of capital. He posited other explanations. One was that the initial introduction of more productive machinery would temporarily raise the rate of surplus value, at least for the capitalist who was the first to employ these methods. As these productive innovations became standard, competition would drive down the prices of the goods produced, so that no additional profit would remain and the rate of surplus value would revert to its previous level. Another argument, seemingly taken from David Ricardo, was that more efficient and productive methods only increased the rate of surplus value if they were employed in the production of goods necessary for working-class consumption. It is clear how this argument works: if mass consumer goods were cheaper, then workers could be paid less, yet still maintain the same standard of living. They could then devote a smaller proportion of the working day to producing goods whose sale would pay their wages, and a larger proportion to goods whose sale provided capitalists with surplus value. One does have to wonder about the limitation to the production of consumer goods. To take an example of a major technological change underway as Marx was writing his economics treatise, a Bessemer converter could transform 3–5 tons of pig iron into steel in fifteen or twenty minutes, a process that took twenty-four hours in a puddling furnace. Would not such an enormous increase in the labor productivity of the producers' goods sector of the economy drive up the rate of surplus value?[33]

In Volume Three, Marx discussed countervailing tendencies, noting that, empirically, the rate of profit had not fallen over the previous three decades. He observed that the period had seen the introduction of high-profit luxury goods industries, and that there had been economies in the use of capital: more efficient steam engines, using less fuel, for instance. Trade with colonies and underdeveloped countries was another way to keep the rate of profit high; but Marx, unlike his successors, did not see such commerce as the life jacket of capitalism. Competition, he asserted, following a line of argument developed by Ricardo, would bring down initially high rates of profit. More generally, Marx saw colonialism as belonging to an earlier phase of capitalism, the pre-1800 era of primal accumulation, when capitalists extracted surplus value by force and violence; it was less relevant to an industrial age, when surplus value could be extracted in more peaceful fashion.[34]

The sheer variety of explanations demonstrated Marx's difficulty with the concept of the falling rate of profit. Most of his final views on the topic are contained in Volume One of *Capital*, written after Volumes Two and Three, even though Volume One did not explicitly address the issue. One explanation Marx gave in Volume One—especially the French and second German editions of the 1870s—was to treat improvements in productivity as the result of scientific and technological discoveries, having no necessary connection to investments. This analysis cut the link between the rising rates of labor productivity and the growing organic composition of capital. Another was to consider whether increases in productivity could raise the rate of surplus value, the rate of profit, and workers' wages simultaneously. Such a development, Marx concluded, would only be possible in a communist economy, never in a capitalist one—a conclusion that could only be reached if one assumed that under capitalism the rate of profit had to fall in the long term.[35]

There was one final and quite different consideration of the matter in a late manuscript fragment, written after 1875. In this very brief consideration, Marx suggested that capitalists would be reluctant to introduce more productive machinery and more efficient forms of production, because these would make their existing facilities obsolete and reduce their rate of profit. It would then fall to socialism to take up the former capitalist task of increasing the productivity of labor. This is an interesting idea—and one could certainly induce many examples of capitalists reluctant to innovate for precisely the reason Marx gave—but it ran contrary to all of Marx's previous thoughts on the topic.[36]

In the end, there was no proof of the tendency of the rate of profit to fall, a noticeable gap in Marx's analysis of the future of a capitalist economy. Although his vision of a capitalist world where wealth grew at one pole and misery at another did not require a falling rate of profit, the dynamics unleashed by that trend were needed in his system to make the bipolar result, with its revolutionary implications, an ineluctable possibility, with no room for mitigation. In postulating a falling rate of profit, Marx was not developing a new idea, but repeating what had been a truism of political economy since the publication of Smith's *Wealth of Nations*, nine decades before the appearance of Volume One of *Capital*. This idea had emerged and gained widespread assent in the late eighteenth- and early nineteenth-century British scene of rapid population growth pressing on limited resources, of halting and limited increases in labor productivity, and of a disruptive introduction of early industrial technology—a gloomy environment, very different from the more prosperous decades following the mid-nineteenth century. Marx's vision of capitalism's future was this transcribed version of capitalism's past, a backward look shared by many political economists of his day.

CLASSICAL POLITICAL ECONOMY FACED the problem of reconciling the labor theory of value with market prices. Marx did not believe that all economically relevant variables were determined by socially necessary labor time; he thought interest rates, for instance, arose from the intersection of supply and demand. He did assert that the price of commodities, and the wages of labor (the price of the commodity labor power), resulted from the socially necessary labor time required for their production and reproduction; the setting of prices by the intersection of supply and demand in the market was a semblance, behind which stood the real determinations of value.[37] Marx had to expose this semblance, explain how the inner logic of value led to its articulation as price.

This "transformation problem," the transformation of value into price, is one faced by all economists—in the twentieth and twenty-first centuries very much a minority—who reject the idea that price and value are identical. The primary representative of this viewpoint in recent decades has been the neo-Ricardian school of the Italian economist Piero Sraffa, whose followers have devised elaborate mathematical formulations of this transformation problem.[38] Marx's own ideas were much simpler; he found them considerably easier to explain than he did the tendency of the rate of profit to fall.

Marx first articulated his solution to the transformation problem in a letter to Engels in 1862, and he reiterated it in Volume Three of *Capital*. The solution began by imagining the sum of all production in an entire capitalist economy, its constant and variable capital, and its rate of surplus value. This would produce an overall rate of profit, which, Marx argued, would, via competition between capitalists and the movement of capital from one business to another, eventually become general. Because the rate of profit was set by the organic composition of capital and the rate of surplus value in the entire economy, in some specific economic branches, whose organic composition differed from the overall average (Marx assumed here a constant rate of surplus value across the economy), goods might sell at a market price above or below their value. This price, the cost of capital, plus the average rate of profit, Marx called the "price of production," and he identified it with Adam Smith's "natural price" of a commodity, David Ricardo's "price of production," and the eighteenth-century French economists, the Physiocrats', *prix nécessaire*. All these concepts referred to the respective economists' reconciliation of the difference between value determined by labor and price determined by the market. As was the case with the tendency of the rate of profit to fall, Marx placed himself squarely in the tradition of political economy, arguing that his work provided the correct explanation for observations made and conclusions long reached but not properly understood.[39]

As the followers of Sraffa have pointed out, Marx's solution to the transformation problem is formally incorrect.[40] But besides their criticism, which involved mathematical techniques not existing in Marx's day and well beyond his own knowledge of mathematics, Marx's solution seems to be very strongly at odds with his observations about the central features of an industrial and capitalist economy. Marx explained that the rate of profit was equalized across different economic sectors by capital flowing from less profitable to more profitable ones. One would expect capitalists to seek out the greatest profit, but what made one sector more profitable than another? In his analysis, Marx assumed that the rate of surplus value was the same across all economic sectors. In other words, a given quantity of labor produced a certain amount of profit. If that were the case, then the rate of profit, which was the ratio of the surplus value to the sum of the constant and the variable capital, was highest where the constant capital was smallest. In his letter to Engels outlining his solution to the transformation problem, Marx compared a textile mill—by the standards of the 1860s, a highly mechanized enterprise—with a large tailoring workshop, a craft operation without machinery or steam power, and asserted that the latter was the more profitable business. "Were the value of $c = 0$," Marx wrote in Volume Three, "the rate of profit would stand at its maximum."[41]

The explicit statement that the least mechanized firms were the most profitable sounds empirically rather dubious, whether considering capitalism in the nineteenth century or capitalism today. Marx's solution to the transformation problem required capitalists to equalize the rate of profit by transferring funds from less profitable to more profitable sectors of the economy, but that would mean from more mechanized to less mechanized ones. It is difficult to see how such a movement of capital could be reconciled with Marx's repeated, analytically crucial observations about the growing social productivity of labor and the increasing organic composition of capital. A possible solution would have been to relax the assumption that the rate of surplus value was the same in all branches of the economy. If the more mechanized sectors had a higher rate of surplus value, then they could have been more profitable than the less mechanized ones, and capital would flow their way. But such an assumption would have undermined Marx's central assertion of a falling rate of profit caused by an increasing organic composition of capital. Marx's analysis of the relationship between value and price, an investigation of a central problem of the political economy of his day, ended up raising still more questions about his entire vision of the future of capitalism.

KARL MARX AND AGRICULTURE together in the same sentence sounds rather odd. Marx's capitalism was of an urban and industrial nature, filled with steam engines, railroads, and textile mills. His cities were dense and burgeoning, teeming with working-class slums. His vision of a capitalist future was more of the same, only more extreme. Sarcastic comments about the "idiocy of rural life" in the *Communist Manifesto*, or about French peasants being like a bunch of potatoes in a sack in *The Eighteenth Brumaire*, do not suggest any sentimental feelings about the countryside or regrets about the dissolution of rural folkways under the impact of a capitalist market economy. If Marx cared little for rural life, the policies of twentieth-century communist governments, claiming to follow his doctrines, have magnified this impression. These governments displayed strong, at times downright genocidal hostility toward farmers, and their agricultural policies generally ended in disaster.

Such a view of Marx as hostile or at best indifferent to the countryside and its denizens ignores the development of his thought. Even though he lived in the world's largest city after 1849, he became steadily more convinced of the significance of agriculture in a capitalist economy and of the importance of social conflict in the countryside for his revolutionary plans. In part, he gained these views through an intensive study of the works of eighteenth- and early nineteenth-century political economists—the French Physiocrats plus Ricardo and Malthus, in particular—for whom the economics of agriculture were crucial to their understanding of the functioning and the patterns of development of the entire economy. Marx's journalism and political engagement also influenced his views. He reported frequently for the *New York Tribune* on agricultural prospects in England and the state of the grain trade. His obsession with Lord Palmerston led to a study of the power of the great Whig landowners. Both through his association with the IWMA and the campaigns of its English affiliates for a more democratic franchise in Great Britain, and via his personal connections to Irish nationalism, Marx became aware of the nature of landlord rule in Ireland, and its ramifications for political and social structures in Britain, the center of global capitalism.

As a result of all these interests, a considerable portion of *Capital*

was devoted to disputed agricultural questions in the political economy of Marx's day, especially the nature of ground rent, as well as the
extent of crop yields and the prospects for increasing them. Marx's
investigations into these topics and his conclusions about them never
made it into the portions of *Capital* published in his lifetime, in part
because he became convinced of the importance of agriculture-related
topics and continued his studies of these until the very end of his life.
But a consideration of the material on agriculture, which was published
as part of Volume Three, illuminates the importance of Marx's predecessors in shaping his own views, and demonstrates, in an unexpected
context, the problems emerging from Marx's ideas about the falling
rate of profit.

Marx relied on conditions in Great Britain not only for his analysis of industrial capitalism but of agricultural capitalism as well. He
pointed to a small number of aristocratic or gentry landowners, renting
out their land to capitalist tenant farmers, who employed large numbers
of propertyless agricultural laborers to cultivate it. This three-class
model—landlord, capitalist farmer, agricultural laborer—made a considerable impression on Marx. In the concluding section of *Capital*, he
talked of the "wage laborers, capitalists and landowners, [who] make
up the three great classes of modern society based on the capitalist
mode of production."[42] This was quite different from the passage in
the *Communist Manifesto*, written some fifteen years earlier, when Marx
and Engels had explained that capitalist society was being divided into
two great classes, the bourgeoisie and the proletariat. The addition of a
class of landowners is compelling evidence of the growing importance
of agriculture and rural society on Marx's thought.

Marx was certainly aware that there were many other forms of
agricultural production, beyond the British model. A brief section of
Capital dealt with the small peasant agriculture of France and Marx's
native Rhineland. Another variant existed in east-central and Eastern
Europe, especially the Russian Empire following the emancipation of

the serfs in 1861: a mix of noble landlords, some directing the cultivation of their own estates, others renting them out to tenants, small peasants, and landless laborers. In European settler societies in Canada, Australia, and the United States, the landowner and the capitalist farmer were the same person. For much of the 1870s, Marx studied these two forms of agricultural production intensively, but never reached the point of writing up an analysis of them.[43]

When political economists investigated farm production in early nineteenth-century Great Britain, they assumed that the good-quality land was already being used at its maximum productivity for agriculture. They then focused on the economic effects of a growing population. The best-known prognosis, one cited ever since, came from Thomas Malthus. Since the best land was already used at its maximum productivity, the only way to increase agricultural output was to cultivate inferior land, whose crop yield would be less than that from the land currently in production, so that food supply would increase less than population did. If that process continued unchecked, the ultimate result would be large-scale starvation.

David Ricardo, Malthus's chief opponent, nonetheless shared a good deal of his enemy's analysis. In Ricardo's economic model, the combination of population growth and the cultivation of inferior land would not lead to starvation, but to rising food prices. Capitalist manufacturers would have to pay their workers more, so the latter had enough to eat, which would tend to reduce the capitalists' profits. (Like Marx's capitalists, who were unable to raise the rate of surplus value, Ricardo's capitalists were unable to introduce more efficient forms of production so that they could pay higher wages and still make larger profits.) Ultimately, this situation would reduce the rate of profit to zero, and lead to the "stationary state," where capitalists did not invest and the economy ceased to grow. The increase in food prices would, in Ricardo's analysis, at first accrue to farmers. Since farmers were tenants, they would bid more for the chance to produce food on the landlords' properties, so that their growing profits would flow into the hands of the landlords as higher rents. The only way out of this gloomy situation, at least temporarily, was to import food from other countries, which is why Ricardo strongly favored the repeal of the Corn Laws that imposed a tariff on imported grain. After his death, his ideas made him the hero of the liberals, radicals, and capitalists of the Anti–Corn Law League, who fought successfully for this repeal.[44]

Marx greatly admired Ricardo, calling him "the greatest economist of the nineteenth century" and the "economist of the modern age." He was rather less positive about Ricardo's rival. Malthus's profound pessimism about the possibility of human progress in any kind of society, his extreme political conservatism, his endorsement of the aristocracy, and his religious vocation (Malthus was, by profession, an Anglican parson) pushed almost every single one of Marx's many buttons. In a lengthy and particularly venomous footnote to Volume One of *Capital*, Marx denounced Malthus's famous essay on population as a "schoolboy's superficial plagiarism, declaimed in the style of a damned, rotten priest, copied from De Foe, Sir James Steuart, Townsend, Franklin, Wallace, etc. containing not a single sentence thought up by him." Malthus's mediocre and mendacious work, Marx went on, "was joyfully greeted by the English oligarchy," seeking a counterrevolutionary response to the progressive doctrines of Condorcet in the age of the French Revolution. Marx then denounced the many Anglican parsons who had taken up the pastime of writing on political economy and compared their work unfavorably to the economic writings of anti-clerical, Enlightened philosophers such as Adam Smith.[45]

Even if Malthus had stolen all his ideas, they still needed refutation, and Marx was quick to provide it. Overpopulation, he asserted, was not caused by the lower classes breeding faster than the food supply could be increased; rather, it was a result of the growing mechanization of production, which offered fewer employment opportunities for the workers. It was useless to improve the working-class condition by the

"Malthusian" practice of birth control. (Malthus, like most conservative Christians, then and now, regarded contraception as deeply sinful, but freethinking political economists, such as John Stuart Mill, advocated it.) Capitalists would simply respond to a decline in the number of workers by expanding mechanization rather than increasing wages. All such "Malthusian" ideas involved, according to Marx, falsely interpreting the social and economic consequences of the accumulation of capital as though they were laws of nature.[46]

For all his personal attacks on Malthus and forthright rejection of his views, Marx remained haunted by the problem of providing adequate food for a growing population. Without a fundamental reform of agriculture, as he observed to Engels in 1851, "Father Malthus will prove to be right." The solution lay in the application of science and technology to agriculture. Just a few months before he shared his doubts about Malthus with Engels, Marx read an article in *The Economist* about putting wires into the ground in a rectangular pattern around a field, to pick up electricity from the atmosphere and improve the soil's fertility. Intrigued by this possibility, he wrote to Engels and to Roland Daniels, his unofficial science adviser, about it. In 1878–79 Marx was already suffering from the tuberculosis that would kill him; yet he spent a substantial proportion of his fast-declining energies taking extensive notes on agricultural chemistry, a long-term interest of his. For anybody steeped in the political economy of early nineteenth-century England it was not so simple to exorcise the Malthusian specter.[47]

Intimately connected to the question of the adequacy of the food supply was the nature of ground rent. In this area of agricultural economics, it was Ricardo rather than Malthus who had Marx's attention. Ricardo had devised the theory of differential rent: the idea that rent on land was equal to the difference in yield between the most fertile and the least fertile piece of land. Farmers received the same price for the crops produced on any piece of land, so the most fertile land would be the most desirable, and farmers would bid up the rent they were willing to pay landlords for the right to work that land, until the prospective rent equaled the difference between the yield on that land and that on the worst land that could produce a crop. Opposing Ricardo's theories were the adherents of absolute rent: the proposition that the rent on a piece of land was equal to the return on the capital invested in it.

Marx's antipathy toward private ownership of land was strong, more pronounced than his dislike of other aspects of capitalist private property. In Volume Three of *Capital*, he noted:

> From the standpoint of a higher economic and social formation the private property of particular individuals in part of the globe will appear as ridiculous as the private property of one person in another person. An entire society, a nation, even all simultaneously existing societies together, are not owners of the earth. They are just its possessors, its usufructors and, as good family fathers, have to pass it on to following generations in an improved condition.[48]

Other capitalists, if taking surplus value from the proletariat, were at least directing an increase in society's production, while landlords were simply extracting surplus value from capitalists without doing anything for it at all: "The capitalist is still an independent functionary in the development of surplus value and surplus product. The landowner, without any activity of his own, only has to divert into his own pocket a growing proportion of surplus value and surplus product."[49]

Landlords, in Marx's view, were monopolists and parasites; compared to them, capitalists were relatively admirable creatures. In his discussion of the relationship between English landlords and their capitalist tenant farmers, Marx described how tenants paid their landlords "tribute," how landlords "blackmailed" the rent out of the tenants and "swindled" them—one of the very few passages in *Capital* showing much sympathy for capitalists. (Admittedly, Marx went on to write that the tenant farmers made up their losses in rent by depressing the wages of agricultural laborers below the subsistence minimum.) What made the situation worse was that the landlords' position was steadily improving. A falling rate of profit, and with it falling rates of interest, consistently raised the price of land.[50]

In these respects, Marx's attitude toward landlords was similar to Ricardo's, definitely no friend of aristocratic and gentry landowners. Some of Ricardo's more radical but still quite pro-capitalist followers even advocated the nationalization of land. Marx accepted Ricardo's ideas about differential rent, and discussed them in some detail. He argued that Ricardo's version was not sweeping enough, depending as it did on bringing into cultivation marginal land; instead, he argued, any difference in the fertility of land would be enough to create a differential rent.[51]

If he endorsed a version of Ricardo's theory of differential rent, Marx also accepted the ideas of Ricardo's opponents about the existence of absolute rent. Yet Ricardo's influence extended to the endorsement of his antagonists' theories, because Marx's theory of absolute rent emerged from his solution of the transformation problem, which involved the differential rate of profit in different branches of the capitalist economy. An average rate of profit, according to Marx, developed because capital flowed from the less profitable to the more profitable branches of the economy, and Marx generally identified the more profitable branches with a lower organic composition of capital.

Compared to industry, agriculture was less mechanized, and more profitable, so that capital would flow into it. Ricardo's landlords, in his theory of differential rent, siphoned off the difference in productivity between the most and least productive land. In a very similar way, Marx's landlords, in his theory of absolute rent, siphoned off the extra profits, the difference between the rate of profit in agriculture and the average rate of profit in all capitalist enterprises. Such a state of affairs would continue until the organic composition of capital in agriculture was the same as the organic composition of capital averaged across all economic sectors. At that point, capital would no longer flow to agriculture, since it was no more profitable than any other economic sector. Absolute rent would cease to exist, although differential rent, reflecting the difference between lands of different fertility, would continue.[52]

This eventual end to absolute rent contradicted an assertion Marx made, following Ricardo, that rents would increase over time and landlords would soak up an ever-increasing proportion of total surplus value. How could this contradiction be resolved? Marx's answer was the role of the natural fertility of the soil: "the increase of social productive power in agriculture only compensates the decline in the power of nature, or does not even compensate it . . . so that in spite of technological development the product does not become cheaper; instead it is prevented from becoming ever more expensive."[53] This was a fundamentally Malthusian argument, that the best land was already being cultivated, and additional cultivation or improved methods could not increase agricultural output enough to make for the increasing demand of a growing population. Marx combined his analysis of agriculture in a capitalist economy with two of his key assertions about the development of capitalism: the equalization of the rate of profit across an entire economy, needed to resolve the transformation problem, and the increasing organic composition of capital. The upshot was a contradictory picture that could only be resolved by borrowing ideas from an economist whose person and theories Marx despised.

THE EXTENDED DISCUSSION OF the economics of farming in *Capital* and the increasing significance Marx gave to agriculture and rural society point to a backward-looking economics, a treatise written in the 1860s, whose central interests and approaches stemmed from circumstances in the first decades of the nineteenth century. Did Marx, the secular prophet, have nothing to say about future developments of capitalism? There were brief passages in *Capital*, primarily in Volume Three, where he took up features of economic life that would rise to considerable importance in the twentieth century and beyond. As is almost always the case with Marx's economic writings, his observations about these features were perceptive and sharply written, but not entirely prophetic.

One such area was corporations, a form of economic organization during the 1860s found primarily among railroads and public utilities. (Engels, in editing Marx's writing on corporations for Volume Three, added a note on the enormous expansion of this form of business in the 1880s and 1890s.) Already critical in his 1850s journalism on the *Crédit Mobilier*, Marx continued this assessment in *Capital*, asserting that such a bank could only exist in France, a country where "neither the credit system nor big industry has developed to its modern height." In more modern countries, such as Great Britain or the United States, it would have been impossible. Far from seeing financial corporations as the capitalist avant-garde, Marx perceived them as marks of economic backwardness.[54]

Marx understood that corporations implied scattered stock ownership, payment of dividends (which he regarded as further evidence of the declining rate of profit), and possibilities for stock speculation and stock swindling. He was also aware of what would later be called the separation of ownership from control, where salaried corporate managers directed firms whose owners were individual stockholders with little influence on business decisions. In his discussion of this separation, Marx considered corporations alongside workers' production cooperatives, both of which he perceived as evidence of the imminence of socialism. In corporations, capital was no longer the possession of individuals, but "social capital, capital of directly associated individuals. . . ." Corporations were the "abolition of capital as private property within the limits of the capitalist mode of production itself." Far from being a new stage of capitalism, corporations in

Marx's view were evidence of capitalism's end—an idea first devised by French socialists of the early nineteenth century, once again a sign of the backward-looking nature of Marx's economic views.[55]

Another feature of twentieth- and twenty-first-century capitalism has been the rise of the service sector in the economy. Marx was certainly aware of the sale of services, and he included them in the German expression *Ware*—yet another reason why "commodities" is a poor translation. If hardly at contemporary levels, services were still a significant part of the nineteenth-century economy. Marx's comment about workers in the service sector was: "From the whore to the Pope, there is a mass of such scum." In a more positive vein, he also included doctors and teachers in that group. Such labor, he asserted, was useful (sometimes, anyway), and those engaged in it were producing, but they were not productive in terms of his analysis of capitalism, for their labor did not generate surplus value. In other words, Marx regarded service workers as mostly self-employed, and transactions with them as examples of the simple exchange of commodities for money. He also considered commercial employees, such as clerks or traveling salesmen. He saw their work as part of the division of labor among capitalists, including manufacturers, wholesalers, retailers, and financiers: all shared in the surplus value workers produced. The common twentieth- and twenty-first-century situation in which capitalists employ workers to produce services rather than goods was outside Marx's intellectual universe.[56]

BASIC CONCEPTS OF MARX'S economics were as linked to early nineteenth-century economists as they were to early nineteenth-century economic circumstances. Marx himself felt that post-Ricardo economic theories were, with very few exceptions, a production of mediocre epigones. But the land of Smith, Malthus, Ricardo, James and John Stuart Mill had nothing to say about Marx's continuation of and challenge to their economic theories. The language barrier was impenetrable: the only English-language notice of *Capital* to appear in Marx's lifetime was one paragraph as part of a review on twenty-two different German-language publications. The anonymous reviewer knew little about political economy and seemed a good deal more interested in a scholarly tome on Romanian poetry.[57] Marx's economic treatises had a greater intellectual impact in central Europe, where readers spoke the language in which he wrote, but most of them rejected the intellectual world of classical political economy that formed the basis of Marx's ideas.

Marx himself was deeply frustrated by the lack of response to his first work, *On the Critique of Political Economy*. He veered between accusing pro-capitalist economists of engaging in a conspiracy of silence to suppress his ideas and condemning his publisher for inept marketing— or, perhaps, for being in on the conspiracy. Marx did succeed in offending his Berlin publisher with his accusations, so that he needed to seek out a new publisher in Hamburg when *Capital* was ready for the press. Although biographers have followed Marx's belief in the lack of interest in his initial work of political economy, that opinion is not entirely correct. The pamphlet sold out its entire printing within a year of publication. It did receive a number of short reviews, by some well-known German economists of the time, generally in specialized business and literary journals, to which Marx in London had no access.

One of these reviews, in Bremen, by the prominent pro–free trade economist and journalist Viktor Böhmert, praised the pamphlet's investigation of monetary theories, but criticized its Hegelian "handling of economic occurrences as moments of a dialectical process . . . a form of expression which . . . exceeds the boundaries of that which one has, by God, alas, allowed authors operating with Hegelian phraseology to make of our good German language." Böhmert wondered why Marx could not use the "opposing genuinely empirical [method] of all the natural sciences." It was an evaluation that emphasized the growing position of positivism in post-1850 German and European thought.[58]

There were no reviews of Marx's book in the German daily newspapers, the major reason he became convinced of a conspiracy of silence against him. Determined not to allow this to happen again, Marx and Engels arranged to have Engels publish anonymous reviews of *Capital* in a wide variety of German dailies. Since those dailies would not tolerate an openly pro-communist review, they discussed what sort of political personas Engels should adopt for the reviews. The whole point of the exercise was to spur a public debate in central Europe about Marx's work.

For all his efforts to get such a debate going, Marx was once again frustrated by the silence of the leading newspapers. By 1867, a German labor movement had come into existence, which greeted the work of a pro-labor and socialist economist with enormous enthusiasm. Johann Baptist von Schweitzer, for all his personal and political differences with Marx, ran a nine-part article series in the *Social Democrat*, providing a detailed account of *Capital*'s contents, and heavily praising its point of view. One of the leading social democrats, Johann Most—later to become an anarchist and flee for the United States—wrote a popular summary of Marx's work under the title *Capital and Labor*, in 1874. Marx, although he inevitably had criticisms, was impressed with the book; he and Engels edited and revised it for a second edition, published in the Saxon city of Chemnitz in 1876.[59]

German economists did review *Capital*, often offering impassioned defenses of private property against Marx's subversive doctrines. But, gradually, another view emerged, at first just via word of mouth, that economists and others with related occupations, such as senior civil servants and statisticians, were sympathetic to Marx's ideas. Ludwig Kugelmann reported that a Berlin academic had been so impressed by

Capital that he wanted to nominate Marx for a professorship of political economy at a German university.

With the passage of time, more favorable comments began to appear in print. This attitude was connected with the rise in central Europe of a group of academics critical of the doctrines of classical political economy. Known as the "Historical School," these economists denounced the abstract theorizing of Smith, Ricardo, and the Mills; they wanted an empirical examination of labor and business conditions, a discussion of the economic effects of institutions, and an analysis of the historically specific circumstances of the development of capitalism in different countries and regions. Instead of leaving the economy to the workings of the market, they advocated government intervention, via wages and hours legislation, health and safety inspections, and, more controversially, the creation of a social insurance system, the revival of the guilds, and the imposition of protective tariffs. From the advocacy of these measures, they came to be known in the 1870s as *Kathedersozialisten*, or "chaired professor socialists"—a distinct exaggeration, since a large majority of them were adherents of the liberal and conservative parties. A few, mostly younger men, above all the economist and sociologist Werner Sombart (later to become famous for posing the question, "Why is there no socialism in the United States?"), were willing to flirt, briefly, with supporting the socialist labor movement.[60]

This reconciliation between Marx's ideas and those of German economists was, essentially, a misunderstanding. Far from rejecting the abstract economic reasoning of Ricardo, Marx strongly endorsed it and devised his own, Hegelianized version of it. More insightful members of the Historical School recognized this feature early on. One of the first scholarly reviews of *Capital*, written in 1869 by Hermann Roesler, a professor at the University of Rostock, praised Marx's historical investigations of the development of capitalism. It also denounced his economic abstractions, noting that Marx's description of labor power was "exactly as Smithianism is accustomed to representing it," and that his labor theory of value was devised "with Ricardo," as "Smith, J. St. Mill," and others of that school had propounded it.[61]

Marx had nothing good to say about Historical School's arsenal of state-sponsored economic remedies, in view of his intense suspicion of any measures taken by an authoritarian Prussian and German government. Even before he became a communist, Marx had been pro–free trade, and he continued to hold this position as a critic of capitalism. If there were to be any interference in the workings of the market, which was leading to the collapse of capitalism, then it would have to come from trade unions and the politically organized labor movement, not from economics professors and German state officials.[62]

Members of the Historical School were not the only later nineteenth-century economists to reject the ideas of classical political economy. More widespread, and more successful in establishing a European and worldwide following, were the marginal utility theorists, who found the problem with classical political economy not in its theoretical abstractions, but in the wrong theoretical abstractions. These economists, whose ideas form the basis of contemporary mainstream economics, rejected the labor theory of value and asserted that the value of a good or service was determined by consumers' subjective appraisal of the usefulness of purchasing an additional one of these goods or services as against the purchase of any other good or service. This viewpoint brought together use value and exchange value, which Marx had so carefully separated. It identified value completely with market price, and perceived the intersection of supply and demand as the determinant of value, rather than labor time as Marx, following the classical political economists, asserted.

Marginal utility theory was just developing in the 1870s. According to the Russian academic Maxim Kovalevsky, then a frequent visitor in the Marx household, Marx was resuming his study of calculus to respond to the ideas of an English economist, William Stanley Jevons, one of the first marginal utility theorists, who deployed this advanced mathematics. Marx never seems to have put his considerations of this new version of economics on paper, but by the time all three volumes of *Capital* had appeared, it had increasingly become the dominant form of economic analysis. In Germany itself, marginal utility theory could make little headway against the Historical School; instead, it was Austria that became a center of marginal utility analysis in the German-speaking world and on the Continent more generally. Eugen von Böhm-Bawerk, one of the leading Austrian economists, wrote a celebrated critique of Marx's ideas in 1895, following the publication of Volume Three of *Capital*. The point at which Böhm-Bawerk struck at Marx was his analysis of the transformation problem, the way that commodities, whose value was derived from the socially necessary labor time needed for their production and reproduction, came to be sold at market prices. Böhm-Bawerk pointed out that in Marx's work this transformation occurred via the establishment of an average rate of profit across different industries, by means of "competition." What, asked the Austrian economist, was this competition, if not the intersection of supply and demand in the market? If this was the case, then prices and values were not determined by labor time, but by market interaction of consumer preferences, as the marginal utility school asserted.[63]

Böhm-Bawerk was not contending, as other contemporaries did, that Marx had gotten the transformation problem wrong, but that a transformation from value to prices was conceptually impossible. His criticism was a declaration that most economists were living in a completely different intellectual world from the one Marx had inhabited. Of course, this applied to Adam Smith, David Ricardo, and James and John Stuart Mill as well, since they too had based their economic analysis on a labor theory of value. Böhm-Bawerk was honest enough to admit this, but most "neoclassical" economists, as partisans of the marginal utility approach came to be known, were not so open about the fundamental differences in their understanding of economics from that of the iconic pioneers of their discipline. They hid these differences by quoting phrases, such as Smith's "invisible hand," generally wrenched completely out of their original context.[64]

By the beginning of the twentieth century, Marx's economics had become unorthodox, fundamentally different from the mainstream, neoclassical version of economics, and also at odds with the chief established alternative to the mainstream, the ideas of the Historical School. Marx's economic conceptions, however, had found a home in the burgeoning early twentieth-century socialist labor movement, as part of that movement's more general rejection of the ideas of the bourgeois society it criticized and rejected. This was not at all what Marx himself had intended. Far from opposing the mainstream political economy of his day, the ideas of Smith, Ricardo, and their followers, Marx had embraced it and promoted his own work as the most advanced and correct version of their approach. His criticisms generally centered on the extent to which political economists were unwilling to develop the ultimate consequences of their ideas. Marx was an orthodox political economist, who rejected most socialist criticisms of Ricardo. He did not want to see his economic writings limited to a ghettoized existence in a labor movement promoting a counterculture to the established bourgeois capitalist world; he had yearned for a public confrontation in the established newspapers, magazines, and scholarly journals of his day, and was frustrated when it failed to materialize.

Marx's basic economic principles, his views about the main lines of economic development, and his conception of the place of his particular economic vision in the public sphere, had all been shaped by the intellectual trends and economic and political circumstances of the first half of the nineteenth century. When his ideas finally percolated into a broader public domain, a good decade after his death, in part as the result of the tireless and painstaking editorial labors of Friedrich Engels, all these circumstances had changed. What was once economic orthodoxy had become outdated and unscientific to the economic mainstream; or, if one prefers, dissenting and unorthodox. What was once the future of economic developments had become their past, and what were once common assumptions of bourgeois society had become the prized possession of a labor movement distant from and hostile to that society.

12

The Private Man

NO SINGLE PERIOD ALLOWS us to peer more insightfully into Marx's personal life than the twenty-five years between 1850 and 1875. During that time, the challenges of being a father and the head of a growing family were in precarious co-existence with the demands posed of an intellectual and political leader. At the end of the quarter century, Marx was increasingly withdrawn from active political life. His surviving children were grown, and the two who were married had made him a grandfather. Plagued by chronic illness, he faced a premature old age, at a time when modern, scientific medicine had yet to make significant inroads into Victorian life. This quarter century of adult maturity is a good time to observe Marx the private man: husband and father, friend and enemy, bourgeois intellectual, German and Jew. Distinctions between private and public are never absolute, and this admittedly commonplace reflection goes double for a passionately engaged figure such as Marx.

MARX WAS MOVED TO reflect on manhood after visiting Karl Schapper on his deathbed in April 1870. In the final stages of tuberculosis, Schapper received his onetime ally and rival, and, as Marx wrote to Engels, "behaved in a truly distinguished manner." While Schapper's wife and son were in the room, he spoke of his impending demise in French, to spare them the details. Remaining true to his principles, Schapper mocked Arnold Ruge, who had gone back on his Young Hegelian atheism and proclaimed a belief in the afterlife, stating sarcastically that if this were true, "the soul of Schapper would give a pounding to the soul of Ruge in the hereafter." Schapper was particularly proud that his family was cared for, in spite of his reduced circumstances: his daughter married, his oldest son with his own business, the younger boys apprenticed to a goldsmith, and his wife as his heir. "'Tell all our people,'" Schapper said to Marx, "'that I have remained true to principles. . . . During the era of reaction I had enough to do, bringing my family through. I have lived as a hard working worker and die as a proletarian.'" Profoundly impressed by Schapper's bearing and demeanor, Marx observed that "The genuinely masculine in his character now once again appears clearly and strikingly."[1]

Schapper's manhood lay in being principled and courageous, remaining loyal to his communist ideas, holding fast to the atheism that was integrally related to them, and not allowing fear of his impending death to weaken his beliefs. Marx's own life embodied these concepts. He, too, remained true to his principles, even when expediency would have dictated otherwise. Marx was not afraid of confronting death, especially by challenging people who had impugned his honor to duels. These challenges were hardly limited to the raucous teenager and touchy young lover, but continued in his years as an adult. Accompanied by Ferdinand Freiligrath and Wilhelm Wolff, he burst into the editorial offices of one German-language London weekly in 1851 and challenged the editor, who had accused Marx of embezzling funds from the refugee committee, to a duel. Twenty years later, then fifty-three years old, he challenged another editor to a duel over printed assertions that he was behind the ostensible atrocities of the

Paris Commune. Although Marx regarded dueling as an archaic, feudal survival, he nonetheless saw it as a way for "individuality to assert its rights" in bourgeois society, and so sometimes a necessity. Marx's endorsement of this expression of masculinity was in line with a very common attitude among Germany's educated middle class, a deeply entrenched social custom that continued until the mass slaughter of the First World War upended previous ideas about the meaning of death-defying courage.[2]

Schapper's courage and loyalty to principle were embedded in his family life. As a man, he was the head of his family. He had supported his wife and children the best he could. Being a loyal and loving husband and father—a man both commanding a household, but also providing for the dependents in it—was another integral feature of manhood as Marx tried to live it.

Marx's marriage to Jenny von Westphalen lay at the center of his life. It had commenced with their wedding day in Kreuznach in 1843 and ended with Jenny's death in 1881. As with any long-married couple, the two had their share of arguments and disagreements, "the worm that is in every marriage," as Jenny wrote. Most of these disputes centered on questions of money, and were most frequent during financial crises. At times the quarrels were severe, and led Marx to regret ever having gotten married. He ventilated his complaints to Engels on a number of occasions. Writing in 1858, he stated, "There is no greater stupidity for people with universal aspirations than to marry and so to betray themselves to the petty wretchedness of domestic and private life."[3]

Yet to all observers, Karl and Jenny remained the picture of a loving and devoted couple. Karl's mature love letters testify to his devotion. One written in 1856, when Jenny was visiting her mother in Trier, encapsulates Karl's love for Jenny, her place in his life, and his ideas about loving relationships between men and women:

Great passions, which, due to the closeness of their object, take the form of small habits, grow and once more reach their natural size through the magic effect of distance. . . . My love of you, as soon as you are distant, appears as . . . a giant, in which all the energies of my spirit and all the characteristics of my heart are crowded together. I feel myself again as a man, because I feel a great passion. The many different perspectives in which we are enveloped by university studies and modern intellectual self-cultivation, and the skepticism, with which we necessarily note the problems with all subjective and objective impressions, are designed to make us all small and weak and whining and indecisive. But the love, not of Feuerbach's human being, not of Moleschott's metabolism, not of the proletariat, but the love of the beloved, namely of you, makes the man once again into a man.[4]

One should not read too much theoretical reflection into a love letter, but Marx was staking out a distinct position for romantic love, separate from and beyond political action, scholarly evaluation, and the class struggle. Love sustained his life, removing him from the doubts and uncertainties, compromises and ambiguities that defined his political and intellectual engagement. His union with Jenny allowed him to be decisive and straightforward, in short, to be nothing less than a fully realized adult male.

With this attitude, Karl could easily have consigned Jenny to a purely domestic sphere, as women of the European and American middle class so often were in the nineteenth century. He could have excluded her from his intellectual and political engagements. But this was evidently not the case. Jenny was Karl's secretary or amanuensis, copying out his manuscripts in a good hand, and handling correspondence when he was ill. She had, as Karl noted shortly after his wife's death, a "passionate interest" in his political strategies and theoretical formulations. Whether she helped her husband devise them is harder to say, especially because Laura and Eleanor Marx burned most of their parents' correspondence after their deaths. Jenny's own, fragmentary memoirs, written in 1865 when Karl was visiting his Dutch relatives, dealt with her husband and his causes, but concentrated on the difficulties and pleasures of their family life together.[5]

Offspring were an integral part of that family life and Marx was proud of his virility and the children resulting from it. One important reason he and Engels were so contemptuous of Moses Hess was that the latter's sexual failings, probably impotence, led Hess's wife to run after lovers and act promiscuously.[6] Equating masculinity with virility proved taxing for women, and Jenny did go through seven pregnancies. The practice of birth control, only becoming common in most European countries during the half century following Marx's death, was in part inspired by the wish to break this equivalence between masculinity and number of offspring.

Jenny and Karl certainly knew about contraception. In August 1844, when Jenny was visiting her mother in Trier with their first child, she wrote to Karl in Paris: "Little Karl, how long will the little doll play a solo role? I fear, I fear, when papa and mama are together once again, living in their marital community of goods, that soon a duo will take the stage. Or should we begin to do it in the good Parisian way?"[7] Like most questions about intimate behavior in the past, it is impossible to know whether Karl and Jenny tried the "good Parisian way" (most probably the practice of withdrawal) and failed to get it to work, or rejected the possibility altogether. In view of Jenny's six pregnancies in the eleven years following the letter, it must have been one or the other.

In Marx's view, manliness meant fatherhood. Nineteenth-century bourgeois fathers have long had a bad press—regarded as domineering, tyrannical, insensitive, unloving, even violent. Friedrich Engels and Moses Hess, both confidants of Marx, had to endure such paternal tyrants. At best, bourgeois fathers appeared as distant authority figures, wrapped up in their work and unavailable to their children. Recent historical studies, though, have tended to rehabilitate fathers, pointing out that at least some of them—even very buttoned up German or Swiss ones—played with their children and were physically affectionate and emotionally accessible.[8] Marx was certainly that sort of father. Visitors to his house as well as his own children commented on his love and affection for them. They noted the way he played with them, told them stories, and read to them. The desolate moods that followed his children's deaths bespoke a paternal love that was anything but distant. Marx profoundly enjoyed the presence of children—not just his own but all children. Wilhelm Liebknecht, who was constantly in the household during the 1850s, remembered Marx as "the most tender father":

> One must have seen Marx with his children to obtain a complete notion of the depths of sentiment and the childlike nature of this hero of *Wissenschaft*. In his free minutes, or while strolling, he brought them along, played the wildest and most lively games with them— in short he was a child among children. On Hampstead Heath we played "cavalry": I hoisted the one little daughter onto my shoulder, Marx took the other, and we competed in jumping and trotting— and from time to time a little riders' battle was delivered.[9]

Memoirs and reminiscences often sentimentalize the past. But the loving letters Marx wrote his daughters while he was visiting Engels in Manchester, and their replies, all the more affectionate for being in stiff schoolgirl English, testify to the close relationship.[10] One of the many things Marx disliked about his son-in-law Charles Longuet was what Marx saw as Longuet's neglect of his children.[11]

All three of Karl and Jenny's surviving children were girls. Karl made no secret of his preference for male offspring, writing to Engels after the birth of his short-lived daughter Franziska in 1851, "My wife alas, delivered a girl and not a boy."[12] But following the heartrending death of his son Edgar, girls were all Karl had. He was determined that they grow up to be proper young ladies, learning French and Italian, taking drawing lessons, practicing piano or singing. Their future was the reason Karl resisted cutting back his household expenses: "a purely proletarian household arrangement . . . would go well, if I were alone with my wife, or if the girls were boys," he explained to Engels. In the mid-1860s, when money flowed more freely, Karl increased his spending on Jenny and Laura, by then young adults, allowing them to have parties and balls.[13]

The upbringing and social life of the Marx daughters were, in these respects, typical of the nineteenth-century educated middle class, in both England and Germany.[14] Some aspects of their lives, though, were a bit more uncommon. Their education, through secondary school, was unusually elaborate, especially considering that in the mid-1860s there were all of twelve girls' secondary schools in London, with a grand total of just 1,000 pupils. Marx's daughters took gymnastics classes, exercising vigorously while wearing bloomers, those scandalous pants promoted by mid-nineteenth-century feminists. Unlike the common nineteenth-century practice of bringing daughters up to be devout, even in otherwise freethinking households, Karl and Jenny raised their daughters as the same outspoken atheists that they were. Karl was more than happy to talk to them about his politics. The oldest daughter, Jenny, began in her teens to serve as her father's secretary, replacing her aging and fatigued mother. She also wrote for left-wing newspapers, expressing her sympathies for Irish nationalism.[15]

The daughters were being prepared for a proper, bourgeois marriage, in which they would have the kind of role their mother played for their father: creating a cultured, artistic home, running the household, and having children, but also understanding and supporting a husband's left-wing political aspirations. Marx had some difficulty balancing these different aspirations for his daughters. Laura, the best-looking of the three (unlike her sisters, she took after her mother rather than her father), became involved in 1866 with Paul Lafargue, a radical French student living in exile, and also a member of the General Council of the International Working Men's Association. Marx made very clear that his daughter's future financial security would have to take precedence over political agreement or emotional attraction. The formal letter he wrote her would-be fiancé was a loud—deafening—warning shot. It began with some words concerning excessive intimacy:

> If you wish to continue your relationship with my daughter, you will have to give up your way of "paying court." . . . The habits of an all-too great intimacy would be all the more inappropriate as both lovers will be residing in the same vicinity during a necessarily extended period of rough hardships and purgatory. . . . In my opinion, true love is expressed in reserve, modesty and even in the shyness of the lover towards his idol, but definitely not in letting loose passion and demonstrations of a premature familiarity. If you offer the justification of your Creole temperament, than I have the duty to interpose my reason between your temperament and my daughter. If you do not know how to express your love to her in a form appropriate to London's latitude, then you will have to content yourself with loving at a distance.

After making it painfully clear that Lafargue was to keep his hands off his daughter, Marx went on to discuss financial matters:

> Before the final arrangements of your relationship to Laura, I must have serious information about your economic circumstances. . . . You know that I have sacrificed my entire fortune in revolutionary struggle. I do not regret it. Quite the opposite. Were I to start my

career over again, I would do the same. Only I would not marry. As much as it is in my power, I wish to keep my daughter from the cliffs on which the life of her mother has been shattered.[16]

The letter mentioned Marx's own life explicitly, but the implicit references were at least as important: his own long engagement to Jenny and their (presumed) premarital sexual relations; his belief, after living with the difficulties his wife faced in their wretched exile existence during the 1850s, and its reprise, following the loss of his correspondent's post with the *New York Tribune*, that women should not have to bear the hardships of political engagement and class struggle. It was a man's duty and a feature of his romantic love to spare his wife the deprivations of his life, and his angry letter to his daughter's fiancé reflected the frustrations of being unable to do so.

Marx did not just send angry letters. He at least contemplated sending Laura off to boarding school to remove her from her passionate lover; and some three months after that letter was written, he had a loud shouting match with Lafargue.[17] In spite of Marx's reluctance, the couple were married, and remained so for almost forty-five years. (Marx's apprehensions about Lafargue's earning potential proved correct, but Engels came to the rescue of the Lafargues as he had to the Marxes.) Jenny Marx married another French political refugee, Charles Longuet, five years after her sister's marriage, although her father raised many of the same objections to her choice as he had to her sister's. Jenny's marriage, however, was cut short by her premature death in 1883.

In spite of their father's fuming, Jenny and Laura Marx fulfilled his expectations. This would not be the case with Eleanor. A decade younger than her sisters, she was kept at home for much of the 1870s to take care of her aging parents—a common fate of youngest children in the nineteenth century. Her life was affected by the late nineteenth-century ideal of the "new woman," who would have a professional career before or as an alternative to marriage, and whose sexuality could be expressed more freely than in the high Victorian era. Eleanor demonstrated these attitudes publicly by sitting alone in a restaurant, reading newspapers, and smoking cigarettes. Running through a number of career options in theater, journalism, and left-wing politics, and a couple of lovers as well, she was driven to suicide in 1898 by her last lover, Edward Aveling, a cad and bounder straight out of Victorian melodrama. Her tragic end, in contrast to the less troubled personal lives of her sisters, suggests that Marx's conflicting expectations for his daughters (both housewives and political activists, subordinate to their men but intellectually self-assured) could no longer be reconciled, at least in avant-garde bohemian circles, at the end of the nineteenth century.[18]

As we have seen, there was another woman in Marx's household besides his wife and daughters. This was of course the servant Lenchen Demuth. She had given Marx a son, albeit one he could never acknowledge. Wilhelm Liebknecht has left an intriguing portrait of her place in the Marx household:

> Lenchen exercised . . . a kind of dictatorship. . . . And Marx bowed to this dictatorship like a lamb. It has been said, that no one is a great man to his valet. To Lenchen, Marx certainly was not. She would have given her life for him, and Frau Marx and each of the children one hundred times over—indeed, she gave him her life—but Marx could never impress her. She knew him, his moods and his weaknesses and she could wrap him around her finger. Was he in such an angry mood, did he storm and rage so much that others were happy to stay far away, Lenchen went into the lion's den, and, if he growled, she read him the law so impressively, that the lion became tame like a lamb.[19]

On the surface, this passage provides a comic portrait of a world turned upside down, the servant, lowliest person in the household, dominating its patriarchal head. On another level, it can be read as Marx's voluntary surrender of his patriarchal authority, to express it all the more clearly. He freely permitted Lenchen Demuth to talk him out of his bad moods. When Liebknecht wrote his reminiscences in 1896, he was part of the leadership circle of the German Social Democratic Party, whose members had recently learned the closely guarded truth about the paternity of Freddy Demuth. With that in mind, Liebknecht's portrayal of the relationship between the master and his servant reads at a deeper but veiled level as if he was describing a subordinate who had a secret hold on her superior, which she used to influence him as no one else could. There was no hint that Lenchen used her power over Marx for purposes of blackmail. Indeed, she died quite poor. But the secret in the midst of the household must have constantly shadowed Karl's patriarchal authority.

Marx's private attitudes about men and women were similar to his public ones. He endorsed women's political participation: women were free to join the IWMA, and Marx solicited female memberships—albeit from the wives of his friends, Dr. Kugelmann and Engels in particular. As Marx was proud to point out, there was a female member of the General Council, the English freethinker Harriet Law. She generally supported Marx's positions, and he approved of her forthright, perhaps not entirely feminine rapping on the table while endorsing his remarks. Marx's comment, though, that "The progress of society can be exactly measured by the societal position of the fair sex (including the ugly ones)" combined ostensible support for women's rights with some actual contempt for women.[20]

Leftists today would denounce these attitudes as repugnant sexism, and late twentieth- and twenty-first-century feminists as a group have not embraced Marx or his ideas warmly. Feminists are sometimes more sympathetic to Engels, who late in his life would attempt, in his book

The Origin of the Family, Private Property, and the State, to integrate women's issues into Marxist doctrine. Engels's private life, his cohabitation with the Manchester factory girls Mary and Lizzie Burns, might seem more emancipated than Marx's proper, bourgeois marriage and his attitudes about his daughters. Yet the printer Stephan Born reported in his memoirs resentment among workers and artisans who knew Engels, seeing his relationship with the factory girls as just another example of a capitalist sexually exploiting his female workers. Engels's own opinions about sexuality appear in a letter he wrote to Marx's friend Ludwig Kugelmann, the gynecologist in Hanover. Advising the doctor to take up horseback riding for health, he continued, "You as a gynecologist are obligated to *Wissenschaft* [to ride] because gynecology is indeed most closely connected with riding and being ridden. In every way, a gynecologist must be firmly in the saddle."[21]

This locker-room attitude was prevalent among the younger bachelors in Marx's circle: Wilhelm Pieper, Wilhelm Liebknecht, Adolf Cluss, and, in a somewhat different way, Ferdinand Lassalle. They all had a wide variety of assorted sexual relationships with prostitutes and working-class women. They all also contracted venereal disease but eventually got married—except Lassalle, who was killed in a duel by the fiancé of his intended before he could marry her.[22] These actual nineteenth-century alternatives to Marx's stuffy, patriarchal marriage and concerns about his daughters' purity seem rather less attractive today.

Among mid-nineteenth-century German communists there existed one marriage of equals: between Fritz and Mathilde Franziska Anneke. He was a Prussian army officer turned communist, she a freelance political journalist—already an unusual, assertive role for a woman. During the 1848 Revolution, they were both communist activists in Cologne, where they jointly edited a left-wing popular newspaper, and tried to remain neutral in the disputes between Marx and Andreas Gottschalk. After fighting on the side of the insurgent governments of southwestern Germany in the spring of 1849 (Mathilde Franziska caused quite a stir by joining her husband in the field), they emigrated to the United States, where they continued their left-wing activism. Fritz was a passionate opponent of slavery and fought in the Union Army during the Civil War, while Mathilde Franziska became an outspoken women's rights advocate, and probably would have played a major role among American feminists, were it not for her refusal, like many left-wing German émigré(e)s, to learn English. As was common among leftists of the time, Fritz opposed the germ theory of disease. As a matter of political principle, he refused to have their two children inoculated against smallpox; tragically, both children died as a result.[23]

Marx, by contrast, had his children vaccinated, and then revaccinated when his wife contracted smallpox. His marriage was not a politicized partnership of equals, but one in which he assumed a dominant patriarchal role. Unlike Fritz Anneke, he separated his public political principles from his private life; his children were fortunate their father did so. Marx's own balancing act of nineteenth-century manifestations of manhood may appear sexist or inappropriate by today's standards, especially when we think of his treatment of Lenchen Demuth. However, compared to many of his contemporaries, Marx comes across as having chosen some of the best possibilities available to a husband and father of the mid-nineteenth-century Anglo-German middle class.

MARX COULD BE WARM, jovial, and hospitable, but also angry, sarcastic, and hostile. He was a true and loyal friend, but a vehement and hateful enemy. Individuals could be almost instantly reassigned from one category to another, as happened to Bruno Bauer, Moses Hess, Arnold Ruge, and Ferdinand Freiligrath. Marx's relations with Ferdinand Lassalle would most likely have ended up the same way, were it not for the latter's untimely death. Those drastic transitions were most common when Marx was a young man, but he was over

forty when he ended his friendship with Freiligrath, and in his old age
when he brought his close and warm friendship with Dr. Kugelmann
to a sudden and abrupt end in the mid-1870s.[24]

These were the actions of a person of strong emotions, both positive and negative, a feature of Marx's personality only strengthened by
the constant stress of his decades of exile. They were also the actions
of a man for whom personal friendship and political affiliation had
become, by the time he was in his thirties, largely identical. In the
1850s and 1860s, when Marx listed members of his party and he or
Jenny recounted their friends, the two groups were composed of the
same people. Jenny did have non-political friends, but Marx did not,
and the new friends he made through the IWMA, to say nothing of his
future sons-in-law, were his political associates.[25]

Friedrich Engels was personally and politically closer to Marx than
any other friends. Marx's reliance on Engels for financial and emotional support is well known and was already recognized by contemporaries. Marx himself was happy to demonstrate publicly his opinion
of his friend and colleague. Discussing members of his "party" in 1853,
Marx stated that Engels was "the only one from whom to expect real
support . . . an authentic universal lexicon, capable of working at any
hour of the day and night, whether drunk or sober, quick as the devil
in writing and understanding." Seven years later, Engels had advanced
to the status of Marx's "alter ego." Particularly around the time of the
publication of *Capital*, the climax of his life's intellectual work, Marx
expressed his gratitude to and admiration for his friend. "Dear boy," he
wrote in February 1866, "in all circumstances I feel more than ever the
good fortune of such a friendship that exists between us. On your side,
you know that no relationship is worth so much to me." The following
year, after delivering his manuscript to the publisher, he assured Engels
that "Without you I could never have brought the work to an end, and
I assure you that it has always weighed on my conscience like the Alps
that primarily for my benefit you have allowed your wonderful forces

to be wasted and to rust in commercial pursuits. Into the bargain, you have had to endure, along with me, all my petty wretchedness."[26]

The benefits of the close relationship were undeniable, but its costs were not insignificant. A central feature of the bond between the two men was the denigration of third parties, not just their political enemies but their potential friends as well. The correspondence between Marx and Engels is filled with nasty and hostile remarks about fellow socialists, from Karl Grün and Moses Hess through August Willich and Ferdinand Lassalle, to Johann Baptist von Schweitzer and Wilhelm Liebknecht, to say nothing of non-communist radicals and democrats. One can only imagine what Marx and Engels said to each other when they met face to face. Sharing hostile remarks, nasty observations, and salacious or scandalous stories about fellow leftists brought them closer together, but also increased their personal and political isolation.

The mature friendship took the form of two closely linked individuals together against the world. The place of each of them in that connection appears in two very different reminiscences. Wilhelm Liebknecht wrote that

> Marx was the most accessible of men, and cheerful and amiable in personal relations. Engels was much gruffer. There was something militarily abrupt in his manner, which called out opposition and contradiction, while Marx in the company of others had something extraordinarily winning. In the editorial office of the "New Rhineland News," everything went smoothly when Marx was there. When Engels took over for him, conflict broke out immediately . . . as I . . . was told. I myself only got into strife with Marx twice, with Engels quite often.[27]

Henry Hyndman, the English socialist intellectual who met Marx toward the end of his life, wrote of their acquaintance that "At first the aggressive, intolerant, and intellectually dominant side of him preponderated; only later did the sympathy and good-nature which underlay his rugged exterior become apparent." Engels lacked those sympathetic sides, being "exacting, suspicious, jealous, and not disinclined to give full weight to the exchange value of his ready cash in his relations with those whom he helped."[28]

These two recollections underscore a common point: in comparison to Marx, Engels was a difficult person, who got along poorly with his fellow leftists. He may have mellowed a bit over the years, especially after Marx's political associates attempted to expel Engels from leftist politics in the 1840s, but his access to that politics ran through Marx. There was an implicit arrangement between the two: Engels would support Marx, and Marx would guarantee Engels a place in the labor movement, where he might otherwise have been shunned.

It would be unfair to say that the two friends had such an instrumentalist understanding of their relationship. Their evident pleasure in each other's company was always apparent to those who knew them, and formed a consistent theme in reminiscences of the two men. Their care for each other appeared not just in their mutual appreciation but in their repeated medical suggestions. Engels's advice to Marx about how to treat his autoimmune disorder, ranging from taking arsenic to reducing the stress in his life, is one good example. On hearing about Engels's persistent illness (possibly mononucleosis) in 1857, Marx dropped everything he was doing and rushed off to the British Museum to research the latest medical opinions on the topic. He recommended his friend take iron, advice the latter did eventually try, although he preferred cod-liver oil. Neither would have done much for Engels's health—except perhaps the vile taste of such remedies temporarily distracting him from his suffering—but the discussion was a way for two men to articulate the depth of their friendship.[29]

Still, Engels's position in the communist movement was, for eighteen years, integrally connected with the money he earned working for Ermen & Engels in Manchester. It might have been an unpleasant pursuit, but was at first relatively lucrative, and after he became a partner, quite opulent. There must have been a temptation for Engels to renounce his radicalism and concentrate on his business as so many of his contemporaries from the 1848 Revolution had done, which would have been a catastrophe for Marx.

Engels's liaison with Mary and Lizzie Burns, a secret life involving a clandestine apartment he shared with the two working-class women quite apart from his ostensible residence, always left him slightly disreputable. It prevented him from making a socially more suitable marriage that would probably have alienated him from his friend and their radical politics.[30] The Burns sisters helped keep Engels, the desk-bound capitalist, a red, and a loyal friend and associate of Marx. Yet his relations with them were interwoven into the one serious break in the friendship during the years after the two friends moved to England.

Marx's letters to Engels were filled with accounts of his wife and children, and Engels's contained repeated queries about the family. Engels also exchanged letters with Jenny von Westphalen, written more formally than the correspondence with Marx, using the German second-person respectful *Sie* rather than the informal *Du*. But until Lizzie Burns's death, Engels's letters almost never contained mention of the Burns sisters, and Marx's, with two very brief exceptions, each of one short sentence, never took note of their existence. In his many visits to Manchester, Marx must have met with the sisters, but he did not commit their names to paper.[31]

This was no doubt a concession to Jenny von Westphalen, who had despised Mary Burns ever since she met her in Brussels in 1845. Marx's balancing act between his wife and his best friend went on for decades; but it came to a crashing end with Mary Burns's death in January 1863, when Marx responded to Engels's letter announcing his companion's demise by asking for money. Engels was appalled at his friend's lack of empathy, so different from Engels's own attitude on the death of Marx's children and the life-threatening illness of his wife. Even Engels's "Philistine acquaintances" had shown "more sympathy and friendship" than did Marx over Mary's death.

Marx's finances had reached another very low point, following the termination of his work as a correspondent for the *New York Tribune*, and his seeming lack of empathy for his friend was partly the result of the emotional strains emerging in his marriage. Jenny had been denouncing her husband for allowing his pride to get the best of him, and refusing to let Engels know how desperate their financial situation was. Without Karl's knowledge, she had written a begging letter to Wilhelm Wolff in Manchester, asking for a few pounds to help pay their bills, infuriating her husband, who saw the letter as undermining his authority as head of household. Jenny's search for money was a response to her husband's plans to resolve the family's financial difficulties by drastically cutting expenses. Since the previous summer, he had been toying with the idea of giving up their Kentish Town house. The two teen-aged daughters, Jenny and Laura, would find work as governesses; Lenchen Demuth would be dismissed; and Karl, his wife, and the eight-year-old Eleanor would move into a small flat in a model working-class housing project. The lives of all the family would have been disrupted, but none more so than Jenny's, who for the first time in her marriage would have had to do the housework herself.

The news of the death of Engels's longtime female companion reached the Marxes on the same day a bailiff was in the house seizing goods their landlord had attached for failure to pay the rent, a sign that Karl had failed in his duties. As a result, Jenny faced the prospect of a future working-class existence without a servant. Showing his sympathies for a woman from the working class whom his wife despised at this time was more than Marx could manage. In writing the letter to Engels that requested money, he was evidently choosing his wife over his friend.[32]

Resolving the break in the friendship required realigning relations between the two households. Financial support from Engels coupled with some timely inheritances meant that the Marxes could keep their home; the older daughters would not become upscale servants, but remain eligible; and their mother would continue to have household help. In return, the Marxes became much more solicitous of Engels's female companion. After Lizzie Burns replaced her sister in Engels's affections, Marx went out of his way to include greetings to her and inquiries about her in his letters. In return, Engels began including news of Lizzie in his letters. Even Jenny Marx eventually sent greetings in a letter to Engels, something inconceivable for Lizzie's sister.[33] When Engels and Lizzie moved to London in 1870, the Marxes socialized with both of them. Some mutual concessions in his family enabled Karl to reconcile the two central personal relationships in his life and his obligations as friend and patriarch.

THE GREAT ANTAGONIST OF the bourgeoisie was distinctly bourgeois in his private life. Rather than making hostile and sarcastic observations about this, as later critics of Marx's ideas would, or declaring the connection irrelevant to Marx's political and economic conceptions, as is typical of his defenders, it would be more helpful to consider Marx as a nineteenth-century Anglo-German bourgeois. He was a figure of his age, a man who endorsed bourgeois cultural and behavioral ideals, struggled with them, and modified them to fit his own circumstances.

To be bourgeois was to have property, income, security. Marx had none of those; their absence was a continuous dead weight in his life. Just before he reached the midcentury point, he wrote to Engels:

> In a few days, I will be 50. If that Prussian lieutenant said to you: "Already 20 years in service and still a lieutenant," so I can say: half a century on my back and still a pauper! How right my mother was! "If Karrell had only made capital, instead of, etc!"[34]

Whether Henriette Marx actually made that oft-quoted remark is doubtful, since she died four years before the publication of *Capital*, and probably before Marx's economic treatise had even acquired that name. Marx's description of his mother, her Dutch accent turning "Karl" into "Karrell," evoked the woman of property, who came to Trier from Amsterdam with her dowry, the owner of house and vineyard, sheets and table linens. She had a fierce hold on the assets Marx wanted and could only acquire after her death. Such an evocation only underlined his feelings of failure about his own acquisition and preservation of property and income for himself and, especially, his family. Marx felt this failure to be properly bourgeois at a most atavistic level. Three years before his fiftieth birthday, Jenny let Engels know confidentially that her husband lay awake every night thinking about his family's impoverished future after he lost the *Tribune* job:

> The worst of it is that during the entire time, even while suffering the greatest pain [from his skin disease] he has had to deal with his fears about money. I now see for the first time how deeply he took the matter to heart. Since the business with America [the end of the *New York Tribune* work] and the drying up of all regular sources of subsistence, he has had no rest. For entire nights, it always went through his head.[35]

His lack of assets and income was shameful—it had to be hidden from the world. As a practical matter, had the Marxes not kept up appearances, creditors would have called in their loans. But some kinds of debt, especially the use of the pawnshop, were particularly shameful—a resort for the working class, not for respectable bourgeois. Rather than going themselves, Karl or Jenny sent Lenchen Demuth to the pawnbroker's for them.[36]

Jenny von Westphalen dealt with shopkeepers, and kept the household accounts. She knew the exact status of the family finances, while her husband did not. When Engels in 1868 provided a regular income for the Marxes, he began with an initial lump-sum payment, to eliminate all their debts. It turned out that Jenny had concealed from Karl £75 of the debts that she was hoping to pay off from the housekeeping money. When her husband discovered this subterfuge, he asserted that "Women evidently always need a guardian to run their affairs."[37] Marx understood that owing money was a shame to him as man by showing his inability to support his family, but could not recognize that it was shameful to his wife as a woman, implying that she was not running their household frugally and efficiently.

Shame about the family finances was closely intertwined with Marx's suspicious attitude toward the engagement of his daughter Laura to Paul Lafargue. Marx tried to hide his financial circumstances from Lafargue's parents. He made desperate efforts to come up with the funds to provide some dowry—any dowry—for his daughter. His inability to do so was another sign of his failure to be sufficiently bourgeois.[38] The belief, found in some interpretations, that Marx was blithe about his debts and cared little for his financial difficulties—sometimes portrayed as a rejection of bourgeois attitudes toward money, sometimes as a rejection of purported Jewish interest in it—bears little resemblance to Marx's own feelings of guilt and shame about his chronic indebtedness, and his difficulties in obtaining a regular income.

Contemporaries understood that a bourgeois professional or academic would have a difficult time in his early years, and Marx's circumstances before he reached the age of thirty were similar to those of other young men of his social class—exacerbated, admittedly, by the early death of his father, his unusually youthful marriage, and his political commitments. His contemporaries generally experienced a gradual improvement in their circumstances as they grew older. This was true for Marx as well, in spite of the additional difficulties of life in foreign exile from the age of thirty-one onward. But the loss of his regular position with the *New York Tribune* undid the family's economic success. Most bourgeois academics and professionals did not experience this kind of midlife setback, which created the profound loss of faith in himself that Marx expressed on his fiftieth birthday.

Another way to look at Marx's position is to consider the financial opportunities available to leftists at the time. In the first two thirds of the nineteenth century, leftist leaders were typically writers—journalists and freelance authors, taking any and every opportunity to make a living with a pen, whether directly connected to their politics or not. By the 1860s, a gradual shift from prominent leftists as authors to left-wing leaders as functionaries of a political party was underway—an occupation that, for all its problems, was more secure and better paid than the thankless task of freelance writing. Marx himself never made this transition, always refusing any leading position in the IWMA, to say nothing of a paid one. Even had he been willing to do so, large left-wing political parties were still in their infancy throughout his lifetime, lacking the dues-paying mass membership to support full-time professional politicians.

There were other possibilities for procuring income, such as appealing to the public for support. Ferdinand Freiligrath's friends in England did this in 1867, after he lost his position as a banker. The appeal, circulated in Germany and among German emigrants worldwide, ultimately brought in over 30,000 talers. Marx found it a repugnant spectacle. His attitude was best summed up by little Jenny's comment, which he quoted proudly: "if her father would do something like that, she would publicly declare him not her father."[39] Marx interpreted these appeals as a form of dependence on charity, holding fiercely to the ideal of personal independence that was consistent with Victorian views of masculinity.

Timely inheritances helped fill some gaps temporarily, but neither the Marxes nor the Westphalens were wealthy enough to leave behind assets that would permanently support a family. What remained as a bourgeois occupation was business, and Marx's own brief brush with the business world came to an end before it ever got started. Instead, there was Engels's business income, on which Marx was, very unhappily, dependent. He told Engels in July 1865: "I assure you that I would rather have my thumbs hacked off than to write you this letter [asking for money]. It is truly crushing to remain dependent for half of one's life."[40]

Marx never commented, however, about his dependence for income on the capitalist exploitation of the workers in the Ermen & Engels textile mill, who were better treated than most millhands but exploited workers, nonetheless. This was not true of his friend, who siphoned off the surplus value. In 1865, as Marx and Engels were breaking with Lassalle's successor, Johann Baptist von Schweitzer, Engels warned Marx that Schweitzer's followers would say, "What does that Engels want, what has he been doing all these years, how can he speak in our name & tell us what we should do, the guy sits in Manchester and exploits the workers, etc."[41] The reactions Engels anticipated seem a little unlikely, since they involved the followers of Ferdinand Lassalle, who with his red silk dressing gowns, dubious connections to a countess, and frequent trips to Swiss spas was not exactly a figure of proletarian rectitude. Rather, they reflected Engels's guilt feelings about his own involvement with a capitalism he hated and wanted to destroy. One of the greatest sacrifices Engels made for Marx by going into his family's textile business was renouncing a clear conscience about how he earned a living.

A POINT EMPHASIZED IN recent studies of the nineteenth-century German bourgeoisie—the German phrase *Bürgertum* is notoriously difficult to translate exactly—is the shaping of that social group by cultural conventions. These included a commitment to industriousness and continuous effort, and a decorous home life well stocked with all the facets of high culture.[42] An adherence to these cultural conventions characterized Marx's private life as well, although sometimes in a distinct form.

Marx had a tremendous capacity for work. He spent twelve-hour days reading Blue Books in the British Museum; he wrote an enormous volume of articles and news reports for the *New York Daily Tribune*. The long hours in meetings of the General Council of the International Working Men's Association, or the bulky manuscripts of his economics treatise, were further testimonies to his labors. Yet for all this toil, Marx's important intellectual projects never came to fruition, or only in truncated form. His chronic financial problems were manifestly distracting and increasingly poor health made completing his work very difficult. But there were also elements of Marx's personality that tended to counteract his best efforts.

One important feature was the disorderly nature of his bohemian life. The scrawled, illegible handwriting, the impenetrable chaos of books and papers (sometimes impenetrable to him as well) that was his study attested to this. He would stay up till all hours and sleep until noon. His work was punctuated by frenetic bursts. He wrote, day and night, followed by a collapse in his health and periods of enforced idleness. None of this was conducive to completing large-scale projects. Marx's actual process of writing was extraordinarily erratic. In a tradition handed down by his Dutch relatives, who had seen him at work on his economic treatise while he was visiting his uncle Lion Philips, "as soon as he had written something down, it was Marx's habit to stand up and to walk around the table, faster and faster, until something occurred to him and he then sat down again to write."[43]

Slow and steady is not the only way to win the race and people who work in bursts and spurts can get a lot done. But there was yet another feature of Marx's personality that impeded the completion of his large-scale efforts. This was his insistence on completeness, on finding every last piece of information, and then rewriting over and over again what he had previously put down in the light of his latest finds. Observations about this feature of his working methods dogged Marx throughout his life. "He reads a lot; he works with uncommon intensity and has a critical talent . . . but he completes nothing, he always breaks off and plunges anew into an endless sea of books," Arnold Ruge noted in 1844. Thirty-five years later, Friedrich Engels, who found this feature of Marx's work-habits extremely frustrating, told him: "I would burn, with pleasure, the Russian publications on agricultural conditions, that, for years, have prevented you from finishing *Capital*!"[44]

If Marx's version of the German middle-class work ethic had its own distinct torqued permutations, his home life followed a more conventional pattern. Both Karl and Jenny insisted on a decorous and proper household: no off-color jokes or slightly risqué songs. Wilhelm Liebknecht remembered stern rebukes about the songs. Karl was very embarrassed if any even remotely sexual topic was brought up in mixed company. His correspondence with Engels certainly contained many such mentions and a reveling in salacious scandals about their political enemies, but there was to be no public discussion of these things in front of women and children. As they got into their teens and early twenties, the two older daughters began to chafe under the cosseted propriety of their parents. After Laura married Lafargue and left home, Jenny, without her parents' consent or even knowledge, took a job as a tutor just so she could get away from the strict atmosphere in the house and her mother's increasingly irritable commands.[45]

Marx's mature public persona was that of a proper and distinguished bourgeois gentleman, as two amusing incidents from the 1860s demonstrate, one emphasizing his respectability to Germans, the other to Englishmen. After seeing to the publication of *Capital*, Marx was returning by ship from Hamburg to London in 1867. On board, he met a "German Fräulein," who appealed to him for help. She was taking the train in England and did not know what to do with her baggage, as it was Sunday, and no porters were allowed to work on Sunday in

England. Chivalrously, Marx escorted her in London until her train left. The young woman, it turned out, was Elisabeth von Puttkamer, Bismarck's niece, "a lively and cultivated girl, but aristocratic and black-white [the Prussian colors] to the tip of her nose." She was astonished to discover that the helpful gentleman was a notorious subversive, but the very fact that an aristocratic young lady turned to Marx for assistance speaks volumes about his outward appearance.[46]

The following year, Marx discovered, upon returning home from a visit to Engels in Manchester, that he had been elected to a largely honorific, minor legal office, Constable of the Vestry of St. Pancras. Both Marx and Engels could not stop laughing about this ridiculously feudal-sounding position, and profoundly enjoyed the advice an acquaintance gave Marx about his election: "I should tell them that I was a foreigner and that they should kiss me in the ars [*sic*]." But, as the acquaintance informed Marx, the office "was an honour much valued by the philistines of St. Pancras," that is, by Marx's own bourgeois neighbors. It says a lot about their opinion of him that they chose him for this honor.[47]

Propriety and decorum went along with a household appreciation of high culture. Marx admired the literary classics: Dante and Cervantes, Goethe and Shakespeare. The works of Shakespeare were, as Eleanor put it, "our house Bible." By the age of six, she had learned long passages from his plays, taking after her older sisters. As the graduate of a German *Gymnasium*, Marx retained an interest in the culture of classical antiquity cultivated there, reading the ancient Greek dramatists in the original. He was no classicist snob and appreciated more recent literature, particularly realist writers: Sir Walter Scott and Alexander Pushkin, Alexandre Dumas and Honoré de Balzac. He was less impressed with German realist novelists (admittedly, the best of them, Theodor Fontane, only began writing fiction after Marx's death), but greatly admired the work of his onetime friend Heinrich Heine, whose poetry and essays were an early form of literary realism. As we have seen, the daughters received music lessons; Marx was familiar with the works of classical musicians, and a great admirer of Bach, although music does not seem to have played the major role in the Marxes' home life that it did for many educated Germans in the nineteenth century.[48]

Very much in contrast to many twentieth- and twenty-first-century leftist intellectuals, Marx had no interest in the artistic avant-garde, or in any variety of popular culture. He relaxed with Shakespeare and Bach, not with popular Victorian fiction or music hall songs. In spite of Engels's efforts to get him up on a horse, Marx engaged in no forms of exercise other than decorously taking long walks. His one substantial free time activity was the eminently intellectual pastime of chess—a game he studied intensively, and sometimes played obsessively. Tellingly, he had a very aggressive, attacking style of play.[49]

Marx's own bourgeois habits form an interesting contrast to those of his closest friend. His illegible and, to judge from the slant of the letters, left-handed scrawl was quite the opposite of Engels's neat and precise clerk's script. Engels's regular working hours and his systematic and methodical approach to political writing were diametrically opposed to Marx's late hours and bursts of intense effort followed by weeks of incapacitating illness. Engels's ability both to earn money and to manage the money he had far exceeded that of his friend.

The contrast between the solid businessman and his bohemian counterpart had its comic moments. In 1870, Engels alerted Marx that he was sure his letters were being intercepted and read by the police. When the letters arrived in Manchester, the four corners of the envelope had not been neatly folded together and sealed, so the seal must have been broken and the envelope incorrectly refolded. In spite of repeated warnings, Marx never responded, presumably evidence that the sloppily sealed envelopes were the result of Marx's carelessness, not the machinations of a vigilant police force.[50]

Far more serious was the effect of Marx's work habits on his economics treatise. Engels's very first letter to Marx implored him to "take care that the material you have gathered is soon tossed out into the world." There followed over the decades a constant stream of admonitions and reminders, all on the same theme: Get the work done! When Engels began his postmortem editing of *Capital*, his only regret was that he had not done more of it: "Had I known, I should have pestered him day and night until it was all finished and printed." What came naturally to Engels presented considerable difficulties to Marx.[51]

The reverse proved true at home, where Marx was highly disciplined. Karl and Jenny's straitlaced household was the antithesis of Engels's lax and relaxed domestic arrangements with the Burns sisters. (No children ever came from those unions, and one does have to wonder whether Engels was better at doing it in "the good Parisian way" or if there were fertility issues involved.) After accompanying her father on shorter visits to Engels, Eleanor Marx upset her mother in 1868 by announcing she would much rather live with him in Manchester than in her parents' stodgy household. The following year, at the age of fourteen, she spent four months with Engels and Lizzie Burns, including a quick trip to Ireland, a visit that was the high point of her young life. One hot summer's day she had a particularly enjoyable experience. Lizzie Burns and her niece, who was the household servant, spent the day with Eleanor, lying on the floor, each wearing a light cotton dress, one petticoat, and no corset or shoes (by Victorian standards, close to naked), drinking wine and beer. Engels appeared that evening, "drunk as jelly." The idea of Jenny von Westphalen lying scantily dressed on the floor drinking with Lenchen Demuth—and the family patriarch tolerating such a spectacle—is inconceivable.[52]

ALTHOUGH IT HAS BECOME a cliché, it is true that the nineteenth-century bourgeoisie was a middle class, perched between the aristocracy and the workers—and Marx's attitudes about class as reflected in his personal life are quite revealing. Although Karl Vogt accused Marx of secretly envying the nobility, this seems extremely unlikely. In the early 1850s, Marx asserted that reactionary, aristocratic government ministers were preferable to petit-bourgeois democrats, but that was a denunciation of the democrats rather than praise of the aristocracy. It would have been odd indeed for someone growing up in a bourgeois Rhineland whose inhabitants did not at all miss the aristocracy of the region, purged by the French Revolution, to have been attracted to the nobility. Marx expressed extreme contempt for this social class, in his writings on ground rent and agriculture in *Capital*, his strange theories about Lord Palmerston and the Whig aristocracy, and his hatred of the Junkers, the Prussian noble landlords, a pillar of the Prussian monarchy he despised. This was not the attitude of someone with any attraction, secret or otherwise, to Europe's hereditary elites. Marx was admittedly married to a noblewoman of sorts, whose visiting cards (a necessity for any proper lady of the time) described her as, "Frau Jenny Marx, née Baroness von Westphalen." At one point, he had to warn her about indiscriminately handing them out because his political enemies might make use of them.[53]

More relevant to the eminently bourgeois communist leader was his relationship with the working class. Even at the height of his political activity in Germany, Marx was a journalist who moved in bourgeois circles. This continued to be the case in exile, especially following the 1850 split in the Communist League. Workers who visited Marx's home in conjunction with their IWMA activities reported on their gracious and friendly reception from all members of the family: the intellectual father, the mother with a title of nobility, and the lively and involved daughters. It did not hurt Marx's relations with the working class that he was a particular kind of bourgeois—a scholar and a learned man, a figure of respect, especially in central Europe—quite unlike Engels, the bourgeois capitalist.[54]

In private, especially in his correspondence with Engels, Marx could be scathing about the working class. Both men referred to the workers organized in mutual benefit and educational societies, trade unions, and nascent socialist political parties—those who came closest to their ideal of class-conscious proletarians—as *die Knoten*, which might be loosely translated as "the knot-heads." It was not a friendly accolade and reflected their frustrations in getting potential supporters to follow their own particular political line. Putting this frustration in terms of the workers' stupidity, though, contained a whiff of bourgeois class prejudice and contempt for less educated and less intelligent manual laborers.[55]

THE POWER OF WHAT we today call ethnic and religious identities was always a blind spot in Marx's political and social theories, although as a practical politician—stirring up the Catholics of the Rhineland against Protestant Prussian rule in 1848–49, or trying to make use of German nationalism for a return to political life following 1859—he was willing to exploit these identities. Two versions of these identities played a distinct role in Marx's private life. One was obvious to him and to his contemporaries: Marx was a German who spent the last thirty-four years of his life living in foreign exile. The other was more subtle: Marx's Jewishness. Sometimes perceived, albeit in very different ways, sometimes altogether unnoticed, it was a concept surprisingly difficult to grasp, both for Marx himself and his contemporaries.

Marx identified himself as a German, usually in a mocking ironic fashion, talking about "we Teutons," and his regrettable but unavoidable affiliation with the German people and the German nation. As was true of his fellow political exiles, Marx's long-term residence in Great Britain weakened his national affiliation and gradually anglicized him. But at times the contrasts between the British and the German way of doing things could also emphasize the German in Marx.[56]

As an economist, Marx found Great Britain to be the model capitalist country. It was efficient, punctual, and productive, greatly superior to a Germany characterized by delayed work and poor-quality products. This attitude carried over into his private life. Marx's apology to his Berlin publisher, Franz Duncker, for having accused him of deliberately delaying the publication of *On the Critique of Political Economy* was an indictment of German business: "For one thing, I have really been gone from Germany for too long and have become accustomed to London conditions, so that I cannot properly appreciate the pace of German business transactions."[57] (This relationship between national character and economy efficiency seems to have gotten reversed over the subsequent 150 years.)

At times, Marx felt a resentment about these comparative conditions. In 1860, the Austrian minister of finance Karl Ludwig von Bruck committed suicide, after accusations of corruption were brought against him. For a sharp critic of matters German, Marx was surprisingly sensitive about English responses, as he wrote to Engels:

> The English naturally harass one now, with Bruck. The day before yesterday one guy annoyed me with it again and asked: "Now, what do you say of Bruck's suicide?" "I'll tell you Sir. In Austria the rogues cut their own throats while in England they cut their people's purses."[58]

These resentments engaged most drastically in the 1850s, probably during the Crimean War. Marx, Edgar Bauer, and Wilhelm Liebknecht had taken part in a pub crawl one night. After considerable consumption, they came to an establishment where a group of Odd Fellows, working-class members of an English lodge, were drinking. At first the encounter went well, and enthusiastic toasts were offered, denouncing "Russian Junkers," since, as Liebknecht pointed out, most Englishmen could not tell the difference between Prussia and Russia. But gradually another mood took over and Edgar Bauer denounced English "snobs," followed by a drunken Marx, who launched into an enthusiastic speech praising German *Wissenschaft* and German music. No other country, Liebknecht remembered him saying, had produced musical artists like Mozart, Handel, Haydn, and Beethoven. Germany was well ahead of England, and only its current wretched economic and political conditions prevented it from being ahead of all other nations, as it one day would be. Liebknecht noted that he had never heard Marx speak English so well. The assembled Odd Fellows were less than happy and turned on their guests with cries of "Damned foreigners!" Just barely escaping a beating, the three émigrés rushed out into the street, where they began throwing rocks at gas lamps, and had to flee again to avoid being arrested by the Bobbies who had appeared to investigate the tumult. Such usually concealed feelings of nationalist resentment might help explain Marx's outbursts at the beginning of the Franco-Prussian War.[59]

In spite of these contretemps, Marx gradually became more anglicized over the decades of the 1850s, 1860s, and 1870s. English phrases crept into his correspondence, although the idea that the letters he exchanged with Engels were a multilingual Tower of Babel is rather exaggerated. Marx used English phrases in his letters primarily as he had used French ones before his move (and afterward for that matter), for emphasis and to express briefly concepts that required a longer and more awkward German exposition. The grammar and syntax of his writing remained distinctly German, and differed considerably from that of his anglicized daughters, who were much more comfortable expressing themselves in both written and verbal form in English or even in French. Marx's own knowledge of French, stemming from his childhood in Trier, was always deeper and more profound than his knowledge of English.[60]

Never having regained his Prussian citizenship, Marx was a stateless person. In 1869, he first floated the idea of changing his legal nationality by becoming a naturalized British subject, making it easier and less risky to travel to the Continent. It took him five years to submit a formal request to that effect, which was turned down. This was after the Paris Commune, and Her Majesty's government was not going to grant its protection to the ostensible sinister mastermind behind that well-publicized outburst of extreme radicalism. Quite unlike their generous policy of granting political asylum, nineteenth-century British governments were very restrictive about naturalizing foreigners and giving them domestic political rights.

The long delay between initial plans and the actual submission of his application reflects some reluctance about taking on a new nationality. Marx was only willing to consider the possibility because changes in the law made it easy to renounce being a British subject after obtaining the condition. As he told Engels, "I am not yet a Freeborn Briton. One naturally resists this sort of thing, as long as current circumstances are acceptable."[61]

EVERYBODY KNOWS THAT MARX was Jewish. They expect that he knew it too, that he understood Jewishness in twentieth- and twenty-first-century terms. Because Marx lacked such a more modern understanding, he is often accused of being an anti-Semite. Rather than reiterating these accusations, or the sometimes rather labored responses of Marx's defenders, it seems more helpful to consider both his attitudes toward his own Jewish ancestry and other people's perceptions of his Jewishness in the light of nineteenth-century understandings of what it meant to be Jewish.

Marx's correspondence was filled with contemptuous remarks about Jews. He often denounced individual Jews as greedy and grasping, but his derisive comments (as we have seen) included a wide range of anti-Semitic observations. They ranged from denigrating Jews as pushy and intrusive to perceiving them as not conforming to classical models of beauty and of melodious voice: "that guttural sound, which the selected people is to some degree cursed with."[62] These observations came to the fore in Marx's descriptions of Ferdinand Lassalle, but he frequently repeated them about much less prominent people. Such remarks by someone of Jewish descent are usually attributed to Jewish self-hatred, accompanied by a denial of Jewish ancestry. Yet Marx was open about his Jewish descent and took a certain perverse pride in it.

The attitude was most clearly expressed in his letters to his uncle Lion Philips, a person Marx greatly admired and who was a father figure to him during his adult life. Marx wrote to Philips in 1864, about the study of a Dutch Orientalist asserting that the Five Books of Moses were not composed by the biblical hero, but after the return of the Jews to Palestine from their Babylonian captivity. In his letter, Marx stated: "Since, however, Darwin has proven our common descent from the apes, scarcely any shock whatsoever can shake 'our pride in our ancestors.'" In another letter to his uncle four years earlier, Marx had talked about "our tribal comrade Benjamin Disraeli."[63] Both of those letters suggest Marx's ironic identification with his own Jewish descent, an attitude not unlike that of Disraeli himself.

In this context, Marx's experiences on a trip from London to the spa town of Karlsbad in 1875 are revealing. One of the passengers in his train compartment leaving London was a "little Yid," a merchant heading for Berlin on business. Writing to Engels to describe his trip, Marx was merciless about his traveling companion's Yiddish-inflected German, the dubious business deals that had led to his being swindled out of £1,700, and his equally dubious plans to get the money back. The description is a stereotypical denunciation of an uncultured and greedy Jew.

Stopping in Frankfurt on his way to Karlsbad, Marx met with Leopold Sonnemann, the publisher of Germany's chief left-wing newspaper, the *Frankfurt News*. The two men discussed the possibility

of political cooperation between the socialists and the radical democrats. As an experienced journalist and editor, Marx greatly admired
Sonnemann's success with his newspaper, attributable to its capitalist
virtues as "the best stock-exchange and commercial sheet in southern
Germany." Sonnemann himself was Jewish, but rather than denouncing him, Marx expressed his respect for this "man of the world."[64]

What distinguished these two encounters in Marx's mind was certainly not the respective individuals' ancestry, their involvement with
capitalism, or even their religion. Rather, it was their cultural affiliations, reflected in their speech, physical appearance, and attitudes
toward the world. Marx's rejection of his travel companion—or more
precisely, his linking of his rejection to the latter's religious and cultural
affiliations—was certainly bigoted, but it also reflected a primarily cultural understanding of Jewish identity.

Such an understanding was common to Marx's contemporaries.
His correspondents had no hesitation in making hostile remarks about
Jews to him and evidently did not feel they were insulting him in doing
so. Few were as drastic as the German émigré radical Albrecht Komp,
who wrote in 1859 of his plans to leave New York, "this Eldorado of
Jewry," and return to Germany; but hostile mentions of Jews occurred
in letters by Engels and Jenny von Westphalen—two people who knew
very well Marx's attitudes and his ancestry.[65]

This understanding of being Jewish as primarily a matter of religious and cultural affiliation was quite pronounced in contemporaries'
attitudes toward Marx's own Jewishness, or lack of it. His political
enemies sometimes condemned him in these terms: Ruge, Proudhon,
and Bakunin all made unflattering denunciations of Marx's Semitic
nature and antecedents. There were also a number of instances when
Marx was treated in a way that made him seem distinctly un-Jewish.
One was the duels. Jews were frequently considered intrinsically lacking in the personal honor needed to take part in a duel: they were not,
as the Germans said, "*satisfaktionsfähig*." Marx's own dueling and his

challenges to meet on the field of honor point to a different identity, or at least reflect his desire to present himself as anything but Jewish.[66]

In private, Arnold Ruge did denounce Marx as Jewish, but in *Two Years in Paris*, his public reckoning with the German communists, Ruge focused his attack on Moses Hess, calling him the "communist rabbi" (a phrase German historians have loved to quote ever since) and telling stories about his smuggling cigars from Belgium into France designed to present Hess as a greedy and conscienceless Jew. Such accusations were absent from Ruge's treatment of Marx in the book, which said nothing of his Jewishness, but instead regretfully explained how a once valued co-worker had been seduced by communist ideas.[67]

Marx's nemesis, Wilhelm Stieber, along with another political policeman, published the indictment in the Cologne Communist Trial under the lurid title *The Communist Conspiracies of the Nineteenth Century*. A 128-page biographical dictionary of Germany's communists, carefully arrayed in alphabetical order, was appended. The entry on Marx contained his "wanted" notice, which described him as "reminding somewhat in speech and external appearance of his Jewish descent." The entry also stated that his late father was a senior official of the Prussian state-owned Saar Basin coal mines, an error that was widely spread and appeared in quite a number of Marx obituaries. It would be hard to think of a more Gentile occupation than that one.[68]

All these perceptions of Marx were compatible with mid-nineteenth-century understandings of Jewishness. These did have a certain somatic component in the form of comments about external Jewish qualities, but even this may have related as much to body language as to actual morphology. Primarily, though, they were tied to religious affiliation and cultural practices. In those respects, Marx did not seem very Jewish. The rise of racial thinking about Jews, accelerated in the 1870s, and generally related to the spread of Darwinian conceptions of human society, would change observers' opinions. Emphasis on Marx's "Semitic" features in favorable reminiscences of him, written from the 1870s to the early twentieth century, are testimony to this change in attitude.[69]

Even some of Germany's earliest racial anti-Semites did not regard Marx-as-Jew to be avoided. When Bruno Bauer, already playing with racial ideas about Jews and European nations more generally, visited England at the end of 1855, he spent hours conversing amiably with Marx about Hegel's *Logic*.[70] Even more remarkable was Marx's encounter with Wilhelm Marr, not just Germany's first prominent racial anti-Semite but the man who invented the phrase "anti-Semitism." By profession a Hamburg journalist, Marr had been politically associated with Ferdinand Lassalle (a strange affiliation for a nascent anti-Semite) and was part of Lassalle's odd scheme to proclaim Schleswig-Holstein annexed to Prussia in the name of the labor movement. Marx was introduced to Marr in 1867, when he was in Hamburg seeing to the publication of the first volume of *Capital*. Marx observed that Marr "in his personal manner . . . is a Lassalle translated into Christian terms, but, naturally, worth much less." This description may have contained a hint of Marr's attitudes toward Jews, and perhaps Marx's low opinion of these attitudes, but it does not suggest any epic confrontation between the two men.[71]

In this respect, Marx's private life appears as fairly conventional for its time. He was patriarchal, prudish, bourgeois, industrious, independent (or trying to be), cultured, respectable, German, with a distinct patina of Jewish background. None of this was out of the ordinary for the middle class of the period. A few aspects of Marx's private life, such as his evident love of children, his rather bohemian work habits, his endorsement of freethinking, even for the women in his life, and his strong emotions, revealed in both friendship and enmity, might have placed him a bit off to one side on the spectrum, but there was little that was drastically unusual. The only way one could tell from Marx's conventional exterior that he was a radical was his chronic financial woes. Even there, the family did its best to keep up appearances, and with the generous and persistent help of Engels was able to become more conventionally bourgeois. Of course, the real question is why anyone should expect private life and public political stances to coalesce. The answer might be that the demonstration of public commitments in private became a measure of individual authenticity in the twentieth century, as it never was during Marx's lifetime.

13

The Veteran

DURING THE TWO YEARS following the suppression of the Paris
Commune, Marx fought his last struggle: a bitter clash over control of
the International Working Men's Association. The contest was physically demanding and time-consuming, but while engaged in gathering
delegates for a political showdown with his anarchist rival Bakunin,
and firing off broadsides against him, Marx was simultaneously working on the second German and French editions of *Capital*. The combined
efforts were too much for his fragile health. He suffered a physical
breakdown in 1873, and had to cease work for months while he sought
medical treatment. On the completion of his cure, Marx's campaign-
ing days lay behind him. Increasingly leaving day-to-day relationships
with radicals and nascent socialist parties to Engels or his sons-in-law,
he cultivated a role as adviser and fount of political wisdom, although,
given his irascible personality, the fierce polemicist sometimes prevailed over the elderly sage. This political role was in line with Marx's
public image after 1870 as a veteran: a protagonist of the great and
far-off upheavals of 1848, a long-term advocate of the working class,
and a predictor of a revolutionary and communist future that he would

not live to see. Marx's private life during his last mortal decade corresponded closely to his public one. He was a doting grandfather, a caring husband during his wife's fatal illness, and, finally, an aging widower in steadily poorer health contemplating his own demise.

THE PARIS COMMUNE MADE Marx a public figure, in a way that he had never been before. His powerful pamphlet defending the insurgent regime brought him to the attention of radical and socialist activists all across Europe. Italian revolutionaries meeting at a banquet in Rome in September 1871 offered a toast to "Carlo Marx, the indefatigable instrument" of the working class. Nearby, in the little town of Macerata, a workers' society chose its three honorary presidents: Garibaldi, Mazzini, and Marx. In view of Marx's and Mazzini's mutual derision, this was not an ideologically consistent decision, but putting Marx on a par with the heroes of Italian leftists was an indication of his public stature.[1]

His visibility radiated well beyond left-wing circles. A newsman from the *New York World* engaged in the new-fangled practice of the journalistic interview with Marx just a month after the suppression of the Commune. Marx's biography was the cover story of the November 11, 1871, issue of Paris's *Illustrated News*, and the story, including his portrait, with the characterization of him as "chief of the International," was reprinted in English, Spanish, Italian, German, and American newspapers. The end of the 1870s saw a new wave of interest in the aging revolutionary. Queen Victoria sent a personal envoy, with the impressive name of Sir Mountstuart Elphinstone Grant Duff, to meet with Marx at the beginning of 1879. A biography appeared in a Dutch collection of lives of prominent men, sort of an early *Who's Who*, and two different British literary and general interest periodicals, *The Contemporary Review* and *Leaders of Modern Thought*, published thumbnail sketches of Marx's life and ideas. American journalists appeared at the house on Maitland Park Road, and even in Ramsgate, when Marx was at the seashore with his family, to interview the revolutionary veteran.[2]

Marx was flattered by the attention paid to him, but annoyed by the many inaccuracies in the biographical accounts and the unwillingness to take his ideas seriously. By far the most sophisticated of these pieces, written by the Scottish journalist John Rae (who would later write a life of Adam Smith), contained a perceptive account of the Young Hegelian roots of Marx's intellectual and political development. The essay was part of an informal series on socialist thinking in Germany. Unlike Rae's two other, equally well informed pieces in the series, the article on Marx contained no description of his economic ideas, continuing what was for Marx a frustrating lack of attention in the country that had invented political economy. Oddly enough, Rae himself began his essay on Marx by noting that very fact.[3]

Even a good decade after the end of the Paris Commune, the revolutionary government that had briefly existed in continental Europe's largest city remained a source of fascination and horror, and the continued interest in Marx was closely linked to his ostensible ties to the Commune. The descriptions based on personal encounters, the newspaper interviews, and the secret report to Queen Victoria emphasized this connection in perverse fashion. Marx's personal appearance was that of an aging Teutonic scholar in his book-lined study, a proper, politely spoken old gentleman, a kindly grandfather playing on the beach with his grandchildren. As Grant Duff noted, "the whole expression rather pleasant than not [is] by no means that of a gentleman who is in the habit of eating babies in their cradles." Yet that very same man, as all the accounts noted, endorsed the Commune and promoted ongoing schemes of upheaval. Such contradictory pictures were all portraits of a veteran revolutionary.

. . .

IF THE PARIS COMMUNE was the source of Marx's expanded public image, it was also at the origin of the struggle for control of the IWMA that would lead to its destruction. The Franco-Prussian War and subsequent revolutionary uprising made the planned 1870 IWMA Congress impossible and also ensured that one could not meet the following year. Marx proposed to hold, instead of a congress, a conference: an informal gathering of delegates from whatever branches of the International could manage to send them. The conference met in September 1871 in closed session, issuing no reports of its proceedings to the press.[4] Officially, it was to deal primarily with organizational matters. It reiterated the IWMA's previous call for sections to gather statistical information on workplaces, approved the creation of exclusively female sections, and devised a standardized organizational structure in which individual local sections in each country were to send representatives to a nationwide "Federal Council," a name emerging from the Commune, where federalist ideas had been very influential. As a distinct organizational novelty, the conference created a Federal Council for England; previously, the General Council had dealt with English affairs.[5]

All IWMA-affiliated societies were to be either regionally based or trade unions; politically oriented sections were prohibited, a proposal aimed at Bakunin's anarchist adherents. If that vague point was not enough, the conference also declared that the General Council would expel any affiliates connected to the International Alliance of Socialist Democracy, Bakunin's onetime front group. For good measure, the conference condemned secret societies, even in countries where government persecution had made the regular functioning of IWMA affiliates impossible. The conference adjudicated the dispute between the pro-Bakunin and anti-Bakunin groups, each claiming to represent the IWMA in francophone Switzerland, but the committee evaluating the opposing claims met at Marx's home, and was so evidently stacked in favor of the anti-Bakunin associations that Paul Robin, who represented the pro-Bakunin ones, stalked out the door, shouting, "I despise you."[6]

The conference issued just one policy recommendation, but it was a very large one. The working class could only act as a class "by constituting itself as a political party, distinct from, and opposed to, all old parties formed by the propertied classes. . . ." It may be hard to grasp how radical a departure this proposal was. At the time of the conference, anything resembling the proposed workers' party only existed in Germany—two actually, the followers of Lassalle, and those of Bebel and Liebknecht. Neither was represented at the conference, and Marx had not shown much faith in the political activities of either one of them. The British trade unionists, with whom he had been closely allied since the founding of the IWMA in 1864, were generally adherents of the Liberal Party—definitely not the recommended workers' party. Of course, Bakunin and his anarchist followers opposed all kinds of political parties. The resolution was a direct slap in their faces.

Compounding the drastic nature of the decision was the process by which it was made. The delegates to the conference were mostly members of the General Council and a random few others: only the Belgian affiliates of the IWMA sent an actual delegation. Members of the General Council, in turn, were co-opted by existing members, which is how Engels, following his move to London, became a member of the Council and corresponding secretary for Italy, Spain, and Portugal. Quite a number of refugees from the Paris Commune, for whom Marx was busy collecting money—his experiences in 1849–50 had taught him about the links between assisting political refugees and drumming up support—had also been co-opted onto the Council. That the conference's decisions were taken in secret only made the whole procedure seem more arbitrary and irregular.[7]

What impelled Marx to take this drastic step, which was sure to conjure up vehement opposition? Engels, with a long history of such backroom maneuvering, had first proposed the idea of a conference

in place of a congress. Marx's worries about the influence of Bakunin
and his followers, busy organizing sections of the IWMA in Southern
Europe, had not diminished. The actions of the anarchist leader during the Franco-Prussian War, when he turned up in Lyon, declared the
state abolished, and proposed to begin burning property documents,
only increased Marx's anxiety about a person with such views gaining
control of the International.[8]

An anti-anarchist move did not have to include drastic policy
changes. Looking back on the events several years later, Engels suggested that from the very beginning the IWMA was a mixture of politically heterogeneous groups that had been willing to work together. But
the revolutionary effect of the Paris Commune led "every tendency" in
the IWMA to exploit the impact of that uprising for its own ends, and
to work to change, fundamentally, the nature of the association. Engels
conveniently excluded from judgment the "German communists" (himself and Marx), who, he asserted, wanted to "go on working on the
basis of the old, comprehensive program."[9] But the London Conference
decision endorsing workers' parties was the very opposite of previous
policy. In the wake of the Commune, Marx and Engels were trying
to reshape, drastically, the IWMA. The possibility that their initiative
would fail, and lead to the dissolution of the organization, was a chance
Marx was prepared to take.

The secret decisions of the London Conference did not remain
secret very long: a member of the General Council, the London-based
German tailor Johann Eccarius, promptly leaked the decisions to the
press. Eccarius had been a long-term ally of Marx and Engels in
the London German Communist Workers' Educational Society, and
the two bourgeois intellectuals had, over the decades, helped him out
financially, assisted him when he was ill, and put him forward for paid
positions in the IWMA and as a journalist. Unlike Marx and Engels,
Eccarius sympathized with the English trade unionists and their ties
to the Liberal Party. His independent stance could be perceived as an

example of the maturity of the working class, able to choose its own political positions, and no longer reliant on the ideas of bourgeois intellectuals. Not surprisingly, Marx and Engels did not see it that way, but took Eccarius's action as a personal insult, and an example of rank ingratitude; they broke off all contact with him.[10]

But once the word was out, opposition to the decisions of the London Conference spread throughout the IWMA. Anarchist groups, such as the pro-Bakunin francophone Swiss sections or the newly formed Italian and Spanish sections, generally under Bakunin's influence, denounced the decisions, and demanded that the General Council be stripped of its powers. The Belgian Federation, not controlled by Bakunin and his followers, also called for a full congress of the IWMA to revise the London Conference decisions.

These were all initiatives from French-speaking or Latin countries, and their declarations opposed to the General Council contained references to malign Prussian influences—in other words, Marx and Engels, neither of whom, in spite of their origins, was exactly pro-Prussian. These assertions, along with the tendency of the Swiss affiliates of the IWMA to break down along German-speaking, pro–General Council and French-speaking, anti–General Council lines, suggest that the nationalist tensions provoked by the Franco-Prussian War could infiltrate the workers' international organization. Other, distinctly non-Latin affiliates joined in condemning the decisions of the London Conference, including the followers of Ferdinand Lassalle, both in Germany and among the German workers in London. Marx and Engels enjoyed the irony of a group known for its support of the Prussian government and its calls for state aid to producers' cooperatives working together with anti-statist anarchists; but their enjoyment did not lessen the opposition. Marx's long-term allies, the British trade union leaders, were becoming steadily more sympathetic to this opposition: although hardly anarchists, in view of their lengthy affiliation with the Liberals, they were no supporters of working-class political parties. The newly formed British Federation quickly became a center of anti–General Council views.

Within a few months of the London Conference, Marx was faced with a full-blown rebellion against the new course of the International he had orchestrated. While Marx and his friends continued to control the General Council, his position in the affiliated societies was quite shaky, since many of his potential allies were gone: the British trade unionists in opposition, the French sections outlawed by the post-Commune conservative government. The German followers of Liebknecht and Bebel had not sent any delegates to the London Conference, paid any dues to the General Council, or shown much interest in further affiliation with the IWMA, leading a frustrated Marx to open correspondence with a local group in Berlin, just to have some say on conditions in Germany. In contrast to the passivity or desertions of Marx's former adherents, Bakunin's followers were busy organizing new sections in Italy and Spain.[11]

There would be no avoiding a congress of the International that would decide the future of the organization. The first eight months of 1872 saw feverish activities by both Marx's and Bakunin's adherents to rally supporters to control the forthcoming congress. Marx struck first, with his polemic, *The Purported Schisms in the International*, officially endorsed by the General Council in its meeting of March 5, 1872. A substantial document, laced with envenomed remarks and discussions of personal scandals, the piece denounced Bakunin and his followers for their introduction of secret society tactics into the IWMA. It recounted, with some relish, the story of Bakunin's close connections to the psychopathic Russian revolutionary Nechayev. Bakunin and his followers struck back with their own polemics, denouncing Marx as a bourgeois, smoking cigarettes in his London villa, while the workers in Europe were fighting for their freedom. They condemned him as an authoritarian German, and contended that his faction of the IWMA was led entirely by Jews. Bakunin, in writing unpublished at the time, denounced Marx as the front man of an international Jewish conspiracy.[12]

Mutual denunciations having set the stage, both sides turned to control of the forthcoming congress. Marx was determined to exploit to the fullest the General Council's statutory authority to set the congress's location. Geneva was the initial choice; Marx's old ally there, Johann Philipp Becker, assured him that he could muster enough working-class supporters to rout the adherents of Bakunin should they try to seize control of the congress by force. This was not an entirely far-fetched precaution, since Bakunin's followers had attacked Nikolai Utin, a pro-Marx Russian political exile, on the streets of Zurich in August 1872, and beaten him almost to death. In the end, Marx decided on The Hague as a better site: physically closer to Germany and the United Kingdom, from which he was expecting friendly delegates, further from the Mediterranean lands that were the base of Bakunin's support. At its meeting on June 11, 1872, the General Council duly chose the Dutch city and set the first Monday in September as the date for the congress to convene.[13]

Well before the time and place had been set, Marx and his associates were hard at work, trying to ensure that they would have a majority of delegates. Italy and Spain were the most difficult spots, since most of their sections had been recently founded by the anarchists. Engels, the General Council's corresponding secretary for the two countries, had only a rudimentary knowledge of their languages. His correspondence with the sections there showed a distinct tendency to degenerate into vituperation of their pro-Bakunin leaders. Marx also had personal representatives in the southern Mediterranean. His son-in-law Paul Lafargue had been forced to flee to Spain to avoid persecution by the French government for his support of the Commune. Lafargue maneuvered skillfully, and was able to make the most of a bad situation, rallying as many of Marx's supporters as he could. In Italy, Marx depended on a young German engineer working in Milan, Theodor Cuno, whom the Italian government quickly expelled from the country. For Cuno, it was the beginning of a lifelong political odyssey that would conclude as a member of a left-wing, multiracial commune in 1930s Louisiana; but his expulsion from Italy sixty years earlier left Marx without any way to gather support.[14]

Marx and Engels had another string in their bow, getting the General Council to refuse to recognize the affiliation of the Italian and Spanish sections on the grounds that they had neither paid their dues nor adhered to the rules of the IWMA. The anarchists were outraged by this political maneuvering, but Marx could point out that the 1869 Basel Congress of the IWMA had granted these powers to the General Council with the enthusiastic support of Bakunin and his followers, as they ruefully admitted. They had probably supported the proposal because they hoped to gain control of the General Council and make use of it for their own ends. In adopting this strategy, Marx was looking forward to what we would today call a credentials fight, hoping to undermine the legitimacy of the anarchist delegations. Engels admitted that this was a risky move, because the IWMA's German affiliates, who would provide crucial votes for Marx, had not paid their dues either.[15]

Marx assiduously cultivated the French refugees from the Paris Commune residing in London, most of whom were followers of the ideas of Louis-Auguste Blanqui, the veteran French revolutionary and devotee of secret societies: not ideal for Marx's cause, but at least opposed to Bakunin. The IWMA affiliates in the United States were also the subject of Marx's appeals: "This congress will decide the life or death of the International," Marx wrote to Friedrich Adolph Sorge, a fellow 1848 revolutionary, then living in Hoboken, New Jersey. "You and at least one other if not two must attend." Sections that could not send delegates should send proxies instead, granting their votes to Marx and his friends. Since attending the Congress, even from European countries much closer to The Hague than New Jersey, was often an enormous financial challenge for potential delegates, Marx proposed that friendly affiliated groups provide him and his associates with proxies. Engels opened his wallet to help supportive delegates in England with travel costs.[16]

By late summer 1872, it was increasingly clear that Marx had out-maneuvered Bakunin. The anarchists were either planning to boycott the Hague Congress altogether, in favor of their own to be held in Neuchâtel, or to put in an appearance in the Netherlands, be outvoted, and then go off to Switzerland. In spite of favorable auspices, Marx was determined to leave nothing to chance. He attended the Congress in person, outfitted with four votes, as a delegate of the General Council, and with proxies from sections in New York, Leipzig, and Mainz. Engels accompanied him, as did Jenny, who attended the sessions of the Congress sitting with her daughter Laura. Marx had never previously been to an IWMA congress; he had consistently refused to attend congresses of the German labor parties, although he received invitations from both the followers of Lassalle and those of Bebel and Liebknecht. The September 1872 Hague Congress of the IWMA was the only time Marx ever left England to attend a political meeting since his arrival there as a refugee in 1849—a clear indication of the great importance he placed in the meeting.[17]

The Congress itself was quite the spectacle. Journalists, report-ing on the proceedings, packed the spectators' galleries. IWMA del-egates were unsure whether to be pleased about the public attention or to suspect the newspapermen as spies for the bourgeoisie. The Dutch government, fearing the gathering of revolutionaries would lead to dis-turbances of public order, stationed soldiers seemingly on every street corner of its capital city. In spite of these apprehensions, there was no repetition of the Commune. Everything proceeded in good-natured and orderly fashion, as one might expect in the Netherlands. The del-egates were followed everywhere by crowds of spectators. Since The Hague had the reputation of being a very conservative and religious city, there was no surprise that some were openly hostile; others were simply curious; to the delegates' astonishment, some were very friendly, singing the *Marseillaise*.[18]

Supporters of Marx caucused before and during the sessions at the Hôtel Picot; those of Bakunin, lacking their leader, who did not appear for the Congress, at the Café National. At the very first sessions on September 2–3, credentials fights all went Marx's way, although the anarchists were "rushing wildly about, shrieking and howling interruptions. . . . One, Cyrille, presenting himself with his hat on before the President, gesticulated dramatically, and, shouting as if he would burst a blood vessel, rushed out." Thomas Mottershead, an English silk weaver and trade union leader, a longtime ally of Marx on the General Council, who had recently broken with him, denounced one of the disputed delegates, the journalist Maltman Barry, as "not a recognized leader of British working men." One might imagine Mottershead making this accusation rather unsteadily, since he was drunk throughout the entire Congress. Marx snapped right back at him that such an accusation was an honor, "for almost every recognized leader of English working men was sold to Gladstone, Morley, Dilke [i.e., the leaders of the Liberal Party] and the others."

Marx's open insult of his old IWMA allies was a drastic step, but also evidence that he had the meeting well under control. His slate for the officers of the Congress handily beat out that of the Bakuninists. Votes on crucial issues—the reaffirmation of the right of the General Council to suspend the membership of affiliated societies, the condemnation of Bakunin's International Alliance of Social Democracy, and the expulsion from the IWMA of Bakunin and his right-hand man, the Swiss anarchist James Guillaume—went Marx's way, and by substantial majorities.[19]

Then, on September 7, the penultimate day of the Congress, Marx dropped a bombshell. Engels rose and proposed that the seat of the

General Council be moved to New York. The delegates sat in startled silence: "It was some time before any one rose to speak. It was a *coup d'état*, and each one looked to his neighbor to break the spell." This newspaper account, from the pro-Marx delegate Maltman Barry, captures well the enormous surprise at the seeming perversity of Marx's proposal to send the central authority of the IWMA across the Atlantic Ocean. Such a move would leave it very far from the action of the group and its European affiliates, especially after Marx had triumphed over his anarchist opponents, and reinforced the Central Council's leadership role within the IWMA. The transfer of the General Council away from London passed by a narrow margin of 26 ayes, 23 nays, and 9 abstentions. In a second vote, New York was chosen as the new site of the General Council with 30 votes, against 14 for London, and 13 abstaining.[20]

Critics, like Eccarius, regarded the move as a sham: "the central box of the International may be hung up at the 10th Ward Hotel New York, and . . . the center of action may be in [Marx's home in] Maitland-park, Haverstock-hill. . . ." He was certainly right about that. Marx and Engels sent detailed instructions to Friedrich Adolf Sorge, the leading figure of the New York General Council, about resolutions the Council was to pass. They refused to send him any of the records of the General Council that it would need to function; sending such documents, Engels stated, was just a "formality."[21]

Admittedly, the New York General Council did not have all that much to do. The Belgian, Spanish, English, Italian, and francophone Swiss federations all refused to correspond with it. Some of these groups remained within the IWMA, while others joined a Bakuninist organization. The French government had prohibited the International and arrested the delegates to a meeting of French affiliates held in the southern city of Toulouse. Followers of Lassalle were working against the IWMA within the German labor movement and among the German workers in London. Neither the official IWMA, now centered in New York, nor the various national and local groups rejecting the New York General Council's authority, nor Bakunin's counter-organization lasted more than a few years. By the late 1870s, all remnants of the IWMA had ceased to exist.[22]

Sending the General Council to New York was no spur-of-the-moment decision. Marx had already been toying with the idea of moving the General Council out of London in the late 1860s. In the run-up to the Hague Congress he made no secret of his plans to resign from the General Council and devote himself to completing his economics treatise. Marx saw himself as the central figure in the IWMA, a viewpoint shared by contemporaries both friendly and hostile. Without his guidance, he feared that the organization would fall into the hands of advocates of a secret society politics he despised, so that his planned resignation could only be accompanied by dismantling or at least downgrading the International. Although repeatedly denying this interpretation in public, Marx's intentions were quite clear to observers at the Congress, and he himself even admitted them in a private conversation with a Paris Commune refugee, who was secretly a French police spy.

Historians sometimes compare the decision to the one Marx made in 1850, when he dispatched the Central Authority of the Communist League from London to Cologne, also a move leading to the organization's demise. Marx had done that because his opponents, led by Willich and Schapper, had gained control of the Communist League in London. By contrast, Marx had been quite successful in retaining control of the IWMA at the 1872 Hague Congress. Admittedly, he had done so by questionable machinations and by forming an alliance with the French Blanquists, a group of secret society supporters whose ideas of politics were fundamentally opposed to those of Marx. The transfer of the General Council to New York, in this line of argument, was a pre-emptive strike, to destroy the IWMA while Marx controlled it, before the anarchists, aggressively organizing in southern Europe, and the secret society revolutionary Blanquists could take it over.[23]

This viewpoint has a lot to say for it, but it is in some ways incomplete, as can be seen in Marx and Engels's relationship with the IWMA following the transfer of the General Council to New York. They did continue to try to get the organization to make decisions, to carry out correspondence with the few loyal sections, and even prepared to attend a planned 1873 IWMA congress in Geneva—at least until it became clear that the sole attendees would be groups from Switzerland, so that the Congress would not be international at all. Why do all this if the point of the transfer to New York was to terminate the IWMA?

An answer lies in Engels's letter to Sorge, refusing to send the records of the General Council. Those records, he wrote, "are absolutely indispensable in the struggle with the Secessionists [i.e., the supporters of Bakunin], in order to be able to answer their lies and slander." After the Hague Congress, Marx worked feverishly on a lengthy pamphlet, officially commissioned by the Congress, detailing the relationship of Bakunin's International Alliance of Social Democracy with the IWMA. The writing culminated in a fulminant attack on Bakunin, describing in lurid detail his connections with Nechayev, his Pan-Slavist ideas, and his secret affiliations with the czar.

Marx, as he looked at Europe following the conclusion of the Franco-Prussian War and the suppression of the Paris Commune, saw the beginning of a new era of reaction not unlike the one that had overtaken the Continent in the 1850s. The IWMA would be unable to function effectively, much as had been the case with the 1848 revolutionaries in the subsequent decade. Under these circumstances, he wrote to Sorge, at the end of September 1873, "it is quite useful for the formal organization of the International to move to the background for the moment . . . so that no idiots . . . or adventurers . . . seize the leadership and compromise the cause." This continued to be the viewpoint

Marx and Engels articulated throughout the entire decade of the 1870s and into the early 1880s; they always opposed any revival of the International as inopportune under the prevailing political circumstances and likely to do more harm than good.[24]

Starting with the suppression of the Paris Commune and moving onward for the next three years, Marx's policies were aimed at creating a legacy: identifying the Commune with his ideas of communist revolution; linking the IWMA to the Commune; and aligning the International with his version of working-class revolutionary politics. Marx took into account that such policies might well lead to the destruction of the IWMA, but he saw the primary value of the group in its image for future revolutionaries, not in its increasingly compromised possibilities of action with present ones. This stance went along with his own advancing age and failing health, making it steadily more difficult for him to carry out all his demanding political and scholarly tasks. Public plans and private concerns converged in a tacit admission that the communist revolution Marx had spent the previous three decades planning and striving toward would not occur in his lifetime. Like the organization he had been instrumental in building and dismantling, the value of Marx's life and work would be in its legacy for the future.

AT THE END OF June 1872, Jenny Marx described the demands on her father's time as he prepared for the Hague Congress of the IWMA. A special meeting (besides the time-consuming regular ones) of the General Council lasted from four in the afternoon until one in the morning. Moments free of IWMA business were taken up with going over the proofs for the second German edition of *Capital* and revising the translation for the French edition. Even after the meeting in the Netherlands, and the transfer of the General Council to New York, Marx found himself still very busy denouncing Bakunin and the anarchists, and working on the French edition of *Capital*.[25]

His health began to deteriorate visibly. He suffered from persistent insomnia; at the Hague Congress, he hardly slept at all. To Adolf Hepner, a German Congress delegate, he looked aged, visibly older than Engels. Following the Congress, new symptoms began to appear: persistent episodes of dizziness and repeated, agonizing headaches. Wilhelm Wolff had shown similar symptoms before suffering a fatal stroke in 1864, and Engels feared that Marx would meet the same fate. Marx's complaints are clinical evidence of an advanced case of hypertension, so Engels's suspicions were probably correct. Engels insisted that Marx consult his former Manchester physician, Eduard Gumpert, whose medical knowledge Marx deeply respected. The doctor's orders were that Marx could write at most four hours a day. For a full restoration of his health he would need an extended stay at a spa, drinking its mineral waters, a nineteenth-century medical treatment enormously popular among the middle and upper classes.[26]

Marx followed this advice, as usual with financial assistance from Engels. In September 1874, he traveled, accompanied by Eleanor, who was having her own health problems, to Karlsbad in the Austrian province of Bohemia, today's Karlovy Varý in the Czech Republic. Marx went slightly incognito, to avoid the attention of the Austrian authorities. He registered at the hotel as Charles Marx, rentier of London, rather than as Dr. Karl Marx, which would have brought a discount on the daily fee the spa guests had to pay. The therapeutic value of drinking the spa's sulfurous thermal waters may be doubted, but the extended rest, complete with daily long walks through the town and the surrounding woods and hills, were a beneficial break from the political controversies and long nights of writing in London, to say nothing of that city's choking, coal-dust-laden air. Marx went back to Karlsbad in 1875 and returned to London, as Engels noted, "completely changed . . . powerful, fresh, cheerful and healthy." The trip was repeated in 1876; in 1877, Marx, accompanied by his wife and Eleanor, chose a smaller spa, Bad Neuenahr, in the Rhineland.[27]

. . .

FOR ALL THE IMPROVEMENT in his health, Marx did not return to his previous life of political activism and immense intellectual effort, but became more of an adviser and observer. His suggestions showed both new elements in his view of the world late in his life, and also long-term continuities in his political thought and vision of the future. Evidence of Marx's views at this time is slimmer than previously, because, unlike the 1850s and 1860s, he was no longer engaging in political polemics or writing regular journalism. Engels lived in London just a short walk away, so their extensive correspondence, a very rich source of Marx's opinions, had been replaced by a daily conversation in Marx's study, or, in nice weather, strolling on Hampstead Heath.

There were some issues that concerned Marx deeply and for which a fair amount of evidence is available. One was the prospect of a new war between the great powers—a possibility that haunted the Continent from the end of the Franco-Prussian War in 1871 onward, although it did take forty-three years before it finally broke out. During the 1848 Revolution and in the following two decades, Marx had been bellicose, seeing a great European war as a spur to revolution and a necessary process for radicalizing revolutions. In the 1870s, he became more skeptical of the prospect, fearing that such a war would have reactionary political consequences, "for a longer or shorter period a useless exhaustion of forces" was how he put it. Engels was more drastic, stating that such a war "would be our greatest misfortune; it could set back the [socialist] movement [in Germany] for twenty years."[28]

There was one exception to this skepticism, involving Marx's long-term bête noire, Russia. Just as the Crimean War of 1853–56, pitting the Western powers against Russia over the future of the Ottoman Empire, had been the major political event of the era of reaction, so a new war over the fate of the Ottoman Empire in Europe at the end of the 1870s drew Marx's attention. This war began with uprisings of the

Slavic peoples of the Balkans against Turkish rule, particularly violent and dramatic in Ottoman Bulgaria. European leftists in general, and veterans of the Revolution of 1848 in particular, were very excited about the Bulgarian Revolution of 1877, which was the first uprising on the Continent after the suppression of the Paris Commune.

Marx was not. He and Engels saw the anti-Ottoman insurgents in the Balkans as tools of Pan-Slavists, trying to expand Russian influence. This attitude only intensified when the czar declared war on the Sultan, and sent his armies marching into the Balkans to liberate the Muslim ruler's Christian subjects, and then to seize the Ottoman capital of Constantinople. This Russo-Turkish War unleashed a furious dispute in English politics. The Liberals, led by William Gladstone, took a distinctly anti-Turkish stance, publicizing the massacres of thousands of Christians by Islamic soldiers suppressing the uprising—the "Bulgarian horrors," in contemporary parlance. Against them were the vigorously anti-Russian Conservatives, and their veteran leader Benjamin Disraeli, who emphasized, in crude form, nationalist hostility. The Tories' efforts to gain popular support for their plans brought the phrase "jingoism" into the English language.[29]

As had been the case during the Crimean War, Marx was vehemently against Russia. But a quarter century later, he lacked his 1850s public platforms: the *New York Tribune* and the newspapers, pamphlets, and public meetings of the followers of David Urquhart, who died in 1877. Still, Marx had other means of influencing the public. He was able to feed information to an Irish Nationalist MP, Keyes O'Cleary, who was out to derail the Liberals. O'Cleary stood up in the House of Commons and asked Gladstone, who was demanding that the Ottoman Empire carry out reforms, why Gladstone was not demanding the same of the Russian Empire—and then detailed a list of evils found in the realm of the czar, provided for him by Marx from Russian émigrés. Marx informed his followers in Germany that the "working class press is not paying enough attention to the Eastern Question"; he provided

Wilhelm Liebknecht with a set of talking points for the debate in the Reichstag, enabling Liebknecht to attack Bismarck for what Marx saw as a perniciously pro-Russian slant to German policies.[30]

Marx's attitudes toward British politics in the 1870s were very much like those of twenty years previously. Although not denouncing Gladstone as a paid agent of the czar, he despised the Liberals as lackeys of Russia, people who "scream and howl to the greater glory of the Tsar, liberator of [oppressed] peoples." By contrast, he greatly admired Disraeli's stand against the Russian Empire, and only regretted that Conservative noblemen in Disraeli's cabinet were taking a pro-czarist stance, and not letting him exercise his talents to the full. Marx was infuriated when the one working-class MP sitting for the Liberal Party, Thomas Burt, actually voted against Disraeli's military appropriations to prepare for action against the Russians. Marx was appalled that a "direct representative of the mine-workers and himself a miner" could "leave their army in the lurch" while bourgeois leftists, such as John Bright, whom Marx had denounced in the 1850s for lack of martial spirit, avoided casting an anti-military vote by scurrying out of the House of Commons.[31]

Inspired by the parties' opinions about war with Russia, Marx developed a more broadly pro-Conservative attitude. He was a strong supporter of Irish nationalism, and a sworn enemy of English landlord rule in Ireland, two issues on which the Conservatives had absolutely contrary positions. Nonetheless, Marx denounced Gladstone's efforts to improve the position of Irish tenant farmers and to reach a compromise with Irish Nationalists as at best halfhearted, and at worst completely fraudulent. Marx's two main British acquaintances during his later years, the journalist Maltman Barry and the eccentric intellectual Henry Hyndman, were both close to the Tories. One of Marx's last written comments on British politics, from a letter to his daughter Jenny in April 1881, less than two years before his death, was full of praise for the brilliant Conservative speakers in Parliament, including Lord Randolph Churchill, whose son, Winston, was then seven years old. The future vehement anti-communist would no doubt have been amused had he known of the communist patriarch's admiration for his father.[32]

Marx's pro-Tory tendencies had already been apparent in the 1850s, but they were magnified by the IWMA British trade unionists' refusal to abandon the Liberals for a workers' party. His stand against Russia in the 1870s was also a continuation of long-term attitudes, but there was a distinct new twist to them, Marx's increasing enthusiasm about the prospects for revolution in that country. Encouraged by the growth of opposition to the czar's regime, and his own personal contacts with Russian radicals, Marx hoped that either a military defeat in the Russo-Turkish War of 1878 or a humiliating retreat before the opposition of other great powers would lead to an inflammatory situation in the realm of the czar. Even after the end of the war and the resolution of the ensuing diplomatic crisis—which did bring a humiliating Russian retreat, as a result of Disraeli's policies—Marx continued to see a Russian revolution on the horizon.

Such revolutions would take place in Russia as a result of wartime defeats, by the Japanese in 1905 and the Germans in 1917, the latter bringing to power the Bolsheviks, a political party endorsing Marx's ideas. The revolution Marx was expecting around 1880 was a different one, a rerun, in the czar's realm of what had happened in France a century earlier. As Engels said about what he and Marx expected in Russia, "First from the court out and constitutional, but that is 1789 before 1793." Marx did have high hopes for the broader European ramifications of a revolution in Russia. "This time the revolution begins in the east," he wrote enthusiastically to Friedrich Sorge in October 1877, "the hitherto intact bulwark and reserve army of counterrevolution." The results of a Russian revolution would be particularly apparent in central Europe: "Defeat of Russia, revolution in Russia—would sound the death-knell of Prussia." Here, Marx was still thinking of the politics of the 1850s, when the Prussian kingdom, the smallest and militarily weakest of the great powers, had been dependent on the czar, whose defeat in the Crimean War heralded the beginning of the end of the era of reaction. After Prussia's victory over France in 1870–71, and the subsequent merger of all the German states into the militarily and diplomatically powerful, Prussian-dominated German Empire, authoritarian German rulers like Bismarck no longer needed the patronage of the czar. If anything, it was the other way around.[33]

Marx's views on the latest economic developments also reflected the influences of the 1850s, particularly his disappointment over the outcome of the global recession of 1857. The decade of the 1870s saw the re-emergence of large-scale economic crises throughout Europe and North America: abrupt stock exchange crashes, followed by deep and severe recessions with very high unemployment and growing labor unrest, such as the 1877 nationwide rail strikes and riots of the unemployed in the United States, which Marx observed with interest. These sharp downturns were the prelude to a twenty- to twenty-five-year period of frequent and more severe recessions, deflationary price declines, and slower economic growth, which economists and historians used to call (the term has gone out of fashion in recent years) the Great Depression of the nineteenth century.[34]

Surprisingly, Marx did not see this chain of economic crises as *the* crisis of capitalism he had so often predicted. Rather, he saw them as "partial" crises, with the terminal crisis still a ways off in the future, presumably after the end of his own life. Marx even hoped that the economic crisis of the 1870s would not be too severe, because he feared that a "premature" crisis would grant capitalism a new lease on life. Instead, he focused his attention on the effects of deflation for agriculture. Collapsing farm prices, he thought, would lead to increasingly vehement class struggles among landlords, capitalist tenant farmers, and agricultural laborers in Great Britain, undermining a central pillar of British society and politics. This focus on British agricultural society and its place in a potential upheaval of the capitalist world was one Marx had already adopted in the more prosperous years of the late 1860s.[35]

The difficult economic environment of the last quarter of the nineteenth century coincided with and encouraged a great expansion of colonial empires. The 1880s saw the "scramble for Africa," as contemporaries put it. Later disciples of Marx, including Lenin, Rosa Luxemburg, and Karl Kautsky, would put imperialism at the center of their analyses of capitalism; but Marx himself, as had been the case with his writings on imperialism in the 1850s, did not perceive the connection. He lived to see the British occupation of Egypt (then an autonomous province of the Ottoman Empire) in 1882, one of the first steps in the scramble for Africa. The very last written comment he made on public affairs, in a letter to Eleanor just two months before his death, concerned this imperialist move. Ignoring financial concerns, such as the money the Egyptian government owed foreign bondholders, the economic and strategic issues connected with the Suez Canal, or even visions of a great British Empire in Africa—which Marx described, sardonically, as daydreams—he focused instead on Russia. There were no British interests involved, Marx insisted: the policy of Gladstone's Liberal government was "just the tool of other, non-British clever schemers," the Russians, who wanted a British occupation of Egypt as a pretext to allow them to seize another Ottoman province, Armenia. This evaluation, shared by Engels, was part of Marx's long-term suspicion of Russian policy, and his equally long-term denunciation of the Liberal Party as a tool of the czar, but very different from future Marxists' understanding of imperialist ventures.[36]

UNTIL SHORTLY BEFORE HIS death, Marx continued to be involved with existing revolutionary movements and nascent socialist parties on the Continent. His interactions with German, French, and

Russian socialists reveal the way he took his own lifetime of political experiences—anchored, more than anything else, by the revolutions of 1848–49—and applied them to the political circumstances coming into existence in Europe during the last quarter of the nineteenth century.

The most important and substantial of these political initiatives involved the German socialists. Marx and Engels purported to be internationalists, Engels stating that he and Marx were "representatives of international socialism," who "belong to the German party barely more than to the French, American or Russian. . . ." Yet for all their internationalism, they could not deny a personal connection to the German labor movement: "We enjoy every victory won in Germany as much as elsewhere, and even more, because the German party has from the very beginning developed in dependence on our theoretical positions."[37]

The creation of a German nation-state in 1871, bringing together Prussia and formerly anti-Prussian kingdoms, such as Saxony and Bavaria, into a federalist German Empire, ended any reason for the separate existences of the pro-Prussian Lassalleans of the General German Workers' Association, and the anti-Prussian Social Democratic Labor Party led by Liebknecht and Bebel. Increasing persecution of both socialist parties by the German government authorities, who no longer saw them as tools in the politics of national unification, made the idea of a merger seem steadily more plausible, an idea strongly endorsed by Marx's close ally Wilhelm Liebknecht.

Representatives of the two groups met and drew up a common program as a precursor to the unity congress, scheduled for the Thuringian city of Gotha in late May 1875. Marx and Engels only learned about this decision, made without any input from them, through the newspapers. It was bad enough that their supporters were agreeing to a merger with the followers of Lassalle, on terms that Marx and Engels regarded as favorable to the latter, but to do so on the basis of a "pernicious and demoralizing . . . program," one "good for nothing but canonizing Lassalle's articles of faith"—that was unbearable. After a detailed discussion with Engels, Marx drew up extensive criticisms, and sent them off to Germany to be circulated among the party leadership. The critique was coupled with an ultimatum: if the merger congress went ahead, on the basis of the draft program, "Engels and I will publish a short declaration, whose content is that we will distance ourselves from this program and have nothing to do with it."[38]

Marx's criticisms, "Marginal Notes on the Program of the German Workers' Party," or "Critique of the Gotha Program," as they are now known, were a savage condemnation of the elements of Lassalle's ideas contained in the draft document. Oddly, one of the major aspects of Marx's anger sounded a lot like the *Communist Manifesto*, the program's assertions that the means of production were a "monopoly of the capitalist class," and that, compared to the workers, the other classes formed "one reactionary mass." Marx's own thinking had changed in the quarter century since the *Manifesto*, and he had come to regard the class of landowners as increasingly important to capitalist society. "In England," Marx noted in his critique, "the capitalist is usually not even the owner of the land on which his factory stands." But these criticisms also had a political point. Marx saw the proposed program as continuing Lassalle's efforts at a political "alliance with the absolutist and feudal enemies of the bourgeoisie," his attempts to cozy up to Bismarck and the authoritarian Prussian government.

The program's endorsement of Lassalle's opposition to trade unions, and support for state-sponsored producers' cooperatives, was also anathema to Marx. Unions were the means for the workers to seize back from the capitalists part of the surplus value they had produced for them. Marx's skepticism of cooperatives was only deepened if they were to be sponsored by Bismarck's authoritarian regime. His dislike of Bismarck was closely linked to the attack on the Gotha Program's rejection of internationalism, its insistence that the working class should strive for its liberation "within the context of the contemporary nation-state." Coming from the man who had recently dissolved the IWMA and opposed efforts at its revival, this might sound odd, but Marx regarded the assertion as yet another concession to Bismarck, who had brought nationalism under his political control.

If the critique dealt first and foremost with Lassallean elements in the Gotha Program, Marx by no means spared the ideas of his own followers, Bebel and Liebknecht. He had little good to say about the program's political demands: the "free state"—a circumlocution for a democratic republic, a demand that could not legally be uttered in Bismarck's Germany—was "nothing but the universally known democratic litany, universal suffrage, direct legislation [by popular initiative], civil liberties, popular militia etc. They are a mere echo of the bourgeois People's Party. . . ." Marx was unhappy with the call for state-sponsored free and equal public education, which he saw as yet another concession to authoritarianism. And the demands for academic freedom and freedom of conscience were just "old slogans of liberalism," and even in the Prussian constitution—not exactly stuff for the program of a revolutionary labor party.

The "Critique of the Gotha Program" was the latest in a series of assertions of Marx's revolutionary strategy that had begun three decades earlier with his essay "On the Jewish Question." A central European revolution would involve a double recurrence of the French Revolution of 1789, both overthrowing the authoritarian Prussian state and organizing the workers to demand a communist regime. Marx had always denounced radical movements that would perform one, but not both, of these revolutionary tasks. In the 1860s, he had lashed out against the anti-capitalist but pro-Prussian Lassalleans, and the anti-Prussian but insufficiently anti-capitalist followers of Liebknecht and Bebel. The merger was bringing the worst features of the two approaches together, "a compromise between these two versions of belief in miracles, equally far from socialism."

In spite of Marx and Engels's ultimatum, the unity congress duly met in Gotha, founding the Socialist Labor Party of Germany, and adopting the draft program. Marx and Engels did not go through with their threat to disavow the newly unified party, ostensibly because the bourgeois press and the workers had misinterpreted the character of the program, seeing it as socialist and revolutionary rather than confused and backward, but this contention was evidently a pretext. Marx was not prepared to denounce the party he saw as his legacy, although in future criticisms he would always blame Liebknecht for having compromised with the Lassalleans and allowed dubious elements into the socialists' ranks.[39]

Marx was very impressed by the united party's performance at the 1877 national elections, when it doubled the socialists' previous vote totals and emerged as a significant political voice against Bismarck. The Iron Chancellor was more than ready for the socialists' challenge. Exploiting two failed attempts in 1877–78 to assassinate the elderly German emperor Wilhelm I, and blaming them on socialist terrorists (in reality, both assassins were mentally ill lone assailants), Bismarck intimidated the liberals and Catholics in the Reichstag into passing a law prohibiting the Socialist Labor Party and public advocacy of its doctrines. This was not the Nazi era, when workers' parties were outlawed and their leaders thrown into concentration camps. In the more gentlemanly nineteenth century, the Socialist Labor Party was prohibited, but running socialist candidates for parliament was not, and otherwise illegal socialist propaganda could be spread with impunity if it was part of an election campaign.[40]

While historians may be consoled by the fact that Hitler's persecution of Germany's socialists was much worse than Bismarck's, nineteenth-century German socialists could not share that attitude. They sought ways to respond to the new unfavorable situation. One party leader, Johann Most, fled the country, and from English exile, with the support of the London Communist Workers' Educational Association, advocated the immediate violent overthrow of the German government. Marx and Engels regarded these appeals as an invitation to the workers to be massacred by the army, but merely reacted with a display of condescension toward the German artisans in London for supporting such stupid notions.[41]

Marx took much more seriously the proposal of the party leadership to start a daily newspaper in Switzerland, but found less amenable its proposed editorial policy, a strong criticism of the socialists' revolutionary aspirations. By praising the violence of the Paris Commune and demanding a showdown with the capitalists, members of the Zurich editorial board asserted, the socialists had driven the liberal middle class into the arms of Bismarck and his reactionary politics. The editors advocated a renunciation of violent revolution, reforming capitalism rather than introducing socialism, class cooperation in place of class struggle, and gaining support across society instead of appealing solely to the working class. This program strongly resembled what would later be dubbed "revisionism," the revision of Marx's doctrines of class struggle and socialist revolution. Eduard Bernstein, author of *Evolutionary Socialism*, the bible of the early twentieth-century revisionists, was one of the members of the exile newspaper editorial board two decades earlier.

Lenin cut his political teeth on the denunciation of revisionism, so it has become a familiar point of Marxism. To Marx in 1879, the idea of a reform-oriented labor party was an unfamiliar political stance, quite unlike the previous forms of socialism, labor organization, and radical politics he had opposed. Lassalle had proposed to organize workers, quite militantly, against the bourgeoisie, although he was willing to take the assistance of the reactionary Prussian government in doing so. English trade unionists had no interest in an independent labor party, but were affiliated with the Liberals. The anti-socialist democrats and republicans of the 1840s were also no adherents of a labor party.

Marx found the proposals as pernicious as they were novel; in the fall of 1879, he and Engels sent a circular letter denouncing them to the leaders of the German Socialist Labor Party. In the circular, the two London veterans used their experiences from 1848 to characterize the new policies: they were the same as those proposed in the midcentury revolution by the petit-bourgeois democrats, the bourgeois democrats, and the True Socialists—three groups that did not get along. This effort to dispose of a new phenomenon by dismissing it as a recurrence of discredited old ones was a sign of the intellectual difficulty Marx and Engels had in dealing with the proposal, but it did not stop them from making a threat:

> As far as we are concerned there is only one way open. For almost forty years now, we have emphasized the class struggle as the fundamental driving force of history, and especially the class struggle between bourgeoisie and proletariat as the great lever of modern social upheaval; it is impossible for us to go together with people who wish to strike this class struggle from the movement. . . . If the new party organ takes a stance corresponding to the bourgeois and not proletarian sentiments of these gentlemen [the members of the editorial board], there will be nothing we can do, as sorry as we will be, but to protest against it publicly, and to dissolve the solidarity, with which we have hitherto shown the German party vis-à-vis foreigners.

The party leadership took this warning more seriously than it had the ones connected with the Gotha Program, dispatching August Bebel and Eduard Bernstein to London in 1880 to convince the revolutionary veterans that the Zurich newspaper was not neglecting the class struggle. The emissaries were successful in their efforts, and Engels went on to write for the newspaper; by that time, the health problems of Marx and his wife made his participation impossible.[42]

What this episode suggested was a gradually developing new revolutionary formulation. For decades, Marx had tried, often with considerable difficulty, to guide German radicals between exclusively opposing Prussian authoritarianism and exclusively opposing capitalism. By the end of the 1870s, he was trying to guide the social democrats between Most's demands for immediate revolution and Bernstein's ideas of a fundamentally reformist workers' movement. This, too, would prove a difficult tightrope for socialist leaders to walk, although most of the tightrope walking would be done by a later generation, fifteen to thirty years after Marx's own death.

Marx treated the German labor movement with angry ultimatums and demands to follow a particular political line. His relationship with the labor movement in France was quite different. Following the electoral and parliamentary victories of supporters of the republican form of government over the monarchists in the late 1870s, French socialists began political organizing. The 1880 amnesty for participants in the Commune allowed exiles to return, including both of Marx's sons-in-law, and to become involved in socialist politics.

French socialists founded a multiplicity of parties and factions; adherents of one of those groups, led by a man named Jules Guesde, became known as "Marxists." Although the term had been used earlier, generally in pejorative fashion, to refer to supporters of Marx in the struggles for control of the IWMA, the designation by Guesde's followers was its first sustained and positive use. Marx was not happy having his name associated with this group of supposed supporters, and told Paul Lafargue, according to Engels's reminiscence, "what is certain is that I myself am not a Marxist." Marx also told Engels that the doctrinaire "Marxists" and "anti-Marxists" alike in France were ruining his stay there while visiting his family in the fall of 1882. Both men saw differences among French socialists as primarily a product of idiosyncrasy, personal vanity, and obscure and unnecessary doctrinal disagreements. Meeting with these socialists in person during visits to his family in 1881 and 1882, Marx encouraged them to put aside such differences. The London exiles treated disagreements among German socialists, by contrast, as important questions of political principle, a difference in attitude testifying to Marx and Engels's political involvement and personal investment in the German labor movement.[43]

Also unlike the case in Germany, Marx's interventions in the French labor movement came at the request of the French socialists themselves. This was true of Marx's relationship with socialists in Russia, although similar circumstances involved a very different country. Marx had lived in France, knew the language well, and had, for decades, perceived France—Paris in particular—as central to his plans for global revolution and a communist future. Russia, by contrast, was for Marx the enemy, the czarist regime suppressing revolutionary movements in Europe and across the world. Opposition to Russia was one of the few political areas where Marx was willing to work with people of very different views, such as David Urquhart. His suspicions of Russia extended to Russian revolutionaries, whom he persistently suspected of being agents of the czar or pan-Slavists, using radical and nationalist ideas to expand czarist power in Eastern Europe. Late in Marx's life his opinions about the revolutions in the Balkans and the Russo-Turkish War of 1877–78 exemplified this viewpoint. The Russian academic Maxim Kovalevsky, who visited Marx in London frequently during the mid-1870s, remembered that Marx's attitude toward Russia "was not essentially different from the prejudice of 1848 revolutionaries . . . who saw in Russia just the bulwark of all kinds of reaction and the strangler of democratic and liberal revolutions."[44]

But interest in Marx and his ideas grew rapidly in Russia. Academics there were intrigued with *On the Critique of Political Economy* and waited anxiously for the main part of Marx's economics treatise to appear. Russian was the first language into which *Capital* was translated. As an oppositional revolutionary movement began to develop in the core provinces of the czar's empire during the 1870s, primarily among university students exposed to Marx's ideas in their studies, its adherents began to turn to Marx for advice.

Marx was, at first, bemused by the favorable reception of his ideas in a country he had repeatedly denounced. By the late 1860s, when he was regarding rural society as steadily more crucial to his revolutionary aspirations, Russia came increasingly to his attention. He studied the social and economic relations in Russian agriculture intensively for the sections on ground rent and farming in the planned second volume of *Capital*. In the 1870s, he developed greater political connections with Russian revolutionaries, both refugees from the Paris Commune and anti-Bakunin exiles in Switzerland. Some very guarded correspondence, often written in English, with false names and cover addresses, began to be exchanged between the veteran socialist in London and potential Russian insurgents. Political exiles and Russian academics abroad made their way to the house on Maitland Park Road.[45]

In 1881, Vera Zasulich, acting on behalf of a group of Russian émigrés in Switzerland, sent a letter to Marx, dealing with the very common practice of Russian peasants holding their village land in common. In view of the discussion in *Capital* of the end of feudalism and the development of capitalist agriculture in Western Europe, the émigré revolutionaries wanted to know the post-revolutionary future of this property form: would rural land have to become private property, as in Western Europe, or was there the possibility of maintaining collective ownership in some future communist society? Marx had already received a similar inquiry from the clandestine, revolutionary committee in St. Petersburg, and had found it filled with difficult implications.

One was theoretical. His stages model of history, outlined in the *Critique of Political Economy*, set out a universal process of social evolution through which all countries would go, albeit at a different pace and at different times. Marx regarded collective ownership of agricultural land in Russia as an earlier, more primitive stage of society, seen in ancient German tribes, or in slowly moving Asian societies. Engels especially, but Marx as well, had always mocked the idea, sometimes

propounded by Russian radicals, that the collective ownership of farm-
land in the czar's empire was a precious and unique form of society, a
sort of Russian gift to a communist future. For Marx and Engels, the
continuing presence of this form of land ownership was archaic and
backward; praise of it was politically pernicious, part of reactionary,
Pan-Slavist schemes.[46]

Marx's reply to Zasulich's letter went through five different lengthy
drafts—a considerable effort at a time when his physical strength was
failing, demonstrating the importance he placed on the topic. In the
end, he just sent her a short note, stating that in Western Europe the
transition was from feudal private property in land to capitalist private
property, so not applicable by analogy to Russia. The peasant commune might serve as a "fulcrum for the social regeneration of Russia," but only if at first "the deleterious influences assailing it from all
sides" were "eliminated." How, exactly, this might happen was specified
a year later, when Marx and Engels wrote a brief preface to a Russian
edition of the *Communist Manifesto*, noting that if a Russian revolution
were a signal for a "proletarian revolution in the West," the two movements might be mutually complementing and common property in land
could "serve as the point of departure for a communist development."[47]
Such formulations, reminiscent of speculations Marx and Engels made
about Western European socialist regimes' reforming colonial empires,
suggest a continuing perception of Russian backwardness. They were
also a reference to an implausible future, since at the time the preface
was written, Marx was enthusiastic about the possibilities for revolution in Russia, but saw the socialist labor movement in Western Europe
as in a relatively early stage of development. It was hard to see how a
Russian revolution would coincide with a Western European workers'
uprising.

In these difficult and repeatedly qualified formulations, Marx was
wrestling with how to reconcile his long-held theories of social development with his growing interest in the revolutionary potential of rural

society, and his desire to remain on good terms with the Russian revolutionaries. In the end, he was equivocal. Future Russian revolutionaries would treat Marx's formulations as tea leaves to be read so as to make their country the central point of a global communist revolution, which, for all Marx's equivocations, was certainly not how he saw things.

THE ELDERLY MARX'S MUSING on the possibilities of revolution in Russia were just one aspect of the views he held, toward the end of his life, on revolution and a post-communist revolutionary future. Some aspects of these views demonstrated a lifelong continuity. Marx's vision of revolution, for instance, was always modeled on the Jacobin phase of the French Revolution. The new-fangled designation of fellow socialists as "comrades," a usage beginning with the followers of Ferdinand Lassalle, was one that Marx rarely employed, and when he did, it was within quotation marks in ironic fashion. Following good Jacobin practice, in the IWMA he was always "Citizen Marx." Another indication of Marx's revolutionary ideals was the closing salutation that appears in most of his letters to Engels, the French word *Salut*. By itself just a common French term, it was also the abbreviated form of the Jacobin greeting, *Salut et Fraternité*. Marx used the full form, or its German version, *Gruß und Handschlag*, in letters to other leftists.[48]

If the echoes of the Jacobin regime of 1793 remained in Marx's revolutionary vocabulary throughout his life, so did his advocacy of political change by means of the violent overthrow of existing governments. There were occasional qualifications, especially the speech he gave at a banquet and public meeting in Amsterdam, the day after the end of the 1872 IWMA Hague Congress. In this speech, for which no written transcript survives and which is known only through summaries printed in Dutch newspapers, Marx asserted that in most countries, the workers would need to seize power via violent revolution, but in some—the United Kingdom, the United States, and perhaps the Netherlands—they could come to power by peaceful, legal means. Marx had addressed this issue the previous year in his interview with an American journalist, R. Landor, of the *New York World*. Landor had suggested that in view of the long history of peaceful political change in Britain, the workers could achieve power without revolution. Marx's reply was:

> I am not so sanguine on that point as you. The English middle class has always shown itself willing enough to accept the verdict of the majority so long as it enjoyed the monopoly of the voting power. But mark me, as soon as it finds itself outvoted on what it considers vital questions, we shall see here a new slave-owner's war.[49]

The workers' peaceful attainment of power which Marx suggested was possible in a few countries would only be a prelude to a violent confrontation, begun by the outvoted capitalists, just as southern slaveholders had begun a civil war when anti-slavery advocates were voted into office in the United States.

If Marx's advocacy of violent revolution persisted, he was also willing to consider new kinds of revolutionary action. His thoughts on this were strongly influenced by the Russian revolutionaries, who had begun a terrorist campaign of killing high government officials. Striking down police chiefs and provincial governors with bullets and explosives, their campaign culminated in 1881 with the assassination by a suicide bomber of Czar Alexander II. Marx fervently endorsed the terrorists' actions and poured scorn on other groups within the Russian revolutionary movement who thought that political organization and propaganda should have priority. Such pro-terrorist sympathies were shared by quite a few of his contemporaries in Western Europe and North America, including Victor Hugo, the American abolitionist Wendell Phillips, and even Mark Twain. But Marx himself did not become a proponent of terrorism as a universal revolutionary strategy.

He endorsed it as effective only against czarist autocracy, a regime that eliminated civil liberties and any possibilities for open political activity. Even for Bismarck's nominally constitutional but authoritarian German Empire, which severely limited possibilities for open, legal politics, Marx opposed terrorist activities. Everyone at Maitland Park Road was very distressed at the news of the assassination attempts on Emperor Wilhelm I, fearing that the socialists really were behind them, and that such measures would be a provocation for severe persecution.[50]

Another newer feature of Marx's views, along with his limited endorsement of revolutionary terrorism, was a willingness to comment publicly on the institutions of a future communist society. From the 1840s onward, Marx had refused to do so, and sharply criticized fellow socialists who did. But in the "Critique of the Gotha Program," he sketched a very brief outline of some key economic features of a communist regime, building on speculations concerning the labor theory of value he had first developed in the unpublished early drafts of *Capital*.

In the initial stages of a communist society, Marx asserted, labor value would be directly expressed: workers would not be paid in money, but in notes denominated in labor time. Pay would correspond to hours worked, after deduction of a "common fund" for investment and maintenance, and could be used to purchase goods, themselves priced according to labor time. "The same quantum of labor that he [the worker] has given society in one form, he receives back in the other." Marx had been thinking about this idea for at least two decades, dating back to observations he made in the *Grundrisse* about the Saint-Simonian proposal for a bank that would issue notes denominated in labor time.

This initial phase of socialism was, for Marx, egalitarian only in the measurement of compensation; other forms of inequality would persist. These would not be class inequalities, for everyone would be a worker. Some individuals could work longer or harder (labor time, Marx noted, would not just be measured in hours worked but also in the intensity of the labor) and would receive more labor time notes. Others would have to support a family on the same labor time pay as those who were single. These were "abuses," but ones that were "unavoidable" in the initial phase of communist society. They would only end after the abolition of the "subordination of individuals in servile form to the division of labor" and the disappearance of the "opposition of intellectual and physical labor." Only in this later phase of communism, when "labor is not just a means of life, but the first necessity of life," and when the development of labor productivity has reached unparalleled heights, could "society write on its flag: from each according to his abilities, to each according to his needs!"

This vision of a communist future echoed Marx's 1840s speculations about the abolition of the division of labor. Once, when Marx was visiting Dr. Kugelmann, another guest mocked the utopian aspects of the vision, asking Marx who would polish boots in his "state of the future." Marx coolly replied, "You will," a snappy retort, but one leaving the question unanswered.[51] In Marx's economic writings, from the *Grundrisse* to the second German edition of *Capital*, written just a few years before the "Critique of the Gotha Program," he offered a different explanation for the abolition of the division of labor through the reduction of the working day to a minimum. The expansion of society's productivity would reduce the amount of time required to be spent in alienated, divided labor and leave more time for individuals' "development of their capabilities in art and *Wissenschaft*." Such a vision of a socialist future embodied the values of an educated nineteenth-century German bourgeois, member of a social group with a very high opinion of art and *Wissenschaft*. Since Marx's day, leisure time in economically advanced societies has greatly expanded, but most people do not use their time free from labor for the exalted purposes Marx expected. Late in his life, Marx replaced one utopian vision of the total abolition of alienated, divided labor with another, that of a humanity devoted to artistic and scholarly pursuits.[52]

When did Marx expect this communist society to emerge? There were some revolutions he thought imminent. In September 1877, he informed his America adherent Adolph Sorge about a forthcoming Russian revolution: "If Mother Nature is not particularly unfavorable to us, we'll experience the jubilation!" Three and a half years later, he congratulated his daughter Jenny on the birth of her son Marcel, stating that the new baby and his contemporaries "have before them the most revolutionary period men ever had to pass through. The bad thing now is to be 'old' so as to be only able to foresee instead of seeing." This opinion was not a family secret, for at about the same time he had told the émigré German ultra-revolutionary Johann Most, "I will not see the triumph of our cause, but you are young enough, you can still live to see the people win the victory."[53] The revolution Marx was expecting imminently was the overthrow of the czar, bringing with it the end of the Prussian monarchy. This would represent the completion of the French Revolution of 1789 in Eastern and central Europe, eliminating authoritarian rulers and establishing democratic and republican, if still capitalist and bourgeois regimes. This new state of affairs, much as Marx had expected since the *Communist Manifesto*, would open the way to a more intensive working-class organization and agitation. His grandson would experience the revolutionary and communist culmination of this organization and agitation, the second repetition of 1789, but Marx himself would not live to see it.

MARX'S VIEW OF REVOLUTION during the last decade of his life continued to be dominated by strong emotions: excitement at the prospect of forthcoming uprisings in Eastern and central Europe, deep regret at realizing that he would not live to see the communist upheaval he had been advocating for decades. By contrast, his private life in the 1870s was placid and pleasant. His two oldest daughters were married and out of the house, and Eleanor was sometimes away, working as a

schoolteacher, so in 1874 Karl and Jenny moved down the block from
No. 1 to No. 41 Maitland Park Road, into a smaller residence. If no longer at home, the daughters remained nearby, because their husbands,
political refugees as a result of the Paris Commune, could not yet return
to France. Charles Longuet taught French at University College. Paul
Lafargue, rather than practicing medicine, went into business printing art engravings, with the financial support of his father-in-law. The
business failed and after some nasty legal skirmishing with Lafargue's
partners, he had to be rescued financially by Engels.

All the Lafargues' children died in infancy. Charles Longuet and his
wife Jenny, in the ten years of their marriage, produced six children,
four of whom reached adulthood. Through them, Marx's descendants
live in France today. The first surviving Longuet child, Jean-Laurent-
Fréderick, born in 1876 and known to the family as Johnny, was, for
Marx, the "apple of my eye." All the child's play in which Karl had so
delighted with his children, he could repeat with his grandchildren.
Jenny von Westphalen was overjoyed as well. "When he [Johnny] in
carriage and four, i.e., the marital perambulator, is brought by, everyone jumps on him and greets him with jubilation, in order to be the first
to receive him, old granny out in front."[54]

Favorable political circumstances brought an end to this family
idyll. With the amnesty of 1880, Charles Longuet returned to France
to write for a newspaper run by Georges Clemenceau—remembered
today as the prime minister who led his country to victory in the First
World War, but at the beginning of his political career a leader of the
extreme left, whom Marx hoped to convert to socialism. Karl and
Jenny were contemplating moving to Paris, to remain close to their
grandchildren. But Jenny would not live long enough for this to be a
possibility. She had been feeling steadily more ill in the late 1870s, and
trips to the seaside and to spas had done nothing for her. By the summer of 1881, diagnosed with cancer, she was permanently bedridden,

under the care of Lenchen Demuth and Karl. With a great effort, she got herself together for a trip to Argentueil, outside Paris, and spent three weeks visiting her daughter and grandchildren, before making a final return to London.[55]

In the fall of 1881, as his wife lay dying, Marx himself fell gravely ill and could rarely leave his bed. Fifteen years later, his daughter Eleanor remembered, in an oft-cited passage, one of her parents' last encounters: "I will never forget the morning when he felt strong enough to go into mother's room. Together they were young again—she a loving girl and he a loving lad, entering into life together—and not an old man broken by illness and a dying old woman, saying farewell for what was left of their lives." In Jenny von Westphalen's final days, her spirits were cheered by seeing, fresh off the press, a copy of the essay by Ernest Belfort Bax praising her husband's work, and receiving the news that in spite of the German government's persecution, the socialists had maintained their position in the 1881 national elections—reminders of the man and his causes to which she had devoted her life. The physical pain of cancer eased by generous doses of morphine, she passed away on December 2, 1881.[56]

Marx was too ill to attend his wife's funeral. Engels gave the eulogy, which concluded with an atheist confession of faith:

> The place where we stand is the best proof that she lived and died in the full conviction of atheist Materialism. Death had no terrors for her. She knew that one day she would have to return, body and mind, to the bosom of that nature from which she had sprung. And we, who now have laid her in her last resting-place, let us cherish her memory and try to be like her.

Better known than Engels's graveside speech is the remark he made to Eleanor on the day of her mother's death: "The Moor has died as well."

Perhaps we should give the last word to Marx, a favorite quotation of his from Epicurus, the subject of his doctoral dissertation: "Death is no misfortune to the deceased, but for those who survive him."[57]

Marx outlived his wife by exactly one year, three months, and twelve days. In that time, his health was in steady decline, with only occasional brief and modest improvements. Almost to the very end, his intellect remained active, and he followed current events, whether Liberal Party meetings in England, prospects for revolution in Russia, or the first experiments with the transmission of electric power. There were even some gestures toward political and intellectual work— meeting with French socialist leaders to mediate their quarrels, and preparing the third German edition of *Capital*—but his declining health made these efforts ever briefer and less effective. Marx had to leave the extensive correspondence with the German Socialist Labor Party leaders to Engels. Even the daily strolls with Engels became too much of an effort, and Marx had some harsh words for his friend's promotion of exercise and fresh air.[58]

Marx's symptoms included pain in breathing; a chronic cough that became steadily more violent and painful, leading to vomiting and hemorrhaging, hoarseness and difficulty in speaking; and, toward the end, loss of appetite and difficulty swallowing. These were all most likely the result of tuberculosis, the disease that had killed his father and four of his siblings. Perhaps it was the very same microbes, since they can lie dormant in the body for decades. Marx also complained of a weakness in one side, an inability to write with correct grammar and spelling, and loss of memory: he could have suffered a small stroke, a result of his high blood pressure. The physicians' treatments, as with Marx's other maladies, only made things worse. There was the inevitable arsenic and the use of inflammatory chemicals to raise blisters on the skin and eliminate moisture—just useless torment. Being sprayed with sulfurous mineral water at least felt pleasant. All these useless treatments were occurring at the very same time that the great German biologist Robert Koch had isolated the tuberculosis bacillus and discovered the cause of the illness.[59]

Physicians attributed Marx's illness to a bad climate, and thought the best cure would be dry air and warm weather. His final year was one lengthy odyssey. He spent the winter 1881–82 on the Isle of Wight, followed by three months in Algiers. He then traveled to Monaco and southern France, spent a final summer with Jenny and the grandchildren in Argenteuil, made a visit to Switzerland in the fall, and then returned to the Isle of Wight. Biographers have often noted that the promised mild weather never seemed to materialize: unseasonable cold and rain dogged Marx in his travels to the sun. Since his physicians linked recovery from his illness to the right climate, Marx's fears, expressed to Engels, that he would never encounter good weather, and his instructions not to let his daughters know about these fears, were a way for Marx to say that he saw his imminent death as inevitable. The ultimate goal of his travels was his demise.[60]

The travels were the one time in Marx's life he left Northern Europe, and his stay in the French colonial capital of Algiers, a favorite destination for Frenchmen suffering from lung diseases, made a particular impression on him. Marx found North Africa's exotic sights fascinating: the view of the sea, the hills, the snow-capped mountains in the background, the profusion of flowers even in winter. He was intrigued by the indigenous population—a man nicknamed "The Moor" meeting real-life Moors for the first time. If only his grandson Johnny could see the inhabitants: "how my little favorite would be astonished, by the Moors, Arabs, Berbers, Turks, Negroes, in a word by this Babel and the costumes, (most of which are poetic) in this Oriental world. . . ."[61]

But Marx would not have been Marx if he had not gone beyond the European fascination with the exotic Orient to critical observations about its social and political conditions. His guide to colonial society was a judge on the court of appeals, a man named Fermé, who had been deported to Algeria for his opposition to Napoleon III, and had married an Arab woman. He informed Marx about the police's habit of torturing arrested Arabs to make them confess, while judges were supposed to know nothing of it. Fermé also explained that when an Arab was convicted of murder, the French colonists "demand that into the bargain a half dozen innocent Arabs have their heads just a little bit cut off." This attitude, Marx thought, was typical of European colonists: "The British and Dutch, however, surpass the French in shameless arrogance, pretension and an atrocious Moloch of anger for retribution towards the 'inferior races.'"

Marx's political associate David Urquhart had always admired the Turks for their dignified bearing and their social customs. Marx's attitude toward the Arabs of Algiers was similar. He admired their noble demeanor, and their ability to look dignified even when dressed in rags or riding on a donkey. He praised their "Absolute equality in their social intercourse . . . not of wealth or position but of personality," noting with a certain sympathy "the hatred against Christians and the hope of an ultimate victory over these infidels. . . ." Unlike Urquhart, Marx was not unconditionally pro-Muslim. He knew that the black African population of Algiers had been slaves of the Arabs until liberated by the French colonial authorities, and thought that for all their personal dignity, social equality, and anti-colonial aspirations, the Arabs of Algeria "will go to the devil without a revolutionary movement."[62]

On leaving Algiers, Marx returned to the South of France and spent several days in, of all places, Monte Carlo. The casinos, with their well-heeled gamblers and bevies of beautiful women ranging from countesses to courtesans, were as exotic as the Moors of Algiers. Listening to the gamblers' constant talk of a "system" that would enable them to break the bank reminded Marx of nothing so much as the "inmates of a madhouse." He went on to make an analogy, which his followers (and not only them) have repeated many times: "For all that, a casino is just child's play, compared to the stock exchange!"[63]

The rest of his voyage was more mundane. During his three months in Argentueil, Marx felt well enough to spend hours playing with the grandchildren, commute by train to nearby Enghien for the sulfur water treatments, and take long walks. The Paris suburb was a favorite of the Impressionists for their open-air painting, and one must wonder if Marx, during this visit, or with his dying wife the previous year, encountered Monet on the banks of the Seine. There followed in September 1882 a trip to Switzerland, accompanied by Laura, for by then Marx felt too weak to travel alone.[64]

The final stage of his journey, a return to the Isle of Wight in the winter of 1882–83, was jolted by the news he received on January 11, 1883, that his daughter Jenny, not yet forty years old, had died of cancer of the bladder. It was a crushing blow: Marx returned to London to die. He spiraled steadily downward in the last two months, losing both his appetite and his ability to swallow, so that toward the end he was subsisting largely on milk spiked with rum. He continued to read, but as his concentration waned, his reading matter went from economics and current events to novels and, finally, to publishers' catalogs. Night sweats and a fever were signs of the relentless progression of his illness, although the doctors continued to believe that if the weather improved, Marx might yet survive.[65]

Like so much of the evidence for Marx's life, the news of his death comes from Engels. He made it a practice to walk over to 41 Maitland Park Road every afternoon after his friend returned from the Isle of Wight. On March 14, 1883, he was greeted by a tearful Lenchen Demuth, who told him that Marx, sitting down in his study after midday dinner, had lost consciousness. Engels went in. He found that his friend had ceased breathing.[66] It was a peaceful end to a life filled with powerful, passionate emotions and strongly held convictions, with great aspirations and equally great setbacks, with adversity and struggle.

14

The Icon

··◦][◦··

THE FUNERAL WAS A modest affair. Just a dozen mourners gathered, three days after Marx's death: besides Engels, there was Eleanor, the two sons-in-law, two friends Marx had met through Engels in Manchester, both scientists, and Wilhelm Liebknecht, who had journeyed to London from the Continent to represent the German social democrats. A small delegation from the London German Workers' Educational Association was led by Friedrich Lessner, one of the defendants in the Cologne Communist Trial, who had moved to London after serving his sentence and become a loyal ally of Marx in the IWMA and among the German artisans. The members of the Workers' Association were themselves aging and declining in numbers; Marx and Engels had been on chronically bad terms with them since the Franco-Prussian War and the dissolution of the International. The absence of most of them made the funeral an intimate occasion for family and friends—who were, in Marx's death as in his life, also his political associates.

Unlike the funeral of Jenny von Westphalen, the memorial service for her husband was overwhelmingly political. Condolence telegrams from French, Russian, and Spanish socialists were read out. Liebknecht spoke, providing the atheist confession of faith Engels had offered at Jenny's funeral. While Engels had emphasized Jenny's private life, especially her atheist convictions in the face of death, Liebknecht's speech sounded a different note—an assertion of atheism in public life, combining *Wissenschaft* and politics. He declared that *Wissenschaft* would liberate humanity from God. Natural science was the first step in this liberation, but the science of society Marx had created and made available to the people would ultimately destroy capitalism, "and with it the idols and lords of the earth, who, as long as they live, will not let God die." Liebknecht's speech ended with a graveside oath, calling on his listeners—not so much the gathered mourners as the readers of the social democrats' clandestine newspaper, in which his speech was printed—to commit themselves to follow on the path Marx had led them, until they reached its goal.

Engels, fittingly, gave the main eulogy. He emphasized Marx as a man of *Wissenschaft*. Unlike Liebknecht's presentation, in which echoes of the Young Hegelians were still evident, Engels evoked a positivist *Wissenschaft*, based on the natural sciences. In a telling and oft-quoted passage, he compared Marx to the scientific hero of the age: "As Darwin discovered the law of the development of organic nature, so Marx discovered the law of development of human history." After representing Marx as a scientist, one who was interested in the latest developments in the study of electricity even in his last days, Engels described his friend as "above all revolutionary. To take part in one way or another in the overthrow of capitalist society and the governing institutions it has created, to take part in the liberation of the modern proletariat . . . that was his life's true profession." To illustrate this, Engels described Marx's journalism in some detail, and his participation in associations in Paris, Brussels, and London, culminating in the International Working Men's Association, "the crowning of all" his work. A bit strangely, Engels said nothing of Marx's chief period of revolutionary activity in 1848–49. He concluded with a heroic apotheosis: Marx was "the best hated, best slandered man of his time," constantly under attack by bourgeois governments, while he was "honored, loved and mourned by millions of revolutionary coworkers, from the mines of Siberia across all of Europe and America to California. . . ."[1]

Marx was laid to rest with his wife in Highgate Cemetery. The original grave was a modest slab; the far larger than life-size bust with which it is now crowned was only placed there by the (now defunct) Communist Party of Great Britain in 1956. The gigantic bust was the physical proof of the transformation of a living human being into an icon, a frozen representation of ideas, political positions, and identities, many of which were only tangentially related to the person's actual life. The eulogies of Marx were an early stage in this process of transformation; indeed, Engels was already experimenting with such representations during the last years of Marx's life.[2] Although the eulogies were evidence of purposeful efforts to shape an image of Marx, the process also occurred in unexpected ways without conscious control.

The obituaries of Marx that appeared in newspapers across Europe and North America within a few days of his death demonstrated, in nascent form, important aspects of his future image. One was the idea of Marx the man of science, the author of a definitive work of political economy. The socialist press certainly emphasized this feature of his life, but even the anti-socialist notices noted the quality and influence of his economic scholarship. The *Arbeiterzeitung* (*Workers' News*) of the German socialist immigrants of Chicago proclaimed: "What Darwin was for the natural sciences, John Buckle [the English positivist historian and advocate of the idea of progress] for the science of history, Marx was for the science of political economy."

A second theme, rather more muted than the first, reflected Marx's Semitic antecedents. British and Dutch newspapers reported his Jewish birth; a Spanish one described him as the descendant of a family of Spanish Jews, with a noticeably Mediterranean appearance, while in Turin he was "one of the handsomest types of the Jewish Slav." The newspaper of the Jewish community of St. Petersburg called him "one of the most gifted sons of the Jewish people," an affiliation noted by the *American Israelite* of Cincinnati, albeit not in quite such glowing terms.

Running through virtually all the obituaries was the idea of Marx's revolutionary life—particularly his engagement in the Revolution of 1848 and his role in the IWMA, with its connections to the Paris Commune. Politically more hostile writers observed that Marx's revolutionary aspirations had all ended in failure: the Prussians had suppressed the midcentury revolution; the IWMA had dissolved. The more favorable accounts compared him with other mid-nineteenth-century revolutionaries, such as Mazzini and Garibaldi, whose aspirations had also been thwarted or only partially achieved. They observed that while the IWMA had succumbed to the double blow of government persecution and factional intrigue, its principles remained to guide the labor movement in the future. One succinct summary came from a most unexpected source, the Cuban nationalist and anti-imperialist leader José Martí. After attending a public memorial meeting for Marx in New York, he wrote that Marx "saw in everyone what he carried in himself: rebellion, highest ideals, struggle."[3] These three features of Marx's obituaries—scientist, Semite, and intransigent revolutionary—would be developed in ever more elaborate fashion over the decades that followed, increasingly creating a frozen image of him.

Marx's persona as scientific revolutionary was very much the creation of Engels, an integral part of his determination to cultivate the legacy of his friend's thought as he understood it. Engels's work had begun in the mid-1870s, as part of another intervention in the politics of the German labor movement. This one was directed against the influence of a lecturer in economics at the University of Berlin, Eugen Dühring, who was busy denouncing Marx's ideas. As part of his disengagement from day-to-day politics, Marx let Engels handle the polemics, although he did offer some advice about economic questions. The upshot, the ponderously entitled *Herr Eugen Dühring's Revolutionizing of* Wissenschaft, generally known, for short, as the "Anti-Dühring," was, in the fashion of Engels, a nasty and unpopular polemic. It was serialized in the Social Democratic Party's flagship newspaper. Party leaders, aware of the bad reactions to the piece, took the precaution of printing the work on an irregular schedule, preferably at times when the fewest people possible would be reading the newspaper, which simply infuriated Engels.[4]

But the work was not just an attack on Dühring; it was also designed to provide a positive representation of Marx's ideas. In 1880, one section was reprinted as a separate piece, "The Development of Socialism from Utopia to *Wissenschaft*," or, as it is usually known in English, "Socialism: Utopian and Scientific." In it, Engels presented Marx's ideas as a positivist science, analogous to Darwin's biology, in which the progress of stages of modes of production in human history corresponded to the progressive evolutionary development of species in natural history, occurring with the same scientifically determined necessity. This version of Marx's ideas was absorbed by an entire generation of socialist intellectuals and political leaders entering public life in the last quarter of the nineteenth century. Karl Kautsky, the Austro-German socialist leader and theorist, who became known as the "Pope of Socialism," the leading Marxist intellectual at the beginning of the twentieth century, asserted that no other work had contributed as much to his understanding of Marx's ideas as the "Anti-Dühring." His understanding of *Capital* and Marx's other major works, Kautsky added, ran through Engels's interpretation of them.[5]

Engels's influence on the shaping of what would come to be called "Marxism" was thus considerable. Norman Levine, the author of a challenging if at times exaggerated study of the differences between Marx's and Engels's ideas, has even suggested that most "Marxism" was really "Engelsism."[6] One need not agree with Levine's contention to assert that Engels's version of Marx's ideas tended to iron out Marx's own ambivalence about positivism, and to pass over his Hegelian criticism of the conceptual understanding of the natural sciences. The earlier, more Hegelian writings, which might have offered a different view of his intellectual universe, were either long out of print and rarely available, or still in manuscript form and quite unknown.

This state of affairs was more than a temporary quirk, because the twelve years between the death of Marx and that of his friend saw the development, for the first time in European history, of a mass labor movement. Nineteen socialist and labor parties were founded in Europe between 1880 and 1896, along with nationwide trade union federations. These groups counted, literally, millions of supporters. The political parties sponsored the creation of a "Second" International in 1889, with far more membership, organizational stability, and international influence than the IWMA ever could have hoped for. Taking over Marx's role as adviser and experienced councilor, Engels worked closely with the leaders of these different socialist organizations, both in their nascent state and as they began to blossom into mass movements.

The combination of a mass labor movement with political and intellectual leaders learning Marx's ideas from Engels's writings created Marxism as an ideology and as a political movement. The place of Marx's ideas in different European socialist parties was greatest in the central and eastern portions of the Continent; to the west, competing anarchist and syndicalist ideas in the Mediterranean countries, and the persistent hegemony of the Liberal Party in the United Kingdom, by no means eliminated this emergent Marxism, but they did restrict its influence. Still, everywhere, evocations of Marx appeared in speeches, newspaper articles, and pamphlets; pictures of the bearded prophet became a common sight.

The influence of Marx's ideas, as inflected by Engels, was particularly pronounced in Germany and Austria-Hungary. There, the positivist and Darwinian version of his theories helped resolve the problem with which Marx himself had wrestled in his 1879 open letter to the German Socialist Party leadership. How could socialists strike a proper balance between implausible demands for immediate revolutionary action, and the abandonment of revolutionary aspirations and the class struggle, in favor of seeking reforms in the existing capitalist society and reconciling social classes? Since the broad sweep of socioeconomic and political developments was moving with scientific inevitability in the direction of socialism, there was no need either to mount dangerous revolutionary challenges to a heavily armed existing order, or to abandon the socialists' principles by compromising with other political parties on reforms. This policy, worked out in loving theoretical detail by Karl Kautsky, became a way for ostensibly revolutionary mass labor movements to co-exist with authoritarian empires in the center of Europe. Increasingly, under the influence of the German social democrats, the largest, best organized, wealthiest, and most influential of the socialist parties, this policy became the operating principle of the Second International.[7]

Further to the east, in the Russian Empire, the very same positivist-inflected Marxism came to play a major role in the socialist movement as well, although there it could be interpreted not only as a justification of political passivity, but as an incentive to radical revolutionary initiatives in a regime lacking the constitutional governmental institutions of central Europe. Lenin, the leader of the most radical element in the Russian socialist movement, was every inch the positivist, repeatedly citing the "Anti-Dühring" and Engels's other theoretical writing, while advocating drastic measures to overthrow the government of the czar. After he and his Bolsheviks succeeded in seizing power in the social and political chaos brought about by the impact of a total war on a Russian state and society not up to its challenges, they founded a Third, Communist International. They brought to it both the Marxist iconography and the positivist, "scientific" Marxism of the late nineteenth- and early twentieth-century European labor movement, spreading it across the globe. As long as both twentieth-century communist and socialist parties identified themselves as Marxist, it was Engels's interpretation of Marxism that they had in mind, which is as significant a point as any in a study of the doctrines called "Marxism." The intellectual challenge to this Marxism, stemming from a greater acquaintance with the more Hegelian texts written by Marx before 1850, those texts generally read in existentialist fashion, began in the 1920s. It reached a degree of intellectual maturity in the last third of the twentieth century, coinciding with the end of Marxist political parties.

BOTH MARX'S OWN IDENTIFICATION with his Jewish background and his contemporaries' identification of him with it were faint throughout most of his life, largely a result of attitudes toward Jews as a group characterized primarily by cultural and religious affiliations. As we have seen, Marx himself generally vehemently rejected these affiliations. In his (few) milder moments, he viewed them ironically. The rise of social Darwinist conceptions of human history and society in the last quarter of the nineteenth century led to a different view of Jews, as a group characterized by common biological descent. Such attitudes were already apparent in the last decade of Marx's life, as interviewers noted his Semitic features, people recalled them in their memoirs, and the obituary of his wife discussed the difficulties of the engagement between Jenny von Westphalen and the young Karl Marx in terms of the latter's "Israelite" ancestry.

In the decades after Marx's death, these attitudes only intensified and increasingly acquired strong political connotations. Anti-Semitism became steadily more popular in right-wing circles, precisely as a new opponent of rightists was coming to the fore: rapidly growing socialist parties and a labor movement, brandishing pictures of Marx and claiming to be inspired by Marx's ideas. In such circumstances, it was logical for right-wing enemies of socialist parties and the labor movement to emphasize Marx's Jewish descent. An extreme example of the culmination of this intellectual and political trend was Adolf Hitler, who made it clear that Jewish Marxism was his deadliest enemy; but the hostile, racialized, and politicized identification of Marx as Jewish was widespread in the first decades of the twentieth century.

One less familiar example might help to make the point. In 1932, the marginal utility theory economists of Austria and Germany met at a conference in Dresden, held, in the wake of the Great Depression, to assert the superiority of their approaches to economics over the ideas of the Historical School and the Marxists. One of the participants, Friedrich von Gottl-Ottlilienfeld, professor of political economy at the University of Berlin, denounced Marx's work as a "cabbalistic solution to the problem of value." Whatever one may think of *Capital*, it is difficult to see it as an example of medieval Jewish mysticism—unless, of course, Marx's racial Jewish identity is taken as self-evident.[8]

The identification of Marx as a Jew did not just proceed from enemies of his doctrine, but at least as much from its adherents. The locus of this development was the Russian Empire, wracked, as Marx had suspected in his last years, by growing social and political discontent. Rather contrary to the way Marx perceived the world, nationalist and socialist demands, particularly among the empire's non-Russian nationalities, coincided instead of conflicted. Disproportionately large numbers of Jews, members of a group with particularly strong grievances about czarist rule, who were increasingly inclined to see themselves in national (and even racial) rather than religious terms, embraced socialist ideas. They understood the man who invented these socialist ideas as one of their own, a sort of Jewish folk hero, if you will.

As might be expected, these ideas were particularly pronounced among supporters of the *Bund*, the Jewish socialist party in the Russian Empire. One of the founders of this Jewish socialist movement, Aron Liberman, originally from Vilna, proclaimed: "In the spirit of our people, the great prophets of our time, such as Marx and Lassalle were educated and developed." In the Russian Revolution of 1905, the *Bund* newspaper announced that "the Jewish proletariat has already received [a political Torah] from Karl Marx and his followers."[9] Jews who joined, also in disproportionate numbers, the socialist parties claiming to represent all the nationalities in the czar's empire often perceived their political affiliation as a way to escape their ethnic and national identity; yet their renunciation of that identity was eased by their perception of the founder of their movement as one of them. These attitudes, along with the Jewish leftists expressing them, were carried over into the communist movement in Europe and North America. They generally manifested themselves in unspoken fashion, or at least in unofficial remarks, since they were hardly compatible with the official party line, to say nothing of the increasing hostility of the USSR toward its Jewish citizens in the decades following the Second World War.[10]

The large role that Jews played in the social and political world of twentieth-century revolution and in the mental world of that revolution's most extreme enemies, combined with an understanding of being Jewish as biological and immutable in nature, gave the iconic representative and titular founder of these revolutionary movements a distinctly Jewish character. But only in retrospect. Marx certainly did not see himself as a Jewish folk hero—to say the least—and disillusioned twentieth-century Jewish leftists have often been disappointed about that. Yet the inverse position of seeing Marx as a twentieth-century anti-Semite, whether of Nazi or Stalinist persuasion, leads to problematic conclusions, since it ignores the nineteenth-century context in which Marx's attitudes—expressed in his writings on the Jewish Question, or in the hostile comments about Jews, prominent and obscure, scattered through his correspondence—were embedded.

THE PERCEPTION OF MARX as practitioner of positivist social science modeled on the natural sciences has some reflection in Marx's own ideas, although it seems rather one-sided, overlooking his doubts about positivist, scientific attitudes, and the distinctly anti-positivist Hegelian underpinnings of so much of his thought. Understanding Marx as a Jew, whether with friendly or hostile intent, almost completely escapes the reality of his own perception and much of the perception of him by his contemporaries—to say nothing of broader understandings of what it meant to be a Jew—prevalent during most of his life. By contrast, the perception of Marx as intransigent and uncompromising, as a revolutionary opponent of the existing social and political order, is much closer to reality.

It is important to understand that a good portion of what was revolutionary and intransigent about Marx was not his advocacy of communism. Although Marx's marriage to Jenny von Westphalen ultimately developed along fairly conventional lines, his passionate courtship, at a young age, of an older woman lacking a dowry was a direct challenge to German bourgeois understandings of proper relations between men and women. Marx's hatred of authoritarian and absolutist monarchies, and the aristocrats, bureaucrats, and military officers through whom they exercised their rule—seen above all in his powerful hostility to both the Prussian kingdom and the Russian Empire—was the prime moving force in his revolutionary activity during 1848–49, and in the popular appeal of his politics then as well. Marx's hatred of Prussia and Russia continued throughout his life, at times taking a bizarre course in his endorsement of David Urquhart's conspiratorial theories about English Whigs and the czar, but remaining consistent. Unlike his fellow 1848 revolutionaries, Arnold Ruge and Ferdinand Freiligrath, who became reconciled to the Prussian kingdom when it proved to be the architect of German national unity, and even accepted pensions offered them by Bismarck, Marx could never tolerate Prussia and continued to hope for its demise down to the end of his life. His last years were enlivened by the hope that the reactionary power of the czar could be destroyed, not by a large-scale war the Western powers were reluctant to wage, but by a revolutionary uprising in Russia itself.

Although most 1848 radicals ultimately came to terms with the political developments of the two decades that followed, there were those who remained loyal to their earlier aspirations. Giuseppe Mazzini and Giuseppe Garibaldi come to mind, and some authors of Marx's obituaries compared him to them. The Hungarian nationalist leader Lajos Kossuth was another figure of the 1848 revolutions who continued to be intransigent and irreconcilable. He never accepted Austrian rule over his homeland, even after the Hungarians attained autonomy in 1867, remaining, like Marx, an exile for the rest of his life. Of course, Mazzini, Garibaldi, and Kossuth were all nationalists, whose appeal might have been limited to members of their national group, especially as European nationalisms became steadily more ethnocentric and mutually hostile over the course of the nineteenth century.

Yet this point should not be overemphasized. Both Mazzini and Garibaldi had trans-European, even transatlantic revolutionary reputations and an equally widespread iconic reach.[11] On the other hand, Marx was for decades very much a German political figure, albeit, as was often the case in the first half of the nineteenth century, deeply involved in émigré politics outside Germany. Marx's plans after 1859 for a political comeback were all centered on Germany, on issues of German nationalism. It was only his involvement with the International Working Men's Association—in some ways even more the dissolution of the group than its foundation—and his defense of the Paris Commune that made him into an international figure. Following his death, Marx's international appeal grew steadily, parallel to the development of a mass labor movement in Europe, while that of the other intransigent veterans of 1848 shrank along national lines.

Marx's communist aspirations, stemming from Hegelian ideas about abolishing distinctions, between individuals and civil society, between oppressed and oppressor, between workers and the alienated product of their labor, were certainly as drastic and as radical as anything he might have thought about Russia and Prussia. But so many of Marx's most radical ideas about a future society remained unpublished—the Paris manuscripts, the so-called *German Ideology*, the *Grundrisse*—or were designed for private circulation, as was the case with the March 1850 circular to the Communist League, and the "Critique of the Gotha Program." Others were brief and cryptic, like the passages on the expansion of productivity in a communist society added to the second edition of *Capital*. Marx did sometimes make radical statements about a communist future, for example in the *Communist Manifesto*, with its concluding comments about communists disdaining to conceal their goals, or in his endorsement in the *New Rhineland News* of the Parisian workers' uprising of June 1848, or his description in *The Civil War in France* of the Paris Commune as the model of a future society. But for most of his major episodes of radical political practice, in Cologne during the Revolution of 1848–49, and in the IWMA, Marx was far more reluctant to provide a picture of a communist regime, and either downplayed his advocacy of communism or cloaked it in ambiguous language. When he openly came out with communist aspirations, it was at the end of two periods of intensified political activity, and a sign that he was contemplating abandoning these activities altogether. By contrast, he never moderated his hostility toward either Russia or Prussia.

Marx also never wavered in his aspirations for a dual recurrence of the French Revolution. First, he envisaged a literal replay in nineteenth-century central and Eastern Europe of the eighteenth-century overthrow of the absolute monarchy in France, generally also including a Jacobin-style republican, revolutionary regime and a great revolutionary war. Following on from this, he foresaw a nineteenth-century revolution analogous in its social dynamics to the French Revolution. The overthrow of the monarchy had led to the replacement of the pre-1789 society of orders with a capitalist society of property owners, dominated by the bourgeoisie; the social revolution would lead from capitalism to communism and replace the rule of the bourgeoisie with that of the proletariat. Marx devised various intellectual and political schemes to connect these two revolutions, which generally proved difficult to implement in practice. The exact contours of the two imagined revolutions and their mutual relationship tended to change over time; the growing importance of tensions in rural society in Marx's plans for an anti-capitalist revolution is certainly striking. What remained constant was the French Revolution and its great moments in 1789 and 1793 as both an image and a model. Marx shared this orientation with fellow revolutionaries of his century but the use of the model of the French Revolution marked a pronounced backward orientation in his thought, a tendency to envisage the future in terms of the past.

Yet if the wellsprings of Marx's revolutionary aspirations were distinctly rooted in his formative years during the first half of the nineteenth century, these aspirations and his intransigence about proceeding toward them, whether openly expressed or hidden for tactical purposes, might be a key to the long-term resonance of his ideas. It is remarkable how advocates of so many different causes were drawn to the man and his doctrines, or what they imagined his doctrines to be. Leaders of the mass labor movements of early twentieth-century Europe, proponents of violent overthrow of the authority of the czar, cadres of global communist revolution, anti-imperialist activists in Asia, Africa, and Latin America in the mid-decades of the twentieth century, or discontented young intellectuals in the consumer society of 1960s Western Europe and North America were all Marxists.

Also proclaiming their Marxism were the leaders of the twentieth-century communist regimes in Europe and Asia. Their plans to wrench the economically underdeveloped countries they ruled into an industrialized and productive future in drastic, violent, and totalitarian fashion could take a downright genocidal turn, as they did in Stalin's USSR and Mao's China. These campaigns of Marxist regimes were reminiscent of nothing in Marx's own writings so much as his descriptions of the brutal British modernization of colonial India or his account, in *Capital*, of the cruel, early phase of capitalist primal accumulation. The later history of those regimes, was that of a bureaucratic despotism, not without certain similarities to the Prussian and czarist realms Marx so despised.

All these Marxisms drew the hostility of supporters of the capitalist status quo, who continue to rage against them and their purported founder two decades and more after the end of the ostensibly Marxist Eastern bloc. Marx's actual ideas and political practice—developed in the matrix of the early nineteenth century, the age of the French Revolution and its aftermath, of Hegel's philosophy and its Young Hegelian critics, of the early industrialization of Great Britain and the theories of political economy emerging from them—had, at most, only partial connections with the ones his latter-day friends and enemies found in his writings. In some ways, the actual intellectual connections were beside the point. Marx's passionately irreconcilable, uncompromising, and intransigent nature has been the feature of his life that has had the deepest and most resonant appeal, and has generated the sharpest rebukes and opposition, down to the present day.

Acknowledgments

·∙⊃[]⊂∙·

As academics do, I have presented parts of this work in the form of
public lectures or conference papers, at the University of Tennessee,
Vanderbilt University, the University of Leipzig, the University of
Gießen, the annual conference of the German Studies Association, and
the St. Louis area German historians' study group. At these and other
venues I have received criticism and advice from many fellow scholars, including Celia Applegate, Harald Bluhm, Warren Breckman,
James Brophy, Markus Denzel, Steven Hochstadt, Kenneth Ledford,
Suzanne Marchand, Jennifer Miller, Jerry Muller, Warren Rosen-
blum, Mark Ruff, Corinna Treitel, Meike Werner, Jonathan Wiesen,
and John Williams.

Special thanks for extraordinary assistance are due to Drs. Brian
Johnson and Lindall Perry of Boone Hospital Center, who generously
put their medical expertise at my disposal. I was fortunate in the people who agreed to read earlier versions of the manuscript and provide
trenchant suggestions for its improvement. Jürgen Herres of the *MEGA*
not only did just that, he also uncovered obscure but very useful material buried in the basement of the Berlin-Brandenburg Academy of Sciences. Friedrich Lenger of the University of Gießen provided the same

kind of excellent advice about the book that I have been receiving from him for almost three decades. Christopher Clark of St. Catherine's College, Cambridge, and Helmut Smith of Vanderbilt University placed their rigorous, scholarly readings at my disposal. Colleagues at the University of Missouri read my manuscript, and I am very grateful for the comments and criticisms of John Frymire, Abdullahi Ibrahim, John Wigger, and, especially, Steven Watts, master biographer. Robert Weil, of Liveright/W. W. Norton, was a rigorous and severe editor. He played a major role in improving the manuscript I submitted and I have only myself to blame for not accepting all his suggestions. This same observation goes for everyone mentioned above: they deserve their share of any praise a reader might want to bestow on the book, but readers' reproaches should be directed to me alone.

My wife, Nancy Katzman, has never taken notes for me or typed my manuscripts, but has been, for a good quarter century, a source of love and inspiration.

The book is dedicated to the memory of my father, Louis Sperber.

Source Collections

··◦⫶◦··

The largest, most comprehensive and most scholarly edition of the works of Marx and Engels is the *Karl Marx Friedrich Engels Gesamtausgabe*, referred to in the notes as *MEGA*. Volumes appearing between 1975 until 1990 were edited by the Institutes of Marxism-Leninism in Moscow and East Berlin, and published by the Dietz Verlag in East Berlin. More recent volumes have been edited by the International Marx Engels Foundation and published by the Akademie Verlag in Berlin.

The *MEGA*, after over thirty-five years of work, is still not complete, so that for some of Marx's writings and correspondence it is necessary to have recourse to other, less comprehensive and less scholarly text editions. Unlike the *MEGA*, in which all material is printed in the language in which it originally appeared, the older editions are monolingual, translating material into the respective languages of publication. Since most of what Marx wrote was in German, the most useful of the older editions is *Karl Marx Friedrich Engels Werke*, 39 vols. plus 2 supplementary vols., edited by the Institut für Marxismus-Leninismus beim ZK der SED (East Berlin: Dietz Verlag, 1956–77), abbreviated in the Notes as *MEW*. For material originally written in English, I used the English-language edition of Marx's and Engels's works, *Karl Marx,*

Friedrich Engels: Collected Works, 50 vols. (New York: International Publishers Co.; Moscow: Progress Publishers, 1975–2004), abbreviated in the Notes as *MECW*. There are three different French-language editions of the collected works, none of which is complete (cf. Attali, *Karl Marx*, p. 548). I have used the version of the Editions Sociales (Paris 1945–) for letters originally written in French (cited as *MEC*) and its volume of the *Poverty of Philosophy* published in 1961 (cited as *MdP*).

There are three other document collections useful for a Marx biography. One is a collection of materials concerning the Communist League, *Der Bund der Kommunisten. Dokumente und Materialien*, 3 vols., edited by the Institutes of Marxism-Leninism in East Berlin and Moscow (East Berlin: Dietz Verlag, 1970–84), cited as *BdK*. Another is the collection concerning the 1872 Congress of the IWMA: *The Hague Congress of the First International September 2–7, 1872*, 2 vols.: Vol. 1, *Minutes and Documents*, Vol. 2, *Reports and Letters*, edited by the Institute of Marxism-Leninism of the C.C., C.P.S.U. (Moscow: Progress Publishers, 1976–78), cited in the Notes as *HCFI*. Finally, for the history of the *Rhineland News*, and Marx's political activity in Cologne more generally, a very helpful edition of sources is *Rheinische Briefe und Akten zur Geschichte der politischen Bewegung 1830–1850*, 3 vols.: Vol. 1 and Vol. 2, part 1, edited by Joseph Hansen (Bonn: Peter Hanstein Verlag, 1919–42); Vol. 2, part 2, and Vol. 3, edited by Heinz Boberach (Cologne & Bonn: Peter Hanstein Verlag 1976; Düsseldorf: Droste Verlag, 1998); this citation is abbreviated as *RhBA*.

Notes

··◦◗▯◖◦··

INTRODUCTION

1 Boris Nicolaievsky and Otto Maénchen-Helfen, *Karl Marx: Man and Fighter*, trans. Gwenda David and Eric Mosbacher (Philadelphia: J. B. Lippincott, 1936), v. The standard life of Marx, and an excellent work, is David McLellan, *Karl Marx: A Biography*, 4th ed. (Houndmills, Basingstoke: Macmillan, 2006). Just a few of the more important or more notorious biographies are Isaiah Berlin, *Karl Marx: His Life and Environment*, 4th ed. (Oxford: Oxford University Press, 1978); Leopold Schwarzschild, *The Red Prussian: The Life and Legend of Karl Marx*, trans. Margaret Wing (New York: Charles Scribner's Sons, 1947); Francis Wheen, *Karl Marx: A Life* (New York: W. W. Norton & Co., 2000); Robert Payne, *Marx* (New York: Simon & Schuster, 1968); Jacques Attali, *Karl Marx, ou l'espirit du monde* (Paris: Librarie générale française, 2007); and Wolfgang Schieder, *Karl Marx als Politiker* (Munich: Piper Verlag, 1991).

2 Eric Hobsbawm, ed., *The Communist Manifesto: A Modern Edition* (London: Verso, 1998), 17–18; http://www.guardian.co.uk/books/2011/jan/16/eric-hobsbawm-trist -hunt-marx, accessed 1/27/11.

3 James Brophy, "Recent Publications of the *Marx-Engels-Gesamtausgabe* (MEGA)," *Central European History* 40 (2007): 523–37.

4 Heiko Oberman, *Luther: Man Between God and the Devil*, trans. Eileen Walliser-Schwarzbart (New Haven: Yale University Press, 1989); Ian Kershaw, *Hitler: A Biography* (New York: W. W. Norton & Co., 2008); Constantin Goschler, *Rudolf Virchow: Mediziner—Anthropologe—Politiker* (Cologne: Böhlau Verlag, 2002); Friedrich Lenger, *Werner Sombart 1863–1941. Eine Biographie* (Munich: C. H. Beck, 1994).

PART I: SHAPING

1: THE SON

1 On the history of the city of Trier, see Heinz Heinen et al., eds., *2000 Jahre Trier*, 3 vols. (Trier: Spee-Verlag, 1985–96); more briefly, Eric David, "Trèves: De la capitale d'empire à la ville moyenne; Une ville moyenne frontalière dans la perspective des occupations françaises successives," *Revue d'Allemagne* 26 (1994): 69–81.

2 Cited in Klaus Gerteis, "Sozialgeschichte der Stadt Trier 1580–1794," in *2000 Jahre Trier*, 3: 61.

3 Most generally, on Jews in old regime Europe, see David Vital, *A People Apart: The Jews in Europe 1789–1939* (Oxford: Oxford University Press, 1999), 1–25; or Jonathan Israel, *European Jewry in the Age of Mercantilism, 1550–1750*, 3rd. ed. (London: Valentine Mitchell & Co., 1998), 165–66.

4 Cilli Kasper-Holtkotte, *Juden im Aufbruch. Zur Sozialgeschichte einer Minderheit im Saar-Mosel-Raum um 1800* (Hanover: Hahnsche Buchhandlung, 1996), is a model monograph on the Jews of Trier and vicinity at the end of the old regime and in the age of the French Revolution.

5 Heinz Monz, *Karl Marx Grundlagen der Entwicklung zu Leben und Werk* (Trier: Nco-Verlag, 1973), 215–18; a family tree of Marx's paternal ancestors is in Manfred Schönke, *Karl und Heinrich Marx und ihre Geschwister: Lebenszeugnisse— Briefe—Dokumente.* (Bonn: Pahl-Rugenstein Nachfolger, 1993), 6–8. Samuel Levi would later move to Trier, to become the rabbi there.

6 On the twenty-year period of the French occupation of Trier, there is the excellent collection of essays and exhibition catalog, Elisabeth Dühr and Christl Lehnert-Leven, eds., *Unter der Trikolore Sous le drapeau tricolore Trier in Frankreich—Napoléon in Trier Trèves en France—Napoléon à Trèves 1794–1814*, 2 vols. (Trier: Städtisches Museum Simeonstift, 2004); a good overview is Michael Müller, "Die Stadt Trier unter französisscher Herrschaft (1794–1814)," in Kurt Düwell and Franz Irsigler, eds., *Trier in der Neuzeit*, Vol. 3 of *2000 Jahre Trier*, 377–98. Any otherwise not explicitly cited assertions about Trier under French rule come from these two works.

7 Quoted in Hans-Ulrich Seifert, "Dialektik der Abklärung—Literarische Gegenentwürfe und deutsch-französische Wechselbeziehungen unter napoleonischer Herrschaft (unter besonderer Berücksichtigung der unveröffentlichten Koresondenz zwischen Charles de Vilers und Johann Hugo Wyttenbach)," in Dühr and Lehnert-Leven, eds., *Unter der Trikolore*, 1: 473.

8 Gabriele B. Clemens, "Die Notabeln der Franzosenzeit," in ibid., 1: 105–80.

9 Elisabeth Wagner, "Die Rückführung des Heiligen Rockes nach Trier und die Heilig-Rock-Wallfahrt im Jahre 1810," in ibid., 1: 419–32; Wolfgang Schieder, *Religion und Revolution. Die Trierer Wallfahrt von 1844* (Vierow: SH-Verlag, 1996).

10 Quoted in Kasper-Holtkotte, *Juden im Aufbruch*, 200.

11 In admirable detail, ibid., 190–433.

12 Quoted in ibid., 383.

13 Ibid., 341–44, 414.

14 Heinz Monz, "Neue Funde zum Lebesnweg von Karl Marx' Vater," *Osnabrücker Mitteilungen* 87 (1981): 59–71; Schönke, *Karl und Heinrich Marx*, 122–27.

15 Luitwin Mallmann, *Französische Juristenbildung im Rheinland 1794–1814. Die Rechtsschule von Koblenz* (Cologne: Böhlau Verlag, 1987), 104–25; Schönke, *Karl und Heinrich Marx*, 127–31.

16 For claims that Heinrich studied law, almost certainly false but often repeated in biographies, see Kasper-Holtkotte, *Juden im Aufbruch*, 383, and Schönke, *Karl und Heinrich Marx*, 123.

17 Mallmann, *Französische Juristenbildung*, 122.

18 For Trier in the initial decades of Prussian rule and during the Revolution of 1848, see Elisabeth Dühr, ed., *"Der Schlimmste Punkt in der Provinz": Demokratische Revolution 1848/49 in Trier und Umgebung* (Trier: Selbstverlag des Städtischen Museums Simeonstift, 1998); Manfred Heimers, "Trier als preußische Bezirkshauptstadt im Vormärz (1814–1848)," in Düwell and Irsigler, eds., *Trier in der Neuzeit*, 399–419; and Jonathan Sperber, *Rhineland Radicals: The Democratic Movement and the Revolution of 1848–1849* (Princeton: Princeton University Press, 1991), 154, 181–83.

19 Clemens, "Die Notablen der Franzosenzeit," in Dühr and Lehnert, eds., *Unter der Trikolore*, 1: 106, 178–79; Monz, *Karl Marx*, 160–68; Karl-Georg Faber, "Verwaltungs- und Justizbeamte auf dem linken Rheinufer während der französischen Herrschaft," in Max Braubach, ed., *Aus Geschichte und Landeskunde: Forschungen und Darstellungen Franz Steinbach zum 65. Geburtstag* (Bonn: L. Röhrscheid Verlag, 1960), 350–88.

20 Schönke, *Karl und Heinrich Marx*, 148, 153–61; Mallmann, *Französische Juristenbildung*, 176–78; Sperber, *Rhineland Radicals*, 38–39, 117–18; Jonathan Sperber, *Property and Civil Society in South-Western Germany 1820–1914* (Oxford: Oxford University Press, 2005), 9–10.

21 Suzanne Zittartz-Weber, *Zwischen Religion und Staat: Die jüdischen Gemeinden in der preußischen Rheinprovinz 1815–1871* (Essen: Klartext Verlag, 2003), 63–74.

22 Monz, *Karl Marx*, 243–45. The exact date is unknown because the Protestant pastor in Trier, in very un-Prussian fashion, was sloppy about keeping the register of baptisms.

23 See, e.g., Jerrold E. Seigel, *Marx's Fate: The Shape of a Life* (Princeton: Princeton University Press, 1978); or, more cosmically, Yuri Slezkine, *The Jewish Century* (Princeton: Princeton University Press, 2004), 63, 83.

24 Wilhelm Füssl, *Professor in der Politik: Friedrich Julius Stahl (1802–1861)* (Göttingen: Vandenhoeck & Ruprecht, 1988); Kasper-Holtkotte, *Juden im Aufbruch*, 432.

25 Stefan Rohrbacher, *Gewalt im Biedermeier: Antijüdische Ausschreitungen im Vormärz und Revolution (1815–1848/49)* (Frankfurt & New York: Campus Verlag, 1990), 94–156.

26 Uri R. Kaufmann, "Ein jüdischer Deutscher: Der Kampf des jungen Gabriel Riesser für die Gleichberechtigung der Juden 1830–1848," *Aschkenas: Zeitschrift für Geschichte und Kultur der Juden* 13 (2003): 211–36.

27 Kasper-Holtkotte, *Juden im Aufbruch*, 432; Schönke, *Karl und Heinrich Marx*, 429–69.

28 Schönke, *Karl und Heinrich Marx*, 294–96, 342; *MEGA* 3/1: 290–91. The only trace of Heinrich's Jewish past in his personal library was one otherwise unspecified "Hebrew book."

29 Lucian Hölscher, *Geschichte der protestantischen Frömmigkeit in Deutschland* (Munich: C. H. Beck, 2005), 215–18; Christoph Weber, *Aufklärung und Orthodoxie am Mittelrhein: 1820–1850* (Munich: Ferdinand Schöningh Verlag, 1973); Wolfgang Schieder, *Religion und Revolution*.

30 Schönke, *Karl und Heinrich Marx*, 142.

31 Jan Gielkens, *Karl Marx und seine niederländischen Verwandten* (Trier: Karl-Marx-Haus, 1999), 32–63. Henriette Presburg's father was not a rabbi, contrary to the assertions of many biographers.

32 Monz, *Karl Marx*, 229–30; Schönke, *Karl und Heinrich Marx*, 4–5; Marian Kaplan, *The Making of the Jewish Middle Class: Women, Family and Identity in Imperial Germany* (New York: Oxford University Press, 1991), 85–99.

33 Schönke, *Karl und Heinrich Marx*, 291, 300. On dowries and their role in marriage, see Sperber, *Property and Civil Society*, 21–31; Kaplan, *Making of the Jewish Middle Class*, 93–98.

34 Schönke, *Karl und Heinrich Marx*, 358.

35 These and many similar quotes are in Gielkens, *Karl Marx und seine niederländischen Verwandten*, 33–34.

36 *MEGA* 3/1: 292, 294–95; Monz, *Karl Marx*, 230–38.

37 Schönke, *Karl und Heinrich Marx*, 188; Kaplan, *Making of the Jewish Middle Class*, 64–81.

38 Family dates are from Monz, *Karl Marx*, 230–38. On the practice of wet-nursing, cf. Kaplan, *The Making of the Jewish Middle Class*, 48–49.

39 Monz, *Karl Marx*, 255–58, Schönke, *Karl und Heinrich Marx*, 166, 170, 175, 180, 188–91, 201, 209, 217–19, 221–24, 297; Jürgen Herres, "Cholera, Armut und eine 'Zwangssteuer' 1830/32: Zur Sozialgeschichte Triers im Vormärz," *Kurtrierisches Jahrbuch* 39 (1990): 161–203.

40 Sources cited in previous note and Gielkens, *Karl Marx und seine niederländischen Verwandten*, 105; Hans-Joachim Henning, *Das westdeutsche Bürgertum in der Epoche der Hochindustrialisierung 1860–1914* (Wiesbaden: Franz Steinver Verlag, 1972), 51–52, 470–72.

41 Wheen, *Karl Marx*, 8.

42 Monz, *Karl Marx*, 297; *MEGA* 3/2: 471.

43 Karl-Ernst Jeismann, *Das preußische Gymnasium in Staat und Gesellschaft*, 2nd ed., 2 vols. (Stuttgart: Klett-Cotta, 1996).

44 Quoted in James C. Albisetti, *Secondary School Reform in Imperial Germany* (Princeton: Princeton University Press, 1983), 47.

45 Wilhelm Liebknecht, *Karl Marx zum Gedächtniß. Ein Lebensabriß und Erinnerungen* (Nuremberg: Wörlein & Co., 1896), 38; *MEGA* 3/11: 380.

46 Monz, *Karl Marx*, 297–316.

47 Ibid., 160–78.

48 James Brophy, *Popular Culture and the Public Sphere in the Rhineland 1800–1850* (Cambridge: Cambridge University Press, 2007), 100–02; Schönke, *Karl und Heinrich Marx*, 230–31; Monz, *Karl Marx*, 135–37.

49 *MEGA* 1/1: 449–52.

50 Monz, *Karl Marx*, 173–74.

51 *MEGA* 1/1: 454–57.

52 Ibid., 3/1: 291–92; Monz, *Karl Marx*, 172–73.

53 Christian Jansen, "Der politische Weg des Trierer Paulskirchenabgeordneten Ludwig Simon (1819–1872) gegen den Strom des nationalistischen 19. Jahrhunderts," in Guido Müller and Jürgen Herres, eds., *Aachen und die westlichen Rheinlande und die Revolution 1848/49* (Aachen: Shaker Verlag, 2000), 279–308.

2: THE STUDENT

1 Christina von Hodenberg, *Die Partei der Unparteiischen. Der Liberalismus der preußischen Richterschaft 1815–1848/49* (Göttingen: Vandenhoeck & Ruprecht, 1996), 103–28; Jeismann, *Das preußische Gymnasium*, 2: 340–42.

2 Hodenberg, *Die Partei*, 105–07; Sperber, *Rhineland Radicals*, 70–72.

3 *MEGA* 3/1: 301.

4 *MEW* 35: 466.

5 Peter Kaup, "Karl Marx als Waffenstudent: Burschenschafter an seinem Lebensweg," *Darstellungen und Quellen zur Geschichte der deutschen Einheitsbewegung im neunzehnten und zwanzigsten Jahrhundert* 15 (1995): 141–68; Brophy, *Popular Culture and the Public Sphere*, 216–52.

6 *MEGA* 3/1: 293, also 296–97.

7 Ibid., 3/1: 299.

8 Ibid., 3/1: 319–20, 331, 337.

9 *MEW* 35: 241–42.

10 On the Westphalen family, see Monz, *Karl Marx*, 319–45, and Lutz Graf Schwerin von Krosigk, *Jenny Marx Liebe und Leid im Schatten von Karl Marx*, 2nd ed. (Wuppertal: Staats-Verlag, 1976), 161–216, from which most of the following account comes.

11 William D. Godsey, Jr., *Nobles and Nations in Central Europe: The Imperial Knights in the Age of Revolution 1750–1850* (Cambridge: Cambridge University Press, 2004), 50–71; Heinz Reif, *Westfälischer Adel 1770–1860: Vom Herrschaftsstand zur regionalen Elite* (Göttingen: Vandenhoeck & Ruprecht, 1979), 188, 551 n. 35.

12 *MEGA* 3/1: 332–33, 347–78.

13 Ibid., 3/1: 331, 740; cf. 396.

14 Ibid., 3/1: 337–38; *MEW* 30: 643.

15 *MEGA* 3/1: 332; Schwerin von Krosigk, *Jenny Marx*, 26–30; Monz, *Karl Marx*, 330.

16 *MEGA* 3/1: 306, 338.

17 Karen Hausen, "'. . . eine Ulme für das schanke Efeu.' Ehepaare im Bildungsbürgertum. Ideale und Wirklichkeit im späten 18. und 19. Jahrhundert," in Ute Frevert, ed., *Bürgerinnen und Bürger: Geschlechterverhältnisse im 19. Jahrhundert* (Göttingen: Vandenhoeck & Ruprecht, 1988), 85–117.

18 *MEGA* 3/1: 45, 300–04, 306, 318–20, 347–48; Schwerin von Krosigk, *Jenny Marx*, 39; Heinrich Gemkow, "Aus dem Leben einer rheinischen Familie im 19. Jahrhundert. Archivalische Funde zu den Familien von Westphalen und Marx," *Jahrbuch für westdeutsche Landesgeschichte* 31 (2008): 498–524.

19 *MEGA* 3/1:301, 303.

20 Ibid., 1/1: 483–703; 3/1: 9–17, 318; Manfred Kliem, *Karl Marx und die Berliner Universität 1836 bis 1841* (East Berlin: Humboldt Universität, 1988), 26–29.

21 In the enormous literature on Hegel and his followers, one particularly useful work is John Edward Toews, *Hegelianism: The Path Toward Dialectical Humanism, 1805–1848* (Cambridge: Cambridge University Press, 1980).

22 Cited in ibid., 91; for Toews's admirable discussion of this point, see 89–94.

23 Letter in *MEGA* 3/1: 9–18.

24 Ibid., 3/1: 17, 303–06, 309–10, 315–17; Kliem, *Karl Marx und die Berliner Universität*, 16.

25 *MEGA* 3/1: 311, 315, 323–30.

26 Ibid., 3/1: 331; Gemkow, "Aus dem Leben," 520–21.

27 Monz, *Karl Marx*, 233; Kliem, *Karl Marx und die Berliner Universität*, 33; McLellan, *Karl Marx*, 27–28; *MEGA* 3/1: 360.

28 *MEGA* 3/1: 297, 330; Ute Frevert, *A Nation in Barracks: Modern Germany, Military Conscription and Civil Society*, trans. Andrew Boreham and Daniel Brückenhaus (Oxford: Berg Publishers, 2004), 50–56.

29 Gielkens, *Karl Marx und seine niederländischen Verwandten*, 138–40.

30 Kliem, *Karl Marx und die Berliner Universität*, 20, 25.

31 Sperber, *Property and Civil Society* 21, 36–37; *MEGA* 3/1: 347–48.

32 Kliem, *Karl Marx und die Berliner Universität*, 65–66.

33 Ibid., 54–55; Schwerin von Krosigk, *Jenny Marx*, 217–19; *MEGA* 3/1: 338.

34 Hans Günther Reissner, *Eduard Gans: Ein Leben im Vormärz* (Tübingen: J. C. B. Mohr, 1965); Reinhard Blänker, Gerhard Göhler, and Norbert Waszek, eds., *Eduard Gans (1797–1839): Politischer Professor zwischen Restauration und Vormärz* (Leipzig: Leipziger Universitätsverlag, 2002).

35 On the Young Hegelians, besides the work of Toews cited above, see Warren Breckman, *Marx, the Young Hegelians and the Origins of Radical Social Theory: Dethroning the*

Self (Cambridge: Cambridge University Press, 1999) and, esp., Wolfgang Eßbach, *Die Junghegelianer. Soziologie einer Intellektuellengruppe* (Munich: Wilhelm Fink, 1988).

36 Eßbach, *Die Junghegelianer*, 30–31 and n. 48.

37 Marilyn Chapin Massey, *Christ Unmasked: The Meaning of* The Life of Jesus *in German Politics* (Chapel Hill: University of North Carolina Press, 1983); Franz Courth, "Die Evangelienkritik des David Friedrich Strauß im Echo seiner Zeitgenossen. Zur Breitenwirkung seines Werkes," in Georg Schwaiger, ed., *Historische Kritik in der Theologie: Beiträge zu ihrer Geschichte* (Göttingen: Vandenhoeck & Ruprecht, 1980), 60–98.

38 Peter C. Caldwell, *Love, Death and Revolution in Central Europe: Ludwig Feuerbach, Moses Hess, Louise Dittmar, Richard Wagner* (New York: St. Martin's Press, 2009), is an excellent introduction to Feuerbach's intellectual world.

39 Cited in Heinz-Herman Brandhorst, *Lutherrezeption und bürgerliche Emanziaption: Studien zum Luther- und Reformationsverständnis im deutschen Vormärz (1815–1848) unter besonderer Berücksichtigung Ludwig Feuerbachs* (Göttingen: Vandenhoeck & Ruprecht, 1981), 72. "Light" was a code word among Germany's liberal Protestants, referring to their advocacy of rationalist and Enlightened ideas.

40 Ibid., 73–90; Stephan Walter, *Demokratisches Denken zwischen Hegel und Marx. Die politische Philosophie Arnold Ruges* (Düsseldorf: Droste Verlag, 1995), 99–143.

41 Eßbach, *Die Junghegelianer*, 66–78.

42 *MEGA* 3/1: 58–60, 416–20.

43 Surprisingly, there is still no complete biography of Bruno Bauer. But for his ideas, and his connections to Marx, see Zvi Rosen, *Bruno Bauer and Karl Marx: The Influence of Bruno Bauer on Marx's Thought* (The Hague: Martinus Nijhoff, 1977); Ruedi Waser, *Autonomie des Selbstbewußtseins. Eine Untersuchung zum Verhältnis von Bruno Bauer und Karl Marx (1835–1843)* (Tübingen: Francke Verlag, 1994); Junji Kanda, "Die Feuerbach-Rezeption des jungen Marx im Licht der Junghegelianismus-Forscshung," in Ursula Reitemeyer, Takayuik Shibata, and Franceso Tomasoni, eds., *Ludwig Feuerbach (1804–1872) Identität und Pluralismus in der globalen Gesellschaft* (New York: Waxmann Münster, 2006), 105–15; and Petra Linzbach, "Die konservative Orientierung Bruno Bauers nach 1848," in Lars Lambrecht, ed., *Osteuropa in den Revolutionen von 1848* (Frankfurt: Peter Lang, 2006), 169–81.

44 *MEGA* 3/1: 17, 335–36, 340–46, 349–50, 352–59; Waser, *Autonomie des Selbstbewußtseins*, 11, 84; Rosen, *Bruno Bauer*, 127; Wheen, *Karl Marx*, 256–57.

45 *MEGA* 1/1: 9–91; a commentary on it is Peter Fenves, "Marx's Doctoral Thesis on Two Greek Atomists and the Post-Kantian Interpretation," *Journal of the History of Ideas* 47 (1986): 433–52.

46 *MEGA* 1/1: 58.

47 Kanda, "Die Feuerbach-Rezeption des jungen Marx," 106–07.

48 *MEGA* 1/1: 11–14.

49 Kliem, *Karl Marx und die Berliner Universität*, 60–62, 80–81.

3: THE EDITOR

1 Schönke, *Karl und Heinrich Marx*, 307–09. On inheritance practices, cf. Sperber, *Property and Civil Society*, 36–63.

2 *MEGA* 3/1: 28, 43.

3 Gielkens, *Marx und seine niederländischen Verwandten*, 135–40; *MEGA* 3/2: 311–12, 365–67.

4 *MEGA* 3/1: 353, 358, 751; Rosen, *Bruno Bauer*, 62–63, 128–31; Waser, *Anatomie des Selbstbewußtseins*, 27.

5 Eßbach, *Die Junghegelianer*, 290–95.

6 Arnold Ruge, *Zwei Jahre in Paris*, 2 vols. (Leipzig: Verlag von Wilhelm Jurany, 1846), 2: 55.

7 *MEGA* 3/1: 342–43, 349–50, 352–53, 358.

8 David Barclay, *Frederick William IV and the Prussian Monarchy, 1840–1861* (Oxford: Clarendon Press, 1995), 52–122; Wolfgang Büttner, "Friedrich Wilhelm IV im Blickpunkt zeitkritischer Vormärzliteratur," *Forum Vormärz Forschung* 10 (2004): 195–207; *MEGA* 3/1: 349–50.

9 Eßbach, *Die Junghegelianer*, 124–31 (quote on 128); Toews, *Hegelianism*, 308–19.

10 Bruno and Edgar Bauer, *Briefwechsel zwischen Bruno Bauer und Edgar Bauer während der Jahre 1839–1842 aus Bonn und Berlin* (Charlottenburg: Verlag von Egbert Bauer, 1844), 192.

11 *MEGA* 3/1: 25.

12 Ibid., 3/1: 24, 26.

13 Ibid., 3/1: 366–67.

14 John Knodel, *Demographic Behavior in the Past: A Study of Fourteen German Village Populations in the Eighteenth and Nineteenth Centuries* (Cambridge: Cambridge University Press, 1988), 185–294.

15 *MEGA* 3/1: 21–30; 370, 372, 375.

16 On the founding and initial development of the *Rhineland News*, see Edmund Silberner, "Moses Hess als Begründer und Redakteur der Rheinischen Zeitung," *Archiv für Sozialgeschichte* 4 (1964): 5–44, and Edmund Siberner, *Moses Hess: Geschichte seines Lebens* (Leiden: E. J. Brill, 1966), 1–102.

17 Christopher Johnson, *Utopian Communism in France: Cabet and the Icarians 1839–1851* (Ithaca, NY: Cornell University Press, 1974), esp. 93–95; Edward Berenson, *Populist Religion and Left-Wing Politics in France, 1830–1852* (Princeton: Princeton University Press, 1984), 36–51; Silberner, *Moses Hess*, 7–9, 20–21, 23–28, 72–74.

18 Joseph Hansen, *Gustav Mevissen: Ein rheinisches Lebensbild 1815–1899*, 2 vols. (Berlin: Georg Reimer, 1906), 1:246.

19 Ibid., 1:246; *RhBA* 1: 466.

20 Götz Langkau and Hans Pelger, *Studien zur Rheinischen Zeitung und zu ihrer Forderung nach Handelsfreiheit und Grundrechten im Deutschen Bund* (Trier: Karl-Marx-Haus, 2003); *RhBA* 1: 15–16, 571–81; Hansen, *Mevissen*, 1: 250–51.

21 Hansen, *Mevissen*, 1: 251–52; Hans-Martin Sass, "Bruno Bauers Idee der 'Rheinischen Zeitung,'" *Zeitschrift für Religions- und Geistesgeschichte* 19 (1967): 321–32.

22 The essay appeared in the supplement to several issues of the *Rhineland News*, from May 5 to May 19, 1842. It is reprinted in *MEGA* 1/1: 121–69.

23 *RhBA* 1: 844.

24 *MEGA* 1/1: 134–35.

25 Ibid., 1/1: 139–40.

26 Ibid., 1/1: 159.

27 Ibid., 1/1: 161.

28 Ibid., 1/1: 153.

29 Ibid., 1/1: 169.

30 Ibid., 1/1: 991–92; *RhBA* 1: 344.

31 It appeared in the supplement to the July 10, 12, and 14, 1842, issues of the *Rhineland News*, and is republished in *MEGA* 1/1: 172–90.

32 Ibid., 3/1: 29.

33 Ibid., 1/1: 182–88.

34 *RhBA* 1: 318, 324–26, 338–41.

35 Ibid., 1: 353–54, 368 n. 1; *MEGA* 3/1: 374.

36 McLellan, *Karl Marx*, 42; Wheen, *Karl Marx*, 36; *MEGA* 3/1: 30–32, 37.

37 *RhBA* 1: 381 n. 1, 330–31, 341–42, 345–46, 361, 389; Silberner, *Moses Hess*, 106–08.

38 Silberner, *Moses Hess*, 96; *MEGA* 3/1: 373.

39 *MEGA* 1/1: 31–32.

40 *RhBA* 1: 373, 388; Langkau and Pelger, *Studien zur* Rheinischen Zeitung, 30–94.

41 Eßbach, *Die Junghegelianer*, 214–26 (an excellent account); *MEGA* 3/1: 37–39, 379–83, 773.

42 *MEGA* 3/1: 64, 386–87, 391, 406.

43 For the separation, from Marx's point of view, see *MEGA* 3/1: 37–39.

44 Langkau and Pelger, *Studien zur* Rheinischen Zeitung, 240–332.

45 *RhBA* 1: 375–76, 389.

46 Ibid., 1: 353 n. 1, 374–75, 389; Wheen, *Karl Marx*, 46; *MEGA* 3/1: 33.

47 *MEGA* 3/1: 33–36, 250; *RhBA* 1: 389.

48 *RhBA* 1: 368–69, 384, 397, 410.

49 *MEGA* 2/2: 99–100.

50 Hansen, *Mevissen*: 1: 264–66; Silberner, *Moses Hess*, 119–21; *RhBA* 1: 411.

51 Cf. *MEGA* 1/1: 240.

52 Ibid., 3/1: 38.

53 Ibid., 1/1: 237–40, 1032–37.

54 *MEGA* 1/1: 199–236.

55 Sperber, *Rhineland Radicals*, 76; Dirk Blasius, *Bürgerliche Gesellschaft und Kriminalität* (Göttingen: Vandenhoeck & Ruprecht, 1976); Heinz Reif, "'Furcht bewahrt das Holz.' Holzdiebstahl und sozialer Konflikt in der ländlichen Gesellschaft 1800–1850 an westfälischen Beispielen," in Heinz Reif, ed., *Räuber Volk und Obrig-*

keit (Frankfurt-am-Main: Suhrkamp Verlag, 1984), 43–99; Bernd-Stefan Grewe, *Der versperrte Wald: Ressourcenmangel in der bayerischen Pfalz (1814–1870)* (Cologne & Vienna: Böhlau Verlag, 2004), 215.

56 Heinz Monz, "Der Waldprozeß der Mark Thalfang als Grundlage für Karl Marx' Kritik an den Debatten um das Holzdiebstahlgesetz," *Jahrbuch für westdeutsche Landesgeschichte* 4 (1977): 395–418.

57 *MEGA* 1/1: 206.

58 Ibid., 1/1: 207.

59 Ibid., 1/1: 296–318; Annette Winter-Tarvainen, "Moselweinkrise und Revolution von 1848," in Dühr, ed., *"Der schlimmste Punkt in der Provinz,"* 439–51.

60 *MEGA* 1/1: 313.

61 Alan Kahan, "Liberalism and Realpolitik in Prussia, 1830–1852: The Case of David Hansemann," *German History* 9 (1991): 280–307.

62 *RhBA* 1: 399–400, 402–09, 472 n. 2, 489–90.

63 Ibid., 1: 412–16, 422–25, 463, 468–69.

64 *MEGA* 1/1: 434–43, 1171–81; *RhBA* 1: 471–72, 492–975, 503–05.

65 *RhBA* 1: 473; Liebknecht, *Karl Marx zum Gedächtniß*, 35–36, 41.

66 *RhBA* 1: 472–73.

67 *BdK* 1:308.

68 *MEGA* 3/10: 346.

4: THE ÉMIGRÉ

1 *MEGA* 3/1: 43.

2 Ibid., 3/1: 43–44, 389, 393, 399–400, 406, 412, 538–39; Walter Grab, *Dr. Wilhelm Schulz aus Darmstadt. Weggefährte von Georg Büchner und Inspirator von Karl Marx* (Frankfurt: Büchergilde Gutenberg, 1987), 234–48; Paul Nerrlich, ed., *Arnold Ruges Briefwechsel und Tagebuchblätter aus den Jahren 1825–1880*, 2 vols. (Berlin: Weidmannsche Buchhandlung, 1886), 1: 295–96, 301, 303, 307, 310–12.

3 *MEGA* 3/1: 44, 397.

4 Monz, *Karl Marx*, illus. 19; Helmut Elsner, "Karl Marx in Kreuznach 1842/43 Daten—Personen—Kreuznacher Exzerpte," in Marion Barzen, ed., *Studien zu Marx's erstem Paris-Aufenthalt und zur Entstehung der* Deutschen Ideologie (Trier: Karl-Marx-Haus, 1990), 110–37; Schöncke, *Karl und Heinrich Marx*, 843–47.

5 Franziska Kugelmann, "Kleine Züge zu dem grossen Charakterbild von Karl Marx," in *Mohr und General*, ed. Institut für Marxismus-Leninismus, 3rd ed. (East Berlin: Dietz Verlag, 1970), 297; McLellan, *Karl Marx*, 62; Wheen, *Karl Marx*, 52; *MEGA* 3/3: 690.

6 The notes Marx took, the so-called Kreuznach excerpts, are published in *MEGA* 4/2: 9–278.

7 Ibid., 3/1: 22.

8 Caldwell, *Love, Death and Revolution*, 28–31.

9 *MEGA* 3/1: 45.

10 Ibid., 1/2: 54–58, 96, 114–19; similarly, 1/2: 8–9, 11, 14–15, 40, 88–89, and esp. 125–26.

11 Ibid., 1/2: 30–33.

12 Cf. the editorial comments in ibid., 1/2: 633–34.

13 Ibid., 4/2: 96.

14 Ruge, *Zwei Jahre in Paris*, 1:4, 47.

15 See Gerhard Lippold, "Marx und die Tolstois in Paris," *Beiträge zur Geschichte der Arbeiterbewegung* 45 (2003): 9–26.

16 Birgit Bublies-Godau, "Parteibildungsprozesse im vormärzlichen Exile: Die deutschen Auslandsvereine in Paris," and François Melis, "August Hermann Ewerbeck—Vermittler demokratischer sozialistischer und kommunistischer Ideen zwischen Frankreich und Deutschland im Pariser Exil," both in *Forum Vormärz Forschung* 10 (2004), 87–147 and 268–95, respectively.

17 Lloyd S. Kramer, *Threshold of a New World: Intellectuals and the Exile Experience in Paris, 1830–1848* (Ithaca & London: Cornell University Press, 1988), 25–27 and passim.

18 Wolfgang Strähl, *Briefe eines Schweizers aus Paris 1835–1836*, ed. Jacques Grandjonc, Waltraud Seidel-Höppner, and Michael Werner (Vaduz: Topos Verlag, 1988).

19 For this, and all not otherwise explicitly referenced details of Marx's time in Paris, see Jacques Grandjonc, "Zu Marx' Aufenthalt in Paris: 11. October 1843–1 Februar 1845," in Marion Barzen, ed., *Studien zu Marx' erstem Paris-Aufenthalt und zur Enstehung der Deutschen Ideologie* (Trier: Karl-Marx-Haus, 1990), 163–212.

20 *MEGA* 3/1: 412; cf. Wheen, *Karl Marx*, 62; McLellan, *Karl Marx*, 73.

21 Grandjonc, "Zu Marx' Aufenthalt," 178–202.

22 *Ruges Briefwechsel und Tagebuchblätter*, 1:313–15, 327, 343, 352.

23 Grandjonc, "Zu Marx' Aufenthalt," 181–82; *Ruges Briefwechsel und Tagebuchblätter*, 341–45, 349–54, 358; *MEGA* 3/1: 426–27, 432–33; McLellan, *Karl Marx*, 89.

24 *MEGA* 3/1: 428–31.

25 Ibid., 3/1: 426–27, 432–33, 437–38, 440–42. A few months later, Marx's Cologne supporters sent along an additional 800 francs, about 115 talers.

26 The pieces are in *MEGA* 3/1: 170–83 and 141–69, respectively.

27 Rosen, *Bruno Bauer and Karl Marx*, 140–41.

28 *MEGA* 1/2: 181–82.

29 See two harsh critics: Dagobert Runes, ed., *A World Without Jews by Karl Marx* (New York: Philosophical Library, 1959), and Paul Lawrence Rose, *Revolutionary Anti-Semitism in Germany from Kant to Wagner* (Princeton: Princeton University Press, 1990), 295–305, and the many other examples cited there. Slightly embarrassed apologists would include McLellan, *Karl Marx*, 78–79; Wheen, *Karl Marx*, 55–57; and Allan Megill, *Karl Marx: The Burden of Reason* (Lanham, MD: Rowman & Littlefield, 2002), 142–48.

30 Bruno Bauer, *Die Judenfrage* (Braunschweig: Druck & Verlag von Friedrich Otto, 1843); and Bruno Bauer, "Die Fähigkeit der heutigen Juden und Christen, frei zu werden," in Georg Herwegh, ed., *Einundzwanzig Bogen aus der Schweiz* (Zurich & Winterthur: Verlag des Literarischen Comptoirs, 1843), 56–57; Nathan Rotenstreich, "For and Against Emancipation: The Bruno Bauer Controversy," *Leo Baeck Institute Yearbook* 4 (1959): 3–36. Marx's own interest in the debate is apparent from *MEW* 2: 91–95, 99–104, 112–25.

31 Bauer, "Die Fähigkeit der heutigen Juden," 59–61.

32 Ibid., 57.

33 Opposition to emancipation: Dagmar Herzog, *Intimacy and Exclusion: Religious Politics in Pre-Revolutionary Baden* (Princeton: Princeton University Press, 1996), 53–72; Reinhard Rürup, *Emanzipation und Antisemitismus* (Göttingen: Vandenhoeck & Ruprecht, 1975), 56–64. A contemporary example by a well-known liberal Protestant theologian is Heinrich Paulus, *Die jüdische Nationalabsonderung nach Ursprung, Folge und Besserungsmitteln* (Heidelberg: Universitätsbuchhandlung von C. F. Winter, 1831); an English translation of excerpts of this work can be found online at http:// germanhistorydocs.ghi-dc.org/sub_document.cfm?document_id=436, accessed 3/13/09. For later liberal Protestant theological attitudes, see Uriel Tal, "Theologische Debatte um das 'Wesen' des Judentums," in Werner E. Mosse and Arnold Paucker, eds., *Juden im Wilhelminischen Deutschland 1890–1914* (Tübingen: J. C. B. Mohr, 1976), 599–632. These attitudes were faithfully, if idiosyncratically, reflected in Bauer, *Die Judenfrage*, 9, 11–12, 17, 21, 31–35, 37–38, 40–41, 43, 46–47, 52.

34 Letter in *MEGA* 3/1: 45–46.

35 Marx mentioned Tocqueville's *On Democracy in America* but explicitly cited the work of Tocqueville's collaborator, Gustave de Beaumont, whose novel *Marie* is known today primarily for its discussion of slavery and race relations rather than for its account of the place of religion in American society.

36 *MEGA* 1/2: 147–48.

37 Ibid., 1/2: 164–69.

38 *MEGA* 1/2: 279–80; Margit Naarmann, "Ländliche Massenarmut und 'jüdischer Wucher.' Zur Etablirung eines Stereotyps," in Ludger Grevelhörster and Wolfgang Maron, eds., *Region und Gesellschaft in Deutschland des 19. und 20. Jahrhunderts* (Vierow: SH-Verlag, 1995), 128–49, quote on 144.

39 Silberner, *Moses Hess*, 184–92; Ruge, *Zwei Jahre in Paris*, 1:34–35; Michael Werner, "Börne, Heine Gans: Drei deutsch-jüdische Intellektuelle zwischen Deutschland und Frankreich im Spannungsfeld von Akkulturation, Politik und Kulturtransfer," in Blänker, Göhler, and Waszek, eds., *Eduard Gans*, 46.

40 Siegbert Prawer, *Heine's Jewish Comedy: A Study of His Portraits of Jews and Judaism* (Oxford: Clarendon Press, 1983); Silberner, *Moses Hess*, 388–427.

41 *MEGA* 3/1: 440–41.

42 *Arnold Ruges Briefwechsel*, 1: 352–53, 362–366; *MEGA* 3/1: 264. The closeness of Marx's relationship to Heine should not be exaggerated; see Jeffrey L. Sammons,

Heinrich Heine: A Modern Biography (Princeton: Princeton University Press, 1979), 260–65.

43 *MEGA* 3/1: 65, 484, 489–90, 496–97; Melis, "August Hermann Ewerbeck," 277–78; *Arnold Ruges Briefwechsel*, 1:359, 382.

44 *MEGA* 1/2: 445–63, 555–66; Ruge, *Zwei Jahre in Paris*, 1:145–46; Jacques Grandjonc, *Marx et les communists allemands à Paris 1844* (Paris: François Maspéro, 1974).

45 In Liebknecht, *Karl Marx zum Gedächtnis*, 6, or Lafargue, "Persönliche Erinnerungen an Karl Marx," in *Mohr und General*, 342, we can see this image being formed.

46 Grandjonc, "Zu Marx' Aufenthalt in Paris," 199–200; McLellan, *Karl Marx*, 256; *MEGA* 3/1: 506–08, 513–15.

47 An earlier example of the perception of the separation of Marx and Engels is in *MEGA* 3/2: 336.

48 The latest biography of Engels, Tristram Hunt, *Marx's General: The Revolutionary Life of Friedrich Engels* (New York: Henry Holt & Co., 2010), is a good introduction and interpretation.

49 *MEGA* 2/1: 388–433.

50 Ibid., 3/1: 339–60, 425–26.

51 *MEGA* 3/1: 437–50, 467–94; Edgar Bauer, *Konfidentenberichte über die europäische Emigration 1852–1861*, ed. Erik Gamby (Trier: Karl-Marx-Haus, 1989), 57; and esp. Hunt, *Marx's General*, 74–112.

52 Grandjonc, "Zu Marx' Aufenthalt," 199–202.

53 *Arnold Ruges Briefwechsel*, 344, 351, 354

54 Liebknecht, *Karl Marx zum Gedächtnis*, 36.

55 *MEGA* 3/1: 262, 272–73.

56 A few samples from the large literature along these lines would include Bertell Ollman, *Alienation: Marx's Conception of Man in Capitalist Society*, 2nd ed. (Cambridge: Cambridge University Press, 1976); István Mészáros, *Marx's Theory of Alienation*, 3rd ed. (London: Merlin, 1972); or Louis Althusser, *For Marx*, trans. Ben Brewster (New York: Pantheon Books, 1969).

57 The manuscripts are in *MEGA* 1/2: 189–444; the passages in question are on 273–74, 284–85, 292–306, 319–22, 397–418, 435–37, 439–44.

58 Excerpts of economists in ibid., 4/2: 301–579.

59 Ibid., 1/2: 195, 871–72.

60 Ibid., 1/2: 202.

61 See Eric Roll, *A History of Economic Thought*, 4th ed. (London: Faber & Faber, 1973), 184–92, 201–11; Terry Peach, *Interpreting Ricardo* (Cambridge: Cambridge University Press, 1993), 104–31.

62 Wilhelm Schulz, *Die Bewegung der Produktion. Eine geschichtlich-statistische Abhandlung*, ed. Wilhelm Kade (Glashütten in Taunus: Verlag Detlev Auvermann, 1974), a reprint of the original edition that appeared in Switzerland in 1843. For Schulz and his influence on Marx, see Grab, *Dr. Wilhelm Schulz*, esp. 257–91.

63 Cf. Schulz, *Bewegung der Produktion*, 60–68, with *MEGA* 1/2: 333–36.

64 Schulz, *Bewegung der Produktion*, 69–72, 172–78.

65 *MEGA* 1/2: 234–35.

66 Engels, after his year in Manchester, certainly knew about repetitive labor in textile mills, but his essay on economics printed in the *Franco-German Yearbooks* was quite enthusiastic about the possibilities for mechanized production and had nothing to say about the negative effects of working with machinery.

67 *MEGA* 1/2: 238–39, 387.

68 Ibid., 3/1: 63.

69 Ibid., 1/2: 240.

70 Ibid., 1/2: 241–42, 271; Zvi Rosen, *Moses Hess und Karl Marx* (Hamburg: Hans Christians Verlag, 1983), 137–58.

71 *MEGA* 1/2: 263.

72 Ibid., 1/2: 289.

73 Ibid., 1/2: 325–26, 701; 3/1: 458, 465, 490, 492, 503, 514, 532; 3/2: 200, 265, 270.

74 Ibid., 3/1: 516, 851–52; Grandjonc, "Zu Marx' Aufenthalt in Paris," 202–03.

75 Cited in François Melis, "Heinrich Bürgers," in Helmut Bleiber, Walter Schmidt, and Susanna Schütz, eds., *Akteure eines Umbruchs: Männer und Frauen der Revolution von 1848/49* (Berlin: Fides-Verlag, 2003), 145.

76 *MEGA* 3/1: 453–54.

77 Ibid., 3/1: 434.

5: THE REVOLUTIONARY

1 Karl Grün, *Die soziale Bewegung in Frankreich und Belgien: Briefe und Studien* (Darmstadt: Druck & Verlag von Carl Wilhelm Leske, 1845), 25.

2 Ibid., 17.

3 Bert Andréas et al., eds., *Association Démocratique ayant pour but l'union et la fraternité de tous les peuples: Eine frühe demokratische Vereinigung in Brüssel 1847–1848* (Trier: Karl-Marx-Haus, 2004), 19–51.

4 *MEGA* 3/1: 479–81, 840; 4/4: 555–59.

5 The notes are in ibid., 4/4; the comment on Mill is on 329.

6 On this secret society, the artisans' group it sponsored, and its eventual transformation into the Communist League, the 3-volume collection of documents *Der Bund der Kommunisten: Dokumente und Materialien* has a lot of information. A narrative history is Martin Hundt, *Geschichte des Bundes der Kommunisten* (Frankfurt & Berlin: Peter Lang, 1993); an excellent, brief English-language account is Christine Lattek's *Revolutionary Refugees: German Socialism in Britain, 1840–1860* (London & New York: Routledge, 2006), 22–41.

7 *Neue Deutsche Biographie*, http://mdz10.bib-bvb.de/zend-bsb/pdf_download.pl, accessed 5/19/09.

8 Lattek, *Revolutionary Refugees*, 23, 33–35; Andréas et al., eds., *Association Démocratique*, 52–56; *MEGA* 3/1: 463, 832; 3/2: 322–23; *BdK* 1: 242, 244–53.

9 *MEGA* 3/1: 513, 525–26; 3/2: 7–8, 15, 205–06, 219, 253–54, 378; Andréas et al., eds., *Association Démocratique*, 108–14; *B∂K* 1: 303–08, 401, 432.

10 *MEGA* 3/2: 12–15, 30–32, 34–39, 53–59, 199–201, 212–14, 219–23, 250–55, 274–78, 305–07, 317–20, 347; *B∂K* 1: 322–36, 386–88.

11 Dieter Dowe, *Aktion und Organisation. Arbeiterbewegung, sozialistische und kommunistische Bewegung in der Preußischen Rheinprovinz 1820–1852* (Hanover: Verlag für Literatur und Zeitgeschehen, 1970), 63–93; *MEGA* 3/1: 270–71, 460, 513–14, 532–33; 3/2: 9–10, 23.

12 *MEGA* 3/1: 259–60, 484–88, 496–99; Silberner, *Moses Hess*, 235.

13 Besides the sources cited in n. 11, see Silberner, *Moses Hess*, 212–26, 235–37; *MEGA* 3/2: 9–10, 25, 185, 189, 193, 208, 225–26, 233–34, 238, 248–49.

14 *MEGA* 3/2: 243–45, 270, 272–73, 284, 286–87, 289–91.

15 Ibid., 3/2: 40, 46–47, 51, 85–86, 106–08, 116–17, 269–70, 332, 343, 354–55, 374, 385.

16 Ibid., 3/1: 261, 269, 446–49, 458.

17 *MEW* 2: 12–16, 53, 59–81, 91–141, 172–223; *MEGA* 3/1: 271–72, 458.

18 *MEW* 2: 37–39, 51–52, 55, 59–63, 85–91, 112–25, 143–51; Wolfgang Mönke, *Die heilige Familie Zur ersten Gemeinschaftsarbeit von Karl Marx und Friedrich Engels* (Glashütten in Taunus: Verlag Detleve Auvermann, 1972), 183, 188, 190, 196–97, 202, 211, 241–42, 262, 280.

19 *MEW* 2: 23–56, 125–31.

20 For this and the details that follow, see *MEW* 3:37–39; Inge Taubert, "Wie entstand die *Deutsche Ideologie* von Karl Marx und Friedrich Engels? Neue Einsichten, Probleme und Streitpunkte," in Barzen, ed., *Studien zu Marx's erstem Paris-Aufenthalt*, 9–109; and Inge Taubert, "Manuskripte und Drucke der 'deutschen Ideologie' (November 1845 bis Juni 1846). Probleme und Ereignisse," *MEGA Studien* 3 (1997): 5–31. There is more information in the other essays in this issue of the journal.

21 *MEW* 3: 78–100; Sylvia Palatschek, *Frauen und Dissens: Frauen im Deutschkatholizimus und in den Freien Gemeinden 1841–1852* (Göttingen: Vandenhoeck & Ruprecht, 1990), 27–30.

22 Eßbach, *Die Junghegelianer*, 292 and passim; "Max Stirner," in the *Stanford Encyclopedia of Philosophy*, online at http://plato.stanford.edu/entries/max-stirner/, accessed 6/9/09.

23 Franz Mehring, *Karl Marx: The Story of His Life*, trans. Edward Fitzgerald (Atlantic Highlands, NJ: Humanities Press, 1981), 110; cf. McLellan, *Karl Marx*, 139; Wheen, *Karl Marx*, 94–95. The materials making up *The German Ideology* have not yet been published in the *MEGA*; a few of the passages dealing with Stirner are in *MEW* 3: 103, 116, 161–63, 206–14, 218–19, 228–42, 318–19, 321, 334–38, 365. Stirner's twentieth-century rehabilitation as a precursor to Nietzsche and a pioneer of libertarianism was not something that contemporaries could have predicted.

24 *MEW* 3: 13–77.

25 Ibid., 3: 21.

26 Ibid., 3: 26–27.

27 Ibid., 3: 69.

28 Ibid., 3: 35.

29 Ibid., 3: 35–36; Rosen, *Moses Hess und Karl Marx*, 68–69, 169–70, 172–73.

30 *MEW* 3: 33.

31 Ibid., 3: 31–35, 50–61, 65–68, 74–76.

32 Ibid., 3: 441; *MEGA* 3/2: 193.

33 *MEW* 3: 442.

34 Ibid., 3: 442–43, 453, 455, 475.

35 Ibid., 3: 442; also 447, 453, 455, 475–77.

36 Ibid., 3: 443, 449, 457–58,

37 Silberner, *Moses Hess*, 226–33.

38 *MEGA* 3/1: 23.

39 Cf. *MdP* 43–54, with Pierre-Joseph Proudhon, *Système de contradictions économiques, ou philosophie de la misère*, 2nd ed., 2 vols. (Paris: Garnier Frères, 1850), 1: 65–80.

40 *MdP* 54–79, 134–51, 160–75.

41 Ibid., 115, 118.

42 *MEGA* 3/2: 72.

43 *MEGA* 3/1: 112, 118–19, 121, 361, 372, 377, 697.

44 Ibid., 3/1: 506–07, 513–14, 517–18; Silberner, *Moses Hess*, 166–71, 236; Stephan Born, *Erinnerungen eines Achtundvierzigers* (Leipzig: Verlag von Georg Heinrich Meyer, 1898), 73–74.

45 *MEGA* 3/1: 251–53, 259.

46 *BdK* 1: 303–05.

47 *MEGA* 3/2: 37–38, 208, 211, 217, 219, 270.

48 *BdK* 1: 307–08; Lattek, *Revolutionary Refugees*, 28–31; *MEGA* 3/1: 477.

49 *MEGA* 3/1: 462–63, 485–86; 3/2: 185–86, 208, 211, 217–18.

50 Cf. ibid., 3/1: 513, with Silberner, *Moses Hess*, 257–58.

51 For Marx's relations with Grün, see Dieter Deichsel, "Die Kritik Karl Grüns: Zur Entstehung und Überlieferung von Teil IV des zweiten Bandes der 'Deutschen Ideologie,'" *MEGA Studien* 3 (1997): 103–53; James Strassmaier, *Karl Grün und die Kommunistische Partei 1845–1848* (Trier: Karl-Marx-Haus, 1973); Eckhard Trox, *Karl Grün (1817–1887). Eine Biographie* (Lüdenscheid: Stadtmuseum Lüdenscheid, 1993), esp. 49–56.

52 *MEGA* 3/2: 8.

53 Ibid., 3/1: 205–07, 228.

54 Ibid., 3/2: 34–36, 43, 51–61, 136, 203, 654–55; Paul Thomas, *Karl Marx and the Anarchists* (London: Routledge, 1980), 211.

55 *MEGA* 3/2: 334–35.

56 Ibid., 3/2: 35–36, 43, 78.

57 Grün, *Die soziale Bewegung*, 6, 20, 22, 244, 305, 380, 433, 445, 447.

58 *MEW* 3: 480–98, 509–20; *MEGA* 3/2: 26, 36, 216, 227–28, 233, 256–57, 279, 334, 342, 347.

59 *MEGA* 3/1: 266, 279–80, 713–15; 3/2: 159; Bert Andréas, Jacques Grandjonc, and Hans Pelger, "Karl Marx' Ausweisung aus Paris und die Niederlassung von Marx und Friedrich Engels in Brüssel im Frühjahr 1845," in Barzen, ed., *Studien zu Marx' erstem Paris-Aufenthalt*, 213–43.

60 *MEGA* 3/2: 10; Heinrich Gemkow, "Helena Demuth (1820–1890). Ein Leben im Schatten anderer. Vom Kindermädchen in Trier zur Hasdame in London," in Irina Hundt, ed., *Vom Salon zur Barrikade: Frauen der Heinezeit* (Stuttgart & Weimar: Verlag J. B. Metzler, 2002), 415–24; Jenny von Westphalen, "Kurze Umrisse eines bewegten Lebens," in *Mohr und General*, 206–07.

61 *MEGA* 3/2: 17.

62 Ibid., 3/1: 484, 509, 531.

63 Ibid., 3/1: 266, 270, 458, 460, 503; 3/2: 10, 225, 234.

64 Ibid., 3/2: 360, 365–67, 375–76.

65 Ibid., 3/1: 283; 3/2: 10, 29, 90, 125, 328, 337–39; Born, *Erinnerungen eines Achtundvierzigers*, 67.

66 *MEGA* 3/2: 211.

67 Ibid., 3/2: 272, 284; also 290.

68 Ibid., 3/2: 202, 346–47.

69 Ibid., 3/2: 273, 282; also 211, 341.

70 Ibid., 3/2: 67.

PART II: STRUGGLE

6: THE INSURGENT

1 *MEGA* 3/2: 90, 327; *BdK* 1: 452–57; Lattek, *Revolutionary Refugees*, 38–41.

2 *BdK* 1: 466–87, 501–24.

3 Ibid., 1: 497, 622–23; *MEGA* 3/2: 96, 358; Andréas et al., eds., *Association Démocratique*, 90–92; Silberner, *Moses Hess*, 273.

4 Andréas et al. eds., *Association Démocratique*, 88–105; *MEGA* 3/2: 99–105, 110.

5 Andréas et al. eds., *Association Démocratique*, 106–32, 473–78, 489, 508–27.

6 *BdK* 1: 528–42, 579–83, 616–18, 624–40; *MEGA* 3/2: 119–21, 125; Lattek, *Revolutionary Refugees*, 40–41.

7 Hundt, *Geschichte des Bundes der Kommunisten*, 339–40; *MEGA* 3/2: 368, 374.

8 Speech in Andréas et al., eds., *Association Démocratique*, 509–27.

9 Deichsel, "Die Kritik Karl Grüns," 131 n. 135.

10 *BdK* 1: 538; *MEGA* 3/2: 115.

11 *MEW* 4: 361–80; *MEGA* 3/2: 122.

12 *MEGA* 3/2: 384.

13 Among the many editions of and commentaries on the *Communist Manifesto*, two stand out: John Toews, ed., *The Communist Manifesto by Karl Marx and Friedrich Engels with Related Documents* (Boston: Bedford/St. Martin's Press, 1999), and Gareth Stedman Jones, ed., *The Communist Manifesto* (London & New York: Penguin Books, 2002). My translations are from *MEW* 4: 461–93.

14 Cf. *MEW* 4:461 with *MEGA* 1/1: 124–25.

15 *MEGA* 1/1: 237–40.

16 In Towes, ed., *The Communist Manifesto*, 68.

17 For a well-known description of Marx as prophet of modernity, see Marshall Berman, *All That Is Solid Melts into Air: The Experience of Modernity* (New York: Simon & Schuster, 1982); a more recent one is at http://www.bookforum.com/inprint/107_10/6686, accessed 1/27/11.

18 *MEW* 4: 479.

19 *MEGA* 1/1: 33, 51–52, 125, 352–53; 1/2: 172; 3/2: 41–42, 96, 141, 564; *MEW* 3: 46.

20 Cf. *MEW* 4: 462–63 with Myriam Bienstock, "Die 'soziale Frage im französisch-deutschen Kulturaustausch: Gans, Marx und die deutsche Saint-Simon Rezeption," in Blänker et al., eds., *Eduard Gans*, 169.

21 *MEW* 4: 373.

22 Ibid., 4: 191–203.

23 Cf. Grün *Die soziale Bewegung*, 212–13, 244, 252, 306.

24 Cf. ibid., 4: 378 and 487.

25 Ibid., 4: 309–59; Heinzen later elaborated his criticisms in *Die Helden des teutschen Kommunismus. Dem Herrn Karl Marx gewidmet* (Bern: Druck & Verlag von Jenni, Sohn, 1848), esp. 1, 13–14, 17, 20–21, 25, 39–40, 51, 62, 74, 104.

26 Rosen, *Moses Hess und Karl Marx*, 115.

27 On the situation and subsequent events, see Andréas, et al., *Association Démocratique*, 133–41, 633–94; Westphalen, "Kurze Umrisse," 207–09.

28 *MEW* 4: 536–38; *MEGA* 3/2: 408, 420, 481, 1023.

29 *MEGA* 3/2: 112–13, 118–19, 127, 389; *BdK* 1: 713–14, 721–23.

30 *MEGA* 3/2: 136, 141, 147; *BdK* 1: 729–30; Ulrike Ruttmann, *Wunschbild-Schreckbild-Trugbild: Rezeption und Instrumentalisierung Frankreichs in der Deutschen Revolution von 1848/49* (Stuttgart: Franz Steiner, 2001), 104–17.

31 Sperber, *Rhineland Radicals*, 297; Dowe, *Aktion und* Organisation, 139; *MEGA* 3/2: 142, 149; *BdK* 1: 741–43, 749, 751–52, 770–71.

32 *MEGA* 3/2: 442.

33 Dowe, *Aktion und Organisation*, 250–53.

34 Klaus Schmidt, *Andreas Gottschalk: Armenarzt und Pionier der Arbeiterbewegung Jude und Protestant* (Cologne: Greven Verlag, 2002); Sperber, *Rhineland Radicals*, 223–31.

35 *BdK* 1: 738, 782.

36 *MEGA* 3/2: 21, 374; Silberner, *Moses Hess*, 17, 100, 193, 271, 285–86.

37 Sperber, *Rhineland Radicals*, 178, 224–28; Ruge, *Zwei Jahre in Paris*, 34–35.

38 François Melis, "Zur Gründungsgeschichte der *Neuen Rheinischen Zeitung*. Neue Dokumente und Fakten," *MEGA Studien* 5 (1998): 3–63; *MEGA* 3/2: 152; 3/7: 199, 209.

39 Marcel Seyppel, *Die Demokratische Gesellschaft in Köln 1848/49: Städtische Gesellschaft und Parteienstehung während der bürgerlichen Revolution* (Cologne: Janus Verlagsgesellschaft, 1991), 125–31; Sperber, *Rhineland Radicals*, 190.

40 *MEGA* 3/3: 121, 123, 125, 133, 149, 151, 193–94, 200, 209, 222–23, 288, 297, 332–33.

41 Gemkow, "Aus dem Leben einer rheinischen Familie," 523; François Melis, "Eine neue Sicht auf die *Neue Rheinische Zeitung*? Zur Edition der MEGA²-Bände I/7–9," *Beiträge zur Marx-Engels-Forschung* n.s. (2005): 121–40; *MEGA* 3/2: 164.

42 Sperber, *Rhineland* Radicals, 212; *MEW* 5: 324.

43 *MEW* 5: 63, 6: 44, 218–20.

44 Ibid., 5: 42, 225.

45 *BdK* 1: 796, 798; *MEW* 5: 82, 94, 104–05, 202, 293–99, 397; 6: 146–50, 286, 431–33, 506; *MEGA* 3/11: 161; Sperber, *Rhineland Radicals*, 268–69.

46 Jonathan Sperber, "'The Persecutor of Evil' in the German Revolution of 1848–1849," in Jeremy D. Popkin, ed., *Media and Revolution: Comparative Perspectives* (Lexington: University Press of Kentucky, 1995), 98–114.

47 *MEW* 5: 112–53; *RhBA* 2/2: 345; Seyppel, *Die Demokratische Gesellschaft*, 129–31; Sperber, *Rhineland Radicals*, 301–02.

48 *BdK* 1: 1122.

49 *Freiheit Arbeit* (Cologne), vol. 1, no. 2, January 18, 1849; cf. Sperber, *Rhineland Radicals*, 229.

50 *MEGA* 3/3: 608; Sperber, *Rhineland Radicals*, 228–31.

51 Seyppel, *Die Demokratische Gesellschaft*, 216–38; Sperber, *Rhineland Radicals*, 314–21.

52 *MEGA* 3/2: 163–65, 169–70, 476, 488, 494–95, 500–01, 516, 527–29; François Melis, "Friedrich Engels' Wanderung durch Frankreich und die Schweiz im Herbst 1848: Neue Erkenntnisse und Hypothesen," *MEGA Studien* 2 (1995): 61–92; Silberner, *Moses Hess*, 296–97; Liebknecht, *Karl Marx zum Gedächtniß*, 110.

53 E.g., *MEGA* 3/2: 168.

54 Ibid., 3/3: 591; Sperber, *Rhineland Radicals*, 322–36.

55 *MEW* 6: 240–57; Dowe, *Aktion und Organisation*, 229; Sperber, *Rhineland Radicals*, 264–65.

56 *MEGA* 3/3: 17, 277.

57 Ibid., 3/2: 164; 3/3: 10–11, 19–22, 187–90; François Melis, *Neue Rheinische Zeitung Organ der Demokratie: Edition unbekannter Nummern, Flugblätter, Druckvarianten und Separatdrucke* (Munich: K. G. Saur, 2000), 35–36; Bauer, *Konfidentenberichte*, 28.

58 Cited in Schmidt, *Andreas Gottschalk*, 122; cf. *MEGA* 3/3: 255.

59 *MEW* 6: 397–423; Sperber, *Rhineland Radicals*, 351–54, 360–64.

60 Ibid., 378–79.

61 Dowe, *Aktion und Organisation*, 229–30.

62 *MEW* 6: 503–6, 519; Melis, *Neue Rheinische Zeitung*, 11, 36–38.

7: THE EXILE

1 *MEGA* 1/10: 37–118.

2 Ibid., 3/3: 30; 3/10: 1136; Sperber, *Rhineland Radicals*, 458; see also Marx's defensive remarks in 1850, quoted in Carl Vogt, *Mein Prozess gegen die Allgemeine Zeitung* (Geneva: Selbstverlag des Verfassers, 1859), 141–56.

3 *MEGA* 3/3: 23, 52, 361–62, 804; *MEW* 6: 523.

4 *MEGA* 3/3: 26, 30, 32, 36, 485, 727.

5 Sperber, *Rhineland Radicals*, 421–23, 457–58, 465; *MEGA* 1/10: 5.

6 Sperber, *Rhineland Radicals*, 410–11; *MEW* 6: 527–28; *MEGA* 3/3: 25.

7 *MEGA* 3/3: 27–29, 36–37, 39, 43, 361, 725, 727.

8 Ibid., 3/3: 36–37, 40, 44, 372, 817–18, 823; Herbert Reiter, *Politisches Asyl im 19. Jahrhundert* (Berlin: Duncker & Humbolt, 1992), 201–06.

9 *MEGA* 3/3: 44, 48, 628–29, 725, 728, 823; Reiter, *Politisches Asyl*, 216–74.

10 *MEGA* 3/3: 44.

11 Ibid., 3/3: 49, 830; 1/10: 6–12.

12 Ibid., 3/4: 109.

13 Ibid., 1/10: 553–54.

14 Ibid., 1/10: 555–59, 563–65, 569–75; 3/3: 65–66, 76–77, 80, 402–03, 509, 512, 547, 554, 570; 3/5: 36, 97; Lattek, *Revolutionary Refugees*, 50; Bauer, *Konfidentenberichte*, 29.

15 *BdK* 1: 969–70; Lattek, *Revolutionary Refugees*, 46–47.

16 *MEGA* 3/3: 60; *BdK* 2: 11, 81–82, 445; Lattek, *Revolutionary Refugees*, 55–56; *BdK* 2: 614–21.

17 *MEGA* 1/10: 560–61; 3/3: 435, 461.

18 Ibid., 3/3: 439, 491, 517, 557, 686, 707–08; 3/4: 13.

19 Ibid., 3/3: 439, 449, 455, 464, 515, 518, 548, 555, 572.

20 Ibid., 3/3: 491–92, 494–95, 572, 603.

21 Ibid., 3/3: 94, 656, 665, 668, 686; 1/10: 447–48, 990–92.

22 Ibid., 3/3: 75, 415, 496, 477.

23 Ibid., 1/10: 254–63.

24 Lattek, *Revolutionary Refugees*, 56–59; *MEGA* 3/3: 51.

25 *MEGA* 1/10: 119–96, quotes on 140 and 192.

26 Ibid., 1/10: 318–20; for another example of denouncing radical democrats, see ibid., 1/10: 202–04.

27 Christian Jansen, *Einheit, Macht und Freiheit. Die Paulskirchenlinke und die deutsche Politik in der nachrevolutionären Epoche 1849–1867* (Düsseldorf: Droste Verlag, 2000), 172–96; Reiter, *Politisches Asyl*, 274–83.

28 *MEGA* 3/3: 27, 733.

29 Ibid., 3/3: 363, 376, 385, 500–01, 571.

30 Ibid., 3/3: 48.

31 Ibid., 3/3: 735.

32 Ibid., 3/4: 143; 3/8: 45; Rosemary Ashton, *Little Germany: Exile and Asylum in Victorian England* (Oxford: Oxford University Press, 1986), 16–24.

33 *MEGA* 3/3: 82, 85, 538–39, 563, 733–35.

34 Ibid., 3/4: 355, 444, 473, 509; 3/5: 184, 305, 472; 3/6: 12.

35 Ibid., 3/3: 372, 374–78; 3/6: 197.

36 Ibid., 3/3: 87–88, 555, 563, 567, 588, 614, 647, 653; 3/4: 83–84, 158, 290; 3/5: 163; 3/6: 16.

37 Ibid., 3/4: 5, 84, 170; 3/5: 163; 3/6: 11–12, 50, 452, 554.

38 Ibid., 3/5: 411.

39 Ibid., 3/6: 11–12.

40 Ibid., 3/4: 555.

41 Ibid., 3/4: 520.

42 Ibid., 3/3: 417.

43 Stanley Nadel, *Little Germany: Ethnicity, Religion, and Class in New York City, 1845–80* (Urbana: University of Illinois Press, 1990); Bruce Levine, *The Spirit of 1848: German Immigrants, Labor Conflict and the Coming of the Civil War* (Urbana: University of Illinois Press, 1992).

44 *MEGA* 3/4: 161, 167–68, 204–05, 276, 415; 3/5: 143, 145–46, 182, 237, 411–12, 468; 3/6: 5, 12, 566. On this very interesting individual, see http://www.adolf-cluss.org/, accessed 12/1/11. *MEGA* 3/5: 486–567 contains correspondence of Cluss giving a good impression of his political abilities and activities.

45 *MEGA* 3/3: 617–18. Just fragments of evidence remain in Marx's and Engels's papers concerning their plans to move to New York: ibid., 3/3: 82, 87, 513–14, 564, 582, 624, 628, 660; 3/4: 103; also a contemporary report, reprinted in Vogt, *Mein Prozess*, 141–56.

46 *MEGA* 3/3: 621–23; Westphalen, "Kurze Umrisse," 214–15.

47 *MEGA* 3/3: 105, 108, 702; 3/4: 141, 291–93, 312–13, 396–71, 432, 464; 3/5: 123–24; Hunt, *Marx's General*, 183, 187–88.

48 *MEGA* 3/3: 99.

49 For just a few initial examples of what would become a years-long practice, see ibid., 3/3: 93, 95; 3/4: 5, 31, 33, 39, 96, 99, 109, 111, 141, 151, 161, 170, 199, 234; 3/5: 40, 43, 45, 65, 68, 78, 92, 111, 125–27.

50 Ibid., 3/3: 91–92; Westphalen, "Kurze Umrisse," 215.

51 *MEGA* 3/5: 89, 92; Westphalen, "Kurze Umrisse," 217.

52 *MEGA* 3/5: 96.

53 Wheen, *Karl Marx*, 171–76; Heinrich Gemkow and Rolf Hecker, "Unbekannte Dokumente über Marx' Sohn Frederick Demuth," *Beiträge zur Geschichte der Arbeiterbewegung* 43 (1994): 43–59.

54 *MEGA* 3/3: 57, 445.

55 Lattek, *Revolutionary Refugees*, 49–54; Jansen, *Einheit, Macht und Freiheit*, 185–93.

56 Quoted in Christian Jansen, ed., *Nach der Revolution 1848/49: Verfolgung, Realpolitik Nationsbildung: Politische Briefe deutscher Liberaler und Demokraten 1849–1861* (Düsseldorf: Droste Verlag, 2004), 42.

57 *BdK* 2: 253–56; Lattek, *Revolutionary Refugees*, 67–82, 110.

58 *MEGA* 3/4: 17; see also ibid., 3/3: 566, 1306; 3/4: 140; 3/6: 58; Bauer, *Konfidentenberichte*, 85.

59 *MEGA* 1/10: 578.

60 Ibid., 3/3: 740; Karl Bittel, ed., *Der Kommunistenprozeß zu Köln 1852 im Spiegel der zeitgenössischen Presse* (East Berlin: Rütten & Loening, 1955), 111–12.

61 *MEGA* 3/5: 157, 190; 3/6: 37–38, 74–75; 3/6: 107; Bauer, *Konfdentenberichte*, 37.

62 Jansen, ed., *Nach der Revolution*, 42; Carl Wermuth and Wilhelm Stieber, *Die Communisten-Verschwörungen des neunzehnten Jahrhunderts*, 2 vols. in 1 (Hildesheim: Georg Olms, 1969), 1: 267.

63 *MEGA* 3/3: 669; 3/4: 76–77, 302.

64 Ibid., 1/10: 491–92; 3/3: 77–78, 582; 3/4: 84, 307; 3/5: 166; 3/6: 186; and esp. 1/10: 491–92; Jansen, ed., *Nach der Revolution*, 205.

65 *MEGA* 3/3: 650; 3/4: 147–49, 187, 706; 3/5: 191; 3/6: 37–38, 110.

66 Ibid., 3/4: 138–39; similarly, 3/5: 191; 3/6: 74–75.

67 Ibid., 3/3: 92, 96, 641–43, 878; 3/4: 46–50, 57–58, 63, 234, 240–41, 555; 3/5: 209; Lattek, *Revolutionary Refugees*, 73–74, 111, 126–27.

68 *MEGA* 3/4: 14–16, 31, 66–67; 3/5: 38–39, 60–61, 68, 82, 85, 106, 111, 115–16, 159–60, 176–75, 178–79, 188, 394, 401, 405–06, 409, 473, 773; 3/6: 37–38; 1/11: 221–311.

69 Ibid., 3/4: 164.

70 Jansen, *Einheit, Macht und Freiheit*, 189–90; Lattek, *Revolutionary Refugees*, 83–109; *MEGA* 3/6: 554.

71 *MEGA* 3/5: 96, 135–36; *BdK* 2: 255; Lattek, *Revolutionar Refugees*, 70.

72 *MEGA* 3/5: 127, 129–30, 135–36, 140, 151, 171; Westphalen, "Kurze Umrisse," 212. In "The Great Men of Exile," Marx only alluded in literary form to Willich's sexual escapades: *MEGA* 1/10: 300–01.

73 Lattek, *Revolutionary Refugees*, 69–82; Bauer, *Konfidentenberichte*, 27, 29–30, 32.

74 Vogt, *Mein Prozess*, 141–56; excerpts from the letter are reprinted in *BdK*, vol. 2.

75 Vogt, *Mein Prozess*, 141–56; cf. *MEGA* 3/4: 37, 41–43.

76 Jansen, ed., *Nach der Revolution*, 88, 205, 241.

77 *MEW* 6: 148–50; *MEGA* 1/10: 302–03.

78 *MEGA* 1/10: 467; 3/4: 157–58, 213, 235; 3/5: 6, 93, 110, 183, 185–86; 3/6: 27.

79 Ibid., 3/3: 584; 3/5: 285. On the question of spies and government agents, particularly illuminating are Jürgen Herres, "Der Kölner Kommunistenprozess von 1852," *Geschichte in Köln* 50 (2003): 133–55, and Ingrid Donner, "Der Anteil von Karl Marx und Friedrich Engels an der Verteidigung der Kölner Kommunistenprozeße 1852," *Marx-Engels-Jahrbuch* 4 (1981): 306–44; also Ernst Hanisch, *Karl Marx und die*

Berichte der österreichischen Geheimpolizei (Trier: Karl-Marx-Haus, 1976); and Lattek, *Revolutionary Refugees*, 154–56.

80 *MEGA* 3/4: 247, 255–58, 355, 473, 490, 502–03, 782; 3/5: 440–41; 3/6: 224, 266.

81 Ibid., 3/5: 38, 307, 342, 382, 390, 395, 411–12, 470–71; 3/6: 269, 272, 277.

82 Ibid., 3/5: 191, 342, 798; 3/6: 37–38, 288, 303, 390–91, 411–12, 438, 474, 496.

83 Ibid., 3/6: 41, 48, 68, 81, 83, 98–99, 111–13, 288, 294, 303, 324–27, 338.

84 Hanisch, *Karl Marx*, 18–30; Vogt, *Mein Prozess*, v–viii.

85 *MEGA* 3/3: 571, 586, 646, 650, 672.

86 Ibid., 3/3: 94, 502–04, 533–35; 3/4: 85, 104, 117, 121, 300–01, 322, 326, 334–35, 344, 368, 373, 375, 385; 3/6: 106; Herres, "Kölner Kommunistenprozess," 142; Seyppel, *Die demokratische Gesellschaft in Köln*, 284.

87 On the Cologne Communist Trial, see the articles by Donner and esp. Herres, in note 79; additional details in Bauer, *Konfidentenberichte*, 76–97.

88 *MEGA* 3/2: 178, 548–49.

89 Ibid., 3/4: 128, 138–39; 3/5: 85; 3/6: 553; 3/7: 31.

90 Ibid., 3/6: 259–60; 3/7: 217; Bittel, *Der Kommunistenprozeß*, 53, 55, 63, 68, 112, 153–56, 158, 224, 248–49.

91 Bittel, *Der Kommunistenprozeß*, 92–103, 119–26, 167–70, 182–88.

92 Ibid., 103 (quote), also 59–62, 67–69, 81–82, 84–90, 160, 179, 188–200, 239–41, 243, 247–48, 255–59, 284–85; *MEGA* 3/4: 146.

93 Bittel, *Der Kommunistenprozeß*, 73–80, 137, 143, 145, 212–34, 291–94; *MEGA* 3/6: 46, 83, 106, 555.

94 *MEGA* 3/6: 352, also 52–54, 56–58, 61, 67–68, 70, 557; Bittel, *Der Kommunistenprozeß*, 119–26, 135–36, 167–70.

95 *MEGA* 3/6: 85, 286, 299–300; Bittel, *Der Kommunistenprozeß*, 135–36; Lattek, *Revolutionary Refugees*, 155–56; Bauer *Confidentenberichte*, 97.

96 *MEGA* 3/6: 66, also 86.

97 Ibid., 1/11: 363–422; 976; 3/6: 51, 55, 78, 88, 132–33, 407, 412–13; Donner, "Der Anteil von Marx und Engels," 318–19; Lattek, *Revolutionary Refugees*, 156–58.

98 *MEGA* 3/4: 259–60, 263–74, 276; 3/5: 56–59, 251–52, 255–58; 1/11: 686–90.

99 Text in ibid., 1/11: 96–189. Two literary analyses are Zvi Tauber, "Representations of Tragedy and Farce in History on Marx's *The Eighteenth Brumaire of Louis Bonaparte*," *Tel Aviver Jahrbuch für deutsche Geschichte* 29 (2000): 127–46; and Martin Harries, "*Homo Alludens*: Marx's Eighteenth Brumaire," *New German Critique* 66 (1995): 35–64.

100 *MEGA* 1/11: 101.

101 Ibid., 1/11: 178; also 110, 179; on the literary allusion, Harries, "*Homo alludens*," 53–55.

102 *MEGA* 1/1: 128.

103 Claude Lévi-Strauss, *Tristes Tropiques*, trans. John and Doreen Weightman (London: Jonathan Cape, 1973), 57.

104 *MEGA* 1/11: 690–96; 3/5: 409, 432; 3/6: 241.

8: THE OBSERVER

1 *MEGA* 3/7: 32, see also 154–55; Lattek, *Revolutionary Refugees*, 159–82.

2 *MEGA* 3/8: 215, similarly, 223.

3 Ibid., 3/4: 41–43; 3/6: 138, 154.

4 Ibid., 3/8: 90, 99, 109, 115, 123, 128–31.

5 Ibid., 3/7: 189, also 182–88, 197, 205; Liebknecht, *Karl Marx zum Gedächtniß*, 74–75. My thanks to Dr. Brian Johnson, of Boone Hospital Center, for his retrospective diagnoses.

6 *MEGA* 3/7: 189; also 197; 3/8: 211; Liebknecht, *Karl Marx zum Gedächtniß*, 74.

7 *MEGA* 3/7: 166, 178, 182; 3/8: 107; 3/9: 122, 126, 174; Liebknecht, *Karl Marx zum Gedächtniß*, 75; Chushichi Tsuzuki, *The Life of Eleanor Marx, 1855–1898: A Socialist Tragedy* (Oxford: Clarendon Press, 1967), 9–13.

8 *MEGA* 3/3: 591; 3/4: 170, 183, 185; 1/11: 3–85.

9 Ibid., 3/5: 163–64; 3/6:11, 118, 133–34, 180; 3/7: 13, 24–25, 55, 300; 3/8: 109; Westphalen, "Kurze Umrisse," 222; Adam Tuchinsky, *Horace Greeley's* New-York Tribune: *Civil War-Era Socialism and the Crisis of Free Labor* (Ithaca & London: Cornell University Press, 2009), 104–07, and passim. The articles for the *New York Tribune* are republished in *MEGA* 1/11–14, and *MECW* 14–18.

10 *MEGA* 3/7: 54, 162–64, 209, 346, 472, 496, 526; 3/8: 33, 71, 262, 272, 596–97; 1/12: 393–442; 1/13: 18–26. The articles for the *New Oder News* are in *MEGA* 1/14.

11 *MEGA* 3/7: 195, 198; 1/13: 368; 1/14: 444–45, 529; 1/25: 408.

12 Ibid., 3/6: 103, 129, 521; 3/7: 5, 26, 31, 62, 91, 98, 119, 452, 521; 3/8: 35, 323–24.

13 Ibid., 3/7: 54.

14 Ibid., 3/7: 182; Liebknecht, *Karl Marx zum Gedächtniß*, 70–73.

15 *MEGA* 3/8: 45, 48, 53, 65; 3/9: 129; 3/10: 181; Westfalen, "Kurze Umrisse," 221–22; Bauer, *Konfidentenberichte*, 224.

16 *MEGA* 3/8: 65–67, 72, 74–75, 88, 90, 127; 3/9: 60–62, 115, 136, 169, 221; 3/9: 44, 48.

17 McLellan, *Karl Marx*, 242–44; Wheen, *Karl Marx*, 180–85.

18 *MEGA* 3/6: 203, 207–08; 3/7: 5, 13, 31, 62, 138, 262, 276, 285; 3/8: 285; 3/10: 289.

19 Ibid., 3/7: 219, 525; 3/8: 103–05, 118–19, 148–49, 192–93, 211, 496; 3/8: 193; 3/9: 8, 11–12, 15, 25, 40, 531.

20 Ibid., 3/6: 203; 3/7: 69, 119–20, 126–28, 133, 138, 156, 158, 201–02, 209, 216, 223, 817–18; 3/8: 107, 323–24; 3/9: 53, 122, 129–30, 134; 3/9: 186–92, 196–200, 220, 224, 235, 386.

21 Ibid., 3/7: 138; 3/8: 107; Francis Sheppard, *London 1800–1870: The Infernal Wen* (Berkeley & Los Angeles: University of California Press, 1971), 211, 217–18, 234–35.

22 *MEGA* 3/9: 188–89.

23 Ibid., 3/7: 55, 300; 3/8: 281.

24 Ibid., 37: 58, 62; more generally, Olive Anderson, *A Liberal State at War: English Politics and Economics During the Crimean War* (London: Macmillan, 1967), 1–28.

25 Hans-Henning Hahn, *Aussenpolitik in der Emigration: die Exildiplomatie Adam Jerzy Czartoryskis 1830–1840* (Munich: Oldenbourg Verlag, 1978), esp. 191–201, 207–17.

26 *MEGA* 3/3: 35, 40, 43, 51–52.

27 Ibid., 1/12: 83, 181–84, 229–30, 235, 243–44, 549–56; 1/13: 14, 56–57, 84–85, 89–90, 292, 268–99, 370–74, 398, 532; 1/14: 61–65, 88–93, 117, 194, 243–45, 268–71, 296–301, 411–15, 425–26, 452, 455–59, 546–49, 567; 3/6: 133.

28 Ibid., 1/12: 336, also 358–59, 468; 1/13: 35–36, 41–42.

29 Anderson, *A Liberal State at War*, 33–93.

30 *MEGA* 1/12: 357–86, 564–65; 1/13: 16, 184–85; 1/14: 652; 3/7: 44, 53, 85, 242; 3/8: 85–86; 3/9: 218–19; 3/11: 19–20, 24; *MEW* 30: 371.

31 *MECW* 15: 27–96; also *MEGA* 1/14: 785–88.

32 Anderson, *A Liberal State at War*, 139–52; "David Urquhart," *Dictionary of National Biography*; Miles Taylor, "The Old Radicalism and the New: David Urquhart and the Politics of Opposition, 1832–1867," in Eugenio Biagini and Alastair J. Reid, eds., *Currents of Radicalism: Popular Radicalism, Organised Labour and Party Politics in Britain, 1850–1914* (Cambridge: Cambridge University Press, 1991), 23–43.

33 *MEGA* 3/6: 130–31; 3/7: 56, 65, 94, 110, 298, 390, 526; 3/8: 6, 19, 36–37, 39, 43, 54–55, 66, 107, 523, 596–97; 3/9: 94; 3/11: 18; Liebknecht, *Karl Marx zum Gedächtniß*, 56–57; Bauer, *Konfidentenberichte*, 164–65.

34 *MEGA* 1/12: 632–33, 1165.

35 Ibid., 1/12: 80.

36 Ibid., 1/13: 90–91, 121–22; Jansen, *Einheit, Macht und Freiheit*, 260–65; Natascha Doll, *Recht, Politik und "Realpolitik" bei August Ludwig von Rochau (1810–1873)* (Frankfurt-am-Main: Vittorio Klostermann, 2005).

37 Jonathan Parry, *The Politics of Patriotism: English Liberalism, National Identity and Europe, 1830–1886* (Cambridge: Cambridge University Press, 2006), 145–57, 195–205, 213–19; K. Theodore Hoppen, *The Mid-Victorian Generation 1846–1886* (Oxford: Oxford University Press, 1998), 198; David Brown, *Palmerston: A Biography* (London: Yale University Press, 2010).

38 *MEGA* 3/7: 372–73; also 331.

39 Ibid., 1/12: 68; 1/13: 81, 359; 1/14: 330–31, 367.

40 Ibid., 1/12: 358–59. More generally, for Marx's opinions on the Whigs and his articles on Palmerston and Russell, 1/12: 357–85; 1/14: 575–602; also 3/6: 133–34.

41 Ibid., 3/7: 44.

42 Ibid., 3/9: 63, 121–25.

43 Ibid., 3/6: 174–76, 179–84; Suzanne Marchand, *German Orientalism in the Age of Empire: Religion, Race, and Scholarship* (New York: Cambridge University Press, 2009).

44 *MEGA* 3/6: 189, 198–200; Bipan Chandra, "Karl Marx, His Theories of Asian Societies and Colonial Rule," *Review* 5 (1981): 13–91.

45 See esp. *MEGA* 1/12: 166, 169–73, 248–53.

46 Ricardo King Sang Mak, *The Future of the Non-Western World in the Social Sciences of Nineteenth Century England* (Frankfurt-am-Main: Peter Lang, 1999), 87–173; cf. also Andrew Zimmermann, *Anthropology and Antihumanism in Imperial Germany* (Chicago: University of Chicago Press, 2001), 38–61.

47 Salahuddin Malik, *1857: War of Independence or Clash of Civilizations? British Public Reactions* (Karachi: Oxford University Press, 2008); *MECW* 15: 329, 363.

48 *MECW* 15: 336–41, 349–56; also *MEGA* 1/12: 179, 217–19; *MECW* 15: 575–79, 587.

49 Philip Harling, *The Waning of "Old Corruption": The Politics of Economical Reform in Britain, 1779–1846* (Oxford: Clarendon Press, 1996); Parry, *Politics of Patriotism*, 184–91.

50 *MEGA* 1/12: 231; *MECW* 15: 309–13, 546–49.

51 *MEGA* 3/8: 458.

52 *MECW* 15: 177–80, 293–96. Marx was aware of the religious contours of the Persian monarchy and showed a detailed knowledge of the difference between Sunni and Shiite Islam.

53 Ibid., 15: 123–29.

54 Ibid., 15: 219–25, 232–35; 16: 13–16, 50, 86; *MEGA* 3/9: 218–19.

55 *MEGA* 3/9: 218–19.

56 Ibid., 1/12: 151–53, 332, 337–39, 344, 445–47, 493–94; 1/14: 37–41, 166–69, 262–63; 3/6: 125, 151, 153–54; 3/7: 18–19, 34–35; 3/8: 8–9, 58–61, 64; Liebknecht, *Karl Marx zum Gedächtnis*, 31.

57 *MEGA* 3/8: 211–12.

58 Ibid., 3/8: 13, 53, 61, 210–11, 221, 223–24; 3/9: 73, 77, 104–07.

59 Ibid., 3/8: 197, 3/9: 65, also 148.

60 *MECW* 15: 109–16, 130–38, 301–04, 400–12; *MEW*: 30: 639.

61 *MEGA* 1/12: 153; 3/8: 48–49, 115, 210; *MECW* 14: 657; 15:8–18, 289–92, 357–59, 499–503.

62 *MEGA* 3/8: 115; *MECW* 15: 19–24, 133, 270–77.

63 *MEGA* 3/8: 217–18; *MECW* 15: 413–18.

64 *MEGA* 3/8: 48–50, 53, 202–04, 229–30; *MECW* 15: 117–29, 379, 387–90.

65 *MEGA* 3/8: 184, 191, 193, 207; also 99, 132, 161, 194–95, 198–99, 210, 216–17, 219–20; 3/9:75.

66 Ibid., 3/9: 155, 221–22, 255–56; *MECW* 16: 54–58, 65–81, 96–109, 115–28.

67 *MEGA* 3/8: 235; 3/9: 9–10, 14, 77, 81, 215–16, 218–19; *MECW* 15: 560–65.

9: THE ACTIVIST

1 Bamberger and Venedey cited in Jansen, *Einheit, Macht und Freiheit*, 304–05; for the debate more generally, see ibid., 288–315, and Harald Biermann, *Ideologie statt Realpolitik: Kleindeutsche Liberale und auswärtige Politik vor der Reichsgründung* (Düsseldorf: Droste Verlag, 2006), 78–118.

2 *MEW* 13: 225–68; *MEGA* 3/9: 322–24.

3 *MEGA* 3/9: 275, 298–99, 332, 341, 427–28; 3/10: 102–03.

4 Ibid., 3/11: 19–20.

5 Ibid., 3/9: 427–28, 430.

6 Lattek, *Revolutionary Refugees*, 192–207; *MEW* 13: 376–79, 384–97, 402–04, 410–16, 428–39, 450–67; *MEGA* 3/9: 428–32, 435–37, 469, 479–80, 482–83, 504–06, 509–10, 513–15, 520–21, 537, 539–47; 3/10: 289; Bauer, *Konfidentenberichte*, 507–08, 519–20.

7 Lattek, *Revolutionary Refugees*, 203; *MEGA* 3/10: 74, 176–77, 325; *MEW* 31: 412; 32: 92.

8 Jansen, *Einheit, Macht und Freiheit*, 294–98.

9 Lattek, *Revolutionary Refugees*, 207–14.

10 *MEGA* 3/9: 481; 3/10: 6–8, 36–38, 46, 49, 56–57, 66, 68, 73–77, 82–83, 87, 96–98, 109–11, 113, 115, 117–19, 130–31, 133–34, 164, 175–79, 178, 186–84, 193–94, 218, 220, 224, 231–35, 237–38, 244–48, 276–78, 316, 319–21, 324–30, 744, 815; 3/11: 141, 251; Vogt, *Mein Prozess*, esp. 138–41; Bauer, *Konfidentenberichte*, 543–44.

11 *MEGA* 3/10: 195–97, 199–200, 203–08, 211–17, 231–33, 252–58, 274–75, 280–96, 314–15, 337–48, 411, 457–58, 462–63, 472, 474, 479, 484–88, 505–07; 3/11: 730–38.

12 McLellan, *Karl Marx*, 289; Wheen, *Karl Marx*, 238.

13 *MEGA* 3/10: 116, 194, 383.

14 Ibid., 3/10: 96.

15 Ibid., 3/10: 175–76, 180–81, 188.

16 Ibid., 3/10: 370, 509–10, 561; 3/11: 135–36, 208.

17 Ibid., 3/11: 112–13, 245.

18 Ibid., 1/18: 58–135; 3/10: 247.

19 Ibid., 1/18: 157–2013; 1/11: 180, 188, 196, 218.

20 Jansen, *Einheit, Macht und Freiheit*, 141–45; *MEGA* 3/10: 457–58; 3/11: 69, 218, 270–71, 361, 373, 1034, 1205–07; *MEW* 31: 668; 33: 203–06, 213–14, 220–21; Bauer, *Konfidentenberichte*, 586–87.

21 *MEGA* 3/10: 214–17, 245–48, 350–58, 439–40, 490–91; 3/11: 53, 67, 84, 100, 103; 3/13: 110.

22 Ibid., 3/10: 180–81, 187.

23 Ibid., 3/10: 115, 170; 3/11: 293, 301, 310–12, 315, 319–20, 322, 902–03.

24 Christopher Clark, *Iron Kingdom: The Rise and Downfall of Prussia, 1600–1947* (Cambridge, MA: Harvard University Press, 2006), 513–17; *MEGA* 3/10: 316–17, 379–80; 3/11: 156, 161, 380; Melis, "Heinrich Bürgers."

25 *MEGA* 3/7: 422; the best biography of this controversial figure is Shlomo Na'amann's *Lassalle* (Hanover: Verlag für Literatur & Zeitgeschehen, 1970).

26 *MEGA* 3/7: 158–59; 3/8: 514; 3/9: 56–58, 96, 113, 130, 227, 322–23, 331, 349–50, 359–60, 369–70, 373, 375, 379–80, 468; 3/10: 43, 76–77, 93, 99, 189, 166, 179–80, 184, 192, 211; 3/11: 485–86, 492–93, 581, 1221.

27 Ibid., 3/3: 377, 404–07, 693; 3/5: 270, 421.

28 Ferdinand Lassalle, "Der italienische Krieg und die Aufgabe Preussens," in *Fer-*

∂inan∂ Laßalle Gesammelte Re∂en un∂ Schriften, ed. Eduard Bernstein, 12 vols. (Berlin: Paul Cassirer, 1919–20): 1: 23–112; MEGA 3/9: 291, 298–99, 411–16, 422–23, 467–68, 481, 484–89; 3/10: 42–43, 79–80, 102–03, 167–70, 178, 191–92, 298–301, 369–70, 396–98, 570, 573; 3/11: 19–20, 148–51, 167–70.

29 MEGA 3/9: 467–68, 485–87.

30 Ibid., 3/3: 465, 535; 3/4: 356, 364, 404–05; 3/6: 359–60, 397; 3/7: 244–45, 247; 3/8: 5, 553–54; 3/10: 302–09.

31 Ibid., and 3/3: 34.

32 Ibid., 3/10: 372; 3/11: 324.

33 For anti-Semitic epithets: ibid., 3/9: 166, 324–25, 329–30, 334, 507; 3/10: 180, 206, 231–32; 3/11: 23, 46, 64, 67–68, 158–59, 347–48, 615–16, 1074; MEW 30: 252; for Marx's view of Lassalle's personality in terms of anti-Semitic stereotypes, see MEGA 3/11: 460–61.

34 MEGA 3/11: 223, 225, 227, 229–31, 233, 236–37, 248–50, 259–60, 266, 270–71, 295.

35 Ibid., 3/11: 334, 360, 417, 463.

36 Ibid., 3/11: 379, 389–90, 402–04, 407, 439–40, 458–61, 463, 469–71.

37 Ibid., 3/9: 219, 229, 246; 3/11: 236–37, 419, 458–61, 463; Schönke, Karl un∂ Heinrich Marx, 759–68, 773–78, 784–85.

38 MEGA 3/11: 422–23, 457, 480.

39 Ibid., 3/11: 400–01, 410–13, 417, 426–32, 434, 437–78, 446, 499, 502–03, 512, 515–17, 539.

40 Ibid., 3/11: 460–61, 468.

41 MEW 30: 249, 252, 257–59, 269–70; MEGA 3/13: 565; Westphalen, "Kurze Umrisse," in Mohr un∂ General, 233–34; Eduard Bernstein, "Erinnerungen an Karl Marx und Friedrich Engels," in ibid., 503–04; Gemkow and Hecker, "Unbekannte Dokumente," 58.

42 MEGA 3/11: 572–73, 581–83, 588, 598; MEW 30: 223–24, 227, 230, 275, 263, 621, 639–41.

43 MEW 30: 249.

44 Ibid., 30: 214, 216, 226, 227, 242, 247, 257, 269–70, 316, 656.

45 Gielkens, Marx un∂ seine nie∂erlän∂ischen Verwan∂ten, 75–76, 178–79; MEW 30: 287, 639–41.

46 MEW 30: 218, 260–61, 272–73, 309–19.

47 Ibid., 30: 376, 380–81, 390, 394–98, 417, 419, 643–44; Wheen, Karl Marx, 266; Gielkens, Marx un∂ seine nie∂erlän∂ischen Verwan∂ten, 62; Monz, Karl Marx, 285–91.

48 MEW 30: 691–94.

49 Ibid., 30: 382, 386; 31: 174, 176, 178, 182–83, 186; MEGA 3/7: 108; 3/13: 54, 56, 80, 305, 470; MEW 31: 176, 184–85, 203, 212–13, 514, 589–90, 595–96; 32: 5, 21–22, 42, 228–29, 390–91, 426, 705–06; S. Shuster, "The Nature and Consequence of Karl Marx's Skin Disease," British Journal of Dermatology 158 (2008): 1–3; http://www.mayoclinic.com/health/hidradenitis-suppurativa/DS00818, accessed 9/28/10; James C. Whorton, The Arsenic Century: How Victorian Britain Was Poisoned at Home,

Work and Play (Oxford: Oxford University Press, 2010), 229–61. My thanks to Dr. Lindall Perry, of Boone Hospital Center, for his dermatological expertise.

50 *MEW* 30: 254–59, 271, 284, 287, 291–92, 294, 298, 300, 354, 361–62, 429–30; *MEGA* 3/13: 432.

51 *MEW* 30: 324–29, 337–38, 340, 371–72; Karl Marx, *Manuskripte über die Polnische Frage (1863–1864)*, ed. Werner Conze and Dieter Hertz-Eichenrode ('S-Gravenhage: Mouton & Co., 1961), 93. The relevant volume of the *MEGA* for this year has not yet been published. The Institute of Marxism-Leninism in East Berlin was planning, in 1980, to print the manuscript as a supplement to its edition of Marx's and Engels's works, but the East German government could not tolerate the publication of an essay by the founder of communism attacking Russia for suppressing a Polish revolution when the government of the USSR was pressing for the suppression of Solidarity in communist Poland.

52 *MEW* 30: 289, 30, 333, 347–78, 353–54, 374–75, 384–87, 408, 421–23, 649–51; Clark, *Iron Kingdom*, 523–31.

53 *MEW* 30: 274–78, 345, 347–78, 351, 356–58, 360, 368–69, 375, 377, 402, 407, 432–33, 630–37.

54 Ibid., 30: 427–29, 432–33; *MEGA* 3/13: 3–4, 7–8, 35–36; more broadly, 3/13: 3–256.

55 *MEGA* 3/11: 464, 500, 508, 554–55, 570, 593–96; 3/13: 4, 7, 41–44.

56 Besides the sources cited in the previous note, see Henryk Katz, *The Emancipation of Labor: A History of the First International* (Westport, CT: Greenwood Press, 1991), 1–14; Julian P. W. Archer, *The First International in France 1864–1872* (Lanham, MD: University Press of America, 1997), 1–24; and Henry Collins and Chimen Abramsky, *Karl Marx and the British Labour Movement* (London: Macmillan & Co., 1965), 14–55.

57 *MEGA* 3/13: 91.

58 Ibid., and Margot Finn, *After Chartism: Class and Nation in English Radical Politics, 1848–1874* (Cambridge: Cambridge University Press, 1993), 222–23; Archer, *First International in France*, 28; Eugenia Stépanova and Irina Bach, "Le conseil général et son role dans l'association internationale des travilleurs," in *La Première Internationale: L'institution, l'implantation et le rayonnement*, ed. Denise Fauvel-Rouif (Paris: Centrale Nationale de la Recherche Scientifique, 1968), 50–71; *MEGA* 1/20: 14–15; 3/13: 83, 177, 181–84, 239, 268, 598–99.

59 *MEGA* 3/13: 42; *MEW* 31: 228–29.

60 *MEGA* 1/20: 187–88; more elaboration on 224–35.

61 *MEGA* 1/20: 449, 505–06, 508, 511; 3/13: 395–98, 401, 409, 433–34; *MEW* 31: 215–16, 282, 516; 32: 59, 367.

62 *MEGA* 1/20: 143–86; 3/13: 466–67, 482–83.

63 Finn, *After Chartism*, 234–61; *MEGA* 3/13: 430, 611–12; *MEW* 31: 197–98, 232, 242–43, 398–400, 493, 495.

64 Boris Nicolaevsky, "Secret Societies and the First International," in Milorad M. Drachkovitch, ed., *The Revolutionary Internationals, 1864–1943* (Stanford, CA: Stan-

ford University Press, 1966), 36–56; Archer, *First International in France*, 28–35; *MEGA* 1/20: 111–14, 121–25, 302, 304, 306–07; 3/13: 207–08, 279–84, 326–37, 341–44, 388; *MEW* 31: 169, 495–96; 32: 97, 99, 114–15, 130–31, 190, 580–81.

65 *MEGA* 3/13: 326; *MEW* 31: 254, 355–56; 32: 17–18.

66 Marx used the phrase "behind the curtains" several times to describe his activity in the IWMA: *MEW* 31: 232, 530; 32: 540.

67 *MEGA* 3/13: 429, 561; *MEW* 31: 247, 253.

68 *MEGA* 3/13: 510; *MEW* 31: 169, 204–05, 346–47, 524–25, 529–30; 32: 134, 143–44, 147, 342–44, 346–47, 492–93, 558–59.

69 *MEW* 30: 429, 432–33, 673; *MEGA* 3/13: 16, 69, 71, 74–79, 82, 84–86, 124, 127, 265.

70 *MEGA* 3/13: 122, 133–34, 180–83, 187–88, 94–95, 197–200, 232. On the post-Lassallean scene and the German labor movement in the second half of the 1860s, see Thomas Welskopp, *Das Banner der Brüderlichkeit. Die deutsche Sozialdemokratie vom Vormärz bis zum Sozialistengesetz* (Bonn: J. H. W. Dietz Nachfolger, 2000), 38–44.

71 Berlin, *Karl Marx*, 156.

72 *MEW* 32: 608–10; similarly, 30: 335; 31: 521.

73 Quoted in Silberner, *Moses Hess*, 520; similarly, 518–19; *MEGA* 3/13: 167–68, 887–88.

74 *MEGA* 1/20: 60–69; 3/13: 52–54, 56, 58, 64–67, 70, 74, 83, 87, 137, 161–63, 181–85, 203–05, 211, 229, 232, 235–38, 241, 247–50, 254–56, 264.

75 *MEGA* 3/11: 305–07; 3/13: 493, 540–41, 544, 554–55, 589–90, 605, 609, 1158–59; *MEW* 31: 492–94, 498; Roger Morgan, *The German Social Democrats and the First International 1864–1872* (Cambridge: Cambridge University Press, 1965).

76 *MEW* 31: 197–98, 200–04, 206–11, 214–21, 226–24, 230–31, 233–36, 514–45; Biermann, *Ideologie statt Realpolitik*, 202–38; Clark, *Iron Kingdom*, 531–46.

77 *MEGA* 3/13: 565–66; *MEW* 31: 290–91, 294; 33: 228–29.

78 *MEW* 31: 240–43.

79 Ibid., 31: 352, 362, 371–72, 497–98, 563, 565, 573–74; 32: 295, 315–16.

80 Ibid., 31: 240–41, 391, 393, 402, 411–12, 573–74; 32: 12–13, 22–24, 28, 64, 68–69, 151, 161–62, 177–78, 183, 187–88, 278–79, 334–35, 341, 356, 360, 380–81, 493, 503, 543, 548, 581, 726, 743–44.

81 Ibid., 32: 76, 141, 155, 158–59, 161–62, 173, 187–88, 212, 219, 221, 252, 281, 293, 313, 339–41, 386, 541, 546, 568–74, 764–66.

82 Ibid., 32: 80, 219; similarly, 289–90, 331–32, 343, 346, 581.

83 Ibid., 32: 127–28, 160, 164–65, 168–73, 179–80, 270–71, 297, 329, 331–32, 313, 347–49, 620–21, 745, 768–69, 772.

84 Ibid., 32: 367–68, 608–10, 679–80.

85 Ibid., 32: 131–34, 357–58.

86 *MEGA* 3/11: 356–57; *MEW* 31: 167–69, 180, 182, 208, 216, 242, 250, 254–59, 262–64, 277–78, 307, 309–11, 318, 321–23, 337, 355–56, 361, 392–93, 401, 403, 520–21; 32: 37–38, 43, 47–48, 62–63, 105, 114, 116, 118, 124, 136–37, 141, 147–48, 167, 172, 193, 197, 205, 209.

87 *MEW* 30: 419–20, 425; 32: 214–18, 625–28.

88 Ibid., 31: 376, 380, 396, 399–40, 412–13; 32: 205, 207, 209, 378–79, 392–93, 409–10, 449, 542–43, 638, 656, 667–69.

89 Ibid., 31: 392; 32: 454, 700, 703, 712, 716.

90 *MEGA* 3/11: 605; 3/13: 25, 43, 214–15, 388, 430–31; *MEW* 31: 337–39, 594; 32: 190.

91 Wolfgang Eckhardt, "Bakunin und Johann Philipp Becker: Eine andere Prespektive auf den Beginn der Auseinandersetzung zwischen Marx und Bakunin in der Ersten Internationale," *Internationale wissenschaftliche Korrespondenz zur Geschichte der deutschen Arbeiterbewegung* 35 (1999): 66–122.

92 *MEW* 32: 474–75, 482–84, 498, 520–21.

93 Ibid., 32: 503–05, 507, 509, 513, 799.

94 Ibid., 31: 283–84, 298–99, 378; 32: 31, 32, 88, 608–10.

95 *MECW* 43: 563.

96 *MEW* 33: 5, 675, 716; *MEGA* 1/21: 1056–61.

97 *MEW* 33: 8–9, 12, 15–17, 23–24, 30, 35, 39–42, 51–53.

98 Ibid., 33: 49–50; *MEGA* 1/21: 245–49.

99 Geoffrey Wawro, *The Franco-Prussian War: The German Conquest of France in 1870–1871* (Cambridge: Cambridge University Press, 2003); *MEW* 33: 55, 176–79, 203–04.

100 *MEW* 33: 54–58, 61–62, 64–65, 146–48, 153–57, 162–65, 167–68, 176–79, 182–83, 191–92.

101 For this and the text that follows on the Paris Commune and its relations with Marx and the IWMA, see Robert Tombs, *The Paris Commune, 1871* (London & New York: Longman, 1999); Robert Thomas, "Enigmatic Writings: Karl Marx's *The Civil War in France* and the Paris Commune of 1871," *History of Political Thought* 18 (1997): 483–511; and Collins and Abramsky, *Marx and the British Labour Movement*, 185–210.

102 *MEW* 33: 200–01, 205–06, 216–17, 226–30; 35: 160.

103 Ibid., 33: 193–95, 196, 203–04, 238, 244, 252; *MEGA* 1/22: 174–77, 227–72.

104 *MEGA* 1/22: 59; Royden Harrison, ed., *The English Defence of the Commune 1871* (London: Merlin Press, 1971), 150, 229, 250, 277.

105 *MEGA* 3/4: 155–56.

106 Ibid., 1/22: 45–50.

PART III: LEGACY

10: THE THEORIST

1 *MEGA* 3/4: 377.

2 John W. Burrow, *The Crisis of Reason: European Thought, 1848–1914* (New Haven: Yale University Press, 2000), 31–56; Andreas Daum, *Wissenschaftspopularisierung im 19. Jahrhundert*, 2nd ed. (Munich: R. Oldenbourg, 2002), 2–5. For the ideas of the two leading positivists, see J. D. Y. Peel, *Herbert Spencer: The Evolution of a Sociolo-*

gist (New York: Basic Books, 1971), and Arline Standley, *Auguste Comte* (Boston: Twayne Publishers, 1981).

3 *MEGA* 3/7: 224; 3/8: 203.

4 Ibid., 1/20: 4; *MEW* 4: 468–69.

5 A classic in this respect is Jacques Barzun, *Darwin, Marx, Wagner: Critique of a Heritage* (Boston: Little, Brown, 1941).

6 This fascinating correspondence is in *MEGA* 3/4: 308–09, 336, 339–41, 345–46, 361–63, 386, 391–92.

7 On Darwin's work and its impact, see Michael Ruse, *The Darwinian Revolution: Science Red in Tooth and Claw*, 2nd ed. (Chicago: University of Chicago Press, 1999); Thomas Glick, ed., *The Comparative Reception of Darwin* (Austin: University of Texas Press, 1974); Alfred Kelly, *The Descent of Darwin: The Popularization of Darwin in Germany, 1860–1914* (Chapel Hill: University of North Carolina Press, 1981); and Daum, *Wissenschaftspopularisierung*, 300–16.

8 *MEGA* 3/10: 127, 770; 3/11: 270–71, 316; *MEW* 31: 586–87; 32: 229; Liebknecht, *Karl Marx zum Gedächtniß*, 50–51.

9 *MEW* 30: 249.

10 *MECW* 43: 217.

11 *MEGA* 2/8: 55; *MEW* 32: 17–18, 685–86; also 202–03.

12 Wheen, *Karl Marx*, 363–69.

13 *MEW* 32: 206, 229.

14 Ibid., 31: 247–49, 256–57, 259, 530; for more on Trémaux, and a contemporary appreciation of his theories, see http://philsci-archive.pitt.edu/3881/, accessed 10/21/10.

15 *MEW* 31: 403–05; *MEGA* 1/21: 38–40.

16 Daum, *Wissenschaftspopularisierung*, 286–99.

17 *MEW* 32: 538–39, 547; *MEGA* 2/8: 55.

18 *MEGA* 2/2: 100–01.

19 *MEW* 32: 42, 51–52, 650.

20 Ibid., 31: 224, 233–34; 32: 91, 302–03; 33: 162, 228–29; Collins and Abramsky, *Marx and the British Labour Movement* passim.

21 *MEGA* 1/11: 121.

22 *MEW* 39: 206.

23 *MECW* 14: 655–56; *MEW* 32: 670.

24 *MECW* 14: 15: 102; similarly, *MEGA* 1/12: 531.

25 *MEW* 15: 453–54.

26 *MECW* 15: 38, 57–59, 62.

27 *MEW* 32: 596; also *MEGA* 1/12: 26, and Alain Desrosières, *The Politics of Large Numbers: A History of Statistical Reasoning*, trans. Camille Naish (Cambridge, MA: Harvard University Press, 1998), 73–91.

28 *MEW* 32: 552–54.

29 The passage from *Capital* is in *MEGA* 2/15: 792.

30 See George Mosse, *Toward the Final Solution: A History of European Racism* (New York: Harper & Row, 1978).

31 Linzbach, "Die konservative Orientierung Bruno Bauers nach 1848"; Silberner, *Moses Hess*, 404–18.

32 *MECW* 43: 449.

33 Ibid., 42: 316; *MEC* 8: 333; *MEW* 32: 198; *MEGA* 2/8: 301. Marx's American associate, Adolf Cluss, wrote a very interesting letter on this point in 1853—*MEGA* 3/6: 515–19.

34 *MEW* 30: 259.

35 Ibid., 30: 372.

36 Ibid., 30: 289; similarly *MEGA* 3/13: 31–32.

37 *MEGA* 3/13: 483; *MEW* 31: 247–49.

38 *MEGA* 1/14: 789–95; 3/7: 227, 235–39, 241–42, 246, 843; 3/10: 362.

39 For characteristic examples of these opposing arguments, see Norman Levine, *The Tragic Deception: Marx Contra Engels* (Santa Barbara, CA: Clio Books, 1975), and John Stanley and Ernest Zimmerman, "On the Alleged Differences Between Marx and Engels," *Political Studies* 33 (1984): 226–48.

40 *MEGA* 3/1: 244–45.

41 Ibid., 3/9: 182; similarly, *MEW* 31: 303–04.

42 *MEGA* 3/13: 362–64.

43 *MEW* 32: 286–87. Equally painful to read is Engels's dialectical explanation of why mathematicians did not understand calculus: ibid., 35: 23–25.

11: THE ECONOMIST

1 Michael Krätke, "'Hier bricht das Manuskript ab.' (Engels) Hat das *Kapital* einen Schluss? Teil I," *Beiträge zur Marx-Engels-Forschung* n.s. 2001: 7–43; *MEW* 34: 307. The editors' introductions to the volumes of Series 2 of the *MEGA*, containing Marx's economic writings, include detailed discussions of their publishing and manuscript history.

2 See, e.g., Mark Meaney, *Capital as Organic Unity: The Role of Hegel's* Science of Logic *in Marx's* Grundrisse (Dodrecht: Kluwer Academic Publishers, 2002), or Enrique Dussel, *Towards an Unknown Marx: A Commentary on the Manuscripts of 1861–63*, trans. Yolanda Angulo (London & New York: Routledge, 2001).

3 *MEGA* 2/1: 226, 440, 697–99.

4 Ibid., 2/8: 100–01.

5 Ibid., 2/15: 40, 46, 169, 190.

6 Ibid., 2/15: 789, 804–05; for Marx's own explanation of the place of Vol. Three in this work, see *MEW* 32: 70–75.

7 Marx's son-in-law had observed this feature of his thought: Lafargue, "Persönliche Erinnerung," in *Mohr und General*, 332–34.

8 These distinctions are developed in *MEGA* 2/8: 63–237.

9 Ibid., 2/8: 130.

10 David Ricardo, *Principles of Political Economy and Taxation*, ed., Michael P. Fogarty (London: J. M. Dent & Sons, 1960), 5–24; John Stuart Mill, *Principles of Political Economy*, 2 vols. (New York: D. Appleton & Co., 1864), 1: 563. Although Mill is known today as a political philosopher, to his contemporaries he was above all an economist.

11 *MEGA* 2/1: 75, 455–56, 474; 2/2: 138–39; 2/3.3: 1020–28; 2/3.4: 1300–01, 1313–14, 1357–58; 2/8: 506–07; Noel Thompson, *The People's Science: The Popular Political Economy of Exploitation and Crisis 1816–34* (Cambridge: Cambridge University Press, 1984), 87–106.

12 *MEGA* 2/8: 191.

13 Ibid., 2/1: 301, 305; 2/8: 210–21.

14 Ibid., 2/8: 378.

15 Ibid., 2/8: 259–60 (on exploitation and extraction of absolute surplus value); more generally, 237–80.

16 Ibid., 2/8: 280–303.

17 Ibid., 2/8: 318.

18 Ibid., 2/8: 574–75, 585–90.

19 Ibid., 2/8: 438–39, 714–22.

20 Ibid., 2/8: 585–608.

21 Ibid., 2/8: 594–95; 2/15: 245–55.

22 Ibid., 2/8: 606.

23 Ibid., 1/12: 276–77, 491–96; 2/2: 608–11; 3/7: 169; *MECW*: 255–61, 430–34, 521–26, 560–65.

24 *MEGA* 2/8: 529.

25 Ibid., 2/8: 712–13.

26 Ibid., 2/8: 44.

27 *MEW* 32: 70–75: an important brief précis of crucial features of Marx's mature economic thought.

28 *MEGA* 2/1: 622; 2/15: 211.

29 Ricardo, *Principles of Political Economy*, 70–72; Mill, *Principles of Political Economy*, 2: 290–322; for Marx's observations on Smith's and Ricardo's theories, see *MEGA* 2/1: 625–30; 2/3.3: 1049–93; 2/15: 211.

30 *MEGA* 2/15: 210–11.

31 Leon Smolinski, "Karl Marx and Mathematical Economics," *Journal of Political Economy* 81 (1973): 1189–1204, esp. 1196–97. The algebraic manuscripts are in *MEGA* 2/14; the relevant equations on p. 3.

32 *MEGA* 2/8: 527–28, 567; 2/15: 222.

33 Ibid., 2/8: 318; 2/15: 203; Ricardo, *Principles of Political Economy*, 80; David Landes, *The Unbound Prometheus: Technological Change and Industrial Development in Western Europe from 1750 to the Present* (Cambridge: Cambridge University Press, 1969), 255.

34 *MEGA* 2/8: 704; 2/15: 229–35; Ricardo, *Principles of Political Economy*, 77–78.

35 *MEGA* 2/8: 315–18, 501–02.

36 Ibid., 2/15: 258. In the relevant passage, Marx talks about goods priced in marks, the currency of the united German Empire, which was only introduced in 1875, so the passage must be later than that date.

37 Ibid., 2/15: 347–48.

38 For an overview of their work and its connections to Marx's theories, see ibid., 2/15: 875–910; some English-language accounts appear in Ricardo Bellofiore, ed., *Marxian Economics: A Reappraisal. Essays on Volume III of* Capital, 2 vols. (Houndmills, Basingstoke: Macmillan, 1998), esp. the essays in Vol. 2.

39 *MEW* 30: 263–67; *MEGA* 2/15: 155–198.

40 They observe that Marx assumed the transformation from value to price only occurred in the "price of production," the price of the goods for sale, the "outputs." Marx overlooked that the "inputs," the constant and variable capital needed to manufacture those goods, were themselves originally outputs, and needed to be transformed from value terms to price terms. Doing this sort of multiple simultaneous transformation requires the use of multiple linear equations and matrix algebra.

41 *MEW* 30: 264; *MEGA* 2/15: 83; earliest formulation, *MEGA* 2/1: 634–35.

42 *MEGA* 2/15: 856, also 607.

43 Ibid., 2/14: 448–54; 2/15: 606–07, 779–88; *MEW* 32: 403–04.

44 Thomas Malthus, *An Essay on the Principle of Population*, ed. Anthony Flew (London: Penguin Books, 1970), 100; Ricardo, *Principles of Political Economy*, 64–76, 80; Donald Winch, *Riches and Poverty: An Intellectual History of Political Economy in Britain 1750–1834* (Cambridge: Cambridge University Press, 1996), 350–71.

45 *MEGA* 2/8: 578–79.

46 Ibid., 2/8: 590–601.

47 Ibid., 3/4: 106–07, 113–14, 183, 356; *MEW* 31: 178–79, 183; 32: 5–6, 51–52; Anneliese Griese, "Die geologischen, mineralogischen und agronchemischen Manuskripten. Ein Beitrag zu ihrer wissenschaft-historischen Einordnung," *Beiträge zur Marx-Engels-Forschung* n.s. (2006): 31–48. Engel's views on Malthus were similar to those of Marx: see *MEGA* 3/13: 362–64; *MEW* 35: 150–51.

48 *MEGA* 2/15: 752.

49 Ibid., 2/15: 626; similarly, 608, 612–13.

50 Ibid., 2/15: 611–17.

51 Ibid., 2/15: 627–722.

52 Ibid., 2/15: 725–49, esp. 736, 738–39, 742, 748–49.

53 Ibid., 2/15: 744.

54 Ibid., 2/15: 428–29, 595; also *MEW* 34: 53.

55 Ibid., 2/15: 427, more generally, 426–32. These six pages on corporations in the *MEGA* edition of Vol. Three of *Capital* might be compared to the 160 pages on agriculture and ground rent, to gain an idea of their relative importance for Marx.

56 Ibid., 2/1: 196, 484; 2/8: 484; 2/15: 285, 293–95. Marx's Protestant upbringing and education, his left-wing sympathies for Italian national unity, and his atheist world-view all contributed to his dim view of the Catholic Church, and its intellectually and politically deeply conservative leader, Pope Pius IX.

57 [Anon.], "German Literature," *Saturday Review of Politics, Literature, Science and Art*, vol. 24, no. 638, January 18, 1869, 96–98; *MEW* 32: 535.

58 Inge Schliebe and Ludmilla Kalinina, "Rezensionen des Marxchen Werkes, 'Zur Kritik der politischen Okonomie aus dem Jahre 1859," *Beiträge zur Marx-Engels-Forschung* 1 (1977): 103–23; *MEGA* 3/9: 437, 442–43, 471, 474, 477, 491, 495, 522, 532–33, 539; 3/10: 31, 42–43.

59 *MEW* 31: 345–46, 370, 377–80, 384–86, 388–89, 403–05, 563, 567–68, 573–74, 577; 32: 9–10, 41, 91–92, 134–35, 186–87, 459, 536–67, 546, 550–51, 554, 589; *MEGA* 1/21: 3–14, 38–45, 68–74; 2/8: 737–87, 1368–73.

60 *MEW* 31: 290–91, 391, 575; 32: 8, 11–12, 30, 187, 459, 538, 749; Erik Grimmer-Solem, *The Rise of Historical Economics and Social Reform in Germany 1864–1894* (Oxford: Clarendon Press, 2003); Albert Schäffle, *Kapitalismus und Socialismus mit besonderer Rücksicht auf Geschäfts- und Vermögensfragen* (Tübingen: Verlag der H. Laupp'schen Buchhandlung, 1870), 308–61, 413–28; Lenger, *Werner Sombart*, 78–114.

61 Johannes Siemes, "Karl Marx im Urteil des sozialen Rechts," *Der Staat* 11 (1972): 376–88.

62 For Engels's skepticism about nascent social insurances schemes, see *MEW* 32: 369–70.

63 Heinz Kurz, "Marginalism, Classicism and Socialism in German-Speaking Coun-tries, 1871–1932," in Ian Steedman, ed., *Socialism and Marginalism in Economics 1870–1930* (London: Routledge, 1995), 7–86; Eugen von Böhm-Bawerk, *Karl Marx and the Close of His System*, trans. Alice McDonald, ed. Paul Sweezey (New York: H. Wolff, 1949), esp. 86–98; Kowalewski, "Erinnerungen an Karl Marx," in *Mohr und General*, 391.

64 http://delong.typepad.com/sdj/2009/11/yet-another-note-on-adam-smiths-invisible -hand-what-it-is-and-what-it-is-not-by-adam-smith.html, accessed 1/6/10.

12: THE PRIVATE MAN

1 *MEW* 32: 485.

2 *MEGA* 3/5: 157; 3/6: 47, 73; 3/9: 168–69; 3/10: 757; Ute Frevert, *Men of Honour: A Social and Cultural History of the Duel*, trans. Anthony Williams (Cambridge: Polity Press, 1995).

3 *MEGA* 3/9: 75; similarly, 3/7: 120.

4 *MEGA* 3/8: 31–32; Westphalen, "Kurze Umrisse," in *Mohr und General*, 212; Eleanor Marx-Aveling, "Karl Marx Lose Blätter," in ibid., 277–79; Lafargue, "Karl Marx," in ibid., 338–40.

5 *MEW* 35: 247–48; Westphalen, "Kurze Umrisse," in *Mohr und General*, 204–36.

6 *MEGA* 3/2: 27–28, 38; 3/3: 28; 3/4: 24; 3/8: 46–47; 3/11: 422–23; 3/13: 415–16, 430, 445; *MEW* 31: 400.

7 *MEGA* 3/1: 441.

8 See Gunilla Frederike-Budde, *Auf dem Weg ins Bürgerleben: Kindheit und Erziehung in deutsche und englischen Bürgerfamilien 1840–1914* (Göttingen: Vandenhoeck & Ruprecht, 1994), 151–66; Albert Tanner, *Arbeitsame Patrioten—wohlanständige Damen: Bürgertum und Bürgerlichkeit in der Schweiz 1840–1914* (Zurich: Orell Füssli, 1995), 226–35; and Anthony Fletcher, *Growing Up in England: The Experience of Childhood, 1600–1914* (London: Yale University Press, 2008), 129–48.

9 Liebknecht, *Karl Marx zum Gedächtnis*, 61, 63; Marx-Aveling, "Karl Marx Lose Blätter," in *Mohr und General*, 271–77; Paul Lafargue, "Persönliche Erinnerungen," in ibid., 336–38.

10 *MEGA* 3/6: 464–67, 3/7: 419; 3/13: 157–58, 491; cf. also 3/5: 381–82.

11 *MEW* 35: 80–81.

12 *MEGA* 3/4: 85; similarly, 3/7: 166; *MEW* 34: 388.

13 *MEGA* 3/8: 107; 3/9: 188–89; 3/13: 510; *MEW* 31: 215–16, 307; Westphalen, "Kurze Umrisse," in *Mohr und General*, 228.

14 Fletcher, *Growing Up in England*, 23–36, 244–58; Ira Spieker, *Bürgerliche Mädchen im 19. Jahrhundert: Erziehung und Bildung in Göttingen 1806–1866* (Göttingen: Volker Schmerse, 1990).

15 *MEGA* 3/13: 147, 429; *MEW* 30: 342; 31: 392, 586–87; 32: 670; *MECW* 43: 449, 552–55, 558–60; Lessner, "Erinnerungen eines Arbeiters an Karl Marx," in *Mohr und General*, 187; Sheppard, *London 1800–1870*, 237.

16 *MEC* 7: 308–09.

17 *MECW* 42: 313; *MEC* 7: 334.

18 Tsuzuki, *The Life of Eleanor Marx* passim; Kugelmann, "Kleine Züge," in *Mohr und General*, 312; Sally Ledger, *The New Woman: Fiction and Feminism at the Fin de Siècle* (New York: St. Martin's Press, 1997).

19 Liebknecht, *Karl Marx zum Gedächtnis*, 69.

20 *MEGA* 3/13: 183, 239; *MEW* 32: 582–83, 597.

21 Born, *Erinnerungen eines Achtundvierzigers*, 74; *MEW* 31: 569; Hunt, *Marx's General*, 303–09.

22 *MEGA* 3/4: 373; 3/7: 13, 18, 129, 235; 3/8: 6–7; 3/9: 156, 232.

23 Wilhelm Schulte, "Fritz Anneke, geb. 1818 Dortmund-gest. 1872 Chicago. Ein Leben für die Freiheit in Deutschland und in den USA," *Beiträge zur Geschichte Dortmunds und der Grafschaft Mark* 57 (1960): 5–100.

24 Kugelmann, "Kleine Züge zu dem grossen Charakterbild," in *Mohr und General*, 315–16.

25 *MEGA* 3/6: 134, 139; 3/8: 223–24; 3/11: 469; *MEW* 30: 655; Westphalen, "Kurze Umrisse," in *Mohr und General*, 219, 223–25.

26 *MEGA* 3/7: 38; 3/11: 227; *MEW* 31: 182–83, 298–99; Lafargue, "Persönliche Erinnerungen," in *Mohr und General*, 342–44; Kugelmann, "Kleine Züge," in ibid., 285.

27 Liebknecht, *Karl Marx zum Gedächtniß*, 110; similarly, Paul Lafargue, "Persönliche Erinnerungen an Friedrich Engels," in *Mohr und General*, 480.

28 Henry Hyndman, *The Record of an Adventurous Life* (New York: The Macmillan Company, 1911), 256, 259.

29 *MEGA* 3/8: 123, 127, 132–33, 139–42.

30 Hunt, *Marx's General*, 201–02.

31 *MEGA* 3/4: 13; *MEW* 30: 304–05, 308.

32 *MEW* 30: 269–70, 312–16, 319.

33 Ibid., 33: 676.

34 Ibid., 32: 75.

35 *MEGA* 3/13: 470–71.

36 Westphalen, "Kurze Umrisse," in *Mohr und General*, 222–23; Liebknecht, *Karl Marx zum Gedächtniß*, 69; Sperber, *Property and Civil Society*, 120.

37 *MEW* 32: 343–44.

38 Ibid., 31: 343, 355–56; 32: 33, 38.

39 Ibid., 31: 301, 307, 385; 32: 26.

40 *MEGA* 3/13: 510.

41 Ibid., 3/13: 232; Hunt, *Marx's General*, 189.

42 Jürgen Kocka, ed., *Bürger und Bürgerlichkeit im 19. Jahrhundert* (Göttingen: Vandenhoeck & Ruprecht, 1987); Manfred Hettling and Stefan-Ludwig Hoffman, *Der bürgerliche Werthimmel: Innenansichten des 19. Jahrhunderts* (Göttingen: Vandenhoeck & Ruprecht, 2000).

43 Gielkens, *Marx und seine niederländischen Verwandten*, 79; *MEW* 32: 385.

44 Ruge, *Briefwechsel und Tagebuchblätter*, 343; Lafargue, "Persönliche Erinnerungen an Friedrich Engels," in *Mohr und General*, 482, 487.

45 Liebknecht, *Karl Marx zum Gedächtniß*, 64–66; Lessner, "Erinnerungen eines Arbeiters," in *Mohr und General*, 186–87; *MEW* 32: 217–18.

46 *MEW* 31: 550–51.

47 Ibid., 32: 107–09.

48 Liebknecht, *Karl Marz zum Gedächtniß*, 42; Marx-Aveling, "Karl Marx Lose Blätter," in *Mohr und General*, 273–74; Kugelmann, "Kleine Züge zum dem grossen Charakterbild," in ibid., 282, 290–91, 297; Lafargue, "Persönliche Erinnerungen," in ibid., 323–25; *MEW* 34: 416.

49 Liebknecht, *Karl Marx zum Gedächtniß*, 66–68; Lafargue, "Persönliche Erinnerungen," in *Mohr und General*, 328–29; for one surviving score of a Marx chess game, see Wheen, *Karl Marx*, 389.

50 *MEW* 32: 464, 469–70, 493–94, 506.

51 *MEGA* 3/1: 245; 3/4: 41–43, 90; 3/6: 139; 3/13: 205, 432, 497; *MEW* 31: 176, 178, 246, 283, 292; 32: 22, 426 ; Hunt, *Marx's General*, 297–98.

52 Tsuzuki, *Life of Eleanor Marx*, 23-24; *MEW* 32: 97, 131.

53 Vogt, *Mein Prozess*, 141-56; *MEW* 30: 671-72.

54 Lessner, "Erinnerungen eines Arbeiters," in *Mohr und General*, 186-88; Lafargue, "Persönliche Erinnerungen," ibid., 339; Anselmo Lorenzo, "Bei Karl Marx," ibid., 375-80.

55 *MEGA* 3/7: 26; 3/9: 294, 428-29, 431, 506, 541-42, 547; 3/10: 180-81, 207; 3/13: 227, 232, 256, 481, 519; *MEW* 30: 340, 345, 357-58; 31: 290-91, 374; 32: 28, 369-70, 380-81; cf. also Kugelmann, "Kleine Züge," in *Mohr und General*, 305.

56 *MEW* 30: 370; 31: 183; cf. Ashton, *Little Germany* passim.

57 *MEGA* 3/9: 477.

58 Ibid., 3/10: 552.

59 Liebknecht, *Karl Marx zum Gedächtniß*, 82-84.

60 Kugelmann, "Kleine Züge," in *Mohr und General*, 296, 309; *MEW* 34: 268.

61 *MEW* 32: 283, 288-89; Andreas Fahrmeir, *Citizenship: The Rise and Fall of a Modern Concept* (London: Yale University Press, 2007), 67-68; Wheen, *Karl Marx*, 356-57.

62 *MECW* 43: 293. Other examples include *MEGA* 3/4: 158, 231; 3/6: 201, 207-08; 3/7: 158; 3/9: 293; 3/11: 6-7, 157, 403-04; 3/13: 157-58, 612-13; *MEW* 31: 368; 34: 96.

63 *MEGA* 3/13: 90; *MEW* 30: 665.

64 *MEW* 34: 8-9.

65 *MEGA* 3/6: 27, 724-26; 3/7: 145-46; 3/9: 401; 3/10: 70-71; 3/13: 31; *MEW* 32: 7, 433.

66 McLellan, *Karl Marx*, 78; Frevert, *Men of Honour*, 113-15; Rainer Wirtz, *"Widersetzlichkieten, Excesse, Crawalle, Tumulte und Skandale"* (Frankfurt-am-Main: Ullstein Verlag, 1981), 130-45.

67 Ruge, *Zwei Jahre in Paris*, 35-44, 139-40. Ruge's attitudes toward Hess seem similar to Marx's toward his 1875 traveling companion.

68 Wermuth and Stieber, *Die Communisten Verschwörungen*, 79-80.

69 Lafargue, "Persönliche Erinnerungen," in *Mohr und General*, 328; Hyndman, *Record of an Adventurous Life*, 248; *MEGA* 1/25: 430.

70 *MEGA* 3/7: 224-26.

71 *MEW* 31: 550; Mosche Zimmermann, *Wilhelm Marr: The Patriarch of Antisemitism* (Oxford: Oxford University Press, 1986).

13: THE VETERAN

1 *MEW* 33: 286, 367-68.

2 *MECW* 44: 576; *MEW* 33: 697; 35: 159, 247-48; *MEGA* 1/22: 451-58; 1/25: 429-43; John Rae, "The Socialism of Karl Marx and the Young Hegelians," *The Contemporary Review* 40 (1881): 585-607.

3 Rae, "The Socialism of Karl Marx," 585; John Rae, "The Socialists of the Chair," *The Contemporary Review* 39 (1881), 232-48, and "Ferdinand Lassalle and German Socialism," ibid., 921-43.

4 *MEGA* 1/22: 594; more generally on the conference, see Katz, *The Emancipation of Labor*, 88–95; Thomas, *Marx and the Anarchists*, 320–22.

5 *MEGA* 1/22: 339–46.

6 *MECW* 44: 266.

7 *MEW* 33: 252, 270.

8 Archer, *The First International in France*, 267–69.

9 *MEW* 33: 642.

10 Ibid., 312: 195; 33: 453–54, 472–76; *MEGA* 3/9: 305–06, 310–11, 316, 319, 364; Westphalen, "Kurze Umrisse," in *Mohr und General*, 337.

11 Katz, *The Emancipation of Labor*, 96–114; Collins and Abramsky, *Karl Marx and the British Labour Movement*, 232–34, 251–59; Thomas, *Karl Marx and the Anarchists*, 321–22; *MECW* 43: 266–70; *MEW* 33: 287–88, 309–11, 314–15, 322–23, 332, 367–68, 377, 392, 484–85, 777–78; *MEC* 12: 133–34.

12 *MEW* 33: 397, 498; 18: 7–51; Thomas, *Karl Marx and the Anarchists*, 322–26; Katz, *The Emancipation of Labor*, 99–100; *HCFI* 2: 438.

13 *MEW* 33: 463, 512–14; *HCFI* 2: 329, 333–36, 355, 362–65, 377–78, 440–48.

14 *MEW* 33: 357, 364–66, 367–68, 379, 387–93, 395–96, 404–07, 426, 446–48, 451, 458–59, 488–90; *HCFI* 2: 373–76, 389–91, 626–33.

15 *MEW* 33: 364–66, 367–68, 372–73, 388–90, 406–07, and esp. 512; *HCFI* 2: 175, 228.

16 *MEW* 33: 491, 494, 497–98, 518–19; *HCFI* 2: 378, 380, 387–88, 396, 398, 401, 410–11, 435, 449–50, 457–59, 483–84, 491–92, 498–99.

17 *MEW* 32: 141, 160–62, 331–32; 33: 518–21; *HCFI* 1: 332; 2: 63, 150, 247, 504–06, 513; more generally on the Congress, Katz, *The Emancipation of Labor*, 128–36.

18 *HCFI* 2: 37–38, 68–71, 90–91, 104, 148, 150, 509.

19 Ibid., 1: 29–46, 70–72, 100–06; 2: 39–48, 57–59, 65–66, 74–77, 83–88, 100–01, 146–49, 153–55, 220–25, 228–31, 236–43, 261–79, 505, 510–12, 516, 519–20.

20 Ibid., 1: 77–81; 2: 59–63, 88–89. Newspaper reports presented results of the voting slightly different from the official minutes.

21 Ibid., 2: 89; *MEW* 33: 572–74.

22 *MEW* 33: 537–41, 551–58, 564–67, 581–87; Katz, *The Emancipation of Labor*, 141–44.

23 *MEW* 33: 477, 501; *MEC* 12: 76, 134; *HCFI* 2: 354, 522; Archer, *First International in France*, 297–99; McLellan, *Karl Marx*, 381.

24 *MEGA* 1/24: 163–283; *MEW* 33: 579, 582–83, 597, 606, 609, 614; 34: 2–22, 212–13, 226–28, 35: 159–61, 274–76.

25 *HCFI* 2: 354; *MEW* 33: 585–87.

26 *HCFI* 2: 526; *MEW* 33: 75–76, 95, 593–94, 607, 627; David Blackbourn, "Fashionable Spa Towns in Nineteenth Century Europe," in Susan Anderson and Bruce Tabb, eds., *Water, Leisure and Culture: European Historical Perspectives* (Oxford: Berg Publishers, 2002), 9–21; http://www.mayoclinic.com/health/high-blood-pressure/DS00100/DSECTION=symptoms, accessed 3/4/11.

27 *MEW* 33: 110–13, 116–17; 34: 6–8, 10–11, 23–27, 52–55, 156–57, 193, 201, 243–44; Tsuzuki, *Eleanor Marx*, 36–38.

28 *MEW* 33: 628, 635; 34: 81, 105, 107–08, 317–19, 431, 463–64.

29 Béla Király and Gale Stokes, eds., *Insurrections, Wars and the Eastern Crisis in the 1870s* (Boulder, CO: Social Science Monographs, 1985); Hopken, *The Mid-Victorian Generation*, 622–27; *MEW* 34: 20, 27–28, 212–16, 525.

30 *MEW* 34: 13, 15, 42–44, 209–11, 217–18, 256–57, 267–68, 317–19.

31 Ibid., 34: 320–21; also 28, 236, 244, 317–19.

32 Ibid., 34: 351–57; 35: 31, 80–81, 178–80, 187, 244, 295–97; Kowalewski, "Erinnerungen an Karl Marx," in *Mohr und General*, 384; Collins and Abramsky, *Marx and the British Labour Movement*, 239; Hyndman, *Record of an Adventurous Life*, 208–25.

33 *MEW* 34: 295–97; 317–19; also 48–49, 107–08, 162–63, 245–46, 316, 437, 445–46; 35: 32, 408, 433, 437.

34 Ibid., 34: 59, 63.

35 Ibid., 34: 145, 607; 35: 121, 123, 415; *MECW* 45: 344, 354–55; 46: 31–32, 40.

36 *MEW* 35: 422; also 104; Engels's opinions: 92–94, 358.

37 Ibid., 34: 420–21, 35: 442–43; also 33: 467; 34: 129–30.

38 Ibid., 34: 125–31, 137–38; *MEGA* 1/25: 9–25; Welskopp, *Banner der Brüderlichkeit*, 44–48, 705–11.

39 *MEW* 34: 54, 156, 159, 413.

40 Ibid., 34: 242–43; Vernon Lidtke, *The Outlawed Party: Social Democracy in Germany, 1878–1890* (Princeton: Princeton University Press, 1966), 55–78.

41 *MEW* 34: 15, 107–08, 302–03, 380, 382–83, 390–91, 410–11, 440; Lidtke, *The Outlawed Party*, 107–17.

42 *MEW* 34: 92, 94–95, 105, 107–08, 305, 379–80, 385–86, 390–93, 410–14, 417–22, 429–30, 432–33; *MEGA* 1/25: 171–85; August Bebel, "Der Kanossagang nach London," and Eduard Bernstein, "Erinnerungen an Karl Marx und Friedrich Engels," both in *Mohr und General*, 490–93, 495–502; Lidtke, *The Outlawed Party*, 89–93.

43 *HCFI* 2: 517; *MEW* 34: 285, 591; 35: 27–28, 40–41, 100, 109–11, 120, 228–34, 388–89; Bernard H. Moss, *The Origins of the French Labor Movement 1830–1914: The Socialism of Skilled Workers* (Berkeley & Los Angeles: University of California Press, 1976), 71–135.

44 Kowalewksi, "Erinnerungen an Karl Marx," in *Mohr und General*, 388.

45 *MEW* 32: 174, 566–67; 33: 469; 34: 78–79, 162–63, 169–72, 207–08, 219–20, 238, 477; 35: 191–93, 195, 408; *MECW* 46: 60–64; *MEGA* 1/25: 969–70; Kowalewski, "Erinnerungen an Karl Marx," in *Mohr und General*, 381–404; Bruno Naarden, *Socialist Europe and Revolutionary Russia: Perception and Prejudice 1848–1923* (Cambridge: Cambridge University Press, 1992), 51–65; Derek Offord, *The Russian Revolutionary Movement in the 1880s* (Cambridge: Cambridge University Press, 1986), 1–35.

46 *MEGA* 1/14: 790; 3/8: 58; *MEW* 32: 42, 197, 437, 443–44, 650; 34: 217–18; *MECW* 44: 487; Naarden, *Socialist Europe and Revolutionary Russia*, 41–48, 65–68.

47 *MEGA* 1/25: 217–42, 295–96, 823–24.

48 Ibid., 3/13: 83; *MEW* 31: 525; 32: 670; 33: 311; 34: 308, 311; 35: 442–43.

49 *HCFI* 2: 34, 637; *MEGA* 1/22: 457–58.

50 *MEW* 34: 174–75, 527–28; 35: 178–80; Naarden, *Socialist Europe and Revolutionary Russia*, 68–75; Kowalewski, "Erinnerungen an Karl Marx," in *Mohr und General*, 398.

51 Kugelmann, "Kleine Züge," in *Mohr und General*, 288.

52 *MEGA* 1/25: 14–15; 2/1: 86–89, 103–04, 581–82; 2/8: 501–02.

53 *MEW* 34: 296; 35: 186; *MECW* 46: 89; Philip Foner, ed., *When Karl Marx Died: Comments in 1883* (New York: International Publishers, 1973), 106.

54 *MEW* 34: 44–45, 343, 526; McLellan, *Karl Marx*, 389–90; Izumi Omura, ed., *Familie Marx privat: Die Foto- und Fragebogen-Alben von Marx' Töchtern Laura und Jenny* (Berlin: Akademie Verlag, 2005), xxvii–viii, 481; Liebknecht, *Karl Marx zum Gedächtnis*, 63–64.

55 *MEW* 34: 52, 315, 422, 432, 440, 454, 477, 616; 35: 7, 11–13, 16, 100, 177, 194, 201, 226; *MECW* 45: 353; 46: 30, 60–61, 91; Hyndman, *Record of an Adventurous Life*, 254; Bebel, "Der Kanossagang nach London," and Bernstein, "Erinnerungen an Karl Marx und Friedrich Engels," in *Mohr und General*, 493 and 504.

56 Liebknecht, *Karl Marx zum Gedächtnis*, 87–88; *MEW* 35: 240–41, 247–48, 250, 274; *MEGA* 1/25: 292.

57 *MEGA* 1/25: 287–88; Liebknecht, *Karl Marx zum Gedächtnis*, 88; *MEW* 35: 460.

58 *MEW* 35: 31–32, 40–44, 104–05, 112–13, 120, 124, 132, 140–41, 243, 247, 255, 265–73, 295–96, 334–36, 337–43, 356–58, 781; *MECW* 46: 52–54.

59 *MEW* 35: 45–46, 50–51, 53, 64–66, 71–72, 75, 83, 99, 105, 123, 132, 140–41, 256, 288–89, 293, 354, 397, 421; *MECW* 43: 338; Lessner, "Erinnerungen eines Arbeiters," and Kowalewski, "Erinnerungen an Karl Marx," in *Mohr und General*, 193 and 400; http://www.emedicinehealth.com/tuberculosis/page3_em.htm, accessed 3/14/11; special thanks to Dr. Brian Johnson, of Boone Hospital Center, for his diagnostic expertise.

60 *MEW* 35: 40, 45, 56, 61, 64–65, 69, 99, 262, 295; Wheen, *Karl Marx*, 377–78.

61 *MEW* 35: 41–42, 54, 293–94, 296, 305–11; *MECW* 46: 230–32.

62 *MEW* 35: 41–42, 54, 57–58, 299–300, 305–11.

63 Ibid., 35: 28–29, 328–29.

64 Ibid., 35: 71–72, 75–76, 80, 85, 91, 95, 111, 331.

65 Ibid., 35: 371, 395, 397–98, 424, 445, 451; *MECW* 46: 440–41, 456; Liebknecht, *Karl Marx zum Gedächtnis*, 89.

66 *MEW* 35: 457, 459–61.

14: THE ICON

1 *MEGA* 1/25: 407–13; *MEW* 34: 295–97; 35: 462.

2 *MEW* 35: 228–34, esp. 232–33.

3 Foner, ed., *When Karl Marx Died*, 75–77, 96, 137, 108, 125, 159, 166, 180, and passim.

4 *MEW* 34:14–15, 36, 39–41, 209, 217, 239, 263–64, 285–86, 315–16, 366, 420–21; Welskopp, *Banner der Brüderlichkeit*, 712–22.

5 *MEGA* 1/27: 131–216, 223–482, 587–626; Hunt, *Marx's General*, 289–95.

6 Levine, *The Tragic Deception*, 228, and passim.

7 Geoff Eley, *Forging Democracy: The History of the Left in Europe, 1850–2000* (Oxford: Oxford University Press, 2002), 62–99; Gary Steenson, *After Marx, Before Lenin: Marxism and Socialist Working-Class Parties in Europe, 1884–1914* (Pittsburgh: University of Pittsburgh Press, 1991); Hunt, *Marx's General*, 317–45.

8 Kershaw, *Hitler*, 150–52; Kurz, "German-Speaking Countries," in Steedman, ed., *Socialism and Marginalism in Economics*, 74; also Slezkine, *The Jewish Century*, 181.

9 Jonathan Frankel, *Prophecy and Politics: Socialism, Nationalism and the Russian Jews, 1862–1917* (Cambridge: Cambridge University Press, 1981), 33, 253.

10 Slezkine, *The Jewish Century*, chaps. 2–4; also Johannes Rogalla von Bieberstein, *"Jüdischer Bolschewismus" Mythos und Realität* (Dresden: Edition Antaios, 2002).

11 Cf. Lucy Riall, *Garibaldi: Invention of a Hero* (New Haven & London: Yale University Press, 2007).

Bibliography

·⊰▯⊱·

Albisetti, James C. *Secondary School Reform in Imperial Germany*. Princeton: Princeton University Press, 1983.

Althusser, Louis. *For Marx*, trans. Ben Brewster. New York: Pantheon Books, 1969.

Anderson, Olive. *A Liberal State at War: English Politics and Economics During the Crimean War*. London: Macmillan, 1967.

Andréas, Bert et al., eds. *Association Démocratique ayant pour but l'union et la fraternité de tous les peuples: Eine frühe demokratische Vereinigung in Brüssel 1847–1848*. Trier: Karl-Marx-Haus, 2004.

——, Jacques Grandjonc, and Hans Pelger. "Karl Marx' Ausweisung aus Paris und die Niederlassung von Marx und Friedrich Engels in Brüssel im Frühjahr 1845." In Marion Barzen, ed., *Studien zu Marx' erstem Paris-Aufenthalt, und zur Entstehung der Deutschen Ideologie*. Trier: Karl-Marx-Haus, 1990.

[Anon]. "German Literature," *Saturday Review of Politics, Literature, Science and Art*, vol. 24, no. 638, January 18, 1869: 96–98.

Archer, Julian P. W. *The First International in France 1864–1872*. Lanham, MD: University Press of America, 1997.

Ashton, Rosemary. *Little Germany: Exile and Asylum in Victorian England*. Oxford: Oxford University Press, 1986.

Attali, Jacques. *Karl Marx, ou L'espirit du monde*. Paris: Librarie générale française, 2007.

Barclay, David. *Frederick William IV and the Prussian Monarchy, 1840–1861*. Oxford: Clarendon Press, 1995.

Barzun, Jacques. *Darwin, Marx, Wagner: Critique of a Heritage*. Boston: Little, Brown, 1941.

Bauer, Bruno. "Die Fähigkeit der heutigen Juden und Christen, frei zu werden." In Georg Herwegh, ed., *Einundzwanzig Bogen aus der Schweiz*. Zurich & Winterthur: Verlag des Literarischen Comptoirs, 1843.

———. *Die Judenfrage*. Braunschweig: Druck & Verlag von Friedrich Otto, 1843.

——— and Edgar Bauer. *Briefwechsel zwischen Bruno Bauer und Edgar Bauer während der Jahre 1839–1842 aus Bonn und Berlin*. Charlottenburg: Verlag von Egbert Bauer, 1844.

Bauer, Edgar. *Konfidentenberichte über die europäische Emigration 1852–1861*, ed. Erik Gamby. Trier: Karl-Marx-Haus, 1989.

Bellofiore, Ricardo, ed. *Marxian Economics: A Reappraisal. Essays on Volume III of Capital*. 2 vols. Houndmills, Basingstoke: Macmillan, 1998.

Berenson, Edward. *Populist Religion and Left-Wing Politics in France, 1830–1852*. Princeton: Princeton University Press, 1984.

Berlin, Isaiah. *Karl Marx: His Life and Environment*. 4th ed. Oxford: Oxford University Press, 1978.

Berman, Marshall. *All That Is Solid Melts into Air: The Experience of Modernity*. New York: Simon & Schuster, 1982.

Biermann, Harald. *Ideologie statt Realpolitik: Kleindeutsche Liberale und auswärtige Politik vor der Reichsgründung*. Düsseldorf: Droste Verlag, 2006.

Bittel, Karl, ed. *Der Kommunistenprozeß zu Köln 1852 im Spiegel der zeitgenössischen Presse*. East Berlin: Rütten & Loening, 1955.

Blackbourn, David. "Fashionable Spa Towns in Nineteenth Century Europe." In Susan Anderson and Bruce Tabb, eds. *Water, Leisure and Culture: European Historical Perspectives*. Oxford: Berg Publishers, 2002.

Blänker, Reinhard, Gerhard Göhler, and Norbert Waszek, eds. *Eduard Gans (1797–1839): Politischer Professor zwischen Restauration und Vormärz*. Leipzig: Leipziger Universitätsverlag, 2002.

Blasius, Dirk. *Bürgerliche Gesellschaft und Kriminalität*. Göttingen: Vandenhoeck & Ruprecht, 1976.

Böhm-Bawerk, Eugen von. *Karl Marx and the Close of His System*, trans. Alice McDonald, ed. Paul Sweezey. New York: H. Wolff, 1949.

Born, Stephan. *Erinnerungen eines Achtundvierzigers*. Leipzig: Verlag von Georg Heinrich Meyer, 1898.

Brandhorst, Heinz-Herman. *Lutherrezeption und bürgerliche Emanziaption: Studien zum Luther- und Reformationsverständnis im deutschen Vormärz (1815–1848) unter besonderer Berücksichtigung Ludwig Feuerbachs*. Göttingen: Vandenhoeck & Ruprecht, 1981.

Breckman, Warren. *Marx, the Young Hegelians and the Origins of Radical Social Theory: Dethroning the Self*. Cambridge: Cambridge University Press, 1999.

Brophy, James. *Popular Culture and the Public Sphere in the Rhineland 1800–1850*. Cambridge: Cambridge University Press, 2007.

———. "Recent Publications of the *Marx-Engels-Gesamtausgabe* (MEGA)," *Central European History* 40 (2007): 523–37.

Brown, David. *Palmerston: A Biography.* London: Yale University Press, 2010.

Bublies-Godau, Birgit. "Parteibildungsprozesse im vormärzlichen Exile: Die deutschen Auslandsvereine in Paris," *Forum Vormärz Forschung* 10 (2004): 87–147.

Burrow, John W. *The Crisis of Reason: European Thought, 1848–1914.* New Haven: Yale University Press, 2000.

Büttner, "Wolfgang. Friedrich Wilhelm IV im Blickpunkt zeitkritischer Vormärzliteratur," *Forum Vormärz Forschung* 10 (2004): 195–207.

Caldwell, Peter C. *Love, Death and Revolution in Central Europe: Ludwig Feuerbach, Moses Hess, Louise Dittmar, Richard Wagner.* New York: St. Martin's Press, 2009.

Clark, Christopher. *Iron Kingdom: The Rise and Downfall of Prussia 1600–1947.* Cambridge, MA: Harvard University Press, 2006.

Collins, Henry, and Chimen Abramsky. *Karl Marx and the British Labour Movement.* London: Macmillan & Co., 1965.

Courth, Franz. "Die Evangelienkritik des David Friedrich Strauß im Echo seiner Zeitgenossen. Zur Breitenwirkung seines Werkes." In Georg Schwaiger, ed., *Historische Kritik in der Theologie: Beiträge zu ihrer Geschichte.* Göttingen: Vandenhoeck & Ruprecht, 1980.

Daum, Andreas. *Wissenschaftspopularisierung im 19. Jahrhundert.* 2nd ed. Munich: R. Oldenbourg, 2002.

David, Eric. "Trèves: De la capitale d'empire à la ville moyenne; Une ville moyenne frontalière dans la perspective des occupations françaises successive," *Revue d'Allemagne* 26 (1994): 69–81.

Deichsel, Dieter. "'Die Kritik Karl Grüns: Zur Entstehung und Überlieferung von Teil IV des zweiten Bandes der 'Deutschen Ideologie,'" *MEGA Studien* 3 (1997): 103–53.

Doll, Natascha. *Recht, Politik und "Realpolitik" bei August Ludwig von Rochau (1810–1873).* Frankfurt-am-Main: Vittorio Klostermann, 2005.

Donner, Ingrid. "Der Anteil von Karl Marx und Friedrich Engels an der Verteidigung der Kölner Kommunistenprozeße 1852," *Marx-Engels-Jahrbuch* 4 (1981): 306–44.

Dühr, Elisabeth, ed. *"Der Schlimmste Punkt in der Provinz": Demokratische Revolution 1848/49 in Trier und Umgebung.* Trier: Selbstverlag des Städtischen Museums Simeonstift, 1998.

—— and Christl Lehnert-Leven, eds. *Unter der Trikolore—Sous le drapeau tricolore Trier in Frankreich—Napoléon in Trier Trèves en France—Napoléon à Trèves 1794–1814.* 2 vols. Trier: Städtisches Museum Simeonstift, 2004.

Dussel, Enrique. *Towards an Unknown Marx: A Commentary on the Manuscripts of 1861–63,* trans. Yolanda Angulo. London & New York: Routledge, 2001.

Eckhardt, Wolfgang. "Bakunin und Johann Philipp Becker: Eine andere Prespektive auf den Beginn der Auseinandersetzung zwischen Marx und Bakunin in der Ersten Internationale," *Internationale wissenschaftliche Korrespondenz zur Geschichte der detuschen Arbeiterbewegung* 35 (1999): 66–122.

Eley, Geoff. *Forging Democracy: The History of the Left in Europe, 1850–2000*. Oxford: Oxford University Press, 2002.

Elsner, "Helmut. Karl Marx in Kreuznach 1842/43 Daten—Personen—Kreuznacher Exzerpte." In Marion Barzen, ed., *Studien zu Marx's erstem Paris-Aufenthalt und zur Entstehung der Deutschen Ideologie*. Trier: Karl-Marx Haus, 1990.

Eßbach, Wolfgang. *Die Junghegelianer. Soziologie einer Intellektuellengruppe*. Munich: Wilhelm Fink, 1988.

Faber, Karl-Georg. "Verwaltungs- und Justizbeamte auf dem linken Rheinufer während der französischen Herrschaft." In Max Braubach, ed., *Aus Geschichte und Landeskunde: Forschungen und Darstellungen Franz Steinbach zum 65. Geburtstag*. Bonn: L. Röhrscheid, 1960.

Fahrmeir, Andreas. *Citizenship: The Rise and Fall of a Modern Concept*. London: Yale University Press, 2007.

Fenves, Peter. "Marx's Doctoral Thesis on Two Greek Atomists and the Post-Kantian Interpretation," *Journal of the History of Ideas* 47 (1986): 433–52.

Finn, Margot. *After Chartism: Class and Nation in English Radical Politics, 1848–1874*. Cambridge: Cambridge University Press, 1993.

Fletcher, Anthony. *Growing Up in England: The Experience of Childhood, 1600–1914*. London: Yale University Press, 2008.

Foner, Philip, ed. *When Karl Marx Died: Comments in 1883*. New York: International Publishers, 1973.

Frankel, Jonathan. *Prophecy and Politics: Socialism, Nationalism and the Russian Jews, 1862–1917*. Cambridge: Cambridge University Press, 1981.

Frevert, Ute. *Men of Honour: A Social and Cultural History of the Duel*, trans. Anthony Williams. Cambridge: Polity Press, 1995.

———. *A Nation in Barracks: Modern Germany, Military Conscription and Civil Society*, trans. Andrew Boreham and Daniel Brückenhaus. Oxford: Berg Publishers, 2004.

Füssl, Wilhelm. *Professor in der Politik: Friedrich Julius Stahl (1802–1861)*. Göttingen: Vandenhoeck & Ruprecht, 1988.

Gemkow, Heinrich. "Aus dem Leben einer rheinischen Familie im 19. Jahrhundert. Archivalische Funde zu den Familien von Westphalen und Marx," *Jahrbuch für westdeutsche Landesgeschichte* 31 (2008): 498–524.

———. "Helena Demuth (1820–1890). Ein Leben im Schatten anderer. Vom Kindermädchen in Trier zur Hausdame in London." In Irina Hundt, ed., *Vom Salon zur Barrikade: Frauen der Heinezeit*. Stuttgart & Weimar: Verlag J. B. Metzler, 2002.

———, and Rolf Hecker. "'Unbekannte Dokumente über Marx' Sohn Frederick Demuth," *Beiträge zur Geschichte der Arbeiterbewegung* 43 (1994): 43–59.

Glick, Thomas, ed. *The Comparative Reception of Darwin*. Austin: University of Texas Press, 1974.

Godsey, William D., Jr. *Nobles and Nations in Central Europe: The Imperial Knights in the Age of Revolution 1750–1850*. Cambridge: Cambridge University Press, 2004.

Goschler, Constantin. *Rudolf Virchow: Mediziner—Anthropologe—Politiker.* Cologne: Böhlau Verlag, 2002.

Grab, Walter. *Dr. Wilhelm Schulz aus Darmstadt. Weggefährte von Georg Büchner und Inspirator von Karl Marx.* Frankfurt-am-Main: Büchergilde Gutenberg, 1987.

Grandjonc, Jacques. *Marx et les communists allemands à Paris 1844.* Paris: François Maspéro, 1974.

——. "Zu Marx' Aufenthalt in Paris: 11. October 1843–1 Februar 1845." In Marion Barzen, ed., *Studien zu Marx' erstem Paris-Aufenthalt und zur Enstehung der* Deutschen Ideologie. Trier: Karl-Marx-Haus, 1990.

Grewe, Bernd-Stefan. *Der versperrte Wald: Ressourcenmangel in der bayerischen Pfalz (1814–1870).* Cologne & Vienna: Böhlau Verlag, 2004.

Griese, Anneliese. "Die geologischen, mineralogischen und agronchemischen Manuskripten. Ein Beitrag zu ihrer wissenschaft-historischen Einordnung," *Beiträge zur Marx-Engels-Forschung* n.s. 2006: 31–48.

Grimmer-Solem, Erik. *The Rise of Historical Economics and Social Reform in Germany 1864–1894.* Oxford: Clarendon Press, 2003.

Grün, Karl. *Die soziale Bewegung in Frankreich und Belgien: Briefe und Studien.* Darmstadt: Druck & Verlag von Carl Wilhelm Leske, 1845.

Hahn, Hans-Henning. *Aussenpolitik in der Emigration: Die Exildiplomatie Adam Jerzy Czartoryski 1830–1840.* Munich: Oldenbourg Verlag, 1978.

Hanisch, Ernst. *Karl Marx und die Berichte der österreichischen Geheimpolizei.* Trier: Karl-Marx-Haus, 1976.

Hansen, Joseph. *Gustav Mevissen: ein rheinisches Lebensbild 1815–1899.* 2 vols. Berlin: Georg Reimer, 1906.

Harling, Philip. *The Waning of "Old Corruption": The Politics of Economical Reform in Britain, 1779–1846.* Oxford: Clarendon Press, 1996.

Harries, Martin. "*Homo Alludens:* Marx's Eighteenth Brumaire," *New German Critique* 66 (1995): 35–64.

Hausen, Karen. "'. . . eine Ulme für das schwanke Efeu.' Ehepaare im Bildungsbürgertum. Ideale und Wirklichkeit im späten 18. und 19. Jahrhundert." In Ute Frevert, ed., *Bürgerinnen und Bürger: Geschlechterverhältnisse im 19. Jahrhundert.* Göttingen: Vandenhoeck & Ruprecht, 1988.

Heinen, Heinz et al., eds. *2000 Jahre Trier.* 3 vols. Trier: Spee-Verlag, 1985–96.

Heinzen, Karl. *Die Helden des teutschen Kommunismus. Dem Herrn Karl Marx Gewidmet.* Bern: Druck & Verlag von Jenni, Sohn, 1848.

Henning, Hans-Joachim. *Das westdeutsche Bürgertum in der Epoche der Hochindustrialisierung 1860–1914.* Wiesbaden: Franz Steinver Verlag, 1972.

Herres, Jürgen. "Cholera, Armut und eine 'Zwangssteuer' 1830/32: Zur Sozialgeschichte Triers im Vormärz," *Kurtrierisches Jahrbuch* 39 (1990): 161–203.

——. "Der Kölner Kommunistenprozess von 1852," *Geschichte in Köln* 50 (2003): 133–55.

Herzog, Dagmar. *Intimacy and Exclusion: Religious Politics in Pre-Revolutionary Baden*. Princeton: Princeton University Press, 1996.

Hettling, Manfred, and Stefan-Ludwig Hoffman. *Der bürgerliche Werthimmel: Innenansichten des 19. Jahrhunderts*. Göttingen: Vandenhoeck & Ruprecht, 2000.

Hobsbawm, Eric, ed. *The Communist Manifesto: A Modern Edition*. London: Verso, 1998.

Hodenberg, Christina von. *Die Partei der Unparteiischen. Der Liberalismus der preußischen Richterschaft 1815–1848/49*. Göttingen: Vandenhoeck & Ruprecht, 1996.

Hölscher, Lucian. *Geschichte der protestantischen Frömmigkeit in Deutschland*. Munich: C. H. Beck, 2005.

Hoppen, K. Theodore. *The Mid-Victorian Generation 1846–1886*. Oxford: Oxford University Press, 1998.

Hundt, Martin. *Geschichte des Bundes der Kommunisten*. Frankfurt-am-Main & Berlin: Peter Lang, 1993.

Hunt, Tristram. *Marx's General: The Revolutionary Life of Friedrich Engels*. New York: Henry Holt & Co., 2010.

Hyndman, Henry. *The Record of an Adventurous Life*. New York: The Macmillan Company, 1911.

Israel, Jonathan. *European Jewry in the Age of Mercantilism, 1550–1750*. 3rd ed. London: Valentine Mitchell & Co., 1998.

Jansen, Christian. *Einheit, Macht und Freiheit. Die Paulskirchenlinke und die deutsche Politik in der nachrevolutionären Epoche 1849–1867*. Düsseldorf: Droste Verlag, 2000.

——. "Der politische Weg des Trierer Paulskirchenabgeordneten Ludwig Simon (1819–1872) gegen den Strom des natinalistischen 19. Jahrhunderts." In Guido Müller and Jürgen Herres, eds., *Aachen und die westlichen Rheinlande und die Revolution 1848/49*. Aachen: Shaker Verlag, 2000.

——, ed. *Nach der Revolution 1848/49: Verfolgung, Realpolitik Nationsbildung: Politische Briefe deutscher Liberaler und Demokraten 1849–1861*. Düsseldorf: Droste Verlag, 2004.

Jeismann, Karl-Ernst. *Das preußische Gymnasium in Staat und Gesellschaft*. 2nd ed. 2 vols. Stuttgart: Klett-Cotta, 1996.

Johnson, Christopher. *Utopian Communism in France: Cabet and the Icarians 1839–1851*. Ithaca, NY: Cornell University Press, 1974.

Jones, Gareth Stedman, ed. *The Communist Manifesto*. London & New York: Penguin Books, 2002.

Kahan, Alan. "Liberalism and Realpolitik in Prussia, 1830–1852: The Case of David Hansemann," *German History* 9 (1991): 280–307.

Kanda, Junji. "Die Feuerbach-Rezeption des jungen Marx im Licht der Junghegelianismus-Forscshung." In Ursula Reitemeyer, Takayuik Shibata, and Franceso Tomasoni, eds. *Ludwig Feuerbach (1804–1872): Identität und Pluralismus in der globalen Gesellschaft*. New York: Waxmann Münster, 2006.

Kaplan, Marian. *The Making of the Jewish Middle Class: Women, Family and Identity in Imperial Germany*. New York: Oxford University Press, 1991.

Kasper-Holtkotte, Cilli. *Juden im Aufbruch. Zur Sozialgeschichte einer Minderheit im Saar-Mosel-Raum um 1800.* Hanover: Verlag Hahnsche Buchhandlung, 1996.

Katz, Henryk. *The Emancipation of Labor: A History of the First International.* Westport, CT: Greenwood Press, 1991.

Kaufmann, Uri R. "Ein jüdischer Deutscher: Der Kampf des jungen Gabriel Riesser für die Gleichberechtigung der Juden 1830–1848," *Aschkenas: Zeitschrift für Geschichte und Kultur der Juden* 13 (2003): 211–36.

Kaup, Peter. "Karl Marx als Waffenstudent: Burschenschafter an seinem Lebensweg," *Darstellungen und Quellen zur Geschichte der deutschen Einheitsbewegung im neunzehnten und zwanzigsten Jahrhundert* 15 (1995): 141–68.

Kelly, Alfred. *The Descent of Darwin: The Popularization of Darwin in Germany 1860–1914.* Chapel Hill: University of North Carolina Press, 1981.

Kershaw, Ian. *Hitler: A Biography.* New York: W. W. Norton & Company, 2008.

Király, Béla, and Gale Stokes, eds. *Insurrections, Wars and the Eastern Crisis in the 1870.* Boulder, CO: Social Science Monographs, 1985.

Kliem, Manfred. *Karl Marx und die Berliner Universität 1836 bis 1841.* East Berlin: Humboldt Universität, 1988.

Knodel, John. *Demographic Behavior in the Past: A Study of Fourteen German Village Populations in the Eighteenth and Nineteenth Centuries.* Cambridge: Cambridge University Press, 1988.

Kocka, Jürgen, ed. *Bürger und Bürgerlichkeit im 19. Jahrhundert.* Göttingen: Vandenhoeck & Ruprecht, 1987.

Kramer, Lloyd S. *Threshold of a New World: Intellectuals and the Exile Experience in Paris, 1830–1848.* Ithaca & London: Cornell University Press, 1988.

Krätke, Michael. "'Hier bricht das Manuskript ab.' (Engels) Hat das *Kapital* einen Schluss? Teil I," *Beiträge zur Marx-Engels-Forschung* n.s. 2001: 7–43.

Kurz, Heinz. "Marginalism, Classicism and Socialism in German-Speaking Countries, 1871–1932." In Ian Steedman, ed., *Socialism and Marginalism in Economics 1870–1930.* London: Routledge, 1995.

Landes, David. *The Unbound Prometheus: Technological Change and Industrial Development in Western Europe from 1750 to the Present.* Cambridge: Cambridge University Press, 1969.

Langkau, Götz, and Hans Pelger. *Studien zur* Rheinischen Zeitung *und zu ihrer Forderung nach Handelsfreiheit und Grundrechten im Deutschen Bund.* Trier: Karl-Marx-Haus, 2003.

Lassalle, Ferdinand. *Gesammelte Reden und Schriften*, ed. Eduard Bernstein. 12 vols. Berlin: Paul Cassirer, 1919–20.

Lattek, Christine. *Revolutionary Refugees: German Socialism in Britain, 1840–1860.* London & New York: Routledge, 2006.

Ledger, Sally. *The New Woman: Fiction and Feminism at the Fin de Siècle.* New York: St. Martin's Press, 1997.

Lenger, Friedrich. *Werner Sombart 1863–1941. Eine Biographie*. Munich: C. H. Beck Verlag, 1994.

Lévi-Strauss, Claude. *Tristes Tropiques*, trans. John and Doreen Weightman. London: Jonathan Cape, 1973.

Levine, Bruce. *The Spirit of 1848: German Immigrants, Labor Conflict and the Coming of the Civil War*. Urbana: University of Illinois Press, 1992.

Levine, Norman. *The Tragic Deception: Marx Contra Engels*. Santa Barbara, CA: Clio Books, 1975.

Liebknecht, Wilhelm. *Karl Marx zum Gedächtniß. Ein Lebensabriß und Erinnerungen*. Nuremberg: Wörlein & Comp., 1896.

Lidtke, Vernon. *The Outlawed Party: Social Democracy in Germany, 1878–1890*. Princeton: Princeton University Press, 1966.

Linzbach, Petra. "Die konservative Orientierung Bruno Bauers nach 1848." In Lars Lambrecht, ed., *Osteuropa in den Revolutionen von 1848*. Frankfurt: Peter Lang, 2006.

Lippold, Gerhard. "Marx und die Tolstois in Paris," *Beiträge zur Geschichte der Arbeiterbewegung* 45 (2003): 9–26.

Mak, Ricardo King Sang. *The Future of the Non-Western World in the Social Sciences of Nineteenth Century England*. Frankfurt-am-Main: Peter Lang, 1999.

Mallmann, Luitwin. *Französische Juristenbildung im Rheinland 1794–1814. Die Rechtsschule von Koblenz*. Cologne: Böhlau Verlag, 1987.

Malthus, Thomas. *An Essay on the Principle of Population*, ed. Anthony Flew. London: Penguin Books, 1970.

Marchand, Suzanne. *German Orientalism in the Age of Empire: Religion, Race, and Scholarship*. New York: Cambridge University Press, 2009.

Marx, Karl. *Manuskripte über die Polnische Frage (1863–1864)*, ed. Werner Conze and Dieter Hertz-Eichenrode. 'S-Gravenhage: Mouton & Co., 1961– .

Massey, Marilyn Chapin. *Christ Unmasked: The Meaning of* The Life of Jesus *in German Politics*. Chapel Hill: University of North Carolina Press, 1983.

McLellan, David. *Karl Marx: A Biography*. 4th ed. Houndmills, Basingstoke: Palgrave Macmillan, 2006.

Meaney, Mark. *Capital as Organic Unity: The Role of Hegel's* Science of Logic *in Marx's* Grundrisse. Dodrecht: Kluwer Academic Publishers, 2002.

Megill, Allan. *Karl Marx: The Burden of Reason*. Lanham, MD: Rowman & Littlefield, 2002.

Mehring, Franz. *Karl Marx: The Story of His Life*, trans. Edward Fitzgerald. Atlantic Highlands, NJ: Humanities Press, 1981.

Melis, François. "August Hermann Ewerbeck—Vermittler demokratischer sozialistischer und kommunistischer Ideen zwischen Frankreich und Deutschland im Pariser Exil," *Forum Vormärz Forschung* 10 (2004): 268–95.

——."Eine neue Sicht auf die *Neue Rheinische Zeitung*? Zur Edition der MEGA²-Bände I/7–9," *Beiträge zur Marx-Engels-Forschung* n.s. (2005): 121–40.

———. "Friedrich Engels' Wanderung durch Frankreich und die Schweiz im Herbst 1848: Neue Erkenntnisse und Hypothesen," *MEGA Studien* 2 (1995): 61–92.

———. "Heinrich Bürgers." In Helmut Bleiber, Walter Schmidt, and Susanna Schütz, eds., *Akteure eines Umbruchs: Männer und Frauen der Revolution von 1848/49*. Berlin: Fides-Verlag, 2003.

———. *Neue Rheinische Zeitung Organ der Demokratie: Edition unbekannater Nummern, Flugblätter, Druckvarianten und Separatdrucke*. Munich: K. G. Saur, 2000.

———. "Zur Gründungsgeschichte der *Neuen Rheinischen Zeitung*. Neue Dokumente und Fakten," *MEGA Studien* 5 (1998): 3–63.

Mészáros, István. *Marx's Theory of Alienation*. 3rd ed. London: Merlin, 1972.

Mill, John Stuart. *Principles of Political Economy*. 2 vols. New York: D. Appleton & Co., 1864.

Mohr und General, ed. Institut für Marxismus-Leninismus. 3rd ed. East Berlin: Dietz Verlag, 1970.

Mönke, Wolfgang. *Die heilige Familie Zur ersten Gemeinschaftsarbeit von Karl Marx und Friedrich Engels*. Glashütten in Taunus: Verlag Detlev Auvermann, 1972.

Monz, Heinz. *Karl Marx Grundlagen der Entwicklung zu Leben und Werk*. Trier: Nco-Verlag, 1973.

———. "Neue Funde zum Lebensweg von Karl Marx' Vater," *Osnabrücker Mitteilungen* 87 (1981): 59–71.

———. "Der Waldprozeß der Mark Thalfang als Grundlage für Karl Marx' Kritik an den Debatten um das Holzdiebstahlgesetz," *Jahrbuch für westdeutsche Landesgeschichte* 4 (1977): 395–418.

Morgan, Roger. *The German Social Democrats and the First International 1864–1872*. Cambridge: Cambridge University Press, 1965.

Moss, Bernard H. *The Origins of the French Labor Movement 1830–1914: The Socialism of Skilled Workers*. Berkeley & Los Angeles: University of California Press, 1976.

Mosse, George. *Toward the Final Solution: A History of European Racism*. New York: Harper & Row, 1978.

Na'amann, Shlomo. *Lassalle*. Hanover: Verlag für Literatur und Zeitgeschehen, 1970.

Naarden, Bruno. *Socialist Europe and Revolutionary Russia: Perception and Prejudice 1848–1923*. Cambridge: Cambridge University Press, 1992.

Naarmann, Margit. "Ländliche Massenarmut und 'jüdischer Wucher.' Zur Etablirung eines Stereotyps." In Ludger Grevelhörster and Wolfgang Maron, eds., *Region und Gesellschaft in Deutschland des 19. und 20. Jahrhunderts*. Vierow: SH-Verlag, 1995.

Nadel, Stanley. *Little Germany: Ethnicity, Religion, and Class in New York City, 1845–80*. Urbana: University of Illinois Press, 1990.

Nerrlich, Paul, ed. *Arnold Ruges Briefwechsel und Tagebuchblätter aus den Jahren 1825–1880*. 2 vols. Berlin: Weidmannsche Buchhandlung, 1886.

Nicolaevsky, Boris. "Secret Societies and the First International." In Milorad M.

Drachkovitch, ed., *The Revolutionary Internationals, 1864–1943*. Stanford, CA: Stanford University Press, 1966.

—— and Otto Maenchen-Helfen. *Karl Marx: Man and Fighter*, trans. Gwenda David and Eric Mosbacher. Philadelphia: J. B. Lippincott, 1936.

Oberman, Heiko. *Luther: Man Between God and the Devil*, trans. Eileen Walliser-Schwarzbart. New Haven: Yale University Press, 1989.

Offord, Derek. *The Russian Revolutionary Movement in the 1880s*. Cambridge: Cambridge University Press, 1986.

Ollman, Bertell. *Alienation: Marx's Conception of Man in Capitalist Society*. 2nd ed. Cambridge: Cambridge University Press, 1976.

Omura, Izumi, ed. *Familie Marx privat: Die Foto- und Fragebogen-Alben von Marx' Töchtern Laura und Jenny*. Berlin: Akademie Verlag, 2005.

Palatschek, Sylvia. *Frauen und Dissens: Frauen im Deutschkatholizimus und in den Freien Gemeinden 1841–1852*. Göttingen: Vandenhoeck & Ruprecht, 1990.

Parry, Jonathan. *The Politics of Patriotism: English Liberalism, National Identity and Europe, 1830–1886*. Cambridge: Cambridge University Press, 2006.

Paulus, Heinrich. *Die jüdische Nationalabsonderung nach Ursprung, Folge und Besserungsmitteln*. Heidelberg: Universitätsbuchhandlung von C. F. Winter, 1831.

Payne, Robert. *Marx*. New York: Simon & Schuster, 1968.

Peach, Terry. *Interpreting Ricardo*. Cambridge: Cambridge University Press, 1993.

Peel, J. D. Y. *Herbert Spencer: The Evolution of a Sociologist*. New York: Basic Books, 1971.

Prawer, Siegbert. *Heine's Jewish Comedy: A Study of His Portraits of Jews and Judaism*, Oxford: Clarendon Press, 1983.

Proudhon, Pierre-Joseph. *Système de contradictions économiques, ou philosophie de la misère*. 2nd edn. 2 vols. Paris: Garnier Frères, 1850.

Rae, John. "Ferdinand Lassalle and German Socialism," *The Contemporary Review* 39 (1881): 921–43.

——. "The Socialism of Karl Marx and the Young Hegelians," *The Contemporary Review* 40 (1881): 585–607.

——. "The Socialists of the Chair," *The Contemporary Review* 39 (1881); 232–48.

Reif, Heinz. "'Furcht bewahrt das Holz.' Holzdiebstahl und sozialer Konflikt in der ländlichen Gesellschaft 1800–1850 an westfälischen Beispielen." In Heinz Reif, ed. *Räuber Volk und Obrigkeit*. Frankfurt-am-Main: Suhrkamp Verlag, 1984.

——. *Westfälischer Adel 1770–1860: vom Herrschaftsstand zur regionalen Elite*. Göttingen: Vandenhoeck & Ruprecht, 1979.

Reissner, Hans Günther. *Eduard Gans: Ein Leben im Vormärz*. Tübingen: J. C. B. Mohr, 1965.

Reiter, Herbert. *Politisches Asyl im 19. Jahrhundert*. Berlin: Duncker & Humblot, 1992.

Ricardo, David. *Principles of Political Economy and Taxation*, ed. Michael P. Fogarty. London: J. M. Dent & Sons, 1960.

Riall, Lucy. *Garibaldi: Invention of a Hero*. New Haven & London: Yale University Press, 2007.

Rogalla von Bieberstein, Johannes. *"Jüdischer Bolschewismus" Mythos und Realität*. Dresden: Edition Antaios, 2002.

Rohrbacher, Stefan. *Gewalt im Biedermeier: Antijüdische Ausschreitungen im Vormärz und Revolution (1815–1848/49)*. Frankfurt-am-Main and New York: Campus Verlag, 1990.

Roll, Eric. *A History of Economic Thought*. 4th ed. London: Faber & Faber, 1973.

Rose, Paul Lawrence. *Revolutionary Anti-Semitism in Germany from Kant to Wagner*. Princeton: Princeton University Press, 1990.

Rosen, Zvi. *Bruno Bauer and Karl Marx: The Influence of Bruno Bauer on Marx's Thought*. The Hague: Martinus Nijhoff, 1977.

——. *Moses Hess und Karl Marx*. Hamburg: Hans Christians Verlag, 1983.

Rotenstreich, Nathan. "For and Against Emancipation: The Bruno Bauer Controversy," *Leo Baeck Institute Yearbook* 4 (1959): 3–36.

Ruge, Arnold. *Zwei Jahre in Paris*. 2 vols. Leipzig: Verlag von Wilhelm Jurany, 1846.

Runes, Dagobert, ed. *A World Without Jews by Karl Marx*. New York: Philosophical Library, 1959.

Rürup, Reinhard. *Emanzipation und Antisemitismus*. Göttingen: Vandenhoeck & Ruprecht, 1975.

Ruse, Michael. *The Darwinian Revolution: Science Red in Tooth and Claw*. 2nd ed. Chicago: University of Chicago Press, 1999.

Ruttmann, Ulrike. *Wunschbild-Schreckbild-Trugbild: Rezeption und Instrumentalisierung Frankreichs in der Deutschen Revolution von 1848/49*. Stuttgart: Franz Steiner Verlag, 2001.

Sammons, Jeffrey L. *Heinrich Heine: A Modern Biography*. Princeton: Princeton University Press, 1979.

Sass, "Hans-Martin. Bruno Bauers Idee der 'Rheinischen Zeitung," *Zeitschrift für Religions- und Geistesgeschichte* 19 (1967): 321–32.

Schäffle, Albert. *Kapitalismus und Socialismus mit besonderer Rücksicht auf Geschäfts- und Vermögensfragen*. Tübingen: Verlag der H. Laupp'schen Buchhandlung, 1870.

Schieder, Wolfgang. *Karl Marx als Politiker*. Munich: Piper Verlag, 1991.

——. *Religion und Revolution. Die Trierer Wallfahrt von 1844*. Vierow: SH-Verlag, 1996.

Schliebe, Inge, and Ludmilla Kalinina. "Rezensionen des Marxchen Werkes, 'Zur Kritik der politischen Ökonomie aus dem Jahre 1859,'" *Beiträge zur Marx-Engels-Forschung* 1 (1977): 103–23.

Schmidt, Klaus. *Andreas Gottschalk: Armenarzt und Pionier der Arbeiterbewegung Jude und Protestant*. Cologne: Greven Verlag, 2002.

Schönke, Manfred. *Karl und Heinrich Marx und ihre Geschwister: Lebenszeugnisse—Briefe—Dokumente*. Bonn: Pahl-Rugenstein Nachfolger, 1993.

Schulte, Wilhelm. "Fritz Anneke, geb. 1818 Dortmund-gest. 1872 Chicago Ein Leben für die Freiheit in Deutschland und in den USA," *Beiträge zur Geschichte Dortmunds und der Grafschaft Mark* 57 (1960): 5–100.

Schulz, Wilhelm. *Die Bewegung der Produktion. Eine geschichtlich-statistische Abhandlung*, ed. Wilhelm Kade. Glashütten in Taunus: Verlag Detlev Auvermann, 1974.

Schwarzschild, Leopold. *The Red Prussian: The Life and Legend of Karl Marx*, trans. Margaret Wing. New York: Charles Scribner's Sons, 1947.

Graf Schwerin von Krosigk, Lutz. *Jenny Marx Liebe und Leid im Schatten von Karl Marx.* 2nd ed. Wuppertal: Staats-Verlag, 1976.

Seigel, Jerrold E. *Marx's Fate: The Shape of a Life*. Princeton: Princeton University Press, 1978.

Seyppel, Marcel. *Die Demokratische Gesellschaft in Köln 1848/49: Städtische Gesellschaft und Parteienstehung während der bürgerlichen Revolution.* Cologne: Janus Verlagsgesellschaft, 1991.

Sheppard, Francis. *London 1800–1870: The Infernal Wen.* Berkeley & Los Angeles: University of California Press, 1971.

Silberner, Edmund. "Moses Hess als Begründer und Redakteur der Rheinischen Zeitung," *Archiv für Sozialgeschichte* 4 (1964): 5–44.

———. *Moses Hess: Geschichte seines Lebens.* Leiden: E. J. Brill, 1966.

Slezkine, Yuri. *The Jewish Century.* Princeton: Princeton University Press, 2004.

Smolinski, Leon. "Karl Marx and Mathematical Economics," *Journal of Political Economy* 81 (1973): 1189–1204.

Sperber, Jonathan. "'The Persecutor of Evil' in the German Revolution of 1848–1849." In Jeremy D. Popkin, ed., *Media and Revolution: Comparative Perspective.* Lexington: University Press of Kentucky, 1995.

———. *Property and Civil Society in South-Western Germany 1820–1914.* Oxford: Oxford University Press, 2005.

———. *Rhineland Radicals: The Democratic Movement and the Revolution of 1848–1849.* Princeton: Princeton University Press, 1991.

Spieker, Ira. *Bürgerliche Mädchen im 19. Jahrhundert: Erziehung und Bildung in Göttingen 1806–1866.* Göttingen: Volker Schmerse, 1990.

Standley, Arline. *Auguste Comte.* Boston: Twayne Publishers, 1981.

Stanley, John, and Ernest Zimmerman. "On the Alleged Differences Between Marx and Engels," *Political Studies* 33 (1984): 226–48.

Steenson, Gary. *After Marx, Before Lenin: Marxism and Socialist Working-Class Parties in Europe, 1884–1914.* Pittsburgh: University of Pittsburgh Press, 1991.

Stépanova, Eugenia, and Irina Bach. "Le conseil général et son role dans l'association internationale des travilleurs." In *La Première Internationale: L'institution, l'implantation et le rayonnement*, ed. Denise Fauvel-Rouif. Paris: Centrale Nationale de la Recherche Scientifique, 1968.

Strähl, Wolfgang. *Briefe eines Schweizers aus Paris 1835–1836*, ed. Jacques Grandjonc, Waltraud Seidel-Höppner, and Michael Werner Vaduz: Topos Verlag, 1988.

Strassmaier, James. *Karl Grün und die Kommunistische Partei 1845–1848*. Trier: Karl-Marx-Haus, 1973.

Tal, Uriel. "Theologische Debatte um das 'Wesen' des Judentums." In Werner E. Mosse and Arnold Paucker, eds., *Judem im Wilhelminischen Deutschland 1890–1914*. Tübingen: J. C. B. Mohr, 1976.

Tanner, Albert. *Arbeitsame Patrioten—wohlanständige Damen: Bürgertum und Bürgerlichkeit in der Schweiz 1840–1914*. Zurich: Orell Füssli Verlag, 1995.

Tauber, Zvi. "Representations of Tragedy and Farce in History on Marx's *The Eighteenth Brumaire of Louis Bonaparte*," *Tel Aviver Jahrbuch für deutsche Geschichte* 29 (2000): 127–46.

Taubert, Inge. "Manuskripte und Drucke der 'deutschen Ideologie' (November 1845 bis Juni 1846). Probleme und Ereignisse," *MEGA Studien* 3 (1997): 5–31.

———. "Wie entstand die *Deutsche Ideologie* von Karl Marx und Friedrich Engels? Neue Einsichten, Probleme und Streitpunkte." In Marion Barzen, ed., *Studien zu Marx's erstem Paris-Aufenthalt und zur Entstehung der* Deutschen Ideologie. Trier: Karl-Marx Haus, 1990.

Taylor, Miles. "The Old Radicalism and the New: David Urquhart and the Politics of Opposition, 1832–1867." In Eugenio Biagini and Alastair J. Reid, eds., *Currents of Radicalism: Popular Radicalism, Organised Labour and Party Politics in Britain, 1850–1914*. Cambridge: Cambridge University Press, 1991.

Thomas, Paul. *Karl Marx and the Anarchists*. London: Routledge, 1980.

Thomas, Robert. "Enigmatic Writings: Karl Marx's *The Civil War in France* and the Paris Commune of 1871," *History of Political Thought* 18 (1997): 483–511.

Toews, John Edward. *Hegelianism: The Path Toward Dialectical Humanism, 1805–1848*. Cambridge: Cambridge University Press, 1980.

———, ed. *The Communist Manifesto by Karl Marx and Friedrich Engels with Related Documents*. Boston: Bedford/St. Martin's Press, 1999.

Thompson, Noel. *The People's Science: The Popular Political Economy of Exploitation and Crisis 1816–34*. Cambridge: Cambridge University Press, 1984.

Tombs, Robert. *The Paris Commune, 1871*. London & New York: Longman, 1999.

Trox, Eckhard. *Karl Grün (1817–1887). Eine Biographie*. Lüdenscheid: Stadtmuseum Lüdenscheid, 1993.

Tsuzuki, Chushichi. *The Life of Eleanor Marx, 1855–1898: A Socialist Tragedy*. Oxford: Clarendon Press, 1967.

Tuchinsky, Adam. *Horace Greeley's* New-York Tribune: *Civil War-Era Socialism and the Crisis of Free Labor*. Ithaca & London: Cornell University Press, 2009.

Vital, David. *A People Apart: The Jews in Europe 1789–1939*. Oxford: Oxford University Press, 1999.

Wheen, Francis. *Karl Marx: A Life*. New York: W. W. Norton & Co., 2000.

Whorton, James C. *The Arsenic Century: How Victorian Britain Was Poisoned at Home, Work and Play*. Oxford: Oxford University Press, 2010.

Winter-Tarvainen, Annette. "Moselweinkrise und Revolution von 1848." In Elisabeth Duhr, ed., *"Der Schlimmste Punkt in der Provinz": Demokratische Revolution 1848/49 in Trier und Umgebung*. Trier: Selbstverlag des Städtischen Museums Simeonstift, 1998.

Wirtz, Rainer. *"Widersetzlichkieten, Excesse, Crawalle, Tumulte und Skandale."* Frankfurt-am-Main: Ullstein Verlag, 1981.

Zimmermann, Andrew. *Anthropology and Antihumanism in Imperial Germany*. Chicago: University of Chicago Press, 2001.

Zimmermann, Mosche. *Wilhelm Marr: The Patriarch of Antisemitism*. Oxford: Oxford University Press, 1986.

Zittartz-Weber, Suzanne. *Zwischen Religion und Staat: Die jüdischen Gemeinden in der preußischen Rheinprovinz 1815–1871*. Essen: Klartext Verlag, 2003.

Index

About the Author

JONATHAN SPERBER is the Curators' Professor of History at the University of Missouri. Author of numerous works on the history of nineteenth-century Europe, including *The European Revolutions, 1848–1851* and *Rhineland Radicals: The Democratic Movement and the Revolution of 1848–1849*, he lives with his family in Columbia, Missouri.